GREAT THINKERS
OF THE
EASTERN WORLD

GREAT THINKERS
OF THE
EASTERN
WORLD

The major thinkers and the philosophical and religious classics
of China, India, Japan, Korea, and the world of Islam

EDITED BY IAN P. MCGREAL

HarperCollins*Publishers*

HarperCollins books may be purchased for educational, business, or sales promotional use. For information, please write: Special Markets Department, HarperCollins Publishers, Inc., 10 East 53rd Street, New York, NY 10022.

FIRST EDITION

Designed by Irving Perkins Associates

Library of Congress Cataloging-In-Publication Data

Great thinkers of the Eastern world : the great thinkers and the
    philosophical and religious classics of China, India, Japan, Korea,
    and the world of Islam / edited by Ian P. McGreal. — 1st ed.
        p. cm.
    Includes bibliographical references and index.
    ISBN 0-06-270085-5
    1. Philosophy, Oriental.   2. Asia—Religion.   3. Philosophers—
Asia.   4. Religious biography—Asia. I. McGreal, Ian Philip,
1919–   .
B5005.G74   1995
181—dc20   94-19418
                                                  CIP

96 97 98 99 PS/RRD 10 9 8 7 6 5 4 3 2

CONTENTS

India

Japan

Korea

The World of Islam

PREFACE

Great Thinkers of the Eastern World presents informative essays on over 100 of the outstanding philosophical and religious thinkers of China, India, Japan, Korea, and the world of Islam. Each article in this book summarizes and discusses the central ideas of an outstanding Eastern thinker (or, in some cases, the ideas of a classic work of great influence whose authorship is unknown). The essays are designed to serve as introductions for the general reader to the distinctive philosophical perspectives of the authors or books discussed.

Each essay begins with pertinent biographical information, a listing of the thinker's major works, and a summary statement of the thinker's major ideas. The body of the essay provides a brief biographical account (where information is available) and a careful account and discussion of the thinker's principal works and intellectual contributions. In most cases the work of a particular author is related to the cultural context in which he or she wrote and the ideas are seen to come out of and to lead into the ideas of other great seminal thinkers. The essay is followed by a Further Reading section that cites translations and studies relating to the subject of the essay.

As an aid to appreciating the development of Eastern thought, the essays are arranged chronologically (insofar as temporal order can be determined or, in some cases, guessed at). Although few readers will begin at page one and proceed to the index at the end of the book, anyone who did so would see the development of Eastern thought as a great creative growth, beginning hundreds of years before the Christian era and coming into modern times.

The staff of forty-one scholars was drawn from leading colleges and universities in the United States and abroad, and they come from departments of philosophy, religion, Asian studies, theology, literature, foreign languages, humanities, political science, and history. Most of them are published authors in the areas of their specialties.

This book is a companion volume to *Great Thinkers of the Western World*, edited by Ian P. McGreal, and published by HarperCollins in the fall of 1992. Together the *Western* and *Eastern* volumes constitute an authoritative guide to the world's great philosophers and to the philosophical and religious classics.

The Western intellectual tradition has been most successful in its study and use of scientific and pragmatic thinking, but for centuries it preoccupied itself excessively with theological and metaphysical speculations (unfortunately with little or no empirical or logical warrant), and it repeatedly made intuitive and logical attempts (in my opinion, bound to be unsuccessful) to discover the foundations of ethics. However, with all its faults, the Western philosophical tradition has been helpful in illuminating the relations between the uses of language and the world in which we presume to find ourselves; it has often been demanding in its examination of the pretenders to wisdom; and it has valiantly defended the systematic search for knowledge, the exercise of benevolence, and the ideal of moderation in the pursuit of happiness.

The Eastern tradition is refreshing in that it is predominantly and forthrightly ethical without purporting to prove what is a matter of commitment and tested cultural practice, and its fundamental message—often appropriately expressed in poetic language—is that one will manage best in this life if one disciplines oneself to go with the *Dao* (*Tao*), that is, to be in harmony with the universe as it is and, accordingly, in harmony with one's fellow human beings.

Of course, to more fully appreciate the depth and

worth of the philosophical literature of the Eastern world, one must actually *read*, at least in translation, the Eastern classics and great modern works. We hope that this book will encourage interested readers, if they have not already done so, to venture out and explore for themselves the intriguing literature of the Eastern mind and spirit.

In the Chinese section we have used both Pinyin (the current system of romanization of the Chinese language) and, in parentheses afterwards whenever a term or name is first used in an essay, the Wade–Giles version. A few names of the great philosophical masters have been latinized—such as Confucius and Mencius—and in such cases we give not only that familiar form but also the Pinyin and the Wade–Giles. (Most published books about the Eastern philosophers—and, accordingly, most library catalogs—use the Wade–Giles method, but newspapers, contemporary books, and contemporary encyclopedias are now employing the Pinyin.)

Most of the essays on Indian, Japanese, Korean, and Islamic thinkers and classics involve the use of diacritical marks (bars, dots, and so forth) to indicate the principal phonetic values for terms and proper names in those languages. For the Indian section we have used a simplified system of romanization of the Sanskrit and Pali terms, as illustrated by the very valuable *Sources of Indian Tradition*, edited by Ainslie T. Embree (Vol. 1) and Stephen Hay (Vol. 2), published by the Columbia University Press, 1988. The Japanese, Korean, and Islamic sections employ diacritical marks as indicated by the authors of the articles, although sometimes reverting to unaccented terms and names once the full notation has been given. Because of space limitations, we have not attempted to explain the use of the marks, but librarians or scholars in Asian studies can help the inquirer to find relevant information about the various systems.

An attempt to standardize the romanization of names and terms from the various languages involved in this book was seriously considered, but two major considerations counted against the making of any such effort. The first consideration is that for each of the several languages involved there are

a number of systems of romanization, some preferred by some scholars, some others preferred by others—and sometimes the loyalty to a system results in a resistance to the changes that would be required by standardization. And then there is the further consideration that some scholars like to use a full-blown system of romanization, others like a simpler system. Some are unhappy if diacriticals are not used; others are disturbed if diacriticals are used at all in a book for the general reader who has no knowledge of the languages and no inclination to pronounce the words. Some like to use diacriticals throughout an article; others like to use the diacriticals for a term once and then proceed to use the name or term free of its markings. As editor, I have attempted to give the contributors free rein and yet to insure consistency within the articles themselves.

A few remarks about the order of the names of the Eastern thinkers. In Chinese the family name (surname) comes *first*, as in the Chinese name Kong Fuzi (Pinyin), K'ung Fu-tzu (Wade–Giles), or Confucius (familiar latinized form): the family name was Kong (K'ung). When referring to the Chinese thinkers, usually more than the family name is used; we do not refer to Confucius as simply Kong (K'ung). However, there are exceptions, of course, as with Mao Zedong (Mao Tsetung), often referred to as simply "Mao," but this is a twentieth-century tendency. Incidentally, the *zi* (*tzu*) element in a proper name, as in Laozi (Lao Tzu), Mozi (Mo Tzu), and Mencius (Mengzi/Meng Tzu) is an honorific term, often translated as "Master"; hence, Master Lao, Master Mo, and Master Meng—and, of course, for Confucius, Master Kong (K'ung). (A further complication is that Chinese proper names sometimes include not only family names and personal names, but also newly adopted names, official names, honorific names, and posthumous names, but we will not elaborate on these practices.)

The practice in the use of Japanese names is like the Chinese: the surname comes first. But there is also the tradition among scholars (not universally followed) of using the personal name of a Japanese thinker in discussing his or her work, and this is sometimes a cause of confusion for those unfamiliar with the tradition.

As to the selection of thinkers and works discussed in this book: we do not presume that this list of great Eastern thinkers is the definitive and final word. We have attempted to focus on the philosophers about whose greatness there is no question, but to represent the various lines of thought and faith exhibited in the countries concerned, we have included some thinkers who are little known to the general public but who, for one reason or another, deserve to be included. Each is worthy of attention and further study.

Of course, it is inevitable that some philosophers regarded by some scholars and critics as clearly being of more importance than those included have been left out; this omission may be deliberate, since judgments of worth differ, but it may be inadvertent because of the difficulty of composing balanced lists that fairly represent the diversity of thought within the various cultures with which we are concerned. Independent study of the thinkers discussed here will surely lead the interested lay reader to discover other thinkers not included in this book, of equal or even greater value to the reader.

The distinguished faculty, independent scholars, and editors contributing to this book have been generously cooperative throughout the laborious process of putting it together; they have worked with me in composing and revising the lists of thinkers to be included; they have been conscientious in their research and the writing of the essays, and they have all served informally as insightful consultants whenever I have queried them. I thank them for their excellent work, and I hope they will be proud of the final product of our joint efforts.

I am especially grateful for the generous assistance I have received, especially with regard to linguistic matters, the selection of contents, and the building of a staff, from scholar contributors Mehdi Aminrazavi, Charles E. Butterworth, Narayan Champawat, Bina Gupta, Ruben Habito, Seyyed Vali Reza Nasr, James Sellmann, Michael Sells and Richard Shek.

Also, I want to thank those who helped me in the initial stages of the project by making suggestions about the list of thinkers and by recommending scholars to be invited to become contributors: Jonathan Spence of Yale University, James C. Dobbins of Oberlin College, David Pankenier of Lehigh University, Kenneth Inada of the University of Buffalo, Paul Groner of the University of Virginia, Roger T. Ames of the University of Hawaii and Editor of *Philosophy East & West,* Kwong-loi Shun of the University of California (Berkeley), Peter Nosco of the University of Southern California, John S. Major, Norman Girardot of Lehigh University, Jeffrey F. Meyer of the University of North Carolina at Charlotte, Benjamin E. Wallacker of the University of California (Davis), William Bodiford of the University of California (Los Angeles), Nicholas Heer of the University of Washington (Seattle), and James D. Redington of Georgetown University. (Although these scholars should be given credit, at least in part, for whatever strengths this book finally developed, they should not, of course, be blamed for its omissions and deficiencies.)

Finally, I want to express my appreciation for the technical help given me by my son Colin McGreal, who managed to convert computer disks of a size and language foreign to my computer into disks with which my computer and I felt comfortable.

Ian P. McGreal

ACKNOWLEDGMENTS

Hundreds of reference books, source books, and texts were used, some of them extensively and repeatedly, in the preparation of *Great Thinkers of the Eastern World*. Without the availability of those books, this latest addition to the literature of Eastern thought would have been, if not impossible, at least inadvisable. We take this opportunity to acknowledge with respectful appreciation the use of the books mentioned in the *Further Reading* sections at the end of the articles on the individual thinkers or classics.

Among those books there are several that have been especially helpful, not only to the contributors, but especially to the editor. The tasks of composing the list of thinkers to be discussed, attempting to resolve disputes occasioned by conflicting data, verifying factual information, considering alternative translations and interpretations of work written and published in other languages, and becoming more familiar with the world of Eastern thought were all facilitated and made possible by recourse to the following outstanding reference works:

A Guide to Oriental Classics, 3rd edition. Edited by Wm. Theodore de Bary, Ainslie Embree, Amy Vladeck Heinrich. New York: Columbia University Press, 1989.

A Source Book in Chinese Philosophy. Translated and compiled by Wing-tsit Chan. Princeton, N.J.: Princeton University Press, 1963, 1969, 1972.

Sources of Chinese Tradition. Introduction to Oriental Civilizations (Wm. Theodore de Bary, series editor.) Compiled by Wm. Theodore de Bary, Wing-tsit Chan, and Burton Watson. With contributions by Yi-pao Mei, Leon Hurvitz, T'ung-tsu Ch'u, Chester Tan, and John Meskill. New York: Columbia University Press, 1960.

A History of Chinese Literature. Herbert A. Giles. With a supplement on the modern period by Liu Wu-chi. New York: Frederick Ungar Publishing Co., 1901, 1967.

Sources of Indian Tradition, 2nd ed. Introduction to Oriental Civilizations (Wm. Theodore de Bary, series editor.) Volume 1: *From the Beginning to 1800,* edited and revised by Ainslie T. Embree (1st edition edited by Wm. Theodore de Bary with A. L. Basham, R. N. Dandekar, Peter Hardy, J. B. Harrison, V. Raghavan, Royal Weiler, and Andrew Yarrow). New York: Columbia University Press, 1988. Volume 2: *Modern India and Pakistan,* edited and revised by Stephen Hay (first edition edited by Wm. Theodore de Bary with Stephen Hay and J. H. Qureshi). New York: Columbia University Press, 1988.

A Source Book in Indian Philosophy. Edited by Sarvepalli Radhakrishnan and Charles A. Moore. Princeton, N.J.: Princeton University Press, 1957.

Sources of Japanese Tradition. Introduction to Oriental Civilizations (Wm. Theodore de Bary, series editor.) Volume 1. Compiled by Ryusaku Tsunoda, Wm. Theodore de Bary, and Donald Keene. New York: Columbia University Press, 1958, 1964.

The Rise of Neo-Confucianism in Korea. Edited by Wm. Theodore de Bary and JaHyun Kim Haboush. New York: Columbia University Press, 1985.

Islamic Life and Thought. Seyyed Hossein Nasr. Albany, N.Y.: State University of New York Press, 1981.

In addition, as noted in a remark following the article "Huineng (Hui-neng)" by Ian P. McGreal, we acknowledge our gratitude to Frank N. Magill and Salem Press for permission to use the article (now slightly revised) that appeared first in *World Philosophy* (5 vols., edited by Frank N. Magill, with Ian P. McGreal, Associate Editor. Englewood Cliffs, N.J.: Salem Press, 1961, 1982), and ap-

peared subsequently in *Masterpieces of World Philosophy* (edited by Frank N. Magill. New York: HarperCollins Publishers, 1990), a one-volume edition abstracted from *World Philosophy*.

CONTRIBUTORS

Mehdi Aminrazavi (*Ph.D., Temple University*). Assistant Professor, Department of Philosophy and Religion, Mary Washington College, Fredericksburg, Virginia.

Nandi Bhatia (*Ph.D., Panjab University*). Program in Comparative Literature, University of Texas, Austin, Texas.

Purnima Bose (*Ph.D., University of Texas*). Assistant Professor, Department of English, Indiana University, Bloomington, Indiana.

Charles E. Butterworth (*Ph.D., University of Chicago*). Professor, Department of Government and Politics, University of Maryland, College Park, Maryland.

Narayan Champawat (*Ph.D., University of California, Los Angeles*). Professor Emeritus, Department of Philosophy, California State University, Northridge, California.

Christopher Key Chapple (*Ph.D., Fordham University*). Professor, Department of Theology, Loyola Marymount University, Los Angeles, California.

Ann-Ping Chin (*Ph.D., Columbia University*). Assistant Professor, Department of Religion, Wesleyan University, Middletown, Connecticut.

William E. Deal (*Ph.D., Harvard University*). Assistant Professor, Department of Religion, Case Western Reserve University, Cleveland, Ohio.

Stephen L. Field (*Ph.D., University of Texas at Austin*). Associate Professor, Department of Modern Languages and Literatures, Trinity University, San Antonio, Texas.

Alan Fox (*Ph.D., Temple University*). Department of Philosophy, University of Delaware, Newark, Delaware.

James L. Fredericks (*Ph.D., University of Chicago*). Assistant Professor, Department of Theological Studies, Loyola Marymount University, Los Angeles, California.

Bina Gupta (*Ph.D., Southern Illinois University*). Professor of Philosophy and Director, South Asia Language and Area Center, University of Missouri, Columbia, Missouri.

Ruben L. F. Habito (*Doctor of Letters Certificate, University of Tokyo*). Professor, Perkins School of Theology, Southern Methodist University, Dallas, Texas.

Steven Heine (*Ph.D., Temple University*). Associate Professor, Religious Studies Program, Pennsylvania State University, University Park, Pennsylvania.

Marcia K. Hermansen (*Ph.D., University of Chicago*). Professor, Department of Religious Studies, San Diego State University, San Diego, California.

Dennis Hirota. Author and editor; head translator, Shin Buddhism Translation Series, Hongwanji International Center, Kyoto, Japan.

Lawrence F. Hundersmarck (*Ph.D., Fordham University*). Professor, Department of Philosophy and Religious Studies, Pace University, White Plains, New York.

Jong Myung Kim (*Ph.D., University of California, Los Angeles*). Department of East Asian Languages and Cultures, University of California, Los Angeles, California.

Russell Kirkland (*Ph.D., Indiana University*). Assistant Professor, Department of Religion, University of Georgia, Athens, Georgia.

Kwang-Sae Lee (*Ph.D., Yale University*). Professor, Department of Philosophy, Kent State University, Kent, Ohio.

Win-chiat Lee (*Ph.D., Princeton University*). Associate Professor, Department of Philosophy, Wake Forest University, Winston-Salem, North Carolina.

Chenyang Li (*Ph.D., University of Connecticut*). Assistant Professor, Department of Philosophy and Religious Studies, Monmouth College, Monmouth, Illinois.

Dan Lusthaus (*Ph.D., Temple University*). Assistant Professor, Department of Philosophy and Religion, Bates College, Lewiston, Maine.

Soho Machida (*Ph.D., University of Pennsylvania*). Assistant Professor, East Asian Studies, Princeton University, Princeton, New Jersey.

Ian P. McGreal (*Ph.D., Brown University*). Professor of Philosophy Emeritus, California State University, Sacramento, California.

Robert E. Morrell (*Ph.D., Stanford University*). Professor, Department of Asian and Near Eastern Languages and Literatures, Washington University in St. Louis, St. Louis, Missouri.

Paul Mundschenk (*Ph.D., Claremont Graduate School*). Professor, Department of Philosophy and Religious Studies, Western Illinois University, Macomb, Illinois.

Randall L. Nadeau (*Ph.D., University of British Columbia*). Assistant Professor, Department of Religion, Trinity University, San Antonio, Texas.

Seyyed Vali Reza Nasr (*Ph.D., Massachusetts Institute of Technology*). Assistant Professor, Department of Political Science, University of San Diego, San Diego, California.

José Pereira (*Ph.D., University of Bombay*). Professor, Department of Theology, Fordham University, Bronx, New York.

Laurel Rasplica Rodd (*Ph.D., University of Michigan*). Associate Professor, Department of East Asian Languages and Literatures, University of Colorado, Boulder, Colorado.

James D. Sellmann (*Ph.D., University of Hawaii*). Assistant Professor, Division of Humanistic Studies, University of Guam, Mangilao, Guam.

Michael A. Sells (*Ph.D., University of Chicago*). Associate Professor, Department of Religion, Haverford College, Haverford, Pennsylvania.

Richard H. Shek (*Ph.D., University of California, Berkeley*). Professor, Department of Humanities, California State University, Sacramento, California.

Daniel P. Sheridan (*Ph.D., Fordham University*). Professor, Department of Religious Studies, Loyola University, New Orleans, Louisiana.

Jae-Ryong Shim (*Ph.D., Columbia University*). Professor, Department of Philosophy, Seoul National University, Seoul, Korea.

George J. Tanabe, Jr. (*Ph.D., Columbia University*). Professor, Department of Religion, University of Hawaii, Honolulu, Hawaii.

S. A. Thornton (*Ph.D., University of Cambridge*). Assistant Professor, Department of History, Arizona State University, Tempe, Arizona.

Mary Evelyn Tucker (*Ph.D., Columbia University*). Associate Professor, Department of Religion, Bucknell University, Lewisburg, Pennsylvania.

Paul Varley (*Ph.D., Columbia University*). Professor, Department of History, University of Hawaii, Honolulu, Hawaii.

Joseph S. Wu (*Ph.D., Southern Illinois University*). Professor, Department of Philosophy, California State University, Sacramento, California.

CHINA

CONFUCIUS (KONGFUZI/K'UNG FU-TZU)

Born: 551 B.C., in the State of Lu, now Shandong (Shantung) Province, China
Died: 479 B.C., in the State of Lu
Major Works: Many classics were attributed to the editorship of Confucius, yet most scholars agree that the only work that can represent the ideas of Confucius is the *Analects* (*Lunyu/Lun-yü*), a collection of notes and quotations written down by his disciples and edited after his death.

Major Ideas

Ren (jen) *or human-heartedness is the highest virtue an individual can attain and this is the ultimate goal of education.*

The path to the attainment of ren *is the practice of* li, *which represents social norms.*

Li *is not something fixed and forever, and is subject to change according to individual situations.*

The principle governing the adoption of li *is* yi, *which means proper character and is a principle of rationality.*

The education of an individual is a preparation for a peacefully ordered society.

The supreme method for governing a nation is ruling people by ren, *the ruler being the model of all his people.*

To govern a society which is out of order, the method of "rectification of names" has to be used; this method can be called "the enforcement of li."

Confucius (Kongfuzi or Kongzi/K'ung Fu-tzu), "Master K'ung," stands out as the most significant figure in Chinese history. His family name is Kong (K'ung), and his given name, Qiu (Ch'iu). His early years were rather uneventful and ordinary. His father died when he was only three. As a result, he was raised by his mother and had to experience poverty and hardship. However, when he was fifteen, he set his mind to becoming a scholar. When he got married he embarked on an official career with the hope of putting his ideas into practice. He was appointed the chief of police in the Department of Justice of Lu. After a short period of time he resigned from this position and devoted himself to teaching.

Accompanied by some of his students, Confucius spent a number of years traveling throughout China, hoping to share his ideas with the local rulers who might hire him and implement his political ideas. However, he was rejected by one after another. Eventually, he gave up hopes of getting a desirable political post and returned to the State of Lu and resigned himself to the position of an edu-cator and teacher. He also spent the remaining years of his life editing what have come to be known as the "Confucian Classics," including such books as *The Book of Poetry*, *The Book of History*, and the *Yi jing* (*I ching*) (*The Book of Changes*).

Although Confucius failed in his pursuit of a political career, his career as an educator and teacher was a tremendous success. People were impressed by his integrity, honesty, and particularly his pleasant personality and his enthusiasm as a teacher. Three thousand people came to study under him and over seventy became well-established scholars. His followers, one generation after another, spread his ideas throughout the country of China. Eventually his ideas won the approval as national ideology in the second century A.D. during the Han dynasty. He became honored as "The Ultimate Sage–Teacher." His philosophic ideas have been taught to not only all traditionally educated Chinese, but also to students in other Asian countries such as Japan, Korea, and Singapore.

The Primacy of the Human Heart

In spite of the apparently fragmentary and aphoristic nature of the *Analects*, Confucius clearly indicated that his philosophic ideas were held together by one single concept. This key concept in Confucius's philosophy is what is called *ren* (*jen*) in Chinese. The term appears in the *Analects* over 100 times. Its etymological meanings and English translations have been a topic of scholarly disputes, yet from the *Analects* we learn that the essence of this concept is love. When Fan Chi (Fan Ch'ih) asked about the meaning of *ren*, Confucius replied, "Love of man" (XII, 22). *Ren*, as love, is by no means the kind of impulsive, instinctive love glorified by the romantics. Nor is it the love of God or God's love for humanity. Nor did Confucius preach love for one's enemies. *Ren* is a strictly natural and humanistic love, based upon spontaneous feelings cultivated through education. Accordingly, *ren* may be defined as the cultivated feeling which marks the distinction between a human being and other forms of biological beings. If we follow this suggested definition, many other fundamental concepts in the philosophy of Confucius can adequately be understood. For example:

Xiao (*hsiao*) (filial piety) means the cultivated feeling toward one's parents.
Di (*ti*) (brotherly love or respect) means the cultivated feeling toward one's contemporaries.
Zhong (*chung*) (loyalty) means the cultivated feeling toward one's superiors, lords, emperors, employers, or one's own country.
Li (rituals, rites, proprieties) means the behavioral norms in terms of which one's cultivated feeling is expressed.
Yi (*i*) (righteousness or proper character) is the habitual practice of expressing one's cultivated feeling at the right times and in the right places.
Junzi (*chün-tzu*) (superior or perfect person) means the kind of person in whom cultivated feeling has attained maximum due development.

There is in the *Analects* a puzzling dialogue which most readers find difficult to understand.

After hearing that a man was called a "man of integrity" for being a witness in the court against his father who stole a sheep, Confucius sighed:

Men of integrity in my community are different. The father conceals for his son and the son for his father, therein integrity is found.

(XIII, 18)

Readers may question why Confucius appears to approve law violation and to encourage dishonesty. In this passage where the language is suggestive rather than assertive, Confucius merely disapproves calling the young man a "man of integrity"; he is not encouraging the concealment of crime. If a reader shares Confucius's central doctrine of "the primacy of the human heart," no such question would even be raised.

Professor Liang Sou-ming, a distinguished philosopher in modern China, in his masterpiece *Eastern and Western Civilizations and Their Philosophies* (1922, not translated into English) defines *ren* as intuition. In spite of the obscure, and perhaps misleading nature of the term "intuition," his definition is significantly illuminating because it suggests the immediacy, directness, and spontaneity of *ren*. *Ren* as intuition is a kind of moral insight that results from an ethical education and a life experience that provides a reliable evaluation of the scene of life. It is not an inborn intuition but one cultivated through the practice of *li*, the attainment of knowledge, and the development of the sense of *yi*.

Socialization and Self-Realization

A character disciplined by *ren* is the ideal in morality and the goal of education. How do we attain this goal? In the *Analects* Confucius provided a very clear answer: the transformational process leading to the realization of *ren* is the practice of *li* (XII, 1). The English translation of *li* has been "rites," "rituals," "proprieties," "ceremonies," "courtesy," "good manners," "politeness," and so on. In its broadest sense, the term includes all moral codes and social institutions. In its fundamental but narrow sense, it means socially acceptable forms of behavior. We are tempted to think that *li* is the product of social evolution or merely customs. However, in the philosophy of Confucius, *li* involves the deliberate devices used by the sages to educate people and maintain social order. This has been explained very clearly in the book of *Li ji* (*Li chi*), in which it becomes clear that *li* has a prescriptive and regulative function.

If the ultimate goal of *li* is to maintain a social and moral order, on what grounds can we say that the practice of *li* may lead to self-realization or the attainment of *ren*? Since *li* is a term for moral codes and social institutions, we are tempted to think that the practice of *li* is to enforce conformity with social norms at the cost of individuality. Here it has to be pointed out that, according to the philosophy of Confucius, an individual is not an isolated entity. Instead, an individual exists only in a set of relations with others. *Li* prescribes the norms of human relations. Apart from one's relations with other human beings, the concept of individuality has no meaning. Thus Confucius said, "In order to establish oneself, one has to establish others.—This is the way of a person of *ren*" (VI, 28). It would seem appropriate to say that, for Confucius, in order to be a fully developed individual, one has to go through the give-and-take process of socialization. Individualization and socialization are but two aspects of the same process. Therefore, the practice of *li* is the way to the realization of *ren*.

Perhaps a reference to Aristotle will help in clarifying Confucius's ideas. For Aristotle, a virtue is a habit or a disposition to act. So, the cultivation of virtues is the development of moral habits. Moral habits are in the forms of *li*, recognized, justified, or purposely devised by the sages. Since *ren* is the cardinal virtue, the development of moral habits through the practice of *li* is, no doubt, the means to the realization of *ren*. In other words, *li* and *ren* form a tight means–ends relation. If a personal character of *jen* is the ultimate goal in the ethical theory of Confucius, then the knowledge and practice of *li* is the path to human perfection. Finally, Confucius observed: "He who does not know *li*

cannot establish himself (attain self-realization)" (XX, 3).

A mistaken concept about *li* is that for Confucius, *li* is something permanent and fixed that cannot be changed at all. In the *Analects*, the textual evidence indicates that Confucius regarded *li* as changing through time and from situation to situation (II, 23; III, 14). It is also a mistake to interpret Confucius as valuing only the ancient *li*.

Confucius said:

> Zhou [Chou] could observe the two preceding dynasties. How exuberant its culture is! I prefer following Zhou [rather than its predecessors].
>
> (III, 14)

This quotation provides a ground for challenging the interpretation that Confucius simply advocated returning to antiquity. Change, for him, is something inevitable and necessary, and is taken as a basic fact. But the desirable form of change is gradual reform rather than violent disruption or unpredictable discontinuity. Abrupt change with unpredictable discontinuity seems beyond the historical process as conceived by Confucius.

Since there is not a single *li* for all relations and occasions, there must be a higher principle governing the adoption of *li*. This higher principle is called *yi*, which has been translated as "righteousness" or "proper character." Confucius never gave a definition to this concept, but he used this term for several times:

> A superior person's attitude toward the society is neither one of a conformist nor one of a rebel but one in accordance with *yi*.
>
> (IV, 10)

> The attainment of wealth and honor through the violation of *yi* is as remote from me as clouds floating in the sky.
>
> (VII, 15)

A superior person is conscious of, and receptive to *yi*, but a petty person is conscious of, and receptive to gains.

(IV, 16)

These examples may well suggest that *yi* is the principle of rationality or the principle of moral reason. The first quotation is clear and self-explanatory. The second and the third seem to suggest an opposition between the morally right and the practically profitable. But a careful reading of the *Analects* will reveal that Confucius did not mean to suggest such an opposition. Rather, he has suggested a principle of priority. *Yi* is morally prior to gains or profit. This means that any profit which is incompatible with *yi* has to be given up. In general, *yi* is a regulative principle governing the adoption of any pattern of behavior according to one's rationality and sense of values. As to whether *yi* is innate or acquired through education, Confucius never gives us a clear answer.

The Kingly Way and the Social Order

The first significant topic in the political philosophy of Confucius is concerned with the methodology of governing. Confucius seemed to have known very little about representative government involving a complex legislative body and effective law enforcement. From his viewpoint, to keep the society in order by legislation and law enforcement is but the very last resort. Even if it is technically possible to establish a comprehensive network of legality, to force people to follow legal procedures, for Confucius, is not the way of the sage–king. The sage–king governs the country without unnecessary complicated binding procedures. Instead, he "governs with morality, as if he were the Northern Star, staying in his position, surrounded by all other planets" (II, 1). This metaphorical statement suggests two points. First, a sage governs with morality instead of law or power. Secondly, a good ruler governs by setting up himself as a model, staying in his own position, being imitated by his subjects and people. Now, our important questions are: (1) What

does it mean by governing with morality? and (2) How is governing by model possible?

We should be reminded that the cardinal virtue of Confucian morality is *ren*, which essentially means love of people. Hence the politics of *ren* occupies the center of Confucius's theory of government. What is implied in the government of *ren* is the principle of nonviolence. In a government of nonviolence, capital punishment has very little place. When a ruler asked Confucius if it would be right to execute those who are evil, Confucius replied,

Why is there a need of capital punishment in your government? If you set your mind toward morality, your people will become moral. The character of the ruler is like the wind, and that of the people, grass. The grass bends when the wind blows upon it.

(XII, 19)

This short passage suggests two main points. First, the government of *ren* de-emphasizes severe punishment imposed upon the wrongdoer or the lawless. Secondly, the wind–grass metaphor suggests that the ruler who serves as a moral model for people will be more effective than one who rules by strict law enforcement. According to Confucius, the right method of governing is not by legislation and law enforcement, but by supervising the moral education of the people.

Moral education should start with the family. The cultivation of *ren* is first accomplished through the development of *xiao* (*hsiao*) (filial piety) and *di* (*ti*) (brotherly love and respect). Yuzi (Yu Tzu) once explained to Confucius that *xiao* and *di* constitute the foundation of *ren* (I, 2). As has been indicated, the cultivation of moral virtues is the process of socialization through the practice of *li*. *Li* occupies the foremost place in moral education which is, in turn, a step toward a good social order. In addition to emphasizing the importance of *li*, Confucius maintained that music and literature are also helpful in the development of one's moral education.

Now the question is, if the people ignore the model set up by the ruler and go beyond the boundaries of *li*, what is to be done then? Confucius resorts to a secondary choice—the method of *zhengming* (*cheng ming*), which is literally translated as "rectification of names." In its narrow sense, this doctrine is the enforcement of *yi* in the use of *li*. Consider music, for example: It would be absurd to use wedding music for a funeral, and it is wrong for a feudal lord to adopt music designed for the emperor's palace. In the broad sense, then, *zhengming* is not only the practice of putting things in order according to their "names," that is, their true natures, but also the enforcement of rationality in all institutional procedures and individual behavior of any kind. When the Duke of Chi asked Confucius about governing, Confucius replied: "Let the lord be the lord, the minister be a minister, the father be a father, and the son be a son" (XIII, 11). This is a very pointed but concise interpretation of this doctrine by Confucius himself. In the negative sense, *zhengming* suggests that one should not be performing the duties (or claiming the rights) which are not his or hers. "When one is not holding a position in the government," explained Confucius, "one is not entitled to participate in governmental administration" (VIII, 14).

Zhengming, however, is an urgent matter only when society is out of order. In an ideal state, names are already rectified, and there is no need for further rectification. "If the society were not out of order, I would not bother to reform it" (XVIII, 6). This is a very sincere confession from Confucius. *Zhengming* becomes an urgent policy only when an ideal government is not realized.

What is the ideal government for Confucius? The ideal government for him is a government of *wuwei* (*wu-wei*) (non-action). But how is a government of non-action possible? The answer is, it is possible through the solid groundwork of moral education. Without the groundwork of morals, no matter how hard the government works to remedy the deficiency, there would still be violence and disorder. The reason is given by Confucius in the following:

If you lead the people with political force and restrict them with law and punishment, they can just avoid law violation, but will have no sense of honor and shame. If you lead them with morality and guide them with *li*, they will develop a sense of honor and shame, and will do good of their own accord.

(II, 3)

This is also a doctrine of appealing to the human heart, the moral nature of the human being. When individuals have attained the full development of *ren*, an ideal society, a society free from crimes, disturbances, and violence, will naturally be realized. This is why the book of *Da xue* (*Ta hsüeh*), *The Great Learning*, says:

When the personal life is cultivated, the family will be regulated; when the family is regulated, the state will be in order; and when the state is in order, there will be peace throughout the world. From the Son of Heaven down to the common people, all must regard cultivation of the personal life as the root or foundation.

This passage sums up an important thesis in the political philosophy of Confucius: Self-realization is a step toward world peace. A peaceful world is the ultimate goal of Confucianism. It is also the sublime ideal of the Chinese cultural tradition, in spite of the fact that there have been wars most of the time throughout the dynasties.

JOSEPH S. WU

Further Reading

Translations

Lau, D. C., ed. and trans. *Analects*. Middlesex, England: Penguin Books, 1979. A very scholarly and accurate translation.

Lin Yutang, ed. and trans. *The Wisdom of Confucius*. New York: Random House, 1938. An excellent anthology of Confucian classics, including Lin Yutang's own translation of the *Analects*.

Waley, Arthur, ed. and trans. *The Analects of Confucius*. London: George Allen & Unwin, 1938. Beautiful translation with literary qualities.

Related Studies

Chan, Wing-tsit, trans. and comp. *A Source Book in Chinese Philosophy*. Princeton, N.J.: Princeton University Press, 1963. This is a splendid source book containing not only generous selections but also very useful historical and critical information; chapter 2 contains an extensive selection from the *Analects*. Professor Chan's contribution to Chinese philosophy in the English-speaking world is well known and appreciated by scholars and laypersons alike.

Chan, Wing-tsit, trans. and comp. "The Evolution of the Confucian Concept of Jen," in *Philosophy East and West*, Vol. IV, No. 4, January 1955, pp. 295–319. The most extensive and scholarly study of the concept of *ren*, the leading idea in the *Analects* and in the Confucian tradition.

Creel, H. G. *Confucius and the Chinese Way*. New York: Harper & Row Publishers, 1960. An extensive study of Confucius by an historian exhibiting top-level scholarship.

Fang, Thome H. *Chinese Philosophy: Its Spirit and Its Development*. Taipei: Linking Publishing Co., Ltd., 1981. An insightful and penetrating interpretation of the Chinese philosophic tradition by a very talented contemporary Chinese philosopher thoroughly educated in Western philosophy.

Fingarette, Herbert. *Confucius—The Secular as Sacred*. New York: Harper & Row Publishers, 1972. Professor Fingarette, a scholar in philosophy of law rather than a specialist in Chinese philosophy, has provided a sophisticated reconstruction of Confucius's philosophy through a concept of *li* that appears very close to the concept of law in Western civilization.

Fung, Yu-lan. *A History of Chinese Philosophy*. Translated by Derk Bodde. 2 vols. Princeton, N.J.: Princeton University Press, 1952–1953. The ideas of the *Analects* in general and the concept of *ren* in particular are clearly presented in the relevant chapter of this scholarly work. Excellent for a beginning reader.

Wu, Joseph. *Clarification and Enlightenment: Essays in Comparative Philosophy*. Washington, D.C.: University Press of America, 1978. Several essays are very helpful in clarifying the central issues of the *Analects*, particularly the following two: "The Son Being Witness Against the Father—A Paradox in the Confucian Analects" and "A Critique of the Maoist Critique of Confucius—A Clarification of *ke chi fu li*."

LAOZI (LAO TZU)

Born: c. sixth century B.C., Juren, in the State of Chu (Ch'u), China
Died: According to some traditions Laozi is immortal and never died. According to other traditions, he left China and the place and time of his death are unknown. According to still other traditions, he died of old age and was buried in China.
Major Work: *Daode jing* (*Tao Te Ching*) (*Classic of the Way and Its Power*)

Major Ideas

Everything in the universe follows certain patterns and processes that escape precise definition; imprecisely this is called Dao (Tao), *the "Way."*

De (Te) (power or virtue) *cannot be strived for, but emerges naturally.*

The best "Way" to act or think is wuwei (wu-wei) (*effortless activity*).

Rather than develop sophistication, erudition, or cunning, one should return to the "uncarved block" or "return to infancy."

All opposites are inseparable, complementary, and mutually supplant each other, including life and death. Life is "softness" and flexibility; death is rigidity and inflexibility.

The most efficient and effective "Way" to overcome problems or adversity is by non-contention or yielding, which is not submission or capitulation, but exercising control by taking the "Way" of least resistance.

Normative and prescriptive ethical and moral systems—such as Confucianism—are symptomatic of basic problems to which they contribute rather than solve.

Although in the West the name Laozi (Lao Tzu) is mainly associated with the text *Daode jing* (*Tao Te Ching*) (sometimes called the *Laozi/Lao Tzu* after its presumed author), the Chinese have long considered Laozi in many other roles as well. Of the many legends that surround him—that he is an immortal, a divine being, author of many books, Buddha's teacher in India—his status as author of the *Daode jing* is both the earliest and most important. Western and Asian scholars have questioned whether the *Daode jing* was in fact authored by one person, whether the text is as old as assigning it to Laozi would require, and even whether Laozi is an historical person at all. Since none of the arguments so far advanced by skeptical scholars are as compelling as their advocates presume, this entry will treat Laozi as the author of the *Daode jing*, but some attention will also be given to his other roles.

Laozi Legends

According to both Daoist (Taoist) and Confucian traditions, Laozi was an elder contemporary of Confucius and the two of them met briefly on several occasions. Both traditions maintain that Confucius was deferential and a bit mystified by Laozi. What, if anything, they discussed has been shrouded in speculative legends. Zhuangzi (Chuang Tzu)—who cannot be taken as a reliable historical witness—claimed that Confucius sought out Laozi to ask questions about ritual (*li*), but that is very unlikely.

Laozi is said to have been born in the village of Juren in the ancient State of Chu (Ch'u). He held a minor post as archivist for the State of Zhou (Chou). Zhou was then in decline, but its former more glorious days were the model for Confucius's ideal state. At some point Laozi grew discontented and decided to leave China, traveling westward. At the frontier the border guard recognized him and refused to let him pass until he had committed his wisdom to writing. In the next two or three weeks Laozi produced the *Daode jing*, a slim volume of eighty-one short chapters consisting of a little over 5,000 Chinese characters. Handing the text over to the guard, he mounted his bull and disappeared westward. Pictures and statues of Laozi riding a bull are still very popular throughout East Asia.

Although all the details of the preceding paragraph have been questioned by scholars, they have been recounted for many centuries with consistency by the Chinese. Not so the details of his death. One popular tradition maintains that after Laozi left China he traveled to India where he instructed Siddhartha Gotama, whom he found sitting under the Bodhi tree; Gotama subsequently reached enlightenment and became the Buddha. A book popular in Daoist circles that in part records the teachings transmitted to Buddha, the *Huahujing* (*Huahu Ching*), attributed to Laozi, has been considered slanderous by Chinese Buddhists ever since it emerged around the third or fourth century A.D. This tradition frequently also asserts that Laozi discovered the secret of immortality and thus never died. He is said to still be wandering with other immortals, or dwelling in some celestial sphere. Perhaps in reaction to this, Zhuangzi describes Laozi's funeral as an event with many weeping mourners, something unseemly for a teacher who was supposed to have taught the non-duality of life and death. His hometown, today called Luyi, long ago constructed a tomb that still attracts visitors where both Laozi and his mother are said to be buried.

As the text *Daode jing* rose in importance, so did the person Laozi. He eventually came to be seen by Daoists as a cosmic, divine figure, connected both to the antediluvian Yellow Emperor (Huangdi/Huang-ti) and to their major deity, Taiyi (T'ai-i) ("Supreme Unity"). In some Daoist circles, the *Daode jing* itself came to be seen as a divine document brought down from the celestial realms millennia before the "historical" Laozi lived.

Interpreting the **Daode jing**

The *Daode jing* is often divided into two parts: part 1 (chapters 1–37) is called the "*Daojing* (*Tao ching*)" ("Classic on *Dao*"); part 2 (chapters 38–81) the "*Dejing* (*De ching*)" ("Classic on *De*"). The earliest extant manuscripts, discovered in a second-century B.C. tomb during the early 1970s, have the second part first, which was the way the Legalists (an ancient Chinese political–philosophical school

that held the *Daode jing* in high esteem) ordered the text. In other respects, despite some minor differences, these early manuscripts agree in large measure with our current versions of the text.

Despite its relative brevity for a Chinese text, it has become of the most important and influential writings ever to appear in China. Its terse, poetic style left it open to a variety of sometimes wildly conflicting interpretations. Thus a word of hermeneutic caution before discussing the text itself. It has been taken many different ways over the last two millennia by its Chinese interpreters, from a politically subversive document by Confucian detractors, to the ultimate metaphysical treatise, to a manual on Daoist Yoga practice, and so forth. At times, like an inkblot test, the interpretations reveal more about the assumptions the reader brought to the text than what the text seems to say.

A prime example of this is the first line of chapter 1, usually (incorrectly) rendered in English as "The *Dao* which can be spoken is not the true eternal *Dao*," which expresses the interpreter's notion of ineffability rather than Laozi's, since the line actually reads: "If a *Dao* can be *Dao*-ed, then it's not always *Dao*." The word *Dao* appears three times in this sentence. The first time its meaning is indeterminate; the second time ("can be *Dao*-ed") refers to *Dao* as an ongoing process; the third time ("always *Dao*" or "fixated *Dao*") refers to *Dao* as a fixed, constant thing. Basically Laozi is saying that the term *Dao* can, when used in a sentence, function either as a verb (process) or as a noun (thing), but not both at the same time. Thus linguistic usage compels us to bifurcate what initially is non-dual. This is reinforced later in the same chapter when he writes: "these pairs emerge together, yet are differently named." In other words, it is not that the *Dao* is ineffable, but rather that language itself always reveals the contrastive polarities of *Dao*'s movement, though if one only pays attention to the surface meaning that movement becomes hidden. The chapter never aims to encourage the reader to pick sides between a speakable *Dao* and an ineffable *Dao*. On the contrary, it and the following chapters strongly advise against reifying the products of dichotomous thinking. But attractive interpretations have a way of permanently infiltrating the main text, so reading the *Daode jing* requires vigilance if one does not want to be improperly swayed by erroneous interpretations.

Commentators

Of the many commentators on the *Daode jing*, three are worthy of note based on their influence on many generations of readers:

Wang Bi (Wang Pi) (A.D. 226–249) wrote during the "Pure Talk" period of Chinese philosophy, when Confucian scholars began to look outside their own tradition for inspiration. Wang Bi found it in the *Daode jing*, which he interpreted as a metaphysical treatise with ethical and political implications. He identified *Dao* with *wu*, the Cosmic Void from which all things emerge and to which they return, such that the essence of all things is this "Nothing." Unethical behaviors and motives should likewise be stripped down to "nothing." *Dao* was emblematic of the basic patterns of reality, which, if one acted in accordance with them, would guarantee one's success and virtue. Since he was at heart a Confucian with an unusual understanding of Laozi (he was the first to read line 1 of the *Daode jing* as a denigration of an "effable *Dao*"), his commentary was ignored until Neo-Confucians revived interest in him around the seventeenth century. Since most of the Chinese scholars in contact with the West over the last two centuries have been Neo-Confucian, Wang Bi's interpretation has strongly colored Western translations and interpretations.

Heshang gong (Ho-shang Kung) ("old man who lives on the river") (first–second century A.D.), like Laozi, has been questioned as an historical personage, and scholars are undecided when the commentary bearing his name was actually written. He interpreted the *Daode jing* as a Yoga manual filled with allusions to breathing exercises, visualizations, internal alchemic practices, and so on that, by developing one's body and mind, helped its readers become realized spiritual and ethical per-

sons. His commentary was by far the most popular and widely read by Daoists and others until the Neo-Confucians bestowed that honor on Wang Bi. Daoists, however, still prefer Heshang gong's commentary.

Hanshan Deqing (Han-shan Te-ch'ing) (1546–1623), a leading Buddhist monk during the Ming dynasty, spent fifteen years of his life carefully composing a commentary on the *Daode jing*, a text he obviously deeply admired and loved. Although Hanshan incorporated elements from Heshang gong's commentary as well as liberal citations from the *Zhuangzi*, he primarily read the *Daode jing* as a metapsychological treatise, identifying *Dao* with the One Mind frequently discussed in Chinese Buddhist literature. His commentary has remained the most popular amongst Buddhists in China, Korea, and Japan.

Throughout these and the other Chinese commentaries, Laozi's open-ended poetic phrases have been seen as containing ethical, political, epistemological, linguistic, psychological, and cosmological dimensions that have not always been clearly delineated. Commentators generally presume that the same sorts of patterns operate in each of these spheres, and they turn to Laozi for elucidation of these basic patterns.

Dao and De

In its most basic sense *Dao* means "the Way things do what they do." There is a Way to cook, a Way to fight, a Way to farm, a Way that water behaves, a Way to tie shoes, a Way that certain thoughts and actions produce effects in the world, and so on. When one "has the Way" to tie shoes, for instance, one can do so effortlessly and effectively. Once done, one forgets about it and moves on; one neither demands nor expects credit or blame, nor lingers on the moment of the act, basking in its glory. On the other hand, if one lacks the Way, one's efforts will prove ineffective and wearisome, perhaps even disastrous.

There are reasons, primordial reasons, for the Way things are:

Dao *produces one.*
One produces two.
Two produces three.
Three produces the ten thousand things.

(CHAPTER 42)

In classical Chinese, the expression "ten thousand things" means "everything," since in ancient times there were roughly 10,000 words, or "named" things. *Dao* is not the One of theosophic speculations. It is the indeterminate condition for there to be anything. Commentators have long disagreed over what the "one, two, and three" of this passage refer to, usually plugging in their favorite cosmological, cosmogonic, or metaphysical model. But probably Laozi intentionally left them open-ended in order to show the pattern by which things proliferate.

There is nowhere that this primordial pattern is not at play:

Something amorphous and consummate existed be-
fore Heaven and Earth.
Solitude! Vast! Standing alone, unaltering. Going
everywhere, yet unthreatened.
It can be considered the Mother of the World.
I don't know its name, so I designate it "Dao."
Compelled to consider it, name it "Great."

(CHAPTER 25)

Though *Dao* is indistinct and undefinable, Laozi describes it in various ways. It can be detected in the dialectical back-and-forth at play everywhere. The perpetual reversion of one contrary to its opposite (called *fan* in Chinese) is "the movement of *Dao*. Softly-yielding is the activity of *Dao*" (chapter 40). Because *Dao* is at play in everything, it cannot be reduced to anything determinate, nor does Laozi insist that one see *Dao* his way.

Laozi knows that even if his readers resonate to his message, heeding its implications is another matter:

My words are very easy to understand, very easy
practice.

Yet no one is the World is able to understand or
practice them.

(CHAPTER 70)

Things do not always go the "Way" they should. Deviating from the natural patterns leads to danger and calamity:

When the world has Dao, *domesticated horses haul*
manure [in the farmlands to fertilize crops].
When the world lacks Dao, *war horses are bred*
around the cities.

(CHAPTER 46)

Yet, unlike the Western Deity who is envisioned as a Law-giver demanding obedience, *Dao* never dictates:

Dao *gives birth to others;* De *rears them; things*
shape them; circumstances complete them.
Therefore there are none among the ten thousand
things that doesn't revere Dao *or honor* De.
Dao *is revered and* De *is honored because they*
never dictate,
always letting [things] be themselves [ziran/tzu-
jan].

(CHAPTER 51)

Dao's unselfish generosity can be an example for people to emulate:

Great Dao . . . *clothes and feeds the ten thousand*
things, but makes no effort to control them.
It is always desireless. . . .
That the ten thousand things return to it even
though it makes no effort to control them, it can
be considered Great.
Since it never insists on its own greatness, therefore
it can accomplish its greatness.

(CHAPTER 34)

De, usually translated "virtue" or "power," is a thing's personal stock of *Dao*, or put another way, it is the natural potential or potency instilled within one. Used as a moral term by Confucians, for Laozi *De* signifies natural abilities that enable things to be their best. But *De* must actualize spontaneously, effortlessly—to endeavor to train or learn it by moralistic interventions will invariably produce consequences opposite to those desired.

Laozi's Critique of Confucianism

Confucianism promotes specific moral values and insists that learning and cultivating those values is the only way to make individuals and society truly human and harmonious. Chief among those values are *ren* (*jen*) (humankind-ness), *yi* (*i*) (appropriateness, or the balancing of the individual with the group), and *li* (social rules, rituals, and etiquette). A Confucian goal is to become a "person of *ren*." For Laozi such moral values and exhortations always prove self-defeating.

Laozi's critique of Confucianism occurs in various places in the *Daode jing*, but perhaps in its most devastating form in chapter 38: "The best *De* doesn't *De*," says Laozi, "therefore it has *De*." What Laozi means is that the best sort of *De* is not something that one deliberately and calculatingly does. It happens spontaneously, naturally. "Lower *De* doesn't lose *De*, therefore it has no *De*." If one always pursues a moral ideal rather than relinquishing it, one will never be moral, or at best, one might be called "lower *De*." As he says in chapter 3, "Holding ideals in high esteem makes the people contentious." Ideals require striving, ascending a valuative ladder; and the ladder has value only if some people are higher than others on it. Among the group that deems the ideal worthwhile there will inevitably be rivalry and competition for the higher berth, those above "looking down" on their fellow strivers. When people are contentious, harmony becomes endangered.

Chapter 38 says that "The best *De* is *wuwei* and without deliberate actions." *Wuwei* is impossible to translate accurately, and the common quietist term "non-action" by which it is frequently rendered does the notion of *wuwei* great violence. Laozi's full phrase, occurring several times in the *Daode jing*, is *wuwei er wu bu wei*, which means

"no action, yet nothing isn't done." *Wei* means not only to act, but also to consider or deem, to do something deliberately with effort. *Wu* is used in this phrase as a negational prefix; the point is not to desist from acting, but to do things effortlessly, without friction or contention, without the ulterior motives of gain or loss, praise or blame, reward or punishment. Putting such considerations aside, there is nothing one cannot do:

Lower De *considers others, and takes deliberate action.*
Higher ren *considers others, but takes no deliberate action.*
Higher yi *considers others, and takes deliberate action.*
Higher li *considers others, but when they don't respond or reciprocate, he rolls up his sleeves to force them [to comply].*

(CHAPTER 38)

Ren is innocuous because it is impotent; it does nothing despite its own intent that something ought to be done. *Yi*, according to Laozi, is equivalent to the "lower *De*" since it deliberately imposes itself on others. For Confucians, *ren* is a feeling of mutual, common humankind-ness between individuals. *Yi* delineates the type of roles incumbent on individuals in particular situations, such that those roles become conducive to the enactment of *ren*. *Li* encodes and fixates the rules that individuals must follow in order for *yi* to transpire appropriately. But Laozi argues that once ineffectual *ren* has degenerated into rules, the conditions for conflict, rebellion, and repression have emerged. By definition a rule is something that prescribes something while proscribing its converse. Moreover, a rule prescribes something that would not be natural otherwise—to prescribe what is natural is redundant. Since rules advise doing something unnatural, there will always be someone who will refuse to comply. For a rule to remain meaningful and not become an empty rule, compliance must be enforced. Although the Confucians justify their moral system by claiming that it provides the means for producing social harmony,

Laozi undermines their justification by showing that it actually produces just the opposite result: rebellion and repression.

Chapter 18 charges that moral values cannot cure social problems, they are merely symptoms that the problems are getting worse:

When the great Dao *is abandoned, then there is* ren
  and yi.
When smartness and erudition emerge, then there is
  great Dissimulation.
When family relations are not harmonious, then
  there is [insistence on] filial piety and kindness.
When a country becomes troubled and rebellious,
  then there is [talk about] the loyalty of ministers.

Rather than teach ideals that will be counterproductive in the end, Laozi proposes we give up *ren* and *yi*, erudition and moral inculcation. Confucianism considers "learning" moral values its top objective. Laozi responds: "Pursuing learning, every day more is acquired. Pursuing *Dao*, every day more is dropped."

The Emphasis on Yin

The terms *yin* and *yang*, considered to be fundamental Daoist concepts, occur only once in the *Daode jing* (chapter 42), but the ideas they encapsulate are in evidence throughout the text. Dividing everything in the world into polar complements, *yin* represents the dark, recessive, soft, feminine, low, contractive, centripedal, short, hollow, empty, and so forth, while *yang* represents the light, dominant, hard, masculine, high, expansive, centrifugal, long, full, solid. All things consist of varying proportions of these two polarities. For instance, a blackboard is *yin* because it is dark, and *yang* because it is hard. Nothing is ever purely one or the other; rather all things are in flux between one pole and its opposite. When *yin* reaches its extreme it reverts to *yang*; when *yang* reaches its extreme it reverts to *yin*. Thus when water (*yin*) is compressed (*yin*), it can become a hydraulic lift strong enough (*yang*) to lift an automobile. If someone exerts (*yang*) themselves for a long time (*yang*), they tire and weaken (*yin*).

For Laozi balance between the poles does not mean static parity, but a dynamic reversion that perpetually counterbalances all propensities toward one extreme or the other. Unfortunately the world tends to privilege the *yang* while ignoring or denigrating the *yin*. The *Daode jing* aims to rebalance things by emphasizing *yin* over *yang*. Feminine images are repeatedly given positions of honor (in chapters 1, 6, 42, 52, and others), and *yin* values are consistently promoted. When men want someone to comply with their will, they resort to force; but a woman only has to lie still to seduce a man (chapter 61). This is *wuwei*, not because it is inaction, but because it is effortless, effective action. Similarly, we tend to think that what makes things useful is their solidity, their concreteness. Laozi reminds us that a wheel's hub is "empty," a jar's usefulness lies in its openness to being filled, a room's usefulness derives from its open space as well its doors and windows; it is the "openness" or emptiness (*xu/hsü*) of things that gives them usefulness (chapter 11). Further, "the softest thing overcomes the hardest" (chapters 43, 78), just as the Grand Canyon was carved out of hard rock by soft water. East Asian martial arts, from judo to Mao Zedong's (Mao Tse-tung) military strategy, have recognized and implemented this principle.

The emphasis on *yin* aims at more than a theory of physics or mechanics:

Human beings are born soft and flexible; when they
  die they are hard and stiff. . . .
Plants arise soft and delicate; when they die they
  are withered and dry.
Thus, the hard and stiff are disciples of death; the
  soft and flexible are disciples of life.
Thus an inflexible army is not victorious; an un-
  bending tree will break.
The stiff and big will be lowered; the soft and
  flexible will rise.

(CHAPTER 76)

Yin and *yang* perpetually displace each other; life and death subsist on each other. Seeds return to their roots, summer returns to winter, but from death (*yin*) life perpetually springs up anew. Recognizing that cycle is enlightenment; ignoring it leads to disaster (chapter 16).

Laozi argues that while at birth a child is soft (*yin*), infants can cry all day and never grow hoarse (a *yang* power); though their bones are soft and pliable, their grip is powerful. As human beings grow and learn, they become habituated and complicated, losing their openness and flexibility. Hence Laozi recommends that we "return to infancy" and become "uncarved blocks." Uncarved blocks are capable of becoming anything; once they're carved, their options have been foreclosed. Returning to open possibilities is empowering *De*. Nothing is deeper or more effective than simplicity.

DAN LUSTHAUS

Further Reading

Translations

Feng, Gia Fu, and Jane English, trans. *Lao Tsu: Tao Te Ching*. New York: Vintage, 1972. The large edition includes beautiful photos and the text evokes the open, suggestive atmosphere of the original Chinese. But avoid the smaller edition edited by Jacob Needleman; his preface and notes are inaccurate, and he has fatally tampered with the translation itself.

Henricks, Robert G., trans. *Lao-Tzu: Te-Tao Ching: A New Translation Based on the Recently Discovered Ma-wang-tui Texts*. New York: Ballantine, 1989. An excellent translation and study of the oldest extant manuscripts of Laozi, comparing them with the standard versions. Transcriptions of the Chinese texts included.

Waley, Arthur. *The Way and Its Power: A Study of the Tao Te Ching and Its Place in Chinese Thought*. New York: Evergreen, 1958. Though the author's translation tends toward paraphrase, Waley was the leading Sinologist of his generation and the accompanying essays were groundbreaking. This was the first work to overturn the Neo-Confucian hegemony on Laozi interpretation and still contains much that is not discussed elsewhere.

Related Studies

Chan, Alan K. L. *Two Visions of the Way: A Study of the Wang Pi and the Ho-shang Kung Commentaries on Lao-Tzu*. Albany, N.Y.: SUNY Press, 1991. Addresses historical, philological, and hermeneutic issues. Examines each commentary separately and then compares them.

Erkes, Eduard. *Ho-shang Kung's Commentary on Lao-tse*. Ascona, Switzerland: Artibus Asiae, 1958. The only English translation of Ho's *Commentary*, it is an idiosyncratic rendition, unfortunately long out of print.

Kaltenmark, Max. *Lao Tzu and Taoism*. Stanford, Calif.: Stanford University Press, 1969. The standard work on Laozi and the tradition that developed from him. Accessible and accurate.

Kohn, Livia. *Taoist Mystical Philosophy: The Scripture of Western Ascension*. Albany, N.Y.: SUNY Press, 1991. An in-depth study and translation of a fifth-century Daoist text representative of literature that treats Laozi as a divine being.

Rump, Ariane. *Commentary on the Lao Tzu by Wang Pi*. Honolulu, Hawaii: University of Hawaii Press, 1979. A translation and short study of one of the most important commentaries on the *Laozi*.

MOZI (MO TZU)

Born: c. 470 B.C., either in the State of Lu, now Shandong (Shantung) Province, or in the State of Song (Sung), now Henan (Honan) Province, China

Died: c. 391 B.C., place unknown

Major Work: *Mozi (Mo Tzu)*. This work was not composed by Mozi, but rather was the product of the Mohist tradition (c. 390–221 B.C.). It contains numerous sayings of Mozi, along with chapters on the later tradition's teaching on defensive warfare (chapters 51–79) and discourses on logical method (chapters 40–45).

Major Ideas

The cause of social disharmony is partiality, the absorption with personal needs or with those of one's own family or state.

Benevolence, the active willing of the good, ought to be directed to all persons.

To love everyone results in the greatest benefit to oneself and to others.

The Will of Heaven is the absolute norm for all humanity and this is the norm of universal love.

All in a hierarchical society derive their position through an identification with the superior.

Simplicity and frugality enhance the available goods for all in the community.

The ritualism and formalism of the Confucians are to be rejected.

Born just after the lifetime of Confucius (d. 479 B.C.) and a contemporary of Socrates (c. 470–399 B.C.), Mozi (or Mo Di/Mo Ti: "Ti" is his private name) attempted to teach the Chinese of his day a philosophy that had as its aim the enhancement of social relatedness. Living at the beginning of an era known as the Warring States period (c. 403–221 B.C.), Mozi's society experienced widespread disintegration, extreme violence, and the extensive exploitation of the many by the powerful few. Like Confucius before him, Mozi struggled to create a comprehensive program of personal and community renewal that aimed at building a unified, productive, and healthy society. What little is known of Mozi from ancient tradition indicates that he personally sought to embody the values of universal love and pacifism. At considerable risk to his person he traveled extensively to prevent conflicts between warring states. Like Confucius and Socrates, Mozi gathered disciples about him, thus giving rise to a Mohist movement that flourished for the next 170 years. This movement, which developed various techniques relating to military defense and logic, would eventually succumb to the dominance of Confucianism. Mohism produced a tradition of humanistic learning embodied in a collection of writings known as *Mozi (Mo Tzu) (The Works of Mozi)*, a work of fifteen books divided into fifty-three chapters. Sinologists have argued that the fundamental teachings of Mozi himself are found in books 2 through 9. It is these sections which contain the founder's views on the utility of universal love, the Will of Heaven, the nature of society, the value of austerity, and his differences with Confucianism.

Universal Love and Its Utility

The social crisis of his times, according to Mozi, stems from selfishness, or what he calls partiality. When the ruler of one state thinks only of gaining advantage over the ruler of another state, or when one family seeks its own ends over all other families, the resulting narcissistic self-preoccupation generates a disease of partiality that destroys society. It is only when partiality is replaced by universality that humankind will know peace. Only when everyone regards any other as another self will all be secure.

The heart of Mozi's teaching is benevolence, an

active willing of the good for others. The impulse to seek the good for one's own parents or children ought to be extended to all parents and all children. The natural identification with one's own community ought to be expanded to other cities and states. Mozi thinks of this benevolence as universal and affirms that when persons fall back into partiality, love is destroyed. According to his philosophy, failure to love all is a failure to love altogether. The love he calls for is to be offered to all equally and with the same degree of intensity.

Throughout the *Mozi*, love (*ai*) and benefit (*li*) are used correlatively because love results in a benefit to others and to oneself. The ruler who seeks the good for all the people will be loved in return. The benefit to the whole community will be peace and harmony. War is rooted in partiality and leads only to general destruction. In universal love, the many will enjoy the fruits of increased fertility and economic reward. Indeed, Mozi argues that few states benefit from aggression compared with the evil and suffering they inflict on millions. Their actions are as condemnable as those of a physician who, having given the same drug to 10,000 people, finds that only 4 or 5 have been cured.

For Mozi the path of universal love offered the greatest happiness for all. Thus, when he was challenged with the claim that his teaching was too idealistic, his response called upon the skeptic to consider which person in the midst of a great conflagration would be of the most value: the one person fetching water to extinguish the fire, or the other still holding onto the fuel of partiality? For Mohism, the right act is what offers benefit, the wrong what generates harm. Human perfection lies in the good works done for others. In these ideas, Mohism foreshadows some elements of the later Western tradition of Utilitarianism, especially in that the good is identified with what is useful in promoting the well-being of persons.

The Will of Heaven

The loss of a unifying standard or norm greatly concerned Mozi. He saw in the society of his day multiple norms, often in conflict, promulgated by many diverse individuals who focused only on their own concerns. The loss of a universal standard by which judgments could be made was another manifestation of the bitter fruit of partiality. The moral standard, Mozi argued, ought to be compatible with the actions of the ancient sage–kings and consistent with the experiences of the common people. To be a valid standard, it must also produce great benefits for the people. The criteria of tradition, experience, and efficacy are all met by the standard of universal benevolence.

Accepting the traditional belief in the existence of Heaven (God), Mozi sought to articulate this divine as a personal will that embodies and actively manifests absolute magnanimity. Heaven listens to all who offer prayers and sacrifices. All good flows from Heaven, the source of all things. As the source of moral order, Heaven bestows all rewards and punishments. Therefore, the good person will obey the Will of Heaven by loving universally. Because of acts of love, the good are inevitably rewarded by Heaven, while those who persist in their partial, unfriendly, and hurtful ways experience calamities sent down from Heaven. Mozi was the first to make extensive use of Heaven's will to enhance the values of universal love. Human beings are called upon to reflect the essence of divine will. To mirror in one's actions the Will of Heaven and to do so out of gratitude for Heaven's gifts is the Mohist ideal.

The Nature of Society

Mozi thought that before the development of the state, human beings lived in a condition of disorder and conflict, a chaotic and violent world like that of animals. To achieve personal and group security, humanity banded together in an effort to establish a harmonious existence. Rejecting all fatalism, Mozi grounds the building of social relationships on the efforts of the human intellect to know the universal norm and the free will to carry it out.

Unity is achieved by the commitment of each to the whole. This unity in diversity is conceptualized in the *Mozi* in the traditional Chinese view of societal hierarchy, with each level of authority deriving its power from a higher level. The emperor (the son of Heaven) is the ultimate authority on earth, deriving his status from his superior, Heaven. All members of the society are related because, in the words of the title of one chapter of the *Mozi*, all "identify with one's superior." The superiors are to be like Heaven, rewarding and punishing as they move their subordinates toward universal love and the mutual sharing of goods. In this way, every level of society is to be in perfect accord with the good of the whole.

Mozi was also among the first thinkers in ancient China to advocate that positions of authority be held only by men of ability. He sought to encourage the development of intellectual and volitional qualities that would bring order to the community. In his view, the glorious past age of the sage–kings was a time when only the worthy and the capable held power. Authority should not be placed in the hands of those whose only qualifications for rule derived from their status as relatives of the powerful.

The Value of Austerity

Simplicity and frugality are advocated by Mozi. Clothing ought to be functional, not decorative, while food has value in its nourishment, not in its attractiveness to the taste. Home decorations ought to be kept at a minimum, for the purpose of a house is shelter. Elaborate funerals that publicly demonstrate the importance of the deceased and the level of affection of the bereaved are to be greatly simplified, with an eye to the purpose of the event, the burial of the remains. Mozi also thought of music as a waste of time and an unnecessary ornamentation. Music, including all the activities of entertainment and pleasure-seeking, distracts people from the more basic pursuits of economic and personal security. In Mozi's view, human effort that aims at the betterment of society does not extend to the products of culture. In the idealized past there was, he thought, little music but much good government, while in his own age the situation was exactly the reverse.

Austerity had a value for Mozi because he thought it reduced consumption and its driving source—greed. Extravagant luxury would soon exhaust the resources of society, resources that were needed to supply the legitimate needs of all. Private property was acceptable, but only if the need to acquire it were tempered by the benevolent impulse to share one's private resources with the less fortunate.

Contrast with Confucianism

Mozi's thought is similar to the Confucian ideals of benevolence (*ren/jen*), the Will of Heaven (*tian zhi/ t'ien chih*), and familial duties (*wu lun*). Both Confucians and Mohists sought to achieve social relatedness through the perfection of individuals in society. They differed, however, on the means by which this perfection could be achieved. Mozi repudiated the Confucian teaching and, as such, stands as the first great heretic of that tradition. Confucius considered the pursuit of music as the expression of a noble life, while Mozi saw it as an expression of vanity. The Confucian concerns with proper ritual (*li*), especially as it pertained to funerals, were criticized as being a waste of time and wealth. Indeed, Mohists thought them positively dangerous, for long mourning periods that forbade sexual relations prevented the building of society. Mozi also condemned the religious agnosticism of the Confucians and warned that their failure to know Heaven's Will doomed them to experience Divine wrath. Finally, the Confucian teaching about fate was thought by Mozi to be an invitation to resignation and passivity.

In response to these attacks, Mencius (Mengzi/ Meng Tzu) (c. 371–289 B.C.) led the Confucian apologetic against the Mohists by condemning their failure to recognize the unique status of one's own king or one's own father. Such a failure to make distinctions based on intimacy and loyalty would lead society to the level of beasts. Mencius charged the Mohists with denial of the special relationship owed to one's father, family, and ruler.

In this attack Mencius was reaffirming the Confucian ideal of love measured within the context of different types of relationships. Confucianism in rejection of Mohism affirmed that seeking the good is expressed within a sphere of personal self-interests and systems of particular loyalties, especially those of family members. If the Mohist doctrine of nondifferentiated love were embraced, the whole of the Confucian system would be undermined.

The rise of the Han dynasty (206 B.C.–A.D. 220) and its complete acceptance of the Confucian ideology spelled doom for Mohism. The lack of interest in culture and its expressions left many to see Mozi's teaching as too austere and the call to universal benevolence as too idealistic. Mozi eventually faded from the memory of the Chinese and we find that by 100 B.C. Sima Qian (Ssu-ma Ch'ien) in his *Records of the Grand Historian of China* (*Shiji/Shih Chi*) devoted only twenty-four words to Mozi.

It would remain for the modern world to rediscover the teachings of Mozi. The scholars of the Qing (Ch'ing) dynasty (A.D. 1644–1912) sought to reconstruct the primary texts, while some Western scholars were motivated to study Mohism because of its apparent similarities to Christianity. In contemporary China, Marxist scholarship is sympathetic to Mohism's repudiation of hereditary hierarchy and finds value in its attention to the promotion and enhancement of goods for the whole society. From the perspective of scholars who examine the history of ideas, Mozi's views emerge in many later philosophical and religious systems. In their original setting, these ideas were integrated and, as such, offered a comprehensive worldview powerful enough to rival Confucianism.

LAWRENCE F. HUNDERSMARCK

Further Reading

Translations

Forke, Alfred. *Me Ti des Sozialethikers und seiner Schüler philosophische Werke*. Berlin: Mitteilungen des Seminars für Orientalische Sprachen (Vols. 23–25), 1922. This is the only complete translation of the whole *Mozi* in any European language. Forke also offers a valuable introductory essay to the thought of Mozi, Mohism, and the manuscript traditions.

Graham, A. C. *Later Mohist Logic, Ethics and Science*. Hong Kong: The Chinese University Press, 1978. A translation of the Logic chapters with a very careful exegesis of Chinese terms.

Mei, Yi-Pao. *The Ethical and Political Works of Motse*. Westport, Conn.: Hyperion Press, 1973. First printed in 1929, this is the most extensive English translation. It offers all the chapters (with the exception of those on logic and defense) that relate to Mozi's thought.

Watson, Burton. *Basic Writings of Mo Tzu, Hsun Tzu, and Han Fei Tzu*. New York: Columbia University Press, 1967. The essentials of Mozi's teaching with a helpful index. Ignoring the synoptic nature of the text, Watson has chosen the single chapter that best illustrates a key idea.

Related Studies

Mei, Yi-Pao. *Motse: The Neglected Rival of Confucius*. Westport, Conn.: Hyperion Press, 1973. This is the most comprehensive overview of Mozi's thought in English. Mei's study divides the material into basic themes, making this an excellent introduction.

Rosemont, Henry, ed. "Studies in Classical Chinese Thought" in the *Journal of the American Academy of Religion* (Thematic Issue, Vol. 47). Chico, Calif.: Scholars Press, September 1979. The article by Robin D. S. Yates on "The Mohists on Warfare: Technology, Technique, and Justification" (pp. 550–603) offers a discussion of the later Mohist views on defensive warfare. This article also demonstrates the difficulties found in the extant chapters on military issues.

Rowley, H. H. *Submission in Suffering and Other Essays on Eastern Thought*. Cardiff, Wales: University of Wales Press, 1951. The last chapter in the book, "The Chinese Philosopher Mo Ti," offers a basic introduction to Mozi, while another chapter compares various Eastern and Western conceptions of the Golden Rule. Rowley, a famous Biblical scholar, argues for Mozi's personalistic theism.

Tseu, Augustinus, A. *The Moral Philosophy of Motzu*. Taiwan: Fu Jen Catholic University Press,

1965. This work sets Mohism in dialogue with English Utilitarianism, Chinese Communism, and Catholic Christianity. Although the author competently presents the main lines of Mozi's thought, the author's own Western philosophical presuppositions need to be recognized by the alert reader.

Yu-lan, Fung. *A History of Chinese Philosophy.* Translated by Derk Bodde. 2 vols. Princeton, N.J.: Princeton University Press, 1952. The first volume offers a short, clear introduction to Mozi and to the later Mohist School through the use of primary texts. Yu-lan's *History* is well-respected, and a reading of his chapters on Confucius and Mencius articulates the contrast between Mohism and Confucianism.

ZHUANGZI (CHUANG TZU)

Born: Fourth century B.C.
Died: Third century B.C.
Major Work: *Zhuangzi* (*Chuang Tzu*)

Major Ideas

Our experience of the world is relative to our perspective.

The world of our experience is constantly transforming.

Therefore we must be wary of our tendency to adopt fixed or dogmatic judgments, evaluations, and standards based on a narrow viewpoint, since this leads to conflict and frustration.

*Optimal experience involves freeing ourselves from slavish commitment to convention; this enables us to see clearly (*ming*) and act spontaneously and unobtrusively (*wuwei/wu-wei*).*

The ideal person is one who is perfectly well-adjusted in this way.

The "genuine person" precedes "genuine knowledge."

Language functions to convey meaning, and the meaning of language is relative to context.

Philosophical disputation, though sometimes stimulating, is a somewhat futile enterprise because "right" and "wrong" cannot be determined through argument.

Death is a natural part of life, one of its infinite transformations.

The first seven chapters of the *Zhuangzi* (*Chuang Tzu*), often called the "Inner Chapters," are generally attributed to Zhuang Zhou (Chuang Chou), who, according to legend, lived in what is now known as Henan (Honan) Province, China, from approximately 370–286 B.C. The rest of the text is often understood to contain fragments of material, some of which are sometimes attributed to the same author as the inner chapters, some of which are attributed to other authors.

The *Zhuangzi* is one of the two most famous primordial texts of what can be called "philosophical Daoism (Taoism)," although its influence is also felt in other traditions of Chinese thought. Its exact relationship to the other basic text, the *Laozi* (*Lao Tzu*), is unclear, though the two texts have a great deal in common. Some scholars have regarded the *Zhuangzi* as a commentary on the *Laozi*, and in some passages this might in fact be the case. But in general the *Zhuangzi* has its own philosophical agenda and is unique in many ways. For various reasons, including the *Zhuangzi*'s apparent reference to passages from the *Laozi* and the apparent literary sophistication of the former relative to the latter, it seems very likely that the *Laozi* in some

form or another predates the *Zhuangzi*. In terms of literary sophistication, the *Zhuangzi* is in a class by itself. In some ways it reinvents the Chinese literary language. It makes reference to dozens of stories, myths, and legends common at the time of its authorship, many of which have been lost to us. But the text reworks these stories, eliciting new meanings and significance from them. These references are sometimes rather obscure, which makes reading the text extremely difficult.

The text has exerted an extremely powerful influence on subsequent forms of Chinese philosophical thought. This is particularly true of Chan (Ch'an) (Zen) Buddhism and later Daoist thought.

Zhuang Zhou, the Author

The only information regarding the ostensible author of the text is suspiciously legendary in nature, and must be regarded as at least somewhat unreliable. However, according to the historian Sima Qian (Ssu-ma Ch'ien) (145–c. 86 B.C.), Zhuangzi's personal name was Zhou (Chou) and he lived from approximately 370–301 B.C. He is said to have come from the district of Meng, located in what is known today as Henan (Honan) Province. He served there as a minor official, eventually resigning his position to return to private life. According to this account, he refused an offer from King Wei of Chu (Ch'u) (r. 339–329 B.C.) to become Prime Minister.

Besides this account, there are many stories in the text which are of an ostensibly autobiographical nature. But the historicity of these stories must be regarded with some suspicion, partly because the work is primarily literary and philosophical and not historical in intent, and partly because much of the text is apparently the work of later authors who might easily have taken literary liberties with the facts.

Guo Xiang and the Text

The *Zhuangzi* was most often associated with, though subordinated to, the *Daode jing* for several hundred years, until the end of the Han dynasty (A.D. 220). At that point, the breakdown of political and cultural unity may have resulted in an increased interest in Zhuangzi's rejection of conventional values, his justification of withdrawal from involvement in and fulfillment of civic responsibility, and his emphasis on seeking alternative, more natural attitudes and lifestyles that facilitate "finding the fit" with the world as a whole.

The text reached its present form, more or less, through the efforts of its most influential editor and commentator, Guo Xiang (Kuo Hsiang, c. A.D. 300). It was likely Guo Xiang, who integrated materials from other sources, divided the book up into its present configuration of chapters, and assigned titles to the chapters. In fact, Guo Xiang's influence is so strong that some scholars sometimes find it difficult to distinguish between the thought of Zhuangzi and the thought of Guo Xiang.

Parts of the text spoof and satirize the more reputable and established philosophical traditions of its time, namely, the Confucians and the Mohists. Zhuangzi's basic attitude toward such philosophical disputation is that it is rather pointless and hairsplitting at best. It solves no problems conclusively, and merely leads to conflict and disagreement.

As we shall see, Zhuangzi's own approach can be described as perspectival, that is, the truth value of any claim is related to context or perspective, and must always be carefully qualified in order to have any validity at all. Zhuangzi suggests that words are like a fish trap—once the meaning is caught, one should forget the words, just as the trap is only useful for catching the fish, but can be put aside once the fish has been caught. Accordingly, the style of the text is very poetic, allegorical, evocative, and mythical.

The text as it exists today, as edited by Guo Xiang, consists of thirty-three chapters. The first seven chapters, called the "Inner Chapters," are relatively consistent in style and attitude. Thus they are often considered by scholars to be the work of the author Zhuang Zhou himself. The next fifteen chapters, described as the "Outer Chapters," and the last eleven chapters, called the "Miscellaneous Chapters," are often considered to be the work of later writers, including works representative of what is known as the "Yangist tradition." These materials are perhaps interspersed with fragments of Zhuangzi's own writings. For the most part they seem to be consistent with the spirit of the inner chapters, yet are often not as artfully written, and at times even seem to have significantly different emphases and concerns.

The text seems pretty clearly to have been composed in layers, though scholars disagree on the exact number of layers involved. In any case the composition of the text seems to span at least three different phases or stages in the evolution of Daoist thought. Furthermore, the text is extremely aphoristic, consisting of short stories, sound bites, and anecdotes. This style lends itself, as is also the case, for example, with Nietzsche in the West, to quotation out of context and the inevitable misunderstandings which subsequently result from such textual abuse. One must be wary when attributing any single outlook to the text as a whole. Still, certain themes emerge, and we will discuss some of these below.

Philosophical Outlook

The *Zhuangzi* is often described as advocating relativism, and there are certainly relativistic elements to be found. But unlike more thoroughgoing forms of relativism, the text gives priority to certain attitudes and behaviors, and thus cannot accurately be dismissed as purely relativistic. At least two different modes of experience are given privilege in the text. With reference to mental states, in several places the text advocates a cognitive condition described as *ming*, or "clarity." Clarity in this case seems to involve the ability to discern subtle distinctions without necessarily evaluating experience in terms of a preferred alternative. Therefore the text should not be thought of as advocating the obliteration of distinctions in an overwhelming experience of mystical oneness, which is how some commentators and scholars read the text.

As for behavior, the text privileges what is called *wuwei*, or "effortless action." This kind of behavior seems to involve minimizing conflict with what is inevitable or unavoidable in our experience, and reducing the friction and drag caused by obstinate commitment to a single preferred outcome.

Thus we might draw the conclusion that the ideal person, whom the text variously describes as "genuine" (*zhenren/chen jen*), "fully realized" (*zhiren/chih-jen*), or "spiritual" (*shenren/shen-jen*), is one who is perfectly well adjusted. That is to say, such a person is balanced and at ease in all kinds of situations, and is not thrown by novelty or unexpected circumstances. An image used by Zhuangzi to illustrate this kind of adjustment is what he calls the "hinge of *Dao*" (*daoshu/tao-shu*). In chapter 2, we find the following claim:

A state in which "this" and "that" no longer find their opposites is called the hinge of the Way. When the hinge is fitted in the socket, it can respond endlessly.

(WATSON, 1964)

Although the presence in the text of privileged modes of experience prevents us from accurately

describing the *Zhuangzi* as thoroughly relativistic, still it does seem to be the case that, for the author Zhuangzi, all truth and valuation are necessarily contextually situated. This means, for example, that what is good for one individual might not be good for another, and the same goes for beauty, truth, usefulness, and so on. And just as this is the case for different individuals, it is also the case for a single individual at different times.

Thus, rather than obstinately clashing with the flux of the world by insisting on maintaining dogmatic and constant standards, one would be better off adjusting one's standards and attitudes in response to the needs of the current situation. One implication of this attitude of "least resistance" (*wuwei*) is that one's resources and overall well-being are best preserved through reducing the friction we experience with the world. The best example from the text to illustrate Zhuangzi's conception of this optimally "frictionless" mode of experience is one found in chapter 3, the story of Cook Ding cutting up an ox for Lord Wen-hui. Cook Ding moves like a dancer, skillfully and in rhythm, and he explains his technique:

What I care about is the Way, which goes beyond all skill. When I first began cutting up oxen, all I could see was the ox itself. After three years I no longer saw the whole ox. And now—I go at it by spirit and don't look with my eyes.

(WATSON, 1964)

The knife that Cook Ding uses is still sharp after nineteen years because it never hits or cuts bone, but slips between the joints. It is not an accident that Lord Wen-hui finds in this not just a lesson on butchering, but a lesson on life.

This concern with preserving one's well-being through conservation of one's natural resources can also be found in the Yangist tradition (and is still one of the basic axioms of Chinese medicine), and suggests a significant Yangist influence on the text. In turn, this is also a factor which contributes to the influence exerted by the *Zhuangzi* on the subsequent development of alchemic longevity movements within the Daoist tradition.

Philosophy of Language

Regarding the use of language, we find the following passage in chapter 2 of the text:

> Words are not just wind. Words have something to say. But if what they have to say is not fixed, then do they really say something? Or do they say nothing? People suppose that words are different from the peeps of baby birds, but is there any difference, or isn't there?
>
> (WATSON, 1964)

According to one reading of this passage, words carry significance, though they don't mean anything in and of themselves, and their meaning is not constant. The meaning of any word is dependent on and in turn contributes to the general context of the sentence, paragraph, or any body of discourse. In other words, words mean nothing out of context but come to have meaning according to how they are used in any given situation. As previously indicated, Zhuangzi compares language to a fish net, which is useful only until a fish is caught but then becomes obsolete and must be forgotten until a new fish, or in this case a new meaning, is sought.

More specifically, Zhuangzi distinguishes between three kinds of language that Burton Watson translates as "imputed words," "repeated words," and "goblet words." The first are words attributed to some great historical or legendary figure, which increases their impact. The second are words which gain credibility simply by being familiar, since we often mistake the merely familiar for the obviously self-evident. The third are words whose meaning changes, which Zhuangzi describes as "words that are no-words." This kind of language constantly refreshes itself, and therefore more accurately conveys meaning. It fills and empties, and thus more closely mirrors the distinctions necessary for understanding.

Death as One More Natural Transformation

Zhuangzi conceives of the world as constantly changing. The adaptive qualities of the perfectly well-adjusted person enable him or her to remain balanced in the midst of this maelstrom of change and transformation. Chapter 18 tells of Huizi's (Hui Tzu's) finding Zhuangzi pounding on a tub and singing shortly after the death of Zhuangzi's wife. When Huizi asks why Zhuangzi reacts in this way, Zhuangzi replies that although like anyone else he grieved when she first died, he thought back to the time before she was born and had no body—and even farther back, to the time before her spirit existed:

> In the midst of the jumble of wonder and mystery a change took place and she had a spirit. Another change and she had a body. Another change and she was born. Now there's another change and she's dead. It's just like the progression of the four seasons. . . .
>
> (WATSON, 1964)

Many conclusions can be reached on the basis of this story, but it seems that death is regarded as a natural part of the ebb and flow of transformations which constitute the movement of the *Dao*. To grieve over death, or to fear one's own death, for that matter, is arbitrarily to evaluate what is inevitable. Of course, this reading is somewhat ironic given the fact that much of the subsequent Daoist tradition comes to seek longevity and immortality, and bases some of its basic models on the *Zhuangzi*.

Zhuangzi is suggesting that it is useless, arbitrary, and foolish to set ourselves against what is natural. We can, he seems to say, choose to adopt different perspectives on experience. Why not choose ones which enable us to see death not as something to be feared and lamented, but as just one more phase in a much larger transformational movement? What is now Zhuangzi's wife was something else before she was Zhuangzi's wife, and what was Zhuangzi's wife will be something else after her death as well.

This is not necessarily to suggest an afterlife or any form of personal immortality. But death in general can be said to lead to new life, just as life in general ends in death. An example of this is the fact that dead matter fertilizes the ground and provides the raw material for other living beings to grow and reproduce. Life goes on, though we may not, and it is possible, the text seems to suggest, to adopt the perspective of life itself which transforms, for example, rather than to adopt the more narrow and limited perspective of a single moment in the transformation of life.

The Fully-Realized Person

One of the most famous stories to be found in the *Zhuangzi* is the one found at the end of chapter 2:

> Once Chuang Chou dreamt he was a butterfly, a butterfly flitting and fluttering around, happy with himself and doing as he pleased. He didn't know he was Chuang Chou. Suddenly he woke up and there he was, solid and unmistakable Chuang Chou. But he didn't know if he was Chuang Chou who had dreamt he was a butterfly, or a butterfly dreaming he was Chuang Chou. Between Chuang Chou and a butterfly there must be some distinction! This is called the Transformation of Things.
>
> (WATSON, 1964)

It is significant that the important image in this story is the butterfly. This image sums up much of Zhuangzi's thought. The butterfly is a symbol of transformation; it follows the breeze yet arrives at the flower; its actions are spontaneous and free; it does not wear itself out fighting the forces of nature.

Zhuangzi uses several different phrases to refer to a person who embodies the *Dao* in this kind of natural and effortless fashion. These terms include "genuine person" (*zhenren*), "ethereal" or "spiri-

tual" person (*shenren*), and "fully realized person" (*zhiren*). Perhaps such a person resembles a butterfly in certain ways. He or she has become balanced and centered and is thus able to experience the pitch and roll of oppositions (*taiji/t'ai chi*) without being thrown off balance by them. The sage can thus fit *in* the world, at the center, in the socket of the hinge, at the fulcrum of all dichotomies. He or she blends in with the surroundings and becomes effectively frictionless, transparent, and unobtrusive.

ALAN FOX

Further Reading

Translations

Chung, Bruya. *Zhuangzi Speaks!* Princeton, N.J.: Princeton University Press, 1992. Beautifully produced translation of Tsai Chih Chung's "classic comics" approach to the Chinese classics. The drawings are appealing and the translation is credible, though somewhat superficial at times.

Feng, English. *Chuang Tsu: The Inner Chapters.* N.Y.: Vintage Books, 1974. A coffee-table volume, with a poetic and useful translation and beautiful photographs to accompany and/or illustrate the text.

Fung, Yu-lan. *A Taoist Classic: Chuang Tzu.* Beijing: Foreign Language Press, 1989. This book is especially useful because it contains references to Guo Xiang's commentary, and the text also includes several of Fung's essays on the text and its authors.

Graham, A. C. *Chuang-tzu: The Inner Chapters.* London: George Allen & Unwin, 1981. Important and insightful translation by one of the giants of classical Chinese philosophy.

Watson, Burton. *Complete Writings of Chuang Tzu.* New York: Columbia University Press, 1968. The best complete translation available. Watson's reading is for the most part careful and elegantly poetic.

Watson, Burton. *Chuang Tzu: Basic Writings.* New York: Columbia University Press, 1964. Same translation as above, but includes only the inner chapters and a few of the later chapters.

Related Studies

Chan, Wing-Tsit, trans. and comp. *A Source Book in Chinese Philosophy*. Princeton, N.J.: Princeton University Press, 1963. Chan provides a thorough, though unevenly translated, collection of primary philosophical materials unavailable elsewhere.

Fung, Yu-lan. *A History of Chinese Philosophy*. 2 vols. Translated by Derk Bodde. Princeton, N.J.: Princeton University Press, 1952. Impressive survey of the history of Chinese thought by one of the most important modern Chinese philosophers.

Graham, A. C. *Disputers of the Tao: Philosophic Argument in Ancient China*. La Salle, Ill.: Open Court Press, 1988. One of the last works of one of the greatest of all scholars of ancient Chinese thought. Problematic and unclear at times, but it is a mature and careful summation of Graham's conclusions over the course of his career.

Wu, Kuang-ming. *Butterfly as Companion*. Albany, N.Y.: State University of New York Press, 1990. A lively and helpful guide to reading the first three chapters of the text. This book contains the Chinese text, a word-for-word translation with glosses, and a series of meditations and essays inspired by the text. Very inviting and thought-provoking.

———. *Chuang-tzu: World Philosopher at Play*. New York: Crossroad, 1982. This book's revolutionary approach to the *Zhuangzi* rejuvenates the text and arrives at new and provocative conclusions and, ultimately, more questions.

MENCIUS (MENGZI/MENG TZU)

Born: 371 B.C., now Shandong (Shantung) Province, China
Died: 289 B.C.
Major Work: *Mengzi* (*Meng Tzu*) (*The Book of Mencius*)

Major Ideas

Human nature is originally good, and moral virtues are innate.
Among all the virtues, ren (jen) *and* yi (i) *are the most important ones.*
In order to have ren *and* yi *fully realized, one must cultivate moral courage from within.*
Politically a ruler should practice the Kingly Way accompanied by the economic system called jing tian (ching t'ien).

If Confucius is compared to Socrates in the West, then Mencius should occupy the position of Plato. Without Plato, Socrates would have been unknown to us, and without Mencius, the crowning position of Confucianism in Chinese culture would not have been realized.

Mencius (Mengzi/Meng Tzu) was born in what is now Shandong (Shantung) Province, in a place very close to the birthplace of Confucius. Like Confucius, he was brought up by his widowed mother. But Mencius's mother was considered a model mother in the history of China, because she managed to move three times for the educational environment of her son. Throughout his youth, he developed a very strong sense of mission to "save the world" by "rectifying men's mind, putting an end to perverse ideas, rejecting deviated conducts, and censoring misleading rhetoric." He expressed himself boldly when he asserted that he simply wanted to become a second Confucius.

Probably because of his sense of mission and his professed commitment to Confucianism, he was later honored as the "second sage" in the history of China. His book *Mencius* from the Tang (T'ang) dynasty on has been honored as a model for prose literature and as a landmark in Chinese philosophy.

Theory of Human Nature

Confucius maintains that human beings are "born alike; it is their habits which carry them far apart."

Confucius never made a judgment on human nature as fundamentally good or evil. Mencius is perhaps the first one who developed a theory of human nature from the moral point of view. For him, all the cardinal virtues such as *ren* (*jen*) (human-heartedness), *yi* (*i*) (righteousness), *li* (courteousness), and *zhi* (*chih*) (wisdom) are innate in our nature. In describing these virtues as "innate," Mencius does not mean that they exist as a priori or before any human experience takes place. Rather, the virtues exist as pure potentials. Mencius uses the term *duan* (*tuan*) or "beginning" to mean this. This means that everyone possesses these virtues "to begin with." If an individual is able to carry these beginnings into full development, the individual can become a sage. Mencius's well-known saying that "Everyone can become a *Yao* or *Shun* [ancient sage–king]" is a logical conclusion of his argument.

Mencius's justification for the claim that moral virtues are innate rests on an empirical argument and an analogy. His empirical argument states that when we observe a little child about to fall into a well, we experience a feeling of distress or alarm, and our natural response is to make an effort immediately to rescue the child. From this example we can conclude that our natural feeling does not allow us to tolerate the suffering of others. Such a feeling is universally innate in all of us, and this is the "beginning" of human-heartedness.

Mencius's analogy was developed when he had a

fierce argument with Gaozi (Kao Tzu) (c. 420–c. 350 B.C.), who maintained that human nature is originally morally neutral. Gaozi proposed to use water as an analogy, and Mencius gladly agreed. Gaozi maintained that human nature is like water; if it is directed to the east, it will flow eastward; if directed to the west, it will flow westward. But Mencius argued that since water always flows downward, human nature is naturally and originally good. (This argument has been criticized as a "faulty analogy" by modern Chinese scholars.)

If Mencius maintains that human nature is originally good, how does he explain the problem of evil? Mencius's answer is that either the individual fails to develop his original potential or he simply loses his original nature. But this is by no means the fault of his original endowment. So, the main goal of education is to "get back" the lost *xin (hsin)* (mind or heart). This concept, no doubt, has influenced the metaphysical theory of human nature in Neo-Confucianism, particularly in the philosophy of Zhu Xi (Chu Hsi).

A Theory of Moral Virtues

Mencius focuses on the moral virtues of *ren* and *yi*. *Ren* is the central concept in the *Analects* of Confucius, while Confucius mentions *yi* only a few times. But Mencius paired *yi* with *ren*. First, he specifically defined *ren* as "the human heart," a definition that serves as the foundation for *ren*'s being translated as "human-heartedness" today. He defines *yi* as "the path a man ought to follow."

In Mencius's moral philosophy, the concept of *yi* plays an even greater role. Etymologically, *yi* means "what is proper." This is very similar to the Aristotelian concept of rightness as the mean, the proper point between excess and deficiency. It is relative to the individual, to the particular situation, and to the desired or anticipated results.

For Mencius, the essence of *yi* lies in the cognition of the absolute validity of the "oughtness" of a situation that requires moral action. When such a moral principle prevails, an individual must comply with it even though his own life has to be

sacrificed. This sublime "oughtness" is very closely related to the categorical imperative of Immanuel Kant and obviously has inspired many martyrs who have sacrificed their own lives because of their uncompromising loyalty to their lord or country. Confucius initiated the theory as a philosophy, but in the hands of Mencius the Master's teaching became inspiration, moving from philosophy to religion, and emphasizing the unity of moral conviction and uncompromising obedient action.

The Metaphysical Journey

As mentioned earlier, Mencius believed that every individual can become a sage. The way to become a sage is to undertake a metaphysical journey, a spiritual path without a god. This spiritual path is the path of "cultivating one's own *qi [ch'i]*." The concept of *qi* is a central concept in all corners of Chinese culture. Its original meaning was "steam," "vapor," or "air." But it has been extended to mean spiritual or material force or impetus. Here "cultivating *qi*" in Mencius has its special contextual meaning.

The phrase "cultivation of *qi*" means almost the same as "development of moral or spiritual power." Such a spiritual power is developed through constant accumulation of righteous deeds and is not to be obtained by occasional moral acts. This is comparable to the Eightfold Path of the Buddha, which integrates right mindfulness and right conduct. Although the Buddha's way aims at freedom from suffering, Mencius emphasizes the categorical moral imperative and regards as irrelevant the practical consequences of the act.

As a result, this metaphysical journey leads to the concept of Mencius's ideal personality, even beyond the idea of the *junzi (chün-tzu)* ("gentleman"). Mencius calls the ideal person *da zhang fu (ta chang fu)*, "a great person." This kind of personality will not be corrupted by wealth or fame, will not be bent by power or force, and will not be moved by poverty or mean conditions. Such a person stands in the correct position under the heavens, and follows the great path of the world.

Political and Economic Thought

Mencius's political ideas follow closely the steps of Confucius, who cherished the ideal of a government of *ren*. Mencius makes a clear distinction between the Kingly Way (*wang dao/wang tao*) and the Way of Power (*ba dao/pa tao*). He defines the Kingly Way by reference to a government or a ruler performing the politics of *ren*, and the Way of Power as shown when the ruler exercises forces over his subjects. So, when he traveled to meet the lords of his time, he usually attempted to persuade them to practice this kind of politics. Unfortunately none of them listened to him, and the Kingly Way remains a sublime unrealized goal for Confucianism.

Mencius was obviously familiar with the history of political institutions of the Zhou (Chou) dynasty. His ideal institution seems to be a modified system of the Golden Age of Zhou that is based on a strict hierarchy, ranking from the emperor in a declining scale. In spite of Mencius's well-known saying about the value of the people, he insisted on the distinction between the ruling class and the ruled and never seemed to approve a "self-governed" and "general participation" type of democracy. Besides, he did not seem to have very much tolerance for foreign (or unorthodox type) institutions, and he was very apologetic about the culture of the Zhou as handed down by Confucius.

Confucius never developed any economic thought, but Mencius did. He developed an ideal way of distributing land, a method that might have been based on the original system of early Zhou. He called for dividing a square mile into nine squares of land which appear like the Chinese character for "well" (*jing/ching*). The middle square remains the public land while the remaining eight are to be distributed to eight families. The eight families are to help in cultivating the public land and the revenue from the harvest will belong to the ruler. According to historians, this type of economic system has never been practiced in the history of China. It is Mencius's innovative idea, but it may have been too innovative to be accepted and practiced.

Mencius's Criticism of Other Philosophers

Throughout the *Book of Mencius* readers find many interesting passages in which Mencius argues against other philosophers. The most notable ones are the arguments against Yang Zhu (Yang Chu) (440–360? B.C.), Xu Xing (Hsü Hsing), and the Mohists.

Yang Zhu is a pioneer of Daoism. He advocates a philosophy of self-preservation, emphasizing the virtue of selfishness. Mencius rejects this position from the viewpoint of an altruism based on the cardinal virtue of *ren* and the traditional concept of social hierarchy. Xu Xing, who represents some ideas of primitive communism, contends that the ruler and the subject should both till the soil. Mencius seriously objects to this, maintaining that the intellectually superior should be the ruler and those who merely develop their capacity for physical labor should be the ruled. A cooperative division of labor has to be based on individual differences: being physically strong or being intellectually superior.

Mozi (Mo Tzu) (c. 470–c. 391 B.C.), a younger contemporary of Confucius, advocated a philosophy of utilitarianism and exercised a powerful influence. The Mohists all rejected long periods of mourning and elaborate funerals. In response to a Mohist's rejection of elaborate funerals, Mencius gave the following reply:

> In ancient times there was no burial of one's parents. When a man's parent died, he simply threw the body into a ditch. When he later passed by, what he saw was that the body was being eaten by the foxes or bitten by the gnats or flies. . . . He could not bear the sight. The feeling of his heart flew out to his face. He then hurried home and came back with baskets and a spade for covering up the body. If the covering up of a human body was the right thing for primitive man, it is quite right today for a filial son or man of *ren* to prepare the funeral for his parents.

This is Mencius's typical defense of Confucianism, an appeal to the primacy of the human heart, where feeling rules supreme. It is perhaps because of this appeal to the permanent nature of the human being that Confucianism has been able to survive throughout the dynasties and the present period.

JOSEPH S. WU

Further Reading

Translations

Chai, Ch'u and Winberg Chai, eds. and trans. *The Humanist Way in Ancient China: Essential Works of Confucianism*. New York: Bantam Books, 1965. This volume includes the "Four Books" (the *Analects*, *The Book of Mencius*, *The Great Learning*, and *The Doctrine of the Mean*) and selections from other classics. Readable translation with helpful notes.

Chan, Wing-tsit, trans. and comp. *A Source Book in Chinese Philosophy*. Princeton, N.J.: Princeton University Press, 1963. An authoritative work with a readable translation. Includes thoughtfully selected chapters from *Mencius*.

Creel, H. G. *Chinese Thought: From Confucius to Mao Tse-tung*. Chicago: University of Chicago Press, 1953. A very lucid introductory text with a good chapter on Mencius.

Fung, Yu-lan. *A History of Chinese Philosophy*. Translated by Derk Bodde. Vol. 1. Princeton, N.J.: Princeton University Press, 1952. An authoritative work with a thorough chapter on Mencius (chapter 6).

Legge, James, ed. and trans. *The Life and Work of Mencius*. Oxford: Clarendon Press, 1895. A biographical account with a very readable translation.

Richards, I. A. *Mencius on the Mind*. London: Kegan Paul, Trench, Trubner & Company, 1932. An illuminating critical treatise employing linguistic methods developed in the West.

Waley, Arthur. *Three Ways of Thought in Ancient China*. London: Allen and Unwin, 1939. Available in paperback. Very helpful introductions, with good translations.

Ware, James, trans. *The Sayings of Mencius*. New York: New American Library, 1960. Readable but not quite accurate translation.

GONGSUN LONG (KUNG-SUN LUNG)

Born: c. 320 B.C.
Died: c. 250 B.C.
Major Work: *Gongsun Longzi* (*Kung-sun Lung Tzu*)

Major Ideas

"A white horse is not a horse" is defensible.

If only the features of a thing can be pointed out, how can the whole thing be pointed out when the whole thing is not a feature of anything?

One and one cannot become two since neither becomes two.

To rectify actuality is to rectify its name.

Gongsun Long (Kung-sun Lung) has long fascinated the logicians and linguists of the West. From the Western point of view, any Chinese thinker who seriously claims that "A white horse is not a horse" must be akin to Zeno of Elea (c. 490–430 B.C.), who argues that the swifter runner (Achilles) cannot overtake the slower runner (the tortoise) once the tortoise has a head start. But Western methods of logical analysis seem to be inadequate to the genius of Gongsun Long: one comes to suspect that the key to understanding Gongsun Long is to rid oneself of the presupposition that he was a logician and to see him as a philosopher of language (with particular attention to the Chinese language).

Very little is known of Gongsun Long, perhaps because his paradoxes, like those of Hui Shi (Hui Shih) (c. 380–300 B.C.), although intriguing, did not relate enough to the fundamental concerns of the Chinese to become a significant part of their intellectual history: most, if not all, of Hui Shi's work is lost, and what remains of Gongsun Long's work only hints at the power of argument that must have bulwarked the profoundly simple but perplexing claims that Gongsun Long persistently pronounced. Gongsun Long was a scholar who ran a school, enjoyed the patronage of rulers, and made something of a nuisance of himself by arguing against war and for pacific means of settling disputes. Whatever immortality he enjoys comes from his wit, not from his use of social or political power.

A White Horse Is Not a Horse

If all we had of Gongsun Long's work were his declarations (not his defenses), we could enjoy inventing his intentions (as we must with some of the corrupted texts that survive). But like Plato, although without Plato's metaphysical addiction, he embedded his paradoxes in dialogue, thereby affording us a glimpse into his ways of reasoning.

The *Gongsun Longzi* (*Kung-sun Lung Tzu*) begins the White Horse Argument with the provocative question, "Is it correct to say that a white horse is not a horse?" and proceeds to argue that the claim that a white horse is not a horse can reasonably be made.

The defense of the claim that it can be correct to say that a white horse is not a horse begins with the argument that

> "Horse" denotes the form and "white" denotes the color. What denotes the color does not denote the form. Therefore we say that a white horse is not a horse.
>
> (CHAN, 1963)

Perhaps Gongsun Long's point here is that since a white horse is whiteness (color) + horse (form), and since the whiteness is not a horse, and since what is only "partly" a horse is not wholly a horse, then a white horse is not a horse.

But Gongsun Long does not specifically argue in

this way. He seems to be calling attention to the fact that more is being mentioned by the expression "white horse" than simply a horse; one factor critical to the description has in itself nothing to do with a horse: in mentioning whiteness, one is not mentioning a horse.

In the dialogue, an objection is registered: Surely if there is a white horse, it cannot be claimed that there is *no* horse; the use of the term "white" cannot change that simple fact.

The response is critical (because it provides the fundamental reason for making the paradoxical claim):

> Ask for a horse, and either a yellow or a black one may answer. Ask for a white horse, and neither the yellow horse nor the black one may answer. If a white horse were a horse, then what is asked in both cases would be the same.

> (CHAN, 1963)

The line of reasoning is clear: In asking for a "white horse," one is not simply asking for a "horse"; if one were to ask for a "horse," then any horse would do—including a yellow or a black one. But the request for what is called a "white horse" can be satisfied only by the delivery of a *white* horse; something yellow or black, although describable as a "horse," will not do. In asking for a "white horse," one is not asking for (just any) "horse"; therefore, a "white horse" is not a "horse" (they are different); therefore, a white horse is not a horse.

The resolution of the paradox could have been made simply (but in a pedestrian way) had Gongsun Long directly explained that the expression "white horse" does not have the same descriptive function as the expression "horse"; in other words, the term "horse" is not a synonym for the term "white horse." (The significant difference between the expression "white horse" and the term "horse" is, of course, the term "white"; the significant difference between a white horse and a horse that is

not white is something that is not a horse: whiteness.)

But to talk of synonyms would have been to obscure a central point worth making—that the *uses* (functions) of descriptive expressions will be affected by deleting parts of expressions from utterances in specific contexts.

The Original Claim and the Western Critique

Even those who do not understand Chinese may find the original claim intriguingly simple: *Bai ma fei ma* (*Pai ma fei ma*)—literally, character by character, "White horse not horse" ("A white horse is not a horse"). The statement, however, is not made *as* a paradox; it is made as a possible claim that can reasonably be defended; it is paradoxical only to those who do not understand why it is made as a claim.

A natural tendency for Western critics, schooled as they are in Platonism (even though most of them do not subscribe to it), has been to assume that Gongsun Long discovered "universals"—abstract properties that may be common to a number of things or may, indeed, not be exemplified at all. The characteristic "whiteness," for example, is common to snow, certain bedsheets, certain whales, and so forth, but the property "genius than which none greater can be conceived" need not be illustrated by an example: perhaps (more likely than not) there is no such genius.

The interpretation that may be called "Western" has been that Gongsun Long was simply calling attention, although in a quixotic way, to what seems to followers of Plato to be obvious: the universal "whiteness" is *not* the universal "horseness"; the universal "white-horseness" is *not* the universal "horseness"; and, finally, a white horse is not the universal "horseness" and is, in that sense, not horse. Hence, in asking for an individual thing bearing the property "white-horseness" one is *not* going to be satisfied with an individual thing bearing the property "horseness" (unless it bears the property "whiteness" as well).

Fung Yu-lan's Appeal to Universals

Even the distinguished Chinese historian Fung Yu-lan, in his *History of Chinese Philosophy* (and *A Short History of Chinese Philosophy*), presents a "Western" (Platonic) interpretation:

Kung-sun Lung seems to emphasize the distinction between the universal, "horseness," and the universal, "white-horseness." The universal, horseness, is the essential attribute of all horses. . . . Such "horseness" is distinct from "white-horseness." That is to say, the horse as such is distinct from the white horse as such. Therefore a white horse is not a horse.

However, Fung also argues that

[in] terms of Western logic, [the] argument emphasizes the difference in the intension of the terms "horse," "white," and "white horse." . . . Since the intension of each of the three terms is different, therefore a white horse is not a horse.

Roughly speaking, the terms differ in meaning; therefore what is meant by "white horse" is *not* what is meant by "horse." (This point can be made without committing oneself to a theory of universals, provided that by the "meaning" of a term one refers to its descriptive—"naming"—function.)

In addition, Fung calls attention to the fact that a request for a "white horse" cannot be satisfied by delivering anything other than a *white horse*: delivering something that would satisfy the simple request for a "horse" would not satisfy the former request: A horse is *not* what would satisfy the request for what is called a "white horse"—and that is why it is claimed that "A white horse is not a horse." (Here the emphasis, to be found in the *Gongsun Longzi*, is on the *uses* of these terms; and this point, like the one having to do with "meanings," can be made without recourse to a theory of universals.)

Other Paradoxes Attributed to Gongsun Long

Scholars differ as to the translation and sense of the "paradoxes" of Gongsun Long. There is also the question as to whether the paradoxes attributed to Gongsun Long are indeed his. (Some scholars even argue that the "paradoxes" are not paradoxes.)

Among other puzzling claims attributed to Gongsun Long are the following:

1. Only the features of things can be pointed out (named) and yet the world (and other wholes) can be named even though the world (or a whole thing) is not itself a feature of anything.
2. One and one cannot become two, since neither becomes two.
3. (Often attributed to Gongsun Long, but a product of forgery.) A hard white stone is not three (hard, white, stone) but two (either hard-stone or white-stone); the features are separate.

The Rectification of Names

Gongsun Long was obviously concerned with problems stemming from the practice necessary to thinking, knowing, and communication—the practice of "naming" things, the art of describing the world. He argues that a "name is to designate an actuality" and that to "rectify is to rectify actuality, and to rectify actuality is to rectify the name corresponding to it."

Surely Gongsun did not "prove" his paradoxes; that is, he did not succeed in showing that a white horse is not a horse nor that a hard white stone is always only two (hard-stone or white-stone), not three. But his lines of argument make it clear that he was not advocating the use of cryptic descriptions, even though, like riddles, they may be explained. He was making a serious effort to resolve problems of naming (describing) things (and the world) and the difficulties one gets into if one makes the wrong suppositions about those uses, especially when there is the problem of distinguishing parts from wholes. It may be said that he was not so much a logician as he was a student of language absorbed in the problem of relating the uses of "names" to an understanding of "actuality," the world of things as we can know it. That this particular absorption did not become infectious, marking a course through the centuries of Chinese thought, is perhaps more an accident of culture than it is a deficiency on the part of Gongsun Long.

IAN P. McGREAL

Further Reading

Translations

Chan, Wing-tsit, trans. and comp. *A Source Book in Chinese Philosophy*. Princeton, N.J.: Princeton University Press, 1963. Chapter 10 of Chan's excellent sourcebook, *Debates on Metaphysical Concepts: The Logicians*, presents most of what is extant of Gongsun Long's work, together with an ample selection of the paradoxes of Hui Shi. The accompanying discussion is very acute and helpful.

de Bary, Wm. Theodore, Wing-tsit Chan, and Burton Watson, comps. *Sources of Chinese Tradition*. In the *Introduction to Oriental Civilizations* series, edited by Wm. Theodore de Bary. New York: Columbia University Press, 1960. Chapter 5, "Logic and Cosmology," contains the paradoxes of Hui Shi and extended selections from the *Gongsun Longzi*.

Related Studies

Fung, Yu-lan. *A Short History of Chinese Philosophy*. Edited by Derk Bodde. New York: The Free Press, Macmillan, 1948; London: Collier-Macmillan, Ltd. Chapter 8, "The School of Names," is a lively and illuminating account of the work of Hui Shi and Gongsun Long.

Graham, A. C. *Disputers of the Tao: Philosophical Argument in Ancient China*. La Salle, Ill.: Open Court Publishing Co., 1989. A brilliant account of Chinese philosophy, with an original and perceptive discussion of Gongsun Long's White Horse argument (in chapter 5, "The Sharpening of Rational Debate: The Sophists"). Appendix 2, "The Relation of Chinese Thought to Chinese Language," is particularly pertinent.

Hansen, Chad. *Language and Logic in Ancient China*. Ann Arbor, Mich.: The University of Michigan Press, 1983. Hansen argues that one need not and should not have recourse to the Platonic view of universals and individuals to understand and criticize Gongsun Long's White Horse argument. He advocates a "mass noun" view of the Chinese language, a nominalistic hypothesis that contends that the Chinese deal only with nouns that point to "stuff" that is uncountable and thereby to objects indicated through the use of such nouns: they have no need for a theory of universals.

XUNZI (HSÜN TZU)

Born: c. 300 B.C.
Died: c. 215 B.C.
Major Work: *Xunzi* (*Hsün Tzu*), in thirty-two chapters, edited by Liu Xiang (Liu Hsiang) (77 B.C.)

Major Ideas

Human nature is evil.

Evil arises from the unchecked expression of desire and emotion.

Human beings are capable of becoming good through the civilizing activities of teachers and rulers.

"Artifice," in the form of laws, education, and public ritual, is the foundation of civil society.

All events have natural causes: religion has no supernatural efficacy, and gods and spirits are the products of superstition and ignorance.

Religious rituals are effective agents of social control and moral persuasion.

Xunzi (Hsün Tzu), "Master Xun," was born Xun Qing (Hsün Ch'ing) in the last years of the Warring States period of the Zhou (Chou) dynasty, and saw near the end of his life the unification of the empire under the First Emperor of the Qin (Ch'in). Among the last of the "Hundred Philosophers" who established the intellectual heritage of China, Xun Qing studied in his thirties and forties with the great thinkers of his day at the renowned Jixia (Chi-hsia) Academy. He served as an adviser to a king and prime minister of the State of Qi (Ch'i) as well as two kings of Qin, and later served as a county magistrate in the State of Chu (Ch'u) (where he eventually retired) and a senior minister in the State of Zhao (Chao). These experiences shaped his writings, which took the form of philosophical argumentation and political persuasion, and addressed issues of character, morality, statecraft, and social organization.

Xunzi idolized Confucius (Kongfuzi/K'ung Fu-tzu), but he was highly critical of the Confucian "schools" of his day. He met a number of these "Confucians" (known as *Ru/Ju*, "scholars" or "ritualists") at the Jixia Academy, and directed many of his strongest polemical arguments against "heterodox *Ru*." The most significant were the followers of Mencius (Mengzi/Meng Tzu), and some of Xunzi's most spirited writing is in refutation of the Mencian interpretation of human nature. The other group that most concerned Xunzi con-

sisted of the followers of Mozi (Mo Tzu, or Mo Di/Mo Ti), who subscribed to the doctrines of social egalitarianism, frugality, religious literalism, and universal love. These doctrines were, for Xunzi, not only naive with regard to human nature and the natural world, but also threatening to the stability of the state. In addition, Xunzi was exposed during his tenure at the Jixia Academy to the works of Shen Buhai (Shen Pu-hai), Yang Zhu (Yang Chu), Hui Shi (Hui Shih), Gongsun Long (Kung-sun Lung), Laozi (Lao Tzu), Zhuangzi (Chuang Tzu), and Zou Yan (Tsou Yen), as well as a number of other thinkers known only through Xunzi's comments on their doctrines. Consequently, Xunzi's writings are an excellent source for the intellectual life of the final years of the Zhou. His own thinking reflects the incorporation or rejection of Mencian Confucianism, Mohist Philosophy, Daoism or Eremeticism, Dialectics or Linguistic Philosophy, Cosmological Theory, and Legalism—the so-called "Six Schools" of pre-Qin philosophy.

Human Nature Is Evil

Xunzi said, "Human nature is evil; goodness is acquired." He is the only major Chinese philosopher ever to have made such a statement; Mencius, who was preoccupied with the issue, did not entertain this position even as a possibility. Writing half a century before, Mencius defended his belief in the

35

goodness of human nature against the position of the philosopher Gaozi (Kao Tzu), that human nature was neither good nor evil. For Mencius, every person has a natural inclination to do good, and this natural inclination is represented by "Four Sprouts" or feelings from which the major Confucian virtues naturally grow: the sprout of compassion grows into "benevolence" (*ren/jen*), the sprout of shame for wrongdoing grows into "morality" (*yi/i*), the sprout of deference grows into "propriety" (*li*), and the sprout of judgment between right and wrong grows into "wisdom" (*zhi/chih*). That is, the traditional Confucian virtues represent the full development of natural human feelings: as long as these feelings are nurtured and grow (Mencius said, "given the right nourishment there is nothing that will not grow"), anyone can become a sage.

It is important to recognize the developmental nature of this process. For the classical Chinese philosophers, "human nature" (*xing/hsing*) is not merely what is innate or given at birth (though these ideas are certainly present in the idea of *xing*), but also what is natural to the development of the person. *Xing*, "human nature," is etymologically related to *sheng*, "life"—the course of life, not only its beginnings. So, *xing* represents the natural development of a person over the whole course of life.

For Xunzi, the natural inclination of a person is the satisfaction of personal, usually selfish, desires. "With life, there is the tendency toward self-benefit." Xunzi agreed with Mencius that humans are basically feeling-oriented, but he did not describe feelings in the same morally positive terms: the "feelings" are not "compassion," "shame," "deference," and so on, but rather the emotions love, hate, pleasure, anger, sorrow, and joy. In response to outside stimuli, these feelings manifest themselves as desires, the satisfaction of which is basically selfish and antisocial. Since human desires are inexhaustible, their natural expression is chaotic and competitive. If persons indulge their feelings without restraint, the result will be wrangling and strife, violence and crime, licentiousness and wantonness.

Whereas for Mencius the natural development of basic human feelings produces virtue or "goodness" (*shan*), Xunzi maintains that the natural development of feelings produces suffering or "evil" (*e/o*). Acts of virtue (benevolence, trustworthiness, filial piety, loyalty to the state, and so on) "are all contrary to a person's *xing* and run counter to the emotions."

Xunzi's is not a doctrine of metaphysical evil, such as that found in the West. Rather, evil is the consequence of the unchecked expression of human emotions and desires. In this sense, human beings tend to be self-interested, animalistic, and unrestrained, and must acquire the ability to harness and control their natural inclinations.

"Artifice"

Despite his view that human nature is evil, Xunzi was thoroughly Confucian in his conviction that human beings are perfectible, that "any man can become a sage." This can be accomplished by the guidance of rulers and teachers, the implementation of universal standards of behavior, and the proper ordering of society. "Goodness is acquired" through a process of gradual "accumulation" of models of behavior from the outside.

The key word employed by Xunzi in this context is *wei*: to contrive, manipulate, or create; to deliberate; and, as a noun, "activity," "construct," or "artifice." Goodness is a human construct, invented by the sage–kings of the early Zhou (Chou) dynasty in the form of laws and rites. These standards of goodness are passed on from rulers to subjects and from teachers to students, and can be cultivated within individuals through education. Xunzi concluded from his negative evaluation of human nature that education is fundamentally a molding process that "civilizes" the young, and that public ritual (*li*) is the primary means for the creation of a prosperous and peaceful culture. *Li* was, of course, a defining idea for Confucius, who emphasized the broader meaning of "propriety" and "decency" in all interactions, and Xunzi's indebtedness to Confucius on this point defined him as a Confucian thinker. In Xunzi's terms, *li* are the rules of proper conduct in both ceremonial and everyday contexts that can shape individuals to think less often of themselves. He does not deny that this is a manipulative, "unnatural" process. Just as straight wood can be shaped into a wheel or dull metal can be sharpened, a person can "become clear in thought and faultless in action" through education and the practice of *li*.

The distinction between the natural and the artificial also applies to the feelings and mind. Although feelings are natural, thought is "artificial" or "contrived," deliberate.

The likes and dislikes, happiness and anger, sadness and joy of the *xing* are called "emotions." When the emotions are aroused and the mind chooses among them, this is called "thought." When the mind is capable of action on the basis of deliberation, this is *wei*.

Deliberation is an "artificial" molding activity that functions to harness emotions and suppress their natural, selfish expression.

This capacity for overcoming natural desires distinguishes persons from animals. It also makes social life possible, as the unchecked expression of emotion would preclude the possibility of civil society. In Xunzi's terms, what distinguishes people from animals is "differentiation," both as a function of rational thought and as the basis for communal existence. "We are not as strong as oxen . . . yet they are used by us. Why? . . . . Because we differentiate among ourselves." Condemning the social egalitarianism of the Daoists and Mohists in the strongest terms, Xunzi underscored the ideals of social hierarchy, division of labor, and clarity of roles described by Xunzi and his Confucian predecessors as the "rectification of names." Successful statecraft involves the proper identification of duties, the creation of models and standards for behavior, and the judicious implementation of rewards and punishments. Within such an environment, goodness can be "constructed" and society made harmonious.

Xunzi's Naturalism

Xunzi was a religious skeptic. He did not believe in ghosts and spirits, omens, or the ability to divine the future based on individual physical characteristics. He refused to acknowledge unseen causes of natural events or political upheaval, or to admit any connection between strange natural events and the success or failure of human endeavors. The greatest wisdom, he said, is to see that the social realm, the realm of the heavens, and the realm of the earth are separate (they form a "triad"); only the first of these can be understood and only human action has moral significance. After a long discussion of strange events, including falling stars, whistling trees, eclipses of the sun and moon, and untimely winds and rains—interpreted by diviners as having profound significance for the state—Xunzi concludes,

Never in history has there been a time when such things did not occur. . . . Marvel at them, but do not fear them!. . . Among all the unusual occurrences, the ones to fear are the man-made disasters. . . . Marvel at them, and fear them as well!

Xunzi's clearest expression of these views appears in a discourse on "Heaven" (*tian/t'ien*). Prior Confucians had conceptualized *tian* in anthropomorphic terms, as guiding human life, rewarding and punishing, delighting in or detesting human acts. Xunzi, perhaps reflecting Daoist influence, described *tian* simply as the order of nature, independent of human behavior in its processes and activities. *Tian*, he said, is impartial, speechless, natural, spontaneous, purposeless, indifferent, unconscious, irrational, and unknowable. "So, a person of depth does not attempt to contemplate it."

This is not to say that Xunzi rejected ceremony or religious ritual, however. He simply rejected an interpretation of religious ritual as "true" or efficacious:

You pray for rain and it rains. For what reason? I say there is no reason. It is as if you had not prayed for rain and it rained anyway.

Yet religious ritual has its positive effects if it is seen for what it truly is—the ordered expression of human emotion and a model of social harmony. Xunzi describes the function of religion as "ornamental" (*wen*), a word that connotes order, pattern, and emotional and aesthetic balance. "Ornament," like "artifice," creates models or paradigms for human life, and religion is part of the general molding process of education. Religious ritual (*li*) gives emotion an appropriate outlet and helps us to overcome our naturally selfish expression of desire. But there is no question of spiritual efficacy.

So, the gentleman regards them as ornamental, the common people as divine. To see them as ornamental is fortunate; to see them as divine is unfortunate.

Lasting Influence

Xunzi never enjoyed the esteem of his greatest intellectual rivals, Mencius and Mozi. He died with the knowledge that the new empire was loathe to implement his traditional models of ceremony and social organization, adopting instead the harsh measures of the Legalist School. His own disciples Han Fei Zi (Han Fei Tzu) and Li Si (Li Ssu) abandoned his teachings in favor of Legalism, and the *Ru* (*Ju*) School was fractured and unable to influence the policies of the Qin emperor.

With the revival and elaboration of Confucian thought during the Han dynasty, Xunzi's interpretation of ritual became normative, and whole passages of his works were copied into the *Book of Rites* (*Li ji/Li chi*). His demystification of "Heaven" was also accepted by Han Confucians such as Wang Chong (Wang Ch'ung), who rejected the belief in gods and ghosts and the ethical interpretation of natural portents. The view that religion has no spiritual efficacy but functions as a positive agent of social control and moral persuasion has been the predominant view of Confucian officialdom throughout Chinese history, and can be traced in the first instance to Xunzi.

As for the issue of human nature, the Mencian view has generally been preferred, and Mencius has enjoyed a much higher status in history. Zhu Xi (Chu Hsi), prime architect of the Neo-Confucian revival in the Song (Sung) dynasty, eschewed Xunzi, and he was largely ignored until modern times. But even before the Song, there was only one commentary written on the *Xunzi* (by Yang Liang of the Tang/T'ang dynasty), compared to nine on the *Book of Mencius*. Nonetheless, the debate between Mencius and Xunzi defined an ongoing dialectic in the history of Chinese thought, and Xunzi's view appears as a subtext in every significant moral treatise.

RANDALL L. NADEAU

Further Reading

Translations

Dubs, Homer H. *The Works of Hsün-tzu*. London: Arthur Probstham, 1928. A generally faithful translation of twenty-three chapters of the *Xunzi*, but now outdated by modern scholarship.

Knoblock, John. *Xunzi: A Translation and Study of the Complete Works*. Stanford, Calif.: Stanford University Press, 1988, 1990. The first two volumes of three projected, to include all thirty-two chapters of the *Xunzi*. The definitive study and translation, thoroughly annotated.

Watson, Burton. *Hsün-tzu: Basic Writings*. New York: Columbia University Press, 1963. The ten most central chapters of the *Xunzi*, by a master translator.

Related Studies

Cua, Antonio S. *Ethical Argumentation: A Study in Hsün Tzu's Moral Epistemology*. Honolulu, Hawaii: University of Hawaii Press, 1985. A philosophical investigation of the work, by a scholar trained in Western philosophy.

Dubs, Homer H. *Hsüntzu: The Moulder of Ancient Confucianism*. London: Arthur Probstham, 1927. A classic brief study, though partly outdated by recent scholarship.

THE SPRING AND AUTUMN ANNALS OF MASTER LU (LÜSHI CHUNQIU/LÜ-SHIH CH'UN-CH'IU)

Author: Presumably compiled by Lu Buwei (Lü Pu-wei) (c. 291–235 B.C.)
Date of Composition: Third century B.C.
Type of Work: Political philosophy, ethics

Major Ideas

Political order depends on the ruler's properly performing seasonal rites.

The teachings of traditional philosophy should be applied according to the seasons of the year.

The ruler must respect and protect his own life.

The ruler must govern with an attitude of public-spiritedness.

The harmony of music provides an important key to uniting cosmological and political order.

The ruler must maintain troops, preparing for a just war.

The ruler's practice of filial piety is necessary to develop loyalty in the people.

Proper timing is of the essence in achieving political order.

The ruler cannot afford to blindly follow tradition; he must respond to present circumstances with innovative practices.

Lu Buwei (Lü Pu-wei) was a very successful merchant from Yangzhai (Yang-Chai), the capital of the State of Han. He skillfully manipulated the royal family of Qin (Ch'in) and worked his way into the Qin court, serving as court tutor and chancellor to King Zhuang-Xiang (Chuang-Hsiang) of Qin (ruled 250–247 B.C.), and Lu Buwei was enfeoffed as Marquis Wenxin (Wen-hsin; "Literary Truth"). When the young King Zheng (Cheng), the First-Emperor-to-be, took the throne in 247 B.C., Lu was promoted to the rank of prime minister (247–237 B.C.), until he was implicated in the Lao Ai Rebellion. Lu Buwei died, possibly by suicide, in exile in 235 B.C.

Lu Buwei's contribution to pre-Qin literature and philosophy is his sponsorship of the *Spring and Autumn Annals of Master Lu*, the *Lüshi chunqiu* (*Lü-shih ch'un-ch'iu*). The work was written and compiled by the numerous guest scholars and retainers who heeded Lu Buwei's call for intellectuals. Lu was probably competing with other states which were compiling their own books, and as the court tutor he may have wanted to develop his own instructional material. The *Annals of Master Lu* impacts Chinese history in two ways. First, it provided the young king of Qin with a practicable philosophical approach for unifying the empire and proclaiming himself First Emperor. Second, the text was an imperial commission and avoided the infamous burning of the books in 213 B.C., and as such it influenced Han dynasty literature, most notably the *Xinxu* (*Hsin-hsü*), *Huainanzi* (*Huai-nan Tzu*), *Chunqiufanlu* (*Ch'un-ch'iu fan-lu*), and others.

The *Annals* is an eclectic philosophical work, drawing from the various teachings of the Late Zhou (Chou) dynasty philosophies. The text contains 160 chapters and is divided into three parts: the "Twelve Chronicles," the "Eight Observations," and the "Six Discussions." The numbers probably had some significance, possibly representing the "three powers"—Heaven, Earth, and human beings.

"The Twelve Chronicles"

The "Twelve Chronicles" is arranged according to the twelve months of the year. The lead chapter of each subdivision of the "Twelve Chronicles" contains the earliest extant source of the "Monthly

Commands" chapter of the *Book of Rites*—one of the five "Confucian Classics." The philosophical relevance of this material is that it provides a grand system of cosmic correlations and explains the significance of the imperial rituals to be performed through the changing seasons of the year. Most importantly, it is proposed in these chapters that the weather will be influenced positively or negatively according to the ruler's performance of the seasonal rites. For example, in the spring the rites of spring must be performed properly for the ice to melt and the planting to begin; if the rites of winter are performed in the spring, it will continue to snow. One of the defining characteristics of Chinese political philosophy is its commitment to the significance of cosmic harmony and its belief that this harmony is based on a reciprocal relationship obtaining between human life and the environment.

Because of the agricultural base of Chinese society, the ruler's political control often depended on weather conditions, which affected the harvest. Although the modern reader may think that this idea that human actions can influence the weather involves a reliance on superstitious magic, the belief seems to contain a profound understanding of an advanced ecological perspective. Government rituals may not affect the environment, but certainly other forms of government policy have contributed to the environmental crisis.

The lead chapters of the "Twelve Chronicles" are followed by four auxiliary chapters for each month; these chapters give the ruler detailed discussions on the art of rulership and self-cultivation. The material is eclectic, drawing from the various teachings, but there is a general pattern that suggests that there is a philosophy for every season. The spring chapters are dominated by Daoist (Taoist) ideas of self-cultivation and governing by non-purposive action (*wuwei/wu-wei*). The summer chapters focus on Confucian ideas of education and ritual music. The autumn chapters deal with military matters, and the winter chapters discuss the Mohist idea of frugal funerals and Legalist ideas of administration.

Two important themes introduced in the spring chapters of the "Twelve Chronicles" that are echoed throughout the text are: the importance of the ruler's respecting and protecting his own life, and the significance of governing with an attitude of public-spiritedness, avoiding selfish exploitation. The title of "Son of Heaven" belongs to the person who is able to nurture life. He establishes offices and officials to assist in nurturing life. Political chaos and the demise of the ruler are brought about when the offices and officials are not regulated properly to do what they were established to do. Things are used to cultivate life; the problem is that confused rulers use life to nurture things. These ancient teachings appear to have relevance for modern life. The text often warns the ruler to take care not to be overindulgent in satiating his senses and desires.

The chapters in the summer months section of the "Twelve Chronicles" develop Confucian ideas of education, ritual, and music. In keeping with Confucian and other moralist teachings good people, even good rulers, need good teachers to serve as advisers. An important part of the Confucian education was ritual and music. Traditionally these are not separate subjects. One cannot perform ritual, especially not imperial rites, without music. Originally there were six "Confucian Classics"; the *Book of Music* is no longer extant. At present the *Annals of Master Lu* contains the earliest extant text on ancient Chinese music. The dominant theme is that the harmony of music provides an important key to uniting cosmological and political order. Traditional Chinese music theory had two scales: a five-tone and a twelve-tone scale. The five-tone scale correlates with the Five Elements theory (*wuxing/wu-hsing*), and the twelve-tone scale correlates with the twelve lunar months. A wise ruler is supposed to recognize that the cosmos vibrates in a musical harmony, and so he should align the court rituals and the government policy according to the cosmic musical harmony to bring social and political order to his state and people.

The chapters in the autumn section of the "Twelve Chronicles" open with a concern for military matters. Traditionally a good ruler was expected to hold off on military attacks until after the autumn harvest so as not to destroy the crops essential to the life of the people. The text argues against disarmament, proposing that a wise ruler must maintain troops, preparing for a just war. The good ruler not only needs troops to defend his own people and state, but the text argues that the virtuous ruler is willing to attack immoral rulers who oppress their own people. It is strongly implied, through various historical examples, that the way to unify the empire and become emperor is by fighting the just war. Although the battles of the State of Qin were not just wars, it was certainly through warfare that King Zheng was able to proclaim himself the First Emperor.

"The Eight Observations"

The "Eight Observations" also contains a wealth of interesting eclectic philosophy. The chapter "Practicing Filial Piety" contains material found in the Han dynasty Confucian text *The Classic of Filial Piety* (*Xiaojing/Hsiao ching*). The ruler's practice of filial piety is necessary to develop loyalty in the people. The traditional saying is that filial sons make loyal ministers. Confucian philosophy assumes that people imitate others. So the ruler must set a good example for the people to emulate. The ruler ought to show proper respect to his own parents to teach the commoners to respect their own parents, and by extension the people will learn to respect and be loyal to their ruler, who is understood to act as a parent to the nation.

A recurring theme through the whole text is the importance of timing. A couple of chapters are entirely devoted to the idea that proper timing is of the essence in achieving political order. The text is primarily concerned with the ruler's appropriating timely action, and this timely action must occur on three levels: the cosmic, the sociopolitical, and the interpersonal. As was noted above, the ruler must perform seasonal rituals to maintain environmental and political order. Lu's *Annals* also contains the earliest extant material from the *Yinyang Wuxing* (Five Elements) School of Zou Yan (Tsou Yen). The Five Elements philosophy

attempts to correlate ancient physics, astronomy, and geography, with political, social, and psychological phenomena.

The second chapter in the first section of the "Eight Observations" argues that the founders of the early dynasties noted the cosmic transformations of the five elements and adjusted the court emblems and policy to match the element. For example, King Wen, founder of the Zhou dynasty, observed that the element fire had come into dominance; so he made fire and its correlated color, red, the symbols of the Zhou. The text points out that the element water would conquer fire. It is interesting to note that after the State of Qin conquered the various states and unified the empire, part of the First Emperor's justification was that he recognized that the element water dominated the cosmos, and that Qin would rule by following the element of water, which extinguished the fire of Zhou. On the political level, the ruler must be sensitive to changes in custom and reform the laws and statutes in a timely fashion to maintain social and political order.

The third and seventh chapters in the second of the "Eight Observations" provide the most detailed discussion on timely action in pre-Qin literature. These two chapters emphasize the importance of observing timely action in the ruler's personal behavior, especially his interpersonal relationships. The recurring theme is that the ruler must await the right time before taking action. Numerous examples are given of rulers and their ministers who had to await the proper opportunity before taking action which led to their success in life or politics. Because timing plays an important role in business, it is not too surprising that Lu Buwei would give timing an important place in his book.

Some scholars have argued that the *Annals* is an anti-Legalist text (see Hsiao Kung-chuan in the "Further Readings" section below). Such an argument not only defies the eclectic nature of the text, but it also ignores the explicit Legalist content. The eclectic character of Lu's *Annals* is to borrow the useful elements from all the traditional teachings concerning the art of rulership. The chapter "Examining the Present" contains material that parallels passages in edicts written later by the notorious Legalist prime minister of Qin, Li Si (Li Ssu), and that chapter may have even been written by Li Si himself since he was in the State of Qin while the text was being compiled. That chapter contains the Legalist idea that a ruler in the present cannot afford to blindly follow tradition, especially not the policy of the early kings, but rather must respond to present circumstances with innovative practices. The idea of not imitating the ancient kings influenced later writers such as Wang Chong (Wang Ch'ung) and even the Daoist commentator Guoxiang (Kuo-hsiang).

The "Six Discussions" section contains important information on ancient Chinese agricultural practices, representing the most comprehensive extant material from the agriculturist school of philosophy. The importance of proper timing in farming and ruling is discussed. Possibly the three sections of Lu's *Annals* were independent attempts to write the definitive text on the art of rulership; each had its shortcomings and thus the three were combined to form one massive eclectic text.

JAMES D. SELLMANN

Further Reading

Translations

Sellmann, James. "The *Lü-shih ch'un-ch'iu*'s Proposal of Governing by Filial Piety," *Asian Culture Quarterly*. Vol. XIII, no. 1, Spring 1985, 43–62. In addition to explicating the philosophical arguments, this article also provides a translation of a chapter from the *Annals of Master Lu*.

———. "On Mobilizing the Military: Arguments for a Just War Theory from the *Lü-shih ch'un-ch'iu*," *Asian Culture Quarterly*. Vol. XI, no. 4, Winter 1983, 26–43. This article also contains a translation.

Watson, Burton. *Early Chinese Literature*. New York: Columbia University Press, 1962, pp. 186–189. This work provides a critical review of the *Annals* and a translation of one chapter.

Wilhelm, Richard. trans. *Frühling und Herbst des Lü Bu We*. Introduction by Wolfgang Bauer.

Düsseldorf: Eugen Diederichs Verlag, 1979. The only complete translation in a Western language.

Related Studies

Bodde, Derk. *China's First Unifier, A Study in the Ch'in Dynasty as seen in the Life of Li Ssu*. Hong Kong: Hong Kong University Press, 1967. This is a valuable source for understanding the spirit of the Qin (Ch'in) dynasty.

Carson, Michael F. *A Concordance to Lü-shih ch'un-ch'iu*. Taipei: Chinese Material Center, 1985. The introduction contains important material on the structure and history of Lu's *Annals*. To study specific concepts in the text, one needs this comprehensive concordance; the other indexes are incomplete.

Chan, Wing-tsit, trans. and comp. *A Source Book in Chinese Philosophy*. Princeton, N.J.: Princeton University Press, 1963. This book provides a general introduction to pre-Qin philosophy, and it uses Lu's *Annals* to explicate Zou Yan's teachings.

Feifel, Eugen. "Review of *Frühling und Herbst des Lu Bu Wei*," *Philosophy East and West*, vol. 25, no. 1, 1975, 112–115.

Fung, Yu-lan. *A History of Chinese Philosophy*. 2 vols. Translated by Derk Bodde. Princeton, N.J.: Princeton University Press, 1952. Volume 1 makes extensive use of Lu's *Annals* to explicate the philosophy of the Hundred Schools, especially Yang Zhu and Zou Yan.

Hsiao, Kung-chuan. *A History of Chinese Political Thought*. Translated by F. Mote. Princeton, N.J.: Princeton University Press, 1979. In part 2, section 3, Hsiao develops the idea that Lu's *Annals* is an anti-Legalist text.

Louton, John. "Concepts of Comprehensiveness and Historical Change on the *Lü-shih ch'un-ch'iu*," in *Explorations in Early Chinese Cosmology*. Edited by H. Rosemont, Jr. Chicago: Scholars Press, 1984, 105–118. Louton argues that the authors of the *Annals of Master Lu* understand historical change as a product of the interaction of humans beings and nature.

Needham, Joseph. *Science and Civilization in*

China, Vol. 2, *History of Scientific Thought.* Cambridge: Cambridge University Press, 1956. This work provides an insightful survey of pre-Qin philosophy. Many of the later volumes cite passages from Lu's *Annals.*

Sellmann, James. "Three Models of Self-Integration (*tzu te*) in Early China," *Philosophy East and West.* 37/4 October 1987, pp. 372–390. This article discusses the concept of "self-integration" in Lu's *Annals.*

———. "Seasonality in the Achievement of *Hsing* in the *Lü-shih ch'un-ch'iu*," *Asian Culture Quarterly.* Vol. XVIII, no. 2, Summer 1990, 42–68. This article explicates the eclectic understanding of human nature in the book and contains numerous passages in translation.

Wylie, A. *Notes on Chinese Literature.* Taipei: Bookcase Shop Ltd. 1970 report, 157–158. Although Wylie surveys a wide range of literature, this work must be read carefully because many of his evaluations are out-of-date; his claim that the *Annals of Master Lu* shows Buddhist influence is definitely wrong.

HAN FEI

Born: c. 280 B.C., the State of Han, China
Died: c. 233 B.C., the State of Qin (Ch'in), China
Major Work: *Han Fei Zi* (*Han Fei Tzu*) (Date of compilation unknown.)

Major Ideas

Human beings are selfish, but they respond to reward and punishment.

Reward and punishment are the main tools of government.

Good government requires law, power, and statecraft.

Clear and well-defined law as made by the ruler should replace the moral norm and serve as the only standard for behavior.

Political power should be held by the king alone and not be shared with either the aristocracy or the ministers.

A good ruler rules through a complex but well-designed bureaucracy, which he controls and manages skillfully.

Order is achieved when names correspond with reality.

In emulation of the way nature without activity produces myriad things, the ideal ruler achieves order without active participation in governing.

Han Fei is the most well-known figure of the Legalist School (*Fa-jia/Fa-chia*). Although Han Fei's ideas were not always original and in many cases owed their origins to his Legalist predecessors, no ancient Chinese philosopher had managed to synthesize and articulate better than Han Fei the complex set of philosophical and practical ideas about government known as Legalism. In short, Legalism, as articulated by Han Fei, advocates government by law founded on the absolute power of the king. It is a very distinctive way of thinking about human nature and government that is fundamentally anti-Confucian with some Daoist (Taoist) affinities.

Han Fei lived in the late Warring States period. Most of what we know about his life comes from Sima Qian's (Ssu-ma Ch'ien's) *Shi Ji* (*Shih Chi*). He was born into a high-ranking aristocratic family in the State of Han in central China. The year of his birth is estimated by some scholars to be around 280 B.C. He studied under the Confucian philosopher Xunzi (Hsün Tzu). Han Fei had as a fellow student a man named Li Si (Li Ssu), who later would serve as the prime minister to the First Emperor of the Qin (Ch'in) dynasty and engineer the

largest and most radical Legalist reform known in Chinese history.

Han Fei attempted to participate in government and volunteered his advice to the king of Han, but without success. Many of Han Fei's essays were written in this period both to express his views on government and to vent his personal frustrations. The king of Han finally decided to send Han Fei as an envoy to the king of Qin when the State of Han was about to be attacked by the State of Qin. This mission to Qin turned out to be Han Fei's journey to his death. Han Fei was imprisoned in the State of Qin and was given poison to drink. He died in the year 233 B.C. Though the king of Qin, the future First Emperor, was a great admirer of Han Fei and had shown interest in employing him, he finally ordered the execution of Han Fei under the advice of his prime minister Li Si, Han Fei's former fellow student, who questioned Han Fei's loyalty to Qin and the advisability of allowing Han Fei to return to Han.

Fifty-five essays, mostly on subjects related to government, were collected after Han Fei's death under the title *Han Fei Zi* (*Han Fei Tzu*). Only a very few of these essays have been disputed as authentic works of Han Fei's.

Selfishness and Government by Reward and Punishment

Han Fei's philosophy was greatly influenced by the great political chaos of the Warring States that resulted from the collapse of the old feudal order of the Zhou (Chou) dynasty. Every state was threatened with war and annexation from without and usurpation from within. It is no surprise that Han Fei's political philosophy focused on how a ruler may preserve his rule through the establishment of order and the prevention of chaos. His Legalist philosophy was offered as an alternative to the Confucian philosophy of government. In Han Fei's view, the Confucian philosophy of government, with its emphasis on moral cultivation and the exercise of customary rites (*li*), is ineffective in establishing order because it is based on an understanding of human nature that is fundamentally flawed.

Han Fei believed that human beings are on the whole self-interested. He saw the calculation of long-term self-interest and profit even in parents' affection for their children. Of course there are benevolent people but, in Han Fei's view, they are the exceptions. And since it is the purpose of government to govern as many people as possible, its principles cannot be based on a view of human psychology that is true only of the exceptions. In fact, in Han Fei's view, even though the calculative selfishness of human beings is the main cause of social and political chaos, it is also what makes government possible. According to Han Fei, people have likes and dislikes and they act selfishly so as to obtain what they like and avoid what they dislike. This is why human beings respond to reward and punishment. Reward and punishment are what Han Fei wittily refers to as "the two handles" of government, as if by manipulating these two handles rulers could simply redirect the actions of their subjects, including making them serve the public and obey the law. Han Fei argues that a virtuous

person is much harder to govern. Since a virtuous person is not motivated by his own selfish gain, he does not respond to reward and punishment. A ruler thus does not have a handle on his virtuous subjects when it comes to making them conform to the law.

This is not to say that Han Fei maintains that Confucians were untruthful when they constantly referred to an earlier antiquity as an exemplary era of the sage–kings, Yao and Shun—an era when moral virtues reportedly reigned. In Han Fei's view, human nature has remained the same through the ages; only the material conditions have changed. According to Han Fei, in early antiquity there had been few people with an abundant supply of resources and hence people could have afforded to be kind and generous to each other, while in his own times there were many people with few supplies and hence they were contentious. In addition, the material primitiveness of antiquity had not allowed one to improve one's living condition much by being in a position of power. With less at stake, people had not been as interested in acquiring power, thus making it easier for ancient emperors to rule with benevolence or to abdicate in deference.

It is clear that Han Fei thought that the difference between his times and the earlier antiquity lay not in the difference between the moral qualities of the people of the two ages, but rather in the changing conditions of human life. Since the conditions of human life had fundamentally changed since antiquity, Han Fei thought it would be futile for the Confucians to advocate the return of the ancient form of government.

Han Fei takes history seriously. On the one hand, he realizes that history involves changing conditions of human life. What worked in the past may not work again in the future. But, on the other hand, Han Fei also combs history for lessons on how to govern. His writings are full of historical examples. Han Fei seems to be quite determined not to repeat the mistakes of the past. But more importantly, Han Fei believes that principles of government are to be discovered from careful observations of the actual workings of human history and cannot be based on the high-sounding abstract ideas preserved in traditional learning.

In Han Fei's account, reward and punishment are necessary tools of government because people do not voluntarily obey the law. Reward and punishment should be used to provide incentives for the subjects to obey the law. Han Fei argues that in order to function effectively as a deterrence, punishment for crimes must be harsh. People may very well be tempted to commit a crime if the consequence of being caught is not unbearable. Thus Han Fei believes that it is inhumane to have lenient punishments for crimes. This is because without a powerful deterrence, crimes will still be committed and punishment will still be applicable. If punishments are so harsh that no one would seriously entertain breaking the law, punishments will never have to be used.

But punishment can act as a deterrence only if crimes are effectively detected. Therefore Han Fei thinks that rewards should be provided for reporting crimes. In addition, he advocates collective responsibility by which one can be held accountable for the crimes committed by one's neighbors. This will presumably bring about mutual surveillance of each other by the subjects themselves and hence extend the long arm of the law without further active policing by the government.

Law, Power, and Statecraft: Three Elements of Good Government

Han Fei's view on good government is a synthesis of the views of several of his Legalist predecessors. Each of these predecessors has stressed one of three elements which Han Fei has come to realize as equally essential for good government, namely, law (*fa*), power (*shi/shih*), and statecraft (*shu*).

From Shang Yang (d. 338 B.C.), the famous statesman and reformer in the State of Qin, Han Fei learned the importance of *fa* (law). What Han Fei means by law is positive law—codified rules of conduct as made by the rulers and promulgated among the people. Law so made and promulgated is to serve as the norm for all behaviors and to replace all other standards of right and wrong, in-

cluding any preconceived moral standards or customary or religious rules of rite. Han Fei repeatedly compares law to the chalk line that carpenters use to tell the straight from the crooked. In this analogy, one can clearly see that Han Fei wants law to serve as a clear, unambiguous, and public standard that will settle any dispute about right and wrong. In this way the Legalist rule of law seeks to standardize societal norms for proper behavior through the decrees of the sovereign.

It is particularly important to standardize norms, Han Fei argues; the lack of clear and indisputable norms will only encourage individuals to make personal gains at the expense of society. Han Fei, like other Legalists, believes that it is of primary importance to standardize measurements. If units of measuring weight or volume are not standardized, one can easily be taken advantage of in commercial transactions. Han Fei also believes that the law should not be changed too often. Too many changes can only add to the confusion that encourages criminal behavior. If it is necessary to change the law, it should be done only with the old law clearly repealed.

This concern for clear and definite public norms explains why Han Fei is critical of Confucian emphasis on personal morality and the customary rules of rites. None of these provides sufficiently clear and definite standards for behavior in Han Fei's view. In fact, Han Fei argues that there are so many disputes among learned gentlemen on what morality and customary rites require that no ordinary citizen can reasonably be expected to rely on these scholars or their teachings for guidance. Han Fei believes that all teachings of proper behavior should be based on the law and magistrates should also act as teachers. All private teachings hence should be banned. Presumably this is the view that the First Emperor later overzealously put into practice by ordering that thousands of Confucian scholars be buried alive and their books burned.

The second essential element of good government, according to Han Fei's account, is *shi* (power), sometimes translated as meaning position or elevation. The importance of power had been stressed by Shen Dao (Shen Tao) (dates unknown).

The idea is that without some kind of awe-inspiring power, even a sage cannot effectively influence people's behavior. But with this political power, even a mediocre ruler can effectively make people act as he wishes. Hence the rule of law will not be possible unless the sovereign has this kind of political leverage to inspire respect and fear in people in order to make them conform to the legal norms he decrees.

Han Fei's view on political power goes even farther. He thinks that this awe-inspiring political power should be wielded by the king alone, in effect elevating the king above everybody else, including the aristocracy. Han Fei's rejection of any sharing of political power is motivated by his observation that the political chaos in many of the warring states was caused by the dispersal of political power throughout the aristocracy.

How does a ruler retain absolute power and remain the sole person politically elevated above everybody else? Han Fei's answer is for the ruler to retain sole control of reward and punishment. If noblemen and ministers do not have their own power to reward and punish people and merely act as the agents of the sovereign in enforcing the law, then they will not be able to manipulate people for their own gains. Ministers and noblemen, in Han Fei's view, are to be deprived of special privileges and equally subject to the law as ordinary citizens.

The third element of good government is *shu* (statecraft), often translated as "method" or "tact." Han Fei was indebted to an earlier prime minister of Han, Shen Buhai (Shen Pu-hai) (d. 337 B.C.), for realizing the importance of statecraft. In Han Fei's view, even though the ruler is to retain the ultimate control of the state, he is also to remain hidden from the day-to-day operation of the government. Laws are enforced and policies are implemented by a bureaucracy that has no political power of its own. For this kind of government to function properly, the ruler needs to be an expert practitioner of the art of personnel management. In Han Fei's view, it is essential for the ruler to know how to use people properly, including how to identify talents and to get people to perform suitable

tasks. The ruler should also know how to manipulate those in his service to achieve desired results. In addition, the ruler needs to be smart in dealing with his own royal household and the nobility as well. Besides ensuring the proper functioning of the government, the purpose of the ruler's expertise in personnel management is to keep all of his subordinates in their place and to prevent them from acquiring any political power.

Han Fei offers much specific practical advice on statecraft. His most important advice, perhaps, is that a ruler should remain inscrutable and refrain from revealing his own likes and dislikes to the ministers to avoid being manipulated by them.

Correspondence Between Names and Reality

Han Fei repeatedly writes that order is achieved when names (*ming*) correspond with reality or actuality (*xing/hsing*). Good government, therefore, seeks to make names correspond with reality. One thing Han Fei means by this is that each government office should also be correctly named by the ruler to describe its duties. Thus the name of each office will very strictly serve as the standard for evaluating performance. Furthermore, a minister should only propose to the ruler exactly what he intends and is capable of accomplishing for each project, not too much and not too little. Overachievement is as punishable as a crime as underachievement. Making names correspond with reality in these ways minimizes chaos by allowing the sovereign and his ministers to know clearly what to expect of each other. It is also considered to be a method of controlling the ministers.

Han Fei prefers very strict correspondence between names and reality as the criterion for evaluating performance because for a ruler to allow the ministers to have discretion in exercising their duties is to loosen the ruler's control over them and in effect to share power with them. This consideration explains why Han Fei praises a former ruler of Han for his bizarre act of executing the keeper of the royal hat for laying a robe on the ruler when he got drunk and fell asleep one night.

The crime committed by the keeper of the royal hat is said to be that of overstepping his office.

Han Fei and Daoism

Han Fei's philosophy is often claimed to have Daoist origins. Besides the presence of Daoist language in several of Han Fei's essays, there are two essays in the *Han Fei Zi* that are specifically commentaries on the *Daode jing* (*Tao-te ching*). However, there have been debates about Han Fei's authorship of some of these Daoist writings. The Daoist influence on Han Fei, if it exists, is primarily on two related points. First, the Daoist ideal of action through inaction is supposed to be achieved in Han Fei's ideal state. When the laws are properly made and the government bureaucracy is in place, the whole state becomes a self-regulating machinery and order is achieved without the ruler's active participation. In this way, the Legalist ruler mimics the way nature produces the myriad things without itself doing anything in particular. Second, the ruler is not supposed to make laws and define offices arbitrarily. These standards are to be based on the objective standard of right and wrong that originates in the *Dao* (*Tao*) of nature. However, like a Daoist sage, the ruler can know the *Dao* only by remaining empty and still. In Legalist terms, this means that when the ruler rules properly, people will be properly employed according to their different talents and abilities. Those who are capable of speaking the truth and those who are capable of putting it into practice will come forth and produce a profound correspondence between names and reality that goes beyond conventions. In this way, the ruler finds inexhaustible wisdom without being wise himself.

Han Fei's ideas are at once well-reasoned and provocative. Though often put into practice in some mitigated form in subsequent eras, these ideas have never entered into the mainstream of Chinese philosophy. Whatever the reason for this may be, Han Fei's fortune in Chinese intellectual history has certainly not been helped by the great disrepute of the First Emperor and his short-lived Qin dynasty.

The collapse of the Qin dynasty has often been seen, by scholars as well as in the popular mind, as due to the great calamities that resulted from the draconian Legalist policies that the First Emperor, after unifying China through conquests in 221 B.C., had put into effect.

WING-CHIAT LEE

Further Reading

Translations

Liao, W. K., trans. *The Complete Works of Han Fei Tzu*. 2 vols. London: Arthur Probstham, 1959. This translation is reliable, but sometimes awkwardly worded. It remains the only English translation of the complete *Han Fei Zi*.

Watson, Burton, trans. *Han Fei Tzu: Basic Writings*. New York: Columbia University Press, 1964. This is an excellent translation of twelve representative essays of Han Fei's, with a useful introduction. Also available as a part of *Basic Writings of Mo Tzu, Hsün Tzu, and Han Fei Tzu* (New York: Columbia University Press, 1967).

Related Studies

Hsiao, Kung-chuan. *A History of Chinese Political Thought*. Translated by F. W. Mote. Princeton, N.J.: Princeton University Press, 1979. Chapter 7, entitled "Lord Shang and Han Fei Tzu," is one of the best comprehensive accounts of Han Fei's thought.

Peerenboom, R. P. *Law and Morality in Ancient China*. Albany, N.Y.: State University of New York Press, 1993. Though this book is primarily a study of the Huang-Lao School, a particular school of Daoism-Legalism, it contains a chapter devoted to the explication of Han Fei. This book is useful for understanding Legalism as a whole and what is at issue between Legalism and other schools of thought in ancient China.

Wang, Hsiao-po. "The Significance of the Concept of *fa* in Han Fei's Thought System." Translated by L. S. Chang. In *Philosophy East and West*, 27, no. 1, January 1977. This article explains the different aspects of Han Fei's conception of government by law.

Wang, Hsia-po, and Leo Chang. *Philosophical Foundations of Han Fei's Political Theory*. Honolulu, Hawaii: University of Hawaii Press, 1986. This monograph is devoted primarily to Han Fei's relation to Daoism.

THE GREAT LEARNING (DA XUE/TA HSÜEH)

Author: Attributed to Zengzi (Tseng Tzu, 505-? B.C.) or Zi Si (Tzu Ssu, 492-431 B.C.)
Date of Composition: Between third and second centuries B.C.
Type of Work: Ethics and social philosophy

Major Ideas

The task of great learning consists of three aims and eight steps:
The three aims are manifesting one's luminous virtue, renewing the people, and abiding in perfect goodness.
The eight steps are the investigation of things, extension of knowledge, sincerity of the will, rectification of the heart, cultivation of the personal life, regulation of the family, national order, and world peace.

The *Great Learning* is one of the Confucian canon called "the Four Books," the other three being the *Analects* (*Lunyu/Lun-yü*) of Confucius (Kongfuzi/K'ung Fu-tzu), the *Book of Mencius* (*Mengzi/Meng Tzu*), and the *Doctrine of the Mean* (*Zhongyong/Chungyung*). Originally it was a chapter of a larger Confucian work, *Li ji* (*Li chi*), the *Book of Rites*, which was first compiled by Dai De (Tai Te) and later reedited by his nephew Dai Sheng (Tai Sheng, fl. 51 B.C.). (Confucius died in 479 B.C.) During the following period of the Warring States (403–221 B.C.) there were many Confucian followers. The *Li ji* consists of works of these followers, either their own teachings or their recording of Confucius's teachings, on proper social behavior and various rites of music performance, mourning, sacrifice, marriage, and filial piety. It is among the five "Confucian Classics" (the *Book of Changes*, the *Book of Odes*, the *Book of History*, the *Book of Rites*, and the *Spring and Autumn Annals*), which remained the central and most important texts in the Confucian tradition until the "Four Books" were selected by Zhu Xi (Chu Hsi, 1130–1200), the great Neo-Confucianist philosopher in the Song (Sung) dynasty (A.D. 960–1279). The authorship of the *Great Learning* remains a question even today. Whereas scholars such as Zhu Xi believed it was written by Confucius's disciple Zengzi (Tseng Tzu), others attributed it to Confucius's grandson, Zi Si (Tzu Ssu). However, the actual work was perhaps not written until the third and second centuries B.C.

The *Great Learning* was not singled out from the *Li ji* as principally significant until the work of the Song Neo-Confucianists. The Cheng brothers of Henan (Honan) Province deserved much credit for giving the *Great Learning* a status of importance independent of the *Li ji*. Cheng Hao (Ch'eng Hao, also called Cheng Ming Dao/Ch'eng Ming-tao, 1032–85) and Cheng Yi (Ch'eng I, also called Cheng Yichuan/Ch'eng I-ch'uan, 1033–1107), both outstanding Confucian scholars and philosophers, set the pattern for Song-Ming Neo-Confucianism. They both made important contributions to the study of the *Great Learning*. Cheng Hao identified the *Great Learning* as a work handed down from Confucius himself. Cheng Yi maintained that "as a gateway to virtue there is nothing as good as the *Great Learning*." Through many years of careful study they arrived at the conclusion that the original text was misordered in Dai Sheng's version. To make the work more systematic and meaningful to students, the Chengs revised the order of the sections in the text taken from the *Li ji*. It was Zhu Xi who finally made the *Great Learning* a Confucian text of canonical importance. Zhu Xi was the most prominent Neo-Confucian philosopher of his time and devoted his lifetime studying the "Confucian Classics." Among numerous Confucian texts, Zhu Xi selected four (the "Four Books"), which he believed contain the kernels of the Confucian teachings, to be the primary curriculum in the Confucian education. After many years of study, Zhu Xi, following the Chengs' lead, further rearranged the text. Zhu divided the text into two parts, a classic portion (consisting of only 205 characters) and a commentary portion. Zhu affirmed that the classic portion may be taken as the words of Confucius, handed down by Zengzi, and the commentary portion was recordings of Zengzi's words by his disciples. According to Zhu, the title, *Great Learning* (*Da Xue*: *da* means big, great, grand; *xue* means learning or study), means "learning for adults." He explained the title of the *Great Learning* as higher education. Zhu Xi maintained that there were two sections in the education of antiquity, the "small learning" and the "great learning." The "small learning" was for children. It consisted in house chores such as cleaning and sweeping, ways of polite conversation and good manners, and refinements of ritual, music, archery, charioteering, calligraphy, and calculation. The "great learning" was for adults. It consisted of extending knowledge through investigating things, cultivating the self, establishing a harmonious household, organizing the state, and bringing tranquility to the whole world. Unlike some scholars, Zhu Xi believed that the *Great Learning* was a text not only for the ruler, but for the common people as well.

Zhu Xi attached profound significance to the *Great Learning*:

> If one does not read the *Great Learning* first, there is no way to grasp the outline of learning and thereby to appreciate fully the subtleties of the *Analects* and the *Book of Mencius*. If one does not then read the *Great Learning* with the *Analects* and the *Book of Mencius*, there is no way to understand thoroughly the thread that runs through the three texts and thereby to get at the essence of the *Doctrine of the Mean*. . . . From this point of view, it is apparent that those who engage in scholarly study must treat the "Four Books" with some urgency and those who study the "Four Books" must begin with the *Great Learning*.

Since the time of Zhu Xi, the *Great Learning*, along with the rest of the "Four Books," has be-

come a canonical work for Confucianism. In the Yuan (Yüan) dynasty (1271–1368) the government made the "Four Books" the primary texts for the civil service examinations and they remained so until early this century.

The Three Aims and the Eight Steps

The *Great Learning* contains the Confucian educational, moral, and political programs, which are best summarized as "Three Aims" and "Eight Steps." The three aims are "manifesting one's luminous virtue," "renewing the people," and "abiding in perfect goodness." The eight steps are "the investigation of things," "extension of knowledge," "sincerity of the will," "rectification of the mind," "cultivation of the personal life," "regulation of the family," "national order," and "world peace." At the core of Confucianism lie two inseparable goals of morality: cultivating the self and ordering the state or society. The Three Aims and Eight Steps best illustrate the way to achieve these goals.

The text starts with the Three Aims of the "great learning." The first is "manifesting one's luminous virtue." Although Confucius's own view on human nature remains unclear in his *Analects*, Confucians generally believed that human beings are born with a virtuous nature. But this nature needs to be manifested through moral education and self-cultivation. Mencius maintained that humans are born with the feeling of commiseration, the feeling of shame, the feeling of deference and compliance, and the feeling of right and wrong. He called these inborn feelings "the four beginnings" of morality. But these feelings, comprising our "original heart," need to be nourished and developed. Moral education aims at the manifestation of this luminous virtue. The commentary supports this aim by enumerating ancient exemplars of taking the manifestation of one's "Heaven-given luminous virtue" as their goal. Both the Sage-King Wen and the Sage-Emperor Yao are said able to manifest their luminous virtue.

The second item in the text reads: "loving the people." This needs little further exposition if one remembers that Confucius himself expounds his cardinal concept *ren* (*jen*), humanity, in terms of "loving the people." However, the commentary centers on the notion of "renewing" or "renovating" the people. Both Cheng Yi and Zhu Xi proposed that the word "love" (*qin/chin*) in the text be read "renew" (*xin/hsin*). In the commentary, there is a quotation of an ancient inscription saying "One should renew oneself, day after day renew oneself, indeed, renew oneself everyday." Another quotation from the *Book of Odes* reads "Zhou is an old state, but the mandate it has received from Heaven is new." These comments are consistent with Cheng Yi's and Zhu Xi's reading of the sentence as "renewing the people," and their reading was accepted by many Confucian scholars.

The idea of "renewing the people" can best be understood by relating it to the third and last aim of the "great learning": "abiding in perfect goodness." If one abides in the perfect or highest goodness, one will never indulge in complacency and will always strive for perfection. The commentary praises the Sage-King Wen:

> He constantly maintained his luminous virtue and regarded with reverence that which he abided.
>
> As a ruler, he abided in humanity. As a minister, he abided in reverence. As a son, he abided in filial piety. As a father, he abided in kindness. And in dealing with the people of the country, he abided in good faith.

In order to achieve such perfection, one needs to keep the effort of continuously renewing oneself. One way to renew oneself is learning. In the *Analects* Confucius said, "Is it not a pleasure to learn and to repeat or practice from time to time what has been learned?" For Confucius a good person is one who learns untiringly and teaches others without being wearied. It is a duty to cultivate oneself and in the meantime to help others cultivate themselves, to renovate oneself and in the meantime to help others renovate themselves toward perfect goodness. This is what Confucius means by saying that

if you wish to establish your own character, also establish the character of others. If you wish to be successful yourself, also help others to be successful.

This is the way of the "great learning."

The Eight Steps

The Eight Steps are as follows: The ancients who wished that all people throughout the world manifest their luminous virtue would first order their states well. Those who wished to order their states well would first regulate their households. Those who wished to regulate their households would first cultivate their personal lives. Those who wished to cultivate their personal lives would first rectify their hearts. Those who wished to rectify their hearts would first make their wills sincere. Those who wished to make their wills sincere would first extend their knowledge. The extension of knowledge consists in the investigation of things. After things are investigated, knowledge is extended; after knowledge is extended, the will becomes sincere; after the will is sincere, the heart is rectified; after the heart is rectified, the personal life is cultivated; after the personal life is cultivated, the household will be regulated; after the household is regulated, the state will be well ordered; and after the state is well ordered, there will be peace throughout the world.

Unlike many Westerners, Confucius did not believe in a division between the private and public sphere. For him, the philosophy of managing a good household and the philosophy of managing a good state are the same. And in order to manage a good household a person must cultivate oneself. To be moral is not merely a matter of choosing to perform a right act. It is rather a long-term commitment to becoming a good person. In this sense, Confucian morality is a person-making morality. It means the cultivation of oneself throughout one's life. Confucius also believed in governing the state by the moral force of role models. In such a way moral education and cultivation at the individual level and morality at the societal level are linked. In this view, while the individual is a small self, the world is a greater self. The two are closely related.

The text reads,

Things have their roots and branches. Affairs have their beginnings and their ends. One comes to know the Way when one knows what is first and what is last.

In the matter of morality, the root is the individual self. From the Son of Heaven (emperor) to the common people, cultivating the self should be the root. The root determines the branches. Others will follow as self-cultivation progresses.

The starting point of self-cultivation is called *gewu* (ko-wu). Although earlier scholars read it differently, Zhu Xi and many of his followers interpreted it as "the investigation of things." According to Zhu Xi, *ge* means "to reach"; *wu* means "things" or "affairs." So *gewu* means "the investigation of things," or more literally, "to reach to the utmost the principle in affairs and things." Investigating things is the way to extend one's knowledge. The idea of *gewu* distinguishes Confucianism from Chan (Ch'an/Zen) Buddhism. They both believe in the goodness of human nature. Although Confucians maintain that humans are born with luminous virtue, Chan Buddhists believe that everyone has a "Buddha nature." But the Confucian way of *gewu* affirms that our perceptual knowledge of the external world leads to the manifestation of luminous virtue. The Chan Buddhist concentrates on the inner mind and regards study of the external world irrelevant to enlightenment.

Following the step of the extension of knowledge is "making the will sincere." According to the commentary, this means "no self-deception." There is a traditional Chinese saying which describes a respectable person as one "familiar with classics and reasonable." When one becomes knowledgeable, one has a good sense of right and wrong. With a good sense of right and wrong, one will have internal motivation to be moral. Without ulterior purposes, a person likes pretty colors and dislikes bad odors. In the same way, a moral person acts morally to meet one's own need and satisfac-

tion. For such a person, a moral act is not a show put on for others to see. Therefore even when one is alone one does the same kind of thing as would be done in front of people. This is the meaning of saying that "the superior man will always be watchful over himself when alone." This is called sincerity of the will. A person without sincerity of the will is an inferior person. An inferior person acts with no moral conscience. In front of people such a person will put on a show to pretend to be moral. But then he or she is always afraid that others will see through his tricks. Only with sincerity of the will can one live at ease.

Having a sincere will is a prerequisite for rectifying one's heart. "Heart" in Chinese (*xin/hsin*) refers also to the mind. With a sincere will a person acts as he or she believes and is thus at ease with oneself. Therefore such a person will have peace of mind and hence the mind will be set right. With a right mind, a person is not biased in one's action.

Resentfulness, fearfulness, and personal likes and dislikes are bases for biases. To rectify one's mind is to rid of these bases for biases. And only if one sets the mind right can he have one's personal life cultivated. After one is cultivated to be a good person, one is qualified to regulate one's family. For Confucius, a good father figure is a good role model for his children. A person of poor or wicked character cannot be a good householder. In turn, the ability of being a good householder is a prerequisite for governing a state well. And governing a state well is the necessary condition for bringing peace to the world.

The commentary explains the relation between regulating the household, ordering the state well, and making the world peaceful:

No one can teach others without being able to teach his own family. Therefore, the ruler, without going beyond his family, accomplished his teaching throughout the state.

It should be noted that, in the Confucian view, the state is not a mechanism for balancing various pressure groups of conflicting interests. Rather, it is an enlarged family with mutual trust among its members. The proper way of governance is setting up a good role model instead of handing out punitive laws. Under these circumstances, if the ruler treats the aged with reverence, the people will tend to practice filial piety. If the ruler treats his own elder brothers with respect, the people will tend to practice brotherly respect. If the ruler treats the young and the helpless with compassion, the people will follow the same course. The *Great Learning* says,

> Therefore the ruler will begin with cultivating his own virtue.
>
> With virtue, he will have the people with him. If he has the people with him, he will have the territory. With territory, he will have wealth. With wealth, he will have resources for expenditure.

In a word, virtue is the root. Everything else is the branch. And this is at the core of the Confucian ethic.

The Three Aims and the Eight Steps define Confucian moral theory. They demonstrate that between personal cultivation and world peace the various steps are closely linked. In a way, the Three Aims and the Eight Steps can be summarized as one, namely self-cultivation. There is no other work which in such a short length presents Confucian ethic so clearly and systematically. It has exercised a tremendous influence on Chinese society. Even today it remains probably the best introduction to Confucianism.

CHENYANG LI

Further Reading

Translations

Chan, Wing-tsit, trans. and comp. "Moral and Social Programs: the *Great Learning*," in *A Source*

Book in Chinese Philosophy. Translated and compiled by Wing-tsit Chan. Princeton, N.J.: Princeton University Press, 1963. A useful introduction to the work, and the *Great Learning* is translated in full, together with Zhu Xi's commentary.

Collie, David, ed. and trans. *The Chinese Classical Works Commonly Called "The Four Books"*. Gainesville, Fla.: Scholars' Facsimiles and Reprints, 1970. (From the Mission Press 1828 edition.) Collie is very critical of Confucianism in some footnotes, but his translation is fairly readable.

Hughes, E. R. *The Great Learning and the Doctrine of the Mean-in-Action: Confucius' Ta Hsüeh*. New York: AMS Press, 1943.

Yutang, Lin, ed. and trans. *The Wisdom of Confucius*. New York: Random House, Inc., 1938. See "Ethics and Politics."

Related Studies

Fung, Yu-lan. *History of Chinese Philosophy*. Vol. 1. Translated by Derk Bodde. London: George Allen & Unwin Ltd., 1937. In chapter 14, section 7, *The Great Learning*, Fung proposes that the work is the offshoot of Xunzi's (Hsün Tzu's) teachings and explains it accordingly.

Gardner, Daniel K. *Chu Hsi and the Ta-Hsüeh*. Cambridge, Mass.: Harvard University Press, 1986. A study of Zhu Xi's contribution to making the *Great Learning* one of the most significant texts in the Confucian tradition. It also includes the Chinese text and an annotated translation of it.

Pound, Ezra. *Confucius: The Great Digest & Unwobbling Pivot*. New York: New Direction Books, 1951. Includes the poet's translation and commentary on what he calls the *The Great Digest*. (The *Unwobbling Pivot* is the *Doctrine of the Mean*.)

THE DOCTRINE OF THE MEAN (ZHONG YONG/CHUNG YUNG)

Author: Attributed to Zi Si (Tzu Ssu) (492–431 B.C.), but author unknown
Date of Composition: Between the third and second centuries B.C.
Type of Work: Metaphysics and ethics

Major Ideas

Heaven and man are an inseparable single oneness.
Being virtuous is to follow the nature with which Heaven has endowed us.
Sincerity is the Way of Heaven and the Way of human morality.
The moral ideal is to become a superior person who exemplifies the Way of the Mean.

The Doctrine of the Mean is one of the Confucian canon called "the Four Books," the other three being the *Analects of Confucius*, the *Book of Mencius*, and the *Great Learning*. Originally it was a chapter of a larger Confucian work, the *Li ji* (*Li Chi*) (the *Book of Rites*), which was first compiled by Dai De (Tai Te) and later reedited by his nephew Dai Sheng (Tai Sheng, fl. 51 B.C.). Confucius died in 479 B.C. During the following period of the Warring States (403–221 B.C.) there were many Confucian followers. *Li ji* consists of works of these followers, either their own teachings, or their recording of Confucius's teachings, on proper social behavior and various rites of music performance, mourning, sacrifice, marriage, filial piety, and other matters. *Li ji* is among the five "Confucian Classics" (the *Book of Changes*, the *Book of Odes*, the *Book of History*, the *Book of Rites*, and the *Spring and Autumn Annals*), which remained the central and most important texts in the Confucian tradition until the "Four Books" were selected by Zhu Xi (Chu Hsi) (1130–1200), the great Neo-Confucianist philosopher in the Song (Sung) dynasty (A.D. 960–1279).

The *Doctrine of the Mean* has been traditionally attributed to the grandson of Confucius, Zi Si (Tzu Ssu). However, text analysis indicates that the work was probably done between the third and second centuries B.C. The *Doctrine of the Mean* was a work of importance independent of the *Li ji* long before Zhu Xi formed the list of the "Four Books." In Ban Gu's (Pan Ku's) (A.D. 32–92) *Yi wen zhi* (*I-wen Chih*), the first extant Chinese bibliography, the *Doctrine of the Mean* was already referred to as an independent treatise. The Liang Emperor Wu Di (Wu Ti) (464–549) allegedly wrote a commentary on it. And the Song Emperor Ren Zong (Jen-tsung) (1010–1063) once presented to one of his ministers a copy of the *Doctrine of the Mean* copied by the emperor in his own calligraphic style.

Along with the other three of the "Four Books," the *Doctrine of the Mean* was a primary text for the competitive nationwide civil service examinations from 1313 until 1905. Zhu Xi attached profound significance to the *Doctrine of the Mean*. Zhu Xi said,

> If one does not read the *Great Learning* first, there is no way to grasp the outline of learning and thereby to appreciate fully the subtleties of the *Analects* and the *Book of Mencius*. If one does not then read the *Great Learning* with the *Analects* and the *Book of Mencius*, there is no way to understand thoroughly the thread that runs through the three texts and thereby to get at the essence of the *Doctrine of the Mean*. Still, if one is not versed in the perfection of the *Doctrine of the Mean*, how can one establish the great foundation or adjust the great invariable relations of man, how can one read the world's books or discuss the world's affairs?

Whereas the *Great Learning* is a concise and systematic presentation of Confucian social philosophy, the *Doctrine of the Mean* provides a metaphysical justification for this philosophy. It is perhaps the most profound, most philosophical, most metaphysical, and most religious text in the whole body of ancient Confucian literature. It is a work in which some major ideas of Confucianism, Daoism (Taoism), and Buddhism converge. In many aspects, it serves as a bridge between the three major Chinese philosophies.

A Note on the Title: The Zhong yong

The Chinese word *zhong* (*chung*) means "central," "unbiased," and derivatively, "proper."

As a guideline for human behavior, the idea of *zhong* means "to do it just right." *Yong* means "ordinary" or "constant." *Zhong yong*, the title, means "central harmony" or "(the Way of) the Mean." Besides being rendered in English as *The Doctrine of the Mean*, the title has also been translated as *The Golden Mean*, *The Golden Medium*, *The Mean-in-action*, *The Central Harmony*, and *The Unwobbling Pivot*.

Morality: Heaven and Man

The Confucian metaphysic is one of an anthropocosmic unity. One way to describe this metaphysic is that Heaven and man are an inseparable single oneness. The *Doctrine of the Mean* begins by stating that

> What Heaven imparts to man is called human nature. To follow this nature is called the Way [*Dao/Tao*]. To cultivate the Way is called education.

Heaven (*tian/t'ien*) is the nonpersonal supreme deity or spiritual reality. The Way of Heaven is invested in human beings and resides in them as their nature. In this sense the Way of Heaven is imminent in us and we are part of Heaven. This is called the "inseparability of Heaven and man." This idea is not only fundamental in Confucianism, but is also

fundamental in Daoism and Chinese Buddhism, hence in Chinese philosophy in general. It is fundamentally different from the Western view on the dichotomy between human beings on the one hand and nature on the other. It also differs from the Judeo-Christian view that God is the creator of man and thus the foundation of human morality. Another way to present the view in the *Doctrine of the Mean* is to say that human beings, by nature, partake in the reality of Heaven. In this regard Confucian humanism is anthropocosmic, not anthropocentric.

The unity of Heaven and man provides a metaphysical basis for Confucian moral philosophy. Most Confucians believe in the goodness of human nature and that this goodness comes from Heaven. The Way of Heaven is the Way of humanity. Confucius wrote in the *Analects* that "Heaven gives birth to virtue in me." Mencius believed that every human being possesses the four beginnings of human-heartedness, righteousness, propriety, and wisdom, and that therefore human nature is good. He said,

> A person who exerts his heart to the utmost knows his nature. A person who knows his nature knows [the Way of] Heaven. To preserve one's heart and to nourish one's nature is to serve Heaven.

Although human beings are born with a good nature invested from Heaven, this good nature needs to be cultivated and developed. Thus, to cultivate oneself to be moral is not merely the way for individuals to be accepted into a community, nor is it merely a way to preserve the society from destruction. Rather, it is to fulfill ourselves as what we really are, to realize our innermost inherent nature, and it is what we are destined to be.

Reality, Sincerity, and Truthfulness

In the *Doctrine of the Mean* the concept that best describes the Heaven-and-human Way is *cheng* (*ch'eng*). The word may be translated as "sincerity," "reality," or "truthfulness." The *Doctrine of the Mean* states that "*cheng* is the Way of Heaven." It also says that absolute *cheng* is ceaseless and lasting. *Cheng* is described as infinite, unlimited, extensive, and deep. It supports all things and can complete all things. Without display *cheng* is prominent, without motion it produces changes, and without action it accomplishes its ends. What is said of *cheng*, the Way of Heaven, is reminiscent of the *Dao* in Laozi's *Daode jing* (Lao Tzu's *Tao Te Ching*). *Cheng* is a process of creativity, or better, it is the dynamic reality itself. This reality is ceaseless, infinite, extensive, and unlimited. It is the beginning and end of everything. It is an active force that works through everything in the universe. To say that reality is dynamic is to say that it is not only a state of being ("lasting") but also a process of becoming ("ceaseless").

When the Way of Heaven works in human beings it gives them humanity. The self-cultivation of the human being, like the development of everything else in the universe, belongs to the ceaseless process of the becoming of *cheng*. The *Doctrine of the Mean* says,

> To think how to be *cheng* is the way of man. He who is [in the state of] *cheng* is one who hits upon what is right without [extra] effort and apprehends without thinking. He is naturally and easily in harmony with the Way. Such a man is a sage. He who tries to be *cheng* is one who chooses the good and holds fast to it.

A person who is cultivated to the utmost goodness is said to have attained possession of *cheng*. Such a person is thus true to his nature. In this sense, *cheng* is also a state of mind and can be understood as "sincerity" or "truthfulness." A person who is sincere about attaining the Way strives for the goodness invested in him by Heaven. Mencius said,

> If a person does not understand goodness he cannot be *cheng* to himself. *Cheng* is the Way

of Heaven and to think how to be *cheng* is the Way to be a [good] person.

Even though Heaven has imparted goodness to us, our self-realization or self-cultivation is not an easy task. It requires sincerity. With sincerity, a person is unswerving in cultivating himself: "Enlightenment results from sincerity."

The Superior Person

A person who is true to oneself is a superior person. The Chinese term *junzi* (*chün-tzu*) is often translated as "gentleman," but since in Confucian texts it is usually used in contrast to *xiao ren* (*hsiao jen*), meaning "small man" or "inferior man," the English expression "superior person" is proper here. "Superior" means "morally superior." The superior person is a role model for other people in self-cultivation.

(In what follows we paraphrase the book's account by using the term "man," understood to mean "person," "human being," male or female.)

Because the superior person is true to himself (or herself), he is "watchful over himself when he is alone." Self-cultivation is primarily an internal process. It does not make any difference whether one is in front of people or alone. However, it is relatively not so different to act morally when people are watching. When we are alone we tend to loosen up and reduce the effort for self-cultivation. To be a superior man, one must be persevering in moral cultivation even when nobody is watching him.

The superior man lives among common people. He enjoys happy union with his wife and children and lives in harmony with his brothers. He is superior because he has a superior moral sense and hence knows how to act properly. He may turn out in any position in the society. He may be in a noble position. Then he does what is proper to a station of wealth and honor. He will not treat his inferiors with contempt. He may be in a humble position. Then he does what is proper to a station of poverty and humbleness. He will not court the favor of the noble and wealthy. He may turn out to be in a difficult and dangerous situation; he will then do what is proper to a station of difficulty and danger. No matter in what situation he finds himself, he will always make the best out of it. Like an archer who, when misses the target, turns around and seeks for the cause of failure within himself, the superior man does not complain against Heaven nor does he blame other people for his lot. The superior man thus lives at ease, enjoying peace of mind, and waits for his own destiny.

Such a person best exemplifies the Mean (*zhong yong*). The *Doctrine of the Mean* explains:

> Before the feelings of pleasure, anger, sorrow, and joy are aroused it is called *zhong* [equilibrium, centrality, mean]. When these feelings are aroused and each and all attain due measure and degree, it is called harmony.

The superior person knows how to attain equilibrium and harmony to the highest degree and will not go astray from the central Way. In other words the superior person is one with unflinching strength. In this regard, Confucius is quoted as follows:

> The superior man maintains harmony [in his nature and conduct] and does not waver. How unflinching is his strength! He stands in the middle position and does not lean to one side. How unflinching is his strength! When the Way prevails in the state, [if he enters public life] he does not change from what he was in private life. How unflinching is his strength! When the Way does not prevail in the state, he does not change even unto death. How unflinching is his strength!

One difference between the superior person and the inferior person is that the superior person follows the Mean while the inferior person departs from it. The Sage-Emperor Shun is an exemplar of the superior man, who, between two extremes, took the Mean and applied it in his dealing with the people. The superior person follows the Way of conscientiousness and altruism. He is conscientious. He is committed to his cause and serious about his internal self-cultivation. He understands that in order to travel to a distant place, one must start from the nearest point; in order to become a morally superior person, he must start with tiny matters in daily life. He is also altruistic (*shu*). This means that he extends his mind to others. When he wants to establish his own character, he also establishes the character of others. Confucius is quoted as criticizing himself for failing to do the four things that characterize the Way of the superior man. The first is to serve one's father as one would expect one's own son to serve oneself. The second is to serve one's ruler as one would expect one's ministers to serve oneself. The third is to serve one's elder brothers as one would expect one's younger brothers to serve oneself. And the fourth is to be the first to treat friends as one would expect them to treat oneself.

Here Confucius uses the method of self-criticism to inspire others to follow the Way of the superior person. He said,

> In practicing ordinary virtues and in the exercise of care in ordinary conversation, when there is deficiency, the superior man never fails to make further effort, and there is excess, never dares to go to the limit. His words correspond to his actions and his actions correspond to his words. Isn't the superior man earnest and genuine?

Finally, the superior person possesses the three virtues, namely wisdom, humanity, and courage. Confucius said,

> Love of learning is akin to wisdom. To practice with vigor is akin to humanity. To know to be shameful is akin to courage. He who knows these three things knows how to cultivate his personal life. Knowing how to cultivate his personal life, he knows how to govern other men. And knowing how to govern other men, he knows how to govern the empire, its state, and the families.

In the Confucian view, the state is not a mechanism of balancing various pressure groups of different interests. It is instead a community of enlarged family endowed with mutual trust. In such a community, the best way to govern is to use the moral forces of role models. The superior person is such a role model. With the virtues of wisdom, humanity, and courage, the superior person is an exemplary person for morality. He is not only a morally superior person himself, he is also devoted to cultivating the Way that Heaven has endowed in every person throughout the world.

The *Doctrine of the Mean* presents a Confucian system of moral metaphysics and philosophy of moral practice. This work has helped shape Chinese civilization for more than two thousand years, and there is no doubt that it will continue to do so in the foreseeable future.

CHENYANG LI

Further Reading

Translations

Chan, Wing-tsit, trans. and comp. "Spiritual Dimensions: the *Doctrine of the Mean*." Chapter 5 in Chan's *A Source Book in Chinese Philosophy*. Translated and compiled by Wing-tsit Chan. Princeton, N.J.: Princeton University Press, 1963.

Collie, David, trans. *Chung Yung or the Golden Medium*. In *The Chinese Classical Works Commonly Called "the Four Books."* Gainesville, Fla.: Scholars' Facsimiles and Reprints, 1970. A reprint of the original Mission Press edition of 1828. Collie is very critical of Confucianism in some footnotes, but the translation, one of the earliest English translations, is fairly readable.

Hughes, E. R. *The Great Learning and the Mean-in-Action: Confucius' Ta Hsüeh*. New York: AMS Press, 1943.

Ku Hungming, trans. "The Central Harmony." In *The Wisdom of Confucius*, edited and with an introduction by Lin Yutang. New York: Random House, Inc., 1938. This translation also appears in *The Wisdom of China and India* (edited by Lin Yutang, New York: Random House, Inc., 1942).

Related Studies

Fung, Yu-lan. *History of Chinese Philosophy*. Volume 1. Translated by Derk Bodde. London: George Allen & Unwin Ltd., 1937. Chapter 14, section 8, is on the *Doctrine of the Mean*.

Pound, Ezra. *Confucius: The Great Digest & Unwobbling Pivot*. Translation and commentary. New York: New Direction Books, 1951.

Tu, Wei-ming. *Centrality and Commonality: An Essay on Confucian Religiousness*. A revised and enlarged edition of *Centrality and Commonality: An Essay on Chung-yung*. Albany, N.Y.: SUNY Press, 1989.

YI JING (I CHING) (BOOK OF CHANGES)

Authors: Unknown. According to tradition, the book was composed in several layers over many centuries. The discovery of the eight component "trigram" (three-line) symbols is attributed to the first of the legendary Five Emperors, Fu Xi (Fu Hsi) (ruled 2852–2737 B.C.). The creation of the sixty-four "hexagram" (six-line) symbols and the composition of the hexagram statements is ascribed to Ji Chang (Chi Ch'ang), posthumously known as King Wen, founder of the Zhou (Chou) dynasty (c. 1027 B.C.). Ji Dan (Chi Tan), younger son of Ji Chang, better known as Zhou Gong (Chou Kung), or the Duke of Zhou, is credited with the formulation of the individual line statements (six per hexagram). Finally, the "Ten Wings," a body of commentaries attached to the above texts, were supposedly written by Confucius (Kongfuzi/K'ung Fu-tzu) (551–479 B.C.).

Date of Composition: Historical events mentioned in the lines of the hexagrams pertain to the period just before and after the founding of the Zhou dynasty, that is, the end of the second and beginning of the first millennium B.C. However, the first recorded reference to the book is much later. A passage dated 672 B.C., from the work of history known as the *Zuozhuan* (*Tso-chuan*), quotes from a divination manual called the *Zhouyi* (*Chou i*), "The Changes of Zhou (Chou)." This text, with its appended commentaries, was finally canonized as the *Yi jing* (the *Book of Change*) in 136 B.C. The commentaries alone date from the third and fourth centuries B.C. Therefore the composition of the *Yi jing* as we now know it spans a period of approximately eight centuries.

Type of Work: Divination manual, philosophy of the cosmos, philosophy of change, ethics

Major Ideas

Hexagrams made up of yin *and* yang *lines can be used as the basis of prognostications.*
The yang *line denotes strength and movement; the* yin *line denotes pliancy and rest.*
There are eight basic trigrams: earth, mountain, water, thunder, heaven, lake, fire, and wood (or wind).
Change is of two different kinds: alternation (the reversal of polar opposites—symbolized in the Yi jing *by the* yang *and* yin *lines)—and transformation (random change, or chance).*
The sequence of hexagrams is a model of the cosmos.

The *Yi jing* (*Book of Changes*) or *Zhou Yi* (*The Changes of Zhou*) was initially a manual of divination, but with the "Ten Wings" appendices attached, the resultant *Yi jing* may be considered a work of philosophy.

It has provided the stimulus for some of the most creative and useful thinking by Chinese seers and scholars, and in both its naive and its sophisticated uses the book has intrigued the Chinese mind and definitively affected the Chinese conception of the cosmos and of the relations of human beings to the continuing changes that are the foreseeable outcome of the universal interplay of opposing natural forces.

At the beginning of the Zhou (Chou) dynasty the Yi jing was consulted as a manual of divination exclusively by kings who believed their questions were being answered by the spirits of their dead ancestors. By the mid-Zhou dynasty (sixth century B.C.) the text of the *Yi jing* was being quoted rhetorically by the aristocracy and court officials to support ethical, political, and other types of arguments. By the end of the Zhou dynasty (late third century B.C.), philosophers believed that those who understood the *Yi jing* could "comprehend the *Dao* [*Tao*] of Heaven and Earth" (Wilhelm). The transformation of the function of the text is a reflection of the evolution of Zhou dynasty Chinese society.

The Yi jing *as Divination Manual*

One of the earliest records pertaining to the practice of divination occurs in the *Shu jing* (*Shu Ching*), or *Book of Documents*:

If you have doubts about any great matter, consult with your own heart; consult with your nobles and officers; consult with the masses of the people; and consult the cracks and the stalks.

(LEGGE)

In other words, if a particular situation were of sufficient import, and if there were doubts in the mind of the ruler as to the proper course to take, then, after availing oneself of all human agencies, divination by "cracks and stalks" (see below) could be undertaken. The prerequisite that doubt must first exist in the ruler's mind was a safeguard that insured a relatively impartial interpretation of the divination results. Moreover, for the impartial diviner no blame would be incurred as a result of action undertaken in the course of the divination. What situations would be considered important enough to merit divination? In the early Zhou dynasty the outcome of battles, the suitability of wedding dates, and the future birth of princes were all appropriate topics of *Yi jing* divination.

When such a situation arose there were at least two types of divination available, the turtle shell (or bone) oracle (the "cracks") and the yarrow stalk (or milfoil) oracle (the "stalks"). Both material objects were thought to be imbued with spiritual qualities and could act as mediums for communication with unseen powers. With the latter method, fifty stalks of the yarrow plant were counted so as to produce a series of six numbers which then corresponded to a particular hexagram of the *Yi jing*. In all ancient societies numbers were magical, and it was the numerological basis of *Yi jing* divination that was supernatural, not the actual text of the oracle. Although the book itself was not scripture, some of its language originated in the sacred ritual of oracle bone divination. Before the discovery at the turn of the century of the bone archives buried at the site of the ancient capital of the Shang dynasty, scholars were ignorant of the intricate terminology of divination that had slowly been lost over the ensuing centuries. In the twentieth century, therefore, a concerted effort has been made to re-cover the "original" meaning of the language of the *Yi jing*.

The major import of recent scholarship lies in the interpretation of what have been called "augur words" and "omens and their prognostications." The omen is usually a record of some randomly occurring natural phenomenon or human action that might prompt a determination of good or bad fortune in the life of the individual. No average person would be capable of making such a determination, but the diviners who interpreted the cracks in turtle shells and the sages who composed the text of the *Yi jing* knew from experience the significance of such omens. They authored the prognostications. Examples of omens appearing in the text are: "The wagon loses a wheel"; "Troops file out in columns"; and "The well is clear." The prognostication consists of an injunction, whereby the inquirer is enjoined to act in a particular manner upon receipt of the specific omen, as well as the augury itself, which determines the good or bad fortune of such action. Examples of omens with attached prognostications are as follows: "Horse carts are rumbling. If you seek a wedding match, by all means go. All signs are favorable"; and "The big wagons are transporting goods. If you are going on a journey, no harm will come."

The Book of Rhetoric

The meaning of another category of augur words transformed dramatically over the time period spanning the evolution of the *Yi jing* from divination manual to book of philosophy. A look at that transformation will provide a better picture of the changing function of the text in Chinese society. In the great majority of hexagram statements the hexagram name is followed by a sentence that usually includes the two expressions *heng* and *zhen* (*chen*). The former is a term indicating that a sacrifice is being offered. The latter is a term meaning "to *inquire* by crack-making" (that is, "to divine"), as in the standard oracle bone formula: "Crack-making on such-and-such a day, Diviner So-and-so inquired. . . ." Taken together the two terms describe the two-stage process whereby divination by stalk-casting was originally under-taken. *Heng* means that the "divination has reached the spirits and that the spirits have communicated their response to the diviner" (Shaughnessy: See *Note*). *Zhen* indicates that the divination rite may proceed. In other words, the first expression indicates that a line of communication has been established between the diviner and the spirit, and the second expression indicates that further inquiry is possible. The diviner would then proceed from the hexagram statement to the appropriate line text. For example, the hexagram statement of hexagram 17, *Sui* (Pursuit), reads as follows: "Primary plea received. Advisable to inquire further. No harm."

As the Zhou dynasty progressed and the power of enfeoffed nobles slowly began to eclipse that of the king, the use of divination, originally a royal prerogative, spread from the capital to the fiefdoms and eventually permeated virtually all of literate society. By the end of the "Spring and Autumn" period (770–476 B.C.) even unlanded gentry were stalk-casting, and uses ranged from medical prognosis to selection of auspicious days for travel. The text of the *Yi jing* was so widely known by then that an individual could allude to particular lines by number, and listeners could spontaneously recall the statement. This familiarity led to ever increasing usage of the text to support one's argument, especially in acts of persuasion, an art that proliferated in the Warring States period (475–221 B.C.), when roving scholars wandered throughout China proclaiming their schemes of government to the contending rulers. Eventually lines were being quoted out of context and interpreted quite liberally by upright officials who needed venerable texts upon which to base their moral instruction.

The didactic function slowly began to influence everyone's understanding of the *Yi jing*, so that eventually much of the original divinatory import was forgotten. The following example will serve to show the extent to which the transformation had progressed. The background is this: Lady Mu Jiang (d. 564 B.C.), the Duchess of Lu, is about to be placed under house arrest for subverting the gov-ernment of her son. Just prior to her incarceration she casts the stalks to determine her future. Her diviner has just interpreted the casting as auspicious, but the Duchess conversely reads the text as a condemnation of her lack of virtue:

> It is said in the *Yi jing*, "*Sui* is great, successful, beneficial, firmly correct, and without blame." Now, that greatness is the lofty eminence of the person; that success is the assemblage of excellence; that beneficialness is the harmony of all righteousness; that firm correctness is the stem of all affairs. . . . *Sui* belongs to one who has those four virtues. What have I to do with it, to whom none of them belongs?

(LEGGE, 1872)

The hexagram statement interpreted here to mean, "great, successful, beneficial, firmly correct, without blame," is none other than the statement interpreted above as "Primary plea received. Advisable to inquire further. No harm." The moralistic interpretation quoted here is the first such record of a hexagram statement being read in such a fashion. But just to show how resilient such readings could be, this particular text appeared verbatim over four centuries later in one of the Ten Wings commentaries of the canonized *Yi jing*. The canonized version of this hexagram formula became the official interpretation and was not seriously challenged until the twentieth century. It was this axiological backdrop that prepared the way for philosophical interpretations of the *Yi jing*.

The Book of Philosophy

The Warring States period was an age when old social norms were collapsing and the search was on for new systems of thought to explain the resulting chaos. This was the era of the "Hundred Schools" and many systems of thought existed, but it was mainly the adherents of the three schools of *Ru* (*Ju*)

(Confucianism), *Dao* (Daoism/Taoism), and *Yinyang* (School of the Yinyang Cosmologists) who took special interest in the *Yi jing*.

As these programs of thought were debated in the intellectual centers of the various kingdoms, venerable texts such as the *Yi jing* were reinterpreted. Confucian moralists concentrated on ethical issues reflected in the social content of the text. Daoists and *Yinyang* theorists were interested in cosmological issues suggested by the numerological and symbolic relations between the graphic matrices. The result was a compendium of seven different commentaries (in ten sections), each of which attempted to picture the *Yi jing* as a coherent system of thought. (Incidentally, modern scholars are almost unanimous in rejecting Confucius [Kongfuzi/Kongzi] as the author of any of the commentaries. There is, in fact, no incontrovertible proof that Confucius even used the *Yi jing*. Although it may be true that his disciples initiated a tradition of *Yi* studies, even this cannot be proven. Until documents to the contrary are unearthed it will have to be assumed that the commentary tradition originated with the Hundred Schools.)

The first commentary, in two sections (first and second wings), is the *Duan Zhuan* (*T'uan Chuan*), or *Commentary on the Hexagram*. For each hexagram, first the name is explained, and then both a moral and a cosmological context is provided for elucidation of the statement. In addition, the *duan* (commentary) attempts to base the prognostications for each hexagram on that figure's unique configuration of spatial lines. That justification includes the following linear relationships. The hexagram matrix consists of six positions, half of which (the first, third, and fifth places, counting from the bottom) are described as superior and half of which (the second, fourth, and sixth places) are described as inferior. Occupying these six relative positions are sequences of two abstract symbols: a solid, or *yang*, line denoting strength and movement, and a broken, or *yin*, line denoting pliancy and rest. When a strong line occupies a superior position, or when a pliant line occupies an inferior position,

order and therefore good fortune is suggested. The converse arrangement suggests disorder and misfortune.

The hexagram matrix can also be divided into two separate trigram matrices. The corresponding lines of each trigram in a given hexagram (lines 1 and 4, 2 and 5, 3 and 6) attract each other if they are occupied by symbols of opposite character. In other words, a *yin*, or broken, line in position 1 of the lower trigram is attracted to a *yang*, or solid, line in position 4 of the upper trigram. This is perceived as auspicious. Finally, the second and fifth places in a hexagram, by virtue of their central position in each trigram, are also perceived as auspicious. For example, hexagram 30, *Li*, or "The Clinging, Fire," is composed of one trigram for fire over another. Fire is composed of one pliant line between two strong lines. The hexagram statement and its *duan* read as follows:

> [Hexagram 30] The Clinging. Perseverance furthers. It brings success. Care of the cow brings good fortune.
>
> [The *Duan*] Clinging means resting on something. Sun and moon cling to heaven. Grain, plants, and trees cling to the soil. Doubled clarity, clinging to what is right, transforms the world and perfects it. The pliant clings to the middle and to what is right, hence it has success. Therefore it is said: "Care of the cow brings good fortune."
>
> (WILHELM, WITH MINOR REVISIONS.)

The second commentary, also in two sections (third and fourth wings), is the *Xiang Zhuan* (*Hsiang Chuan*), or *Commentary on the Images*. It breaks each hexagram down into its component trigrams and deduces the meaning of the former out of the latter. Thus the trigram for earth over the trigram for wood represents hexagram 46, "Pushing Upward" (plants push up through soil). And the trigram for water over the trigram for wood represents hexagram 48, "The Well" (wood sucks up water, the wooden bucket sinks to the bottom of the water well). The *bagua* (*pa kua*), or "eight tri-grams," are as follows:

— —	———	— —	— —
— —	— —	———	— —
— —	— —	— —	———
Earth	Mountain	Water	Thunder

———	— —	———	———
———	———	— —	———
———	———	———	— —
Heaven	Lake	Fire	Wood or Wind

As depicted in the above arrangement, the tri-grams also relate significantly to one another. The top row exhibits a predominance of *yin* and the bottom row a predominance of *yang*. Yet when *yang* and *yin* are unbalanced (in all but Heaven and Earth), a single strong line will rule over two pliant lines, and a single pliant will define the character of two strong lines. Thus, while Earth is called the mother and Heaven is called the father, the remain-ing lower trigrams are daughters and the upper trigrams are sons. Heaven is summer and south; Earth is winter and north. Fire is spring and east; water is fall and west. Nor are the trigrams limited to these primary characteristics. The *Shuogua* (*Shuo Kua*) commentary (*Discussion of the Tri-grams*, eighth wing) expands each of the general trigram categories into as many as twenty distinct terms. For example, the *Shuogua* entry for the earth trigram reads as follows:

> Receptive is the earth, the mother. It is cloth, a kettle, frugality, it is level, it is a cow with a calf, a large wagon, form, the multitude, a shaft. Among the various kinds of soil, it is the black.

(WILHELM, WITH MINOR REVISIONS.)

Discussion of the third commentary, the largest and the most important of the Ten Wings, will be saved for later. The fourth commentary (seventh wing) is the *Wenyan* (*Wen Yen*), or *Elegant Words*. It discusses the hexagram statement, the line state-ments, and the *duan* of only the first two hexa-grams, *Qian* (*Ch'ien*) and *Kun* (*K'un*). It is here that Lady Mu Jiang's moralistic interpretation of the hexagram statement is borrowed from the *Zuo Zhuan*. The fifth commentary (eighth wing), the *Shuogua* (*Shuo Kua*), discusses the eight trigrams. The sixth commentary (ninth wing), the *Xugua* (*Hsü Kua*), or *Hexagram Sequence*, is a gloss on hexagram names which tries to explain why one hexagram follows another. A second version of the *Yi jing* discovered recently in a Han dynasty tomb does not maintain the same order as that in the received text, which may explain why the *Xugua* seems so contrived. The seventh commentary (tenth wing), the *Zagua* (*Tsa Kua*), or *Hexagram Miscellany*, is a poem on the hexagram names.

We now return to the third and most important commentary, with which our discussion will con-clude. Also in two sections (fifth and sixth wings), it is called the *Xici Zhuan* (*Hsi Tz'u Chuan*), *Com-mentary on the Attachments*, or the *Da Zhuan* (*Ta Chuan*), *Great Commentary*. This work, unlike the remainder of the wings, does not consist of line-by-line or hexagram-specific commentaries, but is a collection of essays about the nature of the *Yi jing*. Concepts discussed in these essays constitute a ver-itable metaphysics of "change" upon which the *Yi jing* is based. The term *yi* itself means change; however, since the sequence of hexagrams is a model of the cosmos ("Heaven and Earth"), change in the *Da Zhuan* is discussed from two different perspectives—change in the natural world, the macrocosm, and change in the *Yi jing*, the microcosm. Furthermore, the general concept of change can be subdivided into two different notions—alternation and transformation. Alterna-tion is ordered change—the reversal of bipolar op-posites, which occurs in the *Yi jing* as the alternation of *yin* and *yang* lines, and which occurs in nature as the alternation of day and night or the progression of the four seasons. Transformation, on the other hand, is random change, or chance, which is manifested in the appearance of omens and the occurrence of supernatural phenomena.

Time is also a factor of change, although the *Da*

Zhuan does not analyze this concept in detail. Instead, time is presented as a function of alternation and progression, just as the seasons alternate as the years progress. On the microcosmic level the hexagram is perceived as an analogue of seasonal time. Each of the six positions is defined by its relationship to the other positions, and each of the six lines is limited to one of two poles in an alternating cycle. In the stalk-casting ritual as the hexagram develops from the bottom upwards (mimicking organic growth) each line captures a possible development in the world outside the diviner. In the Zhou dynasty (if the record of the *Zuo Zhuan* is reliable on this point), only one hexagram line text was used to interpret a given situation. So the chance appearance of a given line in a given position, which resulted in a given omen, was analogous to a real-life transformation or occurrence of a supernatural event. The hexagram omen, as such, was a microcosmic model of a unique moment in the life of the inquirer. This is relative, not absolute, time.

The exegetes who pondered the mysteries of the *Yi jing* in the final centuries of the Zhou dynasty had a difficult task before them: to take an often opaque collection of oracular texts and somehow make it into a coherent system of thought. In their attempt to make sense of a largely forgotten tradition, they managed to create a metaphysics that, as far as they were concerned, accounted for the order in the cosmos. This metaphysics gave them the ability to perceive the order in apparent disorder. And with that knowledge they believed that they could predict the future so that the present might be changed accordingly. In the final analysis, this is the change in the *Book of Changes* that has persisted for 3,000 years.

STEPHEN L. FIELD

Further Reading

Translations

Legge, James, trans. *The Yi King*, Vol. 16 of *The Sacred Books of the East*. Edited by F. Max Muller. Oxford: Clarendon Press, 1879. This text is also available as a Dover paperback. The most prolific translator of Chinese classics into English, James Legge was a British missionary to the "Far East" from 1839 until 1873. His translations are still quoted by modern scholars, although he has been criticized for relying extensively on the commentaries of the Song dynasty (960–1279) Neo-Confucian, Zhu Xi (Chu Hsi).

———, trans. *The Ch'un Ts'ew with the Tso Chuen*, in *The Chinese Classics*, Vol. 5, Hong Kong, 1872.

Whincup, Greg, trans. *Rediscovering the* I Ching. Garden City, N.Y.: Doubleday & Company, 1986. A rigorous scholarly translation of the *Yi jing* is not readily available, but this rendition of the *Yi jing* attempts to recover the original meaning. Although Whincup resists the moralistic readings that persisted after the Zhou dynasty, he does include in his translation paraphrases of technical and other aspects of the *Duan, Xiang,* and *Xugua* commentaries.

Wilhelm, Richard, trans. *The I Ching or Book of Changes: The Richard Wilhelm translation rendered into English by Cary F. Baynes.* (Bollingen Series, No. 19). Princeton, N.J.: Princeton University Press, 3rd. ed., revised, 1967. This is the standard English version of the *Yi jing*. Wilhelm translates the complete text, including the Ten Wings, and adds his own commentary.

Further Studies

Smith, Kidder Jr., et al. *Sung Dynasty Uses of the* I Ching. Princeton, N.J.: Princeton University Press, 1990. For those interested in interpretations of the *Yi jing* from the Neo-Confucian period, this book analyzes in detail how four philosophers of the Song dynasty (960–1279) understood the classic.

Wilhelm, Hellmut. *Heaven, Earth, and Man in the Book of Changes.* Seven Eranos Lectures. Seattle: University of Washington Press, 1977. Hellmut was the son of Richard Wilhelm and a *Yi jing* scholar in his own right. This is one of the few English studies of the *Yi jing* prepared for the general public.

Note: In this article the author has profited specifically from the translations by Legge, Whincup, and Wilhelm, and from the studies made by Edward L. Shaugnessy (who provided the interpretation of the significance of the augur terms *heng* and *shen* in his Ph.D. dissertation, "The Composition of the 'Zhouyi,' " Stanford University, 1983), and by Gerald Swanson, whose analysis of change occurs in his article "The Concept of Change in the *Great Treatise*," in *Explorations in Early Chinese Cosmology* (edited by Henry Rosemont, Jr., Chica, Calif.: Scholars Press, 1984).

DONG ZHONGSHU (TUNG CHUNG-SHU)

Born: c. 195 B.C., Guangchuan, China
Died: c. 115 B.C., Guangchuan, China
Major Work: *Luxuriant Dew of the Spring and Autumn Annals* (*Chunqiu fanlu/Ch'un-ch'iu fan-lu*)

Major Ideas

Human life and institutions are subject to universal laws instituted by Heaven.
All phenomena are intricately and dynamically interrelated.
Heaven expressly created humanity to extend and maintain order in the world.
Heaven holds the ruler responsible for the world's status.
Regular and irregular natural events contain symbolic politico-cosmic meaning.

Dong Zhongshu (Tung Chung-shu) was responsible for establishing Confucianism as the theoretical foundation of the inchoate imperial state during the Han dynasty (206 B.C.–A.D. 220). Dong attempted to achieve a coherent system of thought that would provide a rational explanation for the entirety of human experience. Some argue that he was noteworthy more for his effect upon Chinese history than for the profundity of his thought. But such criticisms seem to slight Dong's humanistic trajectory: to him, explaining life really meant explaining human history, and explaining the world really meant explaining how human life should be organized in order to be properly grounded in the fundamental nature of things. In another sense, Dong can be interpreted as a religious theorist, whose speculative thought was informed by certain scriptural notions.

The Background of Dong Zhongshu's Thought

Most classical Chinese thinkers had vaguely agreed that Heaven (*tian/t'ien*) instituted the world and plays some role in human life as well as in the world's ongoing processes. But none of those thinkers articulated any systematic theology; for them, a few basic principles sufficed, primarily as justification of other principles that they considered more pertinent. Dong was, in a sense, working in the other direction: rather than adduce Heaven to support a specific view of human nature, he ad-

duced a specific view of human nature in order to explicate the way in which Heaven had instituted life. Dong's thought ultimately reverted to a teleological philosophy of history.

Those who assess him as a speculative philosopher are sometimes nonplused by Dong's apparent obsession with history and government. In actuality, it is not difficult to understand his thought when one appreciates the context in which he lived. In 221 B.C. the State of Qin (Ch'in), organized according to the totalitarian principles of Legalism, had exterminated its competition and instituted a ruthless new centralized state. In 206 B.C. the Qin government was overthrown, but meanwhile the Chinese had seen their civilization ransacked. Rulers of the subsequent Han period struggled to understand what had happened and why. The collapse of the Qin offered a clear moral and historical lesson: there is justice in the world. But if so, why had the ruthless Qin come to power in the first place? The Han Emperor Wudi was troubled by these questions, and solicited explanations. Dong Zhongshu offered his views in three memorials that are not datable. Fuller and somewhat divergent versions of Dong's thought appear in his principal work, the *Chunqiu fanlu* (*Ch'un-ch'iu fan-lu*) (*Luxuriant Dew of the Spring and Autumn Annals*). However, not only is that text not datable, but modern scholarship has determined that much of it is the work of later hands.

Dong's ultimate goal was to discover universal causative principles that would both explain the past and provide a sound foundation for the future, particularly in the sociopolitical sphere. But unlike thinkers who seek such principles beginning from abstract and a priori assumptions, Dong (like earlier and later Confucians alike) looked instead to his cultural inheritance. He discovered fundamental principles for a complete explanation of life within a text known as the *Chunqiu* (*The Spring and Autumn Annals*) (fifth century B.C.), generally considered the work of Confucius (Kongfuzi/ K'ung Fu-tzu) himself. Some might think it odd that a philosopher should claim to find an explanation of all reality in a text like the *Chunqiu*, which is (at least to the casual observer) merely a laconic chronicle of political events in the long-defunct State of Lu. But at least some Han Confucians saw in the *Chunqiu* the answers to their most pressing questions: it not only had the unimpeachable authority of Confucius himself, but it also provided an idea that suited their most crucial needs, namely the idea that Heaven is at work in worldly events, mandating certain outcomes in the course of human affairs. Dong concluded that by meticulous analysis of the *Chunqiu*, one could discern the precise patterns of Heaven's subtle workings, thereby learning how all of life could be brought into alignment with the divine plan. Such concepts seem analogous to the thought of certain Western religious theorists who see God's plan encoded in the text of the Bible. But in fact Dong's thinking was little different from that of Chinese of Han and later times who saw the keys to Heaven's subtle workings in the *Yi Jing* (*I Ching*), the ancient divination text. Dong was actually following a more typically Confucian path by focusing upon history—in fact, upon the historiographic activities of Confucius himself.

Dong Zhongshu's System of Thought

Dong's vision of the world began with ideas inherited from classical thinkers, such as the Confucian Xunzi (Hsün Tzu). The activity of Heaven and Earth is perfected by Humanity's civilizing activity: Heaven gives birth to things and instills people with moral inclinations (as the classical Confucian Mencius had argued); Earth nourishes things and provides for their material needs; and Humanity completes or perfects all things by maintaining proper patterning (through rites and music). Such patterning is not the product of human invention, but Heaven's own design. Here Dong goes beyond Xunzi: Dong explains and justifies Heaven's patterning through ideas drawn from natural philosophers such as Zou Yan (Tsou Yen), who had explained the world in terms of (1) *yin* and *yang*—two basic aspects of reality within the phenomenal world, seen in all pairs of complementary opposites; and (2) the "Five Forces" (*wuxing/wuhsing*)—cosmic forces metaphorically identified with fire, water, earth, wood, and metal. Dong Zhongshu is generally remembered as the author of a detailed system of correspondences in which everything was correlated to one of the five fundamental forces, so that everything could be shown to be interrelated in an orderly and comprehensible manner. But in his memorials, Dong never actually mentions the Five Forces. Moreover, his system of correspondences remains quite rudimentary; in reality, the elaborate system usually associated with his name was only fully developed in later Han thought. Dong's own real concern was to demonstrate how Humanity's activities might be integrated with the designs of Heaven. To him, the world is not a field of self-contained natural processes, but rather a field in which human life is of central importance, and a field in which Heaven acts; hence "*yang* is Heaven's beneficent power, while the *yin* is Heaven's chastising power."

Dong's immediate concern was with Humanity, which (like all Confucians) he considers nobler than other creatures, for two reasons: (1) only humans display the consciousness and will that we see in Heaven's workings, and (2) only humans interact in terms of "benevolence" (*ren/jen*), "correctness" (*yi/i*), and "wisdom" (*zhi/chih*), the fundamental moral principles articulated by his Confucian predecessors. Though he clearly went beyond those predecessors in his concern with universal processes, Dong placed himself squarely within their tradition by insisting that Humanity "possessed clearly marked patterns for . . . social interaction," and that those patterns are ethical in nature. He also engaged in the Mencius–Xunzi debate over human nature; he agreed with Mencius that we have inherent moral tendencies, but explained them in terms of a theistic teleology: "Heaven, when it constituted human nature, commanded him to practice benevolence and righteousness. . . ." Dong also departed from Mencius's rosy view of human nature:

Mencius evaluates it in comparison with the doings of birds and beasts below, and therefore says that the nature itself is good. I evaluate it in comparison with the doings of the sages above, and therefore I say that the nature is not good.

Hence, like Xunzi, Dong considers the legacy of the sages essential for completing ourselves. It is within the activity of the sages (including Confucius's composition of the *Chunqiu*) that Heaven guides us in carrying out its mandate to bring order to the world.

The contention that human beings are not wholly good in themselves also serves to justify the institution of kingship: the ruler "gives instruction that gives completion to [people's] nature." The king models himself on Heaven by aligning his actions with the natural processes that Heaven has instituted, such as the four seasons. But history shows that each of the three great dynasties (Xia/Hsia, Shang, and Zhou/Chou) had reconfigured certain of its predecessor's patterns, to demonstrate that the "mandate of Heaven" had been transferred to a new ruling house. From that fact Dong concluded that Heaven had actually established not a single invariable pattern, but rather a changing sequence of three sets of patterns. Accordingly, each current ruler must be alert to possible deviations from Heaven's constantly shifting pattern, as intimated by irregular natural events (a concept attested in an edict of early Han times). Here Dong integrates political principles with the idea of a dynamically correlative cosmos, in which actions on the level of humanity (whether proper or improper) stimulate responses on other levels. He sometimes suggests that such responses occur when humanity disrupts the "ethers" (*qi/ch'i*) of *yin* and *yang*. But such "mechanistic" interpretations seem at odds with the more theistic argument that Heaven takes deliberate action to alter the course of human events by warning rulers when they deviate and by transferring the mandate to a new house when appropriate.

Dong Zhongshu's Place in Chinese Intellectual History

Though Dong's thought seems at first rather far removed from that of Confucius, he was, in the final analysis, truly Confucian: his thought was largely an extension of that of Xunzi and Mencius, qualified mainly by his reading of the *Chunqiu*. The overriding issue of his day was to discover universal processes underlying human history, and Xunzi and Mencius had never gone so far. So to make sense of the *Chunqiu* he expanded his field to make use of ideas from classical thinkers such as Zou Yan (Tsou Yen) (305–c. 240 B.C.) and Mozi (Mo-Tzu), as well as from contemporary sources such as the *Yi jing* interpreters and the just-completed *Huainanzi* (*Huai-nan tzu*), which was another attempt to explain all of life along generally Daoist (Taoist) lines. It is notable that Dong shows little trace of the thought of Daoists such as Laozi (Lao Tzu), probably because earlier Han rulers had adopted some of Laozi's political principles. It is here that we see the motivation behind Dong's promotion of "Confucianism." When Dong persuaded Han Emperor Wudi to establish an academy with a "Confucian" curriculum, it was not from sectarian motives. Dong certainly did not reject ideas of non-Confucian provenance: many had great explanatory value. But he was concerned that the authority of the ruler should be solidly grounded in the authority of Heaven, which was codified in the classics that the Confucians had always treasured and promoted. Dong was thus not really concerned to formulate a philosophical "orthodoxy" to which other thinkers had to conform, nor to establish a new "state creed." His goal was essentially the same as that of Mencius: to persuade the ruler of the day to put into effect the moral and institutional principles that had been handed down from the sages of old.

Dong's teachings deeply influenced generations of Han thinkers. His understanding of the world as an interactive cosmos eventually permeated most of Chinese society, and became a fundamental element of the general Chinese worldview. But his utopian vision of a harmonious union of cosmos and polity also inspired other Han officials to produce "revealed" texts wherein Heaven warned that it might withdraw its mandate from the Han. Such ideas inspired not only rebel political movements (which eventually toppled the Han), but also new religious movements, some of which eventually flowed into the Daoist tradition.

RUSSELL KIRKLAND

Further Reading

Fung, Yu-lan. *A History of Chinese Philosophy.* Vol. 2. Translated by Derk Bodde. Princeton, N.J.: Princeton University Press, 1953. Though dated, volume 2 contains the most extensive introduction to Dong's thought available in English, including substantial extracts from his writings. (Quotations from Dong Zhongshu used in this chapter are from this book.)

Hsiao, Kung-chuan. *A History of Chinese Political Thought.* Princeton, N.J.: Princeton University Press, 1979. Includes a briefer but slightly more critical introduction.

Loewe, Michael. "Imperial Sovereignty: Dong Zhongshu's Contribution and his Predecessors," in S. R. Schram, ed., *Foundations and Limits of State Power in China.* London: School of Oriental and African Studies, 1987. A critical assessment by a leading Han historian.

WANG CHONG (WANG CH'UNG)

Born: c. A.D. 27
Died: c. A.D. 97
Major Works: *Lunheng (Lun-heng) (Discursive Equilibrium)*, in eighty-five chapters (A.D. 82–83); chapter 85, an autobiography, mentions three shorter works, none of which survives.

Major Ideas

Natural events have natural causes.

Beliefs in gods, ghosts, and supernatural phenomena are superstitious falsehoods.

There is no correspondence between human events and natural phenomena; the processes of nature are not influenced by human behavior and have no moral significance.

There is no correspondence between moral virtue and personal destiny; fortune and misfortune are the result of fate.

Human nature may be good or evil; those of good nature can become evil, and those of evil nature can become good.

Wang Chong (Wang Ch'ung) was associated with the Imperial College at Luoyang (Lo-yang), the Han capital, where he was exposed to the teachings of a number of competing schools. He served as a minor official in Zhejiang (Che-chiang) and Anhui, but never attained high office. Wang is best known for his monumental work, *Lunheng (Discursive Equilibrium)*, a series of critical essays on the philosophical views and popular beliefs of the times. Employing both empirical evidence and the test of reason, *Lunheng* examines contemporary beliefs in supernaturalism, views of human nature and human destiny, and theories of the correspondence between natural events and human affairs. "Hatred of fictions and falsehoods" was, wrote Wang, the "one phrase" that summarized his teachings, and Wang Chong has been credited with being a rare example of a critical "scientific spirit" in the history of Chinese philosophy.

Wang's style of argumentation in *Lunheng* set a standard for the critical evaluation of evidence. The work draws heavily upon the histories and commentaries of the Zhou (Chou) and Han dynasties, particularly the *Shu jing (Shu-ching) (Book of Documents)*, the *Shiji (Shih-chi) (Historical Records)*, and the *Zuozhuan (Tso-chuan) (A History of the Spring and Autumn Period)*, and subjects their interpretive conclusions to critical scrutiny. The histories contain innumerable reports of marvelous events—astrological anomalies, unusual plants and animals, ghostly apparitions, sudden climatic changes, biological metamorphoses, and hidden treasures—and Wang generally accepts these reports at face value. But he rejects the conclusion that these events are caused by ghosts and spirits, and denies that they have moral significance as cosmic rewards or punishments for human acts. Unlike the *Mozi (Mo Tzu)*, which employed the testimony of the histories as evidence for the retributive activity of Heaven (*tian/t'ien*), ghosts, and spirits, Wang concludes that a rational evaluation of the evidence does not support an anthropomorphic conception of Heaven or the attribution of conscious intention to the dead. He insists on natural explanations for remarkable events.

Naturalism

"The Way of Heaven [*tian/t'ien*] is non-active [*wuwei/wu-wei*]," Wang Chong declares, echoing the naturalistic assertions of the Daoists (Taoists) (in Wang's time, the "School of Huang–Lao") that *tian* is not an intending, willful god, but rather the spontaneous activity of nature. Wang borrows from the *Yinyang* cosmologists of the Han in explaining the "transformations of Heaven" (nature) as the activity of *yin*, *yang*, and the Five Processes or Phases (*wuxing/wu hsing*): the warming of fire, cooling of water, firming of metal, gestating of earth, and maturing of wood. "Heaven's ways are spontaneous [*ziran/tzu-jan*]": nature is self-producing and self-developing, and nothing exists outside the natural order that might act upon it. Most of the *Lunheng* consists of attacks on anthropomorphic conceptions of Heaven and on various forms of supernaturalism (the view that natural events have supernatural causes).

Wang employs two basic arguments to refute supernaturalistic views: the *reductio ad absurdum* and argument from analogy. In a chapter entitled "Comments on Death," Wang reduces the belief in ghosts to a series of logical absurdities. If persons retained physical form after death, then ghosts would be so numerous that "one could barely take a single step without trampling ten"; if the dead truly appeared as ghosts, then they would be stark naked, as "his clothing cannot be said to die with the man"; if ghosts could smell the odor of sacrifices without consuming the food itself, they would wail from hunger and thirst rather than rewarding their benefactors; and if they did eat, they would want to eat every day, not just on designated days of the festival calendar. Elsewhere, in an argument against Daoist immortality adepts who sought "ascension in broad daylight" (a feat credited to the Prince of Huai-nan in the former Han dynasty), Wang observes that "for men to fly, they would have to have feathers"; moreover, such a transformation would have to be observable and incremental—nature has no occurrences of instantaneous metamorphosis. Commenting on hagiographic exaggerations in the widely read biographies of Confucius (Kongfuzi/K'ung Fu-tzu), Wang concludes, "if Confucius could drink one hundred gallons of wine, he would have been a drunkard, not a sage"; and if Confucius knew by prescience or intuition, he would never have asked questions, made mistakes, or traveled to states that rejected him.

Wang argues more forcefully still on the basis of inference from observable analogies. *On creation*: Just as children are not conceived by an act of will, but rather by natural, "spontaneous" intercourse

between men and women, so too the world exists due to natural causes, not the "intentions" of Heaven and Earth. *On sacrifices to Heaven*: "We can observe that Earth has neither a mouth nor eyes, so Heaven, which we cannot see, does not have them either"; "Even if Heaven did have a mouth, it would be too huge to fill"; just as no person can hear an ant, "if Heaven did have ears, it could not hear a man"; and just as beings of different species and persons of different lands speak different languages, "if Heaven did speak, it would speak a 'foreign language.' " *On Heavenly retribution*: Just as "the shaking of branches does not make the wind blow," the injustices of human beings do not cause natural calamities; and just as no one would find fault with one who is ill, calamities are not Heaven-sent reproofs for the mismanagement of human affairs. *On ghosts*: Animals and plants clearly do not become ghosts when they die, so why should humans? Just as ice becomes formless upon melting, or a sack of rice loses its shape when the rice is exhausted, humans become "formless" upon death; just as there is a lack of consciousness in sleep, there is a lack of consciousness in death. Even if there were consciousness after death, it could not possess the clarity of intention that is typically attributed to ghosts: just as an old man finds himself confused and ignorant, his confusion and ignorance would be far greater after death; and just as dreams cannot do physical harm to others, the thoughts of the dead could not harm the living.

Wang Chong and the School of Correspondences

Wang's principal criticisms seem to have been directed at a school of thinkers that was enjoying increasing status in intellectual circles. It is described by Wang as the "School of Change and Reversion," and is known today as the "School of *Yinyang* Cosmology," the "School of Correspondences," or the "New Text School." These scholars combed the classics and histories for examples of "cosmic correspondences" between the activities of nature and the affairs of humankind, such that natural events were interpreted as being divine rewards and punishments for human good and evil. The same principles were employed in making prognostications of future destiny based upon portents discovered in the natural world. Wang Chong refuses to see moral significance in natural events, and argues persuasively against the idea that good fortune is the result of moral virtue or that bad fortune is the result of immoral acts.

Wang Chong insists that Heaven has no anthropomorphic qualities and that there is no consciousness without a body. But he does not deny the existence of marvelous occurrences, which he discusses at length: ghostly apparitions (Wang accepts the evidence of the senses and the testimony of the histories, but denies that apparitions are spirits of the dead); omens and portents indicating future conditions; accurate divination by tortoise shells and milfoil stalks; successful rites to alleviate droughts and floods; biological metamorphoses (insects to plants, animals to humans); dragons, unicorns, phoenixes, demons, and exceptional flora; the appearance of phantasmagoric stellar lights; the eruption of wine springs and the discovery of submerged treasures; and the association of exceptional talents with physiological quirks (the histories give the great sages and worthies a number of exceptional physical characteristics: the Yellow Emperor stayed in the womb for twenty months, Emperor Yao had "the appearance of a cloud," and Confucius had a concave brow; other luminaries were double-toothed, double-browed, or double-jointed).

Wang does not question the veracity of these reports, but he insists on a naturalistic explanation for each. In accounting for these phenomena, Wang assumes the basic views of the *Yinyang* cosmologists: all things are composed of "breath" (*qi/ch'i*), which moves in patterns of "quiescence" (*yin*) and "activity" (*yang*). When in balance, *yin* and *yang* produce the things of the ordered world: *yin* provides their form or body, *yang* their animation or consciousness. But when *yang*, which is associated with the sun and the stars, is "excessive," anomalies appear. Ghosts, demons, dragons, poisonous plants and animals, and other marvels are the prod-

ucts of a natural (albeit exceptional) imbalance of the "breaths" of *yin* and *yang*. They are rare, unpredictable, and often portentous, but they are not supernatural or morally significant, neither auspicious nor inauspicious. "People are afraid of marvels," Wang comments; "therefore they magnify and embellish them." Although such things are admittedly strange, they are not to be feared or invested with significance as rewards or punishments for human behavior.

In particular, Wang rejects the idea that the evil or virtue of emperors and kings can be punished or rewarded by an intending, willful Heaven through the agency of natural events. Floods and droughts are not manifestations of Heaven's "anger" with tyrannous rulers.

The implications of Wang's position must have been threatening to the prevailing ideology of the Han, which recognized an exact correspondence between human affairs and natural events. Wang explicitly admitted the possibility, even the likelihood, that good is not rewarded with prosperity or evil punished with calamity.

Human Nature and Human Destiny

Wang Chong held a number of positions which today would be regarded as pre-scientific, if not superstitious. What is remarkable about Wang, however, is his consistent naturalism. Wang was unceasing in his search for natural explanations for the wonders and anomalies of history and legend. This methodology is especially notable in his analysis of human nature and individual destiny.

Like all things, human beings are composed of the "breaths" of *yin* and *yang*. The breath of *yin* (*yinqi/yin-ch'i*) forms the bones and flesh, the breath of *yang* (*yang-qi*) produces "vitality" and consciousness. Wang describes this *yang-qi* as a kind of "stellar breath," and the human constitution is made up in part of emanations from the stars. Since the constellations continually change their positions relative to the earth, so persons have individual characteristics based on the configurations of the heavens at birth. Moreover, Wang suggests that people are composed of varying quantities of *qi*, and their span of life is determined accordingly. Thus, both character and destiny are determined at birth, and persons are severely limited in the degree to which they can alter either of them.

By "character" (*xing/hsing*), Wang means the moral nature. In contrast to Mengzi (Mencius), who asserted that the *xing* is good, and Xunzi (Hsün Tzu), that the *xing* is evil, Wang Chong believed that the *xing* is good in some and evil in others: what Mencius said of people applied only to those who were "above average," and what Xunzi said of people applied only to those who were "below average." The rest are a mixture of the two. An evil nature can be corrected, however, and Wang Chong is closest to a conventional Confucian position in his belief in the transformative power of education. Thus, character is partly innate, partly cultivated, and governs wisdom, knowledge, and moral virtue.

Although the *Yinyang* cosmologists asserted a correspondence between character and destiny (such that moral virtue leads to an auspicious fate, and moral evil to an inauspicious one), Wang argues for their separation. "Destiny" (*ming*) is determined at birth (by one's "store of *qi*") and by external circumstances (what Wang calls the "accidents" of history, which may overpower the individual destiny with which one is born) and cannot be changed by individual effort. One's fate is predestined and governs life and death, longevity, wealth, social status, and good or bad fortune. In defense of Confucius and the Confucian scholars of his day, Wang insists that failure in the political arena does not reflect negatively on character: the Confucians should be praised for their high standards of moral virtue, a matter of character and self-cultivation, and forgiven for their lack of success, a matter of simple bad luck. Political failure is not divine punishment for moral wrong.

Lasting Influence

Wang Chong did not receive much attention in his times. The Later Han dynasty continued to be dominated by the "School of Correspondences" and its theories of Heavenly retribution, consciousness af-

ter death, and the correlation of natural events and human affairs. There is no commentary on the *Lunheng*, and Wang Chong was not associated with any particular philosophical school in the bibliographical works of the third to ninth centuries (he is listed among the "Miscellaneous Philosophers"). Insofar as he borrowed from Daoist, Confucian, and Cosmological works in his writing, Wang remains difficult to categorize.

Wang has received greatest attention in the last century, and is credited with having demonstrated a "scientific spirit" that was inspiring to the Late Qing/Ch'ing reformers of the nineteenth century and both Republican and Communist historians of the twentieth. Hu Shi (Hu Shih) credited Wang with a "critical scientific spirit" unique in Chinese intellectual history. Fung Yu-lan asserts that Wang "undoubtedly did much to purge China of a great mass of popular superstition"; his critical "scientific spirit . . . makes one regret that it has found no later followers." Qian Mu (Ch'ien Mu) called Wang Chong "China's preeminent logical thinker." Wing-tsit Chan describes Wang as "a thoroughly independent thinker" notable for his:

> critical spirit, skepticism, scientific method, demand for evidence, and revolt against the past . . . His chief contribution to the history of Chinese thought is to clear the atmosphere of superstition and enhance the critical and rational spirit that was already incipient.

Wang has enjoyed similar praise in the West, correcting "the excesses of correlative system-building" at a "low point" in the "debasement" of ancient Chinese thought (A. C. Graham); showing an "astonishingly modern . . . independent spirit" not seen in "any other literary work in human history" (H. G. Creel); and standing as "one of the greatest men of his nation in any age . . . from the point of view of the history of scientific thought" (Joseph Needham). Wang's thorough-going rationalism in the evaluation of evidence and consistent naturalism in accounting for extraordinary events are models of skeptical reasoning, and are representative of naturalistic thinking at its best in the history of Chinese philosophy.

RANDALL L. NADEAU

Further Reading

Translations

Forke, Alfred, trans. *Lun-heng: Philosophical Essays of Wang Ch'ung.* New York: Paragon Books, 1962 (originally published in 1907). This is the only English translation of the work, and is generally quite reliable, though almost completely lacking annotation. Eighty-five chapters (rearranged by the translator) in two volumes.

Related Studies

There are no book-length studies in English. Helpful introductions can be found in volume 2 of Joseph Needham, *Science and Civilization in China* (Cambridge: Cambridge University Press, 1956), and Fung Yu-lan's *History of Chinese Philosophy* (translated by Derk Bodde, Princeton, N.J.: Princeton University Press, 1952). Another useful reference is Wing-tsit Chan's (trans. and comp.) *A Source Book in Chinese Philosophy* (Princeton, N.J.: Princeton University Press, 1963), which contains background information and a selection of translated passages.

LIEZI (LIEH TZU)

Author: Attributed to Liezi (Lieh Tzu) (fifth–fourth century B.C.), but probably not written by him
Date of Composition: c. A.D. 300, contains material from earlier sources
Type of Work: Daoist (Taoist) teachings

Major Ideas

Life and death are part of the natural cycle; one should not cling to either side, but go with the cycle.
Action performed in harmony with the Dao (Tao) requires an attitude of selflessness and purposelessness.
Life is but a dream, and dreams are real.
Practical knowledge and conventional distinctions will only serve to distort one's natural spontaneity.
The world has no limit.
Although people endeavor to achieve by their own efforts, in reality they are destined to get what they achieve.
To live a life of spontaneity and harmony, one must discard preconceptions and conventional standards and comply with the external circumstances.
Life is short, and its true meaning is found in hedonistic self-indulgence.

Liezi is the third major classic of philosophical Daoism (Taoism). As with the other two classics—the *Laozi* (*Lao Tzu*) and the *Zhuangzi* (*Chuang Tzu*), the author and the date of composition of the *Liezi* are obscured by a lack of historical evidence. This obscurity and the fanciful stories surrounding the early Daoist (Taoist) masters are in keeping with the Daoist approach to life: there are no clear answers; the life lived in harmony with *Dao* is full of mystery, obscurity, and creative imagination. Many scholars, Chinese and Western, argue that the man Liezi is a fictitious character. A. C. Graham has brought forward the results of Chinese scholarship along with his own findings and argued convincingly that the text *Liezi* was composed about A.D. 300, shortly before the first commentary of the text was written by Zhang Zhan (Chang Chan, c. A.D. 370). There are a considerable number of passages in the *Liezi* that parallel passages in such texts as the *Zhuangzi*, the *Laozi*, the *Lushi Chunqiu* (*Lü-shih Ch'un-ch'iu*), and *Mozi* (*Mo Tzu*), dated to an earlier period. There may very well have been a Daoist master named Liezi, although, if there was, he probably did not record his teachings in writing; it would not be surprising if his friends recorded stories about him which reflected his teachings and

a later author then used the name "Liezi" to lend a sense of authority to his own work, and included all the stories about Liezi that he could find. Because the name "Daoist" was coined after the *Laozi* and *Zhuangzi* were written, the author of the *Liezi* was the first philosophical Daoist to write deliberately from that perspective.

The earliest mention of the man Liezi is found in chapter 1 of the *Zhuangzi*, where we are told that he could travel for days riding upon the wind. In chapter 7 of the *Zhuangzi*, there is an interesting story (which also occurs in chapter 2 of the *Liezi*) concerning Liezi's early training under his master Huzi (Hu Tzu): Liezi becomes fascinated with the teachings of a shaman and brings the shaman to meet Huzi; Huzi apparently puts himself into various meditative states and ends up scaring the wits out of the shaman, an act which causes Liezi to realize his own foolishness. Thereupon he simplified his life and practice.

The stories concerning Liezi mention that he lived in the State of Zheng (Cheng); some stories relate events when Zichan (Tzu-ch'an, d. 522 B.C.) was prime minister of Zheng; others when Ziyang (Tzu-yang, d. 398 B.C.) was prime minister. Liezi's name was Yukou (Yü-k'ou); "Lie Yukou" is also the title of chapter 32 of the *Zhuangzi*, but only the first passage of that chapter deals with Liezi.

Despite the problems surrounding the historicity of the man and the work attributed to him, the Daoist teachings contained in the book *Liezi* are more clearly presented than those contained in the *Laozi* and the *Zhuangzi*. The text *Liezi* is composed of eight chapters, and aside from the parallel passages found in other texts, the *Liezi* displays a homogeneity of literary style, which would make it the work of one author. It is usually argued that chapter 7, the "Yang Zhu" (Yang Chu) chapter, was written by another author. However, A. C. Graham argues that the Yang Zhu chapter, although different in content, is stylistically consistent with the rest of the text and is probably the work of the same author, but from an earlier hedonistic phase.

Life and Death: A Natural Cycle

The first chapter is entitled "Heaven's Gift." Its theme is a common one in Lao–Zhuang philosophy, namely that life and death are part of the natural cycle of things and, accordingly, one should not cling to life or death, but go with the cycle. This chapter presents a number of reasons for accepting death and even the final destruction of the world. Opposites are complementary and interconnected. So it is with life and death; one cannot exist without the other. For the Daoist, personal identity is an illusion created by social conventions. Clinging to life or death is an obsession of our social illusion. Birth and death are part and parcel of the natural transformations of the cosmic life force *qi* (*ch'i*). According to the *Liezi*, Heaven and Earth will end together with the individual; the particular is another manifestation of the cosmic life force. All things come out of and return to a primordial nothingness; this nothingness is our original home to which we all must return. Because we do not know what is in store for us in death—maybe a greater joy, maybe a rebirth—there is no need to fear death. Finally, since life is full of toil and a burden, one should celebrate death as a well-earned rest.

The Daoist Principle of Action

The "Yellow Emperor" chapter was written to illustrate the Daoist principle of action. Many of the stories are about Liezi, Confucius (Kongfuzi/K'ung Fu-tzu), or Daoist characters. Actions performed in harmony with the *Dao* require an attitude of selflessness and purposelessness. The outward appearance and form of an action are not as important as the attitude and inner realization of the actor, which allows the actor to fuse the external form and the inner attitude.

Various stories are used to illustrate the Daoist theme. For example, the drunk who falls out of a cart is not hurt because he is relaxed and does not brace himself. If wine can give one an inner sense of integrity, then the integrity bestowed by nature should be even better.

There is the story of Liezi displaying his skill at archery: the master challenges him to try it while standing on the edge of a perilous cliff. Up on the cliff Liezi breaks out in a sweat and trembles; the master chastises him. The person who is in harmony with *Dao* does not even quicken his breath when thrown about the universe. The danger one must guard against is within oneself. Self-conscious purposeful action leads to danger. The Daoist acts without self-awareness. This is the action of no action.

Life as Illusion

The third chapter, "King Mu of Zhou," focuses on reality and illusion. The dominant theme here is that life is but a dream, and dreams are real. Unlike other mystical philosophers, the Daoist does not deny the reality of this life and this world; there is no yearning for a higher realm. Daoist mysticism is found in merging with nature. For the *Liezi*, the reality of my life is an illusion or a dream, but it is a necessary illusion. The reality of life is revealed in the dream:

> The breath of all that lives, the appearance of all that has shape, is illusion. . . . It is when

you realize that the illusions and transformations of magic are no different from birth and death that it becomes worthwhile to study magic with you. You and I are also illusions; what is there to study?

The Limitations of Knowledge

"Kongzi" (Confucius) is the title of the fourth chapter. A Daoist literary ploy, especially employed in the *Zhuangzi*, is to use Confucius to criticize Confucian doctrine; this chapter of the *Liezi* uses on the same rhetorical technique. The Confucians rely heavily on education and acquisition of knowledge. The Daoists reject that approach. For the Daoist, practical knowledge and conventional distinctions serve only to distort one's natural spontaneity. Making sharp analytic distinctions is a sign that one is falling out of harmony with the Way.

"The Questions of Tang," the fifth chapter, opens with a few stories of an ancient king Tang and relates other stories from antiquity. The main theme here is that the world has no limit; space and time are infinite. This theme is tied to the Daoist ideas that human judgments and knowledge are limited and dependent on one's perspective. Stories of many marvelous and fanciful things and creatures are told; these stories are not intended to be taken literally, but to defy our common-sense understanding.

The Daoist Idea of Destiny

Chapter 6, "Endeavor and Destiny," opens with a fictitious story of endeavor and destiny personified in discussion. Endeavor represents the way of humans; destiny (*ming*) is the way of nature. Although people attempt to accomplish things entirely by their own efforts, in reality they are destined to achieve whatever it is they accomplish. On the surface, the extreme fatalism present in this chapter appears to lead to apathy and inertia, but a careful reading reveals that this Daoist notion of "destiny," like that of non-action, is sup-

posed to encourage the reader to follow the path of natural spontaneity. The general idea is to get beyond making premeditated actions and just respond to circumstances as they arise, as a good swimmer does who rides the current and does not fight it.

The eighth chapter, "Explaining Conjunctions," is the most heterogeneous of them all. Although it is composed mostly of passages taken from earlier works, it maintains a unifying theme: the conjunction of chance events determines both how one ought to act and what interpretation will be given. The main idea is that to live a life of spontaneity and harmony, one must discard preconceptions and conventional standards and comply with external circumstances. For example, Huzi told Liezi that when Liezi learned how to keep to the rear, then Huzi would start teaching him. Liezi did not understand what he meant, and Huzi told him to observe the example of his own shadow, which complied with the shape of the body. The lesson is that our posture and action should respond to circumstances, rather than follow from our thoughts.

Daoist Hedonism

The title of the seventh chapter, "Yang Zhu," refers to the hermit Yang Zhu (Yang Chu), who was often attacked by the Confucians, especially Mencius (Mengzi/Meng Tzu), for not willingly sacrificing one hair from his shin to save the empire. The teachings of the historical Yang Zhu were supposedly concerned with preserving one's own life, and scholars often hear them being echoed in some of the opening chapters of the *Lushi chunqiu*. The author of the Yang Zhu chapter has expanded the idea of protecting life into a fully developed hedonism. Life is short, and its true meaning is found in hedonistic self-indulgence. In a number of passages it is proposed that the meaning of life is to pursue pleasure in fine clothes, good food, music, and sex. Other passages emphasize that it is not only egoistic pleasure that counts, but also helping others fulfill their pursuit of pleasure is important. Many of the passages contend that overindulgence in pleasure will cause pain, so one must be on guard to not overdo it.

Although there are various passages in the Yang Zhu chapter that advocate the enjoyment of life, the chapter is not totally out of step with the Daoist teachings contained in the text as a whole. If one keeps in mind that Daoist literature cannot be taken at face value in that it holds coded messages, then possibly this also applies to the so-called hedonistic message in this chapter. If non-action and destiny are Daoist codes for living a life of natural spontaneity in harmony with the way of nature, the life of pleasure and enjoyment may also be a code for natural spontaneity. Clearly one dominant idea expressed in different ways in this chapter is that to enjoy life fully one must reject conventional standards, make one's own path through life, and preserve the natural course of one's life by not becoming embroiled in conventional pursuits such as fame, power, and wealth. All this, of course, is a basic Daoist teaching.

JAMES D. SELLMANN

Further Reading

Translation

Graham, A. C. trans. *The Book of Lieh-tzu: A Classic of Tao*. New York: Columbia University Press, 1990. The only complete and authoritative English translation of the *Liezi*. Contains a thirteen-page analytical introduction.

Related Studies

Graham, A. C. "The Date and Composition of *Liehtzu (Liezi),*" *Asian Major*, new series, vol. VIII, part 2, 1961, 139–198. The most thoroughly researched analysis of the date and contents of the *Liezi*.

Kushner, Thomasine. "Yang Chu: Ethical Egoist in Ancient China," *Journal of Chinese Philosophy*. vol. 7, no. 4, December 1980, 319–325. This article attempts to make sense out of the few obscure accounts of Yang Zhu's thought.

GUO XIANG (KUO HSIANG)

Born: Third century in Henan (Honan) Province, China
Died: A.D. 312
Major Work: Zhuangzi zhu (Chuang Tzu chu) (*Commentary on the* Zhuangzi/Chuang Tzu)

Major Ideas

There is a spontaneous order by which things are self-so-ing (ziran/tzu-jan) *and self-transforming* (duhua/tu-hua).
Things are not independent; there is an interpenetration of particulars in nature.
The world is fundamentally a world of change.
True action is the action of non-action (wuwei/wu-wei).
Sagacious wisdom is not ordinary knowledge.

After the period of the "Hundred Schools" during the late Eastern Zhou (Chou) dynasty (c. 771–221 B.C.), the next great flourishing of Daoist (Taoist) philosophy developed at the end of the Later Han dynasty and into the period of political decentralization during the Northern and Southern dynastic period (third to fifth centuries A.D.). Although a blend of Legalist and Confucian philosophies remained the dominant state ideology, there was a resurgence of Daoist religion and philosophy, possibly because of the trying times and political chaos. A number of influences contributed to the renewal: the Seven Sages of the Bamboo Grove and their practice of *qing tan* (*ch'ing t'an*), the art of pure philosophical conversation; the *Xuan Xue* (*Hsüan-hsüeh*), "Mysterious Teachings," represented by Wang Bi's (Wang Pi's) commentary on the *Laozi* (*Lao Tzu*) and the *Yi Jing* (*I Ching*); the *Liezi* (*Lieh Tzu*) and Zhang Zhan's (Chang Chan's) commentary on it; and Xiang Xiu's (Hsiang Hsiu's) and Guo Xiang's (Kuo Hsiang's) commentaries on the *Zhuangzi* (*Chuang Tzu*). The extant text of the *Zhuangzi* and our understanding of it owes much to Xiang Xiu and Guo Xiang. They edited and organized the text from fifty-two to the present thirty-three chapters and wrote the authoritative commentary. According to the *History of the Jin [Chin] Dynasty* biography of Xiang Xiu, he had begun a commentary on the *Zhuangzi* that Guo Xiang continued and enlarged. According to Guo Xiang's biography in the same dynastic history, Guo pla-

giarized Xiang Xiu's commentary. Whereas Zhang Zhan's commentary of the *Liezi* cites Xiang Xiu's commentary of the *Zhuangzi*, those passages usually coincide with what is currently in Guo Xiang's commentary. Because the contributions of Xiang Xiu and Guo Xiang have become intertwined, it would be wise simply to refer to the *Commentary on the* Zhuangzi.

What makes Daoism interesting and also difficult to grasp is its peculiar vision of the world. The obscure poetic style and highly creative imagination expressed in the *Laozi* and *Zhuangzi* make it even more difficult to understand. The Neo-Daoist commentaries attempt to flesh out and clarify those ambiguities; they also bring the Daoist teachings to new heights.

The Dao

The *Commentary on the* Zhuangzi explicates the spontaneous theory of order at work in the *Zhuangzi*. Because of the poetic expression used in the *Laozi* and the *Zhuangzi*, readers are often misled and equate the *Dao* (*Tao*) with a first cause or a personal god who creates nature. The *Commentary* to a passage in *Zhuangzi*, chapter 6, argues otherwise:

> *Dao* is nothing. How can it cause the gods to be divine and the world to be produced? It does not cause the gods to be divine, but they

80

are divine themselves. So *Dao* causes them to be divine by not causing them. *Dao* does not produce the world, but the world produces itself. So *Dao* produces it by not producing it. . . . *Dao* is everywhere, but everywhere it is nothing.

(FUNG, 1933)

Whatever *Dao* is, it certainly is not a god or first cause. Any particular thing—for example, a creature, the world, or a blade of grass—is in fact a complex process of transformation; it is described as being self-produced because there is no one causal antecedent responsible for its existence. A "thing" producing itself does not mean that there are magical or hidden inner powers at work. The nothingness of *Dao* is a rejection of substantialistic thinking; expressed positively, *Dao* is a field of interrelatedness. The spontaneous arising of "things" means that particulars are defined by the contextual processes of their interaction and transformation.

In chapter 14 the *Commentary* argues against simplistic causal understanding:

We may claim that we know the cause of certain things, but there is still the question: what is the cause of these causes? If we continue to ask this question again and again, we have to stop at something that is spontaneously self-produced and is what it is. We cannot ask about the cause of this something. We can only say that it is.

(FUNG, 1933)

The *Commentary* is celebrating the concept of "self-so-ing" (*ziran/tzu-jan*) (or, one might say, "being *so*—the way it is—by itself") and self-transforming (*duhua/tu-hua*), two concepts that had become very popular in the *Xuan Xue* (*Hsüan-hsüeh*) philosophy. Words and translations are misleading; many people think in terms of static concepts. Daoist philosophy attempts to get the reader to think in terms of processes.

If there is no first cause or transcendent princi-

ple, then what brings about order? For the Daoist, there is no order. The world is what it is; we humans impose our value judgments on it and judge it to be order or chaos. Order and chaos are human evaluations and not a reflection of the way things are. The way things are, according to the Daoist vision, is a field network of interrelated processes. Things are what they are through their interpenetration, interdependency, and interaction with others in dynamic processes of transformation. It is the *Commentary* that emphasizes the concept *ziran* (self-so-ing). *Ziran* appears only seven times in the *Zhuangzi*; the *Commentary* makes *ziran* of central importance in understanding the *Zhuangzi*. *Duhua* (self-transforming) does not appear in the text *Zhuangzi*; as a philosophical concept it is a coinage of the *Commentary*.

To say that "things" are self-so-ing and self-transforming is a way of placing emphasis on their interdependency. In explaining the opening passage to chapter 6, the *Commentary* points out the significance that the cosmos and the myriad things have on one's own life. If just one thing is missing, then one would not be born; if just one pattern is incomplete, one's years might be cut short. The *Commentary* is describing the complex network of interpenetration. In a sense there are certain resonances between Daoism and the theory of relativity in physics, but one must take care not to stretch the comparison too far. The Daoist, unlike the physicist, is not concerned with theories or hypothesis testing. In fact the Daoist challenges the whole scientific approach to knowledge, but the Daoist and physicist do share a common vision of the world as a dynamic field of interrelationships.

In Fung Yu-lan's exposition of Guo Xiang's philosophy (see the "Further Readings" below), Guo is presented as a type of determinist and Fung draws parallels between Guo and Marxist historical materialism. Although the comparison serves some heuristic purposes, the reader should be wary of such comparisons. Determinism entails necessary causal relationships, and we have noted that chapter 14 of the *Commentary* contains passages that reject this kind of simplistic causal thinking. In the Daoist web of interrelations anything can, and often does, happen. Under determinism only one thing can happen: that which is determined to occur. If we take the text of the *Commentary* seriously, namely that things just are what they are, self-so and self-produced, then free will and determinism do not apply in the Daoist worldview. I depend on the rest of the world just as those processes depend on me. There is a mutual co-dependency; the world and myself are mutually defining each other. There is a type of freedom in coming to realize the way things are: "Let everything be what it is, and then you have peace."

Change and Transformation

The world is fundamentally processes of change. According to the *Commentary*, there is no force greater than that of change and transformation. Heaven and earth are constantly undergoing renewal; the earth's geography is in a process of change and renewal. Antiquity does not cease; it keeps renewing itself. Things keep changing but we look at them as if they were the same old things. Imperceptibly all things fade away. This process of change applies to myself. Human beings are psychologically habituated to thinking of themselves as always being the same, but the *Commentary* points out that none of us is the same person we used to be. Everything changes. The *Commentary* not only celebrates change in nature, but it also praises change in society.

If human nature is changing, then society is in flux also. In keeping with trends in Legalist philosophy and developments in various Han dynasty philosophers such as Wang Chong (Wang Ch'ung), the *Commentary* argues that the standards and institutions of the early sage–kings cannot be applied to contemporary circumstances. This recognition of the need to change policy stands in direct opposition to Confucian teachings. A passage from the *Commentary* to chapter 9 of the *Zhuangzi* strongly criticizes those who imitate the early kings:

> Those who imitate the sages imitate what they have done. But what they have done is something already past, and therefore cannot meet

the present situation. It is worthless and should not be imitated. The past is dead while the present is living. If one attempts to handle the living with the dead, one certainly will fail.

(FUNG, 1933)

From this passage it should be clear that not all Chinese philosophy is conservative and backward-looking. Like any other culture the Chinese had progressive and reformist thinkers. Another point of interest gleamed from this passage is that unlike Zhuangzi, who seriously questioned the use of institutions and government policy, the *Commentary* is not radical. It only suggests changing social standards to keep up with the changing times.

Acting Without Action

What the Daoists mean by *Dao* is confusing enough—one way to dissolve the riddle is to stop trying to understand it intellectually and "go with the flow" and experience the *Dao* processes. Next to *Dao*, the expression "acting without action" (*wei wuwei/wei wu-wei*) is the second most obscure concept in the Daoist teachings. The *Commentary* sheds considerable light on the subject. Clarifying a passage in chapter 11 of the *Zhuangzi*, the *Commentary* states:

> Without-action (*wuwei*) does not mean doing nothing. Let everything do what it does, and then its character will be satisfied.

Non-action does not mean to take no action at all, but to act naturally and spontaneously. When things or people do what is natural for them, they behave effortlessly. Then there is no purpose driving them to act; non-action is best. To be a Daoist it is not a question of what one does, rather it is a question of *how* one does it. Acting by not acting is really a Daoist expression for realizing a shift in attitude whereby one is not driven by external forces or conventional standards.

There is a paradox here. Because everything is

what it is, self-so and self-transforming, everything is already natural and spontaneous, acting by non-action. A problem arises when human beings impose an artificial will and attempt to make slow horses run fast and fast ones walk slowly. In chapter 9 the *Commentary* proposes that one travel with horses at their own pace; then the horses are "free." The idea is not to let the horses run wild or to think that lying down is better than walking. "Non-action" is an expression for "going with the natural flow."

The paradox is that if what is natural to human beings is to impose their artificial standards, then no one really falls out of harmony with *Dao*; that is, no one really acts unnaturally or with external standards of purposeful action. All actions, then, are acts of non-action. Therefore there is no special need to study Daoism, unless that is what is natural to you. The value of Daoism is to remind oneself to forget. In forgetting one enters the mysterious oneness of heaven and earth.

In the *Laozi* and the *Zhuangzi* there is a clear disdain for and rejection of human knowledge and wisdom, whereas the *Commentary* accepts the validity of original and authentic wisdom and rejects only such knowledge as is imitative. For the *Commentary*, sagacious wisdom is not ordinary conventional knowledge. When scholars interpret the *Zhuangzi* as espousing a "great wisdom," they are in fact following Guo Xiang's idea and not Zhuangzi's. For Guo Xiang, everything is what it is, and so he accepts sagacious wisdom as a reality of the sage. What Guo Xiang rejects is the attainment of knowledge. The sage is wise because it is part of his character to be that way. The attainment of knowledge is a contrived and purposeful activity whereby ignorant people impose willpower, attempting to become something they are not. For chapter 3 of the *Zhuangzi*, the *Commentary* offers its own definition of "knowledge" as "the activity that attempts what is beyond one's natural ability. . . ." The wisdom of the sage is natural and spontaneous for the sage, but not for the ordinary person. The ordinary person attempts to imitate the sage, but this imitation, according to Guo Xiang, is useless, impossible, and potentially harmful.

As we saw above, each situation is unique. Attempting to imitate another's way will not work in one's own circumstances. Because each "thing" is what it is spontaneously, according to its self-so characteristics based on its interrelation with others in the ongoing field of transformation, it is impossible to imitate another, attempting to be what one is not. By attempting to impose an unnatural transformation, like gaining knowledge by imitating others, one might threaten one's natural course and damage one's natural integrity. The fundamental paradox of Daoism begins to emerge again; what if it is my nature or human nature to imitate? Then it would be natural not to be natural. This is a paradox only if we dwell in conventional knowledge. If we practice the art of Daoist forgetting, we do not raise such questions (unless it is one's nature to do so); we just go with the flow.

JAMES D. SELLMANN

Further Readings

de Bary, Wm. Theodore, Wing-tsit Chan, and Burton Watson, comps. *Sources of Chinese Tradition*. New York: Columbia University Press, 1960. Chapter 14, "Neo-Taoism," begins with a discussion of Daoism in philosophy and of "Kuo Hsiang's *Commentary on the Chuang Tzu*," pp. 280–287. Several key passages are translated.

Fung, Yu-lan, trans. *Chuang Tzu, A New Selected Translation with an Exposition of the Philosophy of Kuo Hsiang*. Shanghai: Commercial Press, 1933. The first work in English that attempts to explicate the philosophical thought of the *Commentary*.

———. *A History of Chinese Philosophy*. 2 vols. Translated by Derk Bodde. Princeton, N.J.: Princeton University Press, 1952. Volume 2, chapter 6, part 2 expands on the work presented in the above text; the translations differ slightly.

Ziporyn, Brook. "The Self-so and Its Traces in the Thought of Guo Xiang," *Philosophy East and West*, 43/3, July 1993, pp. 511–539. A helpful discussion of the Daoist idea of "self-so-ing."

JIZANG (CHI-TSANG)

Born: A.D. 549, near present-day Nanjing (Nanking), China
Died: A.D. 623
Major Works: *Zhongguanlun shu* (*Chung-kuan lun-shu*) (*Commentary on the* Mādhyamika shastra); *Erdi zhang* (*Erh ti chang*) (*Essay on the Two Levels of Discourse*); *Bailun shu* (*Pai lun shu*) (*Commentary on the* Shata Shastra); *Shi er men lun shu* (*Shih erh men lun shu*) (*Commentary on the* Twelve Gate Treatise); *Sanlun xuanyi* (*San-lun hsüan-i*) (*Profound Meaning of the* Three Treatises); *Erdi yi* (*Erh ti i*) (*Meaning of the Two Levels of Discourse*); *Dasheng xuanlun* (*Ta sheng hsüan-lun*) (*Treatise on the Mystery of the Mahāyāna*)

Major Ideas

Attachment to or obsessive commitment to any particular viewpoint or viewpoints is a central cause of life's suffering.

To refute what is misleading is to reveal what is correct (or "corrective") because it contributes to the overcoming of attachment to viewpoint.

This refutation can be schematized, among other ways, in terms of the four levels of the two kinds of discourse.

According to the *Further Biographies of Eminent Buddhist Monks*, the Chinese Buddhist monk and scholar Jizang (Chi-tsang) was spiritually precocious, having achieved some degree of attainment by the age of seven through an immediate understanding of a lecture on Buddhism. As this account tells us, he was installed as a monk at that point, and demonstrated a talent for grasping the essence of any particular problem. His literary output was prodigious, and although it indicates an affinity with and sympathy for virtually the entire spectrum of Chinese Buddhist thought, Jizang is most often identified with the Chinese school of Mādhyamika Buddhism, usually called the "Three Treatise School" (*Sanlun zong/San-lun tsung*).

Mādhyamika Buddhism as it appears in the Indian tradition is closely identified with the scholar and monk known as Nāgārjuna, who most likely lived during the second century A.D. His most famous and important work is probably the *Mulamādhyamikakārikās*, or *Verses on the Fundamentals of the Middle Way*. If there is a basic premise behind the work and the tradition it represents, it is that all obsessive viewpoints or commitments of any kind to objects, thoughts, and actions are dysfunctional and are at least in part causes of the basic suffering necessarily associated with the human condition. All claims and propositions, the tradition attempts to demonstrate, are not only logically absurd, but also contribute to *duhkha*, or sorrow.

Mādhyamika studies in China, though, really begin with the work of Kumārajīva (A.D. 344–413), one of the most outstanding translators and transmitters of Buddhist thought to China. His translations of scores of Buddhist, and particularly Mādhyamika, texts have been considered authoritative by many subsequent scholars even up to the present day, and his students and in turn their students became leading figures in the brief but influential evolution of Chinese Mādhyamika. One need only remember that the name of the Mādhyamika tradition in China, the *Sanlun Zong*, means "Three Treatise Tradition," and in fact refers to Kumārajīva's translations of three texts purported to be from the Indian Mādhyamika tradition. These are the *Zhonglun* or *Middle Treatise*, which is a translation of Nāgārjuna's *Mulamādhyamikakārikās*; the *Shi er men lun* or *Twelve Gate Treatise*, which is also believed to be the work of Nāgārjuna; and Aryadeva's *Bai lun* or *Hundred Treatise* (*Sātasāstra*).

Jizang

Jizang lived about 160 years after Kūmarajiva, in the sixth century. Best known for his innovative formulations, the bulk of Jizang's voluminous writings were commentaries on other texts, including the three shastras by Nāgārjuna and Aryadeva from which the Sanlun tradition takes its name, as well as Buddhist sutras and other works. He also often critiqued and analyzed other Buddhist traditions such as Abhidharma, Cheng Shi, and certain Chinese Mahāyāna schools, including the Dilun and Shelun Schools. It is revealing that most of Jizang's works are commentaries on other texts or traditions. Given the ostensible though fundamental reluctance on the part of traditional Mādhyamika to formulate propositional doctrines, however, one might wonder how a writer in the Chinese Mādhyamika tradition, such as Jizang, might have seen his own role. Why was he not guilty of engaging in more *prapanca*, mere wordplay?

For Jizang, the answer can be found in his general methodology of *poxie xianzheng (p'o-hsieh hsien-cheng)*, which might fruitfully be read as "refuting what is misleading, revealing what is corrective," and its specific application in the form of the *sizhong erdi (ssu chung erh ti)*, or "four levels of the two kinds of discourse." In these formulations we most clearly recognize Jizang's insistence that one must never settle on any particular viewpoint or perspective, but that even the so-called "higher discourse" becomes mundane and misleading if it becomes itself a source or object of attachment and fixation. Therefore one must continually reexamine previously established formulations in order to avoid such sedimentations of thought and behavior.

"Refuting What Is Misleading/Revealing What Is Corrective"

The question of the meaning of the phrase *poxie xianzheng* arises because, Jizang claims, and as the practice of the four levels of the two kinds of discourse will be seen to suggest, it is both meaningless and in fact harmful to speak of "true" or "false" in any kind of final or ultimate sense. If this is the case,

then in what sense is Jizang himself justified in using Chinese terms such as *zheng* and its opposite, *xie*, which are often translated as "true" and "false?" Or, as Jizang puts the question:

> If there is no assertion and no denial, and no *zheng* and *xie*, then why is it that [we] write about refuting what is *xie* and revealing what is *zheng*?

For Jizang the term *zheng* cannot be taken as meaning "true" or "correct," but rather "corrective" or "appropriate," since it largely represents the attempt to overcome obsessive commitment to any of the dichotomous distinctions such as "emptiness and being" or "worldly and authentic discourse," found commonly in Chinese Buddhist formulations. At the same time, it must be kept in mind that Jizang is not suggesting that we should *never* make these distinctions—under the proper circumstances they can and do have pedagogical and emotive value. What is apparently being emphasized are the dangers of becoming rigidly committed and attached to any particular set of such distinctions, or the viewpoints which engender them.

However, Buddhism has traditionally recognized a difference between *drsti* or "ontological commitment" and *siddhānta* or "positional commitment." Because the tradition does adopt an outlook, as critical as it may be, even the Mādhyamika is necessarily positionally situated within a traditional perspective. Commentary, since it always remarks on what has been said before, always therefore represents a commitment to a tradition. What is being challenged, then, is the kind of obsession which turns a point of view or perspective into a dogmatic metaphysical fixation. To the extent, therefore, that one becomes committed to one's own point of view as representing "ultimate reality," it becomes necessary to engage in what might be described as "deconstructive" analysis—that is, critical analysis that frees the understanding of language from bondage to the underlying metaphysical commitments of the speaker.

The textual basis for Jizang's emphasis on the

necessity for the further deconstruction of deconstructive language can be found in Kumārajīva's translation of the *Zhonglun*, chapter 13, verse 8:

The Great Sage [Buddha] taught the Dharma of
*   emptiness*
In order to overcome all views.
If one persists in viewing emptiness as an existent
*   [thing],*
Such a one cannot be saved by all the Buddhas.

This passage suggests at least one aspect of Nāgārjuna's understanding of the basic thrust of Buddhist thought and practice, which is the overcoming of attachment or ontological commitment in order to solve the problem of *duhkha* or "suffering." This pragmatic attitude towards truth can be seen in the early Buddhist parable of the raft, which is abandoned once it serves its purpose: even Buddhism is to be abandoned when its purpose has as been achieved.

The problem is that, as Nāgārjuna had anticipated in the previously quoted verse from the *Zhonglun*, there is a tendency to become attached to the effort to become unattached. If one begins to take deconstructive and pedagogically useful notions such as *śunyatā* or "emptiness" as ultimately or fundamentally "true," then one is not only thwarting the cure, one is actually intensifying the illness. This idea also is expressed in another early Buddhist parable, the one concerning the king shot by a poisoned arrow, who wanted to know all kinds of useless information regarding his attacker before allowing the doctor to cure him. As Jizang says:

> It is like water, which is capable of extinguishing fire; if the water itself were to catch on fire, what would one use to extinguish it? Nihilism and eternalism [the two extreme positions] are like the fire, and emptiness is capable of extinguishing them. [But] if one persists in becoming attached to emptiness, there is no medicine which can extinguish this.

The mechanism by which water can be said to "catch on fire" seems to be "persistent attachment." This suggests that even emptiness, which is a cure and not a thing, can itself become poisonous and unhealthy if one allows it to become the object of one's commitment and clinging. This would be equivalent to taking morphine for a back injury, but then continuing its use after the injury has healed. The medicine has become a toxin through the mechanism of addiction. This kind of attachment to the cure is not overcome by additional exposure to the original illness, but rather by revealing the merely provisional or pedagogical nature of the medicine through argument and refutation. Thus, if one develops a fixation on the language of deconstruction, this language itself must be deconstructed. This necessity is described in Buddhist terms as *shunyatā shunyatā*, or the "emptying of emptiness."

The objection is often raised that the progressive deconstructive refutation of all positions is itself a form of nihilism or negativism. But Jizang disagrees, and instead argues that

> One speaks of non-being only because there is initially the illness of [attachment to] being. If the illness of [attachment to] being subsides, then the medicine of emptiness is discarded, and one finally realizes that the holy path has nothing to do with being and non-being. Originally nothing is asserted; subsequently nothing is denied.

Jizang thus seems to reject the charge of nihilism by insisting that no negation would be necessary or even possible without a prior assertion, and that the Mādhyamika deconstruction thus remains a dialectical response to a prior misconception. Although it takes the form of negation or refutation, this is only because the propositions of its opponent are formulated as assertions and affirmations—that is to say, it is meaningful only because it responds to a previous affirmation, proposition, or position. A process by which this progressive deconstruction takes place, enabling the "emptying of emptiness," is described by Jizang as "the four levels of the two kinds of discourse."

The Four Levels of the Two Kinds of Discourse

A central notion which the Chinese Mādhyamika tradition inherits from its Indian predecessors is the idea of the two levels of discourse, sometimes translated as the "two truths." It implies that meaningful discourse can take place on (at least) two levels, which are the *conventional* (or *mundane*) and the *authentic* (or *higher*). That is, language has an everyday reference that is called into question once one analyzes the metaphysical assumptions on which these references are based, and this kind of analysis is liberating in certain ways. In terms of the current discussion, these two levels of discourse could also be described as "tacit acceptance" on the one hand and "deconstruction" on the other.

Jizang says that there are four different ways of understanding this distinction regarding the use of language. That is, the distinction between conventional and liberating forms of discourse can be meaningful in four different ways:

On the *first level*, the naive affirmation of existence is considered conventional, and what is liberating is the idea of nonexistence.

On the *second level*, commitment to any real distinction between existence and emptiness is considered worldly, and the denial of this dichotomy constitutes the higher discourse.

On the *third level*, even the distinction between commitment to and denial of a real distinction between existence and emptiness is regarded as worldly. A standpoint that denies a real distinction between duality and nonduality is then termed an authentic form of discourse.

On the *fourth level*, all of the distinctions made on the previous three levels are repudiated. This level emphasizes that any point of view, no matter how therapeutic and soteriologically effective it may be under certain circumstances, it cannot be said to be ultimately true, and is only of value so long as it serves to discourage or dislodge commitment and attachment. Thus, if one becomes attached to

any such device, it becomes counterproductive and must be discarded.

The apparent intent of this kind of analysis is to emphasize that the way to overcome clinging to a deconstructive strategy is to further deconstruct it. Even though only four levels are described here, there seems to be no point at which one can stop and rest. Jizang's description of the fourth level suggests that even the analytic of the four levels of the two kinds of discourse, like all other Buddhist teaching devices (and in fact all teaching devices whatsoever) is strictly provisional, useful only for a given purpose, and does not express any essentially true or ultimately valid claims about reality.

ALAN FOX

Further Reading

Chan, Wing-tsit, trans. and comp. *A Source Book in Chinese Philosophy*. Princeton, N.J.: Princeton University Press, 1963. Chan provides a thorough, though unevenly translated, collection of primary materials unavailable elsewhere. In fact, since Jizang critiques so many other Buddhist traditions and refers to so many Buddhist texts, he is a frequent source for descriptions of schools and materials throughout the *Source Book*.

Cheng, Hsueh-Li. *Empty Logic: Mādhyamika Buddhism from Chinese Sources*. New York: Philosophical Library, 1984.

———. *Nagarjuna's "Twelve Gate Treatise."* Boston: D. Reidel Publishing Co., 1982. Cheng's two books are among the few to focus on the Chinese Mādhyamika tradition, and this appears to be the only English translation of the "Twelve Gate Treatise" from the Chinese texts.

Fung, Yu-lan. *A History of Chinese Philosophy*. Translated by Derk Bodde. 2 vols. Princeton, N.J.: Princeton University Press, 1952, 1953. Impressive survey of the history of Chinese thought by one of the most important modern Chinese philosophers.

Gadjin, Nagao. *The Foundational Standpoint of Mādhyamika Buddhism*. Translated by John

Keenan. Albany, N.Y.: SUNY Press, 1989. Representative of the best of the Japanese scholarship on the *Sanlun* (Japanese: *sanron*) tradition. The translation is somewhat problematic, but the book has its uses.

Robinson, Richard. *Early Mādhyamika in India and China*. New York: Samuel Weiser Inc., 1978. A very impressive survey of the early Mādhyamika texts and their authors that still holds up after fifteen years as a model for scholars.

Takakusu. *Essentials of Buddhist Philosophy*. Honolulu, Hawaii: University of Hawaii Press, 1956. Though dated, this is a clear and thorough presentation of the basics of the various Buddhist schools as they have been preserved in the Japanese traditions.

XUANZANG (HSÜAN-TSANG)

Born: A.D. 600, Zhenliu (Chenliu) (now Kaifeng), Henan (Honan) Province, China
Died: A.D. 664, Jade Flower Palace Monastery, near Changan (now Xian), China
Major Works: *Xi yu ji (Hsi yü chi) (Record of Western Lands)* (646); *Chengweishi lun (Ch'eng-wei-shih lun)* (*Establishment of the Conciousness-Only System*) (659)

Major Ideas

The Buddhist method requires logic.

Metaphysical notions such as Buddha-nature and Tathāgata-garbha *(Buddha's embryo within all beings) distort basic Buddhist teachings.*

So-called Buddhist absolutes such as Suchness and Unconditioned Dharmas are not real, but are merely linguistic-conceptual creations.

Only what is momentary and produces an observable effect is "real" (dravya)*; the "real" is contrasted with the "erroneous" and the "nominal"* (prajñāpti)*.*

A person's spiritual possibilities are shaped by a combination of inherent and acquired karmic "seeds" that must be brought to fruition.

There is no contradiction between the teachings of Mādhyumika and Yogācāra.

The fame of Xuanzang (Hsüan-tsang), one of the greatest Chinese translators of Indian Buddhist texts, derives in part from his pilgrimage to India and the travelogue he composed after returning to China. His travelogue, *Record of Western Lands*, remains one of our major resources on seventh-century India and Central Asia. During his lifetime, Chinese Buddhism experienced the beginning of a proliferation of competing Buddhist schools and doctrines, many holding views at fundamental odds with their rivals. Many of these schools based themselves on apocryphal texts pretending to be translations of Indian originals as well as authentic texts, into which questionable translations had introduced a host of erroneous ideas that were nonetheless becoming increasingly popular in China and Korea. After returning to China from sixteen years in Central Asia and India, Xuanzang endeavored to bring the Chinese Buddhism of his day back into conformity with what he had learned in India. This he did by retranslating important texts and striving for more accurate renditions, as well as introducing new texts and materials previously unknown in China. Alongside his monumental translation work—seventy-four texts in nineteen years, some of which were quite sizable (including the

Mahā-prajñāpāramitā Sūtra, several thousand pages long)—he trained monks in the complexities of the Yogācāra system and Indian logic, and was the leading advocate for Buddhism at the Chinese imperial court until his death. His translations mark the last major infusion of Indian Buddhist ideas into East Asia.

Xuanzang's Motives for Going to India

By the early seventh century, Chinese Buddhist literature had become a vast sea of translations and original Chinese works representing and supporting many opposing theories and positions, all of which were professedly "Buddhist." Chinese Buddhism in the sixth century could, with some justification, be seen as a battleground between competing versions of Yogācāra Buddhism—the teachings based on the writings of Asanga and Vasubandhu. Details of doctrine, both fine and fundamental, were in perpetual dispute.

While still quite young Xuanzang studied and mastered much of the available Buddhist literature. He was giving lectures to assemblies of monks by the age of thirteen. The Sui dynasty was collapsing and famine and war were spreading death and uncertainty throughout many parts of China, so numerous leading Buddhist scholars and their students converged on Changan, the capitol of the emerging Tang (T'ang) dynasty, where they received support and could practice and teach with relative security. Xuanzang too went to Changan, and after studying with several prominent teachers, gained a reputation for great erudition and original thinking. He came to the conclusion that the many disputes and interpretational conflicts permeating Chinese Buddhism were the result of the unavailability of crucial texts in Chinese translation. In particular, he thought that a complete version of the *Yogācārabhūmi Śāstra*, an encyclopedic description of the stages of the Yogūcūra path to Buddhahood written by Asanga, would resolve all the conflicts. In the sixth century an Indian missionary named Paramārtha (another major translator) had made a partial translation of it. Xuanzang resolved to procure the full text in India and introduce it to China.

Xuanzang in India

Despite the emperor's refusal to grant Xuanzang permission to travel, he left, encountering many hardships along the way as he crossed mountains and desert and faced starvation and murderous robbers; he finally arrived nearly a year later in India. Once there he realized that the disparity between Indian and Chinese Buddhism involved much more than the missing chapters of one text. For over a century Indian Buddhists had become captivated by Dignāga's syllogistic logic, but even though some of Dignāga's epistemological treatises had been translated, Buddhist logic was still unknown in China. Xuanzang also discovered that the intellectual context in which Buddhists disputed and interpreted texts was much more vast and more varied than the Chinese materials had indicated: Buddhist positions were forged in earnest debate with a range of Buddhist and non-Buddhist sects unknown in China, and the terminology of these debates drew their significance and connotations from this rich context. Although in China Yogācāra thought and *Tathāgata-garbha* thought were be-

coming inseparable, in India orthodox Yogācāra seemed to ignore if not outright reject *Tathāgatagarbha* thought. Many of the pivotal notions in Chinese Buddhism (such as the conception of Buddha-nature) and their cardinal texts (for example, *The Awakening of Faith in the Mahāyāna*) were completely unknown in India.

Xuanzang spent many years studying with India's most illustrious Buddhist teachers, visiting holy sites, and debating various advocates of Buddhist and non-Buddhist doctrines, defeating all of them and gaining a reputation as a fierce debater. After one series of debates with two Mādhyamikans (followers of Nāgārjuna's teachings), he composed in Sanskrit a 3,000-verse treatise on "The Non-difference of Mādhyamika and Yogācāra," which is no longer extant. After promising Silabhadra, his mentor at Nalanda University (the central seat of Buddhist learning at that time), to introduce Dignāga's logic to China, he returned in 645 with over 600 Sanskrit texts.

Xuanzang's Translation Project

Hoping to gain valuable tactical military information from Xuanzang, the emperor installed him in a special monastery near the capitol, and assigned some of the leading scholars of the day to assist Xuanzang in his translation projects. Though refusing to provide the emperor with information that might be of military use, he did write a travelogue describing the places he had visited, and especially the Buddhist sites he had visited. This work, *Record of Western Lands*, offers us today our most comprehensive view of the life, customs, manners, geography, and the condition of Buddhism in Central and South Asia in the seventh century.

The scope of materials he translated covers almost the whole range of Buddhist teachings: There are Yogācāra texts with their commentaries; Mādhyamika texts with Yogācārin commentaries; devotional texts (Xuanzang was the first one to associate the notion of "Pure Land"—a realm presided over by a Buddha into which one can be reborn—with Sukhāvatī, the realm of Buddha Amitābha; this "pure land" eventually became the most popular in East Asia); tantric and dhāranī (incantation) texts; logic manuals; major sutras (canonical accounts of the Buddha); Abhidharmic texts (especially the Vaibhāsika abhidharma canon) as well as the *Abhidharma-kosa-bhasya* of Vasubandhu; and a Hindu Vaisesika text. Conspicuously missing are *Tathāgata-garbha* texts. Although comprehensive, his selection of materials was not arbitrary. Rather than compose polemical tracts championing one sectarian viewpoint over another, he presented accurately translated authentic texts that themselves would, he hoped, set the record straight.

Word quickly spread throughout East Asia about Xuanzang: that he had been to India to study Buddhist teachings at their source; that he was uniquely patronized by the Chinese emperor; that he was introducing through his translations new, authentic teachings previously unknown in East Asia. He was the most famous and respected Chinese Buddhist of his day, with students making pilgrimages from Korea and Japan—as well as China—to study with him. His Japanese students carried his teachings back to Japan, establishing the *Hosso* (Dharmacharacteristic) School, which was to be the preeminent Buddhist school there until the advent of Japanese *Tendai* (Chinese: *Tiantai/T'ien-t'ai*), which, through deliberate political machinations, usurped it a few centuries later. Although his teachings spurred interest in Korea, they were eventually syncretized with *Huayan* (*Hua-yen*) and *Son* (*Chan* or *Zen*) teachings, which have dominated Korean Buddhist thought for the last 1,000 years.

The Cheng Weishi Lun (Ch'eng Wei-shih Lun) and Kuiji

In 659 Xuanzang produced his most unusual work. Intending to translate ten separate commentaries on Vasubandhu's *Thirty Verses* at the insistence of his major disciple, Kuiji (K'uei-chi), he instead blended their interpretations and arguments together into a single text. After Xuanzang's death, Kuiji established the *Weishi* (*Wei-shih*) sect, taking the *Cheng weishi lun* as his root text. Kuiji wrote several commentaries to it, most of which are ex-

tant, and his interpretations and expositions have been followed throughout East Asian history as the orthodox reading of the text. There are a number of reasons for being suspicious about Kuiji's claims, however.

Although for Kuiji this text was the singularly most important treatise, there is no evidence that it held any special significance for Xuanzang, who may in fact have regretted amalgamating rather than faithfully translating the original commentaries. The last major text Xuanzang translated was the massive *Mahā-prajñāpāramitā sūtra*. Due to its size and his failing health he considered abridging his translation, but he was tortured by dreams that warned him omitting even a single word would be a grave error. This may likely reflect the remorse left over from his mistreatment of the commentaries he failed to translate faithfully while composing the *Cheng weishi lun*, which he had completed only the year before.

Though Xuanzang's eminence was unassailable, his prestige did not automatically transfer to Kuiji, who had to fight several tenacious rivals, including Fazang (Fa-tsang), a foundational thinker for what was to become the Huayan sect. Historically Fazang proved victorious over Kuiji, since the influence of Xuanzang's orthodox teachings declined rapidly during Kuiji's lifetime.

Even among the followers of Xuanzang there was some dispute over who was his proper heir, and the key justification offered by Kuiji and his supporters for his claim to succeed Xuanzang was his unique access to the *Cheng weishi lun*, based on the presumption that Kuiji alone had been privy to Xuanzang's secret teachings on the text. The rival heir was a Korean monk named Wŏnhyo, whose commentary on *Cheng weishi lun* Kuiji attacked with polemical and vitriolic vigor.

Kuiji's commentary treats *Cheng weishi lun* as a catechism, refuting the erroneous theories of some of the commentaries and promoting the correct interpretation, which, according to Kuiji, was invariably the position of Dharmapāla, a sixth-century Indian Yogācārin. Although the *Cheng Weishi Lun* itself never explicitly attributes any position to any of the Sanskrit authors (in fact, they are never mentioned or named anywhere), Kuiji fastidiously makes such attributions. However, at least in the case of the one Sanskrit commentary still extant against which we can check his attributions—Sthiramati (an important fifth–sixth century Yogācārin)—Kuiji's attributions are fallacious.

An account Kuiji offers of a secret transmission of Dharmapāla's commentary to Xuanzang by a lay-follower of Dharmapāla's while Xuanzang was in India is internally inconsistent and contradicts other contemporary evidence that suggests such a transaction never took place.

Thus, though the East Asian tradition has consistently relied on Kuiji's commentaries for interpreting the text, thereby assuming it presents and champions the view of Dharmapāla, this is probably an exaggeration if not an outright fabrication. Kuiji had much to gain—or so he thought—in garnering exclusive rights to the *Cheng Weishi Lun*, but he may have been overzealous and a bit overly creative in exercising those rights.

Significant Positions in Cheng weishi lun

Using Vasubandhu's *Thirty Verses* for its skeleton structure, the *Cheng Weishi Lun* is an encyclopedic account of orthodox Yogācāra doctrine and its disputes with other Yogācārins as well as non-Yogācārins. It includes detailed discussions of the 8 consciousnesses, 100 dharmas, 3 self-natures, Buddhist causal theories, and the five-step path to Buddhahood (see chapter on Vasubandhu), as well as sundry other topics of concern to Indian and Chinese Buddhists in the seventh century. Since this text is *not* merely a translation (it is much less a translation than is usually assumed), whether or not Kuiji's interpretations are followed, it remains our only source for Xuanzang's own philosophical and doctrinal leanings (aside from *Record of Western Lands*, which is more inspirational than doctrinal or philosophic in tone). Several of its major ideas contrast sharply with ideas that were commonly accepted by Chinese Buddhists at that time.

Although the term *Tathāgata-garbha* never appears in *Cheng weishi lun*, refuting it along with its attendant ideological notions is one of *Cheng*

weishi lun's obvious agendas (which is one reason why advocates of *Tathāgata-garbha* thinking, such as Fazang, attacked Xuanzang's teachings). Chinese *Tathāgata-garbha* rhetoric compared the "pure," "unconditioned" nature of *Tathāgata-garbha* with spatiality, infinitely extended everywhere while neither impeding nor being impeded by anything. *Cheng weishi lun* argues that "spatiality" is a mental construct produced by habitually visualizing some image of spatiality that one has heard about. All "unconditioned" dharmas are similarly linguistic fictions, including one of *Tathāgata-garbha*'s most important synonyms, *tathatā* (Suchness). For many Chinese Buddhists "Suchness" evoked the idea of a metaphysical, subtending reality, clearly accessible only to the enlightened. *Cheng weishi lun* says:

> The unconditioned dharmas are all nominal-fictions established on the basis of Suchness; and Suchness also is a nominal-fictitious term. . . . We are not the same as other schools [who claim] that apart from material-form, mind, etc., there exists a real, permanent dharma called by the name "Suchness." Instead, [we say] the unconditioned dharmas definitely are not real existents.

Cheng weishi lun contrasts three "levels" of reality: (1) the *utterly false and erroneous*, which includes logical chimera, erroneous cognitions (for example, hallucinations), and so forth; (2) the *nominally fictitious*, which are linguistic-conceptual creations mistaken for real existent things (for *Cheng weishi lun* this is a double-edged sword, since although such fictions may lead people to believe in and attach to things that are not the case, the fictions of Buddhist teachings—for example, the concept of Suchness—can help liberate people from the fictitious altogether); and (3) *real existents*, which *Cheng weishi lun* defines as momentary, produced by causes and conditions and producing an observable effect. Thus something permanent and non-observable, such as God or Suchness, is not real, while a moment of conscious sense-perception is real. All three are further defined as "conventionally true." What is "ultimately true" is the flux of mutually dependent, momentary conditions (*paratantra*).

Tathāgata-garbha thought, especially as promulgated by the translator Paramārtha, reified the Mind as the true, subtending, eternal cause of everything, recognition of which constitutes enlightenment. *Cheng weishi lun* sharply distinguishes its own use of the terms "consciousness only" and "mind only" from that idea:

> To oppose false attachment to the view that external to mind and mental-concomitants [*citta caitta*] there are real existent perceptual-objects, we say that only consciousness exists. If you attach to "only consciousness" as something truly existent, that is no different from being attached to external sense-objects, that is, just another dharma-attachment.

External objects are denied in order to focus epistemologically on the fact that whatever is known directly happens only within consciousness. That we are trapped in this narcissistic mirror is the *problem*, not the solution. Breaking this epistemological closure by turning the consciousnesses into "direct cognitions" is *Cheng weishi lun*'s goal.

Finally, the idea the Chinese found most controversial derived from *Cheng weishi lun*'s use of the Yogācāra seed metaphor (see chapter on Vasubandhu). Claiming that each consciousness stream has "seeds" that have inhered in it "beginninglessly," as well as seeds that it acquires through novel experiences (nature versus nurture), *Cheng weishi lun* spells out the classic Yogācāra doctrine of five *gotras* or soteriological "families." The inherent seeds determine one's soteric possibilities. Three of the types represent the three traditional Buddhist images of an enlightened being: *Arhat* (one enlightened by studying Buddhism), *Pratyekabuddha* (one enlightened, unassisted, by discovering the causal principles at work in the world), and *Bodhisattva* (one who is enlightened through the Mahāyāna path). Each of these *gotras* has some but not all of the pure seeds leading to enlightenment, and thus their degree of enlightenment is

determined accordingly. *Arhats* have the least, *Bodhisattvas* more, with *Pratyekabuddhas* in between. Those in possession of the full complement of pure seeds can become Buddhas. The controversial aspect of this model concerns those who utterly lack any pure seeds whatsoever and are thereby incapable of enlightenment. This violated the Chinese Buddhist notion, based on the *Nirvana Sutra* and other scriptures popular in China, that Buddha-nature is universal, so that all beings are capable of enlightenment. No doctrine in *Cheng weishi lun* was more vehemently attacked by opponents than this one.

Xuanzang's Legacy

Of over seventy Buddhist works translated from the Sanskrit by Xuanzang, the one that has remained the most popular, and which has been chanted daily throughout East Asia for over 1,000 years, is the *Heart Sutra*. Famous for its line, "form is emptiness, emptiness is form," it was also what Xuanzang himself chanted at the moment of his death.

His journey to India has continued to excite the East Asian imagination. It was the inspiration for Wu Chengen's (Wu Ch'eng-en's) *Journey to the West* (1592), one of China's most famous and popular novels. In it Xuanzang is accompanied on his journey by a brash, courageous, mischievous, impatient, arrogant, magical monkey (symbolizing the human mind). The novel has been the subject of countless dramatic treatments over the centuries, including a long-running Chinese television serial.

DAN LUSTHAUS

Further Reading

For general readings on Yogācāra thought, see chapter on Vasubandhu.

Translations

Beal, Samuel. *Si-Yu-Ki: Buddhist Records of the Western World*. New York: Paragon Book Reprint, 1968. A readable, useful translation of Xuanzang's *Record of Western Lands*. A classic.

Tat, Wei. *Ch'eng Wei Shih Lun: The Doctrine of Mere-Consciousness*. Hong Kong: The Ch'eng Wei-shih Lun Publication Committee, 1973. The late Tat, a Hong Kong businessman, produced this volume out of devotion to the text. Though the Chinese is on facing pages, the English translation is directly from the French version of Vallée Poussin (see below), minus Vallée Poussin's extensive notes. For those who cannot read French, this is the only other complete Western language version.

Vallée Poussin, Louis de la. *Vijñaptimātratāsiddhi: La Siddhi de Hsuan-tsang*. 2 vols. Paris: Paul Geuthner, 1929. The standard Western translation used by scholars. Vallée Poussin believed Yogācāra was a form of idealism, and translated and paraphrased accordingly. His rendition is very loose in places, relying heavily on Kuiji's commentary.

Related Studies

Li Yung-hsi, trans. *Life of Hsüan-tsang, the Tripitaka Master of the Great Tzu En Monastery: Compiled by Monk Hui-li*. Peking: The Chinese Buddhist Association, 1959. This biography of Xuanzang was written by his contemporary, covering his childhood, his studies, trip to India, and events until his death. A few sections are omitted in this translation, but it is a fine work. Be warned that Li's attempts at reconstructing Sanskrit names are not always accurate.

Waley, Arthur. *The Real Tripitaka*. New York: Macmillan, 1952. A very enjoyable recounting of the life of Xuanzang, containing much information not available elsewhere in English. Waley did this as a companion to his partial translation of *Journey to the West*, which he entitled *Monkey: Folk Novel of China* (New York: Evergreen, 1958). *Monkey* makes delightful, exciting reading.

Yu, Anthony. *The Journey to the West*. 4 vols. Chicago: University of Chicago Press, 1977–83. Yu provides an unabridged translation of the novel. Although not as exciting to read as Waley's version, it is more literally faithful to the original, providing a much broader view of Chinese views and attitudes.

HUINENG

Born: A.D. 638, in present-day Guangdong Province, China
Died: A.D. 713
Major Work: *Liuzu tanjing* (*Liu-tsu t'an-ching*) (*The Platform Scripture of the Sixth Patriarch*)

Major Ideas

Perfect Buddha wisdom is in everyone.
Insight into one's original, pure nature is possible only by putting that nature into practice.
To attain insight into one's Buddha nature, one's mind must be free from attachments and error.
The practice of direct mind leads to sudden enlightenment.
Through no-thought—not being distracted by thought while thinking—one's original nature, the True Reality, is thought.
The original wisdom and such meditation are one.

The *Platform Scripture of the Sixth Patriarch* (*Liuzu Tanjing/Liu-tsu T'an-ching*) is generally regarded as the basic classic of Chan (Ch'an/Zen) Buddhism. The work is reputed to be a record of the teachings of the great Chan master Huineng (Huineng), as expressed in his remarks delivered in the Dafan (Ta-fan) Temple in Shaozhou (Shao-chou) in or about the year 677, as recorded by his disciple Fahai (Fa-hai). The most authentic version of the work is regarded by such scholars as Wing-tsit Chan and Philip B. Yampolsky to be the Dunhuang (Tun-huang) manuscript, found in a cave in Dunhuang, northwest China, in 1900. (Both Chan and Yampolsky have translated the Dunhuang manuscript and have provided copious commentary. See the "Further Reading" section at the end of this chapter.)

Although the details of the life of Huineng are uncertain and some commentators have questioned the authorship of the *Platform Scripture*, the prevailing legends—embellished by commentators over the years—tend to agree on the following biographical items: Huineng was born in 638 into a humble family, the Lu family, originally living in Fanyang and later, at the time of Huineng's birth, in Xinzhou (Hsin-chou) in southwestern Guangdong (Kwangtung) Province. Huineng was a firewood peddler until his early twenties, when he was inspired by a reading of the *Diamond Sutra*; he then

traveled to the north to visit the Fifth Patriarch, who was an exponent of the scripture.

Legend has it that Huineng was appointed Sixth Patriarch after serving a stint under the Fifth Patriarch as a pounder of rice and impressing the Patriarch with a poem, which was requested of all his disciples by the Fifth Patriarch. Huineng's poem was delivered after the following poem was written on the wall by the head monk Shenxiu (Shen-hsiu) (c. 605–706, founder of the Northern School of Chan Buddhism):

The body is the tree of perfect wisdom,
The mind is the stand of a bright mirror.
At all times diligently wipe it.
Do not allow it to become dusty.

Huineng's poem, written after Shenxiu's poem received only a lukewarm reception from the Patriarch, is as follows:

Fundamentally perfect wisdom has no tree.
Nor has the bright mirror any stand.
Buddha-nature is forever clear and pure.
Where is there any dust?

And then he wrote a second verse in which he reversed Shenxiu's imagery:

The mind is the tree of perfect wisdom.
The body is the stand of a bright mirror.
The bright mirror is originally clear and pure.
Where has it been defiled by any dust?

(CHAN, 1963)

Whether or not this story of the contesting poets is true, it appears clear that Huineng did "receive the robe" as Sixth Patriarch in 661, just a few months after arriving in Huangmei to visit the Fifth Patriarch.

In 676, after several years of preaching in southern China, Huineng moved to Canton. He had become a Buddhist priest at the age of thirty-nine. The following year (so the story goes) he was invited to lecture in the Dafan Temple in Shaozhou. There his remarks were recorded by his disciple Fahai (according to the *Platform Scripture*), and the resultant work is, or at least provided the foundation for, the *Platform Scripture*.

Huineng is honored as the Chan Master who initiated the "Southern School" of Chan Buddhism, in opposition to the "Northern School" led by Shenxiu. The Northern School maintained that enlightenment would come gradually as a result of practicing formalized procedures of meditation; the Southern School argued that meditation must be free, a matter of allowing the pure Buddha-nature to reveal itself, and that enlightenment would be sudden. According to Wing-tsit Chan, although this difference of opinion about the speed of enlightenment was present as a matter of emphasis, the two schools differed fundamentally in their concepts of mind, the Northern School maintaining that the mind or Buddha-nature, common to all persons, cannot be differentiated and that its activities are functions of the True Reality, while the Southern School argued that the pure mind can function only in quietude or "calmness," and only after having freed itself from the false or erroneous mind with its attachments to individual thoughts. In any case, the Southern School became the most influential force in the development of Chan Buddhism in China from the ninth century on.

The *Platform Scripture* recounts that the Master

Huineng lectured to more than 10,000 monks, nuns, and followers, all gathered in the lecture hall of the Dafan Temple. His topic was the Dharma (law) of the perfection of Wisdom (of the original, pure wisdom of the Buddha-nature). Huineng begins with an autobiographical account. The material is interesting, but it has little philosophical or religious import. In section 12, Huineng declares that he was determined or predestined to preach to the officials and disciples gathered there in the temple, and he maintains that the teaching is not original with him; it has been handed down by the sages. Sections 13 through 19 contain the fundamental teachings of Huineng. In section 13 Huineng declares that calm meditation and wisdom are a unity, that such meditation is the substance of wisdom, and that wisdom is the function of meditation.

The Buddhist doctrine, here implicit, is that everyone shares the Buddha-nature (wisdom), and if one can turn one's mind inward and not be distracted, one can receive enlightenment. Wisdom and meditation are one in that meditation is regarded as the function or practice of the original nature. Hence, Huineng declares, meditation exists in wisdom, and wisdom is within meditation; neither gives rise to the other. If the mind and words are both good and the internal and external are one, then wisdom and meditation are one.

Huineng next stresses the critical importance of practicing—actively attaining—a straightforward or direct mind. A straightforward mind requires having no attachments and attending to no differentiating characters, thereby realizing that all is one; there is a unity of nature in everything. To achieve such realization in the practice of the straightforward mind is the *samādhi* of oneness, a state of calmness in which one knows all dharmas to be the same. But the calm realization of oneness is not, as some people think, a matter of simply sitting without moving and not allowing erroneous thoughts to rise in the mind. To act in this way is to make oneself insentient, and that is not in accordance with the Way, the *Dao* (*Tao*), which can work freely only if the mind is free from things. If one attempts, as some people do, to view the mind and keep it inactive, one will become radically disturbed and never achieve enlightenment (section 14).

Huineng indirectly criticizes the Northern School in his description of the meditation method that, in effect, renders people insensible and inactive; he continues his criticism in section 16, where he states that the deluded teachers recommend a gradual course to enlightenment, while the enlightened teachers practice the method of sudden enlightenment. In this passage Huineng clearly states that to know one's own mind or to know one's original nature is the same thing, and if people differ in coming to enlightenment, it is because some people are stupid and deluded while others know the method of enlightenment.

Huineng then remarks that everyone has regarded "absence of thought" or "no-thought" as his main doctrine. His remark ties in with what he had just been saying about meditation method, for the doctrine to which he alludes is the meditation method he endorses, a method that came to be identified with the Southern School. Put informally, the statement of method would be "Practice no-thought," and the injunction would make sense if one presumes the point to be that the mind will be open to its nature and able to "think" (intuit) the pure nature common to all within oneself only if it is not distracted by thoughts *about* things, including the thought about achieving enlightenment by not thinking about anything else. The truth is, one cannot achieve awareness even of the Buddha-nature by thinking *about* it.

Huineng speaks of absence of thought as the main doctrine in his method, of "non-form as the substance" and of "non-abiding as the basis" (to follow Yampolsky's translation). He then adds that "Non-form is to be separated from form even when associated with form. No-thought is not to think even when involved in thought," and non-attachment is the original nature of all persons. When involved in the thought consisting in the awareness of original nature (or while succeeding in the practice of freeing the mind), one is not thinking this or that. In that sense the thinking of the original nature is no-thought or absence of thought. As Chan translates a relevant passage,

If one single instant of thought is attached to anything, then every thought will be attached. This is bondage. But if in regard to Dharmas no thought is attached to anything, that is freedom.

To be separated from forms is not to attend to the characters of things; it then happens, so Huineng assures them, that the substance of one's nature is pure. One must not be affected by external objects and one must not turn one's thought to them. But one must, of course, *think*—that is, one must think the pure nature of True Reality. No-thought is free from the error of attending to external things and characters, and free also from all attachment. If your pure nature is allowed to function, as it will if there is the absence of thought, the True Reality will become the substance of thought.

Huineng then speaks of "sitting in meditation" (section 18). He contends that this teaching does not call for looking at the mind or at the purity of one's nature. The objects of such viewing are illusions, and to suppose that one is looking at objects or that there are such objects to look at is to be deluded. However, if delusions are avoided, then the original nature is revealed in its purity. Purity has no form, Huineng argues, and hence one cannot grasp the form of purity and then pass judgment on others. Deluded people are quick to find fault with others because they (the deluded) presume themselves to know the form of purity. By criticizing others, such persons violate the *Dao*, the True Way.

Sitting in meditation, then, is not a matter of looking for forms or characters; sitting in meditation is, rather, to be free and not to allow thoughts to be activated. Hence, Huineng concludes in section 19, true meditation is the achievement of internal calmness and purity. (To "see" the original nature and in purity and freedom to *be* the original nature—to meditate and to be wise—are one and the same. Meditation is the practice of original wisdom; wisdom is the internal subject of meditation.)

The remaining sections of the *Platform Scripture* are concerned with provoking ritualistic attention to the central features of Mahāyāna Buddhism or are taken up with miscellaneous material, most of it probably added by later writers.

Whether or not the ideas represented in the *Platform Scripture* were actually enunciated by Huineng and recorded by Fahai, they represent the central doctrines of the Southern School and are of philosophical and historical interest. In many ways the *Platform Scripture* can be seen as an argument for intuition as a way of enlightenment, in opposition to those who argue for the way of the active intellect and its distinctive mode, analysis.

IAN P. MCGREAL

Further Reading

Translations

Chan, Wing-tsit. *A Source Book in Chinese Philosophy*. Princeton, N.J.: Princeton University Press, 1963. Includes a substantial portion of the *Platform Scripture*, with a very informative introduction; also includes selections from the *Recorded Conversations of Shen-hui*.

————, ed. and trans. *The Platform Scripture*. New York: St. John's University Press, 1963. An unabridged translation of the Dunhuang (Tun-huang) manuscript (probably eighth century), regarded by Chan as the most authentic.

Conze, Edward, ed. and trans. *Buddhist Wisdom Books: The Diamond Sutra and the Heart Sutra*. London: George Allen & Unwin, 1958. A careful translation of two classic scriptures, with copious explanatory notes.

de Bary, Wm. Theodore, Wing-tsit Chan, and Burton Watson, comps. *Sources of Chinese Tradition*. New York: Columbia University Press, 1960. Part of the *Introduction to Oriental Civilizations* series, this excellent source book and commentary provides selections (in chapter 17, "The Meditation School") from the *Platform Sutra*, *Shenhui*, *Yixuan* (*I-Hsüan*), and *Benji* (*Pen-chi*).

Yampolsky, Philip B., ed. and trans. *The Platform Sutra of the Sixth Patriarch: The Text of the Tun-huang Manuscript*. New York: Columbia University Press, 1967. An excellent, informative introduction and translation.

Note: A version of this article as written by Ian P. McGreal, under the title "The Platform Scripture of the Sixth Patriarch," appeared originally in *World Philosophy* (5 vols.), Vol. 2, pp. 591–9, Frank N. Magill, ed., and Ian P. McGreal, assoc. ed., Englewood Cliffs, N.J.: Salem Press, 1982, and subsequently in *Masterpieces of World Philosophy*, pp. 150–6, Frank N. Magill, ed., New York: HarperCollins, 1990. The revised article is used here by permission of Frank N. Magill and Salem Press.

FAZANG (FA-TSANG)

Born: A.D. 643, in Central Asia (Samarkand)

Died: A.D. 712

Major Works: An incredibly prolific writer, Fazang produced more than sixty original works, commentaries on a wide variety of Buddhist texts, and meditation manuals, and participated in at least some of the Buddhist translation projects of his time. Much of his work centers on the exegesis of the *Huayan jing (Hua-yen ching) (Flower Garland Scripture)*, which is sometimes referred to in Sanskrit as the *Avatamsaka Sutra*. A complete list of his works would be impractical, but a few of the major works are:

Huayan wujiao zhang (Hua-yen wu-chiao chang) (Essay on the Five Teachings of the Huayan*); Huayan yihai baimen (Hua-yen i-hai po-men) (The Hundred Gates to the Unfathomable Meaning of the* Huayan*); Huayan fa putixin zhang (Hua-yen fa p'u-t'i-hsin chang) (Essay on the Arousal of the Bodhi Mind in the* Huayan*); Qixinlun yiji (Ch'i-hsin-lun i-chi) (Commentary on the Mahāyāna Awakening of Faith)*

Major Ideas

The world of reality is composed of interpenetrating events linked in causal relations; everything is the cause and effect of everything else.

"Things" in the world are empty of self-being or self-definition, being produced out of the very Suchness of reality itself.

This emptiness is not negative, though, since the reality of empty things is, in fact, the only reality of which it is meaningful to speak.

The history and diversity of the Buddhist tradition can be classified according to five different types of teaching, each accommodating a different spiritual aptitude.

All of these teachings can in turn be described as one of three "vehicles," which can themselves in some sense be described as aspects of the "one vehicle."

Fazang (Fa-tsang) is often regarded as the grand systematizer of a tradition of Chinese Buddhism known as the *Huayan (Hua-yen)* School, named after the *Huayan* or *"Flower Garland Scripture"* (Sanskrit: *Avatamsaka Sutra*). This school flourished during the so-called "Golden Age" of Chinese Buddhism, which culminated during the Tang (T'ang) dynasty (A.D. 618–907). At that time, most of the Buddhist schools in China took as their basis one or another of the Buddhist scriptures, some authentic and some apocryphal. They did not ignore the other scriptures, but each seemed to regard a particular text as the highest expression of the Buddha's teaching. For example, the closest rival of the *Huayan* School, known as *Tiantai (T'ien-t'ai)*, regarded the *Lotus Scripture (Saddharma Pundarīka Sutra)* as the epitome of Buddhist teachings.

The message of the *Huayan Scripture*, as it was developed by the tradition which bears its name, is primarily one of interpenetration and intercausality. The idea of a concrete *Huayan* tradition does not clearly emerge until after Fazang's time, and is somewhat retrospective. However, subsequent commentators and devotees designated Fazang as the third patriarch of the *Huayan* tradition, even though his systematization is perhaps the most sophisticated treatment of the *Huayan* view of the universe. He inherited a number of doctrines from his predecessors, most notably the idea of the "fourfold *dharmadhātu*," which constitutes in some sense the original formulation on which the whole tradition is based.

The term *dharmadhātu* (Sanskrit) or *fajie/fachieh* (Chinese) refers to the realm of events that constitutes the "omniverse." It extends in many dimensions of time and space, and is produced spontaneously and continuously through the interaction of all elements of existence. To speak of the "fourfold" *dharmadhātu* is to suggest that this om-niverse can be seen from four different perspectives. These are:

1. The perspective of phenomena by themselves. This constitutes in some sense a tacit or naive acceptance of the world as it appears to be, namely concrete, discrete, and more or less constant.
2. The perspective of the principle underlying those events, namely the emptiness of self-definition or self-being. The emptiness of an essential nature of things in some sense constitutes their essential nature, paradoxical as this might sound.
3. The perspective of the interpenetration of principle and phenomena. The emptiness of things does not interfere with their reality, and in fact *constitutes* their reality. To be empty is to be real, since to be real is to be part of the web of causality. That is to say, things can be said to exist if and only if they participate in causal relations with all other things. If there were a thing which did not participate in such causal relations, it would have no effect whatsoever on anything, and thus could never be perceived or known, nor could it bring an end to suffering, which is the only meaningful goal of the Buddhist tradition.
4. The perspective of the interpenetration of phenomena with other phenomena. That is to say, since all things are in causal relations with other things, their being overlaps, so to speak, and it is then wrong to conceive of things as separate or discrete. In this sense reality itself can be described as "suchness" or "truly thus." This perspective is sometimes expressed in terms of the "jewelled net of Indra." This image is of a gigantic net, stretching across the sky, with a multifaceted jewel at each junction of the net. Each jewel, then, can be seen reflected in each other jewel. This is a rather holographic image, since each part is seen to contain the whole in some sense.

Fazang was a favorite of the Empress Wu because of his creativity in finding devices for vividly illustrating for her these abstract ideas, two of the most famous of which will now be described. The first of them is the hall of mirrors. Fazang had constructed a room lined with mirrors on all sides and on the ceiling and floor. In the center of the room he placed a candle. Not only was the candle reflected in each of the mirrors, but also each mirror reflected each other mirror, as well as itself reflected in every other mirror. The effect was as if you stood between two mirrors and saw an infinite regress of images, each contained within the other.

The other of his most famous devices was the account of a lion made of gold. The lion seemed to have hair, claws, eyes, and so forth, but all of this was in fact the same substance, gold. This illustrates how the single unique suchness of reality can seem to be differentiated, even though this differentiation is actually nothing more than a superficial and uncritical distinction.

The Ten Mysteries

Fazang characterized the *Huayan* view of the om-niverse in terms of a heuristic device he called the "Ten Mysteries," though some of them overlap. He based his list on previous versions produced by his predecessors, though his is different in various ways.

The "Ten Mysteries" are:

1. Simultaneous completion and mutual correspondence; that is to say, the general and the specific, or the principle and the event, coexist without obstruction.
2. Unimpeded freedom of all things in spatial interrelatedness; this refers to large and small, finite and infinite, and so forth, and implies that any given thing is both large and small, finite and infinite, at the same time, relative to other things.
3. Mutual compatibility and difference between the one and the many; in other words, something is part of a whole while simultaneously being an individual entity.

4. Mutual identification and self-sufficiency of all factors of existence; this refers to the fact that things operate on their own behalf as well as on behalf of the whole, without obstruction.
5. Mutual complementarity of the hidden and the manifest; this refers to an almost gestalt emphasis on the mutual necessity of figure and ground, or event and the background against which it stands out.
6. Mutual compatibility of all things without the slightest loss of individual identity: things do not lose their individuality even when considered to be part of a larger whole.
7. Indra's Net: This image is described earlier.
8. One must rely on phenomena to reveal the principle; that is, since the principle of emptiness and the phenomena which express this principle are nonobstructing, one can find the principle in *any* phenomenon. In other words, a single blade of grass can provoke enlightenment.
9. Distinct existence and mutual inclusion of separate factors of existence in time; that is, each and every factor of existence participates in every other one without loss of individuality.
10. Harmonious interchangeability of principle and phenomena; this refers to the fourfold *dharmadhātu* model discussed earlier.

These Ten Mysteries overlap but offer various ways of understanding the interpenetration of phenomena with principle and with each other without obstruction. In some sense, this can be understood as the relation between a context and the elements which make up the context—the context depends on its elements just as the elements are meaningless outside of a context.

Fazang's Classification of Doctrines

When Buddhism entered China, it did so in an unsystematic and piecemeal fashion. As a result, the tradition was diverse to the point of confusion. It was not immediately clear why there were such differences between different Buddhist doctrines. The Chinese tradition made sense of this diversity by organizing the different teachings into various kinds of categories, based either on the temporal sequence of the teaching, or the sophistication of the teaching, or the method of the teaching, and so on. Fazang's version of this classification, termed *panjiao (p'an-chiao)* or "classification of doctrines," took the form of five different categories of teaching, based on their sophistication and varying accommodation to the limitations of sentient beings. His premise was that since human beings differ in terms of talent for awakening, there must be different teachings to address these individual differences.

The *five categories* of Fazang's classification are:

1. *Hīnayāna*: In the early Buddhist tradition, it was taught that the self does not exist, but that the factors of existence are real.
2. *Initial Mahāyāna*: This includes the early teachings of emptiness as found in the *Prajñāpāramitā* literature and the *Mādhyamika* tradition, as well as the early *Yogācāra* tradition.
3. *Final Mahāyāna*: This includes traditions and texts, such as the *Tathāgata-garbha Sūtra*, the *Lion's Roar of Queen Srimala*, and *The Awakening of Faith in the Mahāyāna*, which speak of the "womb" or "embryo" of Buddhahood (*tathāgata-garbha*) as the matrix from which the world arises.
4. *Sudden Teaching of the One Vehicle*: The term "sudden" here indicates that this teaching makes little or no accommodation for those who lack a special talent for awakening. Later commentators included in this category the Chan tradition, which had not yet really established itself at the time of Fazang.
5. *Comprehensive Teaching of the One Vehicle*: This category specifically refers to the *Huayan* tradition. Fazang believes that the *Huayan* tradition is doctrinally superior to the other schools, which are merely provisional and are incomplete; more precisely, they

make at least some concessions to the limitations of sentient beings.

Fazang's categorization is based on a heuristic, though unconvincing, historical model in which the *Huayan Sutra* was the first Sutra preached by the Buddha while he was still within the throes of his enlightenment. Thus it most closely represents the enlightened view of the omniverse, without modification for the sake of clarity. According to this model, nobody understood a word of the sutra, so at that point the Buddha resorted to a series of teachings which took into consideration the limitations of sentient beings, with the intention of gradually leading them to overcome those limitations. Thus each subsequent teaching renders obsolete the previous ones, though they all continue to function so as to accommodate the greatest number of sentient beings.

Here is one important area in which the *Huayan* School differs from the *Tiantai* School. They both agree that the *Huayan Sutra* was the first sutra preached by the Buddha while still in the glow of the enlightenment experience, and that the Lotus Sutra was one of the last. But for the *Tiantai* School, this makes the Lotus the most valuable and important of the Sutras, since it is the most sophisticated and useful teaching in terms of accomplishing the awakening of sentient beings.

Fazang's Lasting Influence

Fazang's insistence on finding an ontological ground for the operation and generation of the *dharmadhātu* has had a lasting effect on East Asian Buddhism. The priority he placed on the idea of the *Tathāgata-garbha* or "womb of Buddhahood" turned out to set the agenda for the subsequent development of the Mahāyāna tradition as found in China, Korea, and Japan. Even though the *Huayan* School eventually disappears as a separate tradition, its imprint can be found everywhere, especially in such traditions as Chan Buddhism and eventually Japanese Zen. This search for an underlying ontological ground of the omniverse is, ac-

cording to some scholars, entirely contrary to the traditional Indian Buddhist insistence that it makes no sense to speak of fundamental reality and in fact the search for such a bottom line is itself the disease that the Buddhist tradition is attempting to cure. Recently in Japan, a movement within the Buddhist scholastic community has emerged, calling itself "Critical Buddhism," which questions whether East Asian Buddhism can rightfully be called Buddhism at all, because of this apparent discrepancy.

Still, Fazang apparently found it possible to reconcile this apparent discrepancy through appeal to the traditional concept of *upaya* (Chinese: *fangbian/fang pien*), or "skillful means," which refers to the diagnostic and pedagogical skill of the enlightened master, which enables and justifies his use of whatever means are necessary to accomplish the awakening of sentient beings. As long as one does not take the formulation for the fact, one can use whatever teaching devices are at one's disposal to effect the necessary transformation.

ALAN FOX

Further Reading

Chan, Wing-Tsit, trans. and comp. *A Source Book in Chinese Philosophy*. Princeton, N.J.: Princeton University Press, 1963. Chan provides a thorough, though unevenly translated, collection of primary materials unavailable elsewhere.

Chang, Garma C. C. *The Buddhist Teaching of Totality: The Philosophy of Hwa Yen Buddhism*. University Park, Pa.: Penn State Press, 1971. The single most helpful guide to *Huayan* thought and to Buddhist thought in general, including translations of some of the central works and biographies of the central thinkers.

Fung, Yu-lan. *A History of Chinese Philosophy*. Translated by Derk Bodde. 2 vols. Princeton, N.J.: Princeton University Press, 1952, 1953. Impressive survey of the history of Chinese thought by one of the most important modern Chinese philosophers.

Liu, Ming-wood. *The Teaching of Fa-Tsang: An*

Examination of Buddhist Metaphysics. Ann Arbor, Mich.: University Microfilms International, 1979. Very thorough account of the metaphysical aspects of Fazang's thought, as well as other details of his career and of the *Huayan* tradition.

Takakusu. *Essentials of Buddhist Philosophy.* Honolulu, Hawaii: University of Hawaii Press, 1956. Though dated, this is a clear and thorough presentation of the basics of the various Buddhist schools as they have been preserved in the Japanese traditions.

ZHOU DUNYI (CHOU TUN-I)

Born: 1017, Yingdao, in Daozhou, now Hunan
Died: 1073
Major Works: *Taijitu shuo (T'ai-chi-t'u shuo) (An Explanation of the Diagram of the Great Ultimate)*;
Tongshu (T'ung-shu) (Penetrating the Book of Changes)

Major Ideas

The Diagram of the Great Ultimate provides a means to link the metaphysical principles of the universe with moral human nature.

Activity and tranquility mutually generate each other.

Good and bad are the result of human actions in harmony or disharmony with the cosmological structure of the universe.

Sincerity is incipient activating force that assists in determining good and bad.

The mean is the ideal virtue.

A common person can learn to become a sage.

Government must rule by virtue and establish ritual, ceremonies, and music to instruct the people.

The sage modeling Heaven and Earth practices absolute impartiality.

Principle, human nature, and destiny, the cardinal concepts of Neo-Confucian philosophy, are related and are to be treated together.

Zhou Dunyi (Chou Tun-i), also known as Zhou Lianxi or Maoshu, is often considered the "father" of Song (Sung) dynasty (A.D. 960–1279) Neo-Confucianism. The philosophy of the Song is highly eclectic and syncretic. Zhou's success as a Neo-Confucian philosopher is found in his ability to draw in elements of Daoist (Taoist) and Buddhist thought under a chiefly Confucian agenda.

Zhou was born at Yingdao in Daozhou, in present-day Hunan. His uncle, Zhen Xiang (Chen Hsiang), assisted him to become the assistant prefect of Fenning in 1040, and he led an active official career until the year before his death. Some of the important offices he held were: magistrate of various districts (1046–54), prefect staff supervisor (1056–59), professor of the directorate of education and assistant prefect (1061–64). During his last appointment, he built his study, which he named "Stream of Waterfalls" (*lianxi/lien hsi*), after the name of a river near his hometown; his disciples gave him that name posthumously.

Zhou is noted for his profound love of life such that he would not allow the grass outside his window to be cut; he especially loved the lotus flower for its tranquility and purity. The two Cheng (Ch'eng) brothers studied with Zhou (1046–47), and his influence on them has been questioned by A. C. Graham. Zhou esteemed Buddhism and Cheng Yi (Ch'eng I) referred to him as a "poor *Chan* [*Ch'an*; Japanese: *Zen*] fellow." Both Buddhism and Daoism affected his philosophical works. Although Confucian scholars have played down the Buddhist and Daoist influence on Zhou's philosophy, the effect cannot be denied.

Zhou, like Shao Yong (Shao Yung) (1011–77), stood in the respective lineage of Confucian teachers who transmitted various charts that originated with the Daoist master, Chen Tuan (Ch'en T'uan) (906–989). One of the major differences between Zhou and Shao is the role of numerology. Where Zhou employs a purely symbolic interpretation of the Diagram of the Great Ultimate, Shao blends numerology with his interpretations. Shao, like other Neo-Confucians, accepts that there are basic principles governing the universe, and he accepts the same patterns of cosmic generation in the *Book of Changes*, but he introduces the concept of number and numerical formulas into his interpretation.

Another significant difference between Zhou Dunyi and Shao Yong is that Shao, unlike most other Neo-Confucians, does not take an anthropocentric perspective. Zhou and his followers start with human nature and extend their study to the universe. Shao takes the human being as one of many creatures in the universe; though the most important, the human is only one aspect of the natural processes.

Zhou's contribution to Song Neo-Confucian philosophy is twofold. First, he provided a metaphysical and ethical interpretation of the Diagram of the Great Ultimate that served as a cornerstone for much of Song thought. Second, Zhou began a tradition of rational interpretation and revitalized use of the classic *Book of Changes* (*Yi jing/I ching*).

The Diagram of the Great Ultimate

Whereas the Daoist use of the Diagram of the Great Ultimate was probably a kind of alchemic meditative map to work one's way through the forces of nature back to the source, Zhou interprets the diagram in a cosmogonic, metaphysical, and ethical sense. The diagram is a series of symbolic circles. At the top of the diagram is the saying: "The Ultimateless and yet the Great Ultimate" (*wuji er taiji/ wu-chi erh t'ai-chi*). Below that saying is a blank circle, representing the ultimateless. Then comes the Great Ultimate, a circle containing interlocking white and black semicircles showing a dominance of the light of *yang* and movement on the left and the dark of *yin* and quiescence on the right. Below the Great Ultimate, connected by lines, is a square connecting the five phases (*wuxing/wu-hsing*); each phase is represented by a small circle. The *yang* phases are on the left side with fire above and wood below; on the right are the *yin* phases with water above and metal below; the earth phase is naturally at the center. There are lines connecting the five phases and these lines converge on an even smaller circle below the earth phase, parallel to wood and metal at the bottom. That smaller circle represents the alchemic heritage of the diagram, and it is not mentioned in Zhou's commentary. Below the five phases there is another circle marked *qian* (*ch'ien*),

the *yang* male principle on the left, and *kun* (*k'un*), the *yin* female principle on the right, which generates the last circle, representing the production and transformation of the myriad things.

Zhou's claim to fame is that he renders a Confucian interpretation of the diagram that provides Song philosophy with a complex metaphysics, explaining the cosmogonic origins of the world, its cosmological structure, and an explication of human nature and its ethical importance. Beginning at the top Zhou repeats the saying "The Ultimateless and yet the Great Ultimate." He goes on to explain how the Great Ultimate moves to generate the *yang* force, which when exhausted becomes tranquil and generates the *yin* force. *Yin* and *yang*, stillness and motion, mutually generate each other, which reveals the two forms (*liang i/liang yi*). Through the transformations of *yin* and *yang*, the five phases—water, fire, wood, metal, and earth—are formed. When these five forces (*qi/ch'i*) are in harmony, the seasons run their course. When the Ultimateless, the two forms, and the five phases consolidate into a mysterious unity, the male and female are generated, and they in turn engender and transform the myriad things.

Human beings receive these forces in their highest excellence and thereby become intelligent and conscious. The five moral principles of human nature—humanity, rightness, propriety, wisdom, and trustworthiness—develop in reaction to the world; good and bad events occur and, accordingly, the various forms of human conduct. The sage settles conflict according to the mean, correctness, humanity, and rightness; he regards tranquility as fundamental and the highest standard for human beings. Quoting commentary from the *Book of Changes*, Zhou compares the sage and his standards to Heaven and Earth, the sun and moon, and the four seasons. The superior person cultivates the moral principles and enjoys good luck, while the inferior person violates them and has bad luck. Zhou concludes the explanation by praising the *Book of Changes* and claiming that the diagram explains its meaning.

Zhou has clearly borrowed two major Daoist concepts, namely that of the ultimateless (*wuji/wu chi*) and tranquility. This has caused controversy in Neo-Confucian philosophy. Zhu Xi (Chu Hsi) (1130–1200) argued against Lu Xiangshan (Lu Hsiang-shan) (1139–93) that the Ultimateless and the Great Ultimate are not two distinct things, but different phases in the same unity. Zhu also argued that, for Zhou, tranquility and activity are not separable, but always operate together.

Penetrating the Book of Changes

In his *Penetrating the Book of Changes*, Zhou borrows the virtue of sincerity from the *Doctrine of the Mean* to develop further the metaphysical foundation for his ethics. For Zhou, sagehood and sincerity are mutually defining: "Sincerity is the foundation of the sage," and "sagehood is nothing but sincerity. . . ." Sincerity is the source of the five constant virtues and all good activity. Zhou also proposed that sincerity in its original form is nonactive and it is the subtle, incipient activating force that gives rise to good and evil. This claim has generated a fair amount of discussion in Neo-Confucian philosophy. On the surface Zhou appears to contradict himself by proposing that sincerity is the source of human moral goodness and the origin of evil. The traditional Confucian way out of the apparent contradiction is to distinguish human nature as good in substance but sometimes evil in function. Evil arises when human beings fail to adhere to the mean after coming in contact with external things. Thus the mean is the ideal virtue which keeps human moral nature good.

Zhou proposes that one can learn to become a sage. His idea is strongly influenced by Daoist and Buddhist practices. Zhou suggests that the essential way to become a sage is first to learn to concentrate on one thing. This concentration will lead one to have no desires. The state of having no desires will make one empty, tranquil, and straightforward in action. This will cause one to become intelligent and penetrating, which will allow one to become impartial and all-embracing. Then, one is almost a sage.

Concerning proper government, Zhou emphasized traditional Confucian teachings. Government must rule by virtue and establish ritual, ceremonies, and music to instruct the people. The ruler must purify the heart; this means that the ruler must properly practice the virtues of humanity, rightness, propriety, and wisdom. If the ruler develops purity of heart, then men of virtue and skill will come to his court for employment. An important role of government is to establish ritual and ceremonies to regulate and order the people, and to institute music to harmonize them.

The concept of "impartiality" plays a notable role in Zhou's moral teachings. For Zhou, one must first treat oneself impartially in order to be able to treat others impartially. Heaven and Earth are the absolute of impartiality; the sage modeling Heaven and Earth also practices absolute impartiality.

Chapter 22 of *Penetrating the Book of Changes* is entitled "Principle, Human Nature, and Destiny." Although those terms do not appear in the text of that chapter, nevertheless Zhou was the first Song philosopher to advocate that principle (*li*), human nature (*xing/hsing*), and destiny (*ming*) are related and to be treated together. Every major Neo-Confucian philosopher after Zhou further developed the idea expressed in this chapter title and argued for the interrelatedness of principle, nature, and destiny. The seeds of Zhou's philosophy bore fruit with the master Zhu Xi.

JAMES D. SELLMANN

Further Reading

Berling, Judith A. "Paths of Convergence: Interactions of Inner Alchemy Taoism and Neo-Confucianism," *Journal of Chinese Philosophy*, Vol. 6, 1979, pp. 123–147. Berling explicates the Daoist impact on Neo-Confucianism.

Bruce, J. Percy. *Chu Hsi and His Masters*. London: Probsthain, 1923. A useful tracing of philosophical influences on Zhu Xi, including that of Zhou.

Chan, Wing-tsit, trans. and comp. *A Sourcebook in Chinese Philosophy*. Princeton, N.J.: Princeton University Press, 1963. Chapter 28 presents a brief discussion of Zhou and a selection of key passages from the two books.

Chang, Carson. *The Development of Neo-Confucian Thought*. New York: Bookman Associates, 1957. An illuminating survey.

Graham, A. C. *Two Chinese Philosophers: Ch'eng Ming-tao and Ch'eng Yi-ch'uan*. London: Lund Humphries, 1958. Graham argues that Zhou did not influence the Cheng brothers' philosophical development (pp. 152–157).

Fung, Yu-lan. *A History of Chinese Philosophy*. Translated by Derk Bodde. 2 vols. Princeton, N.J.: Princeton University Press, 1952. An excellent critical account of the development of Chinese thought.

Munro, Donald J. *Images of Human Nature: A Sung Portrait*. Princeton, N.J.: Princeton University Press, 1988. This absorbing study of Song philosophy makes reference to Zhou Dunyi.

ZHANG ZAI (CHANG TSAI)

Born: 1020, present-day Kaifeng in Henan (Honan) Province, China
Died: 1077
Major Works: *Zhengmeng (Cheng-meng)* (*Correcting Youthful Ignorance*. Also translated as: *Correct Discipline of Beginners*); *Ximing (Hsi-ming)* (*The Western Inscription*. Part of chapter 17 of the *Zhengmeng*); *Jingxue liku (Ching-hsüeh li-k'u)* (*Assembled Principles of Classical Learning*); *Yishou (I-shou)* (*Comments on the Book of Changes*)

Major Ideas

The ancient economic practice known as the "well-field" system should be revived.
The Great Ultimate is identical with material force (qi/ch'i), *and the cosmogonic origins are traced from material force as substance in the Great Vacuity to material force as function in the Great Harmony.*
Great Vacuity and Great Harmony are the Way (Dao/Tao).
The universe is one; its manifestations are many.
The negative and positive spiritual forces (gui shen/kuei shen) *are the spontaneous activity of the two aspects of material force.*
There is an important distinction to be made between the principle of nature and human desire.
There is mind in the unity of the nature of things and consciousness.
Our nature is the source of all things.
Sincerity implies reality.
There is a reciprocal relationship between developing one's nature and the investigation of things.
Heaven and Earth are our universal parents, and love is the universal virtue.
The person of love has affection for all beings and identifies with Heaven and Earth.

Zhang Zai (Chang Tsai), styled Zihou (Tzu-hou), and called Master Hengqu (Heng-ch'ü) by his contemporaries, was born in the Song (Sung) capital, present-day Kaifeng in Henan (Honan) Province. Because he left there early in life, he is often referred to as a native of Changan, present-day Xi'an (Sian) in Shaanxi (Shensi) Province. Zhang was the son of a prefect. As a youth he loved military arts. At the age of twenty-one he wrote a letter of introduction to the prominent scholar official Fan Zhongyan (Fan Chung-yen) (989–1052), who upon meeting Zhang noted that he was a person of uncommon ability. Fan recommended that Zhang study the *Doctrine of the Mean*, which began his intellectual quest. At first the young Zhang was discouraged with Confucian teaching, and in his studies he concentrated on Buddhism and Daoism (Taoism) for several years. Not finding a suitable answer in those traditions, Zhang returned to the study of Confucianism, especially the *Book of*

Changes and the *Doctrine of the Mean*, which serve as the basis for his Neo-Confucian philosophy.

Zhang received the "presented scholar" degree in 1057 and was appointed a magistrate. When Zhang lectured on the *Book of Changes*, among his students were the soon-to-be-famous scholar statesman Sima Guang (Ssu-ma Kuang) (1019–86), and Zhang's two nephews Cheng Hao (Ch'eng Hao) (also called Cheng Ming Dao/Ch'eng Ming-tao) (1032–85) and Cheng Yi (Ch'eng I) (also called Cheng Yichuan/Ch'eng I-ch'uan) (1033–1107), who later became his critics and were central figures in Song Neo-Confucianism in their own right. In 1069 Zhang pleased the emperor with his orthodox Confucian position on government and was appointed to the position of collator in the imperial library. He eventually resigned because he opposed the radical reforms of Wang Anshi (Wang An-shih) (1021–86). Zhang advocated ancient economic practices and even attempted to revive the practice of the ancient "well-field" system in which eight families till respective plots in a large field divided into nine sections; one section is cultivated collectively and the produce is given to the government. In 1076 Zhang had a compelling dream; he wrote his students about it and was led to compile his teachings, which became his major work, *Correcting Youthful Ignorance* (*Zhengmeng*). In 1077 he was again dissatisfied with politics and resigned as director of the Board of Imperial Sacrifices. He died while returning home from his post.

The Great Ultimate and Material Force

Zhang, like many other Neo-Confucians, received his inspiration from the *Book of Changes*. But unlike them he contributed a different interpretation of the cosmogonic origin. For example, Zhou Dunyi (Chou Tun-i) (1017–73) traces the generation of the universe from the Great Ultimate to the two material forces of *yin* and *yang* and then to the five phases (wood, fire, metal, water, and earth), to the male and female sexes, and to the myriad things. For Shao Yong (Shao Yung) (1011–77), the cosmogony of the universe begins in the Great Ultimate, proceeds through the positive and negative forces of *yin* and *yang*, giving rise to spirit; spirit generates number, which develops form, and form yields concrete things. According to Zhang Zai, the Great Ultimate is identical with material force (*qi/ch'i*). *Yin* and *yang* and the five phases are not generative powers; they are aspects of material force. Before unity occurs, material force as substance is the Great Vacuity. The idea of the Great Vacuity should not be confused with the Buddhist or Daoist ideas of "emptiness" or "non-being." As function, material force is the Great Harmony—the interlocking processes of opposites such as activity and tranquility, or integration and disintegration. The Great Vacuity and the Great Harmony are identified with the Way (*Dao*) and the One.

The key to understanding Zhang Zai's philosophy and one of his major contributions to later Neo-Confucianism is the idea that the universe or material force is one but its manifestations are many. Zhang constantly speaks of the unity in diversity and the diversity in unity. The moral law or Way (*Dao*) is another name for the Great Harmony; the Great Harmony embraces the underlying nature of the processes of interlocking opposites—rising and falling, motion and rest, and so on. Another way to put it is that material force integrates and disintegrates, it attracts and repulses in various ways, but there is only one material force and only one rational principle (*li*) that governs its operation.

Another important contribution Zhang gives to Neo-Confucianism is a demythologized interpretation of the human spirit and of life after death. Before Zhang there were a number of popular conceptions concerning how the ancestral spirits live on in a disembodied state after death. Again obtaining inspiration from the *Book of Changes*, Zhang interprets the negative and positive spiritual forces (*gui shen/kuei shen*) as the spontaneous activity of the two aspects of material force. In substance the material force is one; in function it projects various manifestations. The different shapes and forms found in the universe are the dregs of spiritual transformation. The individual person will come into and go out of existence, but the underlying principle of material force cannot be destroyed. One's coming into existence is the flow of positive spirit (*shen*), and disintegration is the return to negative spirit (*gui*). Thus, for Zhang the personality does not survive death, but there is no total annihilation either. In this way he countered the religious Daoist quest for personal immortality, as well as the Buddhist ideas of transmigration and annihilation.

The Principle of Nature and Heaven

Zhang was the first Neo-Confucian philosopher to draw a distinction between the lower human desires and the higher principle of nature or Heaven (*tianli/t'ien-li*). This idea held prominence in Neo-Confucianism until the Qing (Ch'ing) dynasty. Zhang is also noted for proposing that "in the unity of the nature [of human beings and things] and consciousness, there is the mind." Zhu Xi (Chu Hsi) criticized this idea because it proposes a separation between our human nature and consciousness. Since Zhang seeks unity in diversity, it is not clear just how different human nature and consciousness are. Moreover, Zhang emphasized the central importance of human nature. Human nature is not one's private possession; it is the source of all things. The great person knows and practices the principle of human nature, and thereby loves universally, shares his knowledge, and establishes himself to assist others to establish themselves. There is an important link between human nature and sincerity. For Zhang, as with other Neo-Confucians, sincerity is no longer a human virtue only, but it takes on cosmic and metaphysical significance. Sincerity is the character of reality. Commenting on chapter 25 of *The Doctrine of the Mean*, Zhang wrote,

> By "sincerity resulting from enlightenment" is meant to develop one's nature fully through the investigation of things to the utmost, and by "enlightenment resulting from sincerity" is meant to investigate things to the utmost through fully developing one's nature.

Thus, between developing one's nature to its fullest and the investigation of things, there is a reciprocal relationship.

The Western Inscription

Zhang's essay "The Western Inscription," which takes its name from its having been inscribed on the west wall of the hall in which he lectured, plays an important role in Zhang's thought and later Neo-Confucianism. The major point in the essay is that the universe is united as one family, and love or humanity (*ren/jen*) is the universal virtue. In other words, the person of love has affection for all beings and identifies with the universe—Heaven and Earth.

The essay begins with the grand passage, "Heaven is my father and Earth is my mother, and even such a small creature as I finds an intimate place in their midst."

He continues with the remark that "All people are my brothers and sisters, and all things are my companions." The emphasis is on being obedient to the principles of Heaven and Nature: "To rejoice in Heaven and to have no anxiety—this is filial piety at its purest"; he then adds that whoever disobeys the principle of Nature "violates virtue."

As Wing-tsit Chan points out in his *Source Book in Chinese Philosophy* (from which the quotations given in this chapter are drawn), the "Western Inscription" is often considered the basis of Neo-Confucian ethics, just as Zhou Dunyi's explanation of the diagram of the Great Ultimate is the basis of its metaphysics.

JAMES D. SELLMANN

Further Reading

Bruce, J. Percy. *Chu Hsi and His Masters*. London: Probsthain, 1923. The discussion of Zhu Xi's critique of Zhang is very helpful in bringing out the strengths of both thinkers.

Chan, Wing-Tsit, trans. and comp. *A Source Book in Chinese Philosophy*. Princeton, N.J.: Princeton University Press, 1963. An excellent source of information about the Chinese philosophers; includes extensive passages. Chapter 30, "Chang Tsai's Philosophy of Material Force," presents the key ideas and passages from Zhang. Quotations in this chapter come from Chan.

Chang, Carson. *The Development of Neo-Confucian Thought*. New York: Bookman Associates, 1957. A historical and critical survey of the highlights of Neo-Confucianism.

Fung, Yu-lan. *A History of Chinese Philosophy*. Translated by Derk Bodde. 2 vols. Princeton, N.J.: Princeton University Press, 1952. Fung's work of careful scholarship continues to be a primary source of information on the subject.

Munro, Donald J. *Images of Human Nature: A Sung Portrait*. Princeton, N.J.: Princeton University Press, 1988. A careful study of Song philosophy, with references to Zhang Zai.

T'ang, Chun-i. "Chang Tsai's Theory of Mind and Its Metaphysical Basis," *Philosophy East and West*, Vol. 6, 1956, pp. 113–136. A clear and illuminating critique.

CHENG HAO AND CHENG YI (CH'ENG HAO AND CH'ENG I)

Cheng Hao:
Born: 1032
Died: 1085

Cheng Yi:
Born: 1033
Died: 1107

Major Works: *Er-Cheng quanshu* (*Erh-Ch'eng Ch'üan-shu*) (*The Complete Works of the Two Chengs*). This collection, which has not been translated into English except for brief selections, includes miscellaneous surviving works of the two brothers (commentaries, poems and letters), including the *Yi chuan* (*I ch'uan*) (*Commentary of the Yi jing/I Ching*) by Cheng Yi and the *Cuiyan* (*Ts'ui-yen*) (*Pure Words*), which records conversations of the two brothers.

Major Ideas

There is a reciprocal relationship obtaining between the cultivation of the internal and the external life. Sincerity is the way to unite the inner and the outer.

The proper subjects for study are principle and human nature (xingli xue/hsing-li hsüeh).

The universe is a process of life-giving, and the principle of life-giving is goodness which entails origination.

The Way is constituted in what exists before physical form, and concrete things are constituted in what exists after physical form.

The study of principle to the utmost, the full development of human nature, and the fulfillment of destiny are one.

There is only one principle in the world, and it is identical with human nature.

The substance of all things is found in sincerity and seriousness.

The investigation of things is an important part of self-cultivation and moral development.

Cheng Hao was styled Cheng Mingdao (Ch'eng Ming-tao) and his courtesy name was Bochun; his elder brother Cheng Yi was called Cheng Yichuan (Ch'eng I-ch'uan) and his courtesy name was Zhengshu. Despite their differences, they are often referred to together as the two Cheng brothers or "the two Chengs" because they taught together and their disciples transmitted their works together. They were students of Zhou Dunyi (Chou Tun-i) (1017–73), friends with Shao Yong (Shao Yung) (1011–77), and nephews of Zhang Zai (Chang Tsai) (1020–77). When Zhu Xi (Chu Hsi) (1130–1200) wrote his study of the record of the origin of the school of the Cheng brothers, he lists Zhou Dunyi first, then the Cheng brothers, followed by Shao Yong and Zhang Zai. They are referred to as the "Five Great Masters" of the eleventh century.

Zhu Xi was the first to argue that the Cheng brothers were in the lineage of Zhou Dunyi, and many scholars have followed his precedent. Others, such as Quan Zuwang (Ch'üan Tsu-wang) (1705–55) and more recently A. C. Graham, have denied that Zhou had much influence on them. According to Wing-tsit Chan in *A Source Book in Chinese Philosophy*, the Cheng brothers were strongly influenced by Zhou Dunyi. (It was because of Zhou that they did not take the civil service examination or engage in hunting.) Although they did not make use of Zhou's concept of the Great Ultimate, they did develop his ideas concerning principle (*li*) and the importance of moral cultivation in both the internal and external life. Despite their differences in temperament and philosophy, the Cheng brothers set the pattern for later developments in Song (Sung) philosophy.

Their father was a chief officer. In 1056 they

entered the national university and excelled, quickly making a name for themselves. Cheng Hao received the "presented scholar" degree a year later. He was appointed recordkeeper for a magistrate, and became very famous after saving the dikes, which averted a famine. From 1065 to 1067 he served as a magistrate and won the affection of the people. In 1069 he served as undersecretary to the heir apparent, and the emperor granted him numerous audiences. Cheng Hao opposed the reforms of Wang Anshi (Wang An-shih) (1021–86). He again served as magistrate from 1078 to 1080, but his political enemies had him dismissed. He regained the confidence of the new imperial court, but died before he could take office again.

Cheng Yi received the "presented scholar" degree in 1059. He lived and taught in Luoyang (Loyang) and repeatedly declined appointment to high offices, including a professorship at the Directorate of Education in 1085. The next year Cheng Yi was appointed expositor-in-waiting and delivered many powerful lectures on Confucianism to the emperor, which won him a large following.

Cheng Yi was more temperamental and aggressive that his brother. Because of his critical attacks and uncompromising positions, he gained a number of bitter enemies—chief among them was Su Shi (Su Shih) (1036–1101), leader of the Szechuan group. In 1087 Cheng Yi served as director of the Directorate of Education in the western capital, but resigned within a few months. Censors repeatedly called for his replacement when he was supervisor of the directorate in 1092. In 1097 his enemies made headway against him; his teachings were prohibited, his property was confiscated, and he was banished. Three years later he was pardoned and resumed his position at the directorate. However, by this time government persecution of factions had become severe; he was blacklisted along with his enemy Su Shi and hundreds of other scholars. His followers left him. In 1103 his books were destroyed and his teachings prohibited. The year before he died, he was again pardoned.

The Study of Human Nature and Principle

Illustrating the Neo-Confucian teaching of unity in diversity, the Cheng brothers share basic points and also differ in focus. Because they stressed the study (*xue/hsüeh*) of human nature (*xing/hsing*) and principle (*li*), they are considered the founders of the "School of Nature and Principle" (*xingli xue/hsing-li hsüeh*), which is often used as a label for Neo-Confucianism. They did, however, emphasize different approaches. In a very qualified sense, Cheng Hao put stress on the cultivation of the mind and the subjective, inner life. He laid the foundation for the development of Lu Xiangshan's (Lu Hsiang-shan's) (1139–93) and Wang Yangming's (Wang Yang-ming's) (1472–1529) somewhat "idealistic" tendencies. Cheng Yi, on the other hand, accents self-cultivation through the investigation of things, the study of the external, and laid the foundation for Zhu Xi's philosophy and the somewhat "rationalistic" tendencies of the Cheng–Zhu School. Wing-tsit Chan employs these labels, "idealist" and "rationalist," in an attempt to display the differences between the Cheng brothers. Such Western labels must be used very tentatively; they are not always helpful in describing a European philosopher, much less a Chinese. As Wing-tsit Chan himself points out, for the Cheng brothers there is a reciprocal relationship obtaining between the cultivation of the inner and the outer life that is captured in the famous saying borrowed from the *Book of Changes* and attributed to them both, namely, "seriousness to straighten the internal life and rightness to square the external life." Cheng Hao proposed that sincerity is the means to unite the inner and the outer; Cheng Yi added that our human nature cannot be described properly as either internal or external. Accordingly, distinguishing their philosophical approaches along these lines is at best a provisional heuristic devise.

The Principle of Life-Giving

Although the Cheng brothers did depend heavily on the *Book of Changes* for their cosmology, they did not make use of the concept of the Great Ultimate. In this regard they are unlike Zhou Dunyi, Shao Yong, and Zhang Zai. The Cheng brothers sought their inspiration in an expression from the appendices of the *Book of Changes*: "Change means production and reproduction." The universe, the way of nature, is a process of life-giving. The principle of life-giving is goodness, and goodness entails the idea of origination (*yuan/yüan*). This provides a new understanding in Neo-Confucianism of nature and our place in it. The Cheng brothers made advances beyond Zhou Dunyi's idea of the interaction of *yin* and *yang*, and Zhang Zai's idea of the perpetual interaction of material force. The Cheng brothers appear not to be concerned with a past cosmogonic origin, but rather with the continuous creative generative force of a living universe.

The Cheng brothers' cosmology is heavily influenced by the *Book of Changes* and its appendices, from which they borrowed the concepts "what exists before physical form" (*xingershang/hsing-erh-shang*) and "what exists after physical form" (*xingerxia/hsing-erh-hsia*). Cheng Hao is noted for proposing that the Way is constituted in what exists before physical form, and concrete things are constituted in what exists after physical form. Cheng Hao is quick to point out that although he talks in this manner

> concrete things are the Way and the Way is concrete things. So long as the Way obtains, it does not matter whether it is present or future, or whether it is the self or others.

Cheng Yi's cosmological statement that gained a lot of attention and comment, namely, that "empty and tranquil, and without any sign, and yet all things are luxuriantly present" was taken by Zhu Xi to be an explication of Zhou Dunyi's statement "the Ultimateless and yet the Great Ultimate." In both cases the Cheng brothers draw attention to the immediateness of generation and change; for them, the process of generation is ongoing and continuous. In fact, Cheng Yi criticized the Daoists (Tao-

ists) for proposing that material force comes from vacuity; he says that there is no time sequence. It is not vacuity first and then material force, or *yin* today and *yang* tomorrow. He draws an analogy between one's body and its shadow—both occur simultaneously. This is probably why the Cheng brothers avoid the concept of the Great Ultimate; it implies a sequence of generation, but they see the process of generation as a simultaneous unfolding.

Self-Cultivation

Just as the processes of production and reproduction are continuous and simultaneous, so too is the unfolding of self-cultivation. Cheng Hao contends that the thorough study of principle (*li*), the full development of human nature, and the fulfillment of destiny (*ming*) are achieved simultaneously. There is no time sequence among them. For him, the complete study of principle is not the mere acquisition of knowledge; it entails the fulfillment of one's nature and destiny. Likewise, Cheng Yi proposes that the investigation of principle to the utmost, the complete development of one's nature and the fulfillment of destiny are in fact only one thing: the investigation of principle to the utmost entails the completion of human nature, a process that includes the fulfillment of destiny.

For the Cheng brothers, there is only one principle in the world, and it is identical with human nature. Through material force there are many manifestations of principle, but principle is always one. The myriad forms all constitute one body because they originate from the one principle and contain that principle. What is inherent in things is principle; moral principle is the means by which things are managed. One's self-cultivation and development of the moral virtues are inextricably linked to principle. Cheng Hao says that because there is only one principle in the world, to be serious, humane, or faithful is to be so in accordance with that principle.

In agreement with their uncle, Zhang Zai, the Cheng brothers emphasized the importance of cultivating humanity or humaneness (*ren/jen*). Cheng

Hao argued that a student must first comprehend the nature of human kindness (*ren*). The person of *ren* unites in one body with the myriad things, and the other major virtues, such as rightness, propriety, wisdom, and faithfulness, are all manifestations of *ren*. One's moral duty is to grasp this principle and practice human kindness with sincerity and seriousness.

Cheng Yi argues that unity comes from the practice of *ren*, and that the closest description of what *ren* means is "to be impartial," for although impartiality should not be equated with *ren*, when one makes impartiality the substance of one's being, then one is a person of *ren*. Through the practice of impartiality self and other are united as one. Altruism is the application of *ren*; love is its function. Moreover, according to Cheng Yi, the mind is like seeds, and *ren* is the process of growth.

Again we see that the Cheng brothers' cosmology of production and reproduction is tied into their conception of ethics and moral cultivation. Clearly the Cheng brothers were influenced by their uncle Zhang's essay "The Western Inscription" (see the chapter on Zhang Zai).

The Cheng brothers define *ren* in terms of "seriousness to straighten the internal life and rightness to square the external life." The concept of seriousness (*jing/ching*) plays an important role in their philosophy. The term occurs in the ancient classics, but the Cheng brothers reinterpreted it and raised its significance to new heights. They strongly encouraged their students to avoid Zhou Dunyi's term "tranquility" because it implied Daoist and Buddhist teachings of forgetting. They replaced "tranquility" with the notion of seriousness. For them, "seriousness" entailed attention and awareness, not forgetting. Although they will not allow vacuity and tranquility to be called seriousness, they do propose that one who is serious will be vacuous and tranquil. Their conception of seriousness not only applies to the moral realm of self-cultivation, but also entails a metaphysical and cosmological aspect. That Heaven and Earth are in their respective positions and that change operates in them is none other than seriousness. Because of seriousness, the cosmic processes flow without interruption. The

substance of all things is found in sincerity and seriousness. Seriousness is the basis of all human endeavors. Seriousness is defined as being unselfish which links it back to *ren* and impartiality.

The Investigation of Things

The marked difference between the Cheng brothers is in the emphasis placed on the investigation of things (*gewu/ko-wu*). The term appears in the *Great Learning* (*Da xue/Ta hsüeh*). For Cheng Hao, the investigation of things means to rectify the mind of bad habits. For Cheng Yi, the investigation of things entails the rational logical study and handling of human endeavors; it means the study of principle and as such implies the study of human nature and destiny. Zhu Xi developed Cheng Yi's ideas, and the investigation of things plays an important role in self-cultivation for the Cheng–Zhu philosophy.

The Cheng brothers emphasize unity. The metaphysical, the ethical, the natural, the human, principle, the mind, human nature, destiny, and the self-cultivation of moral virtue are all ultimately linked together. This sense of unity is the guiding light of their philosophic thought. As they themselves proposed: "The highest truth is always resolved into unity, and an essential principle is never a duality."

JAMES D. SELLMANN

Further Reading

Translation

Chan, Wing-tsit, trans. and comp. *A Source Book in Chinese Philosophy*. Princeton, N.J.: Princeton University Press, 1963. An extremely useful sourcebook in which Chan's translations of selected passages are supported by illuminating historical and interpretative comments.

Related Studies

Bruce, J. Percy. *Chu Hsi and His Masters*. London: Probsthain, 1923. In this book the Cheng brothers are discussed in relation to other Chinese thinkers who influenced them and whom they influenced.

Chan, Wing-tsit. "Review of A. C. Graham, *Two Chinese Philosophers: Ch'eng Ming-tao and Ch'eng Yi-ch'uan*," in *Journal of the American Oriental Society*, 79, 1959, pp. 150–155. Chan's review provides a perspective to supplement that expressed by Graham (see below).

Chang, Carson. *The Development of Neo-Confucian Thought*. New York: Bookman Associates, 1957. A helpful survey of the development of Neo-Confucian ideas.

Graham, A. C. *Two Chinese Philosophers: Ch'eng Ming-tao and Ch'eng Yi-ch'uan*. London: Lund Humphries, 1958. A scholarly analysis of the Cheng brothers—their differences and their similarities.

Fung, Yu-lan. *A History of Chinese Philosophy*. Translated by Derk Bodde. 2 vols. Princeton, N.J.: Princeton University Press, 1952. An invaluable account of the history of Chinese thought. See also *A Short History of Chinese Philosophy*, derived from Fung Yu-lan's two-volume work (edited by Derk Bodde, New York and London: The Free Press and Collier-Macmillan, Ltd).

Munro, Donald J. *Images of Human Nature: A Sung Portrait*. Princeton, N.J.: Princeton University Press, 1988. Munro's account of Song philosophy takes note of the work and influence of the Cheng brothers.

ZHU XI (CHU HSI)

Born: 1130, Fujian (Fukien) Province, China
Died: 1200, Fujian
Major Works: *Recorded Sayings*, *Commentary on the "Four Books"*, *Commentary on the* Book of Changes, *Commentary on the* Book of Odes

Major Ideas

Reality has two basic components, li *and* qi (ch'i).
Li *is the principle or form of all existences.*
Qi *is the material force that fills the form.*
Dai ji *is the ultimate principle governing the operating of the universe.*
A human being is endowed with li, *and his or her original nature is good.*
Through interaction with the environment a person can become evil.
The purpose of education is to retain the li *in one's original nature and clean up the pollutants in one's acquired nature.*

Zhu Xi (Chu Hsi, also known as Zu Yuanhui/Chu Yüan-hui) was born in what is now the Province of Fujian (Fukien). He lived in the era during which China was under the attack of invading enemies from the north. The Song (Sung) government was feeble and inefficient. During his employment with the government, Zhu Xi was so critical of the incompetency of the then governmental officials that at various times he was demoted, punished, or fired.

Although Zhu Xi's official life was intermittent and turbulent, his academic achievement and educational contribution were fabulous. He established (or reestablished) the Academy of the White Deer Grotto in Jiangxi Province, and all the prominent scholars of his time were attracted to his lectures. He has become the most influential figure in Chinese philosophy after Confucius (Kong Fuzi/Kongzi). He synthesized Confucius's concept of *ren* (*jen*); Mencius's (Mengzi/Meng Tzu's) concepts of *ren* and *yi* (*i*); the idea of the "investigation of things" in the *Great Learning* (*Da Xue/Ta Hsüeh*); the principle of *cheng* (*ch'eng*) (sincerity) in the *Doctrine of the Mean* (*Zhong Yong/Chung Yung*); the *Yinyang* theory of the Han dynasty; and virtually all the major ideas of Neo-Confucianism in the early Song dynasty.

What made Zhu Xi the most influential figure

after Confucius was his editorship of the "Four Books." He grouped Confucius's *Analects*, *The Book of Mencius* (*Mengzi*), the *Doctrine of the Mean*, and the *Great Learning* (the latter two were originally two chapters of the *Li ji* [*Li chi*] [*The Book of Rites*]), and he wrote extensive commentaries on each of them. His commentaries were insightful and creative. By doing this, he has filled Confucianism with a philosophic life and redefined the major concepts in Confucianism.

The "Four Books" of the Zhu version has become the standard text through the dynasties.

Theory of Reality

Zhu Xi's metaphysics or theory of reality is commonly known as *li-qi* (*li-ch'i*) dualism. *Li* is translated as "reason," "principle," "pattern," "form," or "idea." *Qi* is commonly translated as "material force." *Li* exists in all things, whether animate and inanimate; it transcends space and time and serves as the ultimate reason for the existence of a particular object. Its existence is logically prior to the existence of *qi*. But without *qi*, there is no material embodiment to make possible the existence of *li*. (Zhu's position is different from that of Plato, who maintained that forms exist apart from particular objects that embody those forms. Zhu's view is closer to that of Aristotle, who maintained that forms and matter cannot exist apart from each other.) Zhu Xi believed that all living and nonliving things are endowed with a particular *li* in their existence. For example, human beings share the same *li*, the *li* of being human, while horses share the same *li*, the *li* of being horses.

Qi is the counterpart of *li*; it is attached to *li* and is the element that fills up the form (*li*.) *Qi* serves as the principle of individuation. In other words, it is *qi* that makes an object a unique thing. Although like objects have the same *li*, each individual object is endowed with a unique kind of *qi*. For instance, one person may be tall while another one is short; one horse may be temperamental while another horse is gentle. So, because of different endowments of *qi*, even objects of the same kind may be uniquely different from one another.

In addition to *li* and *qi*, a third concept is required by Zhu to make his metaphysical system complete. This is the concept of *tai ji* (*t'ai chi*), which is usually translated as "the Great Ultimate." *Tai ji* is the highest principle (*li*) governing the universe. It exists in all things of the world. When asked how it is possible for one *tai ji* to exist in all things, Zhu Xi responded with an analogy: "There is only one moon but its light can be seen shining on thousands of lakes and rivers at the same time." For Zhu Xi, *tai ji* not only contains all the principles of the universe, it also contains all the *ji* as well. This concept of *tai ji* is very close to the concept of *Dao* (*Tao*) in Laozi's (Lao Tzu's) *Daode jing* (*Tao-te ching*).

Theory of Human Nature

Zhu Xi inherited from Mencius the belief that human nature is originally good. Zhu Xi's contribution was to establish a metaphysical foundation for such a theory. He makes a distinction between two kinds of nature: original nature and developed nature. The original nature consists of *li* alone. Since it is composed of the principles endowed by nature, it is good. Since every person as a human being is endowed with the same *li*, so all human beings are equally good by virtue of their original nature.

However, humans acquire or develop nature through interaction with the environment and thus acquire different forms of *qi*. As a result, they may fall out of accord with their original good nature and become evil. Zhu Xi attributes evil to *qi*, but he argues that *qi* is not itself necessarily evil. After one's interaction with the environment, one may still maintain one's good nature. This is the importance of education.

Early Confucianism never developed the concept of *xin* (*hsin*), which has been translated as "mind" or "heart." It has to be noted that in Chinese thinking there has never been a demarcation between the intellectually oriented mind and the emotionally inclined heart. The two are integrated, and the proper meaning of the term depends on the context. This is a very important concept in Mahāyāna Buddhism. Since Neo-Confucianism is a synthesis of original Confucianism, Daoism (Taoism), and Buddhism, the concept of *xin* is vital in the theory of human nature.

In the philosophy of Mencius, *ren* constitutes a major part of the original nature of man. But how does *ren* express itself? According to Mencius, it expresses itself in the sensitivity toward the suffering of others. This sensitivity is called *qing* (*ch'ing*) or feeling. According to Chu Hsi, *xin* performs the function of integrating the original nature (*xing*) and the *qing* together. This is a great step forward in philosophical development. *Ren* is the ontological substance and is the *xing* that embodies the *li* embodied in human nature. *Qing* arises in the process of the interaction between the individual and the environment. *Xin* is the name for consciousness in its wholeness integrating *xing* (original nature) and *qing* together. *Xing* is good, but *qing* can be good or evil, depending upon the development of the personality through education.

Theory of Education

In the tradition of Confucianism, the philosophy of education is almost identical with theory of moral education. Cognitive development, logical training, or skill acquirement were considered secondary. In early Confucianism, the primary goal of education is to become a *junzi* (*chün-tzu*), a morally superior person. Neo-Confucianism perpetuates such an ideal. In order to attain such a goal, Zhu Xi adopted the method provided by the *Great Learning*.

The basic principle in moral education for Zhu Xi was to retain in human nature what is originally endowed by *li*, but to clean up the pollutants acquired through harmful interactions between the individual and the environment. The ultimate goal of the *Great Learning* is to create a peaceful world. To create a peaceful world, order must be brought to the nation. In order to bring order to the nation, one has to regulate the family. The regulation of the family requires a well-cultivated personal life. Cultivation of the personal life requires sincere intent. Sincere intent needs the rectification of one's *xin*. Rectification of the *xin* requires attainment of authentic knowledge. The attainment of authentic knowledge requires the examination or investigation of things. So, the investigation of things plays the central role in moral education.

Why is the investigation of things so important to the attainment of such a moral goal? It is because that all the things are the embodiment of all the *li*'s in the universe. The more we investigate things, the closer we are to the reality of the universe and the more we are likely to become one with reality, which is purely good in its very nature. In other words, exhausting the *li*'s through the investigation of things is the same process of exhausting all the *li*'s within our own nature, since our own nature is endowed with the same *li*'s as the myriad things of the universe.

Theory of Ren

Because he was a creative thinker in the Confucian tradition, Zhu Xi's interpretation of *ren* is innovative. In his commentaries on the *Analects*, he established the metaphysical foundation for this concept. In addition, he wrote a treatise on *ren*, in which he relates *ren* to the mind (*xin*) of the universe. The fundamental characteristic of the *xin* of the universe is to produce, to grow, and to benefit the life of myriad things; the human *xin*, then, is to

love, to help others grow, and to benefit the life of others. The mind of the universe contains the *li*'s of altruism, so the human mind contains the *li*'s of loving others.

A common understanding of Zhu Xi's concept of *ren* is based on a remark made in his commentary on the *Analects*. This is his well-known saying that *ren* means the *De* (*Te*) (virtue) of the *xin* (heart), the principle of love. Scholars usually interpret this comment as making a distinction between substance and function. However, the distinction between substance and function in Neo-Confucianism is neither distinct nor clear. It is quite obvious that such an interpretation is the result of the influence of Western philosophy. "The principle of love" is obviously based on the views of Confucius as recorded in the *Analects*. As to "the *De* [virtue] of the heart," this is a very important addition that Zhu Xi contributed to the tradition. Since the human heart contains the *li*'s endowed by nature, the concept of *ren* is established as a concept of the metaphysics of morals.

Criticism of Buddhism

Like his predecessors in the Neo-Confucian tradition, Zhu Xi criticized Buddhism intolerantly. According to Zhu Xi, the Buddhist interpretation of reality is that reality consists in total nothingness, while Confucianism believes in the concreteness of reality. In addition, the Buddhists consider heaven and earth as illusory and thus unreal, a claim that is entirely contrary to fact.

Like his Neo-Confucian predecessors, Zhu Xi was limited in his knowledge of Buddhism and his understanding of Buddhism was very superficial. Because of his limited knowledge, he did not realize that the interpretation of Buddhism as holding to the view of reality as emptiness is the doctrine only of the *Mādhyamika* School; the *Yogācāra* (Consciousness-Only) School, on the other hand, considers reality as being rather than non-being.

Besides, Zhu Xi lacks a good understanding of Chan (Ch'an/Zen) Buddhism, which is the manifestation of the Chinese artistic spirit in the form of a Buddhist religion. As a result, his criticism of

Buddhism is biased, inadequate, and even arbitrary. But a philosopher's misunderstanding and misinterpretation of others is inevitable in the history of philosophy.

JOSEPH S. WU

Further Reading

Translation

Bruce, J. Percy, trans. *The Philosophy of Human Nature by Chu Hsi*. London: Probsthain, 1922. A good translation of chapters 42–48 from the *Zhu Xi Chuanshu* (*Chu Tzu Ch'üan-shu*) (*The Complete Works of Chu Tzu*).

Related Studies

Bruce, J. Percy. *Chu Hsi and His Masters*. London: Probsthain, 1923. A pioneering work in the study of Zhu Xi.

Chan, Wing-tsit, trans. and comp. *A Source Book in Chinese Philosophy*. Princeton, N.J.: Princeton University Press, 1963. Includes extensive selections from Zhu Xi's work. Chan's critical comments on Zhu Xi are very illuminating.

Chang, Carsun. *The Development of Neo-Confucian Thought*. New York: Bookman Associates, 1957. This book contains three chapters on Zhu Xi; informative and interesting.

Creel, H. G. *Chinese Thought: From Confucius to Mao Tse-tung*. Chicago: University of Chicago Press, 1953. A refreshing and stimulating introduction to Chinese thought.

Fung, Yu-lan. *A History of Chinese Philosophy*. Translated by Derk Bodde. 2 vols. Princeton, N.J.: Princeton University Press, 1952, 1953. Includes a very informative chapter on Neo-Confucianism and Zhu Xi.

Needham, Joseph. *Science and Civilization in China*. Vol. II of *History of Scientific Thought* (Cambridge: Cambridge University Press, 1956). Includes a penetrating discussion of Zhu Xi's influence on Western philosophy.

WANG YANGMING (WANG YANG-MING)

Born: 1472, Yue (Yüeh), now Zhejiang (Chekiang) Province
Died: 1529, on a return trip to Yue from Guangxi (Kwangsi)
Major Works: *Chuanxi lu* (*Ch'uan hsi lu*) (*Instructions for Practical Living*), Part I composed in 1514, Part II in 1521–1527; *Daxue wen* (*Ta-hsüeh wen*) (*Questions on the* Great Learning), (1527)

Major Ideas

Any person is capable of becoming a sage.

All persons possess an "innate knowledge of the good"; the source of goodness is within oneself, not introduced from outside.

One's innate goodness is "extended outward" from natural feelings of love for oneself and one's family to one's community and to all other persons, creatures, and things.

Moral action is a natural expression of innate knowledge of the good.

Wang Yangming (born Wang Shouren/Wang Shou-jen) came from a family of accomplished scholars and officials, and was encouraged at a young age to sit for the civil service examinations and to serve in public office. Since 1313, the standard for the examinations had been the Confucian "Four Books" and "Five Classics" as interpreted by the Song (Sung) Neo-Confucian scholar Zhu Xi (Chu Hsi). The intellectual life of the Ming was dominated by Zhu Xi's "School of Principle" (*Lixue/Li-hsüeh*) and the Neo-Confucian educational program. Wang Yangming felt especially constrained by this state-sanctioned orthodoxy, but he could never escape his intellectual indebtedness to it. His personal struggles with both government service and its intellectual basis were defining issues in his life, and his self-questioning, critical spirit had as much of an impact on his times as his mature philosophical thought. Wang is credited with being the guiding light of the "School of Mind" (*Xinxue/Hsin-hsüeh*) or "Ideationist School" of Ming Neo-Confucianism, characterized by a thorough and severe self-scrutiny. Wang's father once said of him that he was "ardent" or "untamed," a quality of character that defined the "Yangming School" for several generations.

Three events typified Wang's struggles. In 1492, at the age of twenty, Wang set out to put Zhu Xi's teachings into practice, through an intense, seven-day meditation in a bamboo grove. Zhu Xi had

written that an intuitive grasp of "Principle" (*li*)—the intelligible order and metaphysical basis for all things—could be found through the disciplined concentration on "external things and affairs." This understanding was fundamental to a true understanding of the self, which, in its basic nature (*xing/hsing*), is indistinguishable from Principle. Wang failed, and this failure precipitated a psychological crisis that resulted in a series of poor performances in the imperial examinations.

The second crisis came in 1502, after Wang had finally succeeded in the examinations and attained high office in the capital. Exhausted from overwork, and overcome by the competitive strains of advancement in the imperial system, he resigned, and for two years abandoned the Confucian program altogether, experimenting with Daoist (Taoist) and Buddhist forms of self-cultivation in a rural retreat. The outcome of this self-imposed exile was a newfound commitment to Confucianism, growing out of an affirmation of "natural feelings" (feelings of attachment to home and family, in particular) which the Daoists and Buddhists both rejected. It was at this point that Wang began to call himself "Yangming," after the grotto in which he had experienced his enlightenment, and to gather disciples.

The third defining event in Wang's life came after a government-imposed exile from 1506 to 1508, when he served as a district magistrate in an "aboriginal" community in southwest China. This experience was an enlightenment to the fundamental goodness and purity of the mind (*xin*) as the source of virtue and the basis of knowledge. Perfect virtue, Wang discovered, is within oneself, not in external things or situations. These principles are the core of Wang's discourse in the *Chuanxi lu* (*Ch'uan-hsi lu*) (*Instructions for Practical Living*), composed after his retirement from public service.

The Innate Knowledge of the Good

The most fundamental difference between Song and Ming Neo-Confucianism, the "School of Principle" and the "School of Mind," is in the method of self-cultivation leading to sagehood (the "Way of the sage," *shengdao* [*sheng-tao*], a common aspiration of all Confucians). For Zhu Xi and the brothers Cheng Yi (Ch'eng I) and Cheng Hao, insight into the underlying Principle (*li*) of the world is attained through the "investigation of things" (*gewu/ko-wu*). *Gewu* involves attentive reflection upon "the principles of things and affairs" through the study of books, the modeling of wise and virtuous individuals, and engagement in public service. This serves to "rectify the mind," that is, to master and control feelings or emotions that lead to subjectivity and selfishness.

Wang Yangming rejects the idea that self-cultivation requires the discovery of external principles. Subjecting Zhu Xi's language to a different interpretation, *gewu* is for Wang the self-rectifying activity of the mind ("rectification" *by* the mind rather than rectification *of* the mind). This implies a fundamentally positive evaluation of feelings, which are not only natural and appropriate, but even basic to the process of self-cultivation. Whereas for Zhu Xi the feelings must be controlled by an external Principle, Wang insists that the feelings are "self-righting" and inherently well-balanced. Wang Yangming reaffirmed the Mencian doctrine of "incipient feelings" as the basis and origin of the cultivation of sagehood. Again and again in the *Chuanxi lu*, Wang emphasizes the capacity of the seeker to realize the natural "equilibrium" or harmony of the mind, a realization that

does not require the "investigation of *external* things and affairs."

In this sense, Wang distinguishes natural feelings from selfish *desires*, which cloud the mind, including the desire for fame, profit, and "life itself." The extirpation of selfish desires is what Wang means by *gewu*.

> [The word *ge*] . . . means to eliminate what is incorrect in the mind so as to preserve the correctness of its original substance.

The "original substance" of the mind is innate knowledge (*liangzhi/liang-chih*), which Wang ties explicitly to the "incipient feelings" of virtue within each individual. *Liangzhi* is the innate capacity to know the good, and so, Wang concludes, "There is no principle outside the mind. . . ." Beginning with the mind, one knows what is right.

The Unity of Knowledge and Action

Rather than inferring from the world what is right and wrong, Wang insists that goodness is found within the mind, and is then "extended" in action. The application of moral judgment to action is called by Wang the "extension of the innate knowledge of the good" (*zhi liangzhi/chih liang-chih*): "to do always in one's life what one's mind says is right and good." Beginning with one's natural feelings of goodness, benevolence is extended outwards to family, friends, the community, and external things. Thus, the "innate knowledge of the good" becomes the basis of a unity between the self and the world. This is known experientially in the sense of identity one feels for all things, from children to strangers and even to tiles and stones. "Even Heaven and Earth cannot exist as Heaven and Earth without the 'innate knowledge of the good' of humankind."

Though Wang's explicit language in the *Chuanxi lu* borders upon a metaphysical "idealism," it is more accurately a dramatic expression of the human creation of value out of the natural harmony of feelings within the mind. In contrast to the empirical, epistemological orientation of Zhu Xi's "in-

vestigation of things," Wang's is closer to an intu-
itionist moral philosophy. Moral value is discovered within the self and then extended outward,
rather than being extrapolated from the underlying
principle (*li*) of external things and affairs.

Wang Yangming's optimistic view of the mind
made him open to learning from every possible
source. He was conversant with Buddhist and Daoist texts, and consistently approached them with a
tolerant and inquisitive attitude. He even urged his
students to "learn from the words of ordinary people"; this is because value is derived not from the
external source of knowledge, but from the inner
response of the mind.

Lasting Influence

Wang Yangming's efforts to distinguish "feelings," which are the naturally good expression of
the mind, from "desires," which cloud the "original clarity" of the mind, set the stage for the intense
introspection and personal fault-finding of the
"Yangming School" of Ming Neo-Confucianism.
For at least 150 years, Chinese intellectual history
was dominated by an emphasis on self-definition,
reflecting on a philosophical level trends towards
individualism and self-determination in the social
and economic spheres.

The Yangming School split into at least eight
sub-schools, within 100 years of Wang's death.
They were divided primarily along two lines, arising from conflicting interpretations of the idea of
the "innate knowledge of the good" (*liangzhi*). The
first ascribed to a moral subjectivism, treating the
mind in its "original nature" as "neither good nor
evil" and relying heavily upon the language of
Chan (Ch'an/Zen) Buddhism in its rejection of
epistemological or moral universals of any kind.
These views were articulated first by Wang Yang-
ming's disciple Wang Ji (Wang Chi) (1498–1583)
and later by members of the Taizhou (T'ai-chou)
School, especially Wang Gen (Wang Ken) (1483?–
1540) and Li Zhi (Li Chih) (1527–1602), who advocated the "natural freedom" of the mind, spontaneous expression of feeling, and celebration of the
"common man." In practical terms, these views

led to a deliberate rejection of "book-learning,"
the civil service examinations and, in some cases,
of government service altogether. Even when engaged in study of the "Classics," they argued, it is
preferable to read them without the use of commentaries, or else to compose one's own commentaries
based on an intuitive response to the texts.

In reaction against the "mad Chan-ism" of the
Taizhou School, members of the Donglin (Tung-
lin) Academy interpreted the "innate knowledge of
the good" as a call to active engagement in public
affairs, drawing upon *universal* standards of virtue
discovered within the mind. These and other Neo-
Confucian "activists" dedicated themselves to
practical concerns and social reform, in contrast to
the abstract metaphysical speculation of the Song
Neo-Confucian "School of Principle." Many of
these thinkers produced autobiographies that are
intensely self-critical, as well as writings concerned with ethics, local administration, and popular education. This wing of the Neo-Confucian
movement was critical of Buddhism, Daoism, and
the "left-wing" followers of the Yangming School.

Wang Yangming exerted his greatest influence
prior to the Qing (Ch'ing) dynasty (1644–1912), but
the Yangming School in Japan (*Yomeigaku*) had a
profound effect upon Tokugawa (1615–1867) culture well into the nineteenth century, and is credited
with being a significant intellectual underpinning
for the Meiji Restoration beginning in 1867.

RANDALL L. NADEAU

Further Reading

Translation

Chan, Wing-tsit, trans. *Instructions for Practical
Living and Other Neo-Confucian Writings by
Wang Yang-ming*. New York: Columbia University Press, 1963. The standard English translation of the *Chuan-xi Lu*, by a master translator
and Neo-Confucian scholar.

Related Studies

Ching, Julia. *To Acquire Wisdom: The Way of Wang
Yang-ming (1492–1529)*. New York: Columbia

University Press, 1976. An introduction to the thought of Wang Yangming in the context of intellectual movements in Song and Ming Neo-Confucianism.

Tu, Wei-ming. *Neo-Confucian Thought in Action:*

Wang Yang-ming's Youth (1472–1509). Berkeley, Calif.: University of California Press, 1976. A lively study that establishes the personal context of many of Wang's principal teachings.

DAI ZHEN (TAI CHEN)

Born: 1724, Xiuning (Hsiu-ning) County, Anhui Province, China
Died: 1777, Beijing (Peking), China
Major Works: *Yuanshan* (*Yüan-shan*) (*Inquiry into Goodness*) (1754–66); (*Mengzi ziyi shuzheng*) (*Meng Tzu tzu-i shu-cheng*) (*An Evidential Study of the Meaning of Terms in the Mencius*) (1772–77)

Major Ideas

The Dao (Tao) (*Way*) *signifies motion and activity, and it is the successive movement of* yin *and* yang.
Nature (xing/hsing) *is an allotment from* yin *and* yang *and the five elemental forces.*
*Blood-and-*qi (-ch'i) (*desire*) *and the knowing mind make up human nature.*
*Morality has its basis in blood-and-*qi *and the knowing mind.*
Principle exists where feelings do not err.
Principle is the principle of differentiation, the internal pattern of things and of human affairs.
The process of understanding begins with empathy and a desire to learn everything about an experience or an aspect of human inquiry.

Within the intellectual world of the eighteenth-century China, where scholarship based on evidential research had been considered an end in itself, Dai Zhen (Tai Chen)—Dai Dongyuan (Tai Tung-yüan)—was an anomaly. The author of numerous studies on ancient texts and a polymath versed in nearly every category of human knowledge, astronomy, mathematics, history, geography, water conservancy, phonology, etymology, and rituals, he consciously tried to disassociate himself from a reputation that honored him as the most accomplished exegete of his time. His private wish was to be taken seriously as a thinker. This was odd since the majority of Qing (Ch'ing) scholars deemed the study of philosophy or any attempt to understand the reason and meaning of things as empty and self-indulgent.

Born in 1724 in the mountainous region of Anhui Province, Dai Zhen was the son of a cloth merchant, a traveling salesman who was too poor to set up shop in his hometown. When Dai Zhen was young, his family could not afford to hire him a private tutor despite evidence that he possessed extraordinary talents, and so he attended a village school for a while and studied on his own. He took enormous pride in what he had gotten on his own without a formal teacher. In fact, after he achieved the status of a prominent scholar, he refused to take

in any disciple with the exception of his younger friend, Duan Yucai (Tuan Yü-ts'ai) (1735–1815), who pestered him repeatedly to accept at least the formal aspect of such a relationship. Dai Zhen never deferred to anyone as his teacher, and he wanted no one to defer to him as teacher. Although some of his contemporaries found this gesture of independence arrogant and even reprehensible, he claimed that he was merely upholding what he believed to be true learning, that it had to be acquired alone and that if one needed instruction or consultation, one should never seek it from above, from one's superior, because only when there is mutuality in scholarly exchange can one reflect and speak without fear or pressure.

By the time Dai Zhen was seventeen, he already knew what he loved—he loved precise scholarship, the kind that was best exemplified by the paleographic studies of the Han, the *Shuo wen jiezi* (*Shuo-wen chieh-tzu*) (*An Explanation of Writing and An Analysis of Characters*) and the *Erya* (*Erh-ya*) (*Progress Toward Correctness*). And he also decided what his lifetime goal was—he intended to focus on "hearing the *Dao* [*Tao*]." By the time he was in his thirties, he began to put the two together, his passion and his purpose. His first philosophical treatise *Inquiry into Goodness* (*Yuan Shan/Yüan-shan*) was completed in 1763 when he was thirty-nine. This was followed by a revision of the *Inquiry* in 1766 and *An Evidential Study of the Meaning of Terms in the* Mencius (*Mengzi ziyi shuzheng/Meng Tzu tzu-i shu-cheng*) in 1777, a work that he finished just months before he died, and one that gave him the greatest satisfaction.

But beginning from his mid-twenties and throughout his life, Dai Zhen had also been writing and publishing on a wide range of subjects—commentaries on ancient mathematics and technology, ancient dialects and dictionaries, works on geography, calendrical science, waterways, and water conservancy. He had been a compiler of local histories and a compiler on the ambitious enterprise commissioned by the Qianlong (Ch'ien-lung) emperor, which was known as the *Complete Library of the Four Treasuries*. His prodigious output was the result of his natural talent and a demonic drive to learn nearly every topic and nearly everything about a topic. He was also under constant financial pressures. In a way Dai Zhen had to adapt his research technique to many types of human inquiry. He did not have any stable source of income, never held a permanent position, and like many Qing scholars and his father before him, he had to peddle his wares to make a living. He attempted the metropolitan examination six times and never passed. Finally in 1775 the Qianlong emperor bestowed the *jinshi* (*chin-shih*) (advanced scholar) degree on him, probably for his contribution to the *Four Treasuries* project.

Dai Zhen was a controversial figure while he was alive and thereafter. He was too fond of ideas at a time when even thinking about them was considered unfashionable and unnecessary; he was too blunt in his criticisms of the philosophy of Cheng Yi (Ch'eng I) (1033–1107) and Zhu Xi (Chu Hsi) (1130–1200), referring to their concept of principle (*li*) as that which "kills people"; he was also accused of plagiarism, of having borrowed another scholar's findings in his study of an ancient classic on waterways called the *Shuijingzhu* (*Shui-ching-chu*). It is difficult to unravel the *Shuijingzhu* controversy. Suspicions of possible wrongdoing did not arise until years after Dai Zhen died, and critics and supporters all have ample evidence to defend

their separate positions. As for his love for the reason and meaning of things *and* his dislike for Cheng Yi and Zhu Xi, the two Confucian thinkers most concerned with the reason and meaning of things, they show that Dai Zhen wanted neither to identify with the philologists of the Han School nor with the philosophers of the Song (Sung) School. He insisted on going his way, which was an attempt to let impeccable scholarship and wide learning throw light on what is inevitable and enduring.

Dai Zhen's Thought

Dai Zhen's thought begins and ends with Mencius (Mengzi/Meng Tzu). The titles of his first and last philosophical works, *Inquiry into Goodness* and *An Evidential Study of the Meaning of Terms in the* Mencius, make this point. But what he understood from Mencius and what he wanted to clarify regarding Mencius's teachings is not the latter's well known theory that human nature is good. What was remarkable about Mencius, he thought, was that he never separated the reason and meaning of things from the things themselves—never separated principle from the event or situation that contains it. Dai Zhen himself said, "Principle exists where feelings do not err." For him this is a correct gloss of Mencius's concept of moral principle (*yili/i-li*).

Both of Dai Zhen's philosophical treatises are about Mencius, but neither one is a commentary on Mencius's work. In the preface of *An Evidential Study of the Meaning of Terms in the* Mencius, Dai Zhen states just why he had to write this book. Just as Mencius had to dispute the doctrines of Yang Zhu (Yang Chu) and Mozi (Mo Tzu), he said that he too had to challenge those erroneous readings of Mencius that had in fact become orthodox interpretations. By "erroneous readings," he was referring to those of Cheng Hao (Ch'eng Hao) (1032–85), Cheng Yi, and Zhu Xi, men whom "most people regarded as sages, worthies, and superior men." In Dai Zhen's view, these Song thinkers had become so accustomed to the ideas of Laozi (Lao Tzu), Zhuangzi (Chuang Tzu), and the Buddhists that they inadvertently used them to get to Mencius, and Dai Zhen felt that it was his responsibility to set things right. His last and most important work is, therefore, primarily a disputation in opposition to the Song interpretations and an attempt to redefine concepts such as the Way, Heavenly Way, principle, human nature, human potentials, and sincerity in light of the Confucian teachings of the Warring States period. The groundwork for his critical efforts was laid in his early book, *Inquiry into Goodness*, where Dai Zhen had already discussed what he meant by "Heavenly Way" and its relation to "what is before form" and "what is within form," as well as the relationship of nature to destiny and what is natural to what is necessary.

In *An Evidential Study of the Meaning of Terms in the* Mencius, he applied the rigorous exegetical method, which he and the eighteenth-century scholars had perfected, to prove that in fact his moral philosophy had a close affinity with that of Confucius (Kong Fuzi/Kongzi) and Mencius; by contrast, Dai Zhen claimed, Cheng Yi and Zhu Xi had been preaching another way all together, by first muddling up principle with the Buddhist and Daoist (Taoist) notion of the spirit and then elevating it to a position of absolute authority. Whether it is the human realm or the cosmic realm, Dai Zhen observed, the Song Confucians had a tendency to separate reality into two categories, the immutable and the changeable, the perfect and the problematic, so that we have reason and *qi*, principle and desires, the moral mind and the human mind. They even analyzed the nature of a person into two parts, physical nature and original nature, the physical tendencies of the body and the principle of the good, which Heaven confers on a person at birth.

In Dai Zhen's view, each person has only one nature, and it is nothing more than his blood-and-*qi* and his knowing mind. Natures are allotments from *yin* and *yang* and the five elemental forces. No two persons can possess identical natures, and natures as such cannot be explained in terms of a single principle, as Cheng Yi and Zhu Xi tried to do in their theory regarding that part of our nature which is conferred by Heaven. Human beings have the potential to be good, Dai Zhen says, not

because they are endowed with the perfect principle, but because their knowing mind can make analogies based on what it knows of itself—what it likes and dislikes—and it has the desire to develop this power to empathize with others to the fullest as it tries to grope for rightness in every situation.

Like Mencius, Dai Zhen finds this desire to be good as no different from the desires for beautiful sights and tasty food, but whereas Mencius explains goodness as a function of our flesh and sentiment, Dai Zhen sees goodness as a function of our flesh and intellect. Although the Chinese character *xin* (*hsin*) refers to heart-and-mind, Mencius gives more weight to the heart, the childlike heart that knows what is good without conscious reflection, while Dai Zhen wagers everything on the mind, on what the mind can do to bring about understanding.

Dai Zhen's credo makes sense in the context of his own likes and dislikes. He loved learning, all learning, especially the difficult kind, because it extended his intellectual potential to the fullest. In *An Evidential Study of the Meaning of Terms in the* Mencius, Dai Zhen compared the growth of the mind to the growth of the body: learning broadens the knowing mind just as food and drink strengthen the body. For him a truly developed mind has wisdom or "divine percipience"; it is able to understand the internal texture of things in the act of seeing the things as they are; it is able to grasp what is necessary in the act of observing what is natural.

However, Dai Zhen detested speculative philosophy and forced reasoning. In his view, a concept such as the Cheng–Zhu notion of principle is purely the product of a mind that yearns for something permanent. When such a mind is given a life of its own and an authority beyond human reach, it can become an instrument of oppression. The strong would claim it for themselves no matter how wrong they might be. The weak could never hope to have it no matter how right they are because at the end it is always the superior who have "reason" and the powerful who win the argument. "When people die because they violated the law," Dai Zhen wrote, "there are those who pity them, but when men die because they have violated principle, who has compassion for them! Alas!"

ANN-PING CHIN

Further Reading

Translations

Ch'eng, Chung-ying, trans. *Tai Chen's Inquiry into Goodness*. Honolulu, Hawaii: East-West Center Press, 1971. A translation of Dai Zhen's *Yuan Shan*.

Chin, Ann-ping and Mansfield Freeman, trans. *Tai Chen on Mencius: Explorations in Words and Meaning*. New Haven, Conn.: Yale University Press, 1990. A translation with detailed annotations of Dai Zhen's *Mengzi ziyi shuzheng* (*Meng Tzu tzu-i shu-cheng*). Also included is a long critical introduction of Dai Zhen's life and times and his principal teachings.

Related Studies

Elman, Benjamin. *From Philosophy to Philology: Intellectual and Social Aspects of Change in Late Imperial China*. Cambridge, Mass.: Harvard University Press, 1984. A critical study of the evidential research movement in the context of late Ming and Qing societies.

Nivison, David. *The Life and Thought of Chang Hsueh-ch'eng*. Stanford, Calif.: Stanford University Press, 1966. A detailed analysis with illuminating insights into the life and thought of the other great eighteenth-century Chinese philosopher, Zhang Xuecheng (Chang Hsüeh-ch'eng) (1738–1801).

KANG YOUWEI (K'ANG YU-WEI)

Born: 1858, Nanhai district of Guangdong (Kwangtung) Province, China
Died: 1927
Major Works: *Xinxue Weijing Kao* (*Hsin Hsüeh Wei Ching K'ao*) (*Study of the Classics Forged During the Hsin Period*) (1891); *Kungzi Gaizhi Kao* (*K'ung Tzu Kai-chih K'ao*) (*Study of Confucius as Reformer*) (1896, published in 1913); *Zhongyong Zhu* (*Chung-yung Chu*) (*Commentary on the* Doctrine of the Mean) (1900); *Lunyu Zhu* (*Lun-yü Chu*) (*Commentary on the* Analects) (1902); *Liyun Zhu* (*Li-yün Chu*) (*Commentary on the* Evolution of Rites) (1913); *Da Tong Shu* (*Ta-t'ung Shu*) (*Book of the Great Unity*) (1935)

Major Ideas

The philosophical texts and ideas written in the "old character" script are false.
Confucius is primarily an institutional reformer.
Confucius is a divine being and founder of a great religion.
World history evolves through three major ages and during each age there are Three Rotations.
"The mind that cannot bear to see the suffering of others" is the core of human nature, the virtue of humanity.
There will be an Age of Great Unity.

Kang Youwei (K'ang Yu-wei) was a native of Nanhai, which was southwest of Canton in Guangdong (Kwangtung) Province. He was born into a highly distinguished scholar–official family and became a precocious student of the "Confucian Classics." At the age of nineteen he became a student of Zhu Jiujiang (Chu Chiu-chiang) (1807–81), a renowned scholar and avid follower of the Lu-Wang School of Neo-Confucianism, founded by Lu Xiangshan (Lu Hsiang-shan) (1139–93) and Wang Yangming (1472–1529), which advocated the practical application of Confucian philosophy. Kang later admitted that his teacher often chastised him for his undue airs of superiority.

At the age of twenty-one, while meditating on the world, Kang had an enlightening experience in which he realized that he was in fact a sage. He began behaving accordingly both in theory, by reshaping the classical tradition, and in practice by proposing political and religious reform. In 1888 he sent a memorial to the Guangxu (Kuang-hsü) emperor (ruled 1875–1908), calling for reform, but the strong conservative faction at court blocked the memorial. In 1891 Kang was teaching in Canton, and Liang Qichao (Liang Ch'i-ch'ao) was one of his disciples. Kang began writing his philosophical works, which would be published later. In 1895, Kang obtained the "presented scholar" degree with distinction, which placed him at the top of the political and intellectual establishment and allowed his ideas to gain some notoriety. In that year China lost the war with Japan. Kang organized students and again petitioned the emperor for reform, but again his memorial was blocked. He became a leader in the Society for the Study of Self-Strengthening.

In 1898, Kang finally received a two-hour audience with the emperor, who was then ready to institute reform. The result was the famous "Hundred Days of Reform" (June 11 to September 20, 1898), during which many imperial edicts were issued calling for sweeping reform. However, when the military commander, Yuan Shikai (Yüan Shih-k'ai) (1858–1916), was ordered to arrest the Empress Dowager, who was the chief opponent to reform, he informed her instead and the reform movement collapsed. The emperor was imprisoned, six leading reformers were executed, and Kang fled to Hong Kong and then to Japan.

For the next sixteen years Kang traveled through the South Seas, America, and Europe. While in Canada in 1899 he founded the Party to Protect the

Emperor. He returned to China after the Republic was established, but because he still advocated a constitutional monarchy, he did not return to prominence. He advocated that Confucianism be established as a state religion; he took part in failed restoration attempts in 1917 and 1924. Although he died in disgrace, he was still referred to as Sage Kang because of his unfailing devotion to Confucianism.

Kang's philosophy did not change drastically during his lifetime, but the spirit of the times did change rapidly. It was due to those changes of the times that Kang is known as both a radical reformer and a reactionary. In the decades before 1900 Kang was known as a radical reformer because China was controlled by a strong conservative element, while he sought social, political, and economic changes. After the Republic was established in 1911, Kang still advocated a constitutional monarchy, which won him the label of reactionary. In both theory and practice Kang's philosophy has had a lasting effect both in China and the West. Among his many achievements as a great thinker, he must be acknowledged as the father of twentieth-century Utopian literature, not only for Chinese philosophy but globally as well.

The Great Unity Philosophy

From his teacher Kang inherited a fundamental tenet of the Lu-Wang School of Neo-Confucianism, namely that the Confucian scholar–official must be both a person of letters and a person of action, that book learning must be complemented by profound action. Although the Qing (Ch'ing) dynasty was clearly in decline throughout the 1800s and the need for reform on all levels was needed, the conservative elements at court had successfully put off all major attempts at reform. Part of Kang's genius was the manner in which he was able to claim an ancient precedent for reform. He made this claim by reinterpreting the "Confucian Classics" and teachings as a reformist philosophy. Kang accomplished this by siding with the New Text School, envisioning Confucius (Kong Fuzi/Kongzi) himself as a reformer, and finally by writ-

ing the "one world" or "great unity" (*datong/ta-t'ung*) philosophy.

Kang was convinced that if he were to have any impact on the ruling conservative faction at court and to maintain his proper place in China's intellectual tradition and development, then he had to argue successfully for the claim that social, political, and institutional reform was part and parcel of the Confucian teachings. Kang argued that the "Confucian Classics" had to be reinterpreted based on the New Text School perspective and that Confucius himself was primarily an institutional reformer.

To understand the New Text School, we have to make an historical digression 2,000 years back to the unification of the empire under the Qin (Ch'in) dynasty (221–206 B.C.).

After the state of Qin unified the empire in 221 B.C., the self-proclaimed First Emperor and his notorious prime minister, Li Si (Li Ssu), instituted the standardization of various practices such as weights and measures, coinage, roads and vehicles, and the written characters in a new style called new script (*jinwen/chin wen*). Li Si's desire to unify everything, especially intellectual thought, led to the 213 B.C. edict to burn private libraries, especially the texts that conflicted with his Legalist practices. Only books dealing with divination, medicine, agriculture, and other nonphilosophical practices were spared. Thus all the pre-Qin classics were destroyed and had to be reconstructed from memory and fragment by scholars after the fall of Qin in 206 B.C. These reconstructed texts were written in the new script and called the "new texts." Dong Zhongshu (Tung Chung-shu) (c. 195–c. 115 B.C.) and others interpreted these texts, relying heavily on supernatural, extravagant, and prognosticative elements. In the Later Han dynasty (A.D. 25–220) texts were discovered (according to legend, in the walls of Confucius's house) written in the pre-Han old script; they are referred to as the "Old Text" because they were written in the old writing style, even though they were found later. (One should not be confused by the labels "new" and "old"; they refer to the script style the characters are written in and not to historical order.) The

so-called Old Text School gave a rational interpretation of the classics and the Confucian teachings. The Old Text approach won out during
the Tang (T'ang) (A.D. 618–907) and Song
(Sung) (A.D. 960–1279) revivals of Confucian philosophy.

Kang Youwei revived the study of the New Text
approach, arguing that the old texts were forged by
Liu Xin (Liu Hsin) (c. 46 B.C.–A.D. 23), and that the
texts written in the new script style were in fact
written by Confucius. By making this move, Kang
lay the foundation for his reinterpretation of the
classics and of Confucius as a reformer; he also
opened an avenue to inspiring Confucianism with
the supernatural, paving the way for its acceptance
as the state religion. Kang believed that, like past
Western nations, China needed a unified state religion. Kang's new text approach did not gain much
backing, and his theory is no longer accepted. However, his idea of reading Confucius as reformer has
been appealed to in the twentieth century.

Kang's philosophical thought is an attempt to
resolve a major problem of the Late Qing dynasty,
namely, how could China adopt Western military
and technological skills without losing her cultural
and moral integrity? Kang's approach to the problem is to accept Confucius and Confucian teachings
as the world's greatest, and while tacitly accepting
Western ideas of evolution, historical progress, social Darwinism, and a blind faith in the positive
progress of technology, he argued that Confucius
was a radical reformer and originator of evolutionary thinking. To create this syncretic blend of Western and Chinese ideas, Kang discredited the
traditional interpretation while maintaining the integrity of Confucius. So Kang argued that Confucian teachings were biased by the petty narrow
views of Xunzi (Hsün Tzu); they were further confused by the forgeries of Liu Xin, and finally dam-
aged by Zhu Xi's (Chu Hsi's) partiality. But Confucius was both a sage and a divine being, according
to Kang, and the truth of his teachings could not be
entirely hidden. That truth was still revealed in the
texts written in the new script and the interpretations of Dong Zhongshu that accompanied those
texts.

Confucius as Divine

According to Kang, Heaven showed mercy on the
plight of human suffering by producing the sagely
king of spiritual intelligence—Confucius. Kang
played up the idea of Confucius as a divine being
with a supernatural divine birth. For Kang, the
genius of Confucius was his ability to reform and
create institutions that, according to Kang, were
actually being used to govern the world. Kang contended that Confucius had actually created new
institutions and reformed old ones for ancient
China by attributing those reforms and institutions
to past sage rulers.

Kang was the first person to propose that Confucius was not only a great political reformer, but
also a great religious founder and leader. Kang
was a powerful evolutionary, syncretic, and universal thinker. Using Confucius as his authority,
Kang developed a philosophical outlook that
merged elements of Chinese and Western religions, philosophies, and sciences. He made
Confucius into a divine being, the founder of a
great religion, master of institutional reform, and
formulator of an evolutionary theory of historical
progress.

The Theory of the Three Ages

The Theory of the Three Ages was actually first
proposed by Dong Zhongshu, but as a cyclic phenomena; Kang appropriated the idea and made it
evolutionary and progressive. He then found passages from the classics that supported it or lent
themselves to being interpreted in that fashion.
Kang advocated that human history was progressive, that individuals living alone in the wilderness
were eventually drawn together, forming clans
which develop into tribes and eventually evolving
into nations. Nations develop through the stages of
autocracy, constitutional monarchy, and finally
into republics. The Confucian virtues, especially
filial piety, the love of father and son, can be extended to all of humanity. When human love truly
becomes universal, the Great Unity will come into
being. Nations will disappear and the individual

will reemerge, but this time in a new higher evolved level of social political order.

According to Kang there is historical progress through the Three Ages and the Three Rotations. The Age of Disorder will give way to the Age of Small Peace, and that will evolve into the Age of Great Peace. Each age contains three rotations, that is, each of the three ages contain itself and elements of the other two ages. So the Age of Disorder is dominated by disorder; it also evolves through a rotation of small peace and great peace, likewise for the Ages of Small Peace and Great Peace. Kang develops geometric exponential developments— the three threes become nine, which expand into eighty-one periods, and those develop into the thousands and innumerable future generations.

Kang argued that there is a point of commonality between Chinese moral teachings and Western philosophy and science. For Kang, the whole universe was tuned to a cosmic harmony. What Western thinkers had called "ether" or what is known as electricity is the same in Confucian thought as material force (*qi/ch'i*) and the breath of humans. This force permeates everything and cannot be cut off. Since everything has this force, there is a principle of attraction in the universe (the magnetic field). The principle of attraction is expressed in human nature as our moral concern for each other—our humanity (*ren/jen*) or what Mencius (Mengzi/Meng Tzu) referred to as "the mind that cannot bear to see the suffering of others." This spirit of human empathy and love holds great promise in store for the future of the human race; it will lead to the age of Great Unity and Great Peace.

Kang blends both a central element of Buddhism (namely that human life is full of suffering) and a key idea of British Utilitarianism (that all creatures desire happiness) with the Confucian conception of moral virtues to create his Utopian image of the age of Great Unity and Peace. Kang accepts the Utilitarian principle that a good person and a good government ought to promote the greatest happiness for the greatest number. Responding to the suffering of his own day, he sought to first identify the causes of suffering and then to eliminate them in order to bring on the age of Great Unity and Peace.

The Forms of Suffering

Kang recognizes that the causes of suffering are innumerable, but he offers a rough classification of six general types that are readily apparent causes of suffering:

> First, there are seven forms of suffering from living: rebirth, death, debilities, life on the frontier, and life as a barbarian, slave, or woman.
>
> Second, there are eight forms of suffering caused by natural disaster: famine, flood, drought, plagues, and so on.
>
> Third, there are the five forms of suffering caused by the forms of life: life as a widow or widower or orphan, illness, poverty, and low status.
>
> Fourth, there are five forms of suffering caused by government: punishment, taxation, conscription, the existence of the state, and the existence of the family.
>
> Fifth, there are eight forms of suffering caused by human feelings: stupidity, hatred, lust, and so on.
>
> Finally, there are five forms of suffering caused by being the object of honor and esteem: wealth, high status, longevity, political power, and finally, existence as a god, sage, immortal, or Buddha.

According to Kang, these various forms of suffering are generated from our making nine types of distinctions: nationality, class, race, physical form (especially male and female), family distinctions, occupations, the sphere of chaos (the irrational), the distinctions between species, and finally the sphere of suffering (suffering itself causes further suffering). Kang sought to eliminate these nine realms of distinctions to rid us of suffering.

The Age of Great Unity

In the age of Great Unity and Peace, everything and everyone would be treated the same; one people, one order, one world, one unity (*datong*).

For Kang, the age of Great Unity means that the world is united as one. There would be no nations, no races, and no wars. The unified world government would work for the improvement of human life. There would be no competition; the world government would regulate agriculture, industry, and commerce. In the age of Great Peace, there would be no rulers, kings, elders, or official ranks or titles. All people would be treated equally. The government would promote and encourage the basic Confucian virtues of wisdom and humanity. Kang envisions a worldwide Utopia without political, social, economic, racial, or sexual distinctions and the strife that follows from such distinctions. Even the family would become an institution of the past; the people would live communally in large public dwellings, eat together in large dining halls, and rear their children communally. Men and women would dress the same. New inventions would appear daily. There would be daily health care and disease would become a thing of the past. Since all desires would be fulfilled, people would attain a state of perfect happiness. The last desire would be earthly immortality. (It is interesting to note that earlier Kang had proposed that immortality was a cause of suffering, but in the age of Great Unity and Peace longevity and even immortality would become a reality and part of the good life.) Kang's Utopian philosophy has had a great impact on twentieth-century Utopian and science fiction literature.

JAMES D. SELLMANN

Further Reading

Translations

Chan, Wing-tsit, trans. and comp. *A Source Book in Chinese Philosophy*. Princeton, N.J.: Princeton University Press, 1963. Chapter 39 provides a good introduction to Kang and a representative selection of his writings.

K'ang, Yu-wei. *Ta T'ung Shu* (*The One World Philosophy of K'ang Yu-wei*). Translated by L. G. Thompson. London: Allen and Unwin, 1958.

Related Studies

Fung, Yu-lan. *A History of Chinese Philosophy*. Translated by Derk Bodde. 2 vols. Princeton, N.J.: Princeton University Press, 1952–53. See also the one-volume paperback edition: *A Short History of Chinese Philosophy* (New York: The Free Press; London: Collier-Macmillan, 1966). A very helpful account in the context of a careful historical survey.

Lo, Jung-pang, ed. *K'ang Yu-wei, 1858–1927, A Symposium*. Seattle, Wash.: University of Washington Press, 1963. Details the life and thought of Kang Youwei.

TAN SITONG (T'AN SSU-T'UNG)

Born: March 10, 1865, Bejing (Peking), China
Died: September 28, 1898, Bejing (Peking), China
Major Work: *Ren xue* (*Jen-hsüeh*) (*An Exposition of Benevolence,* or *A Study of Humanity*) (1896–97)

Major Ideas

China needs to have a transvaluation of values to survive in the modern world.
The teaching of Confucius (Kong Fuzi/Kongzi) is characterized by the central value of benevolence.
Benevolence is characterized by interconnection and non-obstruction.
Mozi's (Mo Tzu's) ideas can help to illustrate Confucian benevolence.
Buddhism is also illustrative of the concept of benevolence.
Christianity is equally demonstrative of the value of benevolence.
Benevolence can be validated by modern science and technological advancement.
Reform in China must follow the ideal of benevolence.

Hailed as a "comet" in the late nineteenth-century Chinese intellectual world, Tan Sitong (T'an Ssu-t'ung) exemplified the brilliance and restlessness of his generation of educated Chinese elite who had to wrestle with the ghost of China's ancient traditions as well as the specter of Western cultural and political domination. Living in that transitional age, Tan made a gallant attempt to reinterpret his own cultural heritage and to synthesize it with the modern scientific culture of the West. At the same time, however, Tan was no mere armchair philosopher engaged in empty speculation and useless contemplation. He was, on the contrary, a man of action, a true patriot who was deeply troubled by the apparent weakness and backwardness of his country when compared with the West. He therefore dedicated himself to fundamental reforms in China and, when his efforts were cut short by the conservative forces, willingly became a martyr for the cause. Tan is remembered by his countrymen as a profound and radical thinker, and a daring and heroic activist who shed his own blood in that ill-fated Reform Movement in 1898.

Though his native place was Liuyang (Liu-yang) county in Hunan Province, Tan Sitong was born in Beijing (Peking) into a scholar–official family on March 10, 1865. His father was then vice director of the Board of Revenues in the central bureaucracy, who later served in various posts in the prov-

inces and eventually became governor of Hubei (Hupeh) Province. Such frequent transfers and different postings of his father allowed the adolescent Tan the opportunity to see a vast stretch of the Chinese empire and to experience different styles of life, including rather wild ones on the frontier. This explains why, in addition to receiving a solid training in classical studies, Tan also managed to acquire a taste for horseback riding, boxing, and swordsmanship, a combination rather rare among his scholarly contemporaries. Moreover, through personal preferences and incidental encounters, Tan was most eclectic in his pursuit of knowledge in his twenties. Even in Confucianism, he did not limit himself to one school of thought or one partisan interpretation, but instead roamed widely throughout the entire spectrum of Confucian scholarship. He also exposed himself to Daoism (Taoism) and the writings of Mozi (Mo Tzu), impressed with the former's carefree attitude and the latter's sense of duty and knight-errantry. His greatest admiration, however, was reserved for Buddhism, especially the Sinicized version of it. He was particularly struck by Buddhism's emphasis on compassion, equality, and equanimity toward death.

From the late 1880s on, Tan Sitong added one more dimension to his already impressive learning. As a result of his father's appointment as governor of Hupeh, then one of the most progressive areas in

China thanks to the enlightened administration of the Governor-General Zhang Zhidong (Chang Chih-tung) (1837–1909), Tan finally had the opportunity to fraternize with scholars who had firsthand knowledge of the West. This occasioned a dramatic widening of his intellectual horizon, which drew him further into a serious inquiry into the secret behind the wealth and power demonstrated by the West. He was attracted to Protestant Christianity, impressed with Jesus' teaching of love and universal brotherhood. At the same time, he was interested in Western science, and began to read voraciously all the translations of Western scientific works put out by the Kiangnan Arsenal in Shanghai. The head of the Translation Bureau at the Arsenal was an Englishman by the name of John Fryer, who had come to China back in 1861 and had spent the following decades propagating Western science in the country that had an illustrious past in technological advancement but had, in recent centuries, lost its momentum and initiative. Tan finally met Fryer in 1893, was duly impressed with the Westerner's knowledge and goodwill, and sought to learn more about the reason behind the success of the West.

Meanwhile, the political situation in China deteriorated further. Despite the modernization program inaugurated in the 1860s, China was increasingly weakened by domestic rebellions and humiliated by external aggression. Western imperialism was encroaching upon her with full force, wantonly violating her sovereignty with demand for extraterritoriality and exacting from her both land and money. The greatest blow to her prestige, however, was inflicted by Japan, a former tributary state. In 1894–95, Japan unceremoniously and resoundingly defeated China in a series of naval battles. This event devastated China's complacency. A fellow Asian country had finally brought home to the Chinese the realization that their nation was in danger of being partitioned and destroyed. Indeed, the validity of China's cultural tradition itself had been called into question.

Deeply agitated by this crisis, Tan came to the conclusion that China had to search deep into her historical past as well as look beyond her territorial boundaries for solutions for her predicament. In other words, she had to reexamine her ancient traditions in the light of her modern needs. She also had to broaden herself to learn from Western institutions and modern scientific discoveries in order to save herself from the real possibility of national and cultural demise. Tan thus became seriously and actively involved in formulating ideas and solutions for political reform and cultural revival. It was in that context and under such conditions that he undertook to write his most celebrated work, *Ren xue* (*Jen-hsüeh*) (*An Exposition of Benevolence*, or *A Study of Humanity*), probably in 1896–97.

As indicated earlier, Tan did not merely advocate ideas for change and reform, he was actually in the thick of it. He helped to found a Reform Society in his native Hunan Province in 1897. In the following year, with the emperor himself committed to fundamental change similar to that launched by Emperor Meiji of Japan several decades earlier, Tan was summoned to the capital for an audience and summarily appointed a fourth-rank secretary in the Grand Council to carry out an avalanche of reform measures. These activities, unfortunately, invited the wrath of the conservative Empress Dowager, who on September 21, 1898, staged a coup d'etat to reclaim control of the government, put the Emperor under house arrest, and proceeded to move against the reformers. Even though Tan had, like some of his cohorts, every opportunity to escape arrest, he refused to flee and told his associates that without shedding blood, there was no hope for China. He wanted to be the first martyr whose death would bring about the birth of a reformed and rejuvenated China. He therefore waited at home for his persecutors. He was arrested on September 25th, and beheaded along with five other prominent reformers three days later at a public execution ground in Beijing. He was only thirty-three years old when he died. His tragic heroism has become legendary among Chinese reformers and revolutionaries alike.

Benevolence and Learning

Tan's heroic martyrdom was followed by the posthumous publication of his major work, the *Ren xue*, which earned him a lasting place in the intellectual history of modern China. The manuscript of the work itself was handed hastily to a friend in the last hectic days before his arrest. It first appeared serially in a Chinese publication in Yokohama, Japan, three months later, and was reprinted by another journal in Shanghai before being published in book form. Composed of two main parts, it contains a potpourri of ideas, explanations, and postulates that are not always successfully integrated (or were even intended to be). It is indicative of a brilliant young mind working in great haste and prompted by a sense of utmost urgency. There are arbitrary twists in meaning, forced arguments, and sometimes outright erroneous and misunderstood notions. Nevertheless, out of this obviously awkward and confused compilation, several salient points can be detected.

The very title of the treatise itself is at once interesting and ambiguous. *Ren xue* may be understood as "An Exposition of Benevolence," which is precisely the title adopted by the translator of this work in its first complete rendition into English, but it can also be interpreted as "Benevolence and Learning," two primary areas of concern outlined by Tan in the preface. Whatever the case may be, there is no question about the centrality of the notion of benevolence in the author's thinking. It needs to be pointed out, of course, that benevolence is the core concept in Confucian teaching.

It is clear from reading the book that Tan has not lost faith with Confucianism at all. What he does find objectionable with the Confucianism of his day is precisely the fact that it has lost sight of its original vision, defined as benevolence. In Tan's opinion, the teaching of Confucius (Kongfuzi/ K'ung Fu-tzu) has been obscured and overshadowed by generations of Chinese rulers and their sycophantic ministers, who have tampered with the message of the sage, turning it into a doctrine of despotic control and patriarchal oppression. The existing ethical norms and social rituals, in particular, are seen by Tan as a complete adulteration of original Confucianism. They are blamed for having created a sociopolitical hierarchy in China since the beginning of imperial times in which the subjects,

the children, and the wives are unmitigatedly exploited and oppressed by their rulers, parents, and husbands, respectively. To recover the original impulse of benevolence in the Confucian teaching, Tan unequivocally calls for the total tearing asunder of the entire network of unequal and discriminatory human relations then prevailing in China.

To Tan, harking back to the quintessential aspect of true Confucianism—benevolence—is critically important for the viability of the tradition in the modern world. He sees the fundamental nature of benevolence as *tong* (*t'ung*) (interconnection, linkage, unimpeded communication, unobstructed penetration). Chinese society, with its political, generational, and gender inequality, has decidedly not been *tong* for all of her imperial history. There is therefore a dire need to rid Confucianism of its distortions and misunderstanding with assistance from other traditions. Tan finds the teaching of Mozi especially helpful in rectifying the situation. Mozi's advocacy of "love without discrimination" (*jian'ai/chien-ai*) and "knight-errantry" (*ren xia/ jen-hsia*) is most illustrative of the spirit of benevolence, as the two best exemplify the quality of *tong* with their emphasis on nonsegregation and camaraderie. Tan also credits Mozi with the stress on learning, especially the study of the natural sciences. As he sees it, Mozi's teaching should be revived to bolster the original spirit of Confucianism.

Buddhism is another tradition which Tan finds compatible with the ideal of benevolence. The Buddha's teaching of compassion is in fact the highest form of benevolence. Compassion implies not being separated from others and the overcoming of the barrier that alienates one person from another. It brings about the realization of the identity of oneself and others. Thus compassion means equality. Buddhist metaphysics also promotes the awareness of the total unity of time, space, and all phenomena. It sees no difference between past, present, and future; nor does it distinguish between here and there. All things are deemed mere creations of the mind, and are therefore ultimately one. This universalistic teaching of the Buddha is the best antidote to the particularism and discrimination fostered by a distorted and adulterated form of Confucianism.

In addition to the indigenous or completely Sinicized traditions discussed above, Tan also detects benevolence in Christianity. Jesus' teaching of loving one's neighbor as oneself and his personal example of willingly dying on the cross to cleanse the sins of all human beings are mentioned by Tan as the clearest indication of benevolence. The Christian doctrine of God being the Father-Creator and humankind being his children inspires Tan to conclude that all are equal and autonomous before God. Tan attributes Western parliamentarianism and participatory democracy to the Christian belief in the sanctity of all individuals and their assumed equality before God. Christianity is thus credited with having given birth to a modern world in which there is *tong* between the ruler and the ruled, as well as between male and female.

Modern Science and Benevolence

Most remarkable is Tan Sitong's exploration into modern science to seek verification of his ideal of benevolence. Inspired by the then-prevailing scientific speculation in the existence of ether, a primordial substance which is believed to permeate the entire universe, Tan proclaims with delight that ether is benevolence, as it brings everything in the cosmos into an all-encompassing whole. Ether enables all the myriad things and phenomena in the universe to form one organic wholeness in which they interpenetrate and fuse together. The highest state of benevolence is *tong*.

This oneness is further made evident by the discovery and use of electricity, whose ubiquitous nature and power of reach must have impressed Tan. Electricity powers the engine of progress and industrial development, making possible easy communication throughout the world via the telegraph, and the manufacture of powerful machines that increase production and enhance living comfort. Another discovery of modern science Tan finds demonstrative of *tong* is mental power. After reading John Fryer's translation of a book written by

Henry Wood, originally entitled *Ideal Suggestion through Mental Photography* but rendered in Chinese as *The Prevention of Disease through Mental Healing*, Tan declares his unbounded faith in the efficacy of the human mind to penetrate all realms and to effect transformation of all phenomena. Indeed, the mind is the link between one person and others, between humankind and other myriad things, and between one planet or one star in a galaxy and the rest of the universe. The activities of the mind overcome all physical barriers to bring all individuals and all things into a harmonious communion. Thus, once again the ability of the mind to form one body with others and all things makes it the epitome of benevolence.

Tan Sitong's analysis of benevolence and its quality of *tong* allows him to propose with clarity and conviction an entire program of reform for China. He envisions a revival of true Confucianism spearheaded by a Martin Luther-like figure. He calls for the reemergence of Mozi's teaching, in particular the two branches that focus on learning and knight-errantry. He sees the need for the ultimate triumph of Buddhism to ensure the widespread practice of compassion. From outside of China, he advocates the appreciation of the Christian ideal of brotherly love and sacrifice, and argues for the serious study of modern science to unleash the power of the mind. His yearning for interconnection and unimpeded linkage prompts him to call for the revamping of Chinese society so that the segregation between the genders and the exploitation of the young by the old can be stopped. Politically, the despotic system of monarchy has to be transformed so that ruler and ruled may be linked together for the purpose of making China strong and wealthy.

Tan and the Modern World

Despite the lack of organization and integration in Tan's work, there is certainly an underlying unity in it. His overarching aim is to make sense of the modern world confronted by China and to provide a theoretical framework for reform in his country. He taps deep into his cultural heritage and explores widely to gather component pieces for that framework. Though steeped in the Confucian tradition, he avoids partisanship and parochialism by first conceding that much of Confucius's teaching has been distorted and adulterated, thus requiring the assistance of other schools of thought to recover its core value. He turns to Mozi and the Buddha for further illustration of the central Confucian value of benevolence. In his desire to salvage what is valuable in China's cultural heritage, he is not narrowly nationalistic. He recognizes and appreciates the value of Christianity and modern science in the illumination of benevolence. He also sees value in the practical application of these foreign creeds and studies, as they ultimately bring about a strong and united world made up of dynamic and informed individuals whose creative energies have been put to full use. He thus pays due admiration to the Faustian-Promethean spirit of the modern West, and hopes that China one day will share that spirit once true benevolence prevails.

Tan feels that he has successfully come up with a perfect and harmonious synthesis of the best in China with the best from the West. But the fact that he finds it necessary to explain and justify his own cultural tradition with modern Western teaching and studies implies that his culture has lost its exclusive grip on him. Confucianism and Chinese culture alone can no longer provide an adequate reference point for the Chinese intellectual of the 1890s. It is a sad fact that may have escaped Tan himself.

RICHARD H. SHEK

Further Reading

Translation

Chan, Sin-wai, trans. *An Exposition of Benevolence: The* Jen-hsüeh *of T'an Ssu-t'ung.* Hong Kong: The Chinese University Press, 1984. A complete English translation of Tan's major work with notes and explanations. The introduction, which provides a synopsis of the work, is also useful.

Related Studies

Chan, Sin-wai. *T'an Ssu-t'ung: An Annotated Bibliography*. Hong Kong: The Chinese University Press, 1980. An authoritative compilation on both Chinese and Western scholarship on Tan Sitong. It also contains useful appendices that detail the chronological development of Tan's thought.

Chang, Hao. "T'an Ssu-t'ung" in *Chinese Intellectuals in Crisis: Search for Order and Meaning, 1890–1911*. Berkeley, Calif.: University of California Press, 1987. An in-depth analysis of Tan Sitong's intellectual quest, from his earliest writing to the *Ren xue*. It puts Tan's thought in the perspective of Neo-Confucian thinking.

Kwong, Luke S. K. "Reflection on an aspect of Modern China in transition: T'an Ssu-t'ung (1865–1898) as a Reformer" in Paul A. Cohen and John E. Schrecker, eds., *Reform in Nineteenth-century China*, pp. 184–193. Cambridge, Mass.: East Asian Research Center, Harvard University, 1976. A psychological probe of the development of Tan's thought. It also points out the limitations of reform ideas.

Shek, Richard H. "Some Western Influences on T'an Ssu-t'ung's Thought" in Paul A. Cohen and John E. Schrecker, eds., *Reform in Nineteenth-century China*, pp. 194–203. Cambridge, Mass.: East Asian Research Center, Harvard University, 1976. A study of a little-noticed area of Tan's philosophy—the influence of Christian missionary writings and translations of scientific works on him.

SUN YAT-SEN (SUN YIXIAN/SUN I-HSIEN)

Born: 1866, Cui-heng (Ts'ui-heng), in Guangdong (Kwangtung) Province, China
Died: 1925, Beijing (Peking, Peiping)
Major Works: *Sun Wen Xue Shuo* (*Sun Wen Hsüeh Shuo*) (*Memoirs of a Chinese Revolutionary: A Program of National Reconstruction for China*) (1918); *Sanmin Zhuyi* (*San Min Chu I*) (*The Three Principles of the People*) (1924); *Jian Guo Dagang* (*Chien Kuo Ta-kang*) (*Fundamentals of National Reconstruction*) (1924)

Major Ideas

The three principles of the people are nationalism, democracy, and "livelihood" (economics).

In order to establish democracy, the principle of equality is required.

Equality does not mean that everyone is created equal; it means that every individual should be given equal opportunity to develop his or her potential to the maximum.

An ideal democracy should include five independent powers: the executive, the legislative, the judicial, the selective, and the supervisory.

A new economics for China should be redistribution of land ownership, practicing the principle that "Land belongs to Farmers."

A new theory of action is to reverse the traditional saying that "to know is easy, but to act is difficult"; this theory of action will help facilitate the revolution of China.

Both Confucius (Kongfuzi/K'ung Fu-tzu) and Mencius (Mengzi/Meng Tzu) had a strong sense of mission to rescue China from falling apart, yet neither succeeded because no opportunities were given to them to try. However, both attained immortality as great sages and thinkers. On the other hand, Dr. Sun Yat-sen has succeeded as a political reformer and a revolutionary, yet his contribution to world philosophy has been obscured by his celebrated career as a political leader. He is Confucius in action, the founder of New China. His practical principles have significantly affected the course of China's history.

Sun Yat-sen's family name is Sun, and Wen is his given name. He was born in a small village called Cui-heng (Ts'ui-heng), north of Macao, in the province of Guangdong (Kwangtung). After several years of traditional schooling in the village, he went to Honolulu, Hawaii, with his elder brother and attended high school there for a few years.

In 1884, Sun went to Hong Kong and entered Government Central School, where he graduated in 1896. He then entered the College of Medicine, where he graduated at the top of his class in July 1872. Realizing the decline of China and the corruption of the Qing (Ch'ing) dynasty, he decided to give up medicine in order to work for the reform of China. He founded the Society for the Revival of China and traveled extensively in China and abroad to raise funds and to recruit members for the society. In 1905 in Tokyo he became the head of the Revolutionary Alliance (which later became the Guomindang [Kuomintang] or National People's Party). He developed the "Three Principles of the People" (nationalism, democracy, and "livelihood" or economics), which served as the philosophic foundation for his vision of new China.

Sun, together with his supporters in the Revolutionary Alliance, planned many uprisings against the Manchu government in different provinces of China, and an uprising on October 10, 1911, in Wuhan (while Sun was in the United States) finally succeeded. Puyi (P'u-i), the Last Emperor of Qing, conceded and stepped down. Sun was elected provisional president of the Republic of China but later resigned in favor of Yuan Shikai (Yüan Shih-k'ai), who was the builder of the Northern Army. Yuan was not satisfied with the title of president and declared himself emperor. A revolt against Yuan was unsuccessful and in 1913 Sun left China and did not return until 1916. Sun and his supporters had to engage in continuous revolutions to clean up the residue forces of imperial China, including some of the warlords in different parts of the country. In 1923 he founded a separate government in Canton. He cooperated with the Communists in the effort to defeat the Japanese invaders, unify China, and prepare the nation for its place in the modern world. Before this effort could be carried through, however, Sun succumbed to poor health and died in Beijing on March 12, 1925. On April 1, 1940, he was given the title "Father of the New China" by the Nationalist government.

A New Vision of Democracy

Having directly observed and experienced the democratic societies of Europe and the United States, Sun was convinced that for China to be saved, a democratic government had to be established. He realized that the Chinese mentality had been formed in its traditional way to expect that government would be in the hands of one or a few people, and that the general public had neither the right nor the duty to participate in the governing process. Accordingly, in many of his lectures he tried to stimulate the masses with his democratic vision and his theory of knowledge and action. He defined politics as "management of affairs of the general public." He firmly believed that every citizen had the right to participate. Such a right is based on the concept of equality.

Sun did not believe that all persons are equal in intellectual or physical capacities; there is no equality in the natural world. So natural inequality is not necessarily an evil. But artificial inequality, or the inequality created by kings and lords, can be the origin of social injustice and thus can cause people to rebel. To avoid unrest or revolution, this artificial type of inequality had to be abolished.

Sun, at the same time, rejected what he called "false equality," which is artificial equality imposed upon what is naturally given. False equality is contrary to natural inequality, and it limits tal-

ented people from excelling. Consequently society must be purged of false equality.

For Sun, true equality is equal opportunity for all people to develop their potentials to the maximum without obstructions or hindrances imposed by the society. He believed that every person should be given an opportunity to realize himself or herself, and he recognized that the realization of the equality of opportunity could be achieved only through education.

Sun's version of democracy was not a direct copy of the Western versions or an imitation of American democracy. In fact, his concept of equality displayed his political originality. His most significant contribution to democracy is found in his "Five Power Democratic System." His democratic system is no doubt based on the American system of three powers, namely, the executive, the legislative, and the judicial branches. But in adopting the American system, Sun created a new form of democracy by blending the American system with traditional Chinese culture. In addition to the three branches, Sun added two more: the selective or the examination branch, and the supervision or control branch.

Chinese culture has had a highly developed examination system for over a thousand years and it has performed the function of selecting competent and qualified people for the government. If the selective function were to fall into the hands of the executive branch, the president or the heads of government units could select personnel as moved by personal relationships. If this selective function is given autonomy, on the other hand, it can limit the executive power and thus insure a greater degree of justice. The supervisory or control branch also had its origin in Chinese culture. In traditional China, the branch performed the supervisory function over officials on all levels of the government and thus acted as the eyes and ears of the emperor. In addition, the branch could even criticize and supervise the emperor from the viewpoint of Confucian philosophy. Sun, therefore, argued for the autonomy of this function, and has proposed this as a separate power for his new political system. This separate function has the power to audit government books, investigate government activities, accept petitions and grievances from the people, impeach government officials for wrongdoing, and reverse government decisions that run counter to the interests of the people.

Theoretically Sun's new version of democracy was not only a likely model for China but also a likely and efficient political model for the world. But it is unfortunate that in 1937, twelve years after his death, the Second Sino-Japanese War broke out and continued until 1945. Before Sun's follower Jiang Jieshi (Chiang Kai-shek) had the opportunity to carry out Sun's plan, the Chinese Communist Army defeated the Guomindang forces and gained control of China.

After Chiang retreated to Taiwan, Sun's political plan was given the opportunity for development and concretization. After Chiang Kai-shek died, Jiang's son Jiang Jinguo (Chiang Ching-kuo) continued to practice Sun's ideology and to modernize Taiwan along basically democratic lines.

A New Economic Theory

Sun was thoroughly familiar with the economic theory of Karl Marx, and his criticism of Marx is perhaps the starting point of his own theory. For Marx, the motivating or energizing force of social progress is class struggle. But for Sun, class struggle is only a symptom of social illness. He criticized Marx as being a pathologist but not a physiologist of society. For Sun, the normal discourse of social progress consists in pursuing livelihood through mutual dependence.

However, Sun was inclined toward socialism to some extent and his economic philosophy is socialistic in nature. The basic principle is redistribution of wealth, but it is not practiced in the Communistic way. Since China is an agriculturally based country, land reform is probably the most vital issue. Sun developed his philosophy for land reform and called his land policy "equalization of land ownership." To begin with, the landlords were required to assess and report the fair market value of their land, with the government having the authority to purchase it. If the landlords overevalu-

ated the value of the land, they had to pay a higher property tax. But if they underreport the value, they were in danger of suffering a loss if the government decided to purchase the land at their self-assessed value. After this initial assessment of value, the appreciated value subsequently would belong to the society since such an appreciation is a result of social prosperity rather than of individual investment or effort. When the government purchased lands from landlords, it would then resell the land to farmers on easy terms. The slogan for this principle was "Land belongs to the farmers." In recent years Taiwan has practiced this land policy and has demonstrated a high degree of success.

In addition to land reform, Sun also developed a policy for the regulation of private capital and a plan for the industrialization of China.

A Theory of Action

There has been a popular saying in traditional China, "To know is not difficult, but to practice is difficult." This saying has been attributed to Fu Yue (Fu Yüeh) of the Shang dynasty, which was in fact in the prehistoric era. According to Sun, the saying has corrupted the Chinese people because it discourages people from engaging in action. To reform a nation or to start a revolution, action is vitally important. In order to facilitate his political activities, he has developed a new theory of action which is just the reverse of this traditional saying.

For Sun, to act is easy, but to know is difficult. Many people have followed a certain custom for a lifetime without knowing why they have acted as they have. Still other people have acted upon impulses without knowing the reasons for their actions. Most persons act without ever having grasped the principles of action. In the main, action can be the result of impulse or habit, but the process of knowing is at a higher level of consciousness, cognition through intellectual discipline or some specialized area of knowledge.

In the history of China, after Fu Yue, the most notable thinker for developing a theory of action was Wang Yangming, who advocated "the unity of knowledge and action." By developing a theory of action that, as Wang Yangming proposed, emphasizes the unity of knowledge and action, Sun has made a significant contribution to modern pragmatic thinking. In some respects his views are in agreement with those of the American philosopher John Dewey (1859–1952), who also developed a sophisticated theory relating knowledge to action. The new thinking in China is built on ancient ideas, but is given new direction by a concern for the systematic resolution of practical problems that relate to the development of both the individual and society. Sun Yat-sen has managed to win the respect of all sides in the revolutionary process that has transformed China.

JOSEPH S. WU

Further Reading

Cantlie, James, and C. Sheridan Jones. *Sun Yat-sen and the Awakening of China.* New York: Revell, 1912. This is a pioneering work on Sun. The chief author Cantlie was in fact Sun's professor in the College of Medicine. He was so impressed with his student's top performance and attractive personality that he became Sun's close friend. When in 1896 Sun was kidnapped by the Chinese legation in London, Cantlie arranged for his rescue through the agency of the Foreign Office.

Cheng, Chu-yuan, ed. *Sun Yat-sen's Doctrine in the Modern World.* Boulder & London: Westview Press, 1989. This is probably the finest scholarly work on Sun Yat-sen in the English publishing world, with eleven articles contributed by twelve scholars. The editor himself is a renowned economist specialized in the economy of China, and is well-versed in Dr. Sun's economic theory and its successful practice in Taiwan.

Ho, Zhongxin. "Sun Yat-sen: Initiator of China's Democracy." *Beijing Review*, 29 (November 10, 1986), 19–22. In spite of the short length of this article, the title and the publishing place should capture readers' attention. Although Sun was a formidable critic of Marxism, the Chinese Communists still respect him as the founder of New China.

Linebarger, Paul. *The Political Doctrines of Sun Yat-sen: An Exposition of the "San Min Chu I."* Baltimore, Md.: Johns Hopkins University Press, 1937. A helpful work by a scholar who has published several books on Sun Yat-sen.

Liu, Yeou-hwa. "A Comparative Study of Dr. Sun Yat-sen's and Montesquieu's Theory of Separation of Powers." Doctoral Dissertation, Claremont Graduate School, San Diego, California, 1983. Available only on microfilm, this is a very valuable study of Sun's political thought.

Williams, Maurice. *Sun Yat-sen Versus Communism. New Evidence Establishing China's Right to the Support of Democratic Nations.* Baltimore, Md.: Williams & Wilkins Co., 1932. This work is very important in explaining Sun's position in relation to Communism.

Wu, Joseph S. "Contemporary Chinese Philosophy outside Mainland China," *International Philosophical Quarterly*, Vol. XIX, No. 4 (December 1979), 451–467. This article provides important information about how Sun's followers developed his economic doctrines in Taiwan.

MAO ZEDONG (MAO TSE-TUNG)

Born: 1893, Shaoshan, Hunan Province, China
Died: 1976, Beijing (Peking), China
Major Works: "On Practice" (1937), "On Contradiction" (1937), "On New Democracy" (1940), "On Literature and Art" (1942), "On the Correct Handling of the Contradictions Among the People" (1957)

Major Ideas

The world is full of contradiction, and dialectics is the method to handle contradictions.

True knowledge can come only from practice, and practice is the sole criterion for truth.

In a semi-colonial and semi-feudal country, socialism can be achieved through two stages: "new-democratic" revolution and socialist revolution.

In a socialist society, the proletarian revolution needs to be continued in order to fight those within the Communist Party who represent the interests of the overthrown bourgeoisie.

Literature and art are tools of political struggle and they must serve the interest of the proletariat and the masses.

Mao Zedong (Mao Tse-tung) was born into an upper-middle peasant family in a southern mountain village, Shaoshan, at a time when the Qing (Ch'ing) dynasty was coming to an end and China was virtually cut into pieces by warlords and Western imperialists. For many people it was a time of searching for answers to revive the thousands-year-old nation. Mao's early life of a typical peasant boy gave him a deep understanding of the reality of China, which was for a long time an agricultural country. This understanding helped Mao a great deal in his later struggles for his career in and outside the party. Educated in the Changsha Normal School, Mao was well versed in Chinese history and literature. He was exposed to Western ideas in his early years. His philosophical thought was formed in the 1930s with much aid from translations of Russian Marxism. As a Chinese Marxist thinker, he was undoubtedly more Chinese than Marxist.

In the philosophical world, Mao is hardly considered an original philosopher. There is no question, however, that he was a profound thinker. As the leader of the Chinese Communist Party and of the People's Republic of China for four decades, Mao's thought has momentously affected both the party and China and has significantly influenced the rest of the world.

"On Contradiction": Mao's Dialectical Methodology and Worldview

Mao's worldview and methodology of philosophy can best be summarized as materialist dialectics. As opposed to idealism, materialism is the view that what is real in the world is material (physical) and exists independently of human consciousness. Mao's dialectics are derived from such Western writers as Hegel, Marx, Engels, Lenin, and Stalin, as well as Chinese Daoism (Taoism). Mao illustrates his dialectic view by contrasting it with the so-called "metaphysical conception." The metaphysical conception, Mao maintains, sees things in the world as "isolated, static, and one-sided." It is the view that changes or development in the world simply involve physical changes of quantity and place and that these changes are caused by external forces. The dialectical view asserts the contrary.

According to the latter, things in the world exist in relation to other things and thus are interrelated. Everything in the world also has its internal cause for its development; this internal cause is an inconsistency within the thing itself, and this contradictoriness is the fundamental cause of a thing's development.

"Contradictoriness" or "contradiction" is a

very broad concept that cannot be defined precisely. As a matter of fact, Mao never gives it a precise definition. It is a Hegelian concept referring to anything that is an unsolved issue—a conflict between social classes, an argument between two people, a daily problem that needs to be solved—all are examples of contradictions. When a contradiction (that is, a problem involving opposition) is solved or resolved, progress is made. The dialectic world outlook holds that contradiction exists in the process of the development of all things and therefore laws of contradiction are universally applicable.

Following Lenin, Mao holds that the most important law of contradiction, hence "the kernel of dialectics," is the law of the Unity of Opposites. It says that the two aspects of a contradiction are interdependent and may switch their positions as the nature of the contradiction changes. In Mao's own words, it is that "Everything divides into two" (*yi fen wei er/i fen wei erh*). This interdependence of the contradictory aspects is present in all things. This thesis is called the universality of contradictoriness. In this sense contradiction is said to be absolute, that is, universal with no exceptions. On the other hand, contradiction is also relative. Namely, it has its particularity. In plain words, this means that every problem (contradiction) is different, has its peculiar nature, and therefore needs to be dealt with in a way that is proper to its particular nature. For example, a contradiction (conflict) between friends and a contradiction (conflict) between enemies have different natures and need to be handled in different ways. The latter is antagonistic and the former is not. Although the latter has to be fought out, the former can perhaps be resolved by a candid talk. However, the nature of a contradiction may change. When a contradiction between friends is not handled properly, they may turn into enemies and face an antagonistic contradiction. By exercising reason and negotiating properly, enemies may change their antagonistic contradiction into a nonantagonistic one. In "On the Correct Handling of the Contradictions Among the People" (the famous "Let a hundred flowers bloom" speech), Mao illustrates what he calls

"correct" ways of handling nonantagonistic contradictions among the people.

Mao is usually given credit for his inventive exposition of the thesis of the principal contradiction and the principal aspect of a contradiction. First, Mao maintains, there are many contradictions in the process of the development of a complex thing; among these contradictions, one must be the principal contradiction, the existence and development of which determines or influences other contradictions. For example, during the Second Sino-Japanese War (1937–1945), there were many contradictions or conflicts between various social groups; the contradiction between the Japanese invader and the Chinese people was the principal one. It played the leading and decisive role and its existence and development determined or influenced the existence and development of other contradictions. The proper methodology for contradiction-solving is to focus on and grasp the principal contradiction and through it to lead the whole thing to develop in the right direction.

Second, within each contradiction one of the two contradictory aspects one must be principal or predominant, and the other secondary or subordinate. The principal aspect always determines the nature of the contradiction. When the two exchange positions, the nature of the contradiction is changed. For example, in a capitalist society the capitalist class and working class exist in a contradictory relationship in which the capitalist class is the principal and therefore dominant aspect. If through a proletarian revolution the working class overthrows the capitalist and puts the working class under the "proletarian dictatorship," the working class will become the principal aspect of the contradiction between the two classes, which is said to continue for a long period of time after the revolution. One important purpose of studying contradictions, Mao holds, is to learn how to analyze and change the nature of a contradiction through changing its principal aspect.

It is difficult to say how valid and useful these doctrines are. For many things can be justified both ways by Mao's dialectics. For instance, China's isolation from the rest of the world from the 1950s through the 1970s was justified by the idea that it is the internal cause of a thing (for example, China's internal affairs) that determines its development; its openness to the world in the 1980s and 1990s is justified by the idea that China's progress depends in good part on relations with other countries (China's economy is connected to that of other countries) and therefore China should not be isolated. (These ideas are held to be the most significant part of Mao's thought and were subjects of required study for decades.)

"On Practice": Theory of Knowledge

"On Practice" is a very short work but perhaps the one which best represents Mao's style—a combination of Marxism with Chinese traditional philosophy. The issue dealt with in this work is the relationship between knowledge and practice, a Chinese philosophical subject of extensive and prolonged discussions for thousands of years. As a dialectic materialist Mao endeavored to achieve a unity of knowledge and practice.

Mao's theory of knowledge is said to be materialist because it relies on practice in the material world. Practice here means experience. Mao believed that our sensual perception of the material world is the origin of all knowledge. Here experience is not merely passive sense experience; it includes active engaging experience, namely practice or activities that change reality. Mao believed that only through personal participation in this kind of reality-changing practice can a person uncover truth. This is one aspect of the dialectic nature of the theory. Another aspect of its dialectics lies in Mao's emphasis on the "deepening movement of cognition." Through experience a person gains perceptual knowledge. This is the first stage of the whole cognitive process. Perceptual knowledge is preliminary and reflects only the separate and therefore superficial aspects of reality.

In the second stage of the cognitive process that is based on perceptual knowledge, concepts are formed through "a sudden change or leap." Conceptual knowledge is rational and logical. Whereas perceptual knowledge reflects only the phenomena of reality, conceptual knowledge is said to grasp the essence of reality. However, conceptual knowledge again needs to be put back into practice for testing and enrichment. Only social practice is the criterion of truth. Mao defines social practice mainly in terms of "the three great movements," namely, material production, class struggle, and scientific research. Thus human cognition, according to Mao, is the prolonged process of movement from practice to cognition and back to practice ad infinitum.

At the end of "On Practice" Mao summarizes his theory of knowledge:

> Discover truth through practice, and again through practice verify and develop truth. Start from perceptual knowledge and actively develop it into rational knowledge; then start from rational knowledge and actively guide revolutionary practice to change both the subjective and the objective world. Practice, knowledge, again practice, and again knowledge. This form repeats itself in endless cycles, and with each cycle the content of practice and knowledge rises to a higher level. Such is the whole of the dialectical-materialist theory of knowledge, and such is the dialectical-materialist theory of the unity of knowing and doing.

Although Mao uses Chinese classic stories to demonstrate his theory, he falls short of explaining exactly how perceptual knowledge is developed into conceptual knowledge. Mao's theory makes sense only if the stages are understood as logical, not actual. In actuality, a person can hardly have any knowledge, perceptual or not, without conceptualization.

Even though presented as a dialectical unity of theory and practice, Mao's theory of knowledge is doubtless practical in character. This characteristic is also evident in his essay "Where Do Correct Ideas Come From?", in which Mao affirms that experience is the only source of knowledge.

On "New Democracy": Political Philosophy

Mao's political and social philosophy is historical materialism. Briefly, it is the Marxist theory that social productive force determines the relations of production, that the economic base determines the superstructure (mainly the state), and that the superstructure, in turn, can enhance or hinder economic development by reacting to the economic base in various ways.

The addition Mao made to Marxism is Mao's theory and practice of how to bring a "semi-feudal and semi-colonial" country like China to socialism. The goal of the Chinese Communist Party, Mao held, was to establish a new society not only with a new politics and a new economy, but also with a new culture. This task had to be accomplished in two steps. The first step was a "new-democratic" revolution, and the second, a socialist revolution. Under usual circumstances, a democratic revolution is a bourgeois revolution against feudalism. But since the Chinese bourgeoisie, Mao argued, were not fully grown and too weak, and their enemies—feudalism and imperialism—were too strong, the Chinese bourgeoisie could not accomplish the historic task of carrying out a democratic revolution. This historic task fell on the shoulders of the Chinese proletariat. Accordingly, in China, the democratic revolution had to be led by the proletariat and therefore it was a "new-democratic" revolution. This revolution, Mao maintained, was to establish "New Democracy," in contrast to the old democracy of the bourgeoisie. It was a new-democratic state under the joint dictatorship of several anti-imperialist and anti-feudalist classes, mainly the proletariat and the revolutionary bourgeoisie. Its leadership, Mao emphasized, had to be the proletariat through their political organization, namely the Communist Party.

The second step was a socialist revolution. The target of the socialist revolution was mainly the bourgeoisie. In such a revolution the proletariat would seize the power of the state and the means of production owned by the bourgeoisie and place the bourgeoisie under the proletarian dictatorship. In such a state, there would be a state and collective economy, and socialist culture would finally be achieved through cultural revolution.

Mao's theory of Chinese revolution is an application of his dialectical theory of contradiction. In the new-democratic revolution period the principal contradiction was between feudalism and imperialism on the one hand and other classes on the other. In the socialist revolution period the principal contradiction was between the bourgeoisie and the working people. The successful implementation of Mao's theory put the Communists into power and established Mao's nearly absolute authority in China for several decades.

In his later years Mao developed a theory of continuous revolution under the proletarian dictatorship. He believed that in a socialist society where the proletariat are the leading class, revolution is still needed because the overthrown bourgeoisie will inevitably select Communist Party officials to represent their interest. Hence the class struggle between the proletariat and bourgeoisie in such a society is represented mainly within the party. Continuous revolution is needed to cleanse the party of these bourgeois representatives. The practice of this theory later proved disastrous to the nation as well as the Party during the so-called "Cultural Revolution" (1966–1976), which turned into virtually a civil war and did not end until Mao died.

In his social and ethical theory, Mao followed the Confucian tradition in stressing the priority of societal interest over individual interest. Individuals must yield to the collective. Individualism and libertarianism must be criticized. A moral person should be willing to benefit others at his or her own expense. Unlike most Confucians, Mao advocated sex equality. He believed that in a socialist society women and men are equals. Women should have the same change in job assignment and should get the same pay as men for doing the same work.

"On Literature and Art"

Although he was a fairly good poet, Mao had little to say on aesthetics. But his philosophy of literature and art had a tremendous impact on contemporary Chinese literature and art. As an historic materialist, Mao believed that literature and art belong to the superstructure of the society and hence necessarily serve the interests of a certain class. In 1942, Mao gave two talks on literature and art in Yenan, then the headquarters of the Chinese Communist Party. There he put forth the idea that literature and artistic works must serve the purpose of the proletarian revolution.

Mao maintained that literature and art must fit well into the whole revolutionary machine as a component part. Writers and artists must stand for the proletariat and the masses, serving as the people's tongue and voice; they must hold the right attitudes toward their own people and the enemy; they must also remember that works of literature and art are to serve the masses—the workers, peasants, and soldiers. In order to accomplish these goals, writers and artists must study Marxism, become Marxists, and identify themselves with the ordinary people. They must learn from the ordinary people, be able to share their feelings, and use their language.

Mao's thought in these talks soon became the official party policy on literature and art. For a long time, perhaps until his death in 1976, political orientation was the primary, if not the sole, criterion for literature and art in China. Writers and artists whose works did not meet the political standard were criticized and silenced.

Undoubtedly Mao was one of the most influential thinkers in China of this century. He was also the most controversial Chinese thinker. Even his followers are widely divided on to what extent he was right and how much he was responsible for China's success and failure for the half century of his domination. Perhaps the full impact of Mao's thought on contemporary China has yet to be realized, and perhaps only history can yield a fair judgment.

CHENYANG LI

Further Reading

Translations

Mao, Tse-tung. *Four Essays on Philosophy*. Peking: Foreign Languages Press, 1966. In addition to "On Practice" and "On Contradiction," this collection also includes "On the Correct Handling of the Contradictions among the People" and "Where Do Correct Ideas Come From?", the latter two essays being applications of the theory which Mao put forth in the former two books.

————. *On New Democracy*. Peking: Foreign Languages Press, 1967. In addition to "On New Democracy," this collection also contains Mao's "Talks at the Yenan Forum on Literature and Art."

————. *Selected Works of Mao Tse-tung*. (5 volumes) Peking: Foreign Languages Press, 1961–1977.

————. *Chairman Mao Talks to the People: Talks and Letters 1956–1971*. Edited with an introduction by Stuart Schram. Translated by John Chinnery and Tieyun. New York: Pantheon Books, 1974. This book contains some of Mao's talks and letters on his theory of continuing revolution under the proletarian dictatorship.

Related Studies

The following biographical and political accounts of Mao present various perspectives on a complex person in a critical period in Chinese history:

Bouc, Alain. *Mao Tse-tung: A Guide to His Thought*. New York: St. Martin's Press, 1977.

Carter, Peter. *Mao*. London: Oxford University Press, 1976.

Fitzgerald, C. P. *Mao Tse-tung and China*. New York: Holmes & Meier Publishers, Inc., 1976.

Karnow, Stanley. *Mao and China*. New York: The Macmillan Company of Canada, Ltd., 1972.

Payne, Robert. *Mao Tse-Tung*. New York: Weybright and Talley, 1969.

Schram, Stuart. *The Thought of Mao Zedong*. New

York: Cambridge University Press, 1989. A useful survey and analysis by one of the leading researchers into Mao's life and thought. His 1967 biography, *Mao Tse-tung*, is an excellent study.

Terrill, Ross. *Mao: A Biography.* New York: Simon & Schuster, 1980; Touchstone Edition (paperback), 1993. A carefully documented, thoughtful, and lively account of Mao's life and thought by the author of *China in Our Time* (1992) and *Madame Mao: The White-Boned Demon* (1984 and 1992).

FUNG YU-LAN

Born: 1895, Henan (Honan) Province, China
Died: 1990, Beijing (Peking), China
Major Works: *History of Chinese Philosophy* (1930, 1934); *New Rationalism (Xin lixue/Hsin li-hsüeh)* (1939); *China's Road to Freedom (Xin shilun/Hsin shih-lun)* (1939); *A New Treatise on the Way of Life (Xin shixun/Hsin shih hsün)* (1940); *A New Treatise on the Nature of Man (Xin yuanren/Hsin yüan-jen)* (1943); *The Spirit of Chinese Philosophy (Xin yuandao/Hsin yüan-tao)* (1944); *A New Treatise on the Methodology of Metaphysics (Xin zhiyan/Hsin chih-yen)* (1946)

Major Ideas

The existence of things is a continuous process of their actualizing the li *by means of the* qi.
There are four spheres of living, namely, the innocent sphere, the utilitarian sphere, the moral sphere, and the transcendent sphere.
The function of philosophy is to help people attain the higher spheres.
There are positive and negative methods in metaphysics; the good philosopher should start with the positive and end with the negative method.

Fung Yu-lan was one of the most outstanding Chinese philosophers and historians of Chinese philosophy in this century. He was born in Henan (Honan) Province. When he was three years old his father passed the civil service examinations and became a county magistrate in Hubei, a neighboring province. While an undergraduate student in Shanghai, Fung became interested in Western philosophy, but to his great disappointment he found his teachers to be poorly grounded in Western thought. In 1915 Fung transferred to Peking University (now Beijing University) in order to study in the department of Western philosophy under a professor who himself had studied philosophy in Germany. Unfortunately, the professor died before Fung could enter the program and so Fung registered in the department of Chinese philosophy, where he acquired a solid foundation in Chinese thought. Later, Fung came to the United States to study and in 1923 received his Ph.D. in philosophy from Columbia University. Subsequently Fung taught philosophy at Qing Hua (Tsing Hua) University, the Southwest Associated University, University of Pennsylvania, University of Hawaii, and Beijing University. Besides professorships, his appointments also included Dean of the College of Humanities at the Southwest Associated University, President of Academic Affairs at Qing Hua University, academician of Chinese Central Academy, and board member of the Philosophy and Social Sciences Section of the Chinese Academy.

In 1949 when the Communists founded the People's Republic, Fung refused to move to Taiwan with the fleeing Nationalists and remained in Beijing. Like many prominent Chinese intellectuals of the time, he later participated in Maoist ideological reform. "I discovered Marxism-Leninism!" he declared. However, Fung was never really converted to Marxism, even though on several occasions he openly repudiated his own philosophy in favor of dialectical materialism. During the Anti-Confucianism Campaign in the 1970s, Fung became an intellectual consultant to a group of radical Communists in the central leadership, among whom was Mao's wife, Jiang Qing (Chiang Ch'ing). This was as close as Fung ever came to realizing his dream of becoming a philosopher-teacher of the ruler. He was a member of the Chinese People's Political Consultative Conference, a nominal advisory body of the Communist government, when he died in 1990 in Beijing.

Fung's own philosophy was developed during 1930s–1940s. Although Fung is best known in the West for his classic two-volume *History of Chinese*

Philosophy, his most original philosophical works are *New Rationalism, China's Road to Freedom, A New Treatise on the Way of Life, A New Treatise on the Nature of Man, The Spirit of Chinese Philosophy*, and *A New Treatise on the Methodology of Metaphysics*. These works constitute the core of his comprehensive philosophical system. Fung called them "the six books at the turning point," meaning that his philosophy marks a great historic social change in China.

Metaphysics: New Rationalism

In Fung's view, the most important contribution of Western philosophy to Chinese philosophy is its method of logical analysis, a method which might remedy a major weakness in traditional Chinese thought. Using this method, Fung developed "a new system," which he called "*Xin li xue/Hsin li hsüeh*," or "New *li xue*." *Li xue*, literally the "School of Principles," refers to the Neo-Confucianism of the Song (Sung) (960–1279) and Ming (1369–1644) dynasties. It was a rationalist school initiated by Cheng Yi (Ch'eng I, 1033–1107) and completed by Zhu Xi (Chu Hsi, 1130–1200). Fung identified himself with this tradition, but called his philosophy "a new tradition," with emphasis on the "new."

Fung's metaphysical system, which is presented mainly in his *New Rationalism*, consists of four main concepts, namely principle (*li*), material force (*qi/ch'i*), the substance of *Dao/Tao* (*Dao ti/Tao t'i*), and the Great Whole (*Da quan/Ta ch'üan*). These four concepts are expressed in a series of propositions with a prima facie presumption that "something exists." The first set of propositions is:

> Any and every thing cannot be but a certain thing. A certain thing cannot but belong to a certain kind of thing. If a certain kind of thing is, then there is that by which that kind of thing is that kind of thing.

The "that by which" (*yi zhao/i chao*) here is the *li* or principle of the kind. Fung explains that, for example, the reason why a mountain is a mountain

is that it possesses that by which a mountain is a mountain. If there are mountains, then there must be the *li* of mountains. Therefore it follows that "there is a thing of a certain kind" implies there is that by which that thing is that kind of thing, namely, there is a *li*. Furthermore, it is possible that there is the *li* of a certain kind of thing without there actually being a thing of that kind, but it is impossible that there is a thing of a certain kind without the *li* by which that thing is a thing of that kind. Therefore, the *li* is logically prior to the actual things of the *li*. Although we can logically infer that if there is not the *li* of a kind of thing, there cannot be a thing of that kind, from the fact that there is not a thing of a certain kind, we cannot infer that there is no such *li*. Therefore there may be more *li*'s than there are kinds of actual things.

Material Force

The second set of propositions starts with the claim that those things that can exist must have that by which they can exist. Logically speaking, things must have that by which they can exist before they do exist. This "that by which" is material force, or *qi*. Because there can be *li* of a kind of thing without there being a thing of that kind, the *li* does not actualize itself. It is the *qi* that actualizes the *li* and realizes actual things. Therefore, we can say that if there is the actualization of *li*, there must be *qi*. The *qi*, as pure matter, is something about which we can say nothing. Only when after it actualizes the *li* in a thing of a certain kind can we speak of it, but by then it is no longer the true, primordial *qi*.

The Great Whole

In the third set of propositions Fung claims that the existence of a thing is the process of actualizing a certain *li* by means of *qi*. All the processes of this actualization taken together are called "the substance of *Dao*." The concept of the substance of *Dao* signifies the nature of the continuous change and constant renewal of the universe. The universe here is not merely the physical universe, but the totality which includes everything that is. The sum total of "all that is" is also called "the Great Whole." The Great Whole contains not only things that have actual being, but also the *li* that has real but not actual being. At this point a paradox arises. As a concept, the Great Whole is an object of thought. But since the object of thought does not include the thought itself, taken as an object of thought the Great Whole is no longer the Great Whole that is supposed to include everything. Therefore, Fung concludes, the Great Whole cannot be thought. However, he insists, one must first attempt to think about the Great Whole in order to realize that it is unthinkable. In his words,

One must think about the unthinkable, yet as soon as one tries to do so, it immediately slips away. This is the most fascinating and also most troublesome aspect of philosophy.

Ethics: Four Spheres of Living

According to Fung, human beings are different from animals in that we are conscious of what we are doing, and this self-consciousness or understanding gives significance to what we do. The various significances which attach to a person's acts constitute what Fung calls the "sphere of living." Because different people, even though doing the same thing, may have different understandings of what they do, there are different significances attached to our lives and therefore various spheres of living. In *A New Treatise on the Nature of Man*, Fung classifies spheres of living into four categories: the innocent sphere, the utilitarian sphere, the moral sphere, and lastly the transcendent sphere. The innocent sphere is the lowest sphere of living. In this sphere a person simply follows the natural instincts or customs of his or her society without being self-conscious of, or clearly understanding, what he or she is doing. Therefore the acts have little or no moral significance.

In the second sphere, the utilitarian sphere, a person may have self-consciousness and be aware of oneself as a distinct individual. Such a person thinks only of the benefit to the self whenever anything is done. This does not necessarily mean that such a person is immoral. The acts may bring benefits to others. But the motivation is self-benefit. The acts are determined by the utility that these acts have for the self.

In the next sphere, the moral sphere, a person is aware that he or she exists only as a member of a whole society. Such a person will do things only for the good of the society. Thus such acts are always moral acts and possess moral significance.

Fung calls the highest sphere "the transcendent sphere." In this sphere a person's consciousness extends beyond the human society to the whole universe. One realizes that the universe is a Great Whole to which one belongs as a part. One thus can identify oneself with the universe and devote one's entire life to its course. Such a person is said to have the "knowledge of Heaven" (*zhi tian/chih t'ien*), to act "in service to Heaven" (*shi tian/shih t'ien*), to be "in unity with Heaven" (*tong tian/t'ung t'ien*), and finally to achieve "enjoyment in Heaven" (*le tian/le t'ien*). The transcendent sphere is Fung's version of the Confucian *ren* (*jen*): humanity.

Fung maintains that the first two spheres represent what human beings are by nature. Primitive and uncultivated people belong to these spheres. The moral sphere and transcendent sphere represent what humans ought to be and are the product of moral cultivation. People in different spheres may do different things. However, the real difference between these spheres is not primarily what people do, but what they think they are doing. People in higher spheres need not accomplish extraordinary things and in fact may achieve no more than do ordinary people. But they act with a higher understanding and hence attach a higher significance to their actions. They live and act in a state of enlightenment. The function of philosophy, according to Fung, is to help people achieve the two higher spheres of living, especially the transcendent sphere. A person cannot live in the moral sphere without understanding the moral principles he lives by, nor can a person live in the transcendent sphere without understanding the *Dao* of the Great Whole. Only philosophy enables a person to attain such understandings. Philosophical concepts such as *li*, *qi*, the substance of *Dao*, and the

Great Whole do not give us positive knowledge about the actual world; however, they have the power to enable us to realize the significance of living and to achieve our highest destiny. Toward the end of *The Spirit of Chinese Philosophy* Fung writes,

> If philosophy can enable men to become sage men [men of the transcendent sphere], then this is the usefulness of philosophy's uselessness. And should this coming to be a sage man be the reaching to the highest of what it means to be a man, this is the usefulness of philosophy's uselessness. This kind of uselessness may rightly be called the highest form of usefulness.

Methodology: The Positive and the Negative

In his *New Treatise on the Methodology of Metaphysics*, Fung maintains that there are two methods of metaphysics. One is the positive method. It is the method that endeavors to emphasize what can be said of the subject of metaphysics. It attempts to give as detailed descriptions and analysis of the subject as possible. The other method is the negative one. By not talking about the subject matter in a positive way, the negative method reveals some aspects of the nature of the subject matter. It reveals the aspects where the positive method cannot accomplish its task. The essence of the negative method is silence.

Fung believes that while in the West metaphysics has been mainly dominated by the positive method, the negative method has prevailed in traditional Chinese philosophy. This is particularly true in Daoism. Both Laozi (Lao Tzu) and Zhuangzi (Chuang Tzu) thought that one cannot learn what *Dao* is but can learn what *Dao* is not. Fung holds that the best way to do metaphysics is to combine the two methods. A good metaphysician should start with the positive method and end with the negative method. If one starts with the negative method, then nothing can be said and nothing can be differentiated. This leads to mysti-

cism. On the other hand, the nature of metaphysics determines that its ultimate object, the Absolute, cannot be described or analyzed. Like the Great Whole, such a concept escapes any analysis or positive descriptions. Yet, the philosopher, by showing that it is unthinkable, gets his idea across to his audience and brings enlightenment to ordinary people.

In *China's Road to Freedom* Fung puts forth his views on the social, political, and cultural reconstruction of Chinese civilization. His *New Treatise on the Way of Life* presents his ethic, and his interpretation of the historical development of Chinese philosophy is found in *The Spirit of Chinese Philosophy* and *History of Chinese Philosophy*. Fung's many other later works are included in his *Collected Works of Three-Pine Hall* (*San-song Tang Quan Ji/San-sung T'ang Ch'üan Chi*), published in the 1980s.

Fung's philosophy is perhaps the most comprehensive and original Neo-Confucianist system in this century. It demonstrates the influence of Western thought on Chinese thought as well as the great vitality of Confucianism. Even though in his later years Fung professed that he only wanted to be an historian of philosophy, in history he will be received primarily as a philosopher.

CHENYANG LI

Further Reading

Fung, Yu-lan. *The Spirit of Chinese Philosophy*. Translated by E. R. Hughes. Westport, Conn.: Greenwood Press, 1970. Chapter 10, "A New System," recapitulates Fung's *New Rationalism*. It also contains a summary of chapter 3 of his *New Treatise on the Nature of Man*.

———. *A Short History of Chinese Philosophy*. Edited by Derk Bodde. New York: MacMillan Publishing Co., Inc., 1948. Chapter 28 briefly summarizes the major parts of his philosophy system. The book itself is an excellent introduction to Chinese philosophy, a condensation of the major work cited below.

————. *History of Chinese Philosophy*. Translated by Derk Bodde. Volumes 1 and 2, Princeton, N.J.: Princeton University Press, 1952–3.

————. *Chuang-Tzu*. Beijing: Foreign Languages Press, 1989. A rewarding study.

Chan, Wing-tsit, trans. and comp. *A Source Book in Chinese Philosophy*. Princeton, N.J.: Princeton University Press, 1963. Chapter 42 is on Fung Yu-lan. It contains brief but insightful comments and discussions by Chan.

Day, Clarence Burton. *The Philosophers of China: Classical and Contemporary*. New York: The Citadel Press, 1962. There is a section on Fung Yu-lan (pp. 330–46), including a short "estimate of Fung Yu-lan."

INDIA

UPANISHADS

Authors: Unknown. The work of many Indian philosophers and teachers.
Date of Composition: c. 600–c. 400 B.C.
Type of Work: Philosophical and religious reflections expressed in prose and poetry. The prose *Upanishads* are: *Brihad-Āranyaka, Chāndogya, Taittirīya, Aitareya, Kaushītaki, Kena, Prashna, Maitri,* and *Māndūkya.* The poetic *Upanishads* are: *Katha, Shvetāshvatara, Īsha,* and *Mundaka.*

Major Ideas

Salvation is achieved through a knowledge of, and union with, the one, absolute Brahman (*the ultimate principle of all reality*), *rather than through rituals and sacrifices as taught by the* Vedas.
All being is created, sustained, and destroyed by Brahman.
The Absolute is beyond all categories of time, space, and causality.
Brahman *as* Ātman *is known to the person as the core self of the person* (ātman).
All that is not divine (māyā) *is created by* Brahman *as acts of divine self-concealment.*
To be entrapped in māyā *deepens ignorance and suffering.*
The Law of Karma, *the universal moral law of cause and effect, determines if there will be a reincarnation back into the world of* māyā.
Yoga, through disciplined efforts, are attempts to experience the divine within the self.
Practices of self-control, detachments, and duties appropriate to one's stage in life seek to overcome selfish individualism.

The word *Upanishad* has its root in three terms: *upa* (near), *ni* (down), and *sad* (to sit). The designation of prose and poetic works as Upanishadic implies that they are based on a "sitting down near" or at the feet of a teacher who, in dialogue with the pupil, examines the fundamental issues of existence. This personal face-to-face encounter with the Wise gave the term *Upanishad* the further connotation of a secret oral teaching passed down through the generations, thus constituting a learned and sacred tradition. The Sanskrit texts that emerge from this oral wisdom tradition of many anonymous sages represent the discussions and opinions of diverse priestly schools all united in their quest for *satyāsya satyam,* the reality of reality. Because of their antiquity and because they contain the essence of the Upanishadic tradition, thirteen works are designated as the *Principal Upanishads.* Collections of "Secret Teachings" have consisted of over 200 other works also called *Upanishads,* but they date mostly from the medieval period. These later works develop the traditions of the original *Upa-nishads* on issues of Yogic practice, asceticism, symbolism, and the various incarnations of the divine.

The *Principal Upanishads,* which serve as the broad foundation of India's philosophical thought, are also known as the *Vedānta,* that is, "the end of the *Veda.*" As Vedānta, the *Upanishads* present themselves as the hidden or real meaning of Vedic religious practice. In fact, they offer a revolutionary shift of focus in ancient Hinduism.

The 1,017 hymns of the *Rig Veda,* a work of great antiquity (c. 1500 B.C.), celebrate the activities of the gods manifested in the natural and the human world. In response to divine power and goodness, the *Vedas* call humanity to acts of sacrifice, prayer, and obedience, believing such devotions will please the deities and thus achieve salvation for the pious. With the *Upanishads,* we see a turn away from the hymnology of god and goddess to an earnest search for one universal reality that sustains the flux of being. This Upanishadic shift is analogous to pre-Socratic thought in the Greek world seeking to find a universal principle in contradistinction to Homeric polytheism. The *Upanishads* seek to discover the unchanging in all that is changing, to accomplish the hope expressed in the prayer of the *Brihad-Āranyaka Upanishad*: "From the unreal lead me to the real, from darkness lead me to light, from death lead me to immortality."

The *Upanishads* critique the ritualistic religion of the *Vedas*, especially the Vedic claim that external acts of piety are able to provide final liberation. Indeed, ritual has the opposite effect of tying a person to the flow of experience and thus causing further entanglement with the sensible world. The *Upanishads* advise the inward journey into the self, rather than the outward movement to the world. While the Vedic tradition rejoiced in the vitality of the universe, the Upanishadic tradition makes a deliberate turn to the human subject, and with this turn offers an intense preoccupation with human consciousness and all that flows from acts of self-reflection. In such acts, the enlightened person realizes that the deepest human longing is for meaning and purpose, an end to human restlessness, a final peace. In a world where all that is good appears to be destroyed by age and death, the seeker longs for the infinite in the finite, the absolute in the relative. Throughout the Upanishadic texts, the fulfillment of this longing is called *Brahman*.

Brahman

In the Vedic tradition, sacred prayers and hymns had the power to create, to cause growth or a swelling (*Brh*) of vitality. The term *Brahman* may have its roots in this idea of dynamic potency and energy that produces and sustains all reality. In the *Vedas*, *Brahman* is tied to the idea of magic formulas, sacred hymns, prayers, and knowledge. The term, therefore, also referred to the class of priests who alone knew the powerful mantras of the Vedic sacrifices. The Upanishadic shift from sacrifices to meditation led to a transference of the term *Brahman* from the office of priest and his power to the supreme power that creates, supports, and rules the whole universe. The *Upanishads* affirm that *Brahman* was the sole source of all thirty-three gods of the earlier Vedic period. The gods, like all crea-

tures, are equally subordinate to the one absolute Lord (*paramēshvara*). All this is prefigured in the words of the *Rig Veda*: "He who is the One existent, sages name variously."

Like the spider who weaves the thread or the fire that gives off the sparks, *Brahman* is the source of all being. He is the eternal that creates the temporal, the one source of the many as an ocean expresses itself in uncountable waves. The essence of the Absolute is dynamic self-expression; vital activity that manifests itself in all the vitality of the cosmos. Once created, the universe is held in being by *Brahman* as he guides all things to Himself. As the reality of all reality, *Brahman* is not only the source and ground of being, but also the cause of its destruction. Everything is lost in *Brahman*, the great infinite devourer, as bubbles return to the sea. *Brahman* is the innermost essence of reality and the case of all diversity. Within all things, He also stands absolutely transcendent of all being as its source and end. In the words of the *Chāndogya Upanishads*, *Brahman* is "The formed and the unformed, the mortal and the immortal, the abiding and the fleeting, the being and the beyond."

The Absolute is beyond all categories of time, space, and natural causality. He is the imperishable One who sees but is not seen, who comprehends all while all fail to comprehend Him. As inexhaustible and unbounded, *Brahman* is incapable of being captured by finite intellects. Our intellectual and sensible categories of space, time, and causality are inadequate for the Absolute. *Brahman*, by containing space, time, and causality remains uncontained within them. All empirical knowledge remains of the finite and, as such, the best it can affirm as it surveys the creation is that *Brahman* is "not this, not this" (*neti, neti*). The *Upanishads*, however, do not proclaim an agnosticism regarding the Absolute but rather that the royal road to knowledge of *Brahman* is knowledge of the self.

Brahman as Ātman

The Absolute of the universe, *Brahman*, is at the same time the ground of the Self (*Ātman*). The claim that *Brahman* is *Ātman* is a claim regarding the essential identity of God and the soul. The famous formula of the *Brihad-Āranyaka*: "*Aham braham asmi* [I am *Brahman*]" is an affirmation that the individual and the world are the manifestation of the same Absolute. The first principle of all being is to be found in human beings; the infinitely great without us is the infinitely great within us. The macrocosmic order is also the microcosmic order. Hinduism, through the *Upanishads*, is affirming that it is possible for every person to achieve what Christianity claims as the unique status of Jesus, perfect humanity and divinity made manifest in human life. The sages of ancient India proclaim no chasm between nature, humanity, and divinity. Here is Upanishadic Monism, that is, all existence is the manifestation of one single universal principle. The enlightened look to the self, to others, and to the whole universe and seeing *Brahman* in joy exclaim: "*Tat tvam asi* [That art thou]." This often repeated formula expresses the movement of thought from the lower level of particularity to the higher one of universality.

In that *Brahman* is absolute truth and pure consciousness, then everything that flows from the consciousness of the self is to some degree an experience of *Brahman*. When a person in an act of self-reflection knows and comprehends the self, the person is also comprehending the whole universe. Knowledge and being are identical, inseparable aspects of the same Absolute. To know truth is to become truth, for the essence of the self is conscious divinity. Thus, self-knowledge, especially intuitive self-knowledge, moves a person ever deeper into the Absolute, for *Ātman* is *Brahman*. This intuitive grasp of Being overcomes the duality of subject and object in a realization of the unity of all reality. Here is Upanishadic Idealism, that is, all existence is the expression of ideas, the manifestation of intellect and known only by intellect.

Another way the *Upanishads* conceptualize the relationship of *Ātman* and *Brahman* is to introduce another term, *purusha*. *Purusha* refers to a specific person with an individual self-consciousness, an ego, a personality, and a body. Throughout the text, we hear a plea to turn from this self-centered *purusha* to the absolute essence of the self. To move from *purusha* to *Ātman/Brahman* in acts of dynamic self-transcendence is to overcome the self-imposed boundaries that separate and differentiate one ego from another and the ego from God. Only in this way is a person able to find release from the illusions, evils, and rebirths of life.

Human Liberation from Māyā

Brahman is not only absolute power and intellect but also perfect bliss, the essence of every good. A person suffers to the degree that what is sought is not fully divine. The pressing problem that underlies the whole of the *Upanishads* is a quest for salvation from all the evils and difficulties of human life. Human liberation or release (*moksha*) is relationship with absolute bliss by overcoming the attachment to all that is not divine (*maya*).

Māyā, like the tricks of a magician, is the veil that hides the Absolute. *Māyā* is not illusion in the sense that the finite does not exist, rather, it is illusion in that the finite, although real, is not the reality of reality. In that all being emerges from *Brahman*, *māyā* is God's act of self-concealment. The *Upanishads* do not explore why God draws this veil over his face, but rather rests content in the affirmation that all beings reveal divine glory, while at the same time conceal the full essence of this glory. Measured by absolute perfection, all that is not *Brahman* falls short and, as such, is referred to as *māyā*, that is, shadows and illusions. *Māyā* has being, but it contains within itself non-being. The pursuit of these illusions—for instance, in the form of desire for wealth, power, or pleasures—all lead to entrapment in *māyā*. To separate one's own ego is likewise *māyā*. All these turns from the eternal to the flow of the finite lead to a life of ignorance and suffering.

The Law of Karma and Reincarnation

The quest for liberation often takes many lifetimes. The infinitely patient *Brahman* calls all humanity to himself in accord with human free will. For some, enlightenment is so completely achieved in their lives that they find complete release (*moksha*) from the flow of births and rebirths (*samsāra*). Others need to be reborn, to be reincarnated, that is, to return to *māyā* to continue to engage in the struggle for perfection.

Karma, a term that means action, is linked to the reincarnation experience as its ultimate cause. The Law of *Karma* affirms that one's next existence will be influenced by one's last existence. We reap what we sow. The theory of reincarnation tied to the Law of *Karma* will be offered in later Hindu tradition to explain the apparent unfair distribution of suffering. Suffering can be seen in this Upanishadic context as purgative, a purification for past lives that challenge the sufferer to overcome all attachment to *māyā*. Likewise, an early death, say that of a child, may be interpreted as all the living necessary for complete perfection. Most importantly, the Law of *Karma* is the claim that there is a universal moral law governing the whole universe akin to universal physical laws of causality. All that happens has a purpose. As the *Katha Upanishad* puts it:

> He who has not understanding, who is un-mindful and ever impure, reaches not the goal, but goes on to transmigration. He, however, who has understanding, who is mindful and ever pure, reaches the goal from which he is born no more.

Therefore, the destiny of the individual depends upon his or her character formed by intellect and will, for everything depends on knowledge (*vidyā*) and acts (*karma*). Thus, "He who knows the *Ātman* overcomes sorrow" (*Chāndogya Upanishad*). Final liberation is a state where even the self-imposed boundaries of individuality are transcended. To eradicate this last illusion of a separate self, where time gives way to timelessness, is the goal of Yoga.

Yoga

The achievement of enlightenment, to know the beyond that is within, requires disciplined effort—a disciplined effort to turn away from the world of the senses, of desire, and of individuality. *Yoga*, from its root *yuj*, implies both a yoke (that is, discipline) and a bond (that is, with *Brahman*). Throughout a process of disciplined concentration, the *yogi* seeks, through numerous techniques of bodily control, to abstract the self from the outside world. By looking within, the yogi desires to get beyond feelings, habits, and desire itself to a point that unifies all experiences. The goal of Yogic practice is complete detachment from *māyā*, complete attachment to *Ātman*. This focused concentration seeks to expand the constrictive self-imposed limits of time, place, and ego until they are all seen to evaporate in the limitless, formless One that is beyond all limits and forms. Yoga seeks to achieve the annihilation of the illusion of a manifold universe, which is why the *Upanishads* tend to elevate the experience of dreamless sleep as an ideal over that of normal, awake consciousness.

Ethics

However, because we must live awake in the world of *māyā*, the *Upanishads* offer guidance regarding the nature of good acts throughout life's journey. The ideal of Upanishadic ethics is self-realization, accomplished only when selfish individuality is overcome. To crave after finite things cannot satisfy the longings for the infinite. Thus the root of cravings must be overcome. Upanishadic ethics places the focus on the inward motive, for the seed of the deed is the motive. Hence the quality of an act tends to be judged by the intensity and quality of a person's self-control, detachment, and renunciation of the objects of desire. "They who seek the *Ātman* by austerity, chastity, faith, and knowledge . . . they do not return" (*Prashna Upanishad*). And elsewhere: "The fool chooses the pleasant out of greed and avarice" (*Katha Upanishad*).

Together with acts of self-denial, the enlightened act with kindness, nonviolence, and compassion. The biblical precept to love thy neighbor as thyself is in the *Upanishads* grounded in Upanishadic ontology. The neighbor is truly the self, for both are *Ātman* at the core. It is only mere illusion that deludes one into thinking of the self as separate from, and threatened by, the other.

A person's duties or obligations (*dharma*) depend upon a person's stage of life, one's toil (*āshrama*). The *Upanishads* delineate four stages of strife where selfishness is slowly rooted out. First, as a student the duty is to have reverence and obedience for the teacher and thus overcome pride. Next, as householder, mothers and fathers overcome self-centeredness as they give themselves to each other and to their children. Third, as old age approaches, a person relinquishes family duties and retires into the forest to meditate and pray. Finally, at the last stage before death, an ascetic person (*sannyāsin*) having experienced all this finite world can offer renounces it completely and seeks to perfect the virtues of chastity, poverty, truthfulness, and compassion. Here the aim is to overcome *samsāra* by a total non-attachment to *māyā*.

In all this, the ethics of the *Upanishads* is focused not primarily on the good of society, although enhancing the good for others is most important, but rather on self-interest in that the ultimate aim is to achieve personal salvation by overcoming attachments. This is why the ascetic wandering *sannyāsin* serves as a paradigm. He who possesses nothing in this world is the witness to, indeed the embodiment of, the claim that all things but *Brahman* pass away.

The Influence of the Upanishads

The struggle in the *Upanishads* to understand the meaning and interrelationship of the one and the many appears not to have had a widespread influence on the masses in its day. The power of the priesthood, sacrifice, and caste continued for the great majority. The lofty mysticism of the *Upanishads* could not compete with more popular mythologies. Vedic polytheism was reluctant to give way to Upanishadic monism. As a popular protest against the Vedic tradition, Buddhism may be judged more successful.

Although its immediate popular impact was slight, the *Upanishads*, by serving as the foun-

tainhead for much of South Asia's symbolic thought, had a very great and long-lasting influence on the history of philosophical and religious ideas. All later attempts to find the invisible in the visible returned to the Upanishadic tradition. Later religious literature would conceptualize *Brahman* as creator, preserver, and destroyer under the names *Brahmā*, *Vishnu*, and *Shiva*. Buddhism, even though it rejects the permanence and immortality of the soul, nevertheless stands within the Upanishadic call for self-realization, the rejection of *māyā*, and the attempt to eradicate cravings and narcissistic self-preoccupation. The extreme asceticism of Jainism could be traced to the Upanishadic indifference toward sensual pleasure. Later Yogic systems would look back to their Upanishadic source as would all conceptions of the unity and wholeness of the universe. The *Bhagavad-Gītā* (c. fourth century B.C.), which could be considered the quintessence of the *Upanishads*, presents the Absolute as personal, manifested in all that is personal and interpersonal. Thus Upanishadic is the *Gītā*'s proverb: "In thyself know thy friend, in thyself know thy enemy." In all these various systems, enlightenment is the key to salvation. They all accept some form of *karma* and rebirth; what is thought and what is done really matters in terms of final liberation. Also, the spirit of tolerance could be said to find its source in the Upanishadic spiritualization of the Vedic tradition, for all religious experiences have value in that they help humanity seek the eternal.

In the ninth century A.D., the influence of the *Upanishads* was greatly intensified—indeed, almost given a new life to the present day—through the efforts of the Hindu sage Shankara (A.D. 788–c. 820). His writings offered a systematic overview of the basic ideas of the *Upanishads* and were labeled *Advaita* because of their non-dualistic character, that is, a rejection of an equal status of matter with spirit. Shankara commentaries celebrate the Upanishadic tradition of pessimism regarding the world, yet express optimism regarding final salvation. This tradition remains fundamental for all Hinduism.

LAWRENCE F. HUNDERSMARCK

Further Reading

Translations

Hume, Robert Ernest. *The Thirteen Principal Upanishads Translated from the Sanskrit*. London: Oxford University Press, 1934. This is a very respected, precise translation. Hume's work also offers a comprehensive fifty-six page annotated bibliography.

Müller, F. Max, trans. *The Upanishads*. Vols. 1 and 15 of *The Sacred Books of the East*. Oxford: Claredon Press, 1879, 1884. This was an early and important translation that helped to popularize the *Upanishads* to the English-speaking world. Today the translation is thought to be somewhat antiquated.

Nikhilananda, Swami. *The Upanishads*. 4 vols. New York: Harper and Brothers, 1949–59. A good translation that offers a running commentary from an Advaitic perspective.

Radhakrishnan, Sarvepalli. *The Principal Upanishads*. New York: Harper and Brothers, 1953. This translation offers the transliterated Sanskrit text along with an excellent introduction to the major Upanishadic themes.

Related Studies

Beidler, William. *The Vision of Self in Early Vedanta*. Delhi: Motilal Banarsidass, 1975. A clear, learned study of the various uses of the term "self," as *purusha*, *Ātman*, and *Brahman*. By way of contrast, this work also offers a helpful discussion on the concept of the self in the *Bhagavad-Gītā*.

Deussen, Paul. *The Philosophy of the Upanishads*. Edinburgh: T. and T. Clark, 1906. This is still considered the standard comprehensive study of all the major philosophical themes by a scholar who is famous for his translation into German of some sixty *Upanishads*.

Keith, Arthur Berriedale. *The Religion and Philosophy of the Veda and Upanishads*. 2 vols. Harvard Oriental Series, vols. 31, 32. Delhi: Motilal Banarsidass, 1925. This important study is helpful in situating the *Upanishads* within, and in contrast to, the Vedic tradition.

Mehta, Rohit. *The Call of the Upanishads*. Bombay: Bharatiya Vidya Bhavan, 1970. A popular and reverent overview of the contents of eleven *Upanishads*.

Ranade, R. D. *A Constructive Survey of Upanishadic Philosophy Being a Systematic Introduction to Indian Metaphysics*. Poona, India: Oriental Book Agency, 1926. This is an easy-to-read general overview. The most helpful aspect of Ranade's work is his detailed index through which the reader can identify all the points made in the book as well as their source in the *Upanishads*.

Sharma, Baldev Raj. *The Concept of Ātman in the Principal Upanisads*. New Delhi: Dinesh Publications, 1972. The author's doctoral dissertation, which traces in a very detailed manner the use of the term *Ātman* in each of the *Principal Upanishads*.

BUDDHA (SIDDHĀRTHA GAUTAMA)

Born: c. 563 B.C., Kapilavastu, India
Died: c. 483 B.C., Kushinagara, India
Major Works: The Buddha's sayings were recollected and written down many years after his death. The *sūtras* (dialogues), which form a part of the Pali *Tripitaka*, are generally conceded to be the closest approximation to what the Buddha actually taught.

Major Ideas

Life in this world is basically one of suffering.
A person's good or bad actions (karma) *result in better or worse reincarnation.*
The highest goal consists in release (nirvāna) *from the cycle of reincarnations.*
Nirvana is achieved by following the Noble Eightfold Path.
Everyone should treat all beings as one would treat oneself.
A Buddhist strives to obtain the happiness of all living beings.
A person should accept a doctrine only if his own experience verifies it.

The Buddha was one among a handful of individuals in the story of mankind in whom humanity reaches its highest fulfillment. His noble character, his penetrating intellect, his love of humanity, and his transcendent wisdom has led to his adoration by millions. He was a philosopher, a doctor of the mind, and a religious leader. His disciples and followers represented a wide spectrum of social classes and included kings, bankers, housewives, and courtesans. The religion he founded spread from India to all of Asia and has enriched the lives of millions for more than twenty-five centuries. So tolerant and gentle was the Buddha's teaching that there is not a single example of persecution or the shedding of a drop of blood in converting people to Buddhism.

India, in the Buddha's time, was undergoing a widespread social transformation. The age of iron had arrived. Smaller states and republics were being taken over by larger, imperialistic states. The established Vedic religion had degenerated into mere ritualism. Society had stratified into rigid caste divisions, with the lower castes bearing the double burden of economic exploitation and social ostracism. Young, bright minds were seeking ideologies that would show individuals how to live meaningfully in an uncertain age.

The first fruit of the new intellectual striving was the philosophy of the *Upanishads*. In this philosophy the ultimate reality underlying the empirical world was designated *Brahman*. *Brahman* is transcendent, pure consciousness. The essence of a human being is also pure consciousness, the *Ātman*. *Brahman* and *Ātman* are one. Through ignorance, *Ātman* gets associated with a body and lives the life of a person. The right and wrong acts committed by a person form his *karma*. Good *karma* results in beneficial results in this life or in a future incarnation. Bad *karma* results in future harm. A person gets born again and again to reap the rewards of his acts. The world of *karma* and reincarnation is called *samsāra*. The ultimate goal, the *summum bonum*, is escape from *samsāra* to the final freedom, *moksha*.

Many bright, energetic young seekers after a new ideology were not satisfied with the Upanishadic philosophy. Although it was a significant departure from the Vedic ritualism, it did not go far enough. The Upanishadic way was tied to the Vedic tradition and its social values. The Buddha belonged to this stream of seekers in the non-Vedic tradition.

Siddhārtha Gautama

The Buddha was born about 563 B.C. His given name was Siddhārtha and the family name was

Gautama. Siddhārtha Gautama also came to be known as Shākyamuni ("Sage of the Shākyas") because he was born in the clan of Shākyas. The Shākyas were a warrior tribe inhabiting an area just below the Himalayan foothills. Gautama's father was a chieftain and Gautama was brought up as a prince. He lived a life of luxury. Even though his father arranged studies and training befitting a future king, Gautama was shielded from the knowledge of the trials of ordinary everyday life. Following tradition, Gautama's father arranged his marriage to Yashodharā, who bore him a son named Rāhula. For Gautama, the luxurious life of the palace was not enough. His father's attempts to shield him from harsh realities of life did not succeed. On his rare visits outside the palace Gautama noticed an old man, a sick man, and a corpse. He realized that the infirmities of old age and the pain of sickness and death highlight the inevitable sufferings of human life. He began wondering if there was a way of life that could conquer suffering and lead to tranquility of mind.

The search for a path that would radically overcome the sufferings inherent in the human condition became the driving force in Gautama's life. He decided to renounce his kingdom and his family and became a wandering ascetic. At first he pursued the path of Yogic meditation with two *Brāhmin* hermits. He succeeded in achieving high planes of meditative consciousness. But he was not satisfied by this path as it did not answer to his quest. Next he tried the path of severe austerities, including suspension of breathing and prolonged fasting. So severe were Gautama's austerities that he came close to death. But this path too did not answer to his quest.

Finally, he resolved to take his seat under the Bodhi Tree facing east and not to arise until he attained enlightenment. On the night of the full moon, Gautama ascended the four stages of trance (*dhyana*). All of the trances were characterized by concentration and accurate cognition. During the last hours of the night, Gautama acquired enlightenment (*Bodhi*) and became the Buddha (the Enlightened One).

The Four Noble Truths

The Buddha had seen the path that leads to the end of all suffering and to liberation (*nirvāna*). He now pondered whether the world was ready for such a deep teaching, but he finally decided to teach his doctrine. He traveled to Sarnath and gave his first sermon in the Deer Park. The Buddha was now thirty-five years old.

His first sermon is called "Turning the Wheel of *Dharma*." The Buddha calls his path the Middle Way, since he rejects both asceticism and hedonism as one-sided extremes.

> There are two extremes in this world, O monks, which the religious wanderer should avoid. What are these two? The pursuit of desires and indulgence in sensual pleasure, which is base, low, depraved, ignoble and unprofitable; and the pursuit after hardship and self-torture, which is painful, ignoble and unprofitable.
>
> There is a middle way, O monks, discovered by the *Tathāgata* [the Buddha], which avoids these two extremes. It brings clear vision and insight, it makes for wisdom and leads to tranquility, awakening, enlightenment, and nirvana . . .

The Buddha proceeds to proclaim his *Four Noble Truths*:

> "Now this, O monks, is the noble truth of pain (*duhkha*): birth is painful, old age is painful, sickness is painful, death is painful, sorrow, lamentation, dejection and despair are painful. Contact with unpleasant things is painful, not getting what one wishes is painful . . . "
> "Now this, O monks, is the noble truth of the cause of pain: that craving which leads to rebirth, combined with pleasure of lust, finding pleasure here and there, namely the craving for pleasure . . . "
> "Now this, O monks, is the noble truth of the cessation of pain: the cessation of that crav-

ing, abandonment, forsaking, release, non-attachment."

"Now this, O monks, is the noble truth of the way that leads to the cessation of pain: this is the *Noble Eightfold Path*, namely, right views, right intention, right speech, right action, right livelihood, right effort, right mindfulness and right concentration . . . "

Like a good physician, the Buddha has diagnosed the malady, found its cause, and prescribed a cure.

Behind this rather simple-sounding diagnosis and prescription lay a profound philosophical discovery. The first part of that discovery is what the Buddha called the "Three Characteristics of Being":

All constituents of being are transitory. Everything is impermanent. Beings come, become and go. What we believe to be enduring objects—physical objects and persons—are nothing but sequences of transitory events. It is our cravings and needs which drive us to create the illusion of permanence. We want to grasp and hold on to objects and persons or we hate and fear them. All this presupposes permanent objects.

All constituents of being are lacking in an ego. Our greatest illusion is that we ourselves are an enduring ego, which persists through a lifetime and even gets reborn. All the attachments of "I" and "mine" flow from this illusion. I, the enduring self, want to grasp and hold pleasures, collect property, fear or love others. But, says the Buddha, there is no enduring I. "I" is just a convenient label for a series of interconnected events.

All constituents of being are painful. According to the Buddha, the impermanent, transitory flux of events can never be the source of real happiness and peace; rather, they engender unhappiness because of our craving nature which can never be satisfied by the impermanent.

The second part of Buddha's philosophical discovery goes beyond impermanence to his theory of causation or the law of dependent origination (*pratītyasamutpāda*):

When this is present, that comes to be; from the arising of this, that arises. When this is absent, that does not come to be; on the cessation of this, that ceases.

In his theory of causation, the Buddha was following the middle path between Eternalism and Annihilationism. The Eternalists, following Vedic teachings, proclaimed that man's true self (*ātman*) is eternal. The Buddha argued against this theory, both because it was unproved and because it fed the flames of human cravings and created unhappiness. The Annihilists, on the other hand, claimed not only that everything was impermanent, but also that there were no connections between events and everything was a chance occurrence. The Buddha saw this to be a mistaken doctrine, both because it was patently false and because if this view was accepted there would be no cure for any disease nor a sure path to liberation.

The Buddha's law of dependent origination is the Middle Way. Everything is impermanent all right, but all happenings are conditioned by others and, in turn, form a condition for other happenings. In short, every event has a cause and causes others. In his "Discourse on Causal Relations" the Buddha mentions four characteristics of causation: (1) objectivity, (2) necessity, (3) invariability, and (4) conditionality. This law of dependent origination, which the Buddha discovered during the night of his enlightenment, forms the fulcrum for his entire system. Not only do his characteristic doctrines such as impermanence, no-self, and suffering flow from the law of dependent origination, but his diagnosis and cure for the sufferings attendant on the human condition are also based on it. This law also enabled the Buddha to give a Buddhist interpretation of the law of *karma* and rebirth. The Buddha conceptualized a person as consisting of five groups (*skandhas*): (1) bodily form, (2) feelings, (3) perceptions, (4) impulses, and (5) consciousness. At any given point in time, a person is a specific configuration of his *skandhas*. His state at a later time is a causal consequence of his earlier state. A potent factor in the causal sequence is a person's moral action. His wrong acts make his later state less favorable, whereas his right acts make it more propitious. This is the Law of *Karma*. Furthermore, this sequence does not end with a person's bodily death. The consciousness factor gets carried over to another newborn body. That is reincarnation with karmic residue. Since human suffering thus persists from life to life, the goal of nirvana, which is liberation from suffering and rebirth, gains supreme importance.

The Noble Eightfold Path

The aim of Buddhist practice is to end transmigration and attain final peace. The most essential and characteristic part of the teaching is a scheme of training and study to attain this aim. The excellent Noble Eightfold Path summarizes the training. The first two items, right views and right intentions, constitute Wisdom; the next three, right speech, right action, and right livelihood, constitute Morality; and the last three, right effort, right mindfulness, and right concentration, constitute Concentration. The movement from Wisdom to Morality to Concentration forms an upward spiral. The aspirant starts with a glimmer of wisdom, which motivates him to morality and beginning level concentration. Concentration, in turn, deepens the wisdom. Greater wisdom strengthens morality, which leads to higher levels of concentration. The growth spiral eventually leads to nirvana.

Buddhist morality is anchored in five principles of conduct. Right Action consists in abstaining from (1) taking life, (2) taking what is not given, (3) misconduct in pleasures, (4) false speech, and (5) intoxicating drink. Right Speech means abstention from telling lies; from backbiting, slander, and talk that may bring about hatred, enmity, and disharmony; from harsh, rude, malicious language; and from idle gossip. Right Livelihood means that one

should abstain from making one's living through a profession that brings harm to others.

These three factors—Right Action, Right Speech, and Right Livelihood—of the Noble Eightfold Path constitute morality. This moral conduct aims at promoting a happy and harmonious life both for the individual and for society. It is the indispensable foundation for all higher attainments.

In the scheme of Buddhist training the most important part is not moral conduct, which though essential is only a preliminary, but meditation, in which the truths about the nature of the universe and one's own being are contemplated and the consciousness becomes gradually abstracted and detached.

One powerful technique of meditation or concentration is called self-possession. It consists in mindfulness (*vipāssana*) meditation on the body, the emotions, thoughts, and *dharmas* (elements), such as the five *skandhas*. For example, the Buddha explains meditating on emotions:

> In this connection, monks, a monk feeling a pleasant emotion understands that he is feeling a pleasant emotion, feeling an unpleasant emotion understands that he is feeling an unpleasant emotion . . . he lives observing the nature of origination of emotions or observing the nature of cessation of emotions . . . thus he lives unattached . . .

Similar directions are given for mindfulness of the body, thoughts, and principles (*dharmas*). The goal is self-possession, leading to non-attachment.

Enlightenment is non-attachment and equanimity. There is no craving, therefore no suffering. Said the Buddha, "Knowledge arose in me and insight: my freedom is certain, this is my last birth, now there is no rebirth." This is nirvana, the Buddhist goal of life. Nirvana has been described as the Great Peace, perfection, extinction. The Buddha said that nirvana is indescribable.

The Buddha was questioned about whether the saint (who has achieved nirvana) exists or does not exist after death. He said that this question and others such as "Is the world eternal or non-eternal?" tend not to edification and therefore are improper. The main problem is suffering and end of suffering. Metaphysical disputes merely distract one from the goal. The Buddha claimed that a person who insists that metaphysical questions be answered before he would follow the path to enlightenment is like a man wounded by a poisoned arrow, who would not let the surgeon remove the arrow until he found out who shot the arrow, what his name was, and so on.

Among the founders of religions the Buddha was the only teacher who did not claim divine authority in any form. He attributed all his realization, attainments, and achievements to human endeavor and human intelligence. His philosophy is entirely based on observation and reasoning. His characteristic doctrines such as impermanence and dependent origination have an empirical justification. His rejection of metaphysical speculation is based on the philosophically sound insight that such questions are unanswerable on the basis of observation. For example, he compares the question "Does the saint exist after death or does he not?" to the question "Does the flame that has gone out, gone north or not?"

Many scholars have claimed that the Buddha was an empiricist and positivist philosopher. This is a dubious claim. Experience, for the Buddha, was a wider concept than ordinary sense perception. The Buddha claimed to have observed his own past lives and the reincarnations of other beings during the trance state before his enlightenment. So experience for the Buddha includes experience during Yogic meditation. Then there is the question whether the Buddha countenanced anything that could be termed unconditional or transcendental. Divergent answers to this question form the nucleus for the two major schools of Buddhism, Theravāda and Mahāyāna.

Theravādins believe that everything is conditioned and impermanent. Nothing is transcendent. Buddha was a human being, though a unique one, exalted above all others. The Theravādin form of religion consists in following the Noble Eightfold Path.

Mahāyānists, on the other hand, believe that there is the unconditional and the transcendent. Only the everyday, empirical world is conditioned and impermanent. They cite the Buddha's claim that nirvana is indescribable, as indicating the existence of the unconditioned. The Mahāyāna goes on to claim that the Buddha himself and many other beings form a part of the transcendental realm, and erects a full-fledged popular religion on that basis.

The Buddha taught his path of liberation for forty-five years. He maintained that only a person who has left the world and become a monk can achieve the final goal of nirvana. He encouraged his followers to form a community that came to be known as the *sangha*. But the Buddha also preached to the lay community, many of whom became his lay followers. It was understood that beyond the immediate aim of individual nirvana lies the objective of the happiness of the whole human society and the still higher objective of the happiness of all living beings. The basic Buddhist precept was to consider all beings as like oneself. Buddhists are encouraged to cultivate a set of four social emotions—friendliness, compassion, sympathetic joy, and impartiality. In a recommended meditation exercise, the meditator is asked to pervade the four directions successively with thought charged with friendliness, compassion, sympathetic joy, and impartiality by considering all beings as one considers oneself and by having thought that by being large, sublime, immeasurable, generous, and nonviolent, pervades the whole universe.

The Buddha's teachings paint a picture of the good society. The most important aspect of this society is that it is classless. All beings are equal before the moral law. The Buddha favored a republican government. His own community (the *sangha*) was organized on the republican model. The Buddha's refusal to appoint a successor and denying for himself the prerogative of exclusive guardianship of the *sangha* underline his republican preference. The Buddha's recommendations for a republican government were that the assembly should be held frequently and should aim at unanimity in its proceedings. Principles to be followed include "Elders should be honored and listened to" and "Women and girls should be protected."

The Buddha was well aware of the fact that republican governments were being replaced by monarchies. For the king, the Buddha recommends a policy of conciliation. The king should consult the wise men of his society frequently. He should uphold the ancient principles, such as honoring the elders. It is the king's duty to provide protection, safety, and shelter for not only the whole of society, but even beasts and birds. Policy of conciliation implies that punishment should be mild and taxes moderate. It is the king's duty to teach his subjects the five principles of good conduct, namely non-violence, non-covetousness, abstinence from sexual misconduct, truthfulness, and temperance. It is the king's duty to prevent poverty, the root of so many evils, by grants to the poor. The three economically productive classes of the society are to be given aid in producing prosperity: The farmers are to be supplied seed and fodder for cattle; traders are to be supplied with capital for their ventures; and the workers are to get decent wages. Ashoka, who ruled from 269 to 232 B.C., became a model emperor by following the precepts of the Buddha.

After forty-five years of strenuous and energetic teaching, the Buddha passed away at the age of eighty.

Everything, whether stationary or movable, is bound to perish in the end. Be ye therefore mindful and vigilant! The time for my entry into Nirvana has arrived! These are my last words.

NARAYAN CHAMPAWAT

Further Reading

Conze, Edward. *Buddhist Thought in India*. London: George Allen and Unwin Ltd., 1962. A careful and clear discussion of the main themes of Buddhist thought by a noted Buddhist scholar; represents the Mahāyānist point of view.

——— , ed. *Buddhist Scriptures*. Harmondsworth: Penguin Books Ltd., 1959. A Buddhist anthology that contains selections from all phases of the central tradition of Buddhism.

Rahula, Walpola. *What the Buddha Taught*. New York: Grove Press, 1974. An excellent, simple, and lucid guide to Buddhist thought by a Buddhist monk from Sri Lanka; represents the Theravādin point of view.

Warder, A. K. *Indian Buddhism*. Delhi: Motilal Banarsidass, 1980. A comprehensive, scholarly treatment of Buddhist thought, using original materials from Pali, Sanskrit, and Chinese writings.

MAHĀVĪRA

Born: Traditional dating of both Svetāmbara and Digāmbara Jainas: 599 B.C.; modern scholarship suggests a birthdate of 540 B.C.; northeast India
Died: Traditional dating of Svetāmbara Jainas: 527 B.C.; Digāmbara Jainas: 510 B.C.; modern scholarship: 468 B.C.; in Bihar, India

Major Ideas

Harmful activities cause the human soul (jīva) *to become mired in* karma.
The goal of human existence is freedom from all karma.
This freedom or isolation leading to perfect knowledge (kevala) *can be attained only through a gradual process of purification.*
This purification can be gained through the practice of nonviolence (ahimsā) *and other vows.*

Vardhamāna, as Mahāvīra was called at birth, was born to a woman of the *Kshatriya* caste named Trisala and her husband, a king named Siddhārtha. According to some accounts, this family followed the nonviolent teachings of an early ascetic teacher named Pārshva, who had died at least 200 years earlier. Vardhāmana, like his contemporary Siddhārtha Gautama, was married (according to the Svetāmbaras) at a young age, but at thirty renounced the world in search of higher meaning. For over twelve years, like other itinerant philosophers of India (*sādhus* or *sannyāsins*), he wandered throughout the Ganges river plain, fasting, meditating, and enduring the assaults of both men and beasts. Due to his efforts, he was given the title "Great Hero" or Mahāvīra, and eventually he attained the state of perfect isolation from all harmful *karma*, a state known as *kevala*. His entry into this state of blessed omniscience qualified him as the twenty-fourth *Tīrthankara* of the Jaina religion, the most recent great teacher of the tradition. His accomplishment was acknowledged by the title *Jina* (Victor), the term from which the name of the Jaina religion is derived.

According to the *Acaranga Sūtra*, the oldest of Jaina texts and dating from the fourth or fifth century B.C., Mahāvīra shared the view that life-forms pervade the elements (earth, water, fire, and air) and plants as well as animals, and that the key to spiritual advancement lies in the avoidance of injury to any life-form. Consequently, after renouncing his worldly ties Mahāvīra devoted himself to rigorous vows, including periodic fasting and silence. In one gruesome tale, his refusal to answer a cowherd's question resulted in the questioner stabbing blades of grass into his ears. Other sufferings that Mahāvīra endured included being struck with sticks and weapons and smeared with dirt. For weeks on end he would neither eat nor drink. Finally, sitting with joined heels in the heat of the sun, he achieved highest knowledge and insight, entering into *kevala*.

For six years, before the time he entered *kevala*, Mahāvīra took as his disciple a fellow wanderer named Makkhali Gosala. Having attained some limited magical powers, Makkhali Gosala proclaimed that he had achieved advanced spiritual status and, when rebuffed by Mahāvīra, he attacked Mahāvīra with his powers of heat (*tapas*). This assault backfired, and Makkhali Gosala later acknowledged Mahāvīra as the true spiritual leader. The followers of Makkhali Gosala, known as Ājivīkas, survived as an independent sect until the thirteenth century. Though only criticisms of the Ājivīkas remain, it seems that they taught a doctrine of spiritual immutability often confused with fatalism.

Although the subject of some dispute, some texts indicate that Mahāvīra followed a lifestyle based on Pārshva's Fourfold Restraint, which might have involved the practice of the four vows, nonviolence (*ahimsā*), truthfulness (*satya*), honesty (*asteya*), and nonpossession (*aparigraha*). According to later tradition, Mahāvīra added a fifth vow of sexual avoidance (*brahmacharya*). Eleven *Brāhman* priests renounced their priestly lifestyle to become followers of the Jina. All eleven disciples or *ganadharas* also achieved *kevala*. According to tradition, during the lifetime of Mahāvīra, Jainism grew to include 14,000 monks, 36,000 nuns, 159,000 laymen, and 318,000 laywomen.

Some 600 years after the death of Mahāvīra the community of Jainas divided into two, with one group traveling south to avoid famine. This group, known as the Digāmbaras, developed its own sacred texts, and insisted on total nudity for all advanced male monks. It furthermore stated that women, by virtue of their physiology, are not equipped to enter into *kevala*, which according to them is reserved only for men. Although the older sect, known as the Svetāmbaras, acknowledges that Mahāvīra and his eleven disciples were naked, they allow their current monastics to wear both an upper and lower robe, and state that women also are capable of achieving liberation. The Svetāmbaras state that Mahāvīra was married, while the Digāmbara tradition states that Mahāvīra remained a bachelor. According to the Digāmbaras, Mahāvīra renounced all possessions, including clothing, on the first day of his retreat from worldly life. According to the Svetāmbara story, thirteen months after he had left home Mahāvīra's loincloth was caught in a thorn bush and fell off, and he never again sought to clothe himself.

Jaina Teachings

Jaina teachings find systematic presentation in the *Tattvārthasūtra* of Umasvati (c. second century A.D.), where the cosmology, ethics, and spiritual path of the Jainas are described in detail. In summary, classical Jaina theory divides the universe into two categories, nonliving (*ajīva*) and living (*jīva*). The former category includes atoms plus principles of physics such as motion, rest, space, and time. The life category, as mentioned earlier, includes the notion that *jīvas* pervade all the elements, plus plants and animals. Each life force

contains energy, consciousness, and bliss, and takes repeated birth within a three-tiered universe. At the lowest level, *jīvas* dwell in hellish realms; in the middle, they exist as elementals, plants, animals, and humans; at the top, they take the form of gods. However, only in the middle realm and as a human can a *jīva* achieve *kevala*.

As a development of the principle of life as given in the *Acaranga Sūtra*, later Jainism teaches a hierarchy of life-forms. The most simple life forms, known as *nigoda*, resemble modern microorganisms, living in moist places and in flesh. Above these are earth bodies, water bodies, fire bodies, and air bodies. The highest grouping of life is found in plants and animals, which are arranged according to the number of senses they possess. All life-forms, including microorganisms and elemental bodies, are said to possess touch. Worms add taste; crawling bugs add smell; flies and moths add sight; water serpents add hearing. Mammals, reptiles, fish, and humans all possess six senses, adding mental capacity to the five senses listed above. Regardless of one's state of life, from a clod of earth to heavenly beings, repeated existence on the wheel of life is certain until one achieves human birth and begins the quest for liberation from *karma*.

The Theory of Karma

The theory of *karma* in Jainism is quite unique, being significantly more developed than *karma* theory in Buddhism or Hinduism. According to Jainism, *karma* is a material, sticky, colorful substance, composed of atoms, that adheres to the life force and prevents ascent to the *siddha loka*, the world of the liberated. This *karma* is attracted to the *jīva* by acts of violence, and the most violent of beings are said to be shrouded with clouds of blackish matter. Beings with increasingly less violent natures are said to be successively cloaked in blue, gray, orangish-red, and yellow *karma*, while the person of nonviolence is said to have only white *karma*. The Jainas further catalogued *karma* in 148 different possible forms known as *prakritis*, ranging from the destructive to the nondestructive, grouped in eight primary categories.

The path to liberation, according to classical Jainism, involves fourteen stages or *gunasthānas*. In the first state, one is mired in ignorance. At the fourth state, one catches a glimpse of liberation and numerous fettering *karmas* are released. In successive states, one takes up the five principal vows (nonviolence, truthfulness, non-stealing, sexual abstinence, and nonpossession) and overcomes the passions. The final state, obtained an instant before death, signifies the elimination of all remaining *karmas*. Today the followers of Jainism live according to the basic precepts that Mahāvīra taught. All Jainas are vegetarians. Members of the lay community traditionally involve themselves only with trades that avoid violence, engaging primarily in commerce, the arts, and publishing. Lay Jainas are known for their periodic fasts, and, on occasion, will wear face masks to avoid inhaling bugs.

Jaina monastics follow a more stringent lifestyle. Depending upon their religious order, they rarely stay in one place for a day or two. They eat only food that is given to them. Members of the Svetāmbara order own a minimum of possessions, while advanced Digāmbara monks own nothing at all, not even clothing. Monks and nuns of both orders carefully sweep the road ahead of them to avoid stepping on insects. In special cases, permission is granted at the end of one's life to fast until the point of death.

The Jaina community is now located primarily in Gujarat and western Rajasthan. Several thousands Jainas have immigrated to America and England. Modern Jainas continue to adapt their lifestyle to Mahāvīra's nonviolent teachings. They have been involved with nuclear disarmament campaigns, the advocacy of vegetarianism, and the release of test animals used in scientific laboratories.

CHRISTOPHER KEY CHAPPLE

Further Reading

Chapple, Christopher Key. *Nonviolence to Animals, Earth, and Self in Asian Traditions*. Albany, N.Y.: SUNY Press, 1993. A summary of the Jaina tradition and examples of modern Jaina practices.

Dundas, Paul. *The Jainas*. London: Routledge, 1992. Comprehensive historical survey of the Jaina tradition.

von Glasenapp, Helmuth. *The Doctrine of Karman in Jain Philosophy*. Bombay: Bai Vijibhai Jivanlal Panalal Charity Fund, 1942. Includes detailed lists of all 148 forms of *karma*.

Jaini, Padmanabh S. *Gender and Salvation: Jaina Debates on the Spiritual Liberation of Women*. Berkeley, Calif.: University of California Press, 1991. Presents Digāmbara and Svetāmbara texts on the title topic.

———. *The Jaina Path of Purification*. Berkeley, Calif.: University of California Press, 1979. Includes detailed descriptions of Jaina spirituality.

Tatia, Nathmal. *Studies in Jaina Philosophy*. Banares, India: Jaina Cultural Research Society, 1951. Excellent summary of Jaina philosophy as found in several traditional texts.

Tobias, Michael. *Life Force: The World of Jainism*. Berkeley, Calif.: Asian Humanities Press, 1992. Provides narrative examples of Jainism as practiced in modern India.

Williams, R. *Jaina Yoga: A Survey of the Mediaeval Sravkacaras*. London: Oxford University Press, 1963. Survey of vows as practiced by Jainas.

BĀDARĀYANA

Born: Probably fifth century B.C., India
Died: Probably fifth century B.C., India
Major Work: *Brahmasūtras* (*Aphorisms on The* Brahman)

Major Ideas

The Vedic Revelation has a unitary object, the Absolute or the Brahman, *a transcendent Being known only through that Revelation.*
The distinctive characteristic of that Being is its emanation of phenomenal reality.
The relation of this Absolute Being to phenomenal reality is one of Difference-in-Identity.

"Teacher of teachers, the splendor of the sacred sciences, Bādarāyana! From him arose the norm of sacred knowledge, for the sake of such beings as the gods." With these words the great Dualist Vedantin Madhva (A.D. 1238–1317) in *Anuvyākhyāna* extols the founder of the Vedantic system, who is evidently the creator of systematic theology itself (some centuries before its reputed inaugurator, Philo Judaeus of Alexandria, c. 15 B.C.–c. A.D. 45), as well as the author of the system's foundational work and the most commented-on text of Hindu theology, the *Brahmasūtras* (*Aphorisms of the* Brahman). Little is known for certain about his life.

Creation of the Vedic Canon

Indian religious thought displayed a preoccupation with system from its beginnings in the *Vedas* (c. fifteenth to ninth century B.C.), in the *Hymn to the Primal Man* (*purushasūkta, Rig Veda*). In that hymn the cosmos, its phenomena, and the human society it enfolds are correlated in their various parts to the several members of the Primal Man, whose dismemberment in the primordial sacrifice (performed by the gods) was the cause of their existence. Here we have a systematic theology of a sort, using images instead of concepts, a veritable *theologia poetica*. As for conceptualized systematic theology, it was foreshadowed in the work of post-Vedic thinkers such as Uddālaka Aruni and Yājñāvalkya, but it could not have arisen in the integrated, all-encompassing and articulate form provided by Bādarāyana before a canon of revela-

tion had been fixed. Hinduism was the first of any religions to establish such a canon, which it did by the eighth century B.C.

This canon turned out to be one vast and amorphous aggregate of ideas and ceremonial prescriptions, embodied in verse and prose, but it was thought there were basically only two themes, the ritual and the Absolute (the *Brahman*). No matter how prolix and verbose it was, the Vedic Revelation (*shruti*)—impersonally originant (*apaurusheya*) and subsisting eternally as subtle sound capable of being heard (*shruta*) only by the sages (*rishis*), and disclosed by them to mankind—was scrupulously and with great effort committed to memory. Writing was unknown, and later, when it came to be known, was judged to be an unworthy vehicle for the transmission of sacred knowledge.

Hindu thinkers soon set themselves to introduce order into the mass of revealed pronouncements. Their work would also need to be memorized, but, not being revealed, it could not demand the same effort at memorization. Their merely human pronouncements would have to be brief; the briefer they were, the better chance they had of being memorized.

To meet the need for brevity, the *sūtra* or aphorism was invented. Literally it means "thread," for it is a mnemonic formula for holding together a complex of concepts (intended to be verbally explained by the teacher), just as a thread holds together beads or jewels. This new literary form, unparalleled anywhere in the world, was used to formulate disciplines in a compact and orderly manner, a form capable of being easily memorized and of recalling to mind the verbal instruction elaborated round it.

Twelve Partial Systematicians of the Vedas

A group of twelve thinkers, evidently contemporaries, appears to have been engaged in ordering the contents of the Vedic Revelation. They described their efforts as "inquiry." As there were two major topics of the *Vedas*—ritual and the *Brahman*—the investigation on ritual was known as *Pūrva Mīmāmsā* (the *Precedent Inquiry*), and that on the *Brahman*, which presupposed ritual, was called *Uttara Mīmāmsā* (the *Subsequent Inquiry*) or *Vedanta* (the end or goal of the *Vedas*). Some of these thinkers—men such as Aitishāyana, Ālekhana, Kāmukāyana, and Lāvukāyana—were engaged exclusively in the *Pūrva Mīmāmsā*. Others—such as Audulomi and Kāshakritsna—seem to have concerned themselves entirely with the *Vedanta*. Others were experts in both *Inquiries*, including Āshmarathya, Ātreya, Bādarāyana himself, Bādari, Jaimini (the organizer of *Pūrva Mīmāmsā*, believed to have been Bādarāyana's own pupil), and Kārshnajini. Both Bādarāyana and Jaimini, who seldom disagree, are the arbiters of the orthodox position in each *Inquiry*, but they also quote themselves, the views they thus express possibly being those that they had held before they became orthodoxy's mouthpieces and systematizers.

Techniques of Systematization

Early systematization of the revealed pronouncements appears to have consisted in *topical classifications* (*adhikaranas*)—for instance, of the sacrifices and rituals—with judgments on the problems that these topics raised. But in due course *principles of interpretation* (*nyāyas*) emerged, which aided in the clear and consistent formulation of such judgments. From the methodical application of principles to topics there arose the *Topical Method* of discussion, the *adhikarana* method, where various views on each topic were propounded, with arguments for and against them, and

a conclusive judgment pronounced. In later Hindu thought this method (subsequently reflected in the *disputatio* of European Scholasticism), had five parts: (1) theme (*visaya*), (2) doubt (*vishaya*), (3) dissentient views (*pūrvapaksha*, or "anterior wing"), (4) orthodox judgment (*siddhānta*, "settled conclusion," also known as *uttarapaksha*, or "posterior wing"), and (5) relevance (*prayojana*).

Although the *sūtra* works composed in accordance with this method were systematic presentations of various features of the Vedic Revelation, they were also (and indeed chiefly) an exegesis on its declarations. In other words, each topic was based on at least one particular revealed utterance, which was known as the *Topical Text* (*vishayavākya*). The text was sometimes alluded to by a *sūtra*'s borrowing a word from the text itself—a cue word that prompted the student, who knew all the revealed texts by heart, about the precise text he was required to recall.

The Comprehensive Systematics of Bādarāyana's Aphorisms on the Brahman

Finally, the *adhikaranas* or topics required organization into a comprehensively ordered work. This was done by assembling them into chapters subdivided into sections. All these techniques of analysis were incorporated by Bādarāyana in his great synthesis, structured into four chapters (each chapter having four sections):

> *Chapter 1. Correlation* or *Order* (*samanvaya*), a synchronization of the pronouncements of Revelation (the *Upanishads*, but also plausibly the *Vedas* themselves) on the *Brahman*.
> *Chapter 2. Non-contradiction* or *Concord* (*avirodha*), a demonstration of the consistency of the Vedantic doctrines on the *Brahman*, and of the *Vedanta*'s invulnerability to attack by hostile systems.
> *Chapter 3. Salvific Means* or *Way* (*sādhana* or *marga*), the means to the attainment of the *Brahman*.
> *Chapter 4. Result* or *Fruit* (*phalam*), the fruition of the *Brahman* thus attained.

The *Brahmasūtras* had a unitary object, the Absolute, to which ritual was subordinated. They were quadripartite in literary form, but were based on a tripartite conceptual pattern, which might be described as Absolute–Emanation–Return. Bādarāyana derived it, at least in part, from the Upanishadic sage Uddālaka Aruni, who first envisaged the primordially existent Being (*sat*) and then the phenomena emanating from it (fire, earth, and water), and ultimately returned to it through absorption. It came to be generally agreed by Vedantins that Reality consisted of three categories: the Absolute (*Brahman*), the individual soul (*jīva*), and material reality (*jada*)—infinite consciousness, finite consciousness, and the unconscious, respectively.

The tripartite pattern was to be used later by systematicians of other religions, as in the monumental works of Catholic systematics—those of Aquinas (c. 1225–74), Scotus (c. 1265–1308), and Suárez (1548–1617). This pattern enabled Bādarāyana to establish the relationship between the three categories which, however, are usually arranged in dichotomies, such as absolute and phenomenal, independent and dependent, and spiritual and material, the members of one dichotomy not being necessarily equivalent to the corresponding ones of another. According to this dichotomous classification, the Absolute would be independent and spiritual, and the individual soul and material reality-dependent, and partly spiritual and partly material. For Bādarāyana these categories, absolute, independent, and spiritual on the one hand, and phenomenal, dependent, and material on the other, were identical in essence and different only in mode. In other words, the relationship between the categories of Reality was neither solely one of Identity or Non-difference (*abheda*), nor entirely one of Difference (*bheda*), but one of Difference-in-Identity (*bhedābheda*).

Bādarāyana's Theology

The Absolute was the supreme (*para*) reality and was identical with the Self (*ātman*): a substance at

once pure Being and pure Consciousness, a substance qualified by attributes, some negative, like infinity, and some positive, like light; a substance whose essence was joy (*ānanda*) and emanatory power. For from it, by a mysterious transformation (*parināma*), emanated the unconscious material world, made up of five elements—space, air, fire, water, and earth. From the last three of these elements were formed material bodies, which were then controlled by indwelling deities or by individual souls (*jīvas*). These souls were the infinitesimal and indivisible particles of the Absolute, which somehow did not sunder its infinite and impartite nature. They participated in the Absolute's consciousness, but possessed their own individual awareness as well.

In addition to being conscious and knowing, the individual souls were agents, enveloped by physical and visible organisms, or bodies, through which they conducted their activity. This activity (*karma*) accumulated and coalesced into a quasi-spiritual and invisible organism, which also functioned as an envelope for each individual soul. The soul, then, was contained in two bodies, the visible Gross Body (*sthūla sarīra*) of flesh and blood, and the invisible Subtle Body (*sūkshma sarīra*) of *karma*. The former was perishable but the latter self-perpetuating; the process of its self-perpetuation, or transmigration (*samsāra*), separated the individual soul from the supreme Self and obstructed its participation in the Self's essential joy. Only through knowledge or gnosis, attainable through meditation (*upāsana*), could this transmigratory process be terminated and liberation attained.

Liberation, the Goal of Man (*purushārtha*), was achieved after death. Once realized, the soul retained its identity, acquiring from the Absolute the power to fulfill its desires, but not to create, conserve, and destroy the world.

The Philosophical Elaboration of the Vedanta

Bādarāyana achieved perfection, but it was a perfection of a limited sort. His *Brahmasūtras* supplied Vedantic systematics with its skeleton only; the nerves, veins, and flesh had to assimilated from elsewhere. The Father of the Vedānta had a keen sense for the symmetrics of a doctrinal organism, but he was unable to interrelate the members (or tenets) of this organism in a philosophical way. In other words, he combined a genius for doctrinal architectonics with a philosophical naiveté. For instance, to the question of how the impartite and spiritual Absolute can change into the multipartite material world, his reply is "as milk transforms into curds."

Indeed, of the three norms of knowledge (*pramāna*), experience (*pratyaksha*), logic or inference (*anumāna*), and Revelation or Word (*shabda*), he assigned primary importance to the latter, which in some strange way he identified with experience. Logic for him served only to refute doctrines contrary to the *Vedas*. However, alongside his Vedanta, there developed systems of thought that made extensive use of logic in elaborating their positions. They formed two groups, the orthodox (*āstika*), those who accept the normativeness of the Vedic canon, and the heterodox (*nāstika*), those who deny that normativeness. The orthodox systems included *Sānkhya* ("Enumerationism"), a dualist cosmology explicating the concepts of bondage and liberation; its companion system *Yoga* ("Methodicism"), the formulator of a meditative technique for realizing that liberation; *Nyāya* ("Logicism"), a system of logic for achieving liberation through clear thinking; and its companion system *Vaisheshika* ("Specificism"), a theory of physics, the specifics of material reality. Prominent among the heterodox systems was Buddhism, whose thinkers evolved a logic of a complexity and refinement rarely equaled and inaugurated a critical philosophy consisting of a dialectic for destroying metaphysics through its own assumptions.

Bādarāyana's successors availed themselves of these forms of speculation to create systems of the Vedānta that are the climax of Indic thought. Into the structure provided by Bādarāyana they assimilated the Sānkhya cosmology, the Yoga meditational technique, the Nyāya logic, the Vaisheshika

physics, and the Buddhist critical epistemology. Their mastery of Buddhist logic suggested to them a counter-dialectic—one calculated to destroy critical philosophy through its own assumptions and thus to reinstate metaphysical and dogmatic thought.

The Vedantic Schools

All these elements were combined to produce a luxuriance of theological systems, which may be classified into three groups: non-sectarian, Vaishnava, and Shaiva, as follows:

Non-sectarian or without clear sectarian affiliation:

Non-dualism (*advaita*) or Absolute Non-dualism (*kevalādvaita*), of Gaudapāda (c. 640–c. 690), Vedantized by Shankara (fl. c. 700–750).

Conditioned Difference-in-Identity (*aupādhikabhedābheda*) of Bhāskara (c. ninth century).

Indivisible or Impartite Non-dualism (*avibhāgādvaita*) of Vijnānabhikshu (sixteenth century).

Vaishnava or of presumed Vaishnava affiliation:

Consciousness Non-dualism (*cidādvaita*), of Yādavaprakāsha (date uncertain).

Immaculate Non-dualism (*vishuddhādvaita*), of Vishnusvāmin (date uncertain).

Qualified Non-dualism (*vishishtādvaita*), of Yāmuna (c. 918–1038), Vedantized by Rāmānuja (c. 1056–1137).

Dualism (*dvaita*) of Madhva (1238–1317).

Innate Difference-in-Identity (*svabhāvikabhedābheda*) of Nimbārka (thirteenth to fourteenth centuries).

Pure Non-dualism (*shuddhādvaita*) of Vallabha (1481–1533).

Inconceivable Difference-in-Identity (*acintyabhedābheda*) of Caitanya (1486–1533).

Differentism (*bhedavāda*) of Shuka (date uncertain). Vaishnava?

Shaiva

Shiva Non-dualism (*shivadvaita*), of Shrīkantha (thirteenth century).
Energy-qualified Non-dualism (*saktivishishtādvaita*), of Shrīpati (fourteenth century).

These systems are modalities of the integrative concept that underlies Bādarāyana's system, the relationship of the phenomenal to the Absolute. This relationship, declares the *Gītā*, was "often celebrated by the sages severally in various hymns and by the well-reasoned and conclusive *Aphorisms of the Brahman* too." In these words, what is perhaps the greatest of Hindu scriptures pays tribute to what is perhaps the greatest work of Hindu theology, and indicates its basic achievement—the incorporation of the mysticism of the inspired pronouncements of the Vedic Revelation in an intellectual, integrated, and comprehensive system.

JOSÉ PEREIRA

Further Reading

Adams, George. *The Structure and Meaning of Bādarāyana's Brahma Sūtras (A Translation and Analysis of Adhyāya 1)*. Delhi: Motilal Banarsidass, 1993.

Ghate, V. S. *The Vedānta. A Study of the Brahmasūtras with the Bhāṣyas of Saṁkara, Rāmānuja, Nimbārka, Madhva and Vallabha*. Poona, India: Government Oriental Series, Class C., No. 1. 1926. The pioneering work in the study of Bādarāyana's thought.

Nakamura, Hajime. *A History of Early Vedānta Philosophy*. Vol. 1. Delhi: Motilal Banarsidass, 1983. Learned and detailed presentation of early Vedanta. Nakamura doubts that Bādarāyana is the author of the *Brahmasūtras*.

Pereira, José. "Bādarāyana: Creator of Systematic Theology." *Religious Studies* (Cambridge, England), 22 (1986): 193–204. Discussion of Bādarāyana's date.

———. *Hindu Theology*. New York: Doubleday, 1976, and Delhi: Motilal Banarsidass, 1991. Translation of thirty-one aphorisms of chapter 1 of Bādarāyana's work (pp. 240–246), along with the *Topical Texts*.

Radhakrishnan, S. *The Brahma Sūtra: The Philosophy of Spiritual Life*. New York: Harper, 1960. Translation of all the *sūtras*, but unreadable, and from a Non-dualist standpoint.

Sharma, B. N. K. *The Brahmasūtras and their Principal Commentaries: A Critical Exposition*. Bombay: Bharatiya Vidya Bhavan. 3 vols: Vol. 1 (1971), vol. 2 (1974), vol. 3 (1978). The most thorough commentary to date on the *Brahmasūtras*, from the Dualist Vedantin point of view, but the Non-dualist and the Qualified Non-dualist positions are also presented.

BHAGAVAD GĪTĀ

Author: Attributed to Vyāsa (dates unknown)
Written: Between fifth and first centuries B.C.
Type of Work: Religious epic, metaphysics, ethics

Major Ideas

Man's true self is ātman, *which is beyond space–time.*
Man's highest goal is moksha, *the release from transmigration in the space–time world of everyday life.*
God is the creator and sustainer of the universe.
One path to release involves doing one's duty without attachment to the fruits of action.
Another path to release consists in loving devotion to God.
True devotion to any deity will lead the devotee to God.

The *Bhagavad Gītā* (*The Song Sung by the Lord*) is one of the great religious classics of the world. It is perhaps the earliest attempt by man to arrive at a comprehensive view of existence. The most important teaching of the *Gītā* is that man can achieve his highest good by action that is not motivated by the desire to obtain some personal benefit, but rather by the desire to do his duty (*dharma*) for its own sake.

The *Bhagavad Gītā* may have been composed as early as the fifth century B.C. or as late as the first century A.D. It is part of the great Indian epic, the *Mahābhārata*. The poem consists of 700 verses divided into eighteen chapters. The *Gītā* is a dialogue between Krishna, an incarnation of God, and Arjuna, a warrior, setting forth a vision of a fulfilling spiritual life. According to the Indian tradition, the *Gītā* embodies the essence of the most sacred Hindu scriptures, the *Vedas*. In a striking image, a Sanskrit verse pictures Krishna as drawing the milk *Gītā* from the *Vedas* (pictured as a cow), for Arjuna the calf.

The *Gītā* has proved to be a very influential work through the ages. Almost all classical Indian philosophers, notably Shankara and Rāmānuja, wrote commentaries on the *Gītā*. So did the contemporary Indian thinkers Sarvepalli Radhakrishnan, Gandhi, and Aurobindo. The *Gītā* was translated into English by Charles Wilkins in 1785. It is now available in more than thirty languages and about 1,000 individual editions.

To understand the teaching of the *Bhagavad Gītā*, it is necessary to place it in its religio-philosophical and cultural context.

The religious life of the Indo-Āryans, who came to India in the middle of the second millennium B.C., centered around the *Vedas*. These holy books represented the revealed wisdom which guided the spiritual life of the Indians. The Vedic way of life was life-affirming. By the middle of the first millennium B.C., there was, however, a significant change. Life came to be viewed as essentially unsatisfactory. A firm belief in *karma* and transmigration added to growing pessimism. If one lifetime is unsatisfactory, an endless chain of rebirth and re-death would be a catastrophe. Thus the state of liberation (*moksha*) from life and death came to be seen as the highest goal of life.

Ātman and Brahman

The *Upanishads*, which are the culmination of the *Vedas*, developed a philosophy with *moksha* as the *summum bonum*. According to the *Upanishads*, the real self of a human being is *Ātman* (spirit), which is not in space and time. The *Ātman* is only contingently and temporarily connected with the body. The whole material universe is founded on *Brahman* (the Universal Spirit). *Brahman* is Being, Consciousness, and Bliss. *Brahman* and *Ātman* are one. Fundamentally, the sorrows of human life are caused by human beings misconceiving their own nature. Although the human self is *Ātman* (spirit), the self identifies itself with the bodily self and thus suffers through cycles of rebirth. When the human being recognizes its true self and the identity of the true self with *Brahman*, the human self is released and is reborn no more.

The teachings of the *Upanishads* created a strange tension within Hindu social life. Hindu morality was based on *Dharma*, eternal laws of moral order. Society was divided into four orders: *Brāhmans* (priests), *Kshtriyas* (warriors), *Vaishyas* (commoners), and *Shudras* (serfs). Each life span was also divided into four stages: student, householder, forest dweller, and hermit. Thus any human being at any point would belong to an order (*varna*) and a stage (*āshrama*). The moral code (*dharma*) would spell out all the duties pertaining to one's *varna-āshrama*. Any person who was dutiful would attain a better and better birth until Heaven was attained. Similarly, those who did evil would descend to Hell, but anyone who exhausted the stored good *karma* would have to leave Heaven and be reborn on Earth, as would the denizens of Hell. Action, therefore, could not provide an escape from the cycle of birth and death. The orthodox tradition said, "Follow your *varna-āshrama dharma*." The *Upanishads* said,

> Following *dharma* will not bring *moksha* [liberation]. The only way to obtain *moksha* is to give up action, become a hermit and seek the highest wisdom of the identity of *ātman* and *Brahman*.

Many of the best of the Hindus left the world of action. The rise of Buddhism added to the same world-negating tendency, for the Buddha too had maintained that life was unsatisfactory and the only way to nirvana lay in leaving the worldly life and becoming a monk.

The teaching of the *Bhagavad Gītā* came as an answer to a life-threatening crisis in Indian society. If the best were to shun action in society, how would society survive? In the *Bhagavad Gītā*, Krishna puts forth a convincing vision of life where a man can follow his *dharma*, perform actions, and

yet escape rebirth and attain liberation. No wonder the *Bhagavad Gītā* became the most revered Hindu scripture.

The Dialogue Between Krishna and Arjuna

The setting of the *Bhagavad Gītā* is a battlefield that symbolizes life itself. The Pandavas and the Kauravas are cousins who have assembled on the battlefield to settle the claim to the kingdom of Hastinapura. The kingdom rightfully belongs to the Pandavas, who are good men. But the evil Kauravas are denying the Pandavas their right. War is the only alternative. Arjuna, the mighty Pandava warrior, is a friend of Krishna, the incarnation of God. As the battle is about to begin, Arjuna loses his resolve. When he notices that winning this war would mean killing his grandfather, his teachers, and his cousins, he lays down his arms and says, "It would be wrong to fight and win at such human cost." Krishna, who has volunteered to be Arjuna's charioteer, now feels called upon to explain to Arjuna why it is his duty to fight. The ensuing dialogue between Krishna and Arjuna constitutes the *Bhagavad Gītā*.

Krishna begins by advising Arjuna that it is his *dharma* (duty) as a warrior to fight a righteous war. Emotional considerations are irrelevant. But as the dialogue proceeds, the teaching gets deeper and deeper, and its scope widens until a whole philosophy of life is set forth.

Krishna's first teaching is that the self Arjuna takes himself to be is not his real self. Arjuna, like most of us, believes that his self (*jīva*) consists of his body and his mind, joined in a very intimate connection. It is *jīva* that suffers and transmigrates. But, says Krishna,

> Your real self is *ātman* [spirit]. *Ātman*, the transcendental self, does not suffer or transmigrate. It is unborn and undying. It is pure consciousness and it is an observer only, never a doer. *Ātman* finds itself lodged in a body and mistakenly identifies itself with *jīva*. All suffering is a result of this misidentification.

When *atman* realizes its true nature, it is released (*moksha*).

Just as the body–mind self is not all there is on the human level, so too empirical reality is not all there is on the macro level of the whole universe. The universe is founded on and sustained by a Supreme Being. The Supreme Being is a pure consciousness, beyond space and time.

Every object in the ordinary, empirical world is composed of three *gunas* (strands). They are *sattva* (goodness), *rajas* (passion), and *tamas* (darkness). Every human being, too, is composed of the three *gunas*, intermixed in a unique proportion. A person's temperament and character expresses his *guna*-nature. In *Brāhmans*, *sattva* predominates and in Warriors, *rajas* predominates. In *Vaishyas* (i.e., traders, farmers, and artisans) we find a mixture of *rajas* and *tamas*, whereas *tamas* rules the serfs.

The moral code (*dharma*) of Hindu society is based on two considerations, promoting the growth and well-being of the individual, and promoting the well-being of society (*lok-samgraha*). *Dharma* is ordained in such a manner that the well-being of the individual and society coincide. Moreover, each person's duty (*sva-dharma*) is based on his *guna*-nature.

Karma Yoga: The Path of Action

Krishna's task, in the *Bhagavad Gītā*, is to show Arjuna his duty and at the same time show him the path to *moksha*. Arjuna is a warrior. It is his *dharma* to fight a just war. His own well-being, as well as society's well-being, requires his doing his duty. He will obtain society's approval, self-esteem, and heaven if he follows the warrior's path. But what about *moksha*? Just doing one's duty may gain Heaven but not *moksha*. According to the *Upanishads*, the only path to liberation was the Path of Knowledge (*Jnāna Yoga*), the knowledge that the *atman* and the Supreme are one and that the empirical world has a lower degree of reality. Krishna does not reject this path. But he says that for people like Arjuna and for most of humanity there is a

better path. This path is called *Karma Yoga* or Path of Action.

Most people act with the desire to gain some personal benefit. The *Gītā* calls the personal benefit derived from an action its fruit. Krishna claims that it is not action itself but action done with attachment to the fruit that binds a person to the wheel of reincarnations. If a person were to act without attachment to its fruit (*nishkāma karma*), his actions would have no karmic consequences. But why act if one is not attached to the fruit of action? Krishna says, "It is for universal well-being [*lok-samgraha*]." He cited himself as a being who has no self-interest, but who nevertheless acts to uphold the world order. The most important moral teaching of the *Bhagavad Gītā* is that of *nishkāma karma*: Everyone should be dutiful (*dharma*) for universal well-being, but without attachment to the fruit of action.

Thus Krishna adds the Path of Action (*Karma Yoga*) to the Path of Knowledge (*Jnāna Yoga*) as a way of obtaining *moksha*. He recommends *Karma Yoga* as being superior because it is conducive to universal well-being and a person's *guna*-nature requires action.

So far we can see how *Karma Yoga* leads to the good by eliminating karmic effects of action, but how does it lead to *moksha*? Remember that *moksha* consists of the recognition of the true nature of the self, which is *atman*. It is the turbulent nature of the mind that conduces to self-forgetfulness. A person pursuing *Karma Yoga* becomes desireless, is not shaken by adversity, and does not restlessly pursue happiness. Such a person is free from affection, fear, and anger, and is unattached and indifferent to benefit or harm. The senses are withdrawn, and one is in the world but not of it. The mind of such a person attains perfect calm. One sees one's true nature as *atman* and is liberated.

Krishna's teachings up to this point have not involved his Godhead. But, in fact, Krishna is the Supreme Being. He is the one who creates and sustains the universe. He is the foundation of the world, which is only a particle of him. He is much more. In the tremendous theophany of chapter 11 when Arjuna asks if he may be vouchsafed the sight of Krishna's universal form, Krishna grants him special vision. Arjuna sees universes being created and destroyed in Krishna's person. The *Gītā* presents the conception of an incarnation of God (*avatāra*). Krishna is an *avatāra* of the Supreme God, *Vishnu*. Krishna says, "Whenever there is a decline of righteousness and lawlessness flourishes, I send forth myself [as an *avatāra*]" (chapter 4, verse 7).

Krishna proclaims yet a third way to *moksha*, the Path of Devotion (*bhakti yoga*). *Bhakti* is a unique relationship between God and man based on mutual love. God is not only the Lord, but also a friend, brother, son, or lover. Krishna played all those roles in his sojourn on this earth. If a man is a true devotee of God, the God will release him from the cycle of reincarnation and give him a place near God. Krishna says to Arjuna,

Do works for Me, make Me your highest goal,
be loyal-in-love to Me, cut off all attachments,
have no hatred for any being at all: for all who
do thus shall come to Me. (chapter 11, verse
55)

The *Bhagavad Gītā*, therefore, sets forth three paths of liberation: Knowledge, Action, and Devotion. Krishna at first suggests that Devotion is best, Action is the next, and Knowledge is third best. However, the *Gītā* is a harmonizing doctrine. In the best Indian tradition, it prefers "both/and" to "either/or," so Krishna ends by saying that the very best way is to combine all of them. In fact, Shankara, one of the outstanding Indian thinkers, did combine all these paths in his life. It is also suggested in the *Gītā* that the best path for a given individual might depend on this *guna*-nature. A *Brāhman* might find the Path of Knowledge best and a warrior might take to the Path of Action more readily. Krishna thought that women and artisans and even serfs might find Devotion more conducive to their nature.

Although the *Bhagavad Gītā* calls for a radical transformation in the life of an individual, it favors social conservatism. A man's duties are defined by the prevailing social norms. Krishna claims that he created the four classes (not castes, since the rigid caste system was a much later development). One's class status imposes its specific duties. Krishna says that it is better to perform one's own duty poorly than to perform another's duty well. He firmly believes that universal well-being results from maintaining the existing social order.

An outstanding feature of the *Bhagavad Gītā* is its religious tolerance. Krishna says, "Whoever with true devotion worships any deity, in him I deepen that devotion; and through it he fulfills his desire" (chapter 7, verse 21).

The book also provides some amelioration for the underprivileged. Krishna says that the Path of Devotion is open to women and to *Vaishyas* and *Shudras*. This opens up the religious life to all. Ram Mohun Roy, the great Indian social reformer, used the *Gītā* in his arguments against the practice of suttee (widow burning). Mahatma Gandhi used the *Gītā* in his crusade against the evils of untouchability.

The *Bhagavad Gītā* is a work devoted to harmonizing diverse points of view. It follows the great Indian tradition of believing that many different points of view can all be true and many different paths can lead to the highest good. Consequently, throughout history different thinkers have been able to appeal to the book to justify their differing positions.

Shankara, the first great commentator on the *Bhagavad Gītā*, was a firm advocate of the Path of Knowledge as the only path to *moksha*. So he interpreted the *Gītā* in such a way that the Path of Action and the Path of Devotion were seen as preparatory to Knowledge. Rāmānuja, on the other hand, was a great devotee of *Vishnu*. His commentary makes the Path of Devotion the highest path and the other two as auxiliary. The American Transcendentalist Henry Thoreau viewed the *Gītā* as giving form to the ideal of Yogic discipline emphasizing solitude, chastity, and austerity. B. C. Tilak, a leader of the Indian nationalist movement, claimed that a follower of the teaching of the *Gītā* would be a committed fighter for India's independence from British rule.

Mahatma Gandhi's use of the *Bhagavad Gītā* is

the most interesting of all. No book was more central to Gandhi's life than the *Bhagavad Gītā*. He constantly referred to it as his "spiritual dictionary" and "the mother who never let [me] down." Gandhi was the greatest apostle of nonviolence since the Buddha. By contrast, Krishna aims at convincing Arjuna that he must fight a war that would be the most violent in India's history. Gandhi resolves the apparent contradiction by his allegorical interpretation of the *Gītā*. The war between the Pandavas and the Kauravas symbolizes the war going on in the heart of every man between good and evil. Krishna's advice to Arjuna is that a man cannot quit the battlefield; he must fight for good and against evil. In order to be a successful fighter a man has to become a man of discipline who has succeeded in controlling his senses and his feelings of attachment and lust. He must become a *Karma Yogin*. Gandhi was such a man.

The *Bhagavad Gītā* has attained its status as a spiritual classic by providing a road map and a guide to countless millions in their difficult journey through the vicissitudes of human life and eventually to their highest good.

NARAYAN CHAMPAWAT

Further Reading

Translations

Radhakrishnan, S. *The Bhagavadgītā*. London: Allen and Unwin, 1948. With an introductory essay, Sanskrit text, English translation, and notes by India's most famous twentieth-century philosopher.

Zaehner, R. C. *The Bhagavad Gītā, with Commentary Based on Original Sources*. London: Oxford University Press, 1969. The most thorough treatment of the *Gītā*. Includes introduction, translation, and commentary with an appendix of main topics.

Related Studies

Minor, Robert. *Modern Indian Interpreters of the Bhagavad Gītā*. Albany, N.Y.: SUNY Press, 1986. The perspectives of Indian scholars illuminate the *Gītā*.

Sharpe, Eric J. *The Universal Gītā*. La Salle, Ill.: Open Court Publishing Co., 1985. A survey of the Western images of the *Bhagavad Gītā*.

PATANJALI

Born: India, date unknown; estimates range from 200 B.C. to A.D. 400
Died: India, date unknown; estimates range from 150 B.C. to A.D. 450
Major Work: *Yoga Sūtras*

Major Ideas

The various ethical and aesthetic practices of India can be synthesized.
The means to achieve Yoga or meditation is restraint of mental fluctuations.
The body and breath can be used to stabilize the mind.
The mind can enter into states of absorption.
Discriminative discernment is the key to liberation.

Meditation is an important aspect of religion in India. Originating perhaps from reinterpretations of Vedic rituals, or possibly stemming from indigenous practices hinted at in the seals of Mohenjodara and Harappa, it was advocated by adherents to various Indian religions: Brahmanical Hinduism, Jainism, and Buddhism. Apparently drawing from several different schools and traditions, Patanjali composed a brief textbook, designed for memorization, in which he summarizes and concatenates several Yogic meditation techniques. This manual was commented upon through the centuries and has become the standard guide for both the theory and practice of meditation in India.

Yoga Sūtras

Patanjali's text, composed in the Sanskrit language, is divided into four sections (*pādas*): Concentration (*samādhi*), Practice (*sādhana*), Empowerment (*vibhūti*), and Isolation (*kaivalyam*). Although some scholars have speculated that he knitted these sections together from five or more earlier texts, the repetition of key themes blends each of these sections with one another. One key theme emphasizes gaining control over the mind. Another involves the cultivation of an ability to discern the difference between the *seer* (one's unchanging true self, referred to as *drashtri*, *ātman*, or *purusha*) and the *seen* (the realm of manifestation and change, referred to as *drishya*, *parināma*, or *prakriti*). When one is able to master the mind and dwell in the state

of "pure seeing," then one is said to achieve what is referred to as a state of isolation (*kaivalyam*), free from negative influence (*akliha karma*), also known as absorption in the "cloud of virtue" (*dharma megha samādhi*).

In the first section of the text, Patanjali lays out his metaphysical, epistemological, and logical premises. He states that thought (*citta vitti*) causes one to stray into the realm of the seen in five forms: valid cognition, error, conceptualization, sleep, or memory. Through the application of dispassion and practice, thought can be restrained (*nirodha*), thus generating the desired state of "abiding in the seer's own form." His metaphysics reflect that of the Sāmkhya School, which, relying on images drawn from Vedic texts, posits a twofold psycho-spiritual reality: the liberated seer and the personality bound to identification with the seen. The ills of the world can be cured by adopting a correct epistemological stance that distances one from attachment to the seen. The logic is driven by a concern to become free from the pervasive suffering (*duhkha*) warned of by both the Buddhists and the followers of Sāmkhya. Above all, Yoga is a soteriological system.

Several practices are advocated by Patanjali to enable one to enter into the Yogic state. Some of these are also found in Buddhism, such as his advocacy of faith, energy, mindfulness, concentration, and wisdom, as well as his listing of friendliness, compassion, happiness, and equanimity. Other practices recommended in the first section include devoting oneself to a meditative ideal (*īshvara-pranidhāna*); chanting; controlling the breathing; cultivating one-pointedness, illumination, or detachment; reflecting on an auspicious dream; or meditating "as desired."

In the second section, he lists two distinct yet overlapping systems: a threefold Yoga including austerity (*tapas*), study, and dedication to a meditative ideal, and the eightfold Yoga for which he is best known. The first phase of this eightfold system entails application of fivefold ethic (*yama*), identical with the ethical system practiced by Jainas: nonviolence, truthfulness, non-stealing, sexual restraint, and non-attachment. Following this, Patanjali lists five positive observances (*niyama*): purity, contentment, austerity, study, and dedication to a meditative ideal, the last three of which are listed earlier as a separate Yoga system. These two fivefold aspects of Yoga practice constitute a prescribed way of being in the world that mitigates the negative influence of worldly action. He then lists two physical modalities of accomplishing Yoga: postures (*āsana*) and breath control (*prānāyāma*). Withdrawal of and control over the senses (*pratyāhāra*) constitute the fifth aspect of the eightfold system, followed by three "inner" limbs: concentration (*dhāranā*), meditation (*dhyāna*), and absorption (*samādhi*).

The various categories of *samādhi* mentioned by Patanjali are of significance for understanding the Yoga system. In his usage of two related terms (*samprajnāta* and *samāpatti*), he first indicates states of concentration associated with thought, reflection, bliss, and a pure sense of ego. He later alludes to a state of absorption wherein the difference between subject and object dissolves. This latter state begins with focusing on an external object (*savitarkā*); this then gives way to a more purified state (*nirvitarkā*). At the next level, internal objects, such as the residues of past action (*samskāra*), serve as the focus, with both a preliminary (*savicāra*) and advanced state (*nirvicāra*) mentioned by Patanjali. All these forms are said to be "with seed," indicating that they hold the potential to stimulate continued detrimental involvement with the "seen" (the realm of manifestation and

change). As skill in *nirvicāra* develops, the influences of past action are worn away and one enters into the state of seedless (*nirbīja*) *samādhi*, a state that in other sections of the text seems to be equated with *kaivalyam*, *dharma megha samādhi*, and the notion of pure seer (*drashtri*).

The Benefits of Yoga

An interesting digression within the thought of Patanjali is his discussion of the powers that accrue during the practice of Yoga. Various benefits are said to arise with the cultivation of the tenfold system of ethics mentioned above in the description of the Noble Eightfold Path. When one is rooted in nonviolence, hostility is said to cease in one's presence. From truthfulness is said to come the ability to speak the future; from the practice of not stealing, great contentment arises; from sexual restraint, vigor; from nonpossession, wisdom regarding the nature and origin of things. From purity comes cheerfulness; from contentment, happiness; from austerity, a perfected body; from study, "union with the desired deity"; and from dedication to the meditative ideal comes the state of *samādhi*. As one turns to the inner limbs of Yoga, the accomplishments and benefits of practice become increasingly esoteric, including such *siddhis* as knowledge of how language works, an ability to remain hidden or to increase one's physical strength, and an understanding of the inner energy centers of the body (*cakras*).

Despite these detours, Patanjali remains true to his central theme advocating control over the mind's processes. In each of his sections, he reminds the reader (or listener) to work at discerning the difference between the ephemeral world of change and the safe refuge of the seer. This knowledge (*viveka khyātir*) holds the key to undoing the influences of past action or *karma*, thereby allowing ascent to the unfettered state of *kaivalyam*.

A Theory of Karma

Of particular interest is Patanjali's theory of *karma*. In the first section he states that various forms of *samādhi* with seed (*sabīja*) serve to counteract the influences (*samskāras*) of past *karma* or action. In the second section, he notes that *karma* is rooted in five afflictions: ignorance, egoism, attraction, aversion, and clinging to life. As long as such *karma* persists, one is subject to future birth and the various sorrows that ensue. The goal of Yoga is to avoid the inevitability of future karmic pain by eliminating affliction and attachment. Patanjali defines the Yogi as one whose *karma* is neither black nor white nor mixed. When one achieves the state of *dharma megha samādhi*, Patanjali states, that afflicted action (*klishta-karma*) ceases; later commentators claim that one then enters into the state of living liberation (*jīvan-mukta*).

The importance of this text is evident from the many times it has been commented upon. The most famous commentary was written by Vyāsa in the sixth or seventh century A.D., followed by commentaries by Vācaspati Mishra (c. A.D. 850), Bhoja Raja (early eleventh century), and Vijnānabhikshu (sixteenth century). The text also was translated into Persian, and commentaries and summaries of Patanjali have been written in Arabic by Al-Biruni.

CHRISTOPHER KEY CHAPPLE

Further Reading

Chapple, Christopher, and Yogi Ananda Viraj (Eugene P. Kelly, Jr.), trans. *The Yoga Sūtras of Patañjali: An Analysis of the Sanskrit with Accompanying English Translation*. Delhi: Sri Satguru Publications, 1990. A grammatical and philosophical analysis of the text, with occasional explanatory comments.

Dasgupta, Surendranath. *Yoga as Philosophy and Religion*. Delhi: Motilal Banarsidass, 1924. A comprehensive summary of Yoga's foundation in Sāmkhya metaphysics and an exposition of Yogic ethics and practice.

Eliade, Mircea. *Patañjali and Yoga*. New York: Schocken Books, 1969. A discussion of Yogic techniques and their relationship to the *Upanishads* and the *Bhagavad Gītā*.

———. *Yoga: Immortality and Freedom*. Princeton, N.J.: Princeton University Press, 1958. A survey of Yoga including its relationship to Brahmanism, Buddhism, Tantrism, and alchemy.

Feuerstein, Georg. *Yoga-Sūtra: An Exercise in the Methodology of Textual Analysis*. New Delhi: Arnold Heinemann, 1979. An excellent analysis of prior textual studies of the *Yoga Sūtras*.

———. *The Yoga-Sūtra of Patañjali: A New Translation and Commentary*. Folkestone, Kent: Dawson, 1979.

Woods, James Haughton. *The Yoga-System of Patañjali*. Delhi: Motilal Banarsidass, 1914. Includes the English translation of Vyāsa's commentary and Vācaspati Mishra's subcommentary.

NĀGĀRJUNA

Born: India, date unknown; between first and second centuries A.D.
Died: India, date unknown; between first and second centuries A.D.
Major Works: *Mūla-madhyamaka-kārikā* (*Verses on the Fundamental Middle Way*), *Vigrāha-vyāvartani* (*Refutation of Objections*)

Major Ideas

All things, ideas, events, and so forth, are "empty," meaning they do not cause or define themselves, but arise and cease due to conditions.

Under close scrutiny even the most rationally constructed positions and systems—including Buddhism—are demonstrably incoherent and irrational.

Things can never adequately be explained either in terms of themselves or in terms of their relations to other things.

No entity arises from itself, from another, from both itself and another, or from neither itself nor another.

All thinking presupposes the categories "identity" and "difference," but these categories are incoherent and have no referent.

Language does not refer to things, but is self-referential.

There are two levels of discourse, the conventional and the ultimate; one learns the latter through the former, and realizes Nirvana *on the basis of the latter.*

Our deepest emotional and existential problems stem from clinging to cognitive positions and presuppositions.

The deep-seated, driving propensity to create the illusion of conceptual order through self-justifying rationalizations can be overcome and eliminated.

Nāgārjuna, one of India's greatest philosophers, lived during a time of great diversity and change for Indian Buddhism. Roughly 500 years after Buddha's death, Buddhist schools were proliferating, debating the whole range of Buddhist doctrines and practices. They were also engaged in serious arguments with non-Buddhist schools. The most important and innovative of these new schools produced a new literature that it claimed went back esoterically to Buddha himself: this new literature was called *Prajñā-Pāramitā* (*Perfection of Wisdom*). Its most distinctive feature was a reanalysis of all the earlier doctrinal models designed to show they all implicitly involved the notion of *shūnyatā* (emptiness). For Buddhists, both the *Prajñā-Pāramitā* literature as well as the notion of emptiness came to be associated with Nāgārjuna; in fact, they became synonymous with his teachings.

Nāgārjuna is the first individual associated by tradition with Mahāyāna Buddhism, the form of Buddhism that developed from the *Prajñā-Pāramitā* literature, dominant today in Tibet, East and Central Asia, and Vietnam. For Mahāyanists, Nāgārjuna is considered second only to Buddha in importance and depth of insight. Although those writings that we can confidently attribute to Nāgārjuna display a quick, sober, logical, and deeply insightful mind, his reputation became so great that soon many fanciful legends were attached to his name.

Legends of Nāgārjuna

Aside from knowing that Nāgārjuna was born in southern India and that he came north to achieve some degree of prominence at Nālandā, the central seat of Buddhist learning until the thirteenth century, all the details we have of his life are deeply embedded in legends. He is reputed to have been a magician and a playboy, who, when caught taking his pleasure with some of the royal ladies by a local king, had a moment of profound remorse, became a monk, and thereafter devoted himself wholeheartedly to Buddhist teachings. Reflecting these sorts of stories, several Tantric and magical texts, such as the *Ratnamāla*, have been ascribed to him.

In the ancient Hindu scripture, *Rig Veda*, numerous myths about Vritra the Dragon describe how, in primordial times, she lived in the depths of the sea holding back all beings in the undifferentiated waters of her belly (*asat*, Nonexistence). Everything was trapped in Nonexistence until the Vedic hero Indra slayed her, splitting open her belly and releasing all the repressed waters and beings, which then flowed out into Existence (*sat*). Buddhists refashioned this psychological cosmogonic story of the actualization of potentialities by discarding the violence and making Nāgārjuna the hero. In the Buddhist version, Nāgārjuna travels deep into the ocean depths to the home of the *Nāgā* King. *Nāgās* are dragonlike beings usually extremely hostile to humans. Nāgārjuna discourses on *Dharma* (Buddhist teachings) with the king, who is so delighted with what Nāgārjuna says that he allows him to return to the surface and gives him the complete corpus of the *Prajñā-Pāramitā* literature as a parting gift, telling Nāgārjuna that these are the authentic words of the Buddha, which he has kept safely locked away in the depths of his ocean lair since Buddha's death, awaiting a sage wise enough to disseminate them to humans.

Nāgārjuna is thus credited with literally bringing this "hidden" literature to light. According to Candrakīrti (eighth century), the most important commentator on Nāgārjuna's works, the myth signifies Nāgārjuna scouring the depths of human ignorance in order to bring the liberating Wisdom of the Buddha to the surface, from the depths of darkness to enlightenment. *Prajñā-Pāramitā* texts continued to be written for many centuries after Nāgārjuna, and many of these were pseudepigraphically attributed to him. In China, the most important of these is the *Dazhi dulun (Ta chih-tu lun)* (*Great Liberating Wisdom Treatise*), which, despite presenting ideas very much at odds with those in Nāgārjuna's main texts,

quickly became a foundational source for East Asian interpretations of Nāgārjuna.

Emptiness

The most important, and most misunderstood, term used by Nāgārjuna is "emptiness." It does *not* mean a cosmic void, nonexistence, a *substratum nihilum*, or a denial of the world(s) of common experience. Nor does it signify a mystical *via negativa*. Rather it signifies the absence of something very precise: *svabhāva*, or self-essence. "Self-essence" is a technical Indian philosophical term denoting anything that creates itself (sui generis), is independent and immutable, possesses an invariant essence, and is self-defining. Usually Hindus also envision self-essential things as eternal. The two most important self-essential things in Hindu thought are God and the Self (or soul).

According to standard Buddhist doctrine, the subtlest, deepest, and most dangerous false view held by humans is the belief in a permanent, independent self. Our sense of "self" derives from "misreading" the causes and conditions of experience. Afraid of death and the possibility of our personal nonexistence, we desperately impute and cling to permanence where there is none, imagining that something permanent subtends the flux of experiential conditions. Rather than recognize causes and conditions for what they are, we hypostatize their obvious effects, often deeming these hypostatized entities to be more real than what we encounter in actual experience. Thus the notion of "self" is symptomatic of our deepest desires and fears. Overcoming that view by seeing that all that comes into existence does so dependent on perpetually changing causes and conditions (*pratītya-samutpāda*) is to "see things as they truly become" (*yathā-bhūtam*).

Buddha had spoken often of a "Middle Way" between extreme views. The two extremes he discussed most often were "Eternalism" and "Annihilationalism," or, put in other terms, "continuity" and "discontinuity." Things (the world, persons, objects) are neither continuous nor discontinuous. Things are neither reducible entirely to their specific causative conditions, nor ever something other than their conditions: this is the Middle Way.

Nāgārjuna understood the basic message of Buddha to be the elimination of all hypostatic theoretizations—abstractions that had been concretized to the point of seeming more real than the conditions from which they had been abstracted. Such views he called *drishti*. For Nāgārjuna, however, the problem of hypostatization was not confined to the notion of self, but was apparent everywhere, since all seemingly rational explanations of the way things are—including the Buddhist explanations of his day—were grounded in conceptual entities that were ultimately unreal (such as self, God, nirvana, and so forth). All our fundamental notions, including time, actions and the agents of action, the characteristics with which things are defined and classified, relations, and so on, all were infiltrated by *drishti*. Nāgārjuna recognized that at bottom *drishti* hinged on the notions of "identity" and "difference." Identity was simply another name for self-essence: a continuous, invariant, self-identical essence. Difference presupposed the very notion of identity that it attempted to negate, since to claim "*X* is different from *Y*" presupposes that *X* and *Y* have determinate identities; and if taken seriously such that "difference" marks the complete absence of all identities, difference would entail such radical discontinuity, disjunction, and lack of intelligibility that even the most mundane things would become incoherent and inexplicable. In his major work, the *Mūla-madhyamaka-kārikā*, Nāgārajuna constructed a methodology for ferreting out *drishti* such that the middle way between identity and difference might be realized. "Empty" signifies what occurs through causes and conditions and is therefore devoid of self-essence. Everything, when seen properly, is devoid of self-essence, and thus "empty." It is the self-essence that is unreal, not the flux of conditions (though Nāgārjuna also warns against hypostatizing "conditions").

Verses on the Fundamental Middle Way

The *Mūla-madhyamaka-kārikā* (*Verses on the Fundamental Middle Way*), in twenty-seven chapters of varying lengths, takes up virtually all fundamental religious, philosophical, and doctrinal issues. The school that founded itself on his teachings, the *Madhyamaka* (the Middle Way-ers), took its name from the title of this text. Written in a precise couplet verse form (and in a style of great poetic beauty), it is at the same time one of the most logically rigorous treatises ever written.

Nāgārjuna employs a strategy designed to force either definitions or relations into at least one of three unsatisfactory consequences: (1) *tautology*, (2) *mutually exclusive contradiction*, and/or (3) *infinite regress*. He implements this strategy by exploiting a fundamental incoherence in the notions of "identity" and "difference," notions without which thinking cannot proceed. Since anything that might be taken under consideration must either be taken by itself (and thus understood in terms of its definition) or in relation to other things, Nāgārjuna's strategy is comprehensive. Nāgārjuna repeatedly demonstrates in the course of his arguments that things can neither be adequately explained in terms of themselves in isolation ($X = X$, a tautology), nor in terms of their relations with other things ($X = Y$, $X \neq Y$, $X \leftrightarrow Y$, and so forth). Moreover, relations are as prone to hypostatization as things. As he says:

> Whatever arises dependent on something other, is neither identical to nor [utterly] different from that other; thus, things neither perish completely nor are they everlasting.

And yet to speak of *X* as related to *Y* requires that they somehow be either the same or different. "Conditional co-arising" (*pratītya-samutpāda*), which all Buddhists take to be the fundamental insight of Buddha's enlightenment, is neither a thing nor a relation for Nāgārjuna since it does not involve either identity or difference.

Since the two options (*X* as "self attempts" and *X* as "related to others") prove to be untenable, to combine the two ("both self and others" or "both *X* and non-*X*") produce only further untenable complications. The notion of "identity in difference," for instance, is incoherent since identity and difference are mutually exclusive; one cannot reify identity while admitting difference. Nonetheless, since both experience and logic depend on and are inseparable from conceiving everything in terms of self and other, this or that, X or non-X (thinking and perceiving are always contrastive), things and relations cannot be simply ignored or rejected out of hand. Thus the position "neither X nor non-X" proves just as unsatisfactory and untenable as the previous three options. These four options (X; non-X; both X and non-X; neither X nor non-X) exhaust all the possibilities for thinking about or describing anything. Since there is no other way to state anything except through one of these four alternatives, all linguistic formulations are invariably problematic. Are words the same or different from their referents?

For instance, chapter 7 examines the notion of "conditioned things," which Buddhists define as "all things characterized by arising, abiding, and ceasing." Nāgārjuna notes these three characteristics must themselves be either conditioned or unconditioned. If the latter, they are incommensurate with conditioning and cannot be used to define it. If the former, they too should be subject to the three characteristics, which entails that arising must arise, abide, and cease. But then the arising of arising must also be conditioned and thus have the three characteristics (arising, abiding, ceasing), and so into infinite regress. What actually initiates arising? Does arising produce itself? Wouldn't it have to already be present to produce itself, in which case further production would be redundant? If arising cannot give rise to itself, how can it account for the arising of anything else? And so on. The more one tries to respond to Nāgārjuna's objections, the more one finds oneself proposing hypostatic explanations.

For Nāgārjuna language is self-referential, tautological. The danger of tautologies—and Nāgārjuna consistently exploits this danger—is that though two different terms are being used to describe an event that is an event precisely because its causal conditions are *not* radically separated, nonetheless because the *terms* are different *they* can be separated and treated as independent entities. This seeming independence is merely a linguistic illusion. For example, one can say "John walks." For Nāgārjuna this is a tautological statement, since without "John" this particular "walking" could not occur, and conversely, without "walks" we would have a different "John" (a cooking John, or a sitting John, or a talking John, and so forth). "John" and "walks" are inseparable, but by separating the two words, one begins to imagine that something called "John" exists independently of walking and that walking exists independently of John.

In fact, grammatically we are compelled to separate nouns from verbs, adjectives from nouns, adverbs from verbs, and so forth. But these linguistic distinctions conceal the actual inseparability of the factors being carved up by distinct words. The danger of this separation is that these separate "entities" are then given invariant identities, and ultimately assigned to universal classes (class of humans, class of walkers, and so forth). So John (noun), even when not walking, is taken to still be John, and thus his essential identity remains unchanged and unaffected by the various activities (verbs) he engages in. But that is untrue. Our activities (*karma*) are perpetually changing us. Once John has been given the status of "unchanging John" (that is, his identity remains constant through time and differing actions) by this simple trick of language, it is a short step to positing an unchanging, invariant identity that is John, that is his "essence" or self (*ātman*), an essence that remains invariant and constant from life to life and even beyond. Noun-verb phrases are tautologies, not relations between separate classes. Metaphysics thus grows out of linguistic fictions.

Because John and walking are not different, it does not follow that they are the same. John is not the only thing that can walk (though "John walks" can only signify the John who walks). To argue they are either the same or different is to fall into one or the other extreme, that is, to lose the "Middle Way."

Nāgārjuna's "Claims"

The other text unquestionably authored by Nāgār-juna is the *Vigrāha-vyāvartanī* (*Refutation of Objections*), consisting of seventy verses with auto-commentary that refute objections raised against his key methodological insight, *shūnyatā* (emptiness), and especially the charge that his dialectic is nihilistic or self-disqualifying. To the charge that if all words are "empty," then his arguments are also empty and thus cannot refute anything, Nāgārjuna responds that emptiness does not mean nonexistence, and that, on the contrary, emptiness is not a denial of the world as such, but rather the reason why the world happens at all. If things really were the frozen, immutable entities philosophers claimed, nothing could change, move, or occur. He explains that his arguments take over the assumptions and assertions of his opponents and then explore their cogency. He makes no counterclaims and thus cannot be refuted.

Several notable "conclusions" are reached in the course of his arguments nonetheless. Nāgārjuna concludes that not the slightest iota of difference can be drawn between *samsāra* (the conditioned cycle of birth and death) and *nirvāna* (the unconditioned). (This conclusion is incessantly misquoted as "*Samsāra* is *nirvāna*." Further, the "notion" of *nirvāna* and the path to its attainment is incoherent. If *nirvāna* is unconditioned, then there can be no conditions that produce it. Hence if Buddhists claim that such and such a practice or meditation "produces" *nirvāna*, then they are stating conditions that produce it, in which case it is not unconditioned. If it is conditioned, it is not *nirvāna*.

Nāgārjuna also introduces an important distinction between two types of ways of looking at things: (1) *samvriti* (conventional), and (2) *paramārtha* (ultimate). He writes: "On the basis of the conventional, the ultimate is taught. On the basis of the ultimate, *nirvāna* is attained." Subsequently, these two were refined by Buddhists over many centuries.

A passage that has attracted much attention is: "Conditioned co-arising is itself emptiness. These are heuristic designations for the middle way."

Finally, Nāgārjuna took seriously the notion of *prapanca*, the cognitive–linguistic proliferation of misconceptions upon which we ground our misunderstandings of the world and the theories (*drishti*) to which we cling to legitimate those misunderstandings. Throughout his writings, Nāgārjuna assures us that conscientious application of the Middle Way will "silence" or "put to rest" *prapanca*. For him that is the equivalent of enlightenment.

DAN LUSTHAUS

Further Reading

Translations

Bhattacarya, Kamakeswar. *The Dialectical Method of Nāgārjuna: Vigrāha vyāvartanī*. An excellent translation, includes the Sanskrit text in Devanagari and roman scripts.

Inada, Kenneth. *Nāgārjuna: A Translation of his* Mūla-madhyamaka-kārikā *with an Introductory Essay*. Tokyo: Hokuseido Press, 1970. Inada's translation is influenced by East Asian translations and interpretations. Includes the Sanskrit text in roman script.

Kalupahana, David J. *Nāgārjuna: The Philosophy of the Middle Way*. Albany, N.Y.: SUNY Press, 1986. Includes romanized Sanskrit text (with frequent errors) and a controversial running commentary that plays up Nāgārjuna's proximity to the earlier Buddhist tradition while narrowing the focus of his intended targets.

Related Studies

Lindtner, Christian. *Nagarjuniana: Studies in the Writings and Philosophy of Nāgārjuna*. Delhi: Motilal Banarsidass, 1987. An important discussion concerning which of Nāgārjuna's works are genuine and which are spurious. Includes Sanskrit and Tibetan versions of some texts, and some English translations.

Ramanan, K. Venkata. *Nāgārjuna's Philosophy as Presented in the* Mahā-Prajnāpāramitā-Shāstra. Delhi: Motilal Banarsidass, 1966. A detailed discussion of the version of "Nāgārjuna" found in the *Dazhi dulun.*

Sprung, Mervyn. *Lucid Exposition of the Middle Way: The Essential Chapters from the* Prasannapadā *of Candrakīrti.* Boulder, Colo.: Prajna Press, 1979. Abridged translation of the most important Indian commentary on the *Mūla-madhyamaka-kārikā.*

Streng, Fredrick J. *Emptiness: A Study in Religious Meaning.* Nashville, Tenn. and New York: Abingdon Press, 1967. The translations in the appendix of *Mūla-madhyamaka-kārikā* and *Vigrāhavyāvartanī* are useful, if occasionally unclear and inaccurate. The body of the book evaluates Nāgārjuna from a Wittgensteinian perspective.

VASUBANDHU

Born: c. fourth century, Purushapura (now Peshawar) in the state of Gāndhāra, northwestern India
Died: c. fourth century
Major Works: *Abhidharma-kosha, Twenty Verses, Thirty Verses (Trimshikā), One Hundred Dharmas Treatise*

Major Ideas

Whatever we are aware of, think about, experience, or conceptualize, occurs to us only within consciousness.
External objects do not exist.
Karma *is collective and consciousness is intersubjective.*
All factors of experience (dharmas) *can be cataloged and analyzed.*
Buddhism is a method for purifying the stream of consciousness from "contaminations" and "defilements."
Each individual has eight types of consciousness, but Enlightenment (or Awakening) requires overturning their basis, such that consciousness is "turned" into unmediated cognition.

Vasubandhu was one of India's most prominent Buddhist philosophers. His prolific writings record an odyssey through the systems of the leading Buddhist schools of his day. Though primarily venerated by later Buddhists as co-founder of the Yogācāra School with his half-brother Asanga, his pre-Yogācāra works as well, such as the *Abhidharma-kosha* and his auto-commentary on it, have continued to be seriously studied until the present day. He wrote commentaries on many Mahāyāna texts, works on logic, devotional poetry, works on Abhidharma classifications, as well as original and innovative philosophical treatises. Many of his writings survive in their original Sanskrit form, but others, particularly his commentaries, are extant only in Chinese or Tibetan translations.

Abhidharma-kosha

Vasubandhu was born into a Hindu family at Purushapura (today called Peshawar) in the state of Gāndhāra in northwestern India, where centuries earlier Buddhist art bearing distinctive signs of Hellenistic influence were produced. At Vasubandhu's time the dominant Buddhist school in Gāndhāra was the Vaibhāshika (also called Sarvāstivāda), because its main text was the *Mahā-Vibhāsha*, a Sarvāstivādin Abhidharma treatise that

spelled out their positions on Buddhist classificatory schema. Vasubandhu studied this school and then traveled to the headquarters of the orthodox branch in Kashmir, studying with the leading teachers there. After returning home, according to tradition, during the day he would lecture on Vaibhāshika doctrine and in the evening distill the day's lectures into a verse. When collected together the 600-plus verses gave a thorough summary of the entire system; he entitled this work *Abhidharma-kosha*.

The *Kosha* categorizes and analyses the basic factors of experience and reality, called *dharmas*. The Vaibhāshika system had seventy-five *dharmas* divided into five major categories:

Eleven types of material forms (the five sense organs and their corresponding objects, plus something called *avijnapti*, which was considered to be a material counterpart to any intention that did not disclose itself through verbal or bodily gestures);
Mind (*citta*);
Forty-six mental associates (attitudes, forms of attention, emotional states, and so forth, which accompany moments of cognition);
Fourteen conditions disassociated from the mind (including linguistic, conceptual, medi-

tational, or moral categories such as grammatical entities, continuity and impermanence, temporary cessation of mental activities [*nirodha-samāpatti*], and accrual or divestiture of *karma*); and

Three unconditioned *dharmas*: spatiality, disjunction from impure *dharmas* by deliberate awareness, and non-arousal of impure *dharmas* due to the absence of their productive conditions.

This scheme was primarily taken as a map of the path towards enlightenment, but in its effort to comprehensively describe all the factors of reality the *Kosha* delved into the full range of Buddhist doctrine, including meditation practices, cosmology, theories of perception, causal theories, the causes and elimination of moral problems, the theory of rebirth, and the qualities of a Buddha. The most important notion, subtending all other discussions in the *Kosha*, is *karma*. *Karma* means "action," and in Buddhism denotes especially intentional actions with moral consequences (as distinguished from physical activity lacking any intention, that being called *kriya* rather than *karma*). "Action" includes cognitive and linguistic acts as well as bodily movements. In rudimentary terms *karma* theory states that present actions are influenced by previous actions and present actions will, in turn, influence future actions. This influence is exerted from moment to moment as well as from life to life. Karmically, an action is either wholesome and beneficial, unwholesome and disadvantageous, or neutral. For instance, a previous "disadvantageous" action is such precisely because it eventually produces negative consequences, just as a current beneficial action is such because it will produce good consequences in the future, and so on. The seventy-five *dharmas* are examined not only in terms of their definitions and interrelations, but most importantly in terms of their karmic qualities, that is, how they affect and are affected by karmic processes. In that way the system becomes more than mere intricate scholarly analysis, it becomes a soteric vehicle.

Apparently Vasubandhu began having second thoughts about Vaibhāshika teachings, since he then wrote a prose commentary to the verses that refuted them by presenting and championing the objections of one of their key opponents, the Sautrāntikas. One key point of dispute between Vaibhāshikas and Sautrāntikas was whether *dharmas* exist in the past and future as well as the present (the Vaibhāshika position) or whether they are discrete, particular moments only existing at the present moment in which they discharge causal efficacy (the Sautrāntika position). The commentary attacked many other Vaibhāshika notions as well. The *Abhidharmakosha-bhāshya*, as the verses with his auto-commentary is called, outraged orthodox Vaibhāshikas, who wrote several treatises that attempted to refute Vasubandhu's critiques.

Vasubandhu's Interim Writings

Vasubandhu remained intellectually and spiritually restless, and continued to refine his Abhidharmic thinking. We do not know the precise order in which his remaining treatises were written (except that the *Trisvabhāva-nirdesha* [*Elaboration of the Three Self-Natures*] was reputedly his last, and his *Twenty Verses* and *Thirty Verses* came near the end), but the general trajectory of his developing ideas can be traced. His *Pancaskandhaprakarana* (*Exposition on the Five Aggregates*) discusses many of the topics covered in the *Abhidharmakosha*, but instead of the *kosha*'s seventy-five *dharmas*, several new ones have been added, and several of the original seventy-five have been dropped. Moreover they are grouped in somewhat different categories. The formulations and definitions of *dharmas* offered here are not yet the full list of "one hundred *dharmas*" that Vasubandhu would write about later in a treatise of that name, but he is clearly moving in that direction.

In his *Karma-siddhi-prakarana* (*Exposition Establishing Karma*), he challenged the views of the Vaibhāshikas and any others who held that *dharmas* might be anything other than momentary. Momentariness basically explained the series of consciousness moments as a casual sequence in which each moment caused its successor. Recog-

nizing that the theory of momentariness had difficulty explaining certain types of continuity—from
one life to the next, the reemergence of a consciousness stream after it has been interrupted in
deep sleep or meditation, and so forth—near the
end of the treatise he introduces the Yogācāra notion of the *ālaya-vijñāna* (storehouse consciousness) in which the "seeds" of previous experiences
are stored subliminally and released into new experiences. The metaphor of seeds being planted in the
consciousness stream by experiences, only to
sprout later (break through from the subliminal into
conscious experience), possibly producing new
seeds that are implanted to be sprouted later, provided a handy model that for Vasubandhu not only
explained continuity between two separate moments of consciousness, but also provided a quasi-
causal explanation for the mechanics of karmic
retribution—that is, it described how an action
done at one time could produce "fruit" at another
time, including across lifetimes. The *ālaya-vijñāna*
also eliminated the need for a theory of a substra-
tive, permanent self that is the doer and recipient of
karma, since, like a stream, it is perpetually changing with ever new conditions from moment to moment. In this treatise Vasubandhu denies that
something at one time can be identical to what
might appear to be the same thing at another time,
since, he claims, it is undergoing changes every
moment, even if so small as to go unnoticed. In
good Buddhist fashion, Vasubandhu argues that
reality consists of a stream of changing causes and
conditions with no permanent entities (such as God
or the soul) anywhere.

Conversion to Mahāyāna and the Thirty Verses

According to tradition, Vasubandhu's half-brother
Asanga, after becoming discontent with the Ma-
hīshāsaka Buddhist teachings he had been studying, went into the forest to meditate for twelve
years, after which he felt no closer to his goal. Then
a *Bodhisattva* named Maitreya appeared to him
from the Tushita Heaven (one of many Buddhist
Heavens, this one particularly important for Yo-

gācāra), and instructed him, dictating five treatises
that became the foundation of the Yogācāra School.
In Mahāyāna Buddhism Maitreya functions as a
type of Messianic figure, the future Buddha who
will come to earth when all sentient beings are
sufficiently enlightened to enter nirvana.

It should be pointed out that although Buddhists
consider Vasubandhu and his brother to be the
founders of Yogācāra, Yogācāric literature such as
the *Samdhinirmocana Sūtra* had been in circulation
for over a century before them. Eventually Asanga
"converted" Vasubandhu to the Yogācāra viewpoint, and Vasubandhu began writing commentaries and treatises in earnest expounding his new
views. One, the *Madhyānta Vibhāga* (*Discourse on
the Middle Between Extremes*) consists of verses by
"Maitreya," accompanied by Vasubandhu's commentary. The text attempts to refashion Nāgārjuna's notion of "emptiness," allowing it to
reinforce rather than negate Yogācāric ideas.

Vasubandhu's *Thirty Verses* (*Trimshika*), despite
its brevity, is one of his most mature works. In
concise verses he sums up his doctrine of *vijñapti-
mātra* (cognitive closure) by defining the Eight-
Consciousnesses theory of Yogācāra in Abhidharmic terms, briefly explaining the Yogācāra
Three-Nature theory, and concluding with a five-
step path to enlightenment. The eight consciousnesses are the five sensory consciousnesses
(seeing, hearing, and so forth), the empirical consciousness, a self-concerned mentality called
manas, and the *ālaya-vijñāna*. Vasubandhu describes each and explains how each can be overcome. The point of *vijñapti-mātra* is not, as many
writers have claimed, to establish a theory of Transcendental Idealism or reify the mind as real. On
the contrary, the stated goal of the *Thirty Verses* is
the extinction of the eight consciousnesses through
an "overturning of their basis" (*āshraya-
paravritti*). Consciousness (*vijñāna*)—which is
"closured" such that what appears to be a real,
external world is nothing more than projected desires and predilections of consciousness—is replaced by direct, immediate cognition (*jñāna*). The
five-step path gradually leads one to this enlightenment, which is described elsewhere in Yogācāric

writings as the transformation of the *ālaya-vijñāna* into the Great Mirror Cognition that, without preference, bias, anticipation, or attachment, accurately reflects everything before it.

The Three-Nature theory, which is treated in many Yogācāra texts (including an independent treatise by Vasubandhu), maintains that there are three "natures" or cognitive realms at play:

The delusional cognitively constructed realm, which is unreal and which posits hypostatic essences or "selves";

The realm of causal dependency, which when mixed with the constructed realm leads one to mistake the products of the flux of causes and conditions for fixed, permanent entities; and

The perfectional realm that functions like Nagarjuna's "emptiness" to remove all traces of hypostatic thinking and cognition. It is an antidote (*pratipaksha*) that "purifies" or cleans the delusional constructions out of the causal realm, which when cleaned of all defilements is "enlightened."

These self-natures are also called the "Three Non-Self-Natures," since they lack fixed, independent, permanent identities and thus should not be hypostatized. The first is intrinsically unreal; the third intrinsically "empty"; and the second (which finally is the only "real" one) is of unfixed nature since it can be "mixed" with either of the other two.

The Twenty Verses

Vasubandhu's most original and philosophically interesting treatise is his *Twenty Verses*. In it he defends Yogācāra from objections by Realists. Yogācāra claims that what we think are external objects are nothing more than mental projections. This has been mistaken for an Idealist position because interpreters focus on the word "object" instead of "external." What Vasubandhu means is that cognition never takes place anywhere except in consciousness. Everything we know we have acquired through sensory experience (in Buddhism

the mind is considered a special type of sense). We are fooled by consciousness into believing that the things we perceive and appropriate within consciousness are actually "outside" our cognitive sphere. Consciousness is driven by karmic intentionalities (the habitual tendencies produced by past actions), and how we perceive is shaped by that conditioning. The goal of Yogācāra is to break out of this cognitive narcissism and finally wake up to things as they are, devoid of erroneous conceptual projections.

The Realist objects that external things must exist because they are consistently located in space and time; furthermore, subjective wishes do not determine objective realities; and, finally, the objective world functions by determinate causal principles. Having stated these objections, Vasubandhu devotes the rest of the text to his response.

Vasubandhu begins by considering the space–time objection. Objects seem to have spatial and temporal qualities even in dreams, although nothing "external" is present. Thus the appearance of cognitive objects does not require an actual object external to the consciousness cognizing it, but without consciousness, nothing whatsoever is cognized.

He then argues that groups, due to collective *karma*, give rise to misperceptions or interpretations in common. According to *karma* theory, it is the consequences of one's own actions (*karma*) that determine what sort of situations one will be "born into" and thus the types of groups with which one will share common views and ways of seeing. Thus Vasubandhu's general point is that how we see things is shaped by previous experience, and since experience is intersubjective, we congregate in groups that see things the way we do (based on similarities in our previous experiences).

In an intriguing example, Vasubandhu argues that the torturing guards in Hell are not real beings, but communal projections by Hell's denizens with which they torture themselves, since it is illogical that one would be born into Hell unless one deserved it based on one's previous actions. If so, then one would not be immune to Hell's tortures; but the guards do not suffer, they mete out suffering. The implication of his argument is that Hell itself is merely a kind of paranoid projection.

The appearance of causal efficacy also occurs in dreams. Moreover, in an erotic dream, even though the erotic "object" is not externally real, it causes an observable physical effect observable in the waking world as well in the dream. Thus our conscious "dreams" can have causal efficacy.

After critiquing Indian atomist theories and explaining his seed theory, Vasubandhu returns to the analogy of dreams when addressing the question "Can we know other minds?" To the claim that other minds are unknowable or at least opaque, Vasubandhu replies that they are knowable, and no more opaque than our own minds are to ourselves. Buddha, who is fully Awakened (Enlightened), knows others' minds more clearly than we know our own. The reason why objects and events seem less clear and less consistent in dreams than when awake is that during sleep the mind is overcome by sleepiness and thus is not "thinking clearly"; therefore, in a dream one does not know that the objects therein are only dream objects until one awakens. To awaken (become enlightened) is to perceive clearly without any mental obstructions. Not only can we know other minds, but we constantly influence each other for better and for worse. Thus *karma* is intersubjective.

DAN LUSTHAUS

Further Reading

Translations

Anacker, Stefan. *Seven Works of Vasubandhu*. Delhi: Motilal Banarsidass, 1984. One of the standard English works on Vasubandhu. Includes a biography that tries to harmonize various traditional accounts with known historical facts. Includes all the important Yogācārin and interim treatises. Each translation is accompanied by helpful essays and notes.

Kochumuttom, Thomas. *A Buddhist Doctrine of Experience: A New Translation and Interpretation of the Works of Vasubandhu the Yogācārin*. Delhi: Motilal Banarsidass, 1982. The other standard work. Kochumuttom argues against the Idealist interpretation of Vasubandhu, instead trying to show in his running commentary to the translations that Vasubandhu is a Critical Realist.

Pruden, Leo, trans. *Abhidharma Kośa Bhāṣyam*. Berkeley, Calif.: Asian Humanities Press, 1988–90, 4 vols. English translation from Louis de la Vallée Poussin's French translation from the Chinese. The only complete English translation of Vasubandhu's encyclopedic work. Includes an introductory essay, indices, and helpful notes.

ĪSHVARAKRISHNA

Born: c. 350
Died: c. 425
Major Work: *Sānkhya Kārikās* (*Verses on the Sānkhya*)

Major Ideas

The truth that liberates is discovered by reason, that is, inference from analogy.

Both Primordial Matter and Spirit are ultimately and uniquely real.

The entire physical universe and all its parts, and also the human experience of that universe, are derived from a single source called prakriti (*Primordial Matter*), *the first cause of the universe.*

Primordial Matter is a single substance that evolves into the multiplicity of the material and psycho-mental universe, and it pervades that universe.

Primordial Matter cannot be experienced; its existence is inferred.

Primordial Matter is made up of three Constituent Processes (gunas), *that is, Intelligibility* (sattva), *Activity* (rajas), *and Inertia* (tamas).

Purusha (*Spirit*) *exists independently of Primordial Matter; it is infinitely multiple.*

Spirit, the final cause of the universe, is the principle for whose sake Primordial Matter evolves into the universe and also into the human psycho-mental experience of it.

Ordinary experience is the confused conjunction and association of the evolutes of Primordial Matter with Spirit.

Liberation or dissociation of Spirit from the evolutes of Primordial Matter is the chief aim of human life; this state of the Spirit is called Isolation (kaivalya).

The *Sānkhya Kārikās* (*Verses on the Sānkhya*) of Īshvarakrishna is the earliest complete text of the Classical Sānkhya, or Distinctionist, School of Indian thought available to us, dating from the beginning of the fifth century A.D. Nevertheless, the Sānkhya, as a recognizable way of philosophical thinking, predates the *Sānkhya Kārikās* by at least a millennium, and is one of the oldest systems of Indian thought. Traces of it can be found in the *Upanishads*, where Sānkhya seems to have had distinctly theistic tendencies. Sānkhya has some remarkable parallels to the ideas of Plotinus (A.D. 205–270) in Western thought.

Although closely related to the development of Yoga and often paired with it, Sānkhya should be understood as a clearly distinct school. Its search for discriminating knowledge should not be confused with Yoga's emphasis on ascetical method. Because of the clarity of Sānkhya's systematic analysis, its influence is pervasive over the whole realm of Indian thought, especially in the area of cosmol-

ogy. Sānkhya's legendary founder was Kapila, but the *Sānkhya Sūtras* attributed to Kapila date from the fifteenth century. Thus the *Sānkhya Kārikās* of Īshvarakrishna, a summary formulation of the Sānkhya tradition as the definitive statement of a very ancient Indian way of thought, may be called the "Classical" Sānkhya.

Of Īshvarakrishna himself almost nothing is known. Important commentaries on the *Sānkhya Kārikās*, a philosophical poem, were composed by Gaudapāda (sixth—or possibly eighth—century A.D.) and the prolific Vācaspati Mishra (tenth century A.D.). A translation of Īshvarakrishna was made into Chinese as early as the sixth century.

Classical Sānkhya is a boldly speculative system of a dualist metaphysics. Contrary to other Indian schools of thought, Sānkhya does not seem to have had religious origins. It does not base itself on the Vedic Revelation. Instead, its basis is a proto-scientific inductive reasoning. The term "Sānkhya" itself means "enumeration." Thus, for Īshvarakrishna, Sānkhya is a true discriminating knowledge of the enumerated supersensual elements of reality that are discovered through a form of inference from analogy. This kind of inference supersedes sensual perception by moving from the world of perceived effects to the unperceived cause, and thus is truly a knowledge of the supersensually real world. This realm of the supersensual is just as real as the perceived world.

Two Principles of Reality

The knowledge taught by Īshvarakrishna, which discriminates between the world of effects and that of causes, is a liberating knowledge. The inferred supersensually real world is composed of two principles of reality. The first principle is Primordial Matter (*prakriti*), a single substance from which evolves the multiplicity of both the physical and the psycho-mental universes. The second principle is Spirit (*purusha*), which is inherently separate from everything that evolves from Primordial Matter, and which is at the same time phenomenally confused with the evolutes of Primordial Matter. Spirit is multiple, not non-dual as maintained by Advaita, since there are many spirits. Primordial Matter and Spirit are diametrically opposed to each other; one is active and the other passive. The evolution of the world takes place, however, through their interaction.

The Three Strands of Primordial Matter

Primordial Matter is the first and substantial cause of the material universe and of the psycho-mental world of experience. For Sānkhya all effects arise from a cause; that cause is Primordial Matter. In proof Īshvarakrishna states that the unity and consistency of the universe points to a single cause; that inferred cause is Primordial Matter. Since an effect is but a modification of a cause, Primordial Matter is all-pervasive in the universe, both in its material and in its psycho-mental evolution.

Primordial Matter is constituted of three strands (*gunas*), that is, Constituent Processes or dynamisms. The Constituent Processes are reciprocally and interdependently opposed to one another. The three Constituent Processes are Intelligibility (*sattva*), Activity (*rajas*), and Inertia (*tamas*). Primordial Matter's Intelligibility is the cause of all that is fine and light; Activity of all that is active; Inertia of all that is coarse and heavy. When these three Constituent Processes are equally balanced, no evolution takes place. When their balance and equilibrium are upset in the disturbing presence of Spirit, evolution begins. This evolution is a transformation, not a new creation, of the original substance of Primordial Matter. Just as evolution can occur, so too can the universe cyclically dissolve back into Primordial Matter.

For Īshvarakrishna, the first to evolve from Primordial Matter is Intellect (*mahat*), the seed of the world Intellect, in its turn, gives rise to the "I"-maker (*ahamkāra*), the principle of individuation. After this the course of evolution splits into a psycho-mental branch and into a physical branch. The psycho-mental branch of evolution is characterized by a predominance of Intelligibility; the physical branch is characterized by a predominance of Inertia. Activity provides the interacting dynamism between the evolutes of Intelligibility and Inertia. The psycho-mental products of evolution are mind (*manas*); the five perceptual organs, namely the senses of smell, taste, sight, touch, and hearing; and the five motor faculties, namely the voice, hands, feet, anus, and genitals. The physical evolutions are the subtle elements (*tanmātras*), namely the essences of smell, taste, color, touch, and sound. From the subtle elements evolve the gross elements (*mahābhūtas*), namely earth, water, fire, air, and ether. Here the primary evolution stops. Everything in the physical and the psycho-mental universes is produced out of these principles. A further secondary evolution also takes place that produces each individual human being in the universe.

Thus Īshvarakrishna to this point has enumerated twenty-four principles of reality. Primordial Matter is an evolvent alone; Intellect, the "I"-maker, and the subtle elements are both evolvents and evolutes (products of evolution); the mind, the perceptual organs, the motor faculties, and the gross elements are only evolutes. The Spirit, the twenty-fifth principle, neither evolves nor is evolved, and is in itself unconnected to Primordial Matter. Thus out of Primordial Matter has evolved both the physical world and the psycho-mental world. The polarities of a universal philosophical problem like the body–mind problem are in Īshvarakrishna's Sānkhya conceived very differently than in most philosophical systems of the West. The difference lies in the conception of Spirit.

Spirit as Final Cause

The existence of Spirit, like that of Primordial Matter, is inferred, but not by an inference from effect to cause. The inference of Spirit is an inference from purpose and design. If Primordial Matter is the material cause of the universe, Spirit is its final cause. The evolution that comes forth from Primordial Matter must have an end that transcends the process itself, that is, Spirit. In addition, Primordial Matter cannot experience its own evolution. Hence the reality for which the evolution takes place, and which experiences the evolution, is Spirit.

Contrary to the view supported by Advaita Vedānta, for Sānkhya Spirit is multiple. On the phenomenal level, the proof for the pluralism of spirits is the variety of experiences. In the liberated state, each spirit is isolated and there is no principle of individuation other than a sheer unexplained facticity of their pluralism. In the context of the later development of Indian thought, this last is a profound weakness in Sānkhya.

Īshvarakrishna explains:

> From the connection of Primordial Matter and Spirit, the evolutes appear as though conscious; and Spirit, innately indifferent, appears as an agent through the action of the Constituent Processes. In order that Spirit see Primordial Matter, and that Primordial Matter be isolated from Spirit, both are linked like a lame and a blind person. From this union is evolution.

The union of Primordial Matter and Spirit is ultimately only an apparent one, but the phenomenal appearance is very real. The ordinary consciousness of a human person is the result of the real appearance of the interaction of Primordial Matter and Spirit, although there is real action here only on the side of Primordial Matter. Bondage consists in ignorance or nondiscrimination of the metaphysical difference of Primordial Matter's evolution of the physical and psycho-mental worlds from the independent reality of Spirit. When the Spirit knows that is has nothing to do with the evolutes of Primordial Matter, it is liberated. As Īshvarakrishna says:

> On separation from the body—Primordial Matter, her purpose realized, having stopped functioning—Spirit attains to an Isolation that is both certain and final.

In Isolation (*kaivalya*) there is no longer any suffering. Furthermore, there is no happiness or pleasure in Isolation since happiness and pleasure are evolutes of Primordial Matter under the predominance of the Constituent Process of Intelligibility. Isolation is a condition of quietude for Spirit since its condition as pure consciousness is finally manifested to itself. It is important to note in this connection that pure consciousness means that Spirit has no intentional objects for its consciousness. Pure consciousness means contentless consciousness with neither a knower nor a known. However, this state of Isolation may begin during the state of embodiment. Hence Īshvarakrishna's Sānkhya, like Shankara's Advaita, teaches the doctrine of living liberation (*jīvan-mukti*).

Īshvarakrishna's Classical Sānkhya preaches the good news of a sublime Isolation reached by a discriminating knowledge. It felt no need of postulating a God (*Bhagavān*) or a single Ultimate Reality (*Brahman*). The Yoga of Patanjali adapts the basic outlines of Sānkhya while it changes its means of achieving liberation. Advaita Vedānta adopts much of the vocabulary and conceptualization of Sānkhya while rejecting its dualism. The later Vaishnava forms of Vedānta adopted its cosmology.

Nevertheless Sānkhya is certainly eccentric

among Indian schools of thought. It would not have taken much for Sānkhya to drop the doctrine of Spirit and become like Buddhism's no-self theory, or to shift toward a simple materialism. It would not have taken much for Sānkhya to simplify the doctrine of the pluralism of spirits into the nondualism of Advaita or to perceive the evolution of Primordial Matter as an illusion. It would not have taken much for Sānkhya to subject the pluralism of spirits to a theistically conceived Lord as the later Vaishnava forms of Vedānta would. Such moves would have meant an epistemological abandonment of Sānkhya's coherence, a rejection of its passive compatibility with Vedic Revelation, or an undermining of its self-reliant non-theism. In the words of Gerald J. Larsen,

> What is striking, however, is the ubiquitous presence of the Sāmkhya network of notions, functioning almost as a kind of cultural "code" (to use a semiotics idiom) to which intellectuals in every phase of cultural life in India have felt a need to respond.

In any case, an understanding of Classical Sānkhya, as formulated by Īshvarakrishna, is necessary for any understanding of Indian religious and philosophical thought.

Daniel P. Sheridan

Further Reading

Keith, A. Berriedale. *A History of the Sāmkhya Philosophy*. Delhi: Nag Publishers, 1975 [1924]. An early study of Sānkhya that has an excellent treatment of Īshvarakrishna.

Larson, Gerald James. *Classical Sāmkhya: An Interpretation of its History and Meaning*. Delhi: Motilal Banarsidass, 1969. A major scholar of Sānkhya brings together interpretation, assessment of the scholarship, and a translation of the *Sānkhya Kārikā* of Īshvarakrishna.

———, and Ram Shankar Bhattacharya, eds. "*Sāmkhya*: A Dualist Tradition in Indian Philosophy." In *Encyclopedia of Indian Philosophy*. Princeton, N.J.: Princeton University Press, 1987. The primary resource for the study of Sānkhya, it includes a summary of all significant texts of Sānkhya.

Pereira, José. *Hindu Theology: A Reader*. Garden City, N.Y.: Doubleday, 1976. This anthology includes a very clear translation of the *Sānkhya Kārikā* of Īshvarakrishna.

Sen Gupta, Anima. *The Evolution of the Sāmkhya School of Thought*. Lucknow, India: Pioneer Press, 1959. An important study of the development of Sānkhya before Īshvarakrishna, with an emphasis on its theistic tendencies.

KUMĀRILA BHATTA

Born: Fl. A.D. 690
Died: c. A.D. 700
Major Works: *Shlokavārtika* (*Exposition on the Verses*) [Commentary on Shabara's *Commentary on Jaimini's* Mīmāmsa Sūtras, Book 1, Chapter 1]; *Tantravārtika* (*Exposition on the Sacred Science*) [Commentary on Shabara's *Commentary on Jaimini's* Mīmāmsa Sūtras, Book 1, Chapters 2–4; Books 2 and 3]; *Tuptika* (*Full Exposition*) [Commentary on Shabara's *Commentary on Jaimini's* Mīmāmsa Sūtras, Books 4–9]

Major Ideas

There are six sources of valid knowledge: perception, inference, verbal testimony, analogy, presumption, and non-perception.

The Vedas *are the only example of verbal testimony in its primary sense.*

Dharma (*enjoined religious observances*) *is taught in the* Vedas.

The enjoined religious observances revealed in the Vedas *could not otherwise be known.*

Enjoined observances are the highest good of human beings.

The Vedas *do not teach anything about history, matters of fact, or empirical knowledge.*

The Vedas *have no author, human or divine; their words are eternal and precede that which they denote.*

There can be no conflict between the enjoined religious observances of the Vedas *and perception or inference.*

The world is real and eternal; it has no creator and is not subject to a cycle of creation and dissolution.

There is a plurality of individual selves.

Liberation from the cycle of death and rebirth is the dissolution of the individual self's relation with the empirical world through the body.

The Hindu school of Pūrva Mīmāmsa (Investigation into the First Part of the *Vedas*) is both the most uncompromising expression of Hindu Orthodoxy's adherence to the *Vedas* and, from the Western point of view, the school of religious and philosophical thought most unique to India. The outlines of its teaching are contained in the *Pūrva Mīmāmsa Sūtras* of Jaimini (fl. A.D. 25) as commented upon by Shabara (fl. A.D. 125). However, the greatest thinker of this school, and indeed of Hindu Orthodoxy, is Kumārila Bhatta, who wrote commentaries on Shabara's *Commentary on Jaimini's Mīmāmsa Sūtras* (seventh century A.D.).

Little is known of Kumārila's life, although he appears in several episodes in the fourteenth- and fifteenth-century biographies of Shankara. Many of the arguments in Kumārila's writings are directed against Buddhism's attack on the Hindu sacrificial system, and his arguments in favor of the *Vedas*

must have contributed to the slow demise of Buddhism in India in the latter half of the first millennium. His teaching also influenced the other orthodox schools of Hinduism that were based on the *Vedas*, mainly that of Advaita Vedānta, even if Advaita developed its own teaching in counterpoint to Kumārila's.

The Vedas as the Means to Liberation

The chief teaching of Pūrva Mīmāmsa as interpreted by Kumārila Bhatta is that the *Vedas* are the authoritative source of liberating knowledge and that the rituals enjoined in the *Vedas* are the means to liberation. All else supports these two points. According to Kumārila, there are six sources of valid knowledge: perception, inference, verbal testimony, analogy, presumption, and non-perception. The first four means of knowledge agree with those taught previously by the Nyāya-Vaisheshika School. The last two are unique contributions of Kumārila and the Bhatta School of Pūrva Mīmāmsa that follows him: presumption and nonperception. Each of these means of valid knowledge has its place in human living, but the supreme means of valid knowledge is verbal testimony (*shabda*).

The primary and only instance of verbal testimony in its truest sense is the *Vedas*. The *Vedas* were not produced by human authorship, according to Kumārila. No human being is mentioned as having composed them, and no one remembers anyone who is claimed to be their author. Nor are the *Vedas* the composition of God. Kumārila saw no need to propose the existence of God since the *Vedas* are eternal; an eternal scripture needs no author or cause. Since the universe is also eternal, there was also no need for God as a creator on the ground of efficient causality.

Kumārila goes on to defend the eternality of the *Vedas* on the basis of a theory of "words." The connection between a word and its meaning is inherent and eternal. He is speaking here specifically of the words of Sanskrit, the perfect and paradigmatic language. The letters, which make up words, do not have parts. They are omnipresent and eternal, given that they exist at a level above their being sounded, almost like Plato's Ideas (eternal forms). What words, which are made of letters, signify is universal. Since universals are eternal, the relationship between words and their universal significance is also eternal.

However, for Kumārila, not all combinations of words are eternally ordered and not all literary compositions are valid verbal testimony—only those that are unauthored. The eternal permanence of words is itself only a negative condition for asserting that the *Vedas* are eternal. Hence the fact that the *Vedas* are made up of words which need to be sounded by speakers cannot be used as an argument against their eternality. The particular arrangement of the words of the *Vedas* is what is asserted to be eternal. This arrangement was constructed neither by a human intelligence nor a divine one. In a way similar to Christian and Muslim

theologians (although, ironically, he does not postulate the existence of God), Kumārila proposes that the knowledge achieved through the exclusive means of verbal testimony is self-evident, that is, self-validating. The truth conveyed by this means of knowledge is true because it comes from a true "means" of knowledge. There is no gratuitous assertion or rhetorical begging of the question here.

According to Kumārila, all the orders of knowledge achieved by the six means of knowledge are intrinsically self-validating, each in its own nonoverlapping order. All doubts or flaws in any of the forms of knowledge are extrinsic and accidental to its inherent and innate truthfulness. The inherent validity of verbal testimony in this case can indeed be clouded, but only through extrinsic circumstances such as being dependent upon the wills of sentient beings capable of deceiving and being deceived.

It is precisely the task of Pūrva Mīmāmsa, as taught by Jaimini and expanded by Kumārila, to draw out the truth and valid knowledge of the *Vedas* by means of valid interpretation, that is, by dissociating the *Vedas*' truth from human misinterpretation by means of reason. The *Vedas* are impersonally and eternally existent and thus capable of expressing transcendent matters, of being the only means so capable because they are untouched by authorship. If a human being or God were the author of the *Vedas*, they would be capable of deception about the highest good of humans. The *Vedas* are thus defectless in their own order as a means of knowledge.

Enjoined Religious Observances

Verbal testimony found in the *Vedas* cannot come into conflict with one of the other valid means of knowledge, such as perception or inference, because the *Vedas* deal with only what is beyond the sensible or beyond what can be inferred. Hence the *Vedas* must be properly interpreted. The purport of the *Vedas* is *dharma*, enjoined religious observances. Kumārila is not speaking here of ethics; the enjoined religious observances cannot be otherwise known. Kumārila says that "there are no assertions in the *Vedas*." Since the *Vedas* are in an eternal order of existence that precedes all phenomena that are historical or empirical, they deal with only the enjoining of the highest good of human beings. The *Vedas'* words do not refer to such things as historical facts or empirical concerns. Since they are not teaching anything perceptible nor inferable, the *Vedas* cannot conflict as means of knowledge with perception or inference.

The chief characteristic of the *Vedas* is the injunction, either positive or negative. Pūrva Mīmāmsa and Kumārila teach hermeneutic methods that interpret all passages in the *Vedas* which are not injunctions as being supportive of injunctions. Thus the central portion of the *Vedas* are the *Brāhmanas* and not the *Upanishads*, as is taught in Vedanta. The purpose of this unique teaching about verbal testimony—revelation—is not to describe what is, but instead what is to be accomplished.

There are some forms of injunctions that do not create meritorious *karma*, but if not performed will create demeritorious *karma*. The more important, optional injunctions are those that if not performed create no demerit, but if performed accrue merit.

The question arises of how an action such as a sacrifice, which once performed is ended, can influence a future event such as liberation from the cycle of death and rebirth. The solution is the Pūrva Mīmāmsa teaching of *apūrva*, the unseen potency. The unseen potency transcends and bridges the temporal distance between the time of the performed sacrifice and the time of merited liberation. The school of Kumārila, in contrast to the opposing Pūrva Mīmāmsa School of Prabhākara, teaches that the enjoined religious observances are in accord with the natural desires of individual human beings. The knowledge, given in the *Vedas*, that the performance of a sacrifice will eventuate in individual liberation from the cycle of death and rebirth is the means to attain fulfillment of human desire. It seems that in earlier Pūrva Mīmāmsa, the aim was to achieve the bliss and happiness of Vedic Heaven (*svarga*). For Kumārila, however, the ultimate aim and good of human life is to attain liberation. This can be achieved only by performing the enjoined sacrifices:

For those who have understood the real nature of the soul, all their past *karmas* having become exhausted through experience, and there being no further karmic residuum left to wipe off, there comes no further body.

Thus Kumārila has no place for the religious practice of *sannyasa*, renunciation of the enjoined religious observances. Liberation, the final escape of the soul from the sufferings of life (by the soul not forming a new relation to a body), is achieved through the enjoined sacrifices. Kumārila, not without ambiguity, states that liberation is essentially a suffering-free state of the soul and does not entail the experience of bliss. On this point at least, Pūrva Mīmāmsa contributed to the development of Shankara's Advaita in the generation after Kumārila. In the fifteenth and sixteenth century some followers of Kumārila's school, under theistic influence, taught that liberation is experientially blissful. In contrast to Advaita, Kumārila is also clear in his teaching about the plurality of individual souls. Liberation is not union with *Brahman*, the ultimate reality.

Kumārila's teaching of Pūrva Mīmāmsa is a powerful use of reasoning and interpretation in order to reconcile the vast diversity of the *Vedas* around a simple insight: *dharma*, the enjoined religious observances of sacrifices, is the inherent teaching of the *Vedas*. In order to do this, the teaching of Pūrva Mīmāmsa was relentlessly realist in epistemology. Only thus could it confront Buddhist idealism and preserve Hindu Orthodoxy. The sacrifices could not be effective in an ideal order, only in a real one. Since the practice of *dharma*, enjoined in the *Vedas*, can liberate one from the cycle of death and rebirth, the doctrine of God is an unnecessary hypothesis. Thus Kumārila and his school of Pūrva Mīmāmsa were the original pragmatists. By means of philosophical reasoning and interpretation, they put the *dharma* in a clearly defined and prescribed realm beyond philosophical probing and questioning. A vast area of human life was allowed for the "secular" realm.

The teaching of Kumārila had a profound historical impact in the further development of Hindu thought. Within a generation the great Shankara would transvaluate the Pūrva Mīmāmsa teaching of *dharma* in a grand subordination that sublated the Vedic injunctions to the great statements about knowledge in the *Upanishads*, while preserving them in non-dualist metaphysics. Hence the charge that Shankara was a crypto-Buddhist is (from the Hindu point of view) groundless, perhaps due to Kumārila.

DANIEL P. SHERIDAN

Further Reading

Translations

Jha, Ganganatha. *Pūrva-Mīmāmsa in Its Sources*. Varanasi, India: Banares Hindu University, 1964. Extensive translation from Kumārila's works, ordered according to topic.

Pereira, José. *Hindu Theology: A Reader*. Garden City, N.Y.: Doubleday, 1976. Contains a translation of a passage of Kumārila's on the "occult power," that is, the unseen potency. In this an-thology, Kumārila is discussed in a theological context.

Radhakrishnan, Sarvepalli, and Charles Moore. *A Sourcebook in Indian Philosophy*. Princeton, N.J.: Princeton University Press, 1957. Contains a translation of Kumārila's writing about the non-creation of the world by God. In this anthology, Kumārila is discussed in a philosophical context.

Related Studies

Dasgupta, Surendranath. *A History of Indian Philosophy*. Volume 1. Cambridge: Cambridge University Press, 1922. A monumental history of Indian philosophy with a lengthy discussion of the philosophical teaching of Pūrva Mīmāmsa, which carefully distinguishes the teaching of Prabhākara from Kumārila.

Hiriyanna, M. *The Essentials of Indian Philosophy*. London: George Allen & Unwin, 1949. Contains a short, accurate, easily understandable chapter on Pūrva Mīmāmsa.

JAYARĀSI BHATTA

Born: Fl. in seventh century A.D., India
Died: Time and place unknown
Major Work: *Tattvopaplavasimha* (*The Lion That Devours All Categories* or *The Upsetting of All Principles*) (seventh century A.D.)

Major Ideas

Perception, inference, and testimony do not lead to knowledge.
There are no gods, supernatural powers, or Ātman.
Moksha is an illusory goal.
It is reasonable to believe that life ends with death and that happiness in this life is the only sensible end.

Jayarāsi Bhatta was a brilliant Indian philosopher who flourished in the seventh century A.D. He belonged to the school of Indian Materialism called Cārvāka or Lokāyata. He holds a special place in the history of Indian philosophy because his work, *Tattvopaplavasimha* (*The Lion That Devours All Categories* or *The Upsetting of All Principles*), is the only extant authentic text of the Cārvāka School.

The Cārvāka was also known as the Lokāyatas, meaning the worldly philosophers (who held that only this world exists) or the Brihasptyas, meaning the followers of Brihaspati. Tradition is not unanimous about who Cārvāka was. The word may be the name of the most important disciple of Brihaspati. It may be a title meaning "one who speaks sweet words," because Cārvāka is said to have taught that man ought to enjoy his life in this world, as there is nothing beyond. We know of some original texts such as *Brahaspatisūtras* (600 B.C.), *Cārvākasūtras*, and *Lokāyatasūtras*. In keeping with Indian philosophical tradition, these texts must have had commentaries explaining their doctrines. But all those original texts are lost to us. Our knowledge of this philosophy comes from Jayarāsi Bhatta's *Tattvopaplavasimha* (seventh century A.D.), and the summaries of Cārvāka given by Mādhva Āchārya in his *Sarvadarshanasamgraha* and Shankara in his *Sarvasiddhāntasamgraha*. From this material, together with references made to the Cārvāka by the rival schools, we are able to reconstruct the metaphysics, epistemology, and ethics of the Cārvāka.

The Cārvāka School held the following opinions, which Giuseppe Tucci (see his *Linee di una storia del materialismo indiano*. Rome: R.A.N. dei Lincei, 1924) gleaned from an exhaustive examination of the relevant sources:

Sacred literature should be disregarded as being false.
There is no deity or supernatural.
There is no immortal soul; nothing exists after death of the body.
Karma is inoperative; it is an illusion.
Everything is derived from material elements (*mahābhūtas*).
Material elements have an immanent force (*svābhāva*).
Intelligence is derived from these elements.
Only direct perception gives true knowledge (*pratyaksha*).
Religious injunctions and the sacerdotal class are useless.
The aim of life is to get the maximum of pleasure.

The Cārvāka were reacting against and challenging the religious and intellectual orthodoxy of their times. The Vedic culture was imbued with a belief in the supernatural. Among the intellectuals, the fundamental metaphysical beliefs led to the primacy of the *Brahman/Ātman*, which underlies and supports all existence. *Brahman* is Being, Consciousness, and Bliss. The highest good is *moksha*, that is, liberation from this world and unity with *Brahman*. The path to *moksha* includes renunciation. Ordinary people believed in the existence of many gods and of forefathers in another world. The way to please the gods and the forefathers was through performances of religious rituals presided over by the *Brāhmans* (priests). Religious practice included copious gifts to the *Brāhmans* and a life of gradually turning away from worldly enjoyments. As the Cārvāka saw it, a strong belief in supernatural existence was the keystone of the Vedic culture. They found it necessary to attack this belief above everything else.

The Cārvāka challenged the orthodox belief in the existence of supernatural Being or Beings by a clever epistemological move. They asked the basic question: How do you *know* that such entities exist?

The Challenge to Inference

In Indian philosophical circles, in those days, three ways of knowing (*prāmanas*) were accepted: (1) perception, (2) inference, and (3) testimony. There are two kinds of perception: *external*, which gives us knowledge of physical objects through the five senses, and *internal*, which gives us knowledge of our own mental states. The Cārvāka accepted *perception* as a valid method for knowledge, but they challenged the acceptability of *inference* as a way of acquiring knowledge.

The standard form of inference accepted by Indian logicians was:

To be proved: *X is P*. [A certain subject, *X*, has a certain predicate.]
   The argument:
(1) *X is M*.
(2) *All M is P*. [If anything is *M*, it is *P*.]
(3) *Therefore, X is P*.

For example:
To be proved: *H is F*. [The hill has fire on it.]
   The argument:
(1) *H is S*. [The hill has smoke on it.]

(2) *All S is F*. [Where there is smoke, there is fire.]
(3) *Therefore, H is F*. [The hill has fire on it.]

The argument about fire on the hill consists of lines (1), (2), and (3). The predicate term of the conclusion, the term *F*, "fire" in our example, is called *sādhya* by Indian logicians and is called the *major term* by Western logicians. The term *S* (the link in the argument), "smoke" in our example, is called *hetu* by Indian logicians and is called the *middle term* by Western logicians. The term *H*, "the hill," the subject term of the conclusion, is called *paksha* by Indian logicians and is called the *minor term* by Western logicians. Universal concomitance is called *vyāpti* by Indian logicians and is defined as a correlation of two terms such that the middle term (*hetu*) is "pervaded" by the major term (*sādhya*).

Evidently, in order to show that the conclusion "*H is F*" (There is fire on the hill) is true, we must know the truth of "*H is S*" (There is smoke on the hill) and the truth of the generalization "*All S is F*" (Where there is smoke, there is fire). The truth of "*H is S*" (There is smoke on the hill) can be ascertained by perception. But, ask the Cārvāka, how are we to know that the universal concomitance between (in this case) *S* and *F* exists? To be sure, we have perceived many instances of the coexistence of smoke and fire, as in the kitchen. But we cannot perceive *all* the instances of smoke accompanied by fire in the past, present, and future, for most of the relevant instances are beyond the reach of our senses.

Since "*All S is F*" (Where there is smoke, there is fire) is equivalent to "*All non-F is non-S*" (Where there is no fire, there is no smoke), we must also examine by perceiving all cases—past, present, and future—of non-*F*'s to make sure that they are non-*S*'s. Obviously the task is impossible.

Furthermore, an invariable connection expressed by a universal proposition of the form as "*All S is F*" can be true only if the generalization is *unconditional*; that is, "Where there is smoke, there is fire" is true as a universal proposition only if there is no qualification that affects the inference from the subject to the predicate, as would be the case were the proposition of the following form

"All *S* is *F* **only if** *C* [a certain condition is met]." The definition of *condition* is such that a *condition* is that which is concomitant with the major term though not constantly accompanying the middle term. Let *C* be a condition. Then it follows from "*F* only if *C*" that:

(1) All *F* is *C* (All instances of fire are instances of *C*) and

(2) If there is at least one case where something is *S* but not *C* (there is smoke but the condition is not met), then it is false that all cases of *S* (smoke) are cases of *F* (fire).

Why, then, does the Cārvāka School claim that a universal proposition cannot be true unless all conditions are absent? We can construct the following argument:

(1) All *S* is *F*.
(2) All *F* is *C*.
(3) *X* is such that *X* is *S* but not *C*.

Then from (1) and (2) it follows that *in all cases if X is S, X is C*. But, line (3) asserts that there is at least one *X* that is an *S* but *not C*. Thus (3) together with (1) and (2) produces the contradiction *S* is *C* (from 1 and 2) and *S* is not *C*. Hence (1) must be false.

Let us look at an example: Suppose we have witnessed many instances of smoking wood in the kitchen, always accompanied by fire. So we believe that:

All smoking wood is wood on fire.

However, unbeknownst to us, wood catches fire only if it is dry. We did not notice this because it so happened that all the cases of concomitance of smoke and fire we noticed were cases of dry wood. Here "the wood's being dry" is a *condition* of smoke's being associated with fire. It fulfills both clauses of the definition of *condition*. The condition, dry wood, is concomitant with the major term, that is:

All wood on fire is dry wood,

and it does not constantly accompany the middle term, that is,

Some smoking wood is not dry wood.

Given these three propositions, then by following the steps of the above-mentioned reasoning we obtain the result that *something is dry wood and not dry wood*; thereby establishing that since there is a *condition*, the universal proposition that (unconditionally) *where there is smoke, there is fire* is false. For the universal proposition to be true, there must be an absence of any condition.

But, says Cārvāka, the knowledge of what the condition is, say dry wood in our example, must here precede the knowledge of its absence. Therefore, it is only when there is knowledge of the condition that knowledge of the universality of the proposition is possible, a knowledge in the form of such a connection between the middle term and major term as is distinguished by the absence of any such condition. On the other hand, the knowledge of the condition depends upon the knowledge of the invariable connection. Thus, Cārvāka concludes gleefully, "We fasten on our opponents as with adamantine glue the thunderbolt-like fallacy of reasoning in a circle" (Mādhava Āchārya, *Sarvadarshanasamgraha*).

Furthermore, the number of such possible conditions, perceptible and imperceptible, is enormous. It would be impossible to examine all the perceptible ones and logically impossible to examine (by perception) the imperceptible ones.

To recapitulate: Can we know the truth of an empirical statement of the kind "There is fire on the hill" in cases where it cannot be established by sense perception? A possible move is to establish it by means of what may be called "causal inference," that is, as the conclusion of an argument of the form given previously. Such an argument is valid; however, in order to claim that the conclusion is true, we must establish the truth of the premises; especially that premise that is a universal proposition. The Cārvāka school produced several arguments to show that the universal proposition cannot be established by perception, the only acceptable means of knowledge.

So far the Cārvāka arguments depend on the examination of instances of *S* and *F* (smoke and fire, to continue with the example). But an opponent could argue that one can gain knowledge of the universal proposition by noticing the relation between the general classes: smoke-ness and fire-ness. But this move will not do it, counter the Cārvāka. First of all, general classes or universals are not perceptible; second, even if there were such a relation between universals, there might arise a doubt about the application of the invariable connection in any given case; it might be that this case is one of *apparent* smoke and therefore not an instance of the appropriate universal class, smoke-ness.

By now, Cārvāka has convincingly argued that the universal proposition cannot be established by perception. Could it be established by either inference or testimony, the other generally accepted means of knowledge?

The Cārvāka claim,

Nor can inference be the means of knowledge of the universal proposition, since in the case of this inference you should require another inference to establish it, and so on, and hence would arise the fallacy of an *ad infinitum* retrogression. (Madhāva Āchārya, *Sarvadarshanasamgraha*)

Testimony cannot be an independent means of knowledge; testimony depends crucially on the reliability of the authority, namely the one providing the testimony. And that reliability has to be established by perception or inference.

Having argued that the truth of a universal proposition cannot be established, the Cārvāka look at the claim that it is reasonable to believe a universal proposition if there has been the experience of a very large number of cases of agreement between the middle term (*hetu*) and the major term (*sādhya*).

But according to the difference of circumstances, time and place, things differ in their power or capacity and thus since the nature and qualities of things are not constant it is not possible that any two entities should be found to agree with each other in all times and all places. Again, an experience of a large number of cases cannot eliminate the possibility of a future failure of agreement. (Jayanta, *Nyāya Manjari*)

This completes the Cārvāka case against the acceptability of causal inference. It is worth noting that Cārvāka anticipated David Hume by 1,000 years or more.

Jayarāsi in his *Tattvopaplavasimha*, after his attack on the acceptability of inference as a source of knowledge, shows that perception cannot be a valid source of knowledge either. The definition of perception requires that perception is non-erroneous. But, argues Jayarāsi, its non-erroneousness cannot be established. Jayarāsi concludes that there are no valid sources of knowledge. We cannot *know* anything about reality.

Jayarāsi represents the extreme end of skepticism inherent in Cārvāka. Jayarāsi claims to have shown that no school of philosophy may set forth its view of reality as knowledge. What then of the claims of the Cārvāka itself? Jayarāsi says that even Cārvāka philosophy cannot be established as knowledge but since it represents common sense, it may be used as a guide to life. All other philosophies going beyond common sense are, of course, untenable.

NARAYAN CHAMPAWAT

Further Reading

Translation

Radhakrishnan S. and Charles A. Moore, eds. *A Sourcebook in Indian Philosophy*. Princeton, N.J.: Princeton University Press, 1957. This anthology contains one chapter from Jayarāsi's book, *Tattvopaplavasimha*.

Related Studies

Chattopadhyaya, Debiprasad. *Lokāyata: A Study in Ancient Indian Materialism*. New Delhi: People's Publishing House, 1964. Best available general treatment of the school of Cārvāka.

Jayatilleke, K. N. *Early Buddhist Theory of Knowledge*. Delhi: Motilal Banarasidass, 1963. Excellent treatment of Cārvāka and Jayarāsi Bhatta as a part of historical review introducing early Buddhism.

GAUDAPĀDA

Born: Place unknown. Fl. in the eighth century
Died: Time and place unknown
Major Works: *Kārikā* (*Exposition*) *on* Māndūkya Upanishad

Major Ideas

Brahman or self is the only reality.
There are three manifestations of the self.
Beyond these three manifestations there is the real self, turīya.
World is only an appearance of the one into many.
Moksha (*release*) *is the highest goal.*
Knowledge and meditation help one realize moksha.

In response to challenges posed by a dualistic interpretation of the *Upanishads* (Hindu scriptural texts), Gaudapāda sought to give a monistic interpretation of these texts. He was the first person, after the Upanishadic seers, to revive the monistic interpretation in a systematic and clear manner.

The dates of Gaudapāda's life are uncertain, and some even question whether such a person ever lived at all. However, tradition regards Gaudapāda as the *paramguru* (teacher's teacher) of Shankara (see the chapter on Shankara in this volume). Tradition maintains that Gaudapāda was the teacher of Govinda, who was Shankara's teacher. Shankara, in his commentary on Gaudapāda's *Kārikā*, credits Gaudapāda for recovering the monistic interpretation from the *Upanishads*. If the tradition is correct, then Gaudapāda must have flourished in the eighth century.

There is a great deal of controversy regarding the degree to which Gaudapāda was influenced by Buddhist thought. Gaudapāda lived at a time when Buddhism was widely prevalent in India. Thus it should come as no surprise that he draws from both Vasubandhu of the Vijnānavāda and Nāgārjuna of the Shūnyavāda Schools of Mahāyāna Buddhism. He draws arguments from the Vijnānavāda tradition to demonstrate the unreality of the world. He uses Nāgārjuna's distinction between two orders of truth to demonstrate that origination from an absolute standpoint is an impossibility. He concurs with Nāgārjuna's denial of causation as a necessary connection. It would be wrong, however, to conclude on the basis of these similarities that Gaudapāda was a crypto-Buddhist, as some scholars claim. It is indeed true that he was well versed in Buddhist doctrines; he accepted these doctrines when they did not conflict with his own monistic principles. He liberally interpreted Buddhist doctrines to cast them in the Advaitic mold.

According to Vedāntins, the first available treatise on Advaita Vedanta is the *Kārikā on* Māndūkya Upanishad written by Gaudapāda. Besides this *Kārikā*, Gaudapāda also wrote commentaries on the Sānkhya system and *Uttara Gīta*. Whether Gaudapāda in fact wrote these commentaries is very difficult to ascertain. T. M. P. Mahadevan, the best known authority on Gaudapāda, raises two other possibilities. First, it is possible that there were more than one Gaudapāda. Second, perhaps the works of other authors might have been attributed to Gaudapāda. There is no evidence to support the thesis that Gaudapāda wrote commentaries other than his *Kārikā*.

Kārikā on Māndūkya Upanishad

Māndūkya Upanishad is one of the ten principal *Upanishads*. The *Upanishads* create an integrative vision that draws together the diverse elements of human experience and the world into a single whole. Such a vision is created with the help of one single principle, and the term *Brahman* designates this principle. The *Upanishads* repeatedly ask: "What is that by knowing which everything becomes known?" The answer is: "*Brahman*." The *Upanishads* further maintain that this fundamental principle of everything is also the essence of the individual (*ātman*). Thus, for the *Upanishads*, *Brahman* is discovered within the *ātman*, or conversely, *ātman* within *Brahman*.

Gaudapāda has written 215 verses known as *Kārikā* to explain the *Māndūkya Upanishad*. The *Kārikā* of Gaudapāda consists of four chapters: (1) *Āgama* (scripture), (2) *Vaitathya* (unreality), (3) *Advaita* (unity), and (4) *Alātashanti* (the extinction of the burning coal). The first chapter explains the text of the *Māndūkya Upanishad*. Here Gaudapāda tries to demonstrate that his views about reality are not only sanctioned by the scriptures, but also by reason. The second gives arguments to explain the phenomenal nature of the world, where duality of names and forms is manifested. The third chapter says that truth is immortal, and that all distinctions are due to *māyā* (nescience). *Māyā* veils the one and projects the many. The fourth develops arguments regarding the reality of *ātman* and the relativity of our everyday experiences. Specifically, it seeks to demonstrate through dialectical reasoning that causation, like all other relations, belongs to the realm of nescience.

Manifestations of the Self

Gaudapāda begins his *Kārikā* with an analysis of three manifestations of the self found in the *Māndūkya Upanishad*: waking, dreaming, and dreamless sleeping. The one and the same self appears as three. In the waking state, the self cognizes external objects. Because the self is in contact with the external objects in this state, its experiences are gross. In the dreaming state, the self experiences objects imprinted upon the mind during the waking experiences. The self in this stage experiences images, and its experience is subtle. In the third, dreamless sleeping, the mind and the senses are quiescent. In this state there is no subject-object distinction, nor distinctions among objects. It is an undifferentiated state; there are no desires; there are no dreams.

Beyond these three manifestations, there is the real self, *turīya*. It is the self per se. It is unseen, non-relational, unspeakable, undefinable, and unthinkable. It is the essence of consciousness. The *Māndūkya Upanishad* calls it the fourth state. For Gaudapāda, however, this state is not one over and above the remaining three; it is, rather, the reality of which the three are appearances. Self is not affected by these illusory manifestations. It is unborn, it is non-dual.

Non-Duality and the Illusoriness of the World

Reality, holds Gaudapāda, is non-dual. The self alone *is*. The multiplicity of names and forms, and the external world that one perceives in everyday experiences, stand in the way of our recognizing the ultimate reality of the non-dual spirit.

The third and the fourth chapters of the *Kārika* seek to demonstrate the unreality of the external world on the analogy of dream experiences. Dream objects are not real, because upon waking up one realizes the unreality of these objects. Dream objects are on par with the contents of erroneous perceptions in waking life. One might mistake a rope for a snake. However, as long as the erroneous perception lasts, it is real enough to frighten the individual undergoing that experience. Thus, both waking and dreaming are equally real from a relative standpoint and equally unreal from the point of view of the truth. When the right knowledge dawns, one realizes that the snake was only illusory. Similarly, dream experiences are real as long as the dream lasts. However, when one returns to the waking stage, one cognizes the unreality of the dream objects. Stated differently, whatever has a beginning or an end is unreal for Gaudapāda. Real, on the other hand, *is*, *was*, and *will be*. The real cannot be subject to change.

Non-dual spirit is the only reality; the world of objects is an illusion. If this is so, the question arises: How or why is the world of illusory appearance created? According to Shankara, *māyā* accounts for the appearance of the world. However, in Gaudapāda's philosophy the term *māyā* does not have a precise connotation. It has been used in a variety of senses. It expresses (1) the inexplicability of the relation that exists between *ātman* and the world, (2) the power or nature of God, and (3) the apparent character of the world.

Gaudapāda maintains that the world is a manifestation of God; it is an expression of his power. "*Ātman* [self], the self-luminous, imagines in himself by himself through his own *māyā*" (Gaudapāda, *Kārikā*). *Māyā*, in this context, is the wonderful power of God; it is inseparable from *ātman*. *Māyā* accounts for the world illusion; *māyā* conditions reality and projects it as the phenomenal world. Reality thus conditioned is known as *Īshvara* (God) or lower *Brahman*. God is both the efficient and the material cause of this world. Accordingly, Gaudapāda in his *Kārikā* rejects the rival themes that account for creation: (1) the world is the manifestation of God's prowess; (2) the world is the manifestation of God's will; (3) the world, like everything, proceeds in time; (4) the world is created for God's enjoyment; and finally (5) the world exists for the sake of God's sport. Gaudapāda rejects all these accounts because the world, for him, is the manifestation of God's nature.

The account of creation given above should not be construed to mean that the world is real, or that it is really created. The fundamental doctrine of Gaudapāda is the doctrine of non-creation (*ajātivāda*). Negatively, it signifies that the phenomenal world is never really created; it only appears to be created. Positively, it signifies that what is real cannot really be created. The real is self-existent; it is neither born, nor does it die.

Finite Self, Bondage, and Liberation

The Upanishadic notion of the identity of the finite self and *Brahman* forms the basis of Gaudapāda's theory of self. Accordingly, Gaudapāda holds that *māyā* is responsible for the misconception that the self is finite. The self in itself is infinite and eternal. However, since the self wrongly identifies itself with the objects that have a beginning and an end, it

is taken to be the many. The individuation of the one into many therefore is not real. Gaudapāda compares the *ātman* to absolute space, and the finite self to space enclosed, say, in a jar; when the jar is destroyed, the limited space in a jar merges into the absolute space. Absolute space is one; the form, purpose, and the names vary according to the limitations imposed upon it. Similarly, there is one absolute self. However, the limitations imposed upon it make it appear as many. The finite self and the absolute self are one, the differences are simply appearances. From a practical point of view, however, we have to treat the two as separate and distinct.

Since the self is deluded by its own ignorance, the removal of ignorance results in freedom from bondage. In such a realization the individual recognizes the *ātman* as the only reality. Such a knowledge is derived from the study of the Vedantic texts. Study of scriptures, detachment from material objects of the senses, and a strong desire for freedom steer an aspirant in the right direction.

Gaudapāda accepts the method of Yoga as a means to release. Intense meditation helps the aspirant get rid of all the obstacles that stand in the way of true knowledge. There are four chief obstacles to right knowledge: lapse of the mind into sleep, preoccupation of the mind on something other than the non-dual self, passion, and satisfaction with the residual impressions of attachment. Gaudapāda subscribes to the equation "*Om* = *Brahman* = Self" found in the *Māndūkya Upanishad*. It signifies what *was*, what *is*, and what *will be*. It is the unmanifest ground of the manifested universe. All this is *Brahman*, of which "aum" is the sound symbol. So, from the point of view of meditation, the meditation on *om* came to be regarded as most important and fruitful. When the mind does not lapse into sleep and dwell on the non-dual self, and is free from passions and attachments, one becomes *Brahman*. It is a state of bliss in which the self alone exists. It is a state where there is no sorrow, no fear, and no plurality, and no return to empirical existence. *Māyā* has been dispelled, and the self has transcended its finitude.

In this connection, one must not lose sight of the fact that since for Gaudapāda the entire world of plurality is simply an appearance, and since nothing ever really comes into being, bondage and release make sense only from a phenomenal point of view. The world, in Gaudapāda's view, is only an appearance of the one into many. It is a transfiguration of the one, not a real transformation. The world, in which the plurality of names and forms is manifested, is an illusory appearance. The self does not really *become* bound; it only *appears* bound. The truth somehow was covered by ignorance. The lifting of the veil of ignorance helps one realize what was always there.

Gaudapāda's interpretation of the scriptures was a turning point in the history of Indian philosophy. He revolutionized Vedānta by introducing the theory of appearance and asserting that non-duality is the true import of the *Upanishads*. He was the first philosopher to expound Advaita Vedānta systematically. The fact that Shankara felt compelled to write a commentary on the *Kārikā* testifies to its author's importance. He was a great preceptor of Advaita, and there is no doubt that Shankara follows him.

BINA GUPTA

Further Reading

Translation

Nikhilananda, Swami, trans. *The Māṇḍukyopaniṣad with Gauḍapāda's Kārikā and Śaṃkara's Commentary*. Mysore, India: Sri Ramakrishna Ashrama, 1974. This work contains a very useful introduction as well as translations of the *Māndūkya Upanishad*, Gaudapāda's *Kārikā*, and Shankara's commentary.

Related Studies

Dasgupta, S. N. *History of Indian Philosophy*. Vol. I. Delhi: Motilal Banarsidass, 1975. The essay on Gaudapāda in this book highlights the important features of Gaudapāda's philosophy in a clear and succinct manner.

Mahadevan, T. M. P. *Gauḍapāda: A Study in Early Advaita*. Madras, India: University of Madras, 1975. The best available source on the philosophy of Gaudapāda.

Radhakrishnan, S. *Indian Philosophy*. Vol. 2. New Delhi: George Allen and Unwin, 1977. This book contains a short essay on Gaudapāda and treats issues of interpretation, epistemology, metaphysics, and ethics.

HARIBHADRA

Born: Traditional date of birth is 459; modern scholarship suggests birthdate of 700; India
Died: Traditional date is 529; modern scholarship suggests date of death at 770; India
Major Works: *Anekāntajayapatākā* (*The Victory Banner of Relativism*), *Ashtakaprakarana* (*The Eightfold Explanation*), *Dhūrtākhyāna* (*The Rogue's Stories*), *Samarāiccakahā* (*The Story of Samarāicca*), *Sāstravārtāsamuccaya* (*The Array of Explanatory Teachings*), *Yogabindu* (*The Seeds of Yoga*), *Yogadrishtisamuccaya* (*An Array of Views on Yoga*)

Major Ideas

Although the Jaina teachings of life force, karma, *and nonviolence are true, there is also truth in other traditions.*

Ultimate reality can be grasped from various perspectives.

The stages of spiritual advancement to be found in the Yoga schools correspond to the fourteen stages to be found in Jainism.

Tolerance of the philosophical and religious views of others is required by the Jaina precept of nonviolence.

The exact or even approximate dates of Haribhadra's life are a matter of dispute (and some scholars have theorized that there were two great thinkers by the name Haribhadra), and hardly anything of the details of his personal life are known. About all that we can state with some assurance is that Haribhadra was born as a Hindu *Brāhman* (or *Brāhmin*) (of the priestly caste) and that he achieved a high degree of learning. There are legends, however, that may hint at some aspects of his personality.

One legend states that at one time he became quite arrogant about his academic accomplishments and tied a string made of gold around his belly to prevent it from bursting from the weight of all his knowledge. Thinking that he had learned all that could be known, he proclaimed that if anyone could tell him something new, he would devote his life to the pursuit of it. It so happened that he overhead a Jaina nun called Yakini reciting a verse that he could not understand. Having been humiliated, he turned first to her and then to her teacher for guidance, thus beginning a long career first as student and then as teacher of Jainism.

In a twelfth-century story told about Haribhadra, two of his nephews were reportedly murdered in a Buddhist monastery for spying on philosophers of the rival faith. In conflict with the Jaina virtue of nonviolence, Haribhadra retaliated by defeating a group of Buddhists in debate and then forcing them into a cauldron of boiling oil, killing them. According to legend, he was then forced to atone for this sin by performing penance as prescribed by his teacher.

Haribhadra's Literary and Philosophical Writings

Haribhadra wrote extensively. Hundreds, if not thousands, of volumes have been attributed to him, and they cover a wide range of issues. His two major *Prākrit* texts are the *Samarāiccakahā*, a literary tale that discusses the workings of *karma*, using as examples such tales as that of the greedy man reborn as a coconut tree, and the *Dhūrtākhyāna*, a satirical critique of Hindu mythology, drawing parallels between wastrel human behavior and similar activities performed by Hindu gods.

In his Sanskrit philosophical texts such as the *Anekāntajayapatākā* and the *Sāstravārtāsamuccaya* he demonstrates his wide grasp of numerous sects of both Hinduism and Buddhism. Although he does not deviate from the core Jaina teachings of life force (*jīva*), *karma*, and nonviolence (see the chapter on Mahāvīra in this volume), he does accept the possibility of truth in other traditions. His work represents one of the earliest cases of overt philosophical tolerance in the Jaina religion. For instance, his *Ashtakaprakarana* lists eight qualities that can be universally applied to the faithful of any tradition: nonviolence, truth, honesty, chastity, detachment, reverence for a teacher, the act of fasting, and knowledge.

Tolerance of the Yoga and Buddhist Schools

Some of Haribhadra's most original thinking is found in his two Sanskrit Yoga treatises, the *Yogadrishtisamuccaya* and the *Yogabindu*. In the former work, Haribhadra provides a comparative analysis of four Yoga schools and aligns their various stages with the fourteen stages of Jaina spiritual advancement. Using Patanjali's eightfold Yoga path (see the chapter on Patanjali in this volume), he develops his own eightfold Yoga scheme, drawing heavily from the goddess imagery prevalent during the era in which he lived. His eight stages bear the names of *Mitrā* (Friendly), *Tārā* (Protector), *Balā* (Power), *Dīprā* (Shining), *Sthirā* (Firm), *Kāntā* (Pleasing), *Prabhā* (Radiant), and *Parā* (Highest) Yoga. These are then correlated with two additional Yoga systems. One is attributed to Bhadanta Bhāskara and is apparently Buddhist in origin, judging from its repeated use of negative terminology. The other is attributed to Bandhu Bhavaddatta, which, from the name of its author and its distinctly Hindu terminology, seems to stem from Vaishnava Hinduism.

Haribhadra indicates that he supports multiple perspectives of ultimate reality, noting that

> With these words—Sadāshivah, Parabrahma, Siddhātma, Tathatā—one refers to it, though the meaning is one in all the various forms.

However, in what amounts to a sociological commentary, he also criticizes certain Yogis who he claims are given over to worldly excess and are "addicted to vanity, decadent pleasures, and cruel behavior." Throughout the text he draws simple parallels between the early stages of Yoga and the beginnings of the Jaina path of liberation, and he implicitly acknowledges that the higher states of Yoga also lead to the Jaina goal of *kaivalya*.

In addition to his positive inclusion of key Buddhist ideas in the *Yogadrishtisamuccaya*, Haribhadra also praises Buddhism in the *Yogabindu*. He states that any great person should be worshipped, even if a Buddha. He states that any gift given to holy person earns merit, and he equates the Buddhist *Bodhisattva* with the Jaina aspirant. He even postulates that the compassion of the *Bodhisattva* in fact makes that person a *tīrthankara*. He refers to the Buddha as a *mahāmuni* or Great Sage.

In summary, Haribhadra is a complex figure. He wrote prolifically. The writings of Haribhadra indicate that he was widely read and that in spite of the implications of later legends that speak of his difficult relationships with Buddhist monks, he appears to have been sympathetic to hearing and considering the positions of various other thinkers. His commitment to seeking out and respecting the views of others serves as a paradigmatic example of the Jaina philosophy of *anekānta* or "manysidedness," which acknowledges the complexity and perspectival nature of human thought. His tolerance of other views may be seen as an extension of the fundamental Jaina precept of nonviolence (*ahimsā*).

CHRISTOPHER KEY CHAPPLE

Further Reading

Translations

Desai, S. M. *Haribhadra's Yoga Works and Psychosynthesis*. Ahmedabad, India: L. D. Institute of Indology, 1983. Translations and commentary.

Dixit, K. K. *The Yogabindu of Acārya Haribhadrasūri*. Ahmedabad, India: Lalbhai Dalpatbhai Bharatiya Sanskriti Vidyamandira, 1968. Sanskrit text with English translation with commentary.

——— . *Yogadisamuccaya and Yogaviṃśikā of Acārya Haribhadrasūri*. Ahmedabad, India: Lalbhai Dalpatbhai Bharatiya Sanskriti Vidyamandira, 1970. Sanskrit text with English translation and commentary.

Related Studies

Dundas, Paul. *The Jains*. London: Routledge, 1992. A superb survey of the Jaina tradition, with several references to Haribhadra.

Granoff, Phyllis. "Jain Lives of Haribhadra: An Inquiry into the Sources and Logic of the Legends." *Journal of Indian Philosophy* 17, no. 2 (1989): 105–128. A critique of stories told about Haribhadra in contrast with his philosophical writings.

Kapadia, H. R. *Anekāntajayapatākā by Haribhadra Sūri*. 2 vols. Baroda, India: Oriental Institute, 1940, 1947. The introduction to volume 1 includes discussion of life and works of Haribhadra.

Tatia, Nathmal. *Studies in Jaina Philosophy*. Banaras, India: Jain Cultural Research Society, 1951. Includes a twelve-page section entitled "Haribhadra's Comparative Studies in Yoga."

Williams, R. "Haribhadra." *Bulletin of the School of Oriental and African Studies, University of London* 28 (1965): 101–111. Discussion of the theory of two Haribhadras.

———. *Jaina Yoga*. Delhi: Motilal Banarsidass, 1963. Discussion of Haribhadra's dates.

SHANKARA

Born: 788, Kāladi, Kerala, South India
Died: 822
Major Works: *Aitareyopanishadbhāshya* (*Commentary on the* Aitareya Upanishad), *Ātmabodha* (Self-knowledge), *Bhagavadgītābhāshya* (*Commentary on the* Bhagavad Gītā), *Brahmasūtrabhāshya* (*Commentary on the* Brahma Sūtra), *Brihadāranyakopanishadbhāshya* (*Commentary on the* Brihadāranyaka Upanishad), *Chāndogyopanishadbhāshya* (*Commentary on the* Chāndogya Upanishad), *Īshopanishadbhāshya* (*Commentary on the* Īsha Upanishad), *Kathopanishadbhāshya* (*Commentary on the* Katha Upanishad), *Kenopanishadbhāshya* (*Commentary on the* Kena Upanishad), *Upadeshasāhasrī* (The Thousand Teachings)

Major Ideas

Reality or Brahman *is non-dual* (advaita).
The world is false.
The world is the product of a creative appearance (māyā).
The self is not-different from Brahman.
It is possible for empirical individual beings to realize Brahman.
In order to realize Brahman, *one must follow the Path of Knowledge* (Jnāna Yoga).
Realization of Brahman (moksha) *is the ultimate goal of human life.*
Moksha *is the realization of one's true nature.*

Shankara was born in Kāladi, a village in Kerala, in 788 into a *Brahmin* family known for its learning. His mother played an important role in shaping his life. Very little is known about his father. Shankara left home at an early age in search of a *guru* (teacher) who could initiate him into *sannyāsa* (renunciation). He joined a hermitage on the bank of the Narmada River and Guru Govinda accepted him as his pupil. There is no record of how long he stayed with Govinda. Suffice to say that Shankara received most of his training under the guidance of Govinda and attained the highest knowledge at a very early age. He traveled across India, debating with opponents and reforming aberrant practices. He died at the early age of thirty-two. Shankara was not only a philosopher; he was a mystic, saint, and poet. An enormous amount of work has been attributed to him. However, there is no doubt that he was the author of the works listed above. His achievements were remarkable, and the short span of his life makes his contributions all the more remarkable.

Among the nine schools of Indian philosophy,

Vedānta has been recognized as the most important and well known. This school bases itself on the teachings of the *Upanishads*, which form the concluding portion of the *Vedas*, the Hindu scriptural texts. Accordingly, the literal meaning of the term *Vedānta* is "the end of the *Vedas*" or "the culmination of the Vedic teachings."

The Vedānta system received its formal expression in the *Brahma Sūtras* (aphorisms dealing with *Brahman* or Reality) of Bādarāyana. These *sūtras* became the source of inspiration among the Vedāntic thinkers. The *sūtras* are brief and lend themselves to a variety of meanings and interpretations. The medieval commentators wrote commentaries on these aphorisms. These commentaries gave rise to different schools within the Vedāntic tradition, of which Advaita, Vishishtādvaita, and Dvaita became the most important. Their primary point of departure was an interpretation of the relation between *Brahman*, the world, and the self.

Shankara was the founder of Advaita Vedānta, the non-dualistic school of Vedānta. It has been and continues to be the most widely known system of

Indian philosophy, both in the East and the West. The entire philosophy of Shankara can be summed up in the following statement: *Brahma satyam, pagan mithyā, jīvo brahmaiva nāparah* (*Brahman* is real, the world is false, the self is not-different from *Brahman*). His major works reiterate this philosophy in different ways. Therefore, in order to get a grip on Shankara's system as a whole, one must begin by reviewing this assertion in Advaitin terms and determining its implications.

Brahman

Brahman, Shankara upholds, is the highest transcendental truth. It is a state of being where all subject–object distinction is obliterated. *Brahman* is devoid of all distinctions; it is without qualities (*nirguna*). It is timeless, unconditioned, and undifferentiated. It is that state of being about which nothing can be affirmed. No positive determination of *Brahman* is possible. (This is very similar to Spinoza's assertion that every determination implies negation: *omnis determinatio est negatio.*)

The *Upanishads* reiterate that the best way to describe *Brahman* is by saying that it is "not this, not this" (*neti, neti*). Apart from *nirguna Brahman*, there is *saguna Brahman*—*Brahman* as interpreted and affirmed by the mind from a limited, empirical standpoint. It is that *Brahman* about which something can be said; it is existence, consciousness, and bliss. In reality, the two *Brahmans* are one and the same. The teaching of Advaita affirm one simple truth: there is one reality, although it is known by different names. Reality has been differently described: pure *Brahman*, determinate *Brahman*, qualified *Brahman*, indeterminate *Brahman*. All these descriptions refer to one and the same reality; they have the same referent, although the senses vary. This is very much like Fregean analysis of the "morning star" and "evening star"; both refer to the planet Venus, although the uses and consequent senses of the terms are different.

Central to Shankara's theory of *Brahman* or reality is the concept of *bādha*, which in the context of his ontology has been construed as "cancellation" or "sublation." Sublation is the mental process of correcting and rectifying errors of judgment. In this process one disvalues—more as a psychological necessity than from a purely logical point of view—a previously held object or content of consciousness on account of its being contradicted by a new experience.

It is important to remember in this context that not all corrections/rectifications constitute sublation. Suppose one believes that a certain hypothesis, say a scientific concept, will work in a certain situation. However, a little later one finds out that it will not. Correction of error has occurred. This, however, is not sublation. Sublation not only requires rejection of an object, or a content of consciousness, but also that such rectification must occur in light of a new judgment to which belief is attached and which replaces the initial judgment.

By using this criterion of sublation, Shankara develops an ontological hierarchy. In his commentary on *Brahma Sutras*, he discusses three orders of existence: (1) absolute existence or reality, (2) empirical existence, and (3) illusory existence.

Absolute existence or reality is that which in principle cannot be sublated by any other experience. The act of sublation presupposes a dualism between the experiencer and the experienced. It involves plurality of objects because sublation juxtaposes one object or content of consciousness against another incompatible object or content of consciousness and judges the first to be of lesser value. The experience of reality is non-dual. Therefore, no other object or content of consciousness could replace it. *Brahman* is the only reality. It sublates everything while remaining unsublatable by any other experience whatsoever.

Empirical existence, "phenomenon" in the terminology of Kant and Plato, is the objective universe, the world of experience, governed by cause and effect. It can only be sublated by the experience of reality or *Brahman*. It persists till the direct knowledge of *Brahman* is attained. The world is only an appearance in Shankara. It is not ultimately real. It is sublated with the experience of *Brahman*.

Illusory existence is the false appearance of something where it does not exist. Illusions, hallucinations, dreams, and wrong perceptions fall under this category. An illusory existence fails to fulfill the functions for everyday empirical truth. For example, a thirsty person passing through a desert runs to a spot to quench his thirst. However, upon reaching that spot he discovers that there is no water there and that his perception of water is nothing but an illusion; it is a mirage. The illusion of a mirage comes to an end when the subject, in light of new experience, realizes that it was not real, it was only a mirage. The illusory existences are sublated by the ordinary empirical standpoint.

Thus, it may be safely said that Shankara upholds what may be termed a synoptic-experiential theory of truth, where (1) truth is determined synoptically, or from the totality of experience, in such a way that it includes both a coherence and a consistency theory; and (2) what is experienced is true until some other experience disvalues it. Dreams or illusions are sublated by normal waking experiences, which in turn are sublated by the experience of *Brahman* or reality. It is easily seen from this nomenclature that what is not "real" is not necessarily "unreal." Real means *real forever*. Real is eternal. *Brahman* is the only reality. Unreal means *unreal forever*. Unreal objects cannot become an object of our experience: for example, a square circle, son of a virgin woman. In order for an object to be sublatable, it must become an object of our experience. Accordingly, unreal is that which neither can nor cannot be sublated by any other experience. It is an absolute nothing; it is non-being. For our purposes then, we will speak of unreal to signify non-being, the apparent to signify all experiences (dreaming and waking) that are sublatable, and the real to signify the experience of reality.

These levels of existence are incommensurable. In this connection one must not lose sight of the fact that this hierarchy holds only from an empirical standpoint. From the standpoint of reality, there is no distinction between appearance and unreality; there is nothing but reality. *Brahman* as reality is nonempirical. It is non-dual. Accordingly, no experience can sublate *Brahman*-experience.

Brahman and the World

If *Brahman* is ultimately the only reality, then the question immediately arises, what precisely is the relationship between *Brahman* and the world? In what sense, if any, can *Brahman* be said to be the creator of the world? Shankara explains the relationship between *Brahman* and the world in terms of *satkāryavāda*: the material effect preexists in the cause. Shankara points out that, logically speaking, if the effect did not somehow preexist in the material cause, then anything should come from anything. However, for Shankara, the effect, though existent in the cause, is only an apparent manifestation of the cause. Accordingly, *Brahman*, the cause, is the only reality; the effect, the world, is only an apparent manifestation of the cause. *Brahman* thus becomes both the material and the efficient cause of the world.

Brahman, in its creative aspect, is known as *Īshvara*, the lord, or the *saguna Brahman*. *Brahman* as *Īshvara* is both the material and the efficient cause of the world. Shankara explains the creation of the world with the help of the Upanishadic concept of *māyā*. Ontologically, *māyā* is the creative power of *Brahman* that accounts for the variety and multiplicity of the phenomenal world. From an epistemological point of view, *māyā* is our ignorance about the difference between reality and appearance. From a psychological point of view, *māyā* is our tendency to regard the real as the apparent, and vice versa.

Since the world in Shankara is apparent, it is therefore different from both real (*Brahman*) and unreal (non-being). It is not real because it is sublatable. It is not unreal because unlike unreal objects, the world has an objective counterpart; it appears to us. The objects of the world, though not ultimately real, possess a different order of reality. This explains why Shankara describes the world as different from the real, the unreal, and the illusory existence.

Although *Brahman* creates the appearance of the world, it itself remains unaffected by the world appearance. Shankara uses the analogy of a magician and his tricks to explain this point. When a magician makes one thing appear as another, spectators are deceived by it. However, the magician himself is not deceived by it. Similarly, *Brahman* is that great magician who conjures up the world appearance and creates the multiplicity of names and forms. Finite individual beings are deceived by this appearance; they mistake appearance for reality. *Brahman* itself is not deceived by this appearance. *Māyā* not only has the power of concealing reality, but also of distorting reality. To put it differently, it is not only that we do not see *Brahman* as *Brahman*, but we perceive it as something else. Once ignorance is destroyed by the knowledge of the real, one is no longer subject to *māyā*. Hence, the next question: How does one dispel ignorance and see *Brahman* as *Brahman*?

Ātman (Soul), Jīva (Finite Individual), and Brahman

Shankara maintains that *ātman* is the innermost self of a person; it is pure formless, undifferentiated consciousness. It is reality, unsublatable by any other experience whatsoever. For Shankara, *Brahman* and *ātman* are one: *tat tvam asi* (that thou art). This Upanishadic saying provides the edifice for his entire philosophy. What is asserted here is that the underlying self of the individual *is Brahman*. It affirms that everything is *Brahman*, that there is no other reality than *Brahman*, although it is known by different names. *Ātman* and *Brahman* are not two different ontological entities, but two different names for the one and the same reality. In the experience of *Brahman*, subject and object coalesce into each other. In this experience one realizes that *Brahman*, the unchanging reality that underlies the external world of names and forms, is also the reality that underlies the internal world of change and appearances. To put it differently, all subject-object distinctions are obliterated; the distinction between the self and non-self vanishes, and one experiences *Brahman* as pure being, consciousness, and bliss.

The empirical finite individual (*jīva*) is a com-

posite of self and not-self. The wrong identification (*adhyāsa*) between the self with the not-self is the basis of our empirical existence. Just as in the snake–rope illusion, the snake is superimposed upon the rope (rope is the immediate datum of consciousness, the snake is an object of past experience, and illusion arises when the snake qualities perceived in the past are superimposed on a given rope); similarly, the individual self superimposes on the pure self, *ātman*, the qualities such as egoism, so that it sees itself as essentially separate from other selves. In other words, finitude and changes, that do not belong to the pure self, are mistakenly superimposed upon it. When one attains the knowledge of reality, ignorance disappears and one realizes *Brahman* as the only reality. This brings us to the next question: How does one attain such knowledge?

Moksha and Jnāna Yoga

Following the Upanishadic tradition, Shankara maintains that *moksha*, the state of freedom from ignorance, is the identity of *ātman* and *Brahman*. This is, and should be, the goal of human endeavor. Initially, the concept of *moksha* was articulated in negative terms, as freedom from the actions that bind a human being in this phenomenal world, as absence of suffering, and so on. However, Shankara was quick to realize that the negative sense of "freedom from" cannot be of highest value for human beings. *Moksha*, in the positive sense, is a state of bliss; it is the realization of our full potentialities. It is discovery of what we are and who we are. It is realization of our true nature. Right knowledge helps one dispel the erroneous identification of the self with the not-self.

Such a knowledge, maintains Shankara, is possible with the help of *Jnāna Yoga*, the Path of Knowledge. Indian philosophers maintain that there are two other paths besides the Path of Knowledge, *Bhakti Yoga*, the path of Devotion, and *Karma Yoga*, the Path of Action. It is generally believed that all Yogas, pursued properly, lead to the same end, namely *moksha*. Shankara, however, maintains that there is a hierarchy among them, and since the realization of *Brahman* is the ultimate aim, he regards the way of knowledge as the highest. For him, devotion to God, leading an ethical life, or surrendering one's actions to God, although no doubt useful, cannot lead to the realization of *Brahman*, the ultimate goal of human endeavors.

The study of the Vedāntic texts destroys one's ignorance. However, before one pursues such a study, one should prepare one's mind in order for the study to be effective. He outlines four qualifications to prepare one's mind: (1) one must be able to distinguish between appearance and reality, the world and *Brahman*; (2) one must give up desires for pleasure and enjoyment, that is, renounce all worldly desires; (3) one must develop qualities such as detachment, patience, and powers of concentration; and (4) one must have a strong desire to attain *moksha*.

After the mind is prepared, one studies the Vedāntic texts with the help of a *guru* who has realized *Brahman*. Such study consists of three steps: (1) listening to the teacher's instructions, (2) understanding the teachings of the *guru* through reasoning until all doubts are removed and one becomes intellectually convinced of the truth; and finally (3) practicing constant meditation. Here one must not overlook the importance of the last step. Intellectual convictions may change; they are not permanent. These intellectual convictions must be transformed so as to form part of one's own immediate experience. With the constant meditation on the great saying of the *Upanishads*, "thou art *Brahman*," one realizes that "I am *Brahman*"; one has the immediate experience of *Brahman*.

Shankara further notes that realization of *Brahman* is possible in this life and body itself. This state is known as *jīvan-mukti*, freedom in this life. In this stage, although the body continues, a person is no longer deceived by it. *Moksha* thus is not something that one looks forward to after death. It is a stage of perfection attained here, freedom while one is still alive. At death, such a person attains *videha-mukti*, the absolute freedom from the cycle of birth and rebirth, a state of equanimity, serenity, and bliss. Attainment of *moksha* is not a new production; it is

the realization of something that was always there. *Moksha* is coming to realize the identity that was forgotten during the embodied existence. It is the realization of one's potentialities as a human being.

Moksha is the highest goal; a liberated person is the ideal of society, and his life is worth emulating. After attaining *moksha* a person helps others attain the same goal and steers them in the right direction. Work is not incompatible with *moksha*; the liberated life is not a life of inactivity as some might assume. Social service is not incomparable with the highest goal of *moksha*. Shankara himself followed this ideal, and other Vedānta philosophers followed this very same path.

At times critics of Advaita maintain that since *Brahman* is the only reality, and the world an illusion, in such an outlook all distinctions between truth and falsehood become meaningless. They contend that morality does not have any place in Advaita. Such an interpretation is based on a confusion between the empirical and the real. An aspirant is bound up in the moral consequences of his or her actions; he or she is subject to ethical judgments. Thus, from an empirical standpoint, until the highest knowledge (*moksha*) is attained, distinctions between true and false are not only meaningful but also very important. It is not an exaggeration to say that in Shankara there are different levels of morality corresponding to different levels of finite individual experiences. Good actions take one closer to *Brahman*, and bad ones away from *Brahman*. It is only when *Brahman* is realized that everything is seen to be a product of ignorance, all forms of analytical reasoning to be without value, and the distinction between good and bad to be meaningless. It is not like Hegel's Absolute coming to know itself, because *Brahman* is never an object of knowledge; *Brahman* simply *is*.

BINA GUPTA

Further Reading

Translations

Deutsch, Eliot A. *Advaita Vedānta: A Philosophical Reconstruction*. Honolulu, Hawaii: University of

Hawaii Press, 1968. This is one of the best introductions available on the philosophy of Shankara.

——— and J. A. B. Van Buitenen. *A Source Book of Advaita Vedānta*. Honolulu, Hawaii: University of Hawaii Press, 1971. This book will help students of Advaita Vedānta to study this school through an examination of its primary sources.

Radhakrishnan, S. and C. A. Moore. *A Source Book of Indian Philosophy*. Princeton, N.J.: University of Princeton, 1957. The general introduction as well as introductions to selections make this volume very helpful.

Related Studies

Puligandla, R. *Fundamentals of Indian Philosophy*. New York: Abingdon Press, 1975. The book introduces students to the problems, methods, and nuances of Indian philosophical systems. It contains a very useful essay on Advaita.

VĀCASPATI MISHRA

Born: 842, Mithila, Modern Bihar, India
Died: Place and date unknown
Major Works: *Bhāmatī* (*"The Lustrous:"* [*Commentary of Shankara's Brahmasūtrabhāshya*]), *Brahmatatt-vasamīksha* (*Examination of the Brahman as Truth*), *Nyāyakanikā* (*Brief Outline of the Nyāya School*), *Tattvabindu* (*Quintessence of the Truth*)

Major Ideas

Brahman is the only reality.
The world is only an appearance.
Brahman *is the content or the object and the* jīva *(finite individual) is the locus of* avidyā *(nescience).*
Hearing the great sayings of the Upanishads *can lead only to mediate knowledge of the self.*
Prasankhyāna *(long-continued contemplation) leads to the immediate knowledge of the self.*

It is generally believed that in the post-Shankara phase of Advaita Vedānta, Mandana, Sureshvara, Padampāda, and Vācaspati started distinct lines of Advaita thought. These lines of thought, though distinct, did not develop independently. They converge at certain points, cross and recross at other points, and raise new philosophical issues of utmost importance, which the later followers of the school attempt to solve. The line of thought initiated by Mandana gave rise to one of the two important schools in the history of Advaita. Vācaspati was the founder of this school of Advaita Vedānta. It is known as the *Bhāmatī* School. Vācaspati in his exposition of Advaita primarily draws from the *Brahmasiddhi* of Mandana Mishrā. The other school, which follows Sureshvara, is known as the Vivarana School (see the chapter on Sureshvara in this volume).

Vācaspati lived in Mithila in the ninth century. His most important work is *Bhāmatī*, which is a commentary on Shankara's *Brahmasūtrabhāshya* (*Commentary on the* Brahma Sūtra). The term *Bhāmatī* etymologically means "the lustrous." This commentary forms the edifice of the school, and the school is named after it. Virtually nothing is known about the life of Vācaspati. He was not a direct disciple of Shankara (see the chapter on Shankara in this volume), and commented not only on Advaita works, but also upon the texts of other orthodox schools of Indian philosophy. He was an independent thinker, and his interpretation of the basic Shankarite worldview is refreshing.

Shankara accounts for the creation of the world with the help of Rig Vedic *māyā*, and uses *māyā* and *avidyā* (nescience) synonymously. Although some of the post-Shankarites, like Sureshvara, were satisfied with this explanation, most of them, like Vācaspati, felt compelled to make a distinction between the two, because in their opinion nescience or ignorance belonging to God must be somehow superior to the one belonging to the finite individual. They could not resist the urge to provide a conceptual construction of the world on the basis of the concept of *māyā*. For the followers of Shankara *māyā* was a principle of creation: it performed a generative function. Its mysteriousness notwithstanding, its workings must be explained rationally. *Avidyā*, on the other hand, performed the functions of obscuring, covering, and concealing the real nature of reality. *Māyā* and its relation to *avidyā* gave rise to a number of questions: If the world is *māyā* and not real, how could it be caused at all? How can *Brahman* as pure consciousness give rise to the material world? What is the locus and the object or content of *avidyā*?

The question whether nescience is one or many also became an issue. Another controversy arose about the relation between *Brahman* and *māyā*. *Māyā* is not real; yet it limits *Brahman* by becoming its limitation. By what process, then, does *māyā* become *Brahman*'s limiting adjunct?

It is impossible to treat all the important problems which Shankara's followers raise for discussion among themselves, not to mention the problems that arose as a result of these discussions. This chapter will be concerned with three key topics: (1) the status of *avidyā*, (2) the removal of *avidyā*, and (3) the status of the *jīva*.

The Status of Avidyā

Following Shankara, Vācaspati maintains that the ultimate reality is one and non-dual. It is pure self, which is pure consciousness or the self-luminous immediate self-revelation that can never be contradicted. It exists forever. Multiplicity of names and forms—the plurality of objects that we see in this world—are only limited appearances of the pure self or *Brahman*. The entire universe is the result of *avidyā* or *ajnāna*, which not only obscures the real nature of the pure self, but makes it appear as something else.

The discussion of the self as opposed to not-self is of utmost importance in the metaphysics of Shankara and his followers, and this distinction plays a very important role in Vācaspati's philosophy as well. Superimposition of the not-self on the self is the cause of *jīva*'s bondage. It covers the totality of one's experience, subjective and objective. The stream of superimpositions and objectifications is beginningless. The stream of indeterminable superimpositions makes us look for the cause of each superimposition in a preceding superimposition. However, there must be an original superimposition. This original superimposition is primal nescience, the root cause. Primal nescience gives rise to derivative nescM, and the individual nescience are products of these derivative nescience. Derivative nescience are sublatable by the right cognition of the objects to which they relate; primal nescience, on the contrary, is sublatable only by knowledge of *Brahman* alone.

In short, Vācaspati articulates *avidyā* as twofold: *avidyā* as a beginningless positive entity, and as a series of beginningless false impressions. In its pos-

itive aspect, it is beginningless, it is primal. In its negative aspect, it is temporary, it is derivative. The causal relation between derivative nescience and its products is different from that between primal and derivative nescience. Primal nescience is the logical ground of the derivative nescience. Primal nescience is one, whereas derivative nescience are many. Primal nescience comes to an end only by *Brahman*-realization. Derivative nescience, on the other hand, are sublatable by other appearances in the empirical realm. In the snake–rope illusion (in which a rope appears to be a snake), the appearance of snake is negated by the cognition of rope; however, from the point of view of reality, both are appearances.

Primal nescience is the material cause of the world. At the time of dissolution, all products of *avidyā* merge in indescribable primal *avidyā*, their root cause, and abide there as potentialities. When dissolution comes to an end, impelled by God's will, these potentialities assume their appropriate names and forms as they had before dissolution. Although creation is impelled by God's will, God's will is conditioned by previous *karmas* and impressions.

Vācaspati, following Mandana, argues for the position that nescience or ignorance resides in many different selves. There are as many nesciences as there are *jīvas* (finite individuals). This makes perfect sense in his view because when a particular *jīva* attains the highest knowledge, nescience comes to an end; however, the nesciences of other *jīvas* continue.

Regarding the locus of nescience, Vācapati argues that the empirical individual, not *Brahman*, is the locus of *avidyā*. For him, the *jīva* is the locus of *avidyā*, because the *jīva*'s illusion is psychological, for which the *jīva* is responsible. This gives rise to a problem: *avidyā* is said to reside in the *jīva* and the *jīva* is said to be a product of *avidyā*. Is this possible? Vācaspati maintains that the *jīva* is the result of a false illusion, the illusion that is the result of a previous false illusion, and so on ad infinitum. In short, psychological ignorance is a chain of beginningless illusions in which each succeeding illusion is the result of its preceding illusion. For Sureshvara, on the other hand, *Brahman* is both the locus and the object of *avidyā*. But, affirms Vācaspati, *Brahman* is pure consciousness, and it is ridiculous to claim that *Brahman* is the locus of nescience.

Regarding the content of nescience, Vācaspati affirms that in an appearance *Brahman* and not-self are wrongly identified. Appearance is sublated by right knowledge. Appearances, in order to be appearances, must be wrongly identified with *Brahman*. Thus *Brahman* is the object of *avidyā*. These appearances are neither real nor unreal. They are not real because they are sublated with the dawn of right knowledge. They are not unreal because they appear; they have an objective counterpart. These appearances belong to the empirical realm and are the product of *avidyā*, which is removed when one attains release.

Removal of Avidyā

Vācaspati concurs with Shankara that knowledge destroys nescience. Performance of appropriate rituals purifies the intellect and produces a desire to know the truth in the aspirant. However, performance of rituals cannot lead to *moksha* (release). The mind must be prepared to receive the truth. The study of the Vedantic texts helps one in that direction.

After the desire to know has been produced, the aspirant goes to a *guru* who is already established in *Brahman*, and practices three steps in the quest for the knowledge of non-dual *Brahman*: (1) hearing, (2) reasoning, and (3) meditating. The aspirant hears the Upanishadic great sayings, such as "Thou art that," reflects on them, and begins uninterrupted meditation accompanied by devotion. Eventually, the seeker of *Brahman* attains *Brahman*; the aspirant has an intuition of *Brahman*. For Vācaspati, this intuition is an immediate cognition. It requires the functioning of the sense-organ, the mind. And this cognition is possible by a long-continued contemplation (*prasankhyāna*).

Although all the followers of Shankara believe that the repeated practice of hearing, reflecting, and meditating is necessary until one is established in the knowledge of "Thou art that," the importance

attached to these three varies. Specifically, there is a great difference of opinion among the followers of Shankara regarding the role that hearing plays as a means to the knowledge of *Brahman*. For Vācaspati, the innate nature of a sentence is to give rise only to mediate knowledge. Therefore, the knowledge arising by hearing these Upanishadic texts and by reflecting on them is only mediate. It no doubt can remove the seeker's ignorance about the existence, nature, and means of attainment of *Brahman*; however, it cannot give rise to the immediate knowledge of *Brahman*. This mediate knowledge of *Brahman* serves as an indirect means to its immediate knowledge, which is gained by meditation. For him, the mind is the primary instrument for the knowledge of *Brahman*. Knowledge becomes immediate through the mind. Therefore, the mind alone is the instrumental cause of the rise of the direct knowledge of *Brahman*. The mind perfected by constant meditation on the meaning of great sayings of the *Upanishads* eliminates all doubts and manifests the identity of "that" and "thou."

In this connection, Vācaspati disagrees with Sureshvara, who contends that it is not the innate nature of a sentence to give rise to only mediate knowledge. Whether a sentence gives rise to mediate knowledge or immediate knowledge depends upon the nature of the object under consideration. If the object is immediate, then, knowledge is immediate. *Brahman* is always immediate and hence the Upanishadic texts can and do give rise to the immediate knowledge of *Brahman*. When nescience is destroyed by knowledge, one attains release. The physical body, however, continues on account of the momentum of the past *karmas*, although the person does not accumulate any more *karmas*.

The Status of the Jīvas (Finite Individuals)

The individual person, for Advaita, is both real and apparent. It is real so far as *ātman* is its ground; it is an appearance so far as it is identified with a body. Regarding the status of the finite individual, Vācaspati upholds the limitation theory that involves the reduction to the finite of the Infinite. Just as space is really one but is divided into particular spaces like the space in a pitcher or a room, similarly self is one; however, on account of limitations it is seen as many. The self limited by its internal organs and other physical features is the *jīva*; when the limiting adjuncts are removed, there is no difference between *jīva* and *Brahman*. He thus disagrees with the Vivarana School, which subscribes to the reflection theory. For them, the *jīva* is a reflection of *ātman* in the mirror of *avidyā*. The reflection is as real as the prototype (*bimba*) since it is in essence the same as the prototype.

Vācaspati rejects the reflection theory. *Brahman* is formless, and hence cannot have any reflection. For him, *Brahman* delimited by nescience is *jīva*. Vācaspati does not subscribe to the reflection theory, because reflection can only be of something that is visible and in what is visible, and neither *Brahman* nor *avidyā* have a visible form.

Vācaspati was not the first Advaitin to propound the theory of *jīva* as the locus of *avidyā*: he borrowed it from Mandana. But his commentaries clarified the obscure areas of Mandana's writings. He was very well aware of the inconsistencies inherent in Mandana's articulation of this theory. The fact that one of the two schools of the post-Shankara phase has been named after his commentary *Bhāmatī* testifies to his importance for the Advaitins.

BINA GUPTA

Further Reading

Translation

Sastri, S. S. and Raja, C. K., eds. and trans. *The Bhāmāti of Vācaspati*, Madras, India: The Theosophical Publishing House, 1933. Provides a translation of the first four sutras of *Brahmasūtrabhāshya*. This book also contains a very long and useful introduction.

Related Studies

Hasurkar, S. S. *Vācaspati Miśra and Advaita Vedānta*. Darbhanga, India: Mithila Institute, 1958. This study highlights the contributions of Vācaspati to the school of Advaita Vedānta. It also provides a historical survey of philosophical conditions that existed in India during its post-Shankara phase.

Mahadevan, T. M. P. *Superimposition in Advaita Vedānta*. New Delhi: Sterling Publishers Pvt. Ltd., 1985. A clear and critical account of the arguments of the various schools of Advaita concerning how the world, an appearance of the real, is a superimposition of the self.

Sharma, C. D. *A Critical Survey of Indian Philosophy*. Delhi: Motilal Banarsidass, 1964. This book contains a short and helpful essay on Mandana.

SURESHVARA

Born: Fl. in the ninth century
Died: Place and time unknown
Major Works: *Brihadāranyakopanishadbhāshya Vārtikā* (*Explanation of the Commentary on the Brihadāranyaka Upanishad*), *Naishkarmyasiddhi* (*Establishment of Non-action*), *Sambandha Vārtikā* (*Explanation of Relations*), *Taittirīyopanishadbhāshya Vārtikā* (*Explanation of the Commentary on the Taittirīya Upanishad*)

Major Ideas

Brahman *is the only reality.*
The world is only an appearance.
Brahman *is the locus as well as the content or the object of* avidyā (*nescience*).
The hearing of the great sayings of the Upanishads *leads to immediate knowledge of the self.*

Of all Shankara's direct disciples, Sureshvara was the most prominent. He has been identified as a distinguished spokesperson of Shankara (see the entry on Shankara in this volume). He successfully defended Shankara's system from the attacks of his opponents and elucidated Shankara's fundamental thesis in a clear and concise manner. Virtually nothing is known about the life of Sureshvara. Tradition takes him to be the direct disciple of Shankara. He flourished in the ninth century. It is believed that in his secular life he was known by the names Mandanamishrā and Visvarūpa. He was the author of two *Vārtikās*: *Brihadāranyakopanishadbhāshya* (*Shankara's Commentary on* Brihadāranyakopanishad) and *Taittirīyopanishadbhāshya* (*Shankara's Commentary on* Taittirīyopanishad).

A *Vārtikā* is a work that examines what is stated explicitly, what is implied, and what is not said clearly in the original work. A *Vārtikā*, in short, performs the threefold function of explaining, supplementing, and offering alternative interpretations of the original text. Sureshvara, in his *Vārtikās*, attempts to vindicate Shankara's philosophy that *Brahman* is real, the world is false, and that the self is not-different from *Brahman*.

Tradition maintains that in his earlier days, he had been an avowed follower of Mīmāmsā, the school that emphasizes the ritualistic aspect of the *Vedas*, and that he had tried to defend the Mīmāmsite interpretation of the *Vedas* in a debate with Shankara that lasted for several days. Shankara defeated him in the debate. Sureshvara accepted the defeat, acknowledged the supremacy of Shankarite worldview, and asked Shankara to initiate him. He then assumed the name Sureshvara, by which he is widely known today. It is said that Shankara wanted Sureshvara to write a *Vārtikā* on his *bhāshya*. However, Shankara's pupils objected on the ground that Sureshvara was formerly a follower of Mīmāmsā and was therefore not competent to do so. Shankara then asked Sureshvara to write an independent treatise on Advaita. This important work, known as *Naishkarmyasiddhi*, is the earliest independent treatise available on Shankara's *bhāshya*. It is much shorter than his *Vārtikās*; it presents the quintessence of Advaita Vedanta in a concise manner.

Brahman

Following Shankara, Sureshvara maintains that *Brahman* or self is the only reality; the world is not real. *Brahman* is unqualified and beyond human comprehension. However, finite mind in its attempt to conceptualize *Brahman* describes it with the help of language. Language has its source in the phenomenal world; it cannot adequately describe that which transcends human perception. Everything in this world is subject to change and destruction except the self. Indeed the very con-

ception of change and destruction presupposes the
self.

According to Shankara, *Brahman* and *ātman*
(self) are identical from the standpoint of reality.
The self is self-luminous; it is not revealed by any
other means; it reveals other objects. It is eternal
consciousness, absolute, and unconditioned. Like
Shankara, Sureshvara contends that though the self
in itself is free, the attributes of the not-self are
superimposed upon it on account of ignorance.
This superimposition takes various forms. When I
say "I am black," I superimpose the attributes of
the body on the self. Similarly, when I say "I am
blind," I superimpose the attributes of the sense-
organ on the self. Sureshvara maintains that the self
is distinguished from the non-self on the basis of
the following three criteria: (1) the self being of the
nature of consciousness is self-established, (2) the
self is devoid of attributes, and (3) the self is immutable; it does not originate and it is not subject to
destruction. Not-self, or the multiplicity of names
and forms that manifests in the world, is only apparent. The world is rooted in *avidyā*.

Avidyā

The term *avidyā*, which has been variously translated as "ignorance," "nescience," and "illusion,"
is one of the most important terms in Shankara's
philosophy, and it plays an equally important role
in Sureshvara's philosophy. This concept accounts
for the apparent diversity of the world. Advaitins
maintain that *Brahman* or reality is one, and the
multiplicity of names and forms, the experience of
diversity that we undergo, is due to *avidyā*.

This gives rise to an interesting problem. If *avidyā* creates the apparent world, whose is *avidyā*?
Nescience or ignorance cannot exist in a vacuum. It
must be ignorance of someone about something
and must have a locus or substratum in which it
resides, and it must refer to some object.

The question regarding the locus and the object
or content of *avidyā* became one of the central
issues between the two main post-Shankara
schools. Both the schools agree that *Brahman* is the
object or content of *avidyā*. However, they vary

regarding the locus of *avidyā*. The Vivarana
School, which follows Sureshvara, maintains that
Brahman is the locus as well as the content of
avidyā. The *Bhāmāti* School, which follows Vacaspati (see the chapter on Vacaspati Mishra in this
volume), maintains that the locus of *avidyā* is *jīva*
(finite individual), although its content is *Brahman*.

Sureshvara argues that although the real self is
forever free, pure, and luminous, it is caught up in
all appearances, because of its erroneous identification with the not-self. *Avidyā* is the root cause
of this erroneous identification. Since this is the
case, the not-self, being itself a product of *avidyā*,
cannot be taken to be its locus or support. To say
ignorance exists in that which is of the nature of
ignorance is meaningless. Additionally, *avidyā*
precedes not-self. It is absurd to claim that whatever is logically and causally prior can be located
in its result. According to Sureshvara, there are
only two categories of human experience, the self
and the non-self. Since the not-self cannot be the
locus of *avidyā*, it follows that the self alone can
be and is its locus.

Sureshvara disagrees with Vacaspati's objection
that since *Brahman* or self is of the nature of knowledge, it cannot be the locus of *avidyā*. This objection, says Sureshvara, is based on a confusion
between the apparent and the real. He reminds his
readers that from the standpoint of *Brahman* or self
there is no *avidyā* at all; it does not exist. The self is
said to be knowledge, not from the phenomenal
standpoint but from the standpoint of reality. Thus,
no contradiction is involved in claiming on the one
hand that the self is the locus of *avidyā* and that it is
knowledge on the other.

For Sureshvara, *Brahman* or self is not only the
locus of *avidyā*, it is also the object or content of
avidyā. Since ignorance is ignorance of the real
nature of the self that transforms itself into the
knower, the known, and the resulting knowledge,
and since *Brahman* or self is regarded as the manifold world of names and forms and since there is no
other object regarding which ignorance is possible,
it is obvious that *Brahman* is also the object of
avidyā. Thus, for Sureshvara, *Brahman* or self is
both the locus and the content of *avidyā*.

Removal of Avidyā

Sureshvara concurs with Shankara in the conviction that an aspirant in quest of *Brahman*-knowledge must possess certain qualifications in order to be eligible for such a study. There are four qualifications: (1) discrimination between the eternal and the noneternal; (2) non-attachment from the results of the actions; (3) development of virtues such as calmness, restraint, forbearance, withdrawal, concentration, and faith; and (4) a longing for *moksha* or release.

After the mind is prepared, the aspirant should go to a qualified *guru* (teacher) who is well-established in *Brahman* to learn the import of the Vedānta teachings. This part of the training consists of three steps: (1) hearing the Vedāntic texts, the texts that teach the unity of *Brahman* and the self; (2) understanding these texts with the help of reasoning so that all the doubts about non-duality are removed; and (3) meditating on what has been heard and ascertained through rational reflection.

Among the followers of Shankara there is a lot of controversy over which of these three steps is the most important. Of the two main post-Shankara schools, the Vivarana, which follows Sureshvara, maintains that hearing the Vedāntic texts leads to the immediate realization of *Brahman*. On the other hand, the *Bhāmāti* School, following Vācaspati, maintains that continued meditation called *prasankhyāna* leads to the realization of *Brahman*.

Sureshvara rejects *Bhāmāti*'s contention in this regard as well. He upholds that just as a person who mistakes a stump of a tree for a human being, when told "This is not a human being but a stump," realizes his error, so the instruction "Thou art that" removes the aspirant's notion of finitude and manifests the self as *Brahman*. There is no time gap between the rise of knowledge and the removal of ignorance. This is not an instance of meditation, but rather a case of right apprehension. Thus, for Sureshvara, great sayings of the *Upanishads*, such as "Thou art that" are the primary means of the immediate knowledge of *Brahman*.

Sureshvara maintains that although reasoning based on the scriptures helps the aspirant discrimi-

nate between the eternal and noneternal, the removal of ignorance that hides the real nature of the self is effected through hearing. Sureshvara reminds his readers of the story "Thou art the tenth" to illustrate how by listening to the scriptural great saying "Thou art that," the aspirant realizes *Brahman*: Once ten young men left home on foot to go to another village. They had to cross a river on their way to their destination; the river was flooded and looked difficult to cross. They decided to wade the swollen stream. Upon reaching the other side of the river, one of these ten young men counted the number in the party in order to make sure that all of them were safe and found to his chagrin there were only nine. The second one counted the number in the party with the same result. A passerby saw that each of them had counted the people in the party excluding himself and pointed out to each one "Thou art the tenth," "Thou art the tenth."

For Sureshvara, "Thou art that" conveys to the seeker the right knowledge of the self immediately. Sureshvara reiterates this view in all three of his major works: *Brihadāranyakopanishadbhāshya Vārtikā*, *Naishkarmyasiddhi*, and *Taittirīyopanishadbhāshya Vārtikā*. Although for Sureshvara the great sayings, and not the mind, are the primary means of the direct knowledge of *Brahman*, he does recognize that mind is an important aid to verbal testimony in the realization of the self. Reflection and meditation remove the obstacles from the seeker's mind and prepare the finite individual to receive immediate knowledge through hearing *Brahman*.

The Status of the Jīva (Finite Individual) After Liberation

Another important question that occupies Sureshvara's attention deals with the status of the *jīva* after liberation. Does the *jīva* (finite individual) after liberation become one with *Īshvara* or *Brahman*?

The *jīva* (finite individual), for Advaita, is both real and apparent. It is real so far as *ātman* is its ground; it is an appearance so far as it is identified with a body. To explain the status of the *jīva* in the phenomenal world, Shankara suggested two theories: (1) *pratibimba vāda*, or the reflection theory, and (2) *avaccheda-vāda*, or the theory of limitation. For the reflection theory, the *jīva* is a reflection of *Brahman* in the mirror of *avidyā*. For the limitation theory, on the other hand, *jīva* is *Brahman* limited by *avidyā*. The first was the theory followed by the Vivarana School and the second was the theory followed by *Bhāmatī*.

For those who maintain that *jīva* is a reflection and *Brahman* simply a prototype of that reflection, the reflection is as real as the prototype (*bimba*), since it is, in essence, the same as the prototype. This is the unique feature of this theory. According to this theory, liberation is articulated in terms of the identity between *jīva* and *Brahman*. One attains that identity; thereupon one becomes a reflection of *ātman*.

Sureshvara advocates what is known as *abhāsāvāda*. This view is very similar to the reflection theory, with one exception: In this interpretation the reflected image is *not* as real as the prototype. The reflected image is in fact different from the prototype and is indescribable either as real or as unreal. Pure consciousness reflected in *avidyā* is *Īshvara* (God), and the pure consciousness reflected in the mind is *jīva*. *Īshvara* and *jīva* as reflected consciousness are different from the prototype and are indescribable either as real or unreal. Thus, whereas according to the reflection theory on attaining identity one realizes that one is essentially identical with the prototype, in Sureshvara's theory the empirical world of names and forms is instantaneously sublated on attaining identity, and *Brahman* shines in its pristine purity as the sole residue.

Sureshvara was the first to expound *abhāsāvāda*. This theory provided ample scope for the Advaitins to reconstruct issues surrounding Shankara's theory of the status of the finite individual.

The fact that the Vivarana School of Advaita follows the line of thought developed by Sureshvara testifies to his importance in the history of Advaita. Although he was not prepared to compromise on the basic non-dualistic perspective of Shankara, he does stress the importance of reconciling the different modes of interpretation. Almost every important philosopher on Advaita resorts to Sureshvara at crucial points, either to vindicate his own position or to criticize other views.

BINA GUPTA

Further Reading

Translations

Alston, A. J., trans. *The Naiṣkarmya Siddhi of Śrī Sureśvara*. London: Shanti Sadan, 1959. This book contains a translation of *Naishkarmyasiddhi* accompanied by a long introduction in which Sureshvara's philosophy is clearly elucidated.

Balasubramanian. R. *The Taittirīyopaniṣadbhaṣya with Sureśvara's Vārtikā*. Madras, India: University of Madras, 1984. Provides a translation of the *Taittirīyopanishadbhashya* and also annotations where necessary. This book contains a very long, useful introduction.

Related Studies

Mahadevan, T. M. P. *Superimposition in Advaita Vedānta*. New Delhi: Sterling Publishers Pvt. Ltd., 1985. A clear and critical explanation of how the world, an appearance of the real, is a superimposition of the self.

Sharma, C. D. *A Critical Survey of Indian Philosophy*. Delhi: Motilal Banarsidass, 1964. Covers major historical developments from the *Vedas* up to the present time, demonstrating the continuity of basic ideas and values.

RĀMĀNUJA

Born: 1017, Shriperumbudur, South India
Died: 1137, Sharīnangam, South India
Major Works: *Shrībhāshya* (*Commentary on the* Brahma Sūtra), *Gītābhāshya* (*Commentary on the* Gītā), *Vedāntasāra* (*The Essence of Vedanta*), *Vedārthasamgraha* (*Compendium of the Vedic Topics*)

Major Ideas

Brahman *is the same as the god of theism.*
The world rooted in Brahman *is as real as* Brahman.
Both matter and selves are eternal.
Souls are many in number.
Souls are essentially alike.
Ignorance is the root cause of our bondage.
Freedom from ignorance is possible through devotion.

Rāmānuja was born in Shriperumbudur, a village in South India, into a *Brahmin* (priestly caste) family. He received his formal training under Yādvaprakāsha, a renowned Vedānta *ācārya* (teacher). Rāmānuja married at an early age of sixteen and after his father's death left home to study with Yādvaprakāsha, who at the time resided in Kāncī. Not much is known about Yādvaprakāsha's life. According to some accounts, however, he probably was a monist. Rāmānuja, on the other hand, was opposed to the monistic interpretation of the *Upanishads* (Hindu scriptural texts). These ideological differences eventually were responsible for Rāmānuja's leaving Yādvaprakāsha and seeking the company of poet–saints such as Yamuna, Mahāpurāna, and Goshthipūrna, and he was greatly influenced by them. These poet-saints of South India were known as *ālvārs*. (The term etymologically means one who has attained a mystic intuitive knowledge of God.) These poet–saints upheld a theistic interpretation of the *Upanishads*, the interpretation that shaped Rāmānuja's philosophical outlook.

Rāmānuja was a theist. He worshipped the god *Vishnu*, to whom he built many temples and *mathas* during his lifetime. The catholic spirit of his religion made it possible for him to acquire a large number of devoted scholars, who carried on his religion and philosophy for centuries to come. Rāmānuja died in 1137.

Rāmānuja was the founder of the school known as Vishishtādvaita Vedānta (qualified non-dualism) in Indian philosophy. Rāmānuja's philosophy is a creative and constructive effort to systematize the teachings of the *Upanishads*, the *Gītā*, and the *Brahmasūtras*. Its chief contribution lies in reconciling the extremes of monism and theism. It is an inquiry into the nature of highest reality, *Brahman*. It also provides a path to the realization of this reality.

It begins by asking the basic Upanishadic question: "What is that by knowing which everything else is known?" The answer is: "*Brahman.*" *Brahman* is knowable; it is realizable.

Brahman

At the outset of his philosophy, Rāmānuja informs us that all knowledge necessarily involves discrimination and differentiation; it is impossible to know an object in its undifferentiated form. The knowable is known as characterized in some form or other by some specific attributes. Since knowledge always involves distinctions, both pure identity and pure difference are unreal. Rāmānuja refuses to divorce the manifold from the one; his unity contains within itself the diversity. He concurs with Shankara (see the chapter on Shankara in this volume) that *Brahman* is real. However, whereas for

Shankara *Brahman* as pure intelligence is devoid of any distinctions—it is pure identity without any difference (*nirguna*)—Rāmānuja's *Brahman* is identity-in-difference. When the *Upanishads* describe *Brahman* as devoid of qualities, they mean that *Brahman* does not have any negative qualities, not that it has no qualities whatsoever. It possesses a number of good characteristics (*saguna*). Existence, consciousness, bliss, knowledge, and truth are some of its attributes. These attributes are responsible for its determinate nature. *Brahman*, for Rāmānuja, is not different from the personal God of theism.

Brahman is an organic unity, a unity that is characterized by diversity. Rāmānuja recognizes three factors as real: *Brahman* or God, soul, and matter. Though equally real, the last two are absolutely dependent on the first. Perhaps the most original aspect of Rāmānuja's philosophy is the rejection of the principle that to be real means to be independent. Although soul and matter in themselves are substances, in relation to God they become his attributes. They are God's body, and he is their soul. Rāmānuja's notion of *aprithak-siddhi* or inseparability explains this relation. The relation of inseparability that obtains between a substance and its qualities may also be found between two substances. Just as qualities are real and cannot exist apart from the substances in which they subsist, similarly matter and soul are parts of *Brahman* and cannot exist without *Brahman*. The soul of a human being, although different from his body, controls and guides the body; similarly, *Brahman*, although different from matter and souls, directs and sustains them. To put it differently, *Brahman* is like a person, and the various selves and material objects constitute its body. Accordingly, Rāmānuja's *Brahman* is not an unqualified identity; it is identity-in-difference, an organic unity, or better yet, an organic union in which one part predominates and controls the other part.

Brahman and the World

Rāmānuja maintains that *Brahman* is real and that the world rooted in *Brahman* is also real. Rāmānuja takes the Upanishadic account of creation literally: the omnipotent God creates the world out of himself. Hindu thought includes the cyclic view that creation is followed eventually by dissolution, then by a new creation. During dissolution, God remains as the cause, with subtle matter and disembodied souls forming his body. This is the causal state of *Brahman*. The entire universe remains in a latent and undifferentiated state. God's will impels this undifferentiated subtle matter to be transformed into gross and disembodied souls into embodied according to their *karmas*. This is the effect state of *Brahman*.

Creation, for Rāmānuja, actually takes place, and the world is as real as *Brahman* itself. Accordingly, Rāmānuja holds that the Upanishadic texts such as "There is no multiplicity here" (*nehu nānā asti kincena*) do not really deny the multiplicity of objects and of names and forms, but rather assert that these objects have no existence apart from *Brahman*. It is indeed true, concedes Rāmānuja, that some Upanishadic texts describe *Brahman* as wielder of a magical power (*māyā*). However, *māyā*, according to Rāmānuja, is the unique power of God by which God creates the wonderful world of objects. He vehemently criticizes Shankara's theory that the world is false; it is a creation of *māyā*. The created world of *Brahman*, for Rāmānuja, is as wonderful as *Brahman* itself.

If someone were to ask "How does the one contain the many?", Rāmānuja in response would put forth the grammatical principle of *sāmānādhikarnya*, or the principle of coordination. According to this rule, words in a sentence having different meanings can denote one and the same thing. Rāmānuja's interpretation of the classical text "This is that *Devadatta*" explains this rule clearly. Rāmānuja holds that the *Devadatta* of the past and the *Devadatta* of the present cannot be entirely identical, because the person as seen at the present and the person as seen in the past are different and have different meanings, yet both refer to the same person. Similarly, unity and diversity, the one and the many, can coexist; they are not contradictories and can be reconciled in a synthetic unity. Accordingly, he does not deny the many; the many, on the contrary, characterizes the one. This rule on the one hand rejects the principle of abstract bare identity and on the other reveals a principle of differentiation at the very center of identity; it demonstrates the reality of the finite self.

Self, Bondage, and Liberation

A finite human being, maintains Rāmānuja, has a body as well as a soul. The material body, although a part of God, is finite. The soul, on the other hand, is eternal, real, and unique. In *samsāra* (embodied existence), the soul wrongly identifies itself with the body on account of *karmas* (past deeds) and ignorance. There are innumerable individual souls; they are qualitatively alike but differ in number.

Freedom from ignorance, *karma*, and embodied existence is possible through work, knowledge, and devotion to God. "Work," for Rāmānuja, means the different rites and rituals prescribed in the *Vedas* according to one's caste and situation in life. These duties must be performed without any desire for the rewards. Disinterested performance of one's duties is the key here. Such a performance destroys the accumulative effects of actions. The study of the *Mīmāmsā* texts (texts that explain how the rites and ceremonies should be performed) is necessary to ensure the right performance of duties. Accordingly, Rāmānuja makes the study of *Mīmāmsā* a necessary prerequisite to the study of Vedānta.

The study of the *Mīmāmsā* texts and the correct performance of one's duties lead one to realize that since sacrificial rites and ritual do not lead to freedom from one's embodied existence, knowledge of Vedānta is necessary. The study of Vedānta is necessary for the development of one's intellectual convictions about the nature of God, the external world, and one's own self. Such a knowledge reveals to the seeker of wisdom that God is the creator, sustainer, and destroyer of the world, and that the soul is a part of God and is controlled by him. Study and reflection further reveal to the aspirant that neither the correct performance of one's duties nor an intellectual knowledge of the real nature of God can lead to freedom from embodiment. Such a

freedom can only be attained by the free, loving grace of God. Accordingly, one should dedicate oneself to the service of God. Rāmānuja, in short, unlike Shankara, maintains that the path of devotion leads one to freedom.

The path of devotion, for Rāmānuja, involves constant meditation, prayer, and devotion to God. Meditation on God as the object of love, accompanied by the performance of daily rites and rituals, removes one's ignorance and destroys past *karmas*. The soul is liberated; it is not reborn again; it shines in its pristine purity.

In this connection, one must not lose sight of the fact that liberation for Rāmānuja cannot be attained by simple human efforts. One might pray to God, meditate, love God with all of one's heart, and even might completely surrender (*prapatti*) oneself to God, but liberation is not possible until God, pleased by one's devotion, chooses to bestow that upon the devotee. In other words, God's help is necessary to attain freedom. God, pleased by the complete surrender of his devotee, destroys his ignorance, and liberates him.

In contrast to Shankara, Rāmānuja argues that the soul does not become identical with God; it merely becomes similar to God. Rāmānuja rejects the notion of complete identity between *Brahman* or God and finite selves. Individual selves are finite and cannot be identical to God in every respect. God not only pervades but controls the entire universe. As the existence of a part is inseparable from the whole, and that of a quality is inseparable from the substance in which it inheres, similarly the existence of a finite self is inseparable from God. Accordingly, his interpretation of the Upanishadic statement "That thou art" is very different from that of Shankara. For Shankara, the relation between "that" and "thou" is one of complete identity. Rāmānuja, on the other hand, maintains that in the Upanishadic statement under consideration, "that" refers to God, the omniscient, omnipotent, all-loving creator of the world, and "thou" refers to God existing in the form of I-consciousness, the finite human consciousness. The identity in this context should be construed to mean an identity between God with certain qualifications and the individual soul with certain other qualifications. To put it differently, God and finite selves are one and the same substance, although they possess different qualities. Hence the name of the system, *Vishishtādvaita* ("qualified identity" or "identity with certain qualifications"). Thus, whereas in the non-dualistic Vedānta of Shankara liberation implies the total effacement of the self, in the qualified non-dualistic Vedānta of Rāmānuja the liberated self lives in eternal communion with God.

Although the Vishishtādvaita of Rāmānuja, like the Advaita of Shankara, maintains that the performance of duties is essential to realizing God, it goes a step further and maintains that such a performance must be accompanied by prayer and devotional worship. Traditionally a person must belong to one of the three higher castes to pursue the path of *moksha*. Rāmānuja recognizes that irrespective of caste and rank, one may follow the pathway prescribed by him to realize the union with God. This accommodating spirit of this system made it possible for it to acquire a large number of followers. The insistence upon the accessibility of the pathway to all persons accounts for the system's wide popularity in India through the ages; it uplifted the lowest caste, and therein lies one of its most important contributions.

BINA GUPTA

Further Reading

Bhatt, S. R. *Studies in Rāmānuja Vedānta.* New Delhi: Heritage Publishers, 1975. In a brief space, the author presents the main points of Rāmānuja's metaphysics.

Sharma, C. D. *A Critical Survey of Indian Philosophy.* New Delhi: Motilal Banarsidass, 1964. This useful book introduces students to the problems, methods, and nuances of Indian philosophical systems. It contains a very helpful essay on Vishishtādvaita.

Srinivasachari, P. N. *The Philosophy of Viśiṣtādvaita.* Madras, India: The Adyar Library and Research Center, 1978. A critical and comprehensive examination of the central features of the philosophy of Vishishtādvaita and its relation to other schools of Vedānta.

Thibaut, George, trans. "The *Vedānta Sūtras* with the Commentary of Rāmānuja." In *The Sacred Books of the East*, Vol. 48. Oxford: The Clarendon Press, 1904. This book provides a translation in English of Rāmānuja's commentary on the *Vedānta Sūtras.* The book is highly technical, suitable primarily for those who wish to do an in-depth study of Rāmānuja's thought.

Varadachari, K. C. *Srī Rāmānuja's Theory of Knowledge.* Madras, Tirumali-Tirupti, India: Devasthanama Press, 1943. Provides a detailed and critical account of Rāmānuja's theory of knowledge.

MADHVA

Born: 1197, Rajatpītha, in the State of Karnataka, South India
Died: 1276, South India
Major Works: *Madhva-bhāshya* (*Commentary on* Brahma-sūtra), *Gītābhāshya* (*Commentary on the* Gītā), *Mahābhārata-tātparya-nirnaya* (*Determination of the Meaning of the* Mahābhārata), *Anubhāshya* (*Short Commentary* [on the *Brahma Sūtra*]), *Anuvyākhyāna* (*Supplemental Explanation* [of the *Brahma Sūtra*])

Major Ideas

The scriptural texts that teach difference convey the real teaching of the Upanishads.
God is the only independent reality.
Matter and souls, although as real as God, are dependent on God.
Souls are many in number.
Ignorance about the true nature of Brahman *is the cause of the soul's bondage.*
Devotion leads to moksha.
Grace is not a gift from God; it must be earned.

Madhva was born into a *Brahmin* (priestly caste) family in 1197, in the city of Rajatpītha, near Udipi, in the Kanara district of the present Karnataka state in South India. No authentic information about the life of Madhva is available. Whatever little we know about him is based on the accounts given in *Madhva-Vijaya*, which contains semi-mythical stories of the lives of Madhva. It is believed that he received his formal training under Achyutapreksha, and was given the name Purnaprajna at the time of initiation. Achyutapreksha was a follower of Shankara (see the chapter on Shankara in this volume), and, like Shankara, believed in a non-dualistic interpretation. Madhva studied Shankara with his teacher. The non-dualistic interpretation of Shankara failed to satisfy him. So he left Achyutapreksha, and studied Vedāntic classics such as the *Ishtasiddhi* of Vimuktātman. Frequent disagreements with Vimuktātman ended this study as well. At this point in his life, he assumed the name Ānandatīrtha.

After several years of independent study of various scriptural texts, Madhva eventually developed his own views, which were diametrically opposed to the views of Shankara. He then assumed the name Madhva, by which he is widely known. He was the author of thirty-seven works, among which the most important are listed above. He worshipped Vishnu as *Brahman* and founded the sect known as sad-Vaishnavism or Brahma-Vaishnavism. He traveled widely in an attempt to convert followers of Shankara to his own doctrines. According to some accounts, he succeeded in converting his teacher Achyutapreksha to his own philosophical outlook.

Madhva was the founder of the school known in the history of Indian thought as Dvaita Vedānta (dualistic Vedānta). The protest against the monism of Shankara was carried much further by Madhva than by Rāmānuja (see the chapter on Rāmānuja in this volume). Whereas for Shankara the texts teaching difference have a practical value in that they steer us in the right direction and lead us to the real teaching of the *Upanishads*, the teaching of nondifference, for Madhva the texts teaching difference convey the true import of the *Upanishads*. His dislike of the Shankarites was so great that he referred to them as "deceitful demons." Madhva expounds a purely theistic philosophy basing it on the dualism of God and the *jīva* on the one hand and the plurality of the universe on the other.

Theory of Knowledge

Madhva's theory of knowledge and perception is the pivot around which his entire philosophy revolves. Everyday perception reveals a world of objects. These objects exist independently of the knower, of our perception of them. Knowledge does not create objects. It simply reveals them as they are. Perception further reveals a distinction between the cognizer and the cognized. His realistic outlook convinced him that these distinctions that are actually cognized ought to be real. Philosophy cannot and should not ignore this fact of common experience. For Madhva, a perception of an object, say a table, implies an awareness of it as being unique, as different from other objects and the self that perceives it. In short, it is not only that we perceive a world of objects and souls, but in reality it is the case that they exist.

One of the most important doctrines of his theory of knowledge is his conception of *sākshin* or witnessing-consciousness. Apart from the five external senses (sight, hearing, smell, taste, and touch) and the internal sense, the mind, Madhva postulates *sākshin* as the seventh sense. Each individual has this witnessing-consciousness. *Sākshin* apprehends everything that occurs to every individual being. It perceives the objects that are presented to the rest of the senses through these senses. Perception here is indirect. It also perceives those objects directly which cannot be perceived by other senses—for example, the five external senses, the mind, and the mental states such as pleasure, pain, time, and space.

Ontology

Madhva accepts the reality of ten categories, namely substance, quality, action, class character, particularity, the qualified, the whole, power, similarity, and nonexistence. We will concentrate on his discussion of substance.

Out of the twenty substances that Madhva enumerates, he accepts, like Rāmānuja, three as the most important: *Brahman* or God, matter, and selves. Since his theory of substance revolves around the notions of difference and dependence, our analysis of Madhva's theory of substance begins with an explication of his notions of difference and dependence.

Difference

The word *dvaita* comes from the Sanskrit root *dvi*, which means two. The term *dvaita* etymologically means duality or dualism. For Madhva, dualism implies difference, which is said to constitute the essence of things. This is another way of saying that each object is unique; each object possesses its own nature, which accounts for one object's difference from another object. In short, difference is not only quantitative, but also qualitative. No two things in the world are alike, no two qualities are alike. Two objects which look like each other are different, because each possesses a self-differentiating characteristic that makes it unique. Thus Madhva's ontology is pluralistic, characterized by qualitative differences.

In terms of the three most important substances, difference may be of five kinds: difference between God and soul, between God and matter, between soul and matter, between one soul and another, and between one form of matter and another. This doctrine of fivefold difference is one of the central features of Dvaita metaphysics.

Dependence

Madhva's theory of dependence is based upon everyday observations. Everything in this world depends on some other thing. The body, for example, depends on the soul; an infant depends on the parents. Thus, dependence of one thing on another is a matter of everyday experience. He extends this principle further and maintains that everything depends on God, though God does not depend on anything.

Madhva, like Rāmānuja, accepts *Brahman* or God, the souls, and matter as real and existing eternally. They are fundamentally different from each other. *Brahman* or God is the only independent reality. God has a divine body and is transcendent. However, since he is the inner controller of all souls, he is also immanent.

Madhva rejects Shankara's *nirguna Brahman* (*Brahman* without characterizations), and accepts *saguna Brahman* (*Brahman* with characterizations) as the ultimate reality. Human nature is such that it yearns for a personal relationship with the supreme person who will listen to his prayers, fulfill his needs, and provide solace and comfort during troubled times. God possesses all positive qualities; for example, existence, consciousness, and bliss. An impersonal *Brahman*, such as that of Shankara, cannot perform these functions. Additionally, in Shankara's interpretation, morality and religion become meaningless. Accordingly, Madhva provides a personal interpretation of the supreme person.

For Madhva the supreme person, *Brahman*, is not different from the God *Vishnu*, the creator, maintainer, and destroyer of the world. Nothing can condition *Brahman*. *Brahman* is an object of knowledge; it is bliss and its creation is also bliss. *Vishnu* (*Lord Nārāyana*) is the ultimate reality; it is the only independent category. God is the real of reals, the truth of truths. Thus, for Madhva, God is neither the limited infinite God of the Nyaya School, nor a being in inseparable relation with matter and selves, an interpretation that one finds in the philosophy of Rāmānuja. He is totally independent, but we depend on him for activity, knowledge, and existence.

God creates the world by his will and brings into existence the world of objects and selves. Objects and selves, though real and eternal and irreducible to each other, are dependent on the first. At the time of dissolution of the world, material objects are transformed into undifferentiated matter and selves into disembodied intelligences by God. (It is important to note in this context that even in the state of dissolution God, matter, and selves remain distinct.)

Soul, Bondage, and Liberation

The individual soul is atomic and real. Consciousness and bliss are intrinsic to it. However, in its embodied state, it is subject to many imperfections on account of *karmas*. The soul identifies itself with the body and sense organs, and thus suffers. Three kinds of souls are distinguished: (1) those who are eternally free; (2) those who have attained freedom from this world; and (3) those who are bound souls.

The third is again subdivided into those who have the power and potency to attain freedom, and those who are not so eligible; some souls are preordained to be saved, whereas others are eternally damned.

God endows souls with free will; accordingly, the individual souls are responsible for their own state of existence in this world. Depending on the kinds of deeds they perform, the souls undergo transmigration. Souls are many in number. Unlike Rāmānuja, for Madhva no two souls are alike. Thus, whereas Rāmānuja advocates qualitative monism and quantitative pluralism of souls, Madhva advocates both qualitative and quantitative pluralism of souls.

Since the immediate cause of bondage is ignorance of the real nature of *Brahman* or God, the soul must acquire knowledge of the real nature of God in order to attain *moksha*. It is important to remember in this context that knowledge by itself does not and cannot remove ignorance; knowledge is only a qualification for release, which in the final analysis depends on God's will. No matter how hard aspirants may try, they cannot gain such an immediate knowledge, unless God chooses to reveal himself to them.

Madhva prescribes definite steps that might lead to such an immediate knowledge. The first step on the path to *moksha* is the cultivation of detachment. Passion for material comforts and luxuries binds one to the world. Cultivation of detachment tones down the soul's attachment to the world and creates in the aspirant a desire for release. An intense study of the scriptures helps one realize the greatness of God and helps the person turn from the world and to God.

This results in devotion to God, which is the second step. Devotion in this context should not be taken to imply occasional moments of devotion, but rather a continuous and persistent devotion to God. Performance of one's actions without any desire for the results of the actions ceases the binding of the souls and takes one closer to attaining *moksha*. Such a purification of one's mind and detachment from one's activities are essential for the practice of devotion and the vision of God.

With the intellectual conviction that *moksha* is

God's gift, one studies the scriptural texts with a *guru*, reflects on what has been studied, and steadily and continuously meditates on the attributes of God. One sees God as the only independent reality; one's doubts and misunderstandings are removed. This is the third step. At this stage of continuous meditation, the aspirant sees God in his or her own reflection, and devotion and knowledge become one continuous process.

The final stage is God's grace, which lifts the veil of ignorance and provides a direct vision of God. God's grace is not simply a gift that he bestows upon the aspirant; rather, the long course that the aspirant pursues enables him or her to earn the grace of God.

Madhva's philosophy represents a unique type of Vedānta; it is in a class by itself. His doctrine of eternal damnation is nowhere to be found in the philosophic—religious literature of India. It is quite possible that he was influenced by the Christian missionaries of his time. His system arose as a reaction against the non-dualistic Vedānta of Shankara. Thus it should come as no surprise that he vehemently criticizes the non-dualistic philosophical outlook. However, in fairness to Shankara, it must be pointed out that Madhva's charge that in Shankara's philosophy religion and morality have not been given their due place is based on a misinterpretation of the Shankarite worldview. In Shankara's levels of being, there is a constant shift between the empirical and the real. From the empirical point of view, the distinction between right and wrong is valid and true, and the finite individual is very much bound to the moral consequences of his actions. Similarly, God, though not the ultimate reality, has practical value, because it is only through the lower that one reaches the higher.

These problems notwithstanding, Madhva's realistic worldview, though not unique, is refreshing. His conception of *sākshin* is one of the most important doctrines of his theory of knowledge, which has provided impetus for further research for the Advaitins and the non-Advaitins alike. Finally, his contention that the lowest caste may study the scriptural texts, and that an inquiry into the nature of *Vishnu* should be the goal of all human beings, irrespective of their caste and economic status, gave Hindu religion a much needed uplift of the lower caste.

BINA GUPTA

Further Reading

Translation

Rao, S. Subba, trans. *Vedāntasūtras with the Commentary of Śrī Madhvācharya*. Tirupati: Sri Vyasa Press, 1936. This translation gives a clear exposition of Madhva's philosophy and its points of agreement and disagreement with other schools of Vedānta.

Related Studies

Ramachandran, T. P. *Dvaita Vedānta*. New Delhi: Arnold-Heinemann, 1976. This book clearly brings out the distinctive contribution of the Dvaita School to Indian philosophy.

Rao, Nagaraja P. *The Epistemology of Advaita Vedānta*. Madras, India: The Adyar Library, 1976. A discussion of some of the important issues surrounding the Dvaita theory of knowledge.

Sharma, B. N. K. *History of the Dvaita School of Vedānta and Its Literature*. Delhi: Motilal Banarsidass, 1960. A comprehensive exposition and creative interpretation of the issues that confront the Dvaita School.

Sharma, C. D. *A Critical Survey of Indian Philosophy*. New Delhi: Motilal Banarsidass, 1964. An introduction to the problems, methods, and nuances of Indian philosophical systems. This book contains a very helpful essay on Dvaita.

JAYATĪRTHA

Born: c. 1365
Died: c. 1388
Major Works: *Nyāyasudha* (*Nectar of Logic*) [Commentary on Madhva's *Anuvyākhyāna Commentary on the* Brahma Sūtras]; *Tattvaprakāshikā* (*Light on the Truth*) [Commentary on Madhva's *Commentary on the* Brahma Sūtras]; *Vādāvali* (*Lineage of Controversies*)

Major Ideas

Madhva is the finest exemplar of one who sees the divinely revealed truth about Ultimate Reality (Brahman), *since his teacher of the meaning of the sacred texts was Vyāsa, their author.*
Madhva's commentaries on the Brahma Sūtras *of Bādarāyana* (Vyāsa) *are therefore authoritative.*
God, Vishnu, is a personal reality, wholly unique, non-dual, independent, and free from contradiction.
The universe is really different from God, who is not its material cause.
The metaphysical postulate of difference is justified by the doctrine of the Inner Witness (sākshin).
The Inner Witness confirms the validity of the three means of valid knowledge: perception, inference, and verbal testimony.
The doctrine of the Specific Difference (vishesha) *explains the real difference between God's being and God's qualities, as well as the difference between one thing and another.*
Other souls are eternally dependent upon God, neither caused nor created, and are either intrinsically good or evil.
The means to the human highest good is devotional meditation, that is, mystical loving contemplation of God, wherein the distinction between God and the soul is maintained.

The Dvaita School of Vedānta was founded by Madhva (1197–1278). Madhva identified God as *Vishnu-Nārāyana*; he was a fierce opponent of Shankara's Vedantic non-dualism, which he felt denigrated the unique personal reality of God. Madhva considered himself a latter-day avatar of Vāyu, *Vishnu*'s son. Hence there is a specifically theological particularity in the Madhva School of Hinduism that must not be forgotten when looking at its philosophical side. A prolific but concise writer, Madhva commented on the basic texts of Vedānta as one who had personally, perhaps mystically, been taught their true meaning by their divine author, Vyāsa, who was an avatar of *Vishnu* himself. Madhva thus spoke with divine authority.

Jayatīrtha (c. 1365–c. 1388), the greatest of the commentators on Madhva, is to Madhva what Vācaspati Mishra was to Shankara; he brought order, development, and final shape to the theological and philosophical writings of Madhva, which were sometimes obscured by the excessive concision of

his writing. So great was the theological brilliance of Jayatīrtha that the rest of the history of the Dvaita School has been one of commentaries and then subcommentaries on Jayatīrtha's commentaries on Madhva's original commentaries. Jayatīrtha's *Nyāyasudha* (*The Nectar of Logic*), is "one of the pinnacles of Indic theological achievement" (Pereira 1976). Jayatīrtha was also the author of a major work in the development of Indian logic. Dvaita Vedānta is a school that holds a strong place for the inspired authority of the master teachers, Madhva and Jayatīrtha.

God and the Material World

For Jayatīrtha, who followed Madhva, in reality there is a fundamental fivefold difference: between God and the material world, between God and conscious souls, between the material world and conscious souls, between soul and soul, and between one material thing and another. God, known only through the revealed scriptures, is *Vishnu-Nārāyana*, personally and inherently eternal and independent. God is the supreme reality uniquely endowed with the fullness of qualities. God is the only independent agent whose will is self-determining.

Although the Advaitins interpreted the texts as suggesting a non-dual relation between God and the world, Madhva and Jayatīrtha's interpretation is that God is one, not two—that is, God is uniquely, independently, and singularly real. Thus and only thus can God sustain by act of will the real existence of everything else. The term *advaita* (non-dualism) found in the scriptures signifies the absolute unity of God, while the term *dvaita* (dualism) signifies the eternal difference between God and all else. But for God's will all else would cease to exist. Everything else depends on God's will for its eternal existence in difference from God. Since this divine will, however, is eternal, the world and conscious souls have existed in this dependent state for all eternity. However, God is not the material cause of the material world nor of the plurality of souls as the other theistic non-Advaitin Vedāntic Schools taught. The material world did not emanate from God but from Primordial Nature (*prakriti*). The plurality of conscious souls is also eternally existent.

Thus, in Jayatīrtha's view, the material world and the plurality of souls, while dependent upon God, are eternally different in their essential nature from God. In the context of Advaita's teaching of nondifference, this metaphysical difference had to be defended. Jayatīrtha applied all of his dialectical brilliance to supporting and defending Madhva's insight. In opposition to this conceptualization of difference, the Advaitins charged that the idea of difference presupposes a knowledge of two entities, which in turn presupposes the idea of difference and so on in an eternal begging of the point. Jayatīrtha counters that the Advaitins are presuming that difference is something in addition to the thing itself. The fact is that each thing exists in its own right, in its very own self-nature. Each thing is identical to itself in such a way that the difference between itself and another thing is due to a special kind of individual identity associated with a "specific difference" (*vishesha*) similar to what the Christian scholastics called "a conceptual distinction with a basis in reality." Ultimately what is called a "difference" is really a reference to the fact that each thing is a unique thing in itself: uniqueness accounts for difference.

Jayatīrtha teaches the same about God. In the plenitude of God's qualities and attributes, there is a difference between the qualities and God's being that is real, but that does not divide God. The problem is common to other monotheistic theologies, both Christian and Muslim. If God's being and God's qualities are identical, not different, it is a tautology to speak of qualities at all. If there is no tautology, and they are not identical, then the qualities of God are real in addition to God's being. This latter result would mean that God is not one. Jayatīrtha, following Madhva's lead, asserts that the qualities of God are identical with God's being, but differ in a real sense because of their specific difference (*vishesha*). There is a conceptual distinction between God's being and God's qualities with a basis in the reality of God because God is self-determining. Furthermore, the specific differences of the qualities of God reveal to human beings aspects of God's being that the sheer fact of God's being itself does not. As Jayatīrtha states:

> In virtue of the Specific [*vishesha*], there is at the same time an infinity of perfections and the *Brahman*'s oneness. As His perfections are infinite, He is endowed with the qualities-and-qualitied relationship; and the unconfused assertion "The *Brahman* and the perfections" is perfectly plausible. (PEREIRA 1976)

The Means of Knowledge

In order to justify the argument that difference may be truly known and not merely be inferred, Jayatīrtha develops Madhva's teaching about the Inner Witness (*sākshin*). There are three accepted, traditional means of knowledge: perception, inference, and verbal testimony. These are "means" or instruments of knowledge. As means of knowledge they in turn must be tested to be validated, that is, discovered to be true. Whatever might test them would likewise in turn have to be tested, and so on in a vicious regression. Tests cannot be tested indefinitely. In fact the testing concludes with the final arbiter of all knowledge, the Inner Witness. The Inner Witness intuits directly. The object known presents itself directly without an instrument or means. Such is the nature of knowledge and it must therefore be invariably correct. The self knows itself by itself, that is, the Inner Witness. All other knowing is secondary since it is carried on by means of an instrument such as perception, inference, or verbal testimony. The truth of these means of knowledge is disclosed in the act of knowing of the Inner Witness.

Jayatīrtha teaches that there are an infinite number of souls, atomic in size, each different from one another. They eternally resemble God in features such as bliss and consciousness. There are three classes of souls: those now bound who will become liberated, those limited to wandering in the cycle of death and rebirth forever, and those doomed to the suffering of hell. Madhva, and Jayatīrtha after him, does not teach that there is universal liberation. Within Hinduism this teaching is unique to the Dvaita School. The bondage of the conscious souls who may be liberated is eternal, extending back into the past, although for some there will be liberation. Consistency is a mark of Madhva and Jayatīrtha, and thus they teach that bondage is dependent upon God's will. Bondage consists in "the uniting of the soul to a subtle body." Bondage is an essential, but potentially removable, real state of the condition of being human.

In addition to bondage there is the ignorance of the soul's essential state of being dependent upon God. This ignorance hides the truth of the soul's dependence from the soul. Liberation from bondage and ignorance is given by the grace of God. Liberation is twofold: It includes knowledge to do away with ignorance and release to do away with bondage to the body in the cycle of death and rebirth. Liberation is the definitive and final act of the soul coming to be its most complete self in the

presence of God. The soul discovers its own finite bliss and consciousness as reflections of the infinite bliss and consciousness of God. This discovery of self is encompassed, and overwhelmed, in the discovery of the immediate vision of God as *Vishnu*. The bliss of seeing God is not a non-suffering, but instead is a positive devotion (*bhakti*) accompanied by bliss. Bliss is a consciously felt joyous experience of the liberated soul.

Devotion

For Jayatīrtha, the only means to liberation from bondage and ignorance is devotion. Devotion is inseparably connected with knowledge: "Since there is an inseparable connection between devotion and knowledge, when one is absent, the other too is absent." When truly known, God is not loved for the sake of the soul, but for God's own sake. At the heart of devotion for Jayatīrtha is the conscious and willing acceptance of the soul's essential dependence upon God. Thus devotion is both the means to liberation as well as the goal of liberation itself.

Nonetheless, Madhva and Jayatīrtha emphasize the necessity for the grace of God even for beginning the practice of devotion as a means to liberation. Without the grace of God, no liberation is possible. God allows, and provides the means for, the conscious soul to love God. Like bondage and ignorance themselves, for Jayatīrtha grace is real. Just as each individual conscious soul is different and distinct, so too will be the extent of its bliss in the heaven of liberation. Jayatīrtha teaches that the mutual rivalry of the state of bondage will be transformed into a state of mutual help in loving God.

Jayatīrtha completed what Madhva had begun. He honed the concepts and categories of Madhva, standardized their definitions, and gave them polemical bite in the dialectical wars with the followers of Shankara, whom Jayatīrtha considered crypto-Buddhists. He both confirmed the established teaching of Madhva and refuted the "demonic" teachings of those who misinterpreted the scriptures. He provided the Dvaita teaching with a balanced and self-sufficient basis in constructive exposition and in critical dialectic. In the whole history of Indian theological and philosophical thought, the arguments of Jayatīrtha and of his follower Vyāsatīrtha (fourteenth century) are perhaps its finest dialectical achievement. In the words of Surendranath Dasgupta, "Jayatīrtha and Vyāsatīrtha present the highest dialectical skill in Indian thought."

DANIEL P. SHERIDAN

Further Reading

Translations

Jayatīrtha. *Vādāvali*. P. Nagaraja Rao, ed. and trans. Adyar, India: Adyar Library, 1943. A complete translation of an independent work of polemical dialectic against Advaita.

Pereira, José. *Hindu Theology: A Reader*. Garden City, N.Y.: Doubleday, 1976. Contains several translated excerpts from Jayatīrtha's commentaries.

Related Studies

Raghavendrachar, H. N. *Brahma-mīmāṃsa. Jijñāsādhikaraṇa*. Mysore, India: University of Mysore, 1965. This is an exhaustive analysis of the first sutras of the *Brahma Sūtras* according to 'the commentaries of Madhva and Jayatīrtha.

Rao, P. Nagaraja. *The Epistemology of Dvaita Vedānta*. Adyar, India: Adyar Library and Research Centre, 1958. Detailed review of Madhva and Jayatīrtha's theory of knowledge.

Sharma, B. N. K. *History of the Dvaita School of Vedānta and Its Literature*. 2d rev. ed. Delhi: Motilal Banarsidass, 1981. Standard historical account of the Dvaita School.

———. *Philosophy of Śrī Madhvācārya*. Revised edition. Delhi: Motilal Banarsidass, 1986. The best synthetic treatment of the philosophical teaching of the school of Madhva and Jayatīrtha.

NĀNAK

Born: 1469, Talwandi (now Nānkana Sahib), India
Died: 1539, Panjab, India
Major Works: *Asa Di Var* [Hymns], *Japji* [Poetry]

Major Ideas

There is one God who is infinite; therefore he cannot die to be reincarnated nor assume human form.

To achieve salvation, it is essential to have a spiritual mentor, a guru.

Renunciation of grihastha *(home), performance of rites and ceremonies, and torment of the body does not lead to enlightenment, but good deeds do.*

All human beings are equal and castes are created by man to retain the superiority of a few.

Repetition of God's name, the Nām, *helps conquer evil.*

Charity, worship, and hard work should be the ethical conduct of life.

Poetry, art, music, and philosophy are important; religion, however, is the highest faculty of attaining spiritual wisdom and knowledge of the eternal truth.

Deeply disturbed by the Hindu–Muslim strife that resulted in unmitigated chaos, religious bigotry on both sides, and exploitation of the poor masses, Nānak attempted to regenerate Indian society by propounding a new faith. This faith was called Sikhism. It preached the monotheism of God, who is the Supreme Being, and the universal brotherhood of man on earth.

It is of little surprise that the teachings of Islam, Hinduism, Sufism, and the Bhakti saints affected Nānak's religious philosophy. Nānak was born in 1469 in the North Indian village of Talwandi, presently called Nānkana Sahib, forty miles from Lahore. The age in which Nānak lived was characterized by political chaos and religious oppression. The rulers of North India were Muslims (first the Lodhi dynasty and later, after 1526, the Mughals). They expressed a relatively low degree of tolerance towards the Hindus, prohibiting public worship and razing numerous Hindu temples to the ground in an attempt to propagate their own religion. Although attempts to spread Islam won a few converts, such intolerance also resulted in an increasingly uncompromising adherence of the Hindus to their own faith. Consequently the Hindu caste system, which created a hierarchical relationships between human beings with the *Brāhmins* (priests) at the top of the hierarchy, followed by the *Kshatriyas* (warriors),

the *Vaishyas* (traders), and the *Shudras* (menial laborers), became more rigid. Similarly, the desire to propagate Islam at the cost of suppressing Hinduism made the implementation of Islamic ideas more stringent. Not only did this wedge aggravate hostilities, but it also denied the basic principle of equality, which is the founding principle of any religion. In this tussle, it was the common man who suffered most of all.

This religious discord caused Nānak to reexamine Islam and Hinduism and question the validity of their religious tenets. In the course of his enquiry, he also turned his attention to the teachings of two other faiths: the Bhakti movement, a religious renaissance that attacked the polytheism and the caste system of the Hindus, and Sufism, which propagated the mysticism of Islam.

Nānak learned about the philosophical ideas of these faiths through extensive travel to various parts of India as well as abroad. Long discourses with Pandits at Hindu places of pilgrimage such as Mathura, Benaras, Gaya, and Jaggannath Puri exposed him to the ideas of Hinduism. His numerous visits to the Sufi establishment at Pak Pattan enlightened him on the teachings of the Sufi saints, and his journey to Mecca and Medina brought him in close contact with Islam.

Nānak's exposure to different religions helped

him to reflect on the existence of humanity and to search for the meaning of life. Instead of blindly accepting the religious ideas of these faiths, he applied reason to them and altered them. He preached that a person's deeds, not caste, would lead to salvation. And he argued that penances, asceticism, and renunciation of the self had no meaning if a person harbors evil intentions towards humanity.

Although Nānak condemned some of the Hindu and Islamic rites and principles, he did not completely discard them. One finds frequent references in his poetry to sacred Hindu texts such as the *Vedas*, the *Shastras*, and the *Puranas*, and allusions to Allah and the Prophet of the Quran. He also used a variety of Hindu and Islamic names such as *Rām*, *Govinda*, *Hari*, *Murāri*, *Rab*, and *Rahim* to address God, the *Sat Kartar* or the True Creator.

Japjī

Nānak's philosophical ideas are crystallized in numerous songs, hymns, and oral discourses called the *Gurbani*, literally meaning the "*guru*'s word," which were composed in a North Indian dialect spoken by the common people. These include *Majh Ki Var*, *Patti*, *Dakhni Onkar*, *Sidh Gosht*, and *Var Malhar*. However, the *Japjī* and *Asa Di Var* are his most important contributions to Panjabi literature and Sikhism, and they express ideas and themes central to Nānak's spiritual and philosophic thought. Nānak's reputation as a philosopher rests largely on these devotional hymns and poetic compositions. The fifth *guru*, Arjan Dev, compiled Nānak's poetry in the *Adi Granth*, which, after the tenth *guru*, Govind Singh, conferred the status of *Guru* on the *Adi Granth*, came to be known as the *Guru Granth Sahib*.

The *Japjī* reveals Nānak's preoccupation with declaring a religion that was monotheistic as opposed to the polytheism of Hinduism. Nānak argues that there is only one God, who is the true creator and the omnipotent master. He is *Nirankar* or formless, infinite, and immortal. Therefore he cannot be reincarnated. Because God is formless, it is impossible to conceive of him in the shape of an idol. (Since people worshipped these idols as God instead of as symbolic representations of God, Nānak disapproved of idol worship.) Nor can God assume human form, because the human body is subject to decay. The proof of God's existence can be found in nature. Since there is only one God, the only way to achieve communion with him is through the *guru*. The *guru* (spiritual teacher) is the prophet or the enlightener, a human representative of God.

Since the *guru* disseminates true consciousness in his disciples, he occupies an important place in Nānak's philosophy. In contrast to the Hindu conception, the *guru* is a teacher and a human being rather than an incarnation of God—one who is to be obeyed and sought for counsel, rather than worshipped. Since the *guru* is God's messenger, the disciples are expected to have faith in him for showing them the true path to God. It is the *guru* who helped human beings realize their own capacity for goodness, helps them see the truth (*sat*) and prevents them from falling into the snare of materialistic falsehood (*asat*). Nānak regarded himself as a *guru* through whom God chose to speak.

The *Japjī* ends with a *Shlok*, the epilogue that emphasizes ethical conduct. Since God is the truth, to be untruthful is to be ungodly, contends Nānak. Only ethical conduct can lead to one's salvation and help human beings to escape the endless cycle of birth and rebirth. Ethical values can be acquired by living among one's people, serving them, and showing them kindness and compassion. One's sins can be purified by repeating the name of God (*Nām*). Ritualistic observances are futile unless one makes an inward journey of the mind and experiences faith and love.

Nānak saw little merit in asceticism, renunciation of worldly life, separation from one's family or home (*grihastha*), the accouterment of special robes, and the painting of the face with ash. Thus one finds in the *Japjī* Nānak's attempts to grapple with the Hindu idea of *karma*—which involves the belief that a person's actions determine man's destiny—and with polytheism as the basis of religion.

Asa Di Var

The underlying theme of *Asa Di Var*, a collection of hymns meant to be sung in the early hours of the morning, concerns the divine achievement of man. A man should be judged on the basis of his actions, not birth. Actions such as honesty, kindness, and compassion will help man attain wisdom and communion with God through the *Satguru* in whom God manifests himself.

Nānak argued that everyone is equal in God's eyes. For him "there is no Hindu; there is no Mussalman." Hence, Nānak vehemently condemned the caste system which, although created on the basis of profession, had in practice created social disparities between people in which the *Shudras* were reduced to the status of untouchables. Nānak's attack on the caste system also came in light of the double standards practiced by some Hindu *Brahmins* who preached the importance of idol worship, wore the saffron mark, and performed religious ceremonies to achieve divine revelation, but did little to free their fellow humans from the shackles of religious and social discrimination. Because everyone is equal, declared Nānak in *Var Malhar*, no one should fear other human beings but only God, the Supreme One.

To create a casteless society Nānak introduced the practice of free *langar* or community kitchens in all Sikh temples and centers. At the *langar*, people sat together irrespective of their castes, and he dined with them. Clearly Nānak's teachings were guided by the spirit of democracy, egalitarianism, and peace and unity among people.

However, merely dining together will not create a casteless society. To treat everyone equally, one has to ward off evil thoughts. The greatest of all evils, according to Nānak, is the ego. Once the ego is conquered, other sins such as anger, greed, lust, pride, and attachment can easily be overcome. Repeating the name of God, the *Nām* (*nāmsimran*), will help conquer these evils. Concentrating on the *Nām* also calms the mind and brings peace and divinity through self-discipline of the mind. Such austerity can also be achieved by listening to hymns, the *kirtan*. Therefore poetry and music are

an important means of attaining spiritual wisdom and communion with God. Nānak's own verses were often sung at religious centers.

Some of the ideas that constituted Nānak's thoughts had been discussed by other faiths. For instance, the Bhakti and the Sufi saints had propagated the principles of equality of mankind, the omnipotence of God, and love for humanity, virtue, kindness, and truth, and had castigated the caste system. However, Nānak was able to communicate his thoughts directly to the common people. He expressed his ideas in a language that could easily be understood by the masses. Thus Nānak's *bani* could serve the purpose of prayer as well as to counsel people directly on how to be good human beings. This is what makes Nānak's contribution to the Eastern world unique. He shunned all forms of religious bigotry, and he rationally selected the aspects of existing faiths that were best suited to the uplift of the common person at a time of socio-religious dissensions. Nor did the masses feel burdened by the thought that their lives would remain spiritually unfulfilled if they did not undertake the pilgrimages required to achieve salvation. The abolition of the caste system in Nānak's religious system made his ideas available to all castes and to men as well as women, giving the suppressed masses a feeling of worthiness and self-confidence. This inspired a positive message of hope towards achieving communal harmony and created a feeling of oneness that helped strengthen the bonds of community at a crucial time in Indian history.

Nānak's philosophy had a considerable impact on his contemporaries and became the basis of the Sikh religion. His nine successors, the last of whom was Guru Govind Singh, emulated his life and fostered the ideas that continue to inspire Sikhs today.

NANDI BHATIA

Further Reading

Translations

Singh, Gopal, trans. and ed. *Sri Guru Granth Sahib: An Anthology*. Calcutta: M. P. Birla Foundations, 1989. Translated from the original Gurmukhi script.

Trump, Ernest. *The Adi Granth, or the Holy Scriptures of the Sikhs*. New Delhi: Munshiram Manoharlal. (1877) 1970. Translated from the original Gurmukhi with introductory essays on Nānak's life; a life sketch of the other Sikh *gurus*; the Sikh religion; and the composition and use of language and meters in the Granth.

Related Studies

Cole, W. Owen. *Sikhism and Its Indian Context 1469–1708: The Attitude of Guru Nānak and Early Sikhism to Indian Religious Beliefs and Practices*. London: Darton, Longman & Todd, 1984. The author explores the philosophy of Nānak and the community that developed as a result of his teachings.

Gill, Pritam Singh. *The Doctrine of Guru Nānak*. Jullundher: New Book Company, 1969. A detailed study of the evolution of Nānak's religious and philosophical ideas.

Grewal, J. S. *Guru Nānak in History*. Chandigarh: Panjab University Press, 1969. The study places the emergence of Nānak's philosophy against the backdrop of the politics, society, and religions of his time.

Puri, J.R. *Guru Nānak: His Mystic Teachings*. Amritsar, India: Radha Soami Satsang Beas, 1982. A detailed analysis of the works of Nānak.

Singh, Gurmukh Nihal, ed. *Guru Nānak, His Life, Time and Teachings*. Delhi: Guru Nānak Foundation, 1969. A collection of essays that provide a detailed analysis of the teachings and philosophical ideas of Nānak. The essays also deal with other religions and provide comparative analyses.

Singh, Ishar. *The Philosophy of Guru Nānak: A Comparative Study*. Vol. 1. Delhi: Atlantic Publishers, 1985. The study analyzes Sikhism on a comparative basis with Hinduism, Jainism, Buddhism, Zoroastrianism, Judaism, Christianity, and Islam.

Singh, Khushwant. *A History of the Sikhs*. Vol. 1: 1469–1839. Delhi: Oxford University Press, 1986. A comprehensive account of the history of the Sikhs from the inception of Sikhism until 1939.

JĪVA GOSVĀMIN

Born: c. 1511, Bengal
Died: c. 1596, in Vrindavana, North India
Major Works: *Bhāgavatasandarbha* (*The Collection of the* Bhāgavata Purāna) [This work has six parts: "Tattvasandarbha" ("Collection on Reality"), "Bhāgavatsandarbha" ("Collection on the Lord"), "Paramātmasandarbha" ("Collection on the Great Soul"), "Krishnasandarbha" ("Collection on Krishna"), "Bhaktisandarbha" ("Collection on Devotion"), and the "Prītisamdarbha" ("Collection on Love")]; *Sarvasamvādini* (*The Harmonization of All*); *Kramasandarbha* (*Commentary on the* Bhāgavata Purāna)

Major Ideas

Scriptural testimony is the only authentic source that knows what is beyond the sensible.
The Bhāgavata Purāna (The History of the Lovers of God) *is the foremost divinely revealed scripture.*
The Bhāgavata Purāna *teaches the path of love* (bhakti) *for God* (Bhagavān).
God is the perfect manifestation of what had been partially known as the Impersonal Absolute (Brahman) *and the Supreme Self* (Paramātman).
God's essential reality is both identical with, and different from, the manifesting powers of God; this difference-in-identity (bhedābheda) *relationship is incomprehensible* (acintya).
This same difference-in-identity relationship characterizes God's relationship to the material universe and to the realm of individual souls.
God is identified with Krishna as revealed in the Bhāgavata Purāna.
Krishna was incarnated so that individual selves might come to know God's most profound nature as love.
The highest good for human beings is their mystical love for God.

In sixteenth century Bengal the ecstatic mystic Caitanya (1486–1533) inspired a revival of Vaishnava devotion to Krishna as represented in his sportful play with the cowherd girls of Vrindāvana. The primary divinely revealed scripture was the *Bhāgavata Purāna*, which teaches the path of mystical love for God and describes Krishna's sports (playful activity). Caitanya was neither a theologian nor a philosopher, and he left only one short verse in writing. He did, however, found at Vrindāvana a lineage of theologians called the six Gosvāmins: Rūpa, Sanāta, Raghunātha Bhatta, Raghunātha Dāsa, Gopāla Bhatta, and Jīva Gosvāmin. This group's prolific literary activity, in genre primarily commentary on the *Bhāgavata Purāna*, provided Caitanya's movement with a firm theological and philosophical base. Of these Gosvāmins the two most significant thinkers are Rūpa Gosvāmin and Jīva Gosvāmin, Rūpa's nephew, whose genius, built on the accomplishments of his uncle, produced one of the great theological syntheses of India.

Three Ways of Apprehending God

For Jīva Gosvāmin, God or the Ultimate Reality may be apprehended in three ways. First, as *Brahman*, the Absolute Reality is understood non-dualistically as without qualities, powers, or sports. This is the way that the followers of the path of Vedāntic knowledge know God. Here Jīva accommodates the truth of the non-dualist tradition of Hinduism. The second way that God is apprehended is as the Supreme Soul (*Paramātman*) that creates the world and is the inner controller of nature and of souls.

This aspect of God is immanent to all other created reality. Here again Jīva accommodates the truth of the difference-in-identity (*bhedābheda*) tradition of Hinduism. Third, the lover of God (*bhakta*) mystically apprehends God (*Bhagavān*) in God's own sports, qualities, and powers.

The way of love for God (*bhakti*) reveals Jīva Gosvāmin's connection to the great theistic and devotional turn that Hinduism made in the medieval period from 1200 to 1700. This theistic dimension of Absolute Reality is God as God truly exists in God's own being, fully personal as Krishna and completely lovable. Thus the inner life of God has an intrinsically human form. This last dimension reveals Jīva Gosvāmin's theological genius since Krishna, if truly the Absolute Reality, is not conceivable without his environment and without his companions as described in the narratives of the *Bhāgavata Purāna*. These he incorporated into his conception of God.

According to the *Bhāgavata Purāna*, Krishna lived in Vrindāvana, Mathurā, and Dvārakā, places known to be in India. If Krishna is God as absolutely conceived, then these well-known places are present to Krishna precisely as intrinsic qualities of God's inner life. So too the many persons whom Krishna encountered in the stories told in the *Bhāgavata Purāna* must be intrinsic qualities of God's inner life. Jīva Gosvāmin conceives of these place and persons as the self-differentiations of God, as displays of the inner power of God's qualities within God's own inner being to God's own inner eye. The qualities are related to God as a power is one with the possessor of the power. Thus the places and persons associated with Krishna have a transcendental and divine reality as expressions of the inner expressive power of Krishna. This inner power constitutes the heavenly world; it illuminates this heavenly world and makes it conscious; and it displays in all its inner differentiations the divine bliss. For Jīva, anthropomorphism is transformed into theomorphism.

Krishna also has an external expressive power that is creative of the world of unconscious material nature. This power creates, evolves, and sustains the material world out of Krishna's own being. A further power of Krishna eternally expresses itself in the plural world of sentient souls or spirits. This power and the souls created by it bridge the distance between God's intrinsic inner life and the unconscious material world exterior to God. The three levels of God's own immanent being, of the unconscious material world, and of the plural world of spirits are thus mutually reflective of God's absolute being.

For Jīva Gosvāmin, Krishna is not a simple avatar as traditionally conceived, that is, a manifestation of God among humans. Krishna's appearance is not so much a "manifestation" of God as it is God's very being. Indeed, Krishna does appear at a certain time in history in the earthly Vrindāvana, but that place is identical with the heavenly Vrindāvana. Krishna's appearance or incarnation at a certain time is, however, due to the unveiling of what was actually there all the time and of what could have been seen at any time by a true lover of God. Krishna unveils his transcendental eternally existent forms for the purpose of showing the individual souls his own inner beauty and splendor, so that they might respond with *bhakti*, that is, with love for God.

Nonetheless, individual souls are as essentially distinct from God as sparks are to a fire. They are eternally pure spirits who may temporarily be connected to unconscious nature through a material body. The material body obscures the soul's ability to see Krishna. In his description of the evolution of the material world Jīva basically follows the outline of the school of Sānkhya with the qualification that Primordial Matter (*prakriti*) is not dualistically distinct from God but instead is the eternal manifestation of the creative power of God. There is thus a consistent motif of God's condescension in Jīva's presentation of the universe, both material and conscious, as reflective and revelatory of God's very being. God's own life as it were has no meaning apart from its expression and culmination in a life that is in form human. Or perhaps it can be said that what in form seems to be human is truly divine.

The Highest Good

For Jīva Gosvāmin, the highest good for human beings is to love God, that is, to be integrated by means of mystical love into the inner life of God. The means to achieve this loving integration is love itself. Jīva encourages the traditional and orthodox practice of *dharma*, the enjoined religious observances of the *Vedas*. Yet it has no meaning except as a preparation for *bhakti*. So too the traditional path of knowledge (*jnāna*) has significance only as a preparation for *bhakti*.

Bhakti as a means consists in the discovery that God's beauty is attractive, that is, lovable. *Bhakti* as an end is an emotional passionate love for God. Liberation consists of loving God. Love for God is not love in a disinterested or altruistic sense, but in the sense of emotional affection. *Bhakti* as a means has several stages of development since it cannot be commanded into being at will. Thus first one must hear about the exploits of Krishna, sing about them, and remember them. To Krishna the devotee must offer respect, greetings, and service. Krishna must be served as a master, served as friend, and finally completely surrendered to.

When these means are accomplished, one is ready for *rāgānugā bhakti*, passion-souled devotion, the imaginative identification with one of the companions of Krishna described in the narratives of the *Bhāgavata Purāna*. Here one is taught to enter into the story itself of Krishna. This practice occasions the arising of the emotion of love for Krishna whereby the devotee completely trusts Krishna, sings of his name, and longs to live in the cities where he lived. When the love has achieved a level where the emotion is completely spontaneous and is completely fixed on Krishna, it is *prema*, the highest form of mystical love for Krishna.

Surrendering to God

According to Jīva, *prema* is characterized by *rasa*, the aesthetic emotional ecstasy of participative delight in the inner beauty of Krishna, the affective transfiguration of all finite sensibility onto a transcendental level, of the finite into the infinite. There are five *rasas*: quietude, surrender to God as a servant, surrender to God as a friend, surrender to God as a son, and surrender to God as a beloved maiden surrenders to her lover. This last is exemplified in the tenth canto of the *Bhāgavata Purāna* in the cowherdesses' erotic love for Krishna. The cowherdesses love Krishna for his own sake and seek for nothing other than his pleasure. They dance with him in an eternal *rasa lila* (passion play). This is the highest summit of the soul's com-

plete unconditional surrender to God, lost in the erotic emotion of ecstatic love. This love is the highest good of human beings, higher even than liberation from the cycle of death and rebirth.

Jīva Gosvāmin's metaphysics is one of *acintya-bhedābheda*, incomprehensible difference-in-identity. The inherent relationship between conscious souls and the material world, and between both and God, is that they are both different and identical. This relationship is like that between cause and effect, whole and part, possessor of power and power. The relationship is one of simultaneous difference and nondifference. Such a relationship, of course, is incomprehensible since it is a relation neither of difference nor or nondifference, but of both. But, according to Jīva, it is a fact that cannot be denied, but is utterly necessary to understand how God could be one and a community at the same time. The incomprehensibility is affirmed on the authority of the sacred scripture. He thus theologically guarantees the simultaneous transcendence and immanence of God.

Jīva Gosvāmin is not afraid of any contradiction because the contradiction would only be apparent. The incomprehensible and supralogical power of God explains the apparent contradiction of the infinite being manifest in the finite, the unlimited in the limited. God cannot be judged on the human principle of contradiction. Contradiction is subsumed in the revealed excellence of God's attractive beauty. The appearance of duality is not due to ignorance, as in Advaita Vedānta, but instead is due to the transcendent creative power of God. Those who are pure of heart can see the whole world for what it is: the expressed nature of God, revealing God as God really is.

DANIEL P. SHERIDAN

Further Reading

Translation

Elkman, Stuart. *Jīva Gosvāmin's Tattvasandarbha: A Study of the Philosophical and Sectarian Development of the Gaudiya Vaisnava Movement.*

Delhi: Motilal Banarsidass, 1986. A clear translation with introduction.

Related Studies

Chakravarti, Sudhindra Chandra. *Philosophical Foundation of Bengal Vaiṣṇavism*. Calcutta: Academic Publishers, 1969. A philosophical study of Bengal Vaishnavism with an emphasis on metaphysics. Includes a comparison to Christianity.

De, Sushil Kumar. *Early History of the Vaiṣṇava Faith and Movement in Bengal from Sanskrit and Bengali Sources*. Calcutta: Firma K. L. Mukhopadhyay, 1961. Monumental work of scholarship treating all phases of the religious and philosophical teaching of the Caitanya School.

VIJNĀNABHIKSHU

Born: Fl. 1550–1600
Died: Probably early seventeenth century
Major Works: *Vijnānāmritabhāshya* (*The Nectar of Knowledge Commentary*) [*Commentary on the* Brahma Sūtras *of Bādarāyana*], *Īshvaragītābhāshya* (*Commentary on the* Bhagavad Gītā), *Sānkhyasāra* (*Quintessence of Sānkhya*), *Sānkhysūtrabhāshya* (*Commentary on the* Sānkhyasūtras [of Kapila]), *Yogasārasamgraha* (*Compendium on the Quintessence of Yoga*), *Yogabhāshyavārttika* (*Explanation of the* Commentary [of Vyāsa] on the Yoga Sūtras)

Major Ideas

The whole truth lies in a synthesis of the truths of all the schools.

Each of the schools of Hindu thought is unfailingly true in its central message and open to error in its peripheral teachings.

Brahman *or God* (Īshvara) *is the ultimate truth and reality; Spirits* (purusha) *and Primordial Matter* (prakriti) *are* Brahman*'s inherent powers.*

Brahman*'s reality is proved through Yogic perception and inference, and the verbal testimony of the scriptures.*

The nature of Brahman *is pure consciousness.*

Brahman *is the Inner Controller* (antaryāmin) *of the many Spirits and Primordial Matter, but it is not to be identified with the Spirits.*

Brahman *and the many Spirits are non-dual* (advaita)—*that is, one—because they belong to the same class having the characteristic of pure consciousness.*

The world evolving from Primordial Matter is not an illusion, since Primordial Matter, like Brahman, *is eternal and real.*

The means to liberation are the ascetical practices of Yoga.

Liberation is achieved when the Spirit discriminates its own existence as pure consciousness from confusion with the evolutes of Primordial Matter.

In the latter half of the sixteenth century, when Vedānta, the explication of the *Upanishads*, was at the height of its authority and the great theistic movements of *bhakti* (love for God) were at their greatest development, Vijnānabhikshu (fl. 1550–1600), as a practitioner of Yoga, preached the concordant truth of all the Orthodox Hindu schools of thought.

In the name of a Vedānta reinvigorated by a return to its sources in the *Upanishads* and the *Vedas*, Vijnānabhikshu brought together Vedānta, Sānkhya, and Yoga in a single theistic synthesis called *avibhāgādvaita* (Indistinguishable Nondualism). This distinctive synthesis of Vedānta, Yoga, and Sānkhya was based on a commentarial enterprise monumental on a scale not seen since the versatile Vācaspati Mishra had written treatises in the ninth century on Advaita, Nyāya, *Pūrva Mīmāmsa*, Sānkhya, and Yoga. Whereas Vācaspati Mishra had commented on each system of thought as an independent, almost academic, exercise, Vijnānabhikshu brought the three schools and their scriptures together in a concordant synthesis, since each by itself did not contain the whole truth.

Vijnānabhikshu's principle of interpretative synthesis is that each orthodox school of thought is true in its central insight, but needs correction in its peripheral teachings. Since the Orthodox Hindu schools are those with a basis in the *Upanishads* and the *Vedas*, Vijnānabhikshu's judgment is that Sānkhya and Yoga are orthodox schools since they are based in the scriptures. As he states:

I therefore conclude that no orthodox system is lacking in authority or is contradictory, as all these systems, in their proper fields, are inabrogateable and are free from discord.

(PEREIRA, 1976)

Vijñānabhikshu thus may lay claim to being the first modern Hindu.

In order to achieve this synthesis, Vijñānabhikshu strongly criticized the Absolute Non-dualism (*kevalādvaita*) of Shankara and his followers. He never misses an opportunity to criticize them as crypto-Buddhists and demonic betrayers of the Vedic tradition. Instead of misinterpreting the *Brahma Sūtras* of Bādarāyana as teaching Absolute Non-dualism, Vijñānabhikshu interprets them as teaching the dualism of Primordial Matter (*prakriti*) and of Spirits (*purushas*), that is, the truth of Sānkhya. At the same time this dualism is contained within the greater non-dualism of Ultimate Reality (*Brahman*) understood as God (*Īshvara*): that is the truth of Vedānta. Liberation of the Spirits from contamination and confusion with the evolutes of Primordial Matter is achieved through the practices of Yogic discipline: that is the truth of Yoga.

Primordial Matter and Spirit are eternally different from each other, but at the same time they are inherent powers which exist on the fundamental ground (*adhishthāna kārana*) of the non-dual *Brahman* of pure consciousness. This is a unique kind of transcendental relationship in which the effects, Primordial Matter and Spirit, subsist in the ground, *Brahman*, in such a way that the effect has no reality apart from the ground without the ground also being effected by its being a cause. Vijñānabhikshu has combined the dualism of Sānkhya and the non-dualism of Vedānta in an Indistinguishable Non-dualism (*avibhāgādvaita*). His Vedānta is thus a difference-in-identity Vedānta like the Vedāntic interpretations of Nimbārka, Rāmānuja, and Jīva Gosvāmin. Where he most differs from them is in his emphasis on Yoga as the means to liberation.

The existence of Ultimate Reality, that is, of God, can be proved through the help of Yogic

perception, inference, and the verbal testimony of the scriptures. Vijñānabhikshu cites the tradition:

"He must be heard of from the words of Revelation, thought about through logical discourse, and, once thought about, must perpetually be meditated upon—these are the causes of the vision of the Self." By "perpetually meditated upon" understand "through the methods of Yogic science."

(PEREIRA, 1976)

For Vijñānabhikshu the most important demonstration is from Yogic perception, but there is also a significant role for an expanded canon of scripture since he cites a wide range of Purānic and Epic texts in support of his teaching and commentary. These scriptural texts treat *Brahman* as an active personal God.

Brahman as Pure Consciousness

The nature of *Brahman* is that of pure consciousness. For Vijñānabhikshu, *Brahman* does not have the qualities of existence, understanding, and bliss that Advaita attributed to *Brahman*. *Brahman* is the basis and support of Primordial Matter and of the Spirits as their Inner Controller (*antaryāmin*). The Spirits are related to *Brahman* as sons to a father or as sparks to a fire. Where the scriptures speak of identity, according to Vijñānabhikshu's method of interpretation, they are speaking of a form of non-difference that is the result of both *Brahman* and the Spirits being of the nature of pure consciousness, that is, members of the class of pure consciousness beings. As Vijñānabhikshu says:

It is therefore certain that the *Brahman* and the souls, related as whole and parts, are in essence consciousness only. This is the definitive doctrine of Vedānta.

(PEREIRA, 1976)

Thus the identity of Indistinguishable Non-difference is one of similarity rather than an identity of being absolutely undivided. Similarly, just as *Brahman* has the quality of being an agent, so too do the Spirits.

During the process of the creation and dissolution of the universe *Brahman* is associated with a coeternal reality called *māyā*, Creative Power, which is conceived of as neither the illusory power nor as the ignorance with which *māyā* is identified in Advaita Vedānta. Creative Power is an evolute of Primordial Matter, which has a difference-in-identity (*bhedābheda*) relationship to *Brahman*. In this way *Brahman*, at a remove, is the material cause of the universe. The created physical universe is a result of the dynamic and willful agency of *Brahman*. It is brought into being at the moment of Primordial Matter's association with Spirits. Through a similar, but different, limitation of *Brahman*'s pure being, *Brahman* is also the efficient cause of the universe.

The Spirits are many for Vijnānabhikshu. He defends this on several grounds. For example, when one human person reaches liberation, why is it that all do not achieve liberation? The reason must be that each Spirit is separate and unique, and therefore there must be more than one Spirit. A generation before Descartes, Vijnānabhikshu also makes use of *"cogito ergo sum"* ("I think, therefore I am"). He states: "The experience 'I know' is a general proof of the existence of Spirit, as no means of knowledge contradicts it" (Pereira 1976).

Just as in Patanjali's Yoga and in Īshvara-krishna's Sānkhya, Vijnānabhikshu teaches that bondage is ignorance, that is, the delusion connected with every Spirit that results from the confusion of what is derived from Primordial Matter with the pure consciousness of the Spirit. Ignorance is real. However, contrary to the longstanding interpretation of Īshvarakrishna's Sānkhya, for Vijnānabhikshu Spirit has real contact with the psycho-mental evolutes of Primordial Spirit. Since Primordial Matter is eternally grounded in *Brahman*, the physical and the psycho-mental universes that evolve from it cannot be illusions, but instead are real. Since the Spirits are also eternal parts of *Brahman*, the confusion that obscures their underlying reality of pure consciousness is also real, even if the

cause of that confusion comes from the evolutes of Primordial Matter.

Liberation and Right Knowledge

Liberation is the achieved state of the Spirit as pure consciousness, a state like God's state of pure consciousness. The practical means to this state is right knowledge. However, as a true Yogin, Vijnānabhikshu teaches that this right knowledge is a Yogic discipline that reaches *asamprajnāta yoga*, that is, the highest Yogic state where the intellect that has comes forth from Primordial Matter is reabsorbed back into Primordial Matter, resulting in the Spirit's not being contaminated by any evolutes from Primordial Matter. The individual Spirit then stands, perfectly and completely isolated, in its natural state of content-free, non-intentional, pure consciousness. In liberation Spirit is eternally isolated but at the same time coexistent with *Brahman*, with which Spirit is inherently similar, that is, Indistinguishable, since *Brahman* is both its material and efficient cause.

The ultimate goal of human life, for Vijnānabhikshu, is Isolation (*kaivalya*). In this state there is a cessation, not of sorrow, but of the experience of sorrow. Sorrow is real in the world. As the world is real and continues to exist, even as a single Spirit achieves Isolation, there is thus no cessation of sorrow. For Vijnānabhikshu, there is a state of living liberation where the individual Spirit, even while embodied, ceases to experience sorrow, and thus is liberated while living. The ultimate state of liberation is not a state of joy, since the mental faculties that might experience joy are evolutes of Primordial Matter from which Spirit has separated in the process of being liberated. Liberation is a state of being different from Primordial Matter, not a state of union with *Brahman*. With regard to the numerous scriptural texts that speak of joy, Vijnānabhiksu says:

Hence, with the denial of the *Brahman*'s nature as joy, the whole group of texts which affirm joy at the moment of liberation are to be understood in the figurative sense of abandonment of sorrow.

(PEREIRA, 1976)

In the sixteenth century Vijñānabhikshu's Vedāntic synthesis of Sānkhya and Yoga stands at the threshold of modern Hinduism and of Neo-Vedānta. This synthesis is the result of Hinduism's inner dynamic, not outside influence. He rescued Vedānta from the crypto-Buddhism of Shankara's Advaita, and restored Sānkhya and Yoga to a place within Vedānta. He reinterprets traditional Sānkhya's atheism in terms of late Vedāntic theism. In justification of the tradition, Vijñānabhikshu maintains that the absence of God in the older texts may be accepted since even in his own view there is no place for God in the achievement of liberation since the Spirit liberates itself through the Yogic discipline. God's function is metaphysical and cosmological rather than soteriological. God is the ground of Primordial Matter's association with Spirits. Oddly, God is the ultimate source of the problem, having brought the universe into being, rather than the source of the solution. The solution is the self-effort of Yoga.

DANIEL P. SHERIDAN

Further Reading

Translations

Pereira, José. *Hindu Theology: A Reader*. Garden City, N.Y.: Doubleday, 1976. This anthology includes a translation of portions of Vijñānabhikshu's *Sānkhyasūtrabhāshya* and the *Vijñānāmritabhāshya*.

Rukmani, T. S. *Yogavārttika of Vijñānabhiksu*. Volume I. *Samādhipada*. New Delhi: Munshiram Manoharlal, 1981. Translation of the first chapter of Vijñānabhikshu's most important work on Yoga.

Related Studies

Dasgupta, Surendranath. "The Philosophy of Vijñāna Bhikṣu." In *A History of Indian Philosophy*, Surendranath Dasgupta, ed. Volume III. Delhi: Motilal Banarsidass. (1922) 1975. A detailed philosophical analysis of Vijñānabhikshu's *Vijñānamritabhāshya* and *Īshvaragītābhāshya*.

Keith, A. Berriedale. *A History of the Sāmkhya Philosophy*. Delhi: Nag Publishers. (1924) 1975. An early study of Sānkhya that has an excellent treatment of Vijñānabhikshu's place in later renaissance Sānkhya.

Larsen, Gerald James, and Ram Shankar Bhattacharya, eds. *Sāmkhya: A Dualist Tradition in Indian Philosophy*. In *Encyclopedia of Indian Philosophy*. Princeton, N.J.: Princeton University Press, 1987. The primary resource for the study of Sānkhya, includes a summary of all the significant texts of Sānkhya, including Vijñānabhikshu's.

MADHUSŪDANA SARASVATĪ

Born: (Fl. in the seventeenth century) Born in Kotalipara, in eastern Bengal.
Died: Date and place unknown
Major Works: *Advaitasiddhi, Siddhāntatattvabindu, Vedāntakalpalatikā*

Major Ideas

Brahman *is the only reality.*
The world is false.
Falsity is neither real nor unreal.
Avidyā (*nescience*) *accounts for the appearance of the world.*
Avidyā *is beginningless, positive, and sublatable knowledge.*
The Path of Devotion leads to moksha (*release*) *faster than does the Path of Knowledge.*

Madhusūdana was the first person in the history of Vedānta to reconcile the metaphysical principles of Advaita with *bhakti*, the Path of Devotion to a personal god. Virtually nothing is known about his life. According to some accounts, he was born in Kotalipara, in eastern Bengal. He took *sannyāsa* (renunciation) at a very early age. Before becoming a monk, he was known as Kamalānayana. He studied Advaita texts under Madhava Sarasvatī and was initiated into *sannyāsa* by Vishveshvara Sarasvatī. He was the author of several works in Advaita (non-dualistic) philosophy. His most famous work is *Advaitasiddhi*, which contains a refutation of the doctrines of Vyāsarajāsvāmin, a follower of the Dvaita (dualistic) School of Vedānta.

Advaitasiddhi attempts to establish Shankara's non-dualism (see the chapter on Shankara in this volume) by refuting the arguments of Vyāsatīrtha, a follower of Madhva's dualistic interpretation (see the chapter on Madhva in this volume). Shankara in his philosophy repeatedly asserts that *Brahman* is the only reality, the world is false, and the finite individual and *Brahman* are nondifferent. In Shankara, *avidyā* (ignorance or nescience) accounts for the falsity of the world. Nescience is positive; it is the cause of all empirical distinctions among the knower, the known, and the knowledge. The manifold world of objects is superimposed on *Brahman* or the pure self, as silver is apparently superimposed on a shell in the shell-silver illusion.

It is not an exaggeration to say that the notion of falsity is the pivot around which the entire Advaita philosophy revolves. The followers of Shankara tried to explain this notion in various ways, because an explanation of this notion was deemed crucial to establishing the non-duality of the Absolute or *Brahman*. Madhusūdana followed in the footsteps of his predecessors. Accordingly, in the first chapter of *Advaitasiddhi*, he seeks to clarify the notion of falsity, its nature and its status. He does so by defending and clarifying the definitions of falsity adduced by previous Advaita teachers. To be specific, he critically analyzes five definitions of falsity to give his readers a clear conception of what this notion entails.

Five Definitions of Falsity

The first definition explains falsity in terms of indescribability, implying that falsity means the absence of both reality and unreality (being and nonbeing) in one and the same locus. For the dualists such a definition is self-contradictory, because there cannot be an absence of both in the same locus; the absence of one necessarily implies the existence of the other. Madhusūdana explains that no self-contradiction is involved here; the absence of reality does not necessarily imply the presence of non-being. Whatever appears is not as real as *Brahman*, though it is empirically real. All appearances are appearances of something and therefore have being. Madhusūdana points out that there is a distinction between falsity and unreality, which the dualists fail to recognize. False appearances have being insofar as they appear, whereas non-being is nonexistent; therefore exclusion of being does not necessarily lead to non-being, and vice versa.

The second definition articulates falsity as an entity that appears in a place where in fact it did not exist, does not exist, and will never exist. Madhusūdana clarifies the meaning and significance of this definition. Both real and unreal in Advaita are unsublatable. Being or *Brahman* cannot be sublated or denied because it is the highest reality. Unreality cannot be sublated or denied because it does not become an object of our experience; it does not become a content of consciousness. On the other hand, the denial of world appearance as in "There is no world appearance here," "There is no world appearance anywhere," does not imply that it can never appear for it to be denied; only unreal or non-being never appears.

The third definition of falsity defines it as that which is sublatable or removable by knowledge. The shell-silver that appears as real is recognized as illusory by knowledge of the shell. Madhusūdana points out that the real meaning of the definition is that falsity is an entity which is sublated by knowledge. The dualists contend that the definition does not make any sense. When a clay jar is destroyed by a heavy metal stick, the jar is destroyed by the metal stick, not by knowledge. Madhusūdana would agree that by the stick, the effect—that is, the jar—is destroyed, but he contends that the jar continues to exist in a latent or potential form in the material cause, that is, in the clay. In other words, in the case under consideration, only the effect is destroyed, not its material cause. On the contrary, when the world appearance is sublated or removed by knowledge, it is removed both as a cause and as an effect.

The fourth definition articulates falsity as "appearance in the same locus of its own absence." Dualists reiterate that if the "absence" in the definition refers to absolute absence, it will lead to dualism. Madhusūdana again brings up the discussion of the different grades of reality and says that no contradiction is involved in asserting both the

existence (real) and nonexistence (unreal) if they belong to different grades of reality.

The fifth definition articulates falsity as that which is different from the real. Falsity is other than the real, yet it appears to be real. Knowledge is said to be valid when it is never contradicted. Madhusūdana reaffirms that only *Brahman*-knowledge is valid since its content is *Brahman*, and it is never contradicted. He further points out that the *Brahman*-knowledge does not possess any defects whatsoever; illusory knowledge, on the other hand, does possess defects and contradictions.

It seems that all the five definitions revolve around one central idea: falsity is that which is negated simply in the locus where it is experienced. Since it is experienced, it is not non-being, and since it is sublated or denied, it is not absolutely real like *Brahman*. The world is false because it is a creation of *avidyā* (nescience or ignorance).

Avidyā (Nescience)

Brahman creates the appearance of the world through the instrumentality of nescience. Nescience not only conceals the real nature of *Brahman*, but makes it appear as something else, namely the world. Madhusūdana concurs with the Advaitin definition that nescience is beginningless, positive, and sublatable knowledge. The non-Advaitins object to this definition on several grounds. Madhusūdana refutes these objections and reestablishes the traditional definition of nescience.

The opponents object to this definition on the grounds that the objects of the world have a beginning in time, therefore the nescience that conceals the consciousness underlying the objects cannot be beginningless. When I perceive a rope as a snake, the nescience that conceals the consciousness conditioned by the rope has a beginning in time. Therefore the traditional definition of nescience is too narrow. Additionally, the opponents point out that it is ridiculous to claim that nescience is a positive entity. Nescience is absence of knowledge; it is simply the negation of knowledge and therefore cannot be a positive entity.

Madhusūdana in response points out that all

forms of nesciences—including even that of a rope which apparently has a beginning in time—are, strictly speaking, beginningless. Nescience is the material cause of the world. Accordingly, it cannot be said to have a beginning in time. Its substratum is beginningless pure consciousness; therefore all forms of nesciences that seem to begin in time in point of fact are beginningless. If the nescience is taken to begin in time, then we will have to look for the cause of this nescience, in another nescience, and so on ad infinitum. Hence in order to avoid an infinite regression, the nescience must be regarded as beginningless. Additionally, says Madhusūdana, when the Advaitins contend that nescience is a positive entity, they do not mean to suggest that nescience has the same level of reality as *Brahman*. Nescience is sublated by knowledge. It is called positive simply because it is not non-being like the horns of a hare. Non-being does not have an objective counterpart; it is never experienced. Nescience accounts for the plurality of names and forms in this world. Therefore it cannot be regarded as negative. A negative nescience cannot serve as the material cause of the objects that we perceive in this world.

Madhusūdana, following Shankarites, draws our attention to the fact that nescience is directly intuited by perception, therefore perception attests to its existence. Perceptions, such as "I am ignorant," "I do not know myself or others," and "I do not know the significance of the scriptures" testify to the presence of positive beginningless nescience. Such uniform experiences will not be possible in the absence of some persistent object that exists in and through all these experiences. Nescience for Madhusūdana is indescribable. "Indescribability" must not be construed to mean absence of description in general. It simply means that nescience can neither be described as real nor unreal. It is not real because *Brahman* is the only reality. It is not unreal, because to be unreal is to be nonexistent, whereas nescience appears and accounts for the apparent world. It continues until it is removed by the truth, when the non-dual self is revealed.

Removal of Avidyā (*Avidyā-Nivritti*)

Advaitins have given different explanations of the nature of *avidyā-nivritti*. The basic issue is: Is *avidyā-nivritti* identical with *Brahman* realization? In response, Madhusūdana says, "Yes."

Some Advaitins maintain that *avidyā-nivritti* is neither identical with *Brahman* nor indescribable. *Avidyā-nivritti* is not real, they say, because *Brahman* is the only reality and acceptance of *avidyā-nivritti* as real would go against their non-dualistic metaphysics. Nor is *avidyā-nivritti* unreal because the unreal is non-being. It cannot both be real and unreal at the same time because that is contradictory. It is not indescribable since what is indescribable is the result of *avidyā*, and *avidyā* and *avidyā-nivritti* cannot coexist in the same locus. Accordingly, they conclude that *avidyā-nivritti* is different from *Brahman*.

Madhusūdana criticizes these views. He maintains that if *avidyā-nivritti* is taken to be different from *Brahman*, then in order that *avidyā-nivritti* may manifest, it will have to be associated with *Brahman*, the only self-luminous reality. However, *Brahman* is supra-relational and therefore it does not, and cannot, have any kind of relation with *avidyā-nivritti*. We will then be forced to admit a superimposed relation between *Brahman* and *avidyā-nivritti*. However, all superimpositions are made possible by *avidyā*. In concrete terms, this would amount to admitting that *avidyā-nivritti* is superimposed on *Brahman* through *avidyā*, which is another way of saying that it is indescribable. Accordingly, concludes Madhusūdana, *avidyā-nivritti* is identical with *Brahman* realization.

Brahman realization, or *moksha*, in Advaita Vedānta is not an attainment of something new. When one speaks of attaining *Brahman*, the term "attaining" is used figuratively. When nescience is removed, the non-dual self is revealed. *Moksha* is the realization that the self is forever blissful, pure existence and pure consciousness. Madhusūdana, following Advaitins, maintains that it is possible to attain *moksha* while embodied. Such a person is called *jivanmuktā*. The body continues because of the momentum of the previous *prārabdha karmas* (the impressions of *karmas* that are bearing fruits in this present life). When *pārabdha karmas* are totally exhausted, one attains *videhamukti*, disembodied liberation.

It is important to bear in mind that for Madhusūdana, unlike Shankara, the Path of Devotion, like the Path of Knowledge, leads to *moksha*. The *Bhāgavata Purāna* was the source of his inspiration in this regard. Madhusūdana maintains that Krishna is an incarnation of *nirguna* (attributeless) *Brahman*. As a matter of fact, for Madhusūdana, out of the two paths—the Path of Devotion and the Path of Knowledge—the Path of Devotion leads to *moksha* faster than the Path of Knowledge. Perhaps this is because the Path of Devotion (*bhakti yoga*) dominated the intellectual climate of India in his day.

Although Madhusūdana was very accommodating to other worldviews regarding the path that leads to *moksha*, he was uncompromising regarding Advaitin metaphysics. He deserves the credit of acknowledging the Path of Knowledge as well as the Path of Devotion, something unheard of in the Advaitin tradition.

BINA GUPTA

Further Reading

Dasgupta, S. M. *History of Indian Philosophy*. Vol. IV. Delhi: Motilal Banarsidass, 1975. This book contains a chapter on the controversy between the followers of the dualistic school (for example, Vyāsatīrtha) and the followers of Shankara (for example, Madhusūdana).

Gupta, Sanjukta. *Studies in the Philosophy of Madhusūdana Sarasvatī*. Calcutta: Sanskrit Pustak Bhandar, 1966. An account of the philosophy of Madhusūdana that highlights the issues surrounding Advaitin metaphysics, epistemology, and ethics.

Mishra, Harmohan. *A Study in Advaita Epistemology*. Delhi: Parimal Publications, 1990. A study of Advaita epistemology as expounded by Madhusūdana Sarasvatī in his *Advaitasiddhi*.

DHARMARĀJA ADHVARIN

Born: (Fl. in the seventeenth century) Khandaramanikkam, Tanjor district, South India
Died: Date and place unknown
Major Work: *Vedānta Paribhāshā*

Major Ideas

Non-dual consciousness is the only reality.
Non-dual consciousness splits into the cognizer, the cognition, and the object that is cognized.
Perception, inference, comparison, postulation, verbal testimony, and non-apprehension are the six sources (pramānas) *of knowledge.*
These six pramānas *are applicable only in the phenomenal world.*
Pramānas *cannot lead to the highest truth* moksha (*release*).

Dharmarāja's *Vedānta Paribhāshā* is a well-known work on Advaita epistemology. The book provides for the first time a systematic exposition and defense of the Advaita theory of knowledge. Shankara does not treat epistemological issues separately, but rather interweaves them with metaphysical considerations. Therefore, although a great deal of work has been done on different facets of Advaita philosophy, very little attention has been paid to its epistemology. One possible explanation for this phenomenon is Advaitic taxonomy. Prior to Dharmarāja's *Vedānta Paribhāshā* neither metaphysical nor epistemological issues were treated separately. It is because of Dharmarāja's efforts that epistemology began to be treated as a separate discipline in the Indian philosophical context.

Dharmarāja was a native of Khandaramanikkam village in the Tanjor district of South India. There is a difference of opinion regarding the time period in which Dharmarāja lived. Some notable Indian scholars, including Sarvepalli Radhakrishnan and S. N. Dasgupta, maintain that Dharmarāja flourished in the sixteenth century. However, more recent scholarship on Dharmarāja's work indicates that he flourished in the seventeenth century. According to tradition, it is believed that as a young student Dharmarāja was a contemporary of Madhusūdana Sarasvatī, who lived in the seventeenth century (see the chapter on Madhusūdana Sarasvatī in this volume). Most Indian scholars, including Radhakrishnan, now accept this view. Dharmarāja

is the author of several unpublished manuscripts on Nyāya (one of the nine schools of Indian philosophy). His only published work is *Vedānta Paribhāshā*, which deals with Advaita epistemology.

Advaita Vedānta, the non-dualistic school of Advaita, is primarily explicated by Shankara (see the chapter on Shankara in this volume). It has been and continues to be the most widely read and accepted school of Indian philosophy. It makes the most enigmatic assertions about reality, the nature of the world, and our perception of it: *Brahman* is real, the world is false, and the individual self is none other than *Brahman* or non-dual consciousness. Since *Brahman*'s non-duality is inconsistent with the plurality of the empirical world, what is the status of this duality? How and why do the real and the not-real become interrelated, and hence confused? How does the non-dual consciousness split into the cognizer, cognition, and the object that is cognized? What is it to be a knower, and what is involved in knowing? The purpose of epistemology in Vedānta is not simply to ask the question from a theoretical point of view, but to "see" the answer.

Advaita Vedānta recognizes six distinct means of knowledge (*pramānas*): perception, inference, comparison, postulation, verbal testimony, and non-apprehension. *Vedānta Paribhāshā* discusses these means of knowledge in its attempt to provide an answer to the basic epistemological question: How do we know? It offers its readers an analysis of ontological problems in Advaita as well as of important issues surrounding Advaita epistemology.

Vedānta Paribhāshā contains eight chapters. The first six chapters provide an in-depth analysis of the means of valid knowledge and discusses the nature, source, and validity of knowledge. The last two chapters provide an analysis of the subject matter and the goal of Advaitic inquiry. The book is written from the Vivarana point of view (see the chapter on Sureshvara in this volume) rather than the *Bhāmatī* perspective (see the chapter on Vācaspati Mishra in this volume).

Perception (Pratyaksha)

The term *pratyaksha* is derived from the roots *prati* (to, before, near) and *aksha* (sense organ) or *akshi* (eye). So etymologically the term signifies what is "present to or before the eyes or any other sense organ." It refers to sense perception as a means of immediate or direct knowledge of an object. Broadly speaking, the Advaitins make a distinction between two kinds of perceptions: external and internal. Perception by any of the five sense organs (sight, hearing, touch, taste, and smell) is classified as external, and perceptions of pleasure, pain, love, hate, and so on as internal.

Dharmarāja concurs with the view that perception is immediate consciousness. However, for him, sensory perception is not the only means of immediate cognition: the immediacy of cognition does not depend on its being caused by sense organs. God, for example, has no senses, but those who believe in God believe that he has immediate knowledge of things.

The theory of perception that Dharmarāja develops is a kind of identity theory: in perceptual cognition, the subject and the object achieve a kind of identity. The Advaita theory of identity is a corollary of its metaphysics: only *Brahman* or pure consciousness is real; it is all-pervading, undifferentiated consciousness. Pure consciousness is also pure existence or being, and any assertions made about the latter are equally applicable to the former. Just as a clay pitcher does not have any independent existence apart from the clay, sim-

ilarly the plurality of objects do not have any independent existence apart from pure consciousness, their source. In other words, these objects, though real empirically, are not real in themselves. The same can be said about the pure consciousness in a cognitive relation, which involves elements such as subject, object, and their relation. These elements are real insofar as they refer to pure consciousness, but are not real in themselves. Dharmarāja reiterates that as identical in essence with pure consciousness, these three terms of a cognitive relation refer to one and the same reality.

Accordingly, pure consciousness, from an empirical point of view, becomes threefold: the cognizer-consciousness, the means-of-cognition consciousness, and the object-consciousness. From the perspective of pure consciousness, these divisions are only apparent and not real; the plurality of objects is only apparently independent of the subject, but not truly independent.

This is how Dharmarāja explains the notion of immediacy in Advaita. The immediacy of knowledge does not depend on its arising from the senses, as is generally maintained, but rather on the object that is presented. The immediacy of the object presented to the consciousness that apprehends it makes it possible for knowledge to be perceptual. Although the phenomenal world rests on a distinction between the cognition and the content, no such distinction exists in the immediate consciousness of *Brahman*. Pure consciousness, accordingly, is the criterion of the perceptibility of objects. Since the cognizer-consciousness and the object-consciousness of, for example, a pitcher share the same consciousness, in the perception of a pitcher, the pitcher becomes "immediate." Perception thus is of utmost importance, because the knowledge obtained there is immediate, which is different from the non-perceptual knowledge obtained by inference, comparison, and postulation.

Inference, Comparison, Postulation, Verbal Testimony, and Non-Cognition

The next means of valid knowledge is inference (*anumāna*). Here Dharmarāja draws attention to the fact that valid inferential knowledge is necessarily linked with a universal relation and its recognition. Consider the following example, typical of Indian philosophers, including Dharmarāja:

> Whatever is smoky is fiery; for example, a kitchen.
> The hill is smoky.
> Therefore, the hill is fiery.

The knowledge that all smoky objects are fiery is called the knowledge of universal relation. This universal relation must have been cognized on a previous occasion and must be cognized, or better yet, re-cognized, in this particular instance (the hill) for inferential knowledge to occur. Cognition of a universal relation, though necessary, is not a sufficient condition of inferential knowledge. However, the cognition as well as the re-cognition of a universal relation together constitute the necessary and sufficient conditions of knowledge.

Knowledge obtained from comparison (*upamāna*) yields knowledge derived from judgments of similarity: a remembered object is like a perceived one. Judgments founded on comparison are of the kind "Y is like X," where X is immediately perceived and Y is an object perceived on a previous occasion that becomes the content of consciousness in the form of memory. Dharmarāja considers a typical instance of comparison given by Indian philosophers. A person has a *gau* (domestic cow), knows what it looks like, and has the capacity to apply its features to other cows. Upon running into a *gavaya* (wild cow) in a forest he says, "The *gavaya* resembles my *gau*." Dharmarāja emphasizes that one has thus gained new or better knowledge not about *gavaya*, but rather about the *gau*, since the person has a better understanding of the body of a *gau*.

Knowledge obtained from postulation (*arthāpatti*) involves the assuming or postulating of a fact in order to make another fact intelligible. Dharmarāja again explains this means of knowledge with the help of a typical example given in Indian philosophy. A man fasts during the day. However, he continues to gain weight or does not lose weight.

One must assume, barring physiological problems, that he eats at night, because there is no way of reconciling fasting and the gaining of weight.

For Dharmarāja, verbal testimony "is a means of valid knowledge in which the relation among the meanings of the words that is the object of its intention is not contradicted by any other means of valid knowledge." He further informs his readers that a sentence is the unit of a verbal testimony. In other words, a sentence signifies more than the constituent words that compose it. To grasp the significance of a sentence, one must know not only the meanings of the constituent words, but also the relation among the meanings of the words that are conjoined syntactically. The apprehension of this relation is called the verbal cognition and if it is not contradicted, it is considered to be valid.

Words, says Dharmarāja, have primary meanings as well as secondary meanings. Primary meaning is something that is directly meant by a word. A word in its primary meaning signifies a universal and not the particular in which it inheres. For example, the word "cow" means "a being possessed of cowness." A universal, in other words, is not an entity that stands over and above the individuals—rather, it refers to the essential characteristics that are common to all members of that class. Thus, whereas the universals or class characteristics constitute the primary meanings of words, the individuals constitute their secondary meanings. A secondary meaning is something that is implied by a word. If the primary meanings of the words of a sentence does not adequately explain the import, then one looks for implied meanings. Very often the principle of seeking a secondary meaning is employed to harmonize scriptural statements with one's own philosophical position. For example, in construing the meaning of the sentence "Thou art that," the primary meanings of "thou" as "the individual consciousness" and of "that" as the "pure consciousness" are discarded; they are taken in their secondary meanings: the consciousness that underlies pure consciousness is the same consciousness that underlies the individual consciousness, thereby declaring that the text affirms the identity of non-dual pure consciousness.

Finally, non-apprehension (*anupālabdhi*) is the only means of the cognition of nonexistence. It yields knowledge of absence where an object would be immediately perceived if it were there. Not every instance of the non-apprehension of something, however, proves its nonexistence. A person may not see a chair in a dark room, but this failure to perceive by no means indicates that the chair is not there. Hence, for non-apprehension to be a sign of absence, the attempt at apprehension must be under appropriate conditions (namely, conditions sufficient to perception).

In connection with the six *pramāṇas* accepted by the Advaitins and discussed by Dharmarāja, it must be pointed out that they have limited applicability. Each of the six *pramāṇas* has its own sphere of operation. They do not contradict one another. They are "true" only in the phenomenal world and cannot establish any final or ultimate truth. There are two forms of knowledge: higher knowledge (*parāvidyā*) and lower knowledge (*aparāvidyā*). The first is the knowledge of the absolute; it is sui generis. It is attained all at once, immediately, intuitively. The second is the knowledge of the empirical world of names and forms, where *pramāṇas* are operative. All *pramāṇas* hold sway as the "ultimate" until *Brahman* is realized, because when *Brahman* is realized nothing remains to be known. To Dharmarāja goes the credit of clearly demonstrating the insufficiency and the relative nature of the six *pramāṇas* in Advaita, thereby paving the way for their transcendence in *Brahman*, the pure knowledge.

BINA GUPTA

Further Reading

Translation

Madhvananda, Swami. *Vedānta Paribhāṣā*. Calcutta: The Ramakrishna Mission, 1972. This is a readable translation of the entire *Vedānta Paribhāsha*.

Related Studies

Datta, D. M. *Six Ways of Knowing*. Calcutta: University of Calcutta, 1972. This book discusses Advaita epistemology critically and compares it with that of other schools of Indian philosophy.

Gupta, Bina. *Perceiving in Advaita Vedanta: Epistemological Analysis and Interpretation*. Lewisburg, Pa.: Bucknell University Press, 1991. A critical analysis of the epistemological issues inherent in the Advaita two-tiered theory of the knowing and the known. The primary focus of investigation is Dharmarāja's chapter on perception in the *Vedānta Paribhāsha*.

Satprakashanada, Swami. *Methods of Knowledge*. Calcutta: Advaita Ashrama, 1974. The author presents important issues surrounding Advaita epistemology in relation to that of other schools of Indian and Western thought.

RABINDRANATH TAGORE

Born: 1861, Calcutta, India
Died: 1941, Calcutta, India
Major Works: *Gitānjali* (1912), *Sādhnā* (1913), *Personality* (1917), *Gorā* (1924), *The Religion of Man* (1931)

Major Ideas

The Supreme One is personality and creates the world and its people for self-expression.
The Supreme and humanity are related by mutual love.
The same stream of life runs throughout the universe.
The whole objective of the human being is to free the personality from the contraction of self in desire into the expression of soul in love.
Religion should establish unity in diversity.
Modern civilization has gathered its wealth and missed its well-being.
True education must aim at freedom from ignorance of the laws of the universe and freedom from passion and prejudice.

Rabindranath Tagore has been acclaimed as perhaps the greatest literary figure in history. In sheer quantity of work, few writers can equal him. His writings include more than 1,000 poems and over 2,000 songs; in addition, he wrote thirty-eight plays, twelve novels, 200 short stories, and innumerable essays covering every important social, political, and cultural issue of his time. He was awarded the Nobel Prize for Literature (1913), the first such award to an Asian. His short stories are compared favorably to those of Chekhov and Maupassant. Not satisfied with just writing literary works, he also produced and directed plays and dance–dramas and acted on the stage. The songs he composed and set to music came to be known as *Rabindra Sangeet* (*Rabindra Music*) and are sung by workers and farmers, boatmen and society ladies, amateur and professional singers. During India's struggle for freedom, young martyrs went up the gallows singing snatches of a Tagore song. Tagore has the unique distinction of having his songs chosen as the national anthems of two nations, India and Bangladesh. His lifelong interest in education led to his founding a school for children (Shantiniketan) and a university (Visva-Bharati). In fact, he was affectionately called *Gurudev* (Revered Teacher). In his old age, he took to drawing and painting and produced 2,500 pictures. His work

was exhibited, with success, in Europe and India. Tagore's own life was a perfect example of his philosophy of creativity, harmony, love, and joy.

Rabindranath Tagore was born into a very distinguished Bengali family. His grandfather, Dwārkānath (1794–1846), became one of Calcutta's leading business magnates and cultural leaders. "Prince" Dwārkānath was a friend of Raja Rāmmohun Roy, the architect of the Indian Renaissance. Rabindranath's father, Debendranath (1817–1905), although competent in business affairs, was spiritually inclined and spent much of his time in religious pursuits. He was called *Mahārishi* (the Great Sage). Debendranath had a large family, fifteen children in all. Rabindranath was the fourteenth and, since a younger brother died shortly after, also the youngest child.

The Tagores lived in an exciting ambience of culture, music, and amateur theatricals. Hence young Rabindranath was drawn to the arts. His most important childhood experience was a tour of the Western Himalayas with his father. Rabindranath was then twelve. The beauty of nature, the religious personality of his father, and the daily recital of verses from the *Upanishads* made an indelible impression.

Rabindranath did not take to formal education. He was in and out of public schools; even the tutors at home could not "educate" him. Later, his attempt to obtain an education at the University of London was inconclusive. Rabindranath was a self-taught man.

He started writing poetry in his early teens. In 1882 when Rabindranath was twenty-one, his first major volume of poetry, *Sandhyā Sangeet* (*Evening Songs*), was published. This was the beginning of a steady stream of poems that flowed from "the Poet" (as he was called) throughout his long life. His last poem was composed five days before his death.

In 1890, his father put Tagore in charge of the family estates. Living on a riverboat on the Ganges, he came in close contact with ordinary village folk. His observations form the basis of many of his short stories. During this period his sympathies for the poor widened, and he initiated Rural Community Development projects.

Years of sadness followed. His father, his wife, a son, a daughter, and a close associate died between 1902 and 1907. But Tagore braced himself and remained engaged in his literary work, his national work for Indian emancipation, and his educational work at his school.

In 1912 his most famous book of poems, *Gitānjali*, was published in England. In 1913, he was awarded the Nobel Prize in Literature. Soon Tagore became an international celebrity. He undertook lecture tours in the United States, Europe, South America, China, Japan, Malaya, Indonesia, Iran, and Iraq. He was knighted by the British crown in 1915, but he returned his knighthood in 1919 as a protest against the British massacre of unarmed civilians in Amritsar.

After a long and distinguished life of creative work and national service as well as being a voice for love and international harmony all around the world, the Poet breathed his last at the age of eighty. He had dictated his last poem only five days before his death on August 7, 1941.

The Supreme Being and the Call for Love

The philosophy of Rabindranath Tagore is founded on a poet's vision of Reality. It is harmonious with India's traditions; after all, the Indian word for

philosophy is *darsana*, which means vision. Tagore says,

> When I was eighteen, a sudden spring breeze of religious experience came to my life for the first time and passed away leaving in my memory a direct message of spiritual reality. (*My Reminiscences*)

The kernel of the Poet's worldview is present in this experience. The Supreme Being is a spiritual reality. The Supreme sends a message to Man; it says: "I love you and I ask for your love. We both need each other's love for self-realization. I have created nature as a stage for our love play. The beauty of nature will open your heart to love and, thereby, you will attain your highest good."

Tagore's philosophy springs from the teachings of the *Upanishads*. He was well aware of the fact that a major tenet of the Upanishadic teachings was the primacy of the impersonal Absolute. He accepted this teaching but went on to assert that the impersonal Absolute presents itself to Man as a Divine Personality. Limitation of the Unlimited (the Supreme) is personality. God (the Supreme) is personal when he creates.

Tagore's philosophy starts with the premise that there is a Supreme Being. He says that the vision of the Supreme One is a direct and immediate intuition. We feel God as we feel light. He also claims that joy is a criterion of truth. Hence, the joy we feel in our vision of the Supreme is evidence that the Supreme exists. Man has three sources of knowledge: (1) senses, (2) intellect, and (3) feeling. By senses man knows the world, by intellect man discovers science and logic-centered philosophy, but it is by feeling that man discovers the Supreme Person.

Tagore objects to the traditional Advaita–Vedāntist view that the Supreme, who is perfect, is formless and impersonal. If the formless had been the real perfection, the form would have found no place in the universe. Since there is form, the formless must have fulfilled itself in form. Moreover, if the Supreme creates form, then it must be a personality since creativity is the defining feature of personality.

The Supreme Person creates the world of forms as *lila* (play). But to what end? Its own self-realization. Self-realization consists in obtaining the highest good. Love is the highest good. God (the Supreme Person) creates human beings in order to realize the bliss of love, which is possible only if lover and beloved are separate entities. Thus the self-sundering of the Infinite to create duality for its own realization:

> Thus it is that thy joy in me is so full. Thus it is that thou hast come down to me. O thou lord of all heavens, where would be thy love if I were not? . . .
>
> And for this, thou who art the King of kings has decked thyself in beauty to captivate my heart. And for this thy love loses itself in the love of thy lover, and there art thou seen in the perfect union of two. (*Gitānjali*)

The Human Being and Nature

Tagore believed that nature is created both as man's home and also as an instrument which, through its beauty, awakens the human heart and directs it towards the Beloved (the Supreme). Just as an artist creates a work of art both to express and evoke a certain mood (*rasa*), the Supreme Person creates the world of nature to evoke love in the human being. According to Tagore, the fundamental fact about "man" (the human being) is his dual nature. Man is Earth's child and Heaven's heir. Like the lotus, which has its roots in mud but its flower in clear sunlight, man has a finite pole in the world of necessity and an infinite pole in aspirations towards divinity. Tagore calls man the "angel of surplus" since the spirit of man has an enormous surplus far in excess of the requirements of the biological animal in man. Civilization is the product of surplus in man. Science, philosophy, art, religion—all these are made possible by this surplus. It enables man to surpass his biological inheritance. Tagore also applies his concept of surplus to the Supreme and says

that the Supreme is boundless in his superfluity, which expresses itself in world process.

At his least developed level, the human being is a desiring animal. The tendency is to desire things and people for self-aggrandizement. If one persists in this path, it will prove fatal to one's true well-being: "When I desire another, it is I who am caught in the coil." The whole object of the human being is to free the personality from the contraction of self in desire into the expression of soul in love.

> "Prisoner, tell me, who was it that bound you?"
>
> "It was I," said the prisoner, "who forged this chain very carefully. I thought my invincible power would hold the world captive leaving me in a freedom undisturbed. Thus night and day I worked at the chain with huge fires and cruel hard strokes. When at last the work was done and the links were complete and unbreakable, I found that it held me in its grip." (*Gitānjali*)

Sādhnā

Sādhnā, the true realization of life, leads from love of self to love of others—family, friends, humans, animals, trees. To love God is to love the entire creation. We move from duality to unity: "The same stream of life that runs through my veins night and day runs through the world and dances in rhythmic measures" (*Gitānjali*).

Tagore says,

> We can look at our self in its two different aspects. The self which displays itself and the self which transcends itself . . . The lamp contains its oil, which it holds securely in its close grasp . . . Thus it is separate from all objects around itself and is miserly. But when lighted it finds its meaning at once; its relation with things far and near is established, and it freely sacrifices its fund of oil to feed the flame. . . . Such a lamp is our self. (*Sādhnā*)

The Ideal human being, according to Tagore, fulfills the demands of life and meets all his social obligations. Tagore did not favor the path of renunciation. Those entirely engrossed in the world and those who deny the world are equally doomed.

Tagore advocated the religion of humanity. To have a religious life, a person must live by one's *dharma*, one's essential quality. This means one must respond to the love-call of the Supreme with love; love for God includes love for humanity and all of nature. Religion is love, harmony, simplicity. "While God waits for his temple to be built of love, men bring stones." Tagore was against idolatry, superstition, and religious fragmentation. In a letter, he wrote, "We must go beyond all narrow bounds and look towards the day when Buddha, Christ and Mohammad will become one." His was the ideal of Universal Humanity.

As a bipolar being, the human being must engage externally in coping with nature and internally in developing spiritually. Early in human history the Indian sages, who lived in forest-hermitages and enjoyed intimacy with nature, developed a spiritual philosophy (although material progress was not neglected). By contrast, Western civilization was developed in the cities and therefore emphasized the external goal of conquest of nature (although spiritual progress was not neglected). As time went on, each civilization went off in the wrong direction. The West succumbed to the love of power and material goods and India succumbed to empty spirituality. Bengal in the late nineteenth century, in the times of Tagore's youth, was the place where the worst of the West and India combined to produce cultural disaster. Tagore's social and political philosophy developed against that background.

Tagore keenly felt the social evils of his society—poverty, superstition, untouchability, oppression of women—and he fought against all of them. At the same time, he did not fall victim to the emotional reaction of his time, which found the West to be the source of all evil. He welcomed Western science and Western beliefs in individual worth, freedom, and democracy. He believed that it was Indian society's many failings that enabled the British to rule India. Even before Gandhi, Tagore started Rural Community Development programs to help farmers help themselves.

During Tagore's lifetime, Western civilization became increasingly self-destructive, a tendency culminating in the two World Wars. Tagore was keenly aware of its failings, and in his writings he emphasized his cherished values: unity in diversity, harmony, creativity, and interiority.

Nationalism, which in modern times had deteriorated from patriotism to chauvinism, drew Tagore's censure. He believed that nationalism was individual selfishness raised to a higher level. Just as a human being must rise from self-centeredness to love for all, countries too must grow to love other cultures and nations. Tagore prays:

*Where the mind is without fear and the head is held
 high;*
Where knowledge is free;
*Where the world has not been broken up into frag-
 ments by narrow domestic walls; . . .*
*Where the clear stream of reason has not lost its
 way into the dreary desert sand of dead habit; . . .*
*Where the mind is led forward by thee into ever-
 widening thought and action—*
*Into that heaven of freedom, my Father, let my
 country awake. (Gitānjali)*

Tagore's love for children and his own childhood experiences encouraged his lifelong commitment to education. He felt that traditional schools imprison children. Children are born with a power to be happy and to make others happy. But in our schools they are like flowers pressed between book leaves. Even further smothering of creativity results from teaching children, not in their mother tongue, but in a foreign language (which is English in India).

Tagore decided to start a school modeled after the ancient hermitage schools of India. He called his school *Shāntiniketan* (The Abode of Peace):

I tried my best to develop in the children of my school the freshness of their feeling for Nature, a sensitiveness of soul in their relationship with their human surroundings, with the help of literature, festive ceremonials and also the religious teaching which enjoins us to come to the nearer presence of the world through the soul, thus to gain it more than can be measured—like gaining an instrument in truth by bringing out its music. (*The Religion of Man*)

Tagore also believed in teaching through manual work. There was a garden and handicraft shop attached to the school. Tagore's ecological concerns were manifested by tree planting ceremonies.

Later Tagore widened his educational commitment by founding a university—Visva-Bharati—where he sought to create unity in diversity by having an international faculty. Tagore kept embarking on strenuous lecture tours and dramatic tours to finance his education enterprises throughout his later years. He saw his two schools as his lasting concrete legacy.

Tagore's ideal was the Universal Human Being—rational, humane, creative, and spiritual. He was himself such a person. His most dominant single quality, which might explain his personality and his genius, was *love*; he was first, last, and above all else a lover. The Poet sang:

My breath will cease,
With these my parting words:
"How much I have loved!"

NARAYAN CHAMPAWAT

Further Reading

Chakravarty, Amiya, ed. *A Tagore Reader*. New York: Macmillan, 1961. An anthology of Tagore's writings intended to offer a fairly comprehensive view of Tagore's contribution to our times.

Kripalani, Krishna. *Rabindranath Tagore: A Biography*. New York: Grove Press, 1962. Best English biography, by a scholar well acquainted with the Tagore family.

Tagore, Rabindranath. *Collected Poems and Plays*. New York: Macmillan, 1936.

Thomson, E. J. *Rabindranath Tagore: Poet and Dramatist*. 2d ed. London: Oxford University Press, 1948. First detailed study of Tagore's work in these genres.

MOHANDAS KARAMCHAND GANDHI

Born: 1869, Porbandar, India
Died: 1948, New Delhi, India
Major Works: *The Story of My Experiments with Truth* (1927), *Satyāgraha in South Africa* (1938), *Selections from Gandhi* (edited by N. K. Bose) (1948)

Major Ideas

Truth is God.
Man's chief goal is self-realization.
Love is the supreme value of life.
Satyāgraha *(civil disobedience) is the only sure way to fight injustice.*
Essence of all religions is ethical action.
All principal religions are equal and are all true.
Politics cannot be separated from spiritual values.
All men are brothers because they possess the same soul.

Mohandas Karamchand Gandhi was the foremost spiritual and political leader of the twentieth century. He was called the *Mahatma* (Great Soul). Albert Einstein said of Gandhi, "Generations to come will scarcely believe that such a one as this walked the earth in flesh and blood." His ambition, Gandhi said, was "to wipe every tear from every eye." Although not a great original thinker, he collected ideas from all religious traditions, especially Hinduism, and fashioned a unique and forceful philosophy of life. His life was an embodiment of his philosophy. His greatest achievement was the creation of a new instrument of social action, namely *satyāgraha*, also known as civil disobedience.

Gandhi was born on October 2, 1869, in Porbandar, India. His parents belonged to the *Vaishya* (merchant) caste of Hindus. His father was a minister of a small Indian princely state. His parents were devotees of the Hindu god, *Vishnu*. There was a strong Jain presence in his community. There were frequent religious ceremonies and recitations of Hindu scriptures. Gandhi's mother was especially devout and undertook frequent fasts and penances. Young Gandhi learned from her the importance of self-suffering (*tapasya*). His father had Hindu, Jain, Muslim, and Zoroastrian friends, and their vigorous but friendly discussions taught

Gandhi religious tolerance. His mind absorbed such sayings as "Only those who feel the sorrow of others are true devotees of *Vishnu*" and "But the truly noble know all men are one, / And return with gladness good for evil done."

Gandhi was a shy, serious boy. Even as a child he resisted temptations to cheat and to lie. He was profoundly influenced by a play, *Harishchandra*, in which the hero, very much like Job, maintains his truthfulness and integrity in the face of superhuman ordeals. To follow truth was the one ideal that inspired young Gandhi.

When Gandhi was thirteen years old, he was married to Kasturba, a girl of the same age. Their parents had arranged the marriage according to custom. The Gandhis had four children and a happy marriage.

When Gandhi was fifteen, he stole some gold to help his elder brother. Conscience-stricken, he made a full, written confession. He had the courage to accept suffering. His father, upon reading the confession, cried and forgave him. It was Gandhi's first lesson in the power of truth to arouse love and the power of love to reform the heart.

At the age of nineteen, Gandhi left for England to qualify for the bar. Before leaving India, he made a pledge to his mother that he would not touch wine, women, and meat. It was in London that

Gandhi began developing his philosophy of life. He found a rational basis for his instinctive vegetarianism. He studied the New Testament, Buddha's teaching, and the Indian religious classic, the *Bhagavad Gītā*. He said,

My young mind tried to unify the teachings of the *Gītā*, *The Light of Asia* and the *Sermon on the Mount*. That renunciation was the highest form of religion appealed to me greatly.

He returned to India in 1891 to practice law, but as a barrister he met with little success. He was too shy to be an adequate advocate. However, as time went on, he developed an excellent technique for adjudicating conflicting interests of the litigants and settling cases out of court. He realized that the true function of a lawyer was to unite parties riven asunder. Gandhi was developing and applying his method of truth and *ahimsā* (nonviolence) to legal practice.

Gandhi went to South Africa in 1893 as a lawyer. It was there that Gandhi's experiments with his life came to fruition. He studied widely. Tolstoy's *The Kingdom of God Is Within You*, Ruskin's *Unto this Last*, and the *Bhagavad Gītā* were the three books that had a decisive influence on Gandhi's thought. He experimented with communal living at the Phoenix Farm and the Tolstoy Farm. But above all, he committed his life to fighting injustice.

Satyagrahā: Truth, Nonviolence, and Self-Suffering

When victimized by injustice in South Africa, Gandhi faced the greatest challenge of his life. Traditionally there were two ways to deal with injustice: you either continued being a victim or you fought back with violence. His ethical nature would not allow the passive alternative. Injustice corrupts the soul, both of the victim and the one who is unjust. It would be doubly wrong, then, to do nothing. Fighting back with violence is no solution either. Violence begets violence. The original perpetrator of injustice now feels victimized and feels justified in responding with violence. Gandhi sought a third

way. His three basic values, truth, nonviolence, and self-suffering, combined in his response, which he called *satyāgraha*. The basic idea was to bring an end to injustice by changing the heart of the wrongdoer by awakening, through love and self-suffering, his sense of justice.

Gandhi experimented with *satyāgraha* both in South Africa and as a leader of the Indian nationalist movement in India. Looking at his various *satyāgraha* movements, one can discern an ideal pattern. The first step is always a careful marshaling of all the facts, leading to negotiation and possibly arbitration. One is to stay open to communication. Each side in a conflict has only a partial view. It needs the critical perspective of the other to sort out truth from untruth. If arbitration fails, the *satyāgrahi* (one leading the *satyāgraha*) prepares the group for direct action. One has to be prepared to suffer without attacking the opponent, to offer love in response to emotional and physical violence. Now the *satyāgrahi* announces his planned direct action and persists in action, accepting all adversity, until the issue is resolved to mutual satisfaction. In a Gandhian fight, you can claim to have won only if your opponent can say the same.

In *satyāgraha*, Gandhi has shown the world a new form of conflict resolution which can be applied to conflicts between nations, between oppressed minorities and their governments, between social groups, and even between individuals. It is a hard path to follow, but the only one that can result in lasting solutions.

Gandhi's *satyāgraha* movements in South Africa were trailblazing events. Their success paved the way for Gandhi's return to India in 1915. Within five years, he became the leader of the Indian nationalist movement.

In 1917, Gandhi led a *satyāgraha* movement in Champaran, which resulted in the amelioration of the wretched conditions of the indigo farmers. In 1918, Gandhi led a *satyāgraha* movement in Ahmedabad on behalf of the textile workers. He led three major *satyāgraha* movements against the British rule in India: (1) the noncooperation movement (1920–22), in response to the Jalianwallah Massacre; (2) the 1930–32 movement, which began with the famous salt march; and (3) the Quit India movement (1940–42). He was jailed three times and spent seven years in prison for political activity. His *satyāgraha* movements raised the consciousness of the Indian masses and made British rule more and more untenable, both morally and practically. Finally, Great Britain had to grant India freedom in 1947. Thanks to Gandhi's gospel of *ahimsā* (nonviolence), Great Britain and India had the friendliest transfer of power from the ruler to the ruled in human history.

God Is Truth, Truth Is God

Gandhi was not a theoretician and his ideas developed only in response to problems faced in action. He was committed to truth in the sense of being truthful and being true to one's word even as a child. Later he came to see that truth covers all ethical action. As his intellect matured, he accepted the Hindu metaphysics that claim that Reality is spiritual and moral. Being both *is* and has value. Moral order is built into the structure of the universe. Unethical action is just as much a violation of Truth as making a false statement. Hence, Gandhi's slogan: *God is Truth*, where God is equated with ultimate Reality. Later Gandhi came to realize that many people doubt the existence of God, whereas Gandhi felt that nobody could deny the basic value of ethical action. Since epistemologically Truth seemed more certain than God, Gandhi changed his basic position from *God is Truth* to *Truth is God*.

Truth is the highest good. Since human beings are fallible creatures, they cannot be sure of knowing Truth as such. Gandhi accepted the Jain theory of the many-sidedness of truth (*anekāntvāda*). Hence the necessity for open-mindedness and soul-searching. In critical situations, Gandhi relied on his "inner voice," which he believed was tuned to the call of Truth through long practice.

Truth is best served by love. If a person's actions are motivated by love for every creature in the universe, those actions will be conducive to the highest Good. Hence, love is the cardinal virtue.

Gandhi took the word, *ahimsā*, which means nonviolence, and expanded its meaning so that *ahimsā* is not just refraining from injuring others, but positively enhancing their well-being; in fact, loving them. The secret of Gandhi's immense popularity and effectiveness was the fact that those who came into contact with him saw him as an embodiment of love and caring.

Gandhi believed in egolessness as the highest personal virtue. He found that the teachings of the *Bhagavad Gītā* best expressed his point of view. The central message of the *Gītā* is *nishkāma karma*, that is, acting without attachment to the fruits of action. Such action expresses love and self-surrender. It leads to egolessness. Gandhi believed that the ego-self must be reduced to zero in order to see God. He believed in a life of renunciation of personal benefits. Consequently, Gandhi was extremely modest, unassuming, and owned no property.

Gandhi took to heart Lord Krishna's message in the *Bhagavad Gītā* that everyone must act in order to "maintain the world." Social action was Gandhi's life. His activities were grounded in two basic beliefs: (1) All human beings are brothers because they possess the same *ātman* or soul; hence, to exploit or injure another is to do violence to oneself. (2) All human beings are basically good. This belief was not a psychological hypothesis but a metaphysical certainty. If Reality is truth and goodness, then untruth and evil must be unreal and illusory. The Real within man must eventually show its goodness. Hence, Gandhi's unshakable conviction that *satyāgraha* would eventually succeed.

Given these beliefs, one can see why Gandhi was one of history's most famous and committed fighters for justice and equality. In South Africa and India he fought against the injustice of colonialism and racial prejudice. Within Hindu society, he fought for equality for women and *harijans* (untouchables). He fought for economic justice for labor and peasants. He also believed in the equality of religions. Having studied Hinduism, Christianity, Islam, Jainism, and Buddhism, he came to the conclusion that all principal religions are equal and are all true. The essence of all religions is not dogmatic truth, but ethical action based on self-surrender. Gandhi's prayer meetings always included recitations from many different religions. Hindu–Muslim unity became the main theme of Gandhi's later life, and he gave his life in pursuit of that aim. He was assassinated by a Hindu fanatic in 1948.

Although Gandhi became famous for broad social action, he was, in fact, even more committed to individual self-development. He aimed at *sarvodaya*: everyone's self-realization. He experimented incessantly with health, diet, restraint of sex, and communal living. He founded several *āshrams*, places where people live in voluntary simplicity in order to pursue self-realization. He gathered men and women of different castes and religions and encouraged them to live in equality and with simplicity. Everyone was expected to do physical labor. Animals were lovingly incorporated in the life of the community.

Gandhi's ashrams provide a model for an ideal life. Diet, clothing, health practices—every aspect of life should be instrumental in increasing egolessness. Physical labor should be a necessary discipline. Equality and love should be the norm. A man living the Gandhian life should reach out to his society and impart the same values not only by preaching but also by providing a living example.

Gandhi's economic ideas were unorthodox and are widely misunderstood. Gandhi was not unequivocally anti-industrialization, but he was against unbridled economic expansion. He saw very clearly that modern economic thinking, in its headlong pursuit of an ever-higher material standard of living, has forgotten that human values include much more than material prosperity. In fact, material prosperity can become a hindrance to self-realization. Gandhi was convinced, and for good reasons, that modern man was headed for disaster. He wanted desperately to convince us to reconsider our economic policies. He believed that small is beautiful and that economics should take account of human values. Economic policy must, first of all, ensure that no one in this world goes hungry or homeless. Coexistence of riches and star-

vation is an obscenity. That is why he worked to created cottage industries and cooperatives in Indian villages. The spinning wheel was a symbol of voluntary simplicity and self-reliance. Although he fought economic inequality, he was also against welfarism. No able-bodied person should live on charity; everyone must earn their bread with their own labor. But he did not believe in expropriation of the wealth of the rich—that would be violence, not *ahimsā*. So he evolved the theory of Trusteeship, that is, the rich should act as the trustees of their wealth, which they should use for social uplift.

Politically, he believed in the decentralization of power. The base of political power should be small community groups patterned after the village *panchayats* of traditional India. The state must have minimum power consistent with the aim of *sarvodaya*, universal self-realization. *Ahimsā* should rule all political relationships.

Gandhi was an incarnation of nonviolence, voluntary simplicity, and tolerance. In a world exploding with violence, mesmerized by complexity, and dazed by intolerance, his life is a beacon of hope. His technique of *satyāgraha* is an invaluable gift to mankind. Humanity will be saved only when more leaders can say with Gandhi, "All my activities have risen from my insatiable love of mankind."

NARAYAN CHAMPAWAT

Further Reading

Bondurant, Joan. *Conquest of Violence*. Berkeley, Calif.: University of California Press, 1965. A penetrating analysis of Gandhian techniques of nonviolent action.

Chatterjee, Margaret. *Gandhi's Religious Thought*. Notre Dame, Ind.: University of Notre Dame Press, 1983. An excellent account of Gandhi's philosophy.

Fischer, Louis. *The Life of Mahatma Gandhi*. New York: Harper, 1950. A complete and intimate portrait of Gandhi's life.

Iyer, Raghavan N. *The Moral and Political Thought of Mahatma Gandhi*. Oxford: Oxford University Press, 1973. A fine statement of Gandhi's philosophy of political action.

AUROBINDO

Born: 1892, Calcutta, India
Died: 1950, Pondicherry, India
Major Works: *The Life Divine* (1949), *Letters on Yoga* (1971), *The Supramental Manifestation* (1972)
[Dates are for publications in book form.]

Major Ideas

India is not an ordinary nation, but, along with her spiritual heritage, is an integral part of the ongoing process of Divine evolution toward a situation in which human life will become the Life Divine—a perfect expression of the Divine Essence.

The Life Divine is not a world-denying ascetic withdrawal, but includes an active participation in human affairs.

Divine evolution is the aftermath of a process of involution wherein the Unmanifest Absolute made itself manifest in several levels of reality including mind, life, and matter.

Human beings have the capacity to assist the process of evolution toward the Life Divine through Yoga and other spiritual disciplines.

Knowledge of the Divine, however, is unavailable by rational means because the Divine in its essence is indeterminable by such means and inexpressible by language.

On Sunday, January 19, 1908, Aravinda Acroyd Ghose, now known universally as Sri Aurobindo or simply as Aurobindo, rose to speak to an eager and spirited crowd at Mahajan Wadi, Bombay. It was a time of intense nationalist fervor in much of India, a time when agitation against the hated foreign Raj had reached its highest point to date. Aurobindo was in the forefront of the nationalist movement, a leader of the group that came to be known as the Extremists—those who wanted the British out once and for all. But Aurobindo's vision of an independent India was categorically different from that of most of his Extremist colleagues, for he was convinced India was unique among the world's nations, and that even her struggle for independence must be deeply imbued with spiritual elements.

India's Spiritual Heritage and Destiny

The crowd in Bombay that January day consisted mainly of young men anxious to get on with the excitement of nationalist agitation, but Aurobindo challenged them to think much more deeply and thoroughly about the wave of nationalism that had engulfed them and which was sweeping them along toward something they envisioned only vaguely. Aurobindo's resolve that day was nothing less than the creation of an entirely new vision of the nationalist goal and the process that would yield that goal.

The essence of Aurobindo's message was that nationalism in India was not really a political program, but a creed, a religion of Divine origins. He chided those in the movement who were nationalists in what he called the European sense, meaning they wanted simply to replace the foreign rulers with themselves and other Indians. They needed to see nationalism as necessary only so that the great truths of India's ancient tradition might again be made available to save the whole world. This was the point: Indian freedom was necessary for the benefit of the whole human community. Even at this point, then, Aurobindo's vision was global in scope.

His vision became fully articulated into a philosophical structure and system of Yoga after he retired from active participation in political life, but while the ideas expressed in the midst of heated political agitation were more thoroughly developed later on, the core remains the same. The core rests upon a clear perception that spirituality is the most important thing for each individual, for the life of any community, for the nation of India herself, and—through India—for the whole world. The development of that spirituality, however, never means retreat from active participation in the affairs of the world. The two must be integrated for either to be complete. The January 1908 message was not a call to abandon political action, but a plea to place it squarely and securely upon a spiritual base, a base articulated in the spiritual tradition of India, a base that would serve the welfare of all the world through the liberated Indian nation. This basic vision informs the rest of his thought.

Childhood to King's College, Cambridge

Aurobindo was born Aravinda Acroyd Ghose at 4:30 A.M. on August 15, 1872, at 12 Lower Circular Road, Calcutta. His father, Dr. Krishnadhan Ghose, was one of those nineteenth-century Indians so enamored of the West that he felt India should reconstruct herself after the English model. As such, his plan was to shape his three eldest sons into young Anglophiles who would dedicate their lives to the great work of transforming Indian society along English lines. The children were spoken to in English, sent to an English-medium school, and, when Aurobindo was only seven, the three boys were taken to Manchester, England, and left in the care of the Reverend William H. Drewett in order that they might be brought up in the manner of English children. The Reverend Drewett taught the boys Greek and Latin, but nothing about their native land. Later Aurobindo attended St. Paul's School in London and King's College, Cambridge, where he earned his bachelor's degree in classics. At his father's command, he also become a probationer for the Indian Civil Service (the I.C.S.), and all signs pointed toward the fulfillment of Dr. Ghose's vision and plan.

The signs, however, were all external. By the time he had finished his work at Cambridge, Aurobindo had become a radical revolutionary who wanted to do nothing more than to help end British colonial rule in his homeland—not to return home as a servant of the Raj. Although he had developed

a real (and lasting) love for much of Western culture, especially its literary heritage, he also came face to face with the blatant racism and cultural chauvinism that permeated the British attitude toward India. In short, he understood and vehemently rejected the very fact of colonialism, which tacitly declared anything and anyone British to be inherently superior to anything and anyone Indian. He knew India needed social change, but he also knew the pernicious belittlement inherent in the colonial situation threatened his country's very soul. How could he return to India a member of the I.C.S., the very organ of British rule? Perhaps it was chance, perhaps luck, perhaps design: in any case, Aurobindo was dismissed from the I.C.S. for failing the riding test, and so returned to India in January 1893 having secured a position with the Maharaja of the State of Baroda in what is now Gujarat.

India: Revolution and Yoga

Aurobindo arrived in India, a bright, intense, English-bred intellectual drawn to politics and the colonial situation. Put differently, he was a misplaced don, an academic athlete yearning to play King's College games. His Cambridge classmate K. G. Deshpande edited a dual-language Bombay newspaper called the *Indu-Prakash*, and he invited Aurobindo to write a series of articles entitled "New Lamps for Old," in order to leaven the discussion of the English-educated Indian community. The articles present a brilliant caricature of the servile attitude of most Indians towards Englishmen, and equally scathing descriptions of the individuals England sent out to administer their paternalistic sovereignty. Beyond his wit and sarcasm, however, there is genuine and insightful criticism of the substance of colonialism, especially as it made impact upon the character and the inner life of Indians.

Aurobindo actually admired much of the British national character as it expressed itself in courage, energy, and pluck. He wanted to see change in India along Western lines, but he knew it had to come from the initiative of Indians who had first to summon up their own courage, energy, and pluck. But colonialism's very nature generated a sense of belittlement in many educated Indians—the very ones who would have to create, organize, and bring to fruition any changes that would actually be effective in India. Indians needed something upon which to base their own sense of identity and pride. Inevitably, it was religion, and Aurobindo became one of the earliest to articulate the glories of India's spiritual tradition in the service of political nationalism.

Before that could happen, he had to discover and experience the essence of that tradition himself. When he first returned to India he was an academic who relished his own abilities to wax poetic about the greatness of his homeland, but he was as Anglicized as any Indian around. He knew *about* Indian spirituality, of course, but, ironically, he shared the common Western view that Yoga and other spiritual disciplines are other-worldly, life-denying, and fuzzy-minded. Then, through the prodding of his friend Deshpande, he tried simple *āsanas* (postures) and *pranayama* (breath control), the basics of *hatha yoga*, and responded like the proverbial duck to water. In a short time his experiences convinced him that contrary to his expectations, Yoga itself could be used to generate the power needed to free his country from English domination.

There were three basic elements in his experiences with Yoga and Indian spirituality during the period when Aurobindo remained active in nationalist agitation. First, the *pranāyāma* and *āsanas* produced the almost tangible results Aurobindo described as a kind of electric power around his head, a vigorous revival of his writing powers, and great health. Second, Aurobindo saw for the first time what he called the "living presence" of God when he looked at an image of the goddess Kali, an event which undermined his previous skepticism about the gods. Finally, under the guidance of a holy man in Bombay, Aurobindo experienced the "silent *Brahman* consciousness," that level of consciousness in the Hindu tradition in which one experiences direct union with *Brahman*, the Absolute, the Divine. Taken together, these experiences meant that Aurobindo no longer simply talked *about* In-

dian spirituality: it engulfed and transformed him such that at last he really was an *Indian*, a true son of Indian spiritual tradition, and he saw himself, India, and the world in a whole new light.

Aurobindo's involvement in the nationalist agitation against the British landed him in jail for a year during 1908–09. Later, when it became evident he would be imprisoned again, he fled to Pondicherry, a French-held territory in South India, arriving there in April 1910. He never left, but devoted the remaining forty years of his life to spiritual work. An *āshram*, or spiritual community, gradually formed around him, and it was within this context as Yogi and spiritual guide to others that his major ideas were articulated.

The Full Vision: Thoughts of a Yogi

There is some truth in the conventional claim that the Western and Eastern worlds differ in what they mean by philosophical inquiry. Although the differences can easily be overplayed, it is true that in the East the thinker's life is expected to reflect the assertions articulated in his or her philosophical formulations and explanations to a much greater degree than in the West where philosophy is viewed as a very abstract enterprise. Indeed, because Aurobindo was so familiar with the Western approach to philosophy, he adamantly denied he was a philosopher at all. What that means for us is that although his thought does contain conceptual structures designed to describe the basic nature of reality, the point of studying his ideas from Aurobindo's own perspective is to change one's whole way of being, to move along in one's inner journey, to transform one's *self*. Intellectual comprehension is not only insufficient, ultimately it has little actual value.

Much of Aurobindo's thought was first articulated in the philosophical journal *Arya*, which began publication August 15, 1914 (Aurobindo's forty-second birthday), at the suggestion and with the financial backing of Paul and Mira Richard, a French couple who had come to Pondicherry and who were deeply impressed with Aurobindo. The stated purpose of the journal was the formation of a vast synthesis of knowledge that would harmonize the diverse religions of humankind. Publication continued until 1921. Almost all Aurobindo's major works first appeared serially in the *Arya*, including *The Life Divine*, *The Synthesis of Yoga*, *Essays on the Gītā*, and *A Defense of Indian Culture*, among many others. Most of his basic philosophical worldview is contained in *The Life Divine*.

The Richards left the journal in 1915, but Mira returned in April 1920 and never left. Eventually she became the practical leader of the *Aurobindo Ashram*, the community of Aurobindo disciples that grew to about 25 by 1926, reached 80 by 1928, and has about 2,000 members today. In time Aurobindo came to believe that Mira Richard was an incarnation of the Divine as female, the Divine Mother, and she was and is referred to as "The Mother" by Aurobindo followers. He also said that his consciousness and the consciousness of the Mother were identical, which does not mean that they shared precisely the same thoughts, but that each had attained the same level of spiritual awareness. Understanding Aurobindo's ideas pertaining to levels of consciousness is tantamount to understanding the heart of his worldview.

Aurobindo's Worldview

According to Aurobindo, Reality in its essence is non-dual (*advaita*), and although it is indeterminable conceptually and verbally, it is apprehensible through direct experience, level by level. Hence there is a very imprecise separation in Aurobindo's thought between descriptions of the levels of Reality on the one hand, and the levels of human consciousness of that Reality on the other. It is easy to reify Aurobindo's concepts into a concrete hierarchy describing Reality itself, but that is a trap that should be avoided. In the final analysis, his descriptions are attempts to articulate his own experiences.

From those experiences, and in harmony with the Hindu tradition, Aurobindo concludes that at the top, in its Essence, Absolute Reality, *Brahman*, is *Sat* (being), *Chit* (consciousness), and *Ānanda* (bliss), which he usually writes as *Saccidānanda*.

Saccidānanda is first *Sat*, or Pure Existence, infinite, eternal, and indefinable. Being and Becoming are both fundamental aspects of *Sat*, for Reality is not static. *Saccidānanda* is also *Chit*, or consciousness-force. This idea derives from Aurobindo's sense that all existence ultimately comes down to a movement of energy, a Force, and this Force is a conscious Force. Third, *Saccidānanda* is *Ānanda*, absolute delight or eternal and unlimited bliss. Hence, in sum, we find a positive vision of ultimate reality—the Absolute, *Brahman*, is a Conscious Existence whose consciousness is limitless bliss.

Aurobindo is aware that most human beings do not experience life as characterized by profound consciousness and bliss. Nonetheless, his long-term view remains very optimistic. He believes that the basic movement of the phenomenal world is a spiritual evolution of consciousness, in Matter, towards the situation in which all material forms will reveal the indwelling spirit. In this situation, human life too will be a perfect mirror of the Divine; human life will *be* the Life Divine. In short, the whole movement of the unfolding cosmos is a movement towards universal Divine Consciousness. This evolution is taking place as the opposite phase of the Divine process of involution, which saw the topmost level descend into inert matter. Aurobindo's descriptions of the levels of that descent illuminate his vision, then, of both the levels of human consciousness and the hierarchy of Reality itself.

At the top is the Supreme *Unmanifest Saccidānanda*, for, in the final analysis, Reality is beyond its manifestations. Next comes *Saccidānanda made manifest*, and it is here we can say its nature is being, consciousness, and bliss. Then there is "Supermind," which is direct truth-consciousness: it is the possession of truth, not the construction of that truth. It is the consciousness by which the Divine knows its own essence and manifestations, which means it is consciousness that yields automatic action in harmony with Divine essence. Supermind-consciousness is in a sense oblivious to the dichotomy of thing in the manifest universe even while it acts within that universe. A crude analogy would be a case of someone's acting in the light of pure unselfish love where the distinctions between self, action, and the beloved are not made.

"Overmind"-consciousness is next, a kind of bridge between Supermind and the lower levels of the human mind, which see and act conditionally in accordance with the multiplicities of the world. Overmind-consciousness knows the unity of things, but action is deliberate, not automatic as in Supermind-consciousness.

Below Overmind and above ordinary consciousness are various levels of awareness to which Aurobindo gave names but which he saw as arbitrary in number. Intuitive mind is a direct encounter with truth, but only in moments of illumination rather than the consciousness of Supermind, which is definitive and immutable. Illumined Mind and Higher Mind are similar to one another, but Higher Mind is a tentative awareness of Unity in that it is still grounded in conceptual thought; Illumined Mind is more integrated, more visionary.

Normal waking consciousness is the level of Mind that brings us trouble because it operates from the perspective of the single individual and assumes the multiplicity of things to be elemental. The multiplicity of things is real, but the level of Mind is unable to see the connectedness of things which to Aurobindo is more basic, more essential. In short, Mind does not know the Whole but mistakes its own individuality as being its defining characteristic in relation to everything else.

It is problematic to conceptualize the levels below Mind in terms of human consciousness, for what remains are Psyche (or Soul), Life, and Matter. Life is the energy that by definition animates every living thing, animal or vegetable, and Matter is the material stuff of the cosmos. Aurobindo postulates Psyche as that which represents the presence of the Divine in all life-forms, but says that it also creates desires in and for the individual, thus separating him or her from the Whole. Because Psyche is the Divine spark, however, when its essence manifests within the individual, it acts in just the opposite way, facilitating the spiritual evolution of that individual.

The purpose of human life, then, is to evolve

spiritually upward toward Supramental consciousness, and human beings have the capacity to help or to hinder this process for the whole of the human community. In essence, when an individual attains, say, to Overmental consciousness, then Overmind itself descends to the level of human consciousness in a way that goes well beyond the spiritual accomplishment of the individual. A specific example of this was Aurobindo's own "Day of Siddhi" (*siddhi* is psychic or spiritual power) on November 24, 1926, when he experienced the descent of Overmind-consciousness, an event which convinced him he was part of the process of the Divine in its self-manifestation.

The way in which a person participates in this process of Divine self-manifestation is through the practice of Yoga. Aurobindo called his system Integral Yoga, not because it was something entirely new, but because it integrates the classical Yogas of devotion, work, and knowledge from the Hindu tradition. In addition, it integrates meditative practices with other activities. In short, Aurobindo realized that people are different from one another and thus no one way is suitable for everyone. In theory, then, anything we do can be part of our Yoga, our spiritual practice. Finally, Integral Yoga implies the integration of spiritual practice with regular activity in the world.

We have come full circle from that day in Bombay in January 1908. During his period of full involvement in the nationalist movement, Aurobindo realized the need to integrate spirituality with worldly activity. His forty years as a Yogi in Pondicherry saw many developments in his thought, but that essential realization never left him.

PAUL MUNDSCHENK

Further Reading

Aurobindo. *Birth Centenary Library*. Pondicherry, India: Sri Aurobindo Ashram Press, 1972. All Aurobindo's works are collected here in a thirty-volume set for the seriously interested reader.
Bruteau, Beatrice. *Worthy Is the World: The Hindu*

Philosophy of Sri Aurobindo. Rutherford, N.J.: Fairleigh Dickinson University Press, 1971. A thorough and insightful study of Aurobindo's vision approached as a philosophical system.

Iyengar, K. R. Srinivasa. *Sri Aurobindo: A Biography and a History*. 2 vols. Pondicherry, India: Sri Aurobindo Centre of Education, 1972. Doubtless the most complete and detailed biography of Aurobindo available to date, although it is clear Iyengar writes from the perspective of a disciple.

McDermott, Robert A., ed. *The Essential Aurobindo*. New York: Schocken Books, 1973. A solid overview of Aurobindo's thought by topics. McDermott provides a brief introduction to each topic, then fills it out with five or six pieces from Aurobindo's writings.

———, ed. *Six Pillars: Introductions to the Major Works of Sri Aurobindo*. Chambersburg, Pa.: Wilson Books, 1974. Excellent analytical essays on six of Aurobindo's major works, including *The Life Divine*.

Minor, Robert N. *Sri Aurobindo: The Perfect and the Good*. Columbia, Mo.: South Asia Books, 1978. A painstaking and insightful analysis of Aurobindo's thought approached within the context of religion and ethics.

Satprem. *Sri Aurobindo or the Adventure of Consciousness*. New York: Harper and Row, 1974. An extensive commentary on several aspects of Aurobindo's Integral Yoga system. Satprem is also a disciple, and is looked upon as a very accomplished Yogin within Aurobindo circles.

K. C. BHATTACHARYYA

Born: 1875, Serampur, West Bengal, India
Died: 1949, Serampur, India
Major Works: *Studies in Vedāntism* (1907), *The Subject as Freedom* (1930), "The Concept of Philosophy," "The Absolute and Its Alternative Forms," "The Concept of Value" (1939)

Major Ideas

The Absolute is indefinite.
The Absolute is freedom.
The Absolute is whatever is free from the "implicational dualism" of content and consciousness.
The Absolute is alternation of Truth, Freedom, and Value.

K. C. (Krishnachandra) Bhattacharyya was born on May 12, 1875, in Serampur, West Bengal, India. He came from a *Brahmin* family of Sanskrit scholars. Therefore, at a very early age he was introduced to ancient Indian scriptures, such as the *Vedas* and the *Upanishads*. He completed a local school in Serampur and then went to Presidency College, Calcutta, for his undergraduate work. He was a very bright student, but his unwillingness to appease British administrators prevented him from securing a position commensurate with his abilities. He held a variety of teaching and administrative positions and retired at the age of fifty-five as the principal of a small college. After retirement from that position, he became a professor of philosophy at Calcutta University, then the Director of the Indian Institute of Philosophy at Amalner, and finally the George V Professor of Mental and Moral Philosophy at Calcutta University. He died on December 11, 1949.

Bhattacharyya was the foremost among contemporary Indian thinkers to attempt to construct a comprehensive philosophical worldview of his own out of elements of Eastern and Western philosophy. He carefully studied ancient Indian philosophical schools: Advaita Vedānta, Sānkhya Yoga, and Jainism. He was also very well versed in classical German philosophies, especially Kant and Hegel. He did not owe allegiance to any particular school, and therefore was not concerned with either the maintenance or the defense of any particular Eastern or Western school of philosophy. In his

philosophy one finds an assimilation of both Eastern and Western philosophies.

A careful study of Bhattacharyya's philosophy reveals that his thoughts have passed through three distinct stages of development. The first stage extends from 1914 to 1918, during which he published three papers: "Some Aspects of Negation," "The Place of the Indefinite in Logic," and "The Definition of Relation as a Category of Existence." The second stage extends from 1925 to 1934, during which he published five papers and one monograph. The papers are "Śamkara's Doctrine of *Māyā*," "Knowledge and Truth," "Correction of Error as a Logical Process," "Fact and the Thought of the Fact," and "The False and the Subjective." He also published his monograph *The Subject as Freedom* during this period. The third stage, the shortest of the three, lasted a little more than a year (1939) during which he published three papers: "The Concept of Philosophy," "The Absolute and Its Alternative Forms," and "The Concept of Value."

First Phase: The Absolute as Indefinite

The search for the Absolute has been the primary concern of Indian philosophy from the *Upanishads* (600–300 B.C.) to the Neo-Vedānta of the twentieth century via the classical Vedānta of Shankara, Rāmānuja, and Madhva (see the chapters on these three individuals in this volume). By focusing on the concept of the Absolute, we not only get a better understanding of how Bhattacharyya's philosophy fits into Indian philosophy historically, but we also are provided with a framework within which to understand the development of Bhattacharyya's philosophy through three distinct phases. In the first phase, he describes the Absolute as "indefinite," in the second as "subject," and in the third as "alternation."

The *Upanishads*, the early texts of the Hindu tradition, identify a single, comprehensive, fundamental principle by the knowing of which everything else in this world becomes known. The typical designation for this principle is *Brahman* or the Absolute. The Absolute defies all characterizations. The *Brihadāranyaka Upanishad* holds that there is no other or better description of *Brahman* than by describing it negatively as *neti*, *neti* (not this, not this). In the classical tradition of Shankara, non-dualist Vedānta, *Brahman* or the Absolute is that state where all subject–object distinction is obliterated. *Brahman* or the Absolute is pure consciousness; it simply is. Bhattacharyya takes for his point of departure this consciousness, which transcends both the subjective and the objective. Since this principle cannot be defined in terms of the objective and its correlate the subjective, he designates it the indefinite. The Absolute is not limited and therefore not definite; it can only be indefinite. To put it differently, both the subjective and the objective belong to the realm of the definite, and that which transcends both is the indefinite.

Bhattacharyya is not unique in the history of philosophy in claiming that the Absolute is indefinite. One finds it in Plato's "nothing," the *māyā* (nescience) of Advaita Vedānta, the "void" of the Buddhists, and the "unknowable" of Kant. All of them, with the exception of Kant, take the indefinite to be a positive entity, a real among reals. Kant brings out the transcendental character of the indefinite; however, this indefinite for him is an unknowable reality.

Bhattacharyya points out that the unknowable can be treated neither as reality nor as thinkable. Every definite content of experience implies an indefinite out of which it is carved. The indefinite creates a fundamental distinction between the definite and the indefinite, the known and the unknown. He expresses this in the principle: "The indefinite *is not* and *is* indefinite at once," or "The indefinite and definite are and are not one." As a mode of the indefinite, the definite also embodies the indefinite. In short, the goal of Bhattacharyya's philosophy was not to ascertain whether the Absolute exists; it was, rather, to understand the Absolute. It is understood paradoxically as that which cannot be understood, namely, the indefinite; both indefinite (not comprehensible) and definite (somehow comprehensible) at once. Bhattacharyya, however, does not rest satisfied with this logical approach; he is led eventually to a psychological approach: although the Absolute as indefinite cannot be an object of our experience, as the basis of all objects it is understood as the subject of our experience. This brings him to the second phase in which the Absolute as indefinite is construed as the Absolute as subject.

Second Phase: The Absolute as Subject

In this phase the Absolute as the indefinite emerges as the Absolute subject that transcends both the subject and the object. Here the Absolute is reached via a series of denials.

In this phase, Bhattacharyya begins with subjectivity, articulating it as an awareness of the subject's distinction from the object. He distinguishes three stages of subjectivity: bodily subjectivity, psychic subjectivity, and spiritual subjectivity. In the first stage the self identifies itself with the body. In the second, the self identifies itself with the images and the thoughts. In the third stage initially there is a feeling of freedom from all actual and possible thoughts; this is followed by introspection where there is the awareness of the subject as "I," which eventually leads one beyond introspection to complete subjectivity or freedom.

The different stages of subjectivity are reached progressively: the denial of the preceding gives rise to the succeeding until there is nothing left to deny or supersede. At every stage there is an inner demand to go beyond that stage. It is important to note that introspection of the subject as the "I" is the realization of the free nature of the subject, where one has an awareness of the subject's freedom. However, this awareness must be denied to make way for complete freedom. Bhattacharyya here is making an important distinction between the subject as *free* and the subject as *freedom*, the former being the introspective stage of subjectivity and the latter the ultimate stage—the ideal—the subject's ultimate goal.

At this point, one might wonder why assume this subjective attitude? Assuming that it leads to freedom, can one not make a case for the objective attitude? These issues form the subject matter of the third phase, the Absolute as alternation.

Third Phase: The Absolute as Alternation

At the outset of his paper "The Concept of the Absolute and Its Alternative Forms," Bhattacharyya informs his readers that philosophy begins in reflective consciousness, which entails an awareness of the relationship between reflective consciousness and its content. Reflective consciousness and its content imply each other, and he calls this relation "implicational dualism." The concept of the Absolute must be understood by reference to this implicational dualism.

Implicational dualism between consciousness and its content or between its subject and object is of three kinds, corresponding to three forms of consciousness: knowing, willing, and feeling. In knowing the content is not constituted by consciousness, in willing it is constituted by consciousness, and in feeling the content constitutes a sort of unity with consciousness. As a result, each has its own formulation of the Absolute.

The first is the Absolute of knowing. In this Absolute, the content determines consciousness; knowledge does not determine truth, truth determines knowledge. In knowing, the object known, in some sense, is independent. The being of the object is free from any reference of knowing. This is a kind of epistemological realism in which the particular act of knowing does not construct the object that is known.

The second is the Absolute of willing. In this Absolute the content is constituted by willing. Willing is active; it is constructive. In the absence of willing, this Absolute is nothing; it is understood as a negation of being. Willing, as a matter of fact, is willing of itself, which in reality is its denial. When a will is satisfied, it is superseded, and in that sense denied.

The third is the Absolute of feeling. In this Absolute consciousness and content determine each other; content is constituted by a sort of unity between feeling and the felt content. In other words, there is a unity free from the duality of content and consciousness. It is a content that is "indefinitely other than consciousness" or consciousness that is "indefinitely other than content." The term "indefinitely" for Bhattacharyya signifies that the Absolute of feeling is indifferent to both being and nonbeing, and accordingly, the Absolute is transcendent.

All this yields an interesting result. The Absolute of knowing may be understood as Truth, the Absolute of willing as Freedom, and the Absolute of feeling as Value. Philosophy, for Bhattacharyya, is a rational analysis of experience in the sense of conceptual clarification, sorting, and ordering of epistemological, metaphysical, ethical, and aesthetic symbols. It is a progress toward the Absolute. The triple Absolute is the prototype of three subjective functions. In everyday experiences, one finds a mixture of these three functions. However, each experience can be purified of the accretions of the other functions and can become pure or Absolute. Absolute knowing is apprehension purged of all noncognitive elements; it is an apprehension of the object-in-itself. Absolute willing is willing purged of all objective elements. Absolute feeling is feeling purged of all cognitive and volitional elements. Each Absolute is a pure experience, that is, positively an actualization of the unique nature of each function, and negatively, a lack of confusion or mixture with other functions. For him, the Absolute is the alternation of these three functions. There are three alternative Absolutes, which cannot be synthesized into one.

Bhattacharyya's conception of the Absolutes is a corollary of the logic of alternation that he advocates. It is a logic of choice, commitment, and coexistence. In our everyday discourse we are presented with alternatives, and we must choose, not because one alternative is correct and the other false, but because we must choose, and having chosen, we must abide by our choice. Bhattacharyya rejects inclusive disjunction (either/or, perhaps both) and accepts exclusive disjunction (either/or, but not both). Alternation, so important in practice, is equally important in theory. With the logic of alternation, Bhattacharyya rejects philosophies that claim that their philosophy is the only true philosophy. For him, there are different paths that lead to different goals, and each goal is Absolute in itself. No Absolute is superior to any other; the ways of the Absolute diverge, but one is not preferable to the other. When one is accepted, the others are automatically rejected. These are genuine alternatives. The Absolute is an alternative of truth, freedom, or value.

Bhattacharyya never clarifies how one conceives of the Absolute in its alternative nature in the ordinary sense of "either/or" while at the same time it remains as an Absolute. This problem notwithstanding, his conception of alternation is a unique and original contribution to philosophy. His goal was not to build a system of philosophy. His philosophy is a kind of living organism in which new material is assimilated and digested, and then grows into a new form. The phases of his thought are not exclusive formulations of his philosophy, they are alternatives. Only by distinguishing among phases is one able to integrate the various facets of his thought and appreciate its organic character. He was widely read in both Eastern and Western philosophy. His philosophy goes a long way toward removing the popular Western misconception that Indian philosophy is exclusively mystical and that it is unscientific and nonrational.

BINA GUPTA

Further Reading

Bhattacharyya Gopinath, ed. *Studies in Philosophy*. 2 vols. Calcutta: Progressive Publishers, 1956 (Vol. I), 1958 (Vol. II). These two volumes contain all the published and a few of the previously unpublished writings of Krishnachandra Bhattacharyya. Each selection contains a useful introduction. Volume I consists of interpretive essays on classical Indian philosophies; volume II contains essays dealing with Professor Bhattacharyya's own philosophy.

Bhattacharyya, K. C. *Studies in Vedāntism*. Calcutta: Calcutta University Press, 1907. This book deals with his method of constructive interpretation. He employs this method to make Vedantism more accessible to modern students of philosophy.

———. *The Subject as Freedom*. Amalner, Bombay: Indian Institute of Philosophy, 1930. This monograph is the first systematic formulation of Bhattacharyya's doctrine of the Absolute.

Burch, George B. *Search for the Absolute in Neo-Vedānta*. Honolulu, Hawaii: The University Press of Hawaii, 1976. This book is clearly written and manages to make sense out of subtle and complicated concepts in K. C. Bhattacharyya's philosophy.

Gupta, Bina. "Alternative Forms of the Absolute: Truth, Freedom, and Value in K. C. Bhattacharyya." *International Studies in Philosophy*, 20 (1980): 291–306. In a clear and critical manner, the author discusses the important issues surrounding Bhattacharyya's conception of the Absolute.

Lal, B. K. *Contemporary Indian Philosophy*. Delhi: Motilal Banarsidass, 1973. The book contains a very helpful essay on Bhattacharyya's philosophy.

SARVEPALLI RADHAKRISHNAN

Born: 1888, near Madras, India
Died: 1975, Madras, India
Major Works: *Indian Philosophy* (1923, 1927), *The Hindu View of Life* (1927), *An Idealist View of Life* (1932), *Eastern Religions and Western Thought* (1939), *The Brahma Sūtras* (1959)

Major Ideas

Monistic Idealism is the most satisfactory philosophy.
Intuition enables us to know Reality directly.
Religious experience is the foundation of true religion.
The Real is the Absolute Spirit and man's true self is one with the Absolute Spirit.
Man's final value is spiritual freedom and selfless service is the way to it.
There are many ways to the same one God.
All human beings are of the same divine essence and therefore of equal worth and entitled to the same fundamental rights.

Sarvepalli Radhakrishnan was India's most eminent twentieth-century philosopher. He was a philosophical bilinguist, having the rare qualification of being equally versed in the European and Asiatic tradition. He created a philosophical East–West synthesis. He was a world leader in comparative religion and comparative philosophy. He sought to revitalize idealist philosophy as an answer to the crisis of world civilization and aspired to be a midwife to the world's unborn soul. He exemplified the idea of the philosopher–king by rising from professor of philosophy at Calcutta and Oxford to become the president of India. He was widely admired as a master of the English language, a spellbinding orator, a dynamic leader, and a generous human being.

Radhakrishnan was brought up and educated in colonial India where Christian missionaries proclaimed Christianity to be the only true religion and portrayed Hinduism as being seriously defective. In his first published works, Radhakrishnan defended the Hindu theory of *karma* and the ethics of Vedānta. The doctrine of *karma* asserts that the rule of law (*rita*) which governs the universe also includes the world of morals. As you sow, so shall you reap. The advantages and liabilities inherent to a given life are the consequences of the good or evil deeds of previous lives. By making an agent's suf-

ferings the consequences of his own past misdeeds, the theory of *karma* solves the notorious problem of evil. The agent himself, not God, causes evil. But *karma* does not entail fatalism nor a negation of freedom. Using an analogy from the games of cards, Radhakrishnan contended that the hand dealt to the player is determined by past *karma*, but he is free to play the game as he wishes. Turning to the ethics of Vedānta, Radhakrishnan argued that critics of the Hinduism were mistaken in claiming that Vedānta is life-negating. This world is the field where one enacts the drama of soul's salvation. This is done not by renouncing the world but acting in it. However, one must act so as to fulfill one's duty without any attachment to the fruits of one's actions. Man's highest duty is selfless service and love (*ahimsā*). Spiritual experience convinces a person that all of creation, human and nonhuman, participates in the Absolute Spirit and therefore has value. Hence, man's duty is to work for universal salvation.

Radhakrishnan's first major work, the monumental *Indian Philosophy*, was a two-volume history published in Muirhead's distinguished *Library of Philosophy* series. It was a remarkable achievement. It was the first book to present a panorama of Indian thought to the English-speaking world, especially England, where it was widely believed that there was no such serious subject as Indian philosophy. Radhakrishnan established the respectability of Indian philosophy throughout the world. Even the editors of the *Encyclopaedia Britannica* asked Radhakrishnan to contribute the first separate article ever on the topic of Indian philosophy for its fourteenth edition.

In 1921, Radhakrishnan was appointed George V Professor of Philosophy at Calcutta University. This was the most prestigious chair in India. Radhakrishnan's fame was spreading in India and England and he was invited to present the 1926 Upton Lectures in Comparative Religion at Manchester College, Oxford. The lectures were subsequently published under the title *The Hindu View of Life* (1927).

The Hindu View of Life

In his lectures Radhakrishnan answered the many Christian critics of Hinduism by formulating his interpretation of the essence of Hinduism. Hinduism is a way of life rather than a dogmatic creed. Its foundation is spiritual experience. Through meditative practices, one has direct experience of the Absolute Spirit (*Brahman*). This experience brings home the unity of the individual self and the Absolute Self. Attaining one's deepest self by losing one's selfish ego becomes the supreme goal.

To the religious consciousness, the Absolute Spirit (*Brahman*) appears as the personal God (*Īshvara*). Monism, that is, belief in one Supreme Reality, is transformed into monotheism. Ultimately there is only one God, but he is symbolized in many forms. The One is analyzed into three elements of personality: cognition is represented by *Brahma*, the supreme knower; emotion is represented by *Vishnu*, the great lover; and will is represented by *Shiva*, the perfect will. The power and glory of feminine creativity is represented by the Great Goddess, *Devi*. Every Hindu is encouraged to choose a personal God, *Ishtadevata*, who best symbolized God for him. After all, there is only one God, and all the gods are his symbolic representations. Whichever form of God a devotee worships, he ultimately worships the same

God. What counts is the devotee's heart, not his creed.

Since Hinduism is a way of life it needs to provide guidance to man throughout his life span. Hindu society is organized so as to enable all of its members to know their respective duties, appropriate to their station in life, and eventually to attain their highest good.

Man has four goals in life: wealth or material well-being (*artha*), cultural and artistic life (*kāma*), righteousness (*dharma*), and spiritual freedom (*moksha*). Material well-being (*artha*) is seen as a precondition for a harmonious family life and social stability. Man does not live by bread alone, but he cannot live without it either. Cultural and artistic life and enjoyment of sensual pleasures (*kāma*) are seen as contributing to the normal fulfillment of one aspect of human personality. However, pursuit of wealth and pleasure must be directed by morality (*dharma*). While pursuing these goals, morality directs man to slowly give up his ego-centeredness. The eventual goal of morality is action without attachment to the fruit of action (*nishkāma karma*). When this stage is reached, a person is ready to pursue the final goal, spiritual freedom (*moksha*).

Hinduism divides individual human life in four stages (*āshramas*), each with its specific goals and practices. The first period of life is training (*brahmacarya*), when one learns to discipline the body and the mind. One learns the arts and sciences which will be useful in later life. The second stage is that of the householder (*garhastha*). A person is encouraged to marry and found a family. A well-balanced sex life is seen as a part of healthy living. The householder is expected to make a success of his profession and finally prepare his sons and daughters for a successful life. In the third stage (*vānaprastha*), the responsibilities of home are given up. When one's bodily powers wane, it is time to depart to the forest and prepare oneself for the true life of the spirit. The last stage of life is that of a *sannyāsin*, when a person lives in solitude and undertakes meditation practices in order to attain spiritual freedom. Such a person has achieved total detachment from worldly aims and developed a spirit of equanimity. He dwells in love and walks in righteousness. He aims at the spiritual freedom of all.

Having successfully presented the Hindu view of life as an example of true religion, Radhakrishnan set himself the task of providing a philosophy as an underpinning for a true world religion. He intended to combine the best of his Indian Vedāntic tradition with the best of Western philosophic thought in a new synthesis.

The Idealist View of Life

Radhakrishnan expounded his philosophy of integral experience in his Hibbert Lectures at the Universities of London and Manchester in 1929. His greatest work, *An Idealist View of Life* (1932), was based on these lectures.

Radhakrishnan remarks upon the spectacular success of science in modern times and notices that most current philosophies, using scientific knowledge as a paradigm, recognize only two sources of knowledge (*pramānas*), namely sense-perception and logic. But Radhakrishnan insists that human beings have yet another way of knowing, a third *pramāna*, which he calls intuition. In fact, he claims that intuition is the fundamental source of cognition, since in intuition the whole of our mind is functioning integrally. Sense-perception and logic are only partial functions of the mind. In any cognitive situation our mind, as a whole, integrally grasps the object by being one with it. Intuitive knowledge arises from an intimate fusion of mind with reality. It is knowledge by being and not by senses or by symbols. It is the awareness of things by identity. Intuitive knowledge is the knowledge by which we see things as they are, as unique individuals and not as members of a class or units in a crowd. Furthermore, intuitive knowledge is self-certifying; the knower has complete certainty.

Integral experience is a vision, which must then be tested by logic and sense experience. Also, the richness and value of integral experience depends upon the "preparedness" that the subject brings to the object. The highest reach of integral experience is the mystic vision of the Absolute Spirit, in which the subject–object duality is transcended. The experience is self-certifying and the subject finds it to be incommunicable. There are no concepts in our language to describe it, but the subject knows that the foundation of the universe is the Absolute Spirit and it is of the same nature as his own deepest self. The experience transforms the person's life, and he becomes a changed man, a saint, a seer, one who has achieved spiritual freedom.

Radhakrishnan is fully aware of the fact that if his new *pramāna*, integral experience or intuition, only justified spiritual knowledge as the foundation of a true religion, it would be a case of special pleading. He wants his philosophy to have a wider scope. So he argues that in all branches of human endeavor, such as science, art, and morality, intuition is basic. A scientist sees the basic structures of his objects of inquiry (physical phenomena) by intuitive insight. The better his preparation, the better the theory. Only then does logic and sense experience come into play. In art, too, the artist embraces his subject in a non-dual unity and then endeavors to translate the vision in some physical medium. The greater his genius and preparation, the greater the art. In a truly aesthetic experience, the viewer becomes one with the art object and finds it distressingly hard to communicate his experience. In morality, too, we need to become one with the object to see the right course. Moral heroes are persons who use integral experience rather than conventional rules.

Radhakrishnan feels justified in believing that he has presented us with a new theory of knowledge that will provide us with an adequate philosophy. The fundamental questions of philosophy have to do with the nature of Being and Value. Radhakrishnan proposes that the answer lies in spiritual or mystical experience. Such experience reveals to us that Being is Absolute Spirit and that the Absolute and the individual self are one. The same experience reveals the highest value to be the full recognition of that oneness (*moksha*). The nature of the Absolute is incommunicable. But logic tells us that the real must be full and changeless. Here Radhakrishnan has to face up to the difficulty encountered by all monistic idealists such as Shankara and the Western philosopher F. H. Bradley (1846–

1924), namely the relation between the changeless Absolute Spirit and the ever-changing world. In answer, Radhakrishnan claims that the world is the translation of one specific possibility of the Infinite Spirit. Why is this possibility being realized? The answer cannot be given; it is a mystery (*māyā*). God is the Absolute Spirit from the cosmic or human end. This view is Radhakrishnan's *via media* between the pantheistic view that the world is God and the traditional Vedāntic view that God, the Divine Person, is an illusion (*māyā*).

Radhakrishnan's thesis that God is the Absolute Spirit from the human point of view makes room for his passionate advocacy of religious tolerance. Many different views of God can be justifiably maintained, since there is no truth of the matter. Creeds are unimportant; conduct is all. By love and righteousness all men can advance to the same spiritual goal, namely the unitary, spiritual experience of the Absolute Spirit. There are many paths to the same goals and each person should take the one most suited to his individual nature.

Eastern Religions and Western Thought

In 1936, Radhakrishnan was appointed Spalding Professor of Eastern Religion and Ethics at Oxford University. He was the first Indian and the first Asian to hold a chair at Oxford. His best work in comparative religion is found in his *Eastern Religions and Western Thought* (1939).

It was Radhakrishnan's contention that there is one perennial and universal philosophy that is found in all lands and cultures, in the seers of the *Upanishads* and the Buddha, Plato and Plotinus, Hillel and Philo Judaeus of Alexandria, Jesus and Paul, and medieval mystics of Islam. It is this spirit that binds continents and unites the ages that can save us from the meaninglessness of modern culture.

Radhakrishnan drew a distinction between true religion, which is based on spiritual experience, and dogmatic religion, which relies on authority. Every historical religion is a mixture of true and dogmatic religion. Hinduism has a much larger proportion of true religion than does Christianity;

hence the Hindu tolerance of different creeds. Radhakrishnan also stressed that no one need change the religion he was born into; he only needs to conform his conduct to the call of true religion. True religion unites, whereas dogmatic religion divides. The progress of science and a world united by technology has made dogmatic religions obsolete. Only the resurgence of true religion will allow humanity to rediscover its inner life and its authentic values. That represents the best hope for the fragmented and hostile national, religious, and cultural groups to unite as the human family.

Radhakrishnan's belief that both philosophy and true religion are committed to changing the world naturally led him to pioneer educational reform. He saw universities as the means to a new world and higher education as an instrument in solving India's and the world's problems. The object of education is to bring forth the ethical man, the man in whom all the capacities—spiritual, intellectual, and physical—are fully developed. He was the vice-chancellor of Andhra University and later Benares Hindu University. He was the most sought-after university convocation speaker. He stressed that being truly educated means having the light to see the truth and the strength to make it prevail.

It was only natural that a man of Radhakrishnan's vision for social service be drawn into political action after Indian independence. He served as India's ambassador to the USSR from 1949 to 1952 and as India's vice-president from 1952 to 1962, and finally rose to the high office of president of India from 1962 to 1967. During those years he felt called upon to clarify his social and political philosophy.

The cornerstone of Radhakrishnan's social philosophy was the axiom, flowing from his Idealist metaphysics, that all human beings are of the same divine essence and therefore of equal worth and entitled to the same fundamental rights. The human individual is the highest, most concrete embodiment of the Spirit on earth and anything that hurts his individuality or damages his dignity is morally wrong. Whatever is conductive to self-realization is good. He was a passionate advocate of freedom in the fullest sense of that term. The state that governs least is the best. Democracy requires the equal right of all to the development of such capacity for good as nature has endowed them with. Taking all in all, in this imperfect world, democratic government is the most satisfactory, since it rests on the consent of the governed. However, freedom for minority groups must be assured.

He was convinced that social justice was not possible without economic justice. He opposed capitalism because concentration of economic power is not just. He also opposed communism and fascism since all forms of regimentation and total-itarianism deny freedom and rights of man. He sought to find a middle way to social democracy. He opposed violence and supported a gradual trans-formation as opposed to the status quo or revolu-tion. He was a dedicated advocate of India's independence and saw Mahatma Gandhi as the model leader of political change.

Radhakrishnan was a passionate believer in an in-ternational state. He had witnessed the destructive fury of narrow nationalistic states in the World Wars. He had been a member of the International Commis-sion for Intellectual Cooperation (1931–39) set up by the League of Nations, and the President of the United Nations Educational, Scientific and Cultural Organization (UNESCO) (1952–54). He worked for and advocated international cooperation all his adult life. As Indian ambassador to the USSR, he tried to mitigate the excesses of the Cold War be-tween the West and Russia. Having seen the destruc-tiveness of nationalism, he was convinced that if man is to survive, the world must be organized on the basis of an international state in which the differ-ences need not be fused, but they need not conflict.

In spite of his heavy involvement in political life, Radhakrishnan continued his philosophical work. He published his commentary on the *Bhagavad Gītā* (1948) and the *Upanishads* (1953). It was traditional for the great philosophers in the Advaita tradition to write commentaries on all three of the great Vedānta classics—the *Bhagavad Gītā*, the *Upanishads*, and the *Brahma Sūtras*. Radhakrish-nan published his commentary on the *Brahma Sūtras* in 1959, and took his place in the pantheon as the greatest exponent of Vedanta in the twentieth century.

NARAYAN CHAMPAWAT

Further Reading

Arapura, J. G. *Radhakrishnan and Integral Experi-ence.* New York: Asia Publishing House, 1966. The most useful full-length study of Radhakrish-nan's philosophy.

Gopal, Sarvepalli. *Radhakrishnan, A Biography.* London: Unwin Hyman Ltd. 1989. Excellent sympathetic and incisive biography by his son

McDermott, Robert A. *Radhakrishnan.* New York: E.P. Dutton and Company, 1970. Selected writ-ings by Radhakrishnan on philosophy, religion, and culture.

Schilpp, Paul A., ed. *The Philosophy of Sarvepalli Radhakrishnan.* Library of Living Philosophers. New York: Tudor Publishing Company, 1952. Several excellent articles by outstanding philos-ophers with Radhakrishnan's "Reply to Critics" and his autobiographical "Confession."

JAWAHARLAL NEHRU

Born: 1889, Allahabad, India
Died: 1964, Delhi, India
Major Works: *Soviet Russia* (1928), *Statements, Speeches and Writings* (1929), *Letters from a Father to His Daughter* (1930), *Glimpses of World History* (1934), *An Autobiography* (1936), *The Discovery of India* (1946)

Major Ideas

The state governs by coercion at the physical, ideological, and economic levels.
No state will willingly give up power unless effective pressure is brought to bear on it.
The use of satyāgraha, *nonviolent noncooperation, as a means of struggle for Indian independence should not become an end in itself.*
The Indian state should be based on secular, socialist, and democratic principles.

Responding to the triple challenges of a feudal *zamindari* land system, a burgeoning native capitalist class, and the British colonization of India, Jawaharlal Nehru dedicated himself to the Indian nationalist movement as it was embodied in the Indian National Congress Party. As a result of his nationalist activities, the British authorities detained him on nine occasions; he would spend more than eight years in prison, where he would author the bulk of his writings.

It was during his seventh imprisonment in 1934—served in Dehra Dun Goal—that Nehru penned *An Autobiography*. Nehru's autobiography breaks with the conventions of the autobiographical genre. It is less an account of his personal life than it is an outline of the major intellectual, philosophical, and political currents that informed his participation in the nationalist movement. Indeed, although the first four chapters describe his childhood and education, the rest of the book focuses on his evolving political ideas based on his experiences in the Congress Party and the political contacts he made internationally. Nehru does not divulge many details of his family life; references to his wife Kamala and daughter Indira are infrequent. When he does speak of Kamala, it is either in the context of her involvement with Congress or in connection with her health, which necessitated treatment abroad. In writing of his family members, he devotes the most space to his father, Mo-

tilal Nehru, who was prominent in the Indian National Congress and known for his moderate views. But these passages do not present intimate glimpses of the father–son relationship. In these sections, Nehru elaborates the political differences between them and describes how Motilal came to support Indian self-rule over dominion status.

It should come as no surprise, then, that *An Autobiography* primarily dwells on aspects of the independence movement such as the major characters, the ideological differences among them, and the tactics utilized in the struggle. As the chapter titles indicate, many of them can stand as independent articles on the issues of Nehru's day: "Wanderings Among Kisans" (9), "Non-cooperation" (10), "Nonviolence and the Doctrine of the Sword" (12), "Communalism" (19), "No-Tax Campaign" (52), "Delhi Pact" (29), "Democracy East and West" (60). Since Nehru wrote his autobiography in prison, he did not have access to other written sources and had to rely on his memory alone to reconstruct events. Though he contradicts himself in places, the historical and philosophical scope of *An Autobiography* is remarkable.

Jawaharlal Nehru grew up in a joint-family household in the city of his birth, Allahabad. He received his early education at home under the guidance of English governesses and tutors. The visits of nationalist leaders, combined with his avid interest in current world events (particularly England's Second Boer War of 1889–1902 in Africa and the Russo–Japanese War of 1904–05), suffused young Nehru with the vague desire to liberate India from British rule. In 1905, however, he was sent to England for his schooling, where he attended Harrow for two years (1905–07) and moved on to Trinity College of Cambridge University to pursue a course in the natural sciences (1907–10). His studies finally ended with a course in law at the Inner Temple in London (1910–12).

After his return to India in 1912, Nehru became a member of the Allahabad High Court. During this year he also attended the annual session of the Indian National Congress as a delegate. The Congress was then, as Nehru described it, "a moderate group, meeting annually, passing some feeble resolutions, and attracting little attention." In 1919, General Dyer's massacre of several hundred Indians peacefully protesting the Rowlatt Acts (which allowed for detention without trial) at Jallianwala Bagh in Amritsar galvanized Nehru to leave his law practice and become a full-time congressional worker. The Jallianwala Bagh massacre convinced him that the practice of law and public service were irreconcilable under colonialism. Nehru served as a deputy on a "Committee of Inquiry" into the Jallianwala Bagh massacre and came into much contact with Mahatma Gandhi during this period.

Satyāgraha: The Nonviolent, Noncooperation Movement

Gandhi had begun to take a more active role in Congress and had introduced a resolution—in a special session of Congress at Calcutta in the autumn of 1920—of noncooperation with the British authorities. The resolution passed, but it alienated some staunch supporters of constitutional methods. Noncooperation, under Gandhi's tutelage, helped transform Congress from an upper-class elite organization to one capable of mobilizing mass support. Noncooperation, or *satyāgraha* as it came to be called, was predicated on the concept of nonviolence (*ahimsā*). Its methods included the boycott of foreign goods (particularly textiles), sit-ins,

protest marches (such as the salt march to Dandi), and demonstrations.

Though Nehru recognized noncooperation as an effective tactic in the struggle for national liberation, he did not embrace nonviolence as an end in itself as Gandhi had. Gandhi's decision to withdraw from the noncooperation movement in the wake of the massacre of policemen by peasants in Chauri Chaura during 1922 drew criticism from Nehru. Condemning the murders as "a deplorable occurrence," Nehru nonetheless felt that the national movement should not be derailed by sporadic acts of violence. He believed that it was impossible to insist that all Indians would remain nonviolent in the face of extreme provocation from the police and the infiltration of the movement by agents provocateurs. So while Nehru advocated nonviolence as a means of struggle, he never lost sight of the ends of national liberation.

Theory of the State

Nehru recognized—as Marxist thinkers before him—that the state itself was a coercive force based on violence. In *An Autobiography* Nehru characterizes state violence as having three manifestations: (1) actual physical violence ("of the armed forces"); (2) ideological violence ("the far more dangerous violence, more subtly exercised, of . . . false propaganda, direct and indirect through education, Press, etc., religious"); and (3) the violence of "economic destitution and starvation."

The British colonial state, which had economically underdeveloped India and had used force to crush peaceful demonstrations, embodied state violence at its most explicit. Given its coercive nature, no state would willingly give up power unless effective pressure was exercised. But the colonial state did not hold a monopoly on violence and coercion. Nehru believed that all "government and social life necessitate some coercion." Within newly independent countries, for instance, state coercion would protect the rights of minority groups—such as Muslims and *Dalits* (untouchables)—by curbing individual or group "tendencies which are inherently selfish and likely to injure society."

Contradictions in Nationalism

Nehru realized that even within anti-colonial movements nationalism could be a contradictory force. According to him, for nationalism to realize its goal of freedom from external domination, it had to unify people around the cause of anti-imperialism. To appeal to as broad a spectrum of people as possible, nationalism had to forego potentially divisive issues of social justice. In doing so, nationalism often spoke in the name of everybody. For example, the main nationalist organization in India, Congress, claimed to represent the entire nation. Nehru understood that this claim was, in his words,

> untenable, for no political organization can represent conflicting interests without reducing itself to a flabby and unmeaning mass with no distinctive and distinguishing features.

Congress could represent only those individuals who agreed with its aims and philosophies. But insofar as its national anti-imperialist agenda offered a wide basis for agreement, Nehru believed that the organization "did represent in varying degrees the vast majority of the people of India."

Nehru defined nationalism "as essentially an anti-feeling" which "feeds and fattens on hatred and anger against other national groups, and especially against the foreign rulers of a subject country." (However, anti-English sentiment in Congress did not so much develop into a racial hatred against individual Britons as it did into a condemnation of the colonial system.) Given the nature of nationalism, it could be hijacked by reactionary forces who could define "the nation" in exclusive terms. The British had earlier created separate electorates for different religious communities in an effort to divide Indians and to justify the continuation of colonial rule on the basis that they were the only ones capable of protecting minority communities and maintaining law and order. Nationalists began to identify the nation with parochial sectarian (in India referred to as "communal") identities. Many of the congressional leaders utilized Hindu myths and idioms

within their speeches. As a result, many Muslims felt alienated from the party.

Differences with Gandhi

Acknowledging Gandhi's ability "to cast a spell on all classes and groups of people and" draw "them into one motley crowd struggling in one direction," Nehru often found himself in fundamental disagreement with some of Gandhi's ideas. Nonetheless the two men shared a profound respect for one another in spite of their philosophical differences. Nehru did not always approve of Gandhi's political idiom. Gandhi, though adamant in his condemnation of communalism, drew on Hindu symbolism in his speeches. Nehru explained, "some of Gandhi's phrases sometimes jarred upon me—thus his frequent reference to *Rāma Raj* as a golden age which was to return."

Gandhi's concept of *Rāma Raj*, a return to the type of rule of the Hindu epic God *Rāma*, troubled Nehru on two counts: first, the use of Hindu myth smacked of religious revivalism, and second, the concept of *Rāma Raj* represented a social order of extreme economic inequality. For Gandhi, *Rāma Raj* represented a golden age in which each individual would forego material luxuries (such as motorized transportation) and embrace a "simple peasant life." By accepting an ascetic lifestyle, the individual would realize "real happiness" and increase her or his "capacity for service" to society.

Nehru completely disagreed with this philosophy. By the late 1920s and early 1930s he had come to subscribe to Marxist interpretations of history. He became convinced that an independent India would have to change the feudal *zamindari* land system, as well as challenge the structure of capitalism. Nehru disliked Gandhi's romantic elevation of poverty and suffering. Everybody, he believed, should have the right to economic well-being. People could develop to their full potential only if their physical needs were met. Rather than bring everyone's standard of living down to that of the "simple peasant," Nehru felt that everyone had the right to a decent standard of living. Unlike Gandhi, who romanticized peasant culture, Nehru believed that peasants should have access to "urban cultural facilities" in the rural areas. He thought Gandhi was misguided in prioritizing personal salvation and sin over that of the general welfare of society as a whole.

In spite of his ideological leanings towards Marxism, Nehru did not align himself with the Communists, for he felt that they had erroneously applied an analysis of the European labor context to the Indian one. Indian Communists had focused their energies on organizing the urban industrial proletariat to the neglect of organizing the rural peasants. Further, Nehru felt that the Communists unfairly criticized the Congress for being too bourgeois in outlook. The Indian National Congress was, in fact, made up of people from a bourgeois-class background but, as its name implied, Nehru pointed out, "its objective so far has been, not a change of the social order, but political independence." Comments such as this one indicate that Nehru thought that the national issue had to take precedence over the class one; once independence had been gained, then India could turn to solving the problem of economic inequality.

Though Nehru articulated a class analysis of the nationalist movement, he did not offer a specific program in his autobiography to challenge either the structures of the *zamindari* land system or capitalism. Instead, he urged his readers to study conditions in India and different manifestations of socialism abroad. Nehru observed,

If socialism is to be built up in India, it will have to grow out of Indian conditions, and the closest study of these conditions is essential.

PURNIMA BOSE

Further Reading

Akbar, M. J. *Nehru: The Making of India*. London: Viking Penguin Inc., 1988. A comprehensive biography of Nehru.

Alphonso-Karkala, John B. *Jawaharlal Nehru*. Boston: Twayne Publishers, 1975. A thorough discussion of Nehru's works in relation to his life.

Chatterjee, Partha. *Nationalist Thought and the Colonial World: A Derivative Discourse*. London: Zed Books Ltd., 1986. Chatterjee analyzes Nehru in relation to Indian nationalism in general and Gandhi in particular.

Nehru, Jawaharlal. *An Autobiography*. London: The Bodley Head, 1958. All quotations in this chapter are from this edition.

Zakaria, Rafiq, ed. *A Study of Nehru*. Calcutta: Rupa & Co., 1989. This book offers a wide selection of perspectives on Nehru, such as those of well-known politicians outside of India, academics, and Nehru's family members.

JAPAN

SHŌTOKU TAISHI

Born: 574, Emperor Yōmei's (Iware no Ike no He no) Namitsuki Palace, Nara Prefecture, Japan
Died: 622, Empress Suiko's Toyura Palace, Nara Prefecture, Japan
Major Works: *Jūshichijō kempō* (*Seventeen-Article Constitution*) (604), *Sangyō gisho* (*Commentaries on Three Sūtras*), *Shōmangyō gisho* (*Commentary on the Sūtra of Queen Shrīmālā*) (c. 609–611), *Yuimakyō gisho* (*Commentary on the* Vimalakirtī Sūtra) (c. 612–613), *Hokkekyō gisho* (*Commentary on the* Lotus Sūtra) (c. 614–615)

Major Ideas

Buddhism provides the ideal basis for a universal state, complemented by Confucian precepts to promote harmony, the source of sound social organization.

The common social good is the ultimate rationale for government rather than divine mandate or the legalistic "inalienable rights" of citizens.

Since all men are influenced by partisan interests and human reasoning is seriously limited in its ability to distinguish right from wrong, important issues must be decided through consensus.

A contemporary of the prophet Muhammad (c. 570–632), Crown Prince Shōtoku has been traditionally venerated as the sage ruler who led Japan from semiliterate tribalism into political unity and cultural greatness. Never emperor, he was entrusted in 593, at age nineteen, with control of the government under the reign of his aunt, Empress Suiko. His thought was an amalgam of Chinese Mahāyāna Buddhism just as it was about to flower after centuries of assimilation, traditional Han Confucianism, and indigenous Japanese traditions; what it appropriated from abroad was shaped by the vision of a universal state, comparable to that of India's great king Aśoka (r. 268–232 B.C.). Later centuries would venerate Prince Shōtoku as the very incarnation of the *Bodhisattva* Kannon.

The Crown Prince, known in his lifetime as Umayado ("Horse Stable Door"), supported the Soga clan (to which he was related through two grandmothers), mainly against the Nakatomi traditional ritualists and the Mononobe military clan, who were decisively defeated in 587. After the assassination of Emperor Sujin in 592, Empress Suiko assumed the throne the following year under Soga auspices, with Crown Prince Shōtoku assigned to perform its administrative functions.

In this period of great political instability and intrigue, Japan was fortunate to have a leader of broad vision to lay the foundations for a unified state beyond clan rivalry. China had only become reunified under the Sui dynasty in 589, after four centuries of fragmentation since the collapse of the Later Han dynasty. Although Han Confucianism still provided a theoretical framework for many of the practical details of government, its credibility as a self-sufficient political philosophy had fallen with the Han, and the Neo-Confucian reformulation was only beginning to take shape. Chinese Buddhism under the Sui and Tang (T'ang) was to be the spirit behind the great cultural flowerings of the Sui, Tang, and Song (Sung), although its importance tends to be minimized by modern historians who are the heirs of centuries of Confucian monopoly on official scholarship.

At this pivotal moment in seventh-century China and Japan, Shōtoku and his Soga allies strongly promoted Buddhist ideals and institutions as the ideological basis for a new progressive government utilizing the practical social precepts of Confucianism. Mahāyāna ideals of accommodation and its explicit recognition of the Two Truths—two fundamental modes of apprehending human experience—easily permits support of complementary social philosophies. In contrast, Confucian thinkers in both China and Japan have almost always been antagonistic to Buddhism.

The Seventeen-Article Constitution

Although the short *Seventeen-Article Constitution* (*Jūshichijō kempō*) (604) is the most famous work attributed to Prince Shōtoku, it was first recorded more than a century after it was composed, in the *Chronicles of Japan* (*Nihon Shoki*) (720). (None of the *Three Commentaries* discussed below is even mentioned in the *Chronicles*; the earliest reference to Shōtoku as their author is 747.) Whatever the historical facts surrounding their creation, the *Constitution* and the *Commentaries* came to symbolize a sea change in Japan's history, the inspiration for the following century of major political reconstruction, including the Taika Reform of 645.

The use of the designation *Constitution* (*kempō*) is sometimes challenged on the grounds that is it a set of moral injunctions rather than a Western-style statement of rights based on the notion of a social contract to which subsequent laws must conform. But the institutions of one society rarely parallel those of another exactly, so the word seems adequate as long as we remain alert to the differences in word usage.

Shōtoku appeals neither to "self-evident truths" nor (as he could have, given his lineage) to some Divine Right of Kings as the basis for law. He begins by stating pragmatically that if society is to work efficiently for the good of all, then people must restrain factionalism and learn to work together:

> Harmony is to be valued, and an avoidance of wanton opposition to be honored. . . . All men are influenced by partisanship, and there are few who are intelligent. But when . . . there is concord in the discussion of business, right views of things spontaneously gain acceptance. Then what is there which cannot be accomplished? (Article 1)

This optimism that people can be persuaded to resolve their differences by appeals to harmony and the common good is in marked contrast to Western views that factions can be controlled only legally by a balance of powers.

Although Prince Shōtoku, founder of numerous temples and writer of *sūtra* commentaries, is known to have been as a staunch supporter of Buddhism, we might hastily infer from the inclusion of so many social injunctions that the *Constitution* is little more than a reworking of Han Confucian social philosophy. But scholars such as Nakamura Hajime have pointed out that this ideal of "harmony" (*wa*) to which these practical virtues converge has its source in Buddhist rather than Confucian thought. Moreover, in Article 2 Shōtoku enjoins people to reverence Buddhism as their final refuge, and reminds them of the limits of reasoning a characteristically Buddhist reservation contrasting with Confucian rationalism:

> How can anyone lay down a rule by which to distinguish right from wrong? For we are all, one with another, wise and foolish, like a ring which has no end. (Article 9)

How, then, are we to determine the right course of action? By consensus, a procedure still alive and well in Japan:

> Decisions on important matters should not be made by one person alone. They should be discussed with many. . . . In the case of weighty matters, when there is a suspicion that they may miscarry, . . . one should arrange matters in concert with others. (Article 17)

Many of the other articles might appear to be textbook elaborations of the "Five Constant [Virtues]" (Chinese: *wu chang/wu ch'ang*; Japanese: *gojō*), which Confucianism prescribes as norms of social behavior:

> *Benevolence* (Chinese: *ren/jen*; Japanese: *jin*): "Men of this kind [sycophants] are all wanting in fidelity to their lord, and in benevolence towards the people" (Article 6). "Let the people be employed [in forced labor] at seasonable times. . .From Spring to Autumn, when they are engaged in agriculture or with the mulberry trees, the people should not be so

employed. For if they do not attend to agriculture, what will they have to eat? If they do not attend to the mulberry trees, what will they do for clothing?" (Article 16)

Righteousness (Chinese: *yi/i*; Japanese: *gi*): "Deal impartially with the suits which are submitted to you" (Article 5). "Give clear appreciation to merit and demerit, and deal out to each its sure reward or punishment" (Article 11).

Propriety in Demeanor (Chinese: *li*; Japanese: *ri*): "When the people behave with decorum, the government of the commonwealth proceeds of itself" (Article 4).

Wisdom (Chinese: *zhi/chih*; Japanese: *chi*): "On all occasions, be they urgent or the reverse, meet but with a wise man, and they will of themselves be amenable" (Article 7). "If we do not find wise men and sages, wherewithal shall the country be governed?" (Article 14)

Good Faith (Chinese: *xin/hsin*; Japanese: *shin*): "In everything let there be good faith, for in it surely consists the good and the bad, success and failure" (Article 9).

The axiom, "Chastise that which is evil and encourage that which is good [*kanzen chōaku*]" (Article 6), employed by some from the Heian through the Edo periods as grounds for subordinating literature to morality and social responsibility, finds its first Japanese formulation in the *Constitution*, although it appears in Chinese writings as far back as *Tso's Commentary* (Chinese: *Zuo Zhuan/ Tso chuan*; Japanese: *Saden*) (second century B.C.). But in the end, all are subordinate to the central ideal of a universal unifying harmony which takes into account human limitations.

Commentaries on Three Sūtras

The first reference to the presence of Buddhism in Japan is 538 (formerly believed to be 552), only a few decades before Shōtoku was born. The elaborate ecclesiastical establishments of Nara and Heian would emerge only centuries later, and even Chinese Buddhism was still developing its own

distinct forms. Kumārajīva's definitive and prolific translations of *sūtras* and commentaries, including the *Lotus*, appeared in the early fifth century A.D., the Tian Tai (T'ien t'ai) School's Zhi Yi (Chinese: Chih-i; Japanese: Chigi) (538–597) was Shōtoku's slightly older contemporary, and Zen's Sixth Patriarch, Huineng (Chinese: Hui-neng; Japanese: Enō) (638–713), was nowhere in sight. It is in this context that we must view Prince Shōtoku's Buddhism.

The *Sangyō gisho*, composed in Chinese, perhaps c. 609–615, consists of commentaries on two Chinese translations of Kumārajīva: (1) the *Lotus Sūtra*, (2) the *Vimalakīrti Sūtra*; and (3) Gunabhadra's early version of the *Sūtra of Queen Shrīmālā*. Scholars have pointed out that Shōtoku's *Lotus* commentary largely follows a well-known interpretation by the monk Fa Yun (Chinese: Fa-yün; Japanese: Hōun) (467–529), later challenged by Tien Tai's Zhi Yi, whose thought underlies Japanese Tendai. Shōtoku's *Vimalakīrti* commentary is seen to reflect the ideas of Zhi Zang (Chinese: Chih-tsang; Japanese: Chizō) (458–522), and the *Shrīmālā* commentary, those of Seng Min (Chinese: Seng-min; Japanese: Sōmin) (467–527). These three Chinese commentators, all famous in their day, were known as the "Three Great Teachers of the Liang Dynasty"; Shōtoku's three commentaries are seen to reflect late Six Dynasties thought of southern Chinese Buddhism. Recently among the Dun Huang (Tun-huang) manuscripts a text has been uncovered whose contents are remarkably similar to Shōtoku's *Shrīmālā* commentary, which may have been its inspiration.

Although Prince Shōtoku's three commentaries may be derivative, this is no fault of scholastic traditions, whose concern is to clarify the obscure rather than to demonstrate the originality of the author. What is astonishing is that they were composed at all, given the fact that few Japanese at the time were literate, and Shōtoku was first and foremost an active political leader rather than a reclusive scholar–monk. Whatever Prince Shōtoku's personal interest or understanding may have been of such abstruse notions as the *Vimalakīrti Sūtra*'s "Dharma-Door of Nonduality," it is reasonable to assume for most of those who heard him lecture, at

Empress Suiko's request, on the *Sūtra of Queen Shrīmālā* (in 606, according to the *Chronicles*), the significant point of the *sūtra* was its portrayal an enlightened ruler who attained complete understanding of the Mahāyāna.

In the *Vimalakīrti Sūtra* could be found assurances that spiritual attainment was not the monopoly of the clergy, but could be realized by a devout layman. And the popular *Lotus Sūtra*, with its emphasis on the Buddha's variety of doctrinal accommodations (Indian: *upāya*; Japanese: *hōben*), provided a convincing basis for the ideal of universal harmony advanced by the *Seventeen-Article Constitution*.

As a cultural hero who led Japan onto the stage of world history, Crown Prince Shōtoku and his accomplishments remain politically controversial to this day. But reinterpretation is the fate of all who leave a lasting mark on the thought and institutions of a society.

ROBERT E. MORRRELL

Further Reading

Translation

Aston, W. G. *Sources of Japanese Tradition*. Vol. 1. Compiled by Ryusaku Tsunoda, Wm. Theodore de Bary, and Donald Keene. New York: Columbia University Press, 1964 (1958), pp. 48–51. W. G. Aston's original translation (1896) may be found in his *Nihongi: Chronicles of Japan from the Earliest Times to* A.D. *697* (London: George Allen & Unwin, 1956). The passages quoted in this chapter are drawn from the *Sources of Japanese Tradition*.

Related Studies

Nakamura, Hajime. "The Ideal of a Universal State and Its Philosophical Basis—Prince Shōtoku and His Successors." Chapter 1 in Nakamura's *A History of the Development of Japanese Thought*, Vol. 1. Tokyo: Kokusai Bunka Shinkokai, 1967. Discussion with some selections.

Hanayama, Shinshō. "Prince Shōtoku and Japanese Buddhism," *Philosophical Studies of Japan*, Volume IV, 1963, pp. 23–48. Discussion with some selections; see also his *Hokke gisho* (Tokyo: Iwanami Bunko, 1983 [1975]. 2 vols. Chinese original with Japanese rendering.).

Swanson, Paul L. *Foundations of T'ien-T'ai Philosophy: The Flowering of the Two Truths Theory in Chinese Buddhism*. Berkeley, Calif.: Asian Humanities Press, 1989. References to Fa Yun (Fa-yün), Zhi Zang (Chih-tsang), and Seng Min (Seng-min), about whom few readings are available in English.

Wayman, Alex and Hideko. *The Lion's Roar of Queen Śrīmālā*. New York: Columbia University Press, 1974. English translation of the *Shōmangyō*.

KŪKAI

Born: 774, Zentsūji, Shikoku, Japan
Died: 835, Mt. Kōya, Japan
Major Works: *Indications of the Goals of the Three Teachings* (797), *The Difference Between Exoteric and Esoteric Buddhism* (814), *Attaining Enlightenment in This Very Existence* (817), *The Meanings of Sound, Word, and Reality* (817), *The Precious Key to the Secret Treasury* (830)

Major Ideas

Enlightenment is attainable in this bodily existence.
All phenomena, as objects of sense and thought, reveal the transcendent Buddha.
Words recited as a mantra *articulate the reality of the Buddha.*
The grace of the Buddha is conferred through meditation, mantra, *and* mudra.

When Kyoto became the new capital of Japan in 794, Kūkai, then a young man of twenty, was in a privileged position to help shape a new intellectual and religious culture for an imperial court anxious to improve upon the old order in the previous capitals of Nara and Nagaoka.

Born into an aristocratic family on the island of Shikoku, Kūkai was tutored in the Chinese classics by his uncle, who was also the tutor to the crown prince of that time. He continued his largely Confucian studies at the government college in Kyoto to prepare for a career as an official. Though an able student, he left the college at some point in order to study and practice Buddhism. At the age of twenty-three, he wrote his first major work, *Indications of the Goals of the Three Teachings*, and argued for the superiority of Buddhism over Daoism (Taoism) and Confucianism.

Buddhism had already been in Japan for over 250 years and had provided the primary methods and diction for philosophical inquiries. In the old capital of Nara there were magnificent temples associated with the six different philosophical schools imported from China. Together these schools represented a mixture of Hīnayāna and Mahāyāna ideas, the most important of which were the doctrine of emptiness of the Sanron School, the Hossō or Mind Only School's notion that phenomena make sense only as productions of the mind, and the view of the Kegon School that all things are interrelated in one grand interfusion. Kūkai's study of Buddhism included a wide spectrum of Buddhist doctrines, and in his own typology of philosophies, which he set forth in *The Precious Key to the Secret Treasury*, each of these different schools had a place in an intellectual and religious hierarchy leading up to what would be his own school of Buddhism—Shingon.

Shingon (True Word) Buddhism was one of the later Mahāyāna developments in India and was introduced to China by Indian and Central Asian monks as a school in the early eighth century. The school, which is regarded as an Esoteric or Tantric form of Buddhism, did not survive much longer after the time of Hui-guo (Hui-kuo) (746–805), one of the first of the indigenous Chinese patriarchs. Along with Saichō (767–822), the founder of Tendai Buddhism in Japan, Kūkai was one of the fortunate few to be chosen to accompany an official mission to China in 804. Traveling all the way to the Chinese capital of Changan (Ch'ang-an), Kūkai studied with Hui-guo for three years and returned to Japan an accomplished expert of Esoteric Buddhism.

Revered for his expertise not only as a Buddhist master but as a poet, ritualist, calligrapher, social worker, educator, and philosopher, Kūkai established the Shingon School at Mt. Kōya, far in the mountains to the south of Kyoto. He was also active in Kyoto as the reviver of Tōji, a major temple in the capital, and spent the rest of life promoting Shingon Buddhism in a wide variety of ways.

Many legends have been told of the great accomplishments of the Master, who is now believed to have escaped a final death by sitting in eternal meditation in his mausoleum. Although Kūkai, posthumously known as Kōbō Daishi (Great Master of the Extensive Teaching), is worshipped today as a deity, the human teacher is revered primarily for his religious and philosophical insights expressed with clarity and literary grace in a large corpus of writings.

Enlightenment

The ultimate goal of all forms of Buddhism is enlightenment, a perfect state of mind and being that has been explained in many different ways. Most often enlightenment was understood in terms of some basic teaching such as the Four Noble Truths, which call for the eradication of desire, the cause of dissatisfaction and suffering. Since desire is fundamentally rooted in life itself, its eradication would entail the end of existence. The attainment of the ideal objective of enlightenment through the extinction of desire was such a difficult if not impossible goal that it was widely regarded to be an objective that could be realized only after many reincarnations. The ultimate goal was difficult to reach, but practitioners have nearly an endless succession of lifetimes to achieve it.

Reflecting the broader Mahāyāna confidence that enlightenment was not such a distant and difficult goal, Kūkai agreed with the Shingon claim that enlightenment was possible in one's own lifetime. This was a most optimistic forecast of the time it will take, and, essentially, the usual view that many lifetimes are required was abandoned. One can be enlightened in the present moment.

Great optimism is also evident in Kūkai's anthropology by which human nature is viewed as being fundamentally, if only potentially, perfect. Other Mahāyāna schools express the same conviction with ideas about the widespread and possibly universal endowment of all beings with the Buddha-nature. When Kūkai says that enlighten-

ment is possible in this existence, he not only means that living beings can be enlightened now, but also that it is with one's own body that the perfect state of being can be realized. This is implicit in all of the other Mahāyāna claims that all beings possess the Buddha-nature, or even more forcefully that they are Buddhas, but the explicit emphasis on the body pushes this line of thinking to the furthest point possible in a religion that places a high priority on some form of monastic discipline: the physical body, normally a major obstacle with all of its passions, is now the vessel of enlightenment.

Although there were some later schools of Shingon, such as the famous Tachikawa School, that advocated sexual relations as the expression of enlightenment, Kūkai took a more conservative view and explained enlightenment in this existence in terms of the metaphysics of oneness.

That everything inheres in everything else is another widely held Mahāyāna idea affirmed by Kūkai. To say that enlightenment is possible in this bodily existence is to say that there is no distinction to be made between ordinary beings and enlightened Buddhas. The doctrinal expression of this conviction of the innate interrelatedness of all things with all things took many different forms, such as non-duality, emptiness, and the intrinsically pure mind. In his *Attaining Enlightenment in This Very Existence*, Kūkai explained the essential unity of all things through an analysis of how the six great elements of the universe (earth, water, fire, wind, space, and consciousness) constitute all Buddhas and ordinary beings. The elements are interfused with each other in an eternal state of harmony, and therefore the body filled with passion is identical with the enlightened body of the Buddha.

Although the literal interpretation of this idea led to the practice of mummifying and worshipping the bodies of so-called dead masters (and Kūkai himself is said to be physically sitting in eternal meditation in his mausoleum on Mt. Kōya), Kūkai advocated meditative insight as the proper means for understanding what otherwise would be a preposterous proposition.

Phenomena

Using the same reasoning that established total harmony, Kūkai explained phenomena as being nothing other than sacred things. Here Kūkai followed basic Kegon doctrine, but gave it a Shingon twist. Although other schools, even as they insisted on total harmony, reserved a place for making a distinction between sacred and secular in the form of a transcendent, formless and imageless body of the Buddha (*hosshin*) that in no way could be identified with anything in the world, Kūkai argued in his *The Difference Between Exoteric and Esoteric Buddhism* that even the transcendent body of the Buddha manifests itself in the world. Even the world of sound—the wind in the pines or the call of a bird, for instance—are preachings of the Buddha.

It is not only the natural world but also the world of art and artifice that can express the highest truths. Art relies on the senses, and Kūkai, true to his confidence in the functions of the body, recommended the use of music, painting, calligraphy, sculpture, and poetry in the ritual attempt to increase one's capacity for understanding or experiencing the propositions of harmony by which a bug is a Buddha or a painted mandala the universe. Contrary to those who held that words were not adequate for expressing the truth that transcend words and even thinking itself, Kūkai was convinced as a man of letters as well as a priest, that language had mysterious powers of revelation.

Language

Words, according to Kūkai in his *The Meanings of Sound, Word, and Reality*, are formed by sound vibrations. Every sound–word has a corresponding reality, and every reality has a sound–word. Although words always point to some kind of reality, the realities themselves may be articulated for the purpose of deception or may be inspired by dreams and hallucinations. The proper or improper use of language depends on the intention and mentality of the speaker as well as on the right manipulation of words. On a superficial level, it is possible to have a sound–word combination that fails to indicate a reality, which might then be said to have transcended words, but this occurs only because of a wrong correlation between the sound and the word.

Even the reality of the Buddha (*hosshin*), which other schools regard as being beyond the reach of words, can be correlated to a wide variety of a special sound–words called *mantras*. A *mantra* is a True Word (*shingon*) because it denotes the reality of the Buddhas without distortion. Consisting of a single syllable or whole sentences, *mantras* sometimes have meanings, or they may be a meaningless stringing together of sounds. Chanting a *mantra* sets up the right sound–word that articulates the reality of the Buddhas for the duration of the sound.

At times Kūkai expressed the common view that ultimate reality transcends language, but in his theory of language he exhibited great confidence in words as indicators of realities in the human world and the realms of the Buddhas.

Grace

Despite all of the emphasis placed on the identity between ordinary beings and the Buddha, Kūkai knew that a real separation still remained. The Buddha does stand apart from people, and for ordinary believers it is more practical and rational to understand that what is required is a communion between the two different parties rather than an experience of exact identity. This communion takes place through the practice of meditation, the recitation of *mantras*, and the formation of ritual hand gestures called *mudras*, a kind of sign language. Through these mediating practices, the Buddha bestows a saving grace that is received and retained by the practitioner.

The ideas and practices imported from China and interpreted by Kūkai formed the basis of the Shingon School in Japan, and wielded an enormous influence on the other schools of Buddhism. The Tendai School adopted much of it through the efforts of teachers who, like Kūkai, went to China, and it too is now classed as an Esoteric kind of Buddhism. Even the austere Zen sects adopted Shingon ideas and practices, all of which were based on Kūkai's confidence that people, their phenomenal world, their language, and the caring Buddhas were intertwined in mutual relationships that will lead to the attainment of perfect enlightenment.

GEORGE J. TANABE, JR.

Further Reading

Hakeda, Yoshito, trans. *Kūkai: Major Works*. New York: Columbia University Press, 1972. Kūkai's major writings are translated in this definitive work, which also contains a biography of the man and a study of his thought.

Kitagawa, Joseph. *Religion in Japanese History*. New York: Columbia University Press, 1966. This general introduction to religion in Japan contains good material on the history of Shingon.

Kiyota, Minoru. *Shingon Buddhism: Theory and Practice*. Los Angeles: Buddhist Books International, 1978. Somewhat technical, this book is a good exposition of Shingon philosophy and the theoretical basis for its practices.

Yamasaki, Taikō. *Shingon: Japanese Esoteric Buddhism*. Boston: Shambala, 1988. Translated and adapted from the Japanese by Richard and Cynthia Peterson, this book provides a brief historical overview and detailed explanations of Shingon theory and practice.

GENSHIN (ESHIN SŌZU)

Born: 942, Taima, Japan
Died: 1017, Mt. Hiei's Yokawa area, Japan
Major Works: *Ōjōyōshū* (*The Essentials for Birth in Amida's Paradise*) (985), *Kanjin ryaku yōshū* (*Essentials of Self-Insight*) (997), *Hongakusan shaku* (*Essay on [Ryōgen's] Hymn to Original Enlightenment*), *Shinnyo kan* (*Seeing Thusness*), *The Yokawa hōgo* (*Yokawa Tract*)

Major Ideas

Meditation on the Buddha Amida with recitation of His Name (nembutsu), *a complementary practice, ensures birth in His Pure Land of Supreme Bliss* (Gokuraku Jōdo)—*our best, but not the only possible, hope for religious salvation during the period of the Latter Days of the Law* (mappō).

Enlightenment is immanent/intrinsic (hongaku) *to sentient beings and is realized by revealing what is already present* (though unrecognized because of ignorance [mumyō]), *rather than being acquired from without.*

The Tendai monk Genshin is the dominant presence in Japanese Buddhist thought during the four centuries between Shingon's Kūkai (Kōbō Daishi, 774–835), Tendai's Saichō (Dengyō Daishi, 767–822), and the Kamakura "reformers" of the thirteenth century: the Pure Land Amidists Hōnen (Genkū), (1133–1212), Shinran (1173–1262), and Ippen (1239–89); Zen's Eisai (Yōsai) (1141–1215) and Dōgen (1200–53); and Nichiren (1222–82), founder of the sect which now bears his name.

In addition to being the representative Tendai Amidist who anticipated the Kamakura Pure Land movements, Genshin (or Eshin) was the leader of Tendai's Eshin-ryū School, which maintained the Intrinsic Enlightenment (*hongaku*) position against the Actualized/Gradual Enlightenment (*shikaku*) views of the Danna-ryū School of Kakuun (953–1007). Both Genshin and Kakuun were disciples of Ryōgen (Jie Daishi, 912–985), who has the dubious distinction of having been the first to employ the temple mercenaries, "monk–soldiers" (*sōhei*), in a dispute with the Gion Shrine. (See Genshin's *Essay on [Ryōgen's] Hymn to Original Enlightenment [Hongakusan shaku]*.)

The Essentials for Birth in Amida's Paradise

Genshin is especially noted for the *Essentials for Birth in Amida's Paradise* (popularly known as the *Essentials of Salvation*), a work in ten divisions which begins by describing the sufferings to be encountered within the Six Paths of transmigration and thus the reasons for "Abhorring and Departing from this Defiled World" (*Onriedo*). This first division includes the vividly Dantean description of the tortures of the Buddhist hells, which inspired the genre of "hell scenes" (*jigoku hensō*) that haunted the medieval Japanese imagination. Even its title appears as a topic (*dai*) in such poems as the following by the Tendai prelate and historian Jien (1155–1225) several centuries later:

Mina hito no	The very thought
Saranu wakare no	Of all those painful farewells
Omou koso	Which none can avoid
Ukiyo wo itou	Is itself enough to engender
Kagiri narikere.	Distaste for this floating world.

The second division, "Longing for the Pure Land," reveals the bliss of the Amida's Paradise of Supreme Bliss (*Gokuraku Jōdo*), and of the possibility of our reaching this Pure Land after death through meditation on the Buddha Amida (*Amita*, "The Infinite One": an East Asian conflation of the Buddhas *Amitāyus*, "Infinite Life," and *Amitābha*) as the human capacity for attaining enlightenment declined with the approach of the Latter Days of the *Dharma* (*mappō jidai*), the onset of which was calculated to begin in A.D. 1052. These descriptions, in turn, inspired the genre of Amidist Descent (*raigō*) pictures of Amida and his retinue coming to welcome the soul of the dying devotee into Paradise.

The remaining eight divisions discuss such issues as the scriptural authorities for Genshin's position, and the "Proper Practice of Nembutsu" (4), an elaborate five-part proposal based on the *Treatise on the Pure Land* (*Sukhāvatīvyūhōpadeśa*), attributed to Vasubandhu (fifth century A.D.), which is a marked contrast to the later Kamakura period simplifications.

While the *Ōjōyōshū* was composed in Chinese to be read by Genshin's scholarly colleagues, his short 491-character *Yokawa Tract* (*Yokawa hōgo*) is a short summary of his position written in simple Japanese for the lay reader. Genshin retired to live at the Eshin-in in Mt. Hiei's Yokawa district about the year 967 and appears as the model for the Priest of Yokawa late in the *Tale of Genji*. The brief appeal to a popular audience is an early example of the vernacular tract (*kana hōgo*):

> Delusive thinking has ever been a basic trait of the unenlightened person [*bombu*]. He experiences no other state of mind. But when at the time of death he performs the *nembutsu* fully aware that he is a deluded unenlightened creature, he will be vouchsafed a welcome by Amida and will sit upon a lotus pedestal. Then indeed will he abandon his delusive thinking, and the mind of enlightenment [*satori no kokoro*] will be manifest. The *nembutsu* which emerges from within delusive thinking is pure as the lotus untainted by mud; and there can be no doubt that the devotee will be born in the Pure Land.

The language here, as in the *Ōjōyōshū*, suggests that the Pure Land is to be understood quite literally as a physical location, rather than as a metaphor for a state of awareness within meditation. Elsewhere, however, as in "a sister work, the *Kanjin ryaku yōshū* [*Essentials of Self-Insight*], the Pure Land position is subordinated to the Tendai teaching on

immediate realization of Buddhahood through deep meditations." (See Andrews, 1973, p. 41.)

The easy movement between literal and figurative understandings of religious myth often tantalizes the student of Buddhism. The problem is partly related to differences of opinion on the question of whether the goal of Buddhist religious practice is immanent or transcendent. Somehow we must reconcile Genshin's vivid and apparently literal descriptions of hells and heavens with his role as leader of the Eshin School, which the maintained position of traditional Tendai practice based on the Intrinsic Enlightenment (*hongaku*) view that any Pure Land was within rather than external.

Intrinsic Enlightenment

The past decade has produced a bookshelf of studies on the philosophies of Chinese and Japanese Buddhism reaching well beyond traditional sectarian accounts. A central issue is the doctrine that enlightenment is intrinsic to the nature of sentient beings and that religious practice is thus merely a revealing of what has always be present, if unrealized. The notion has an early formulation in scriptures of the fourth century A.D., which speak of the Womb of Buddhahood (Indian: *tathāgata-garbha*; Chinese: *ru lai zang/ju-lai-tsang*; Japanese: *nyorizō*), the primal awareness accessed through meditation that is the very ground of our being, although the basic Buddhist insistence on no permanent self or substance resists its reification into a kind of Hindu *ātman*. In choosing among the wealth of English equivalents proposed by scholars, this consideration may lead us to favor "intrinsic to" over, say, "immanent" (implying a *thing* within), or "original" (with temporal overtones). An unfriendly technical vocabulary in half a dozen languages, as well as textual and doctrinal distinctions (necessary though they may be for precise historical understanding), tends to obscure a fairly straightforward conceptual model.

The identification of apparent opposites often found in the literature of the Mahāyāna—"form is no other than emptiness, emptiness is no other than form" (*Heart of Wisdom Sūtra*), *nirvāna* = the phenomenal world of *samsāra*—can be significantly demystified by reference to the Mind Only (Yuishiki, Hossō; Yogācāra, Vijñānavāda) model for the Two Truths theory. However thorough the Mādhyamika critique against any permanent self or substance, consciousness is an irreducible given. This consciousness, pure awareness, or mind, is not merely a blank tablet or logical starting point for some kind of Cartesian or Lockean epistemological system, but that mind-ground which, undefiled, is Buddhahood itself and whose modifications are our experience of the phenomenal world:

> There are not two different spheres or sets of objects to which these [concepts] apply. . . . The relation between the Absolute and phenomena is not that of otherness; the Absolute, looked at through the categories of Reason (thought-forms), is the world of phenomena; and phenomena, devoid of the falsifying thought-forms, are the Absolute.

> (MURTI, 1960)

Accordingly, the world of birth-and-death and the world of *nirvana*—and all other apparent polarities—are not two, but thinking makes it so.

The origin of the term Intrinsic Awakening (or Original Enlightenment) (*hongaku*) to supersede Womb of Buddhahood (*tathāgata-garbha*) is usually traced to the *Treatise on the Awakening of Faith in the Mahāyāna*, a fifth- or sixth-century work formerly attributed to the famous second-century poet, Aśvaghosa (J. Memyō). Neither Sanskrit nor Tibetan versions exist today, but the earlier translation from Sanskrit (*Mahāyāna-sraddotpādā-śāstra*) to Chinese by Paramārtha (J. Shintai, 499–569) has been more influential than the version by Śiksānda (J. Jikusānanda, 652–710) (English translations by Yoshito Hakeda and D. T. Suzuki, respectively). Fazang (Fa-tsang) (J. Hōzō, 643–712), founder of the Chinese Garland (Chinese: Hua-yen; Japanese: Kegon) Sect, incorporated ideas from the *Treatise* and the *Garland Sūtra*; and later in Japan Shingon's Kūkai highly regarded the *Explanation of the Mahāyāna*, a commentary based largely on the *Treatise* and formerly attributed to Nāgārjuna. But Intrinsic Awakening thought found a particularly congenial home in Tendai, and progressed from there to Tendai's offspring in Kamakura Buddhism, some of whom (for example, Hōnen and Dōgen) defined their new programs by rejecting or at least radically reinterpreting it.

Shinran includes only two Japanese representatives, Genshin and Hōnen, in his list of Seven Eminent Monks (*shichi kōsō*), a select group considered to be the forerunners of the True Pure Land Sect (Jōdo Shinshū). Japanese Pure Land thought was eventually dominated by the views of Kamakura and later movements which arose out of, but in opposition to, their Tendai antecedents; subsequent scholarship inevitably colors our understanding of Genshin's position, which is defined in relation to these sectarian histories. Here he is portrayed as still falling short of full understanding.

Objections reveal something of both sides of an issue. Genshin had argued that, given the times, devotion to Amida was the *best*, though not the *only* possible route to salvation. Moreover, his emphasis on meditation as the primary sense of the *nembutsu*—with calling on the name of Amida merely a complementary practice—clearly indicated a leaning to good works ("self power," or *jiriki*) rather than humble faith in Amida's Vow, and betrayed his continuing commitment to traditional Tendai Amidism. We may even wonder if Genshin's colorful visualizations of the hells and heavens may ultimately have been simply Skillful Means (*hōben*) to lead us not to some external, transcendent paradise, but rather to the Western Pure Land which, like the Kingdom of God within, is a dramatic metaphor for the Enlightenment intrinsic in all sentient beings.

ROBERT E. MORRELL

Further Reading

Translations

Reischauer, A. K. "Genshin's Ōjō Yōshu: Collected Essays on Birth into Paradise," *Transactions of the Asiatic Society of Japan*. 2d ser., vol.

7, 1930, pp. 16–97. Translation of the popular first two divisions.

Tsunoda, Ryusaku, Wm. Theodore de Bary, and Donald Keene, comps. *Sources of Japanese Tradition*. Vol. 1. New York: Columbia University Press, 1964 (1958). Pages 192 to 197 are translations by Philip Yampolsky of selections from the first two divisions of the *Ōjōyōshū*.

Related Studies

Andrews, Allan A. *The Teachings Essential for Rebirth: A Study of Genshin's Ōjōyōshu*. Tokyo: Sophia University Press, 1973.

Hakeda, Yoshito S., trans. *The Awakening of Faith*. New York: Columbia University Press, 1967.

Kiyota, Minoru. "Buddhist Devotional Meditation: A Study of the *Sukhāvatīvyūhōpadeśa*." In *Mahāyāna Buddhist Meditation: Theory and Practice*. Edited by Minoru Kiyota. Honolulu, Hawaii: The University Press of Hawaii, 1978. Translation included.

Morrell, Robert E. *Early Kamakura Buddhism: A Minority Report*. Berkeley, Calif.: Asian Humanities Press, 1986, pp. 13–22. Includes translation of Genshin's *Yokawa Tract*.

Murti, T. R. V. *The Central Philosophy of Buddhism: A Study of the Mādhyamika System*. 2d ed. London: Allen and Unwin, 1960.

Swanson, Paul L. *Foundations of T'ien-T'ai Philosophy: The Flowering of the Two Truths Theory in Chinese Buddhism*. Berkeley, Calif.: Asian Humanities Press, 1989.

Tamura, Yoshirō. "Japanese Culture and the Tendai Concept of Original Enlightenment," *Japanese Journal of Religious Studies*. 14, June–September 1987, pp. 2–3. Special issue edited by Paul L. Swanson, "Tendai Buddhism in Japan." See also "Critique of Original Awakening Thought in Shōshin and Dōgen," *Japanese Journal of Religious Studies*, 11, June–September 1984, pp. 2–3. Together these two articles give a concise, lucid overview of the issues and influence of *hongaku* thought, especially in Japan. This important Japanese authority also edits the three Intrinsic Enlightenment items (listed under "Major Works") in Tada Kōryū et al., eds., *Tendai hongakuron. Nihon Shisō Taikei 9* (Tokyo: Iwanami Shoten, 1973).

Ui, Hakuju. "A Study of Japanese Tendai Buddhism." In *Philosophical Studies of Japan*. Vol. 1. Tokyo: Japan Society for the Promotion of Science, 1959. Useful but rather turgid outline of the Eshin and Danna Schools.

HŌNEN

Born: 1133, Okayama, Japan
Died: 1212, Kyoto, Japan
Major Works: *Senchakushū (Selected Passages on the Original Vow)* (1198), *One Page Testament* (1212)

Major Ideas

The decline of Buddhism is a cosmic process working itself out in history.
Religious practices, except for the nembutsu, *should be discarded.*
Nembutsu *or "mindfulness on" Amida Buddha requires only recitation, not meditation.*
Amida's original vow has a mystical power to replace practice as the means for gaining rebirth into the Pure Land.

Hōnen's lifetime spans one of the most significant eras of Japanese history in which political power was divided between courtiers in Kyoto and warriors in the new capital of Kamakura. It was also a time when many of the Buddhist sects that still flourish today were established as new schools. As the founder of the Pure Land Sect, Hōnen takes his place among the other first patriarchs of new schools: Dōgen (Sōtō Zen), Eisai (or Yosai) (Rinzai Zen), Shinran (True Pure Land), and Nichiren. Most of these leaders were trained in Tendai doctrine and practice at Mt. Hiei, and it was primarily against the then-dominant schools of Tendai and Shingon as well as the older philosophical schools of the Nara period (646–794) that they reacted and defined themselves as new.

Hōnen himself started his priestly career as a Tendai monk, and gained early renown for reading through the entire Buddhist canon several times. He was a master of the tradition he would abandon in favor of his Pure Land teaching.

Long before Hōnen's establishment of the Pure Land Sect, ideas and practices about the Pure Land, the perfect realm into which one could be reborn, had been an important part of Japanese Buddhism in general. Using the basic ideas of *karma* and rebirth, Buddhists had long believed that the performance of meritorious acts produced good karmic effects that would bring about rebirth into the Pure Land. Particularly effective were good religious acts such as chanting sutras, meditating, observing the precepts, making offerings to temples, reciting mantras, and so forth. There was merit in surfeit: the greater the scale or number of performances, the greater the karmic merit. One of the most popular practices was the repetition of the phrase, "All praise to Amida Buddha," a chant known as the *nembutsu*, which literally means "mindfulness on" Amida Buddha. As a Tendai monk, Hōnen was steeped in all of these ideas and practices.

Sometime around the year 1175, Hōnen, after a long time of doubt and contemplation, came to the radical conclusion that all religious practices, except for the *nembutsu*, should be discarded. Knowing what a controversial position this would be to take publicly, Hōnen discussed his secret insight with only a few of his trusted disciples. In 1198 he wrote his manifesto titled *Selected Passages on the Original Vow*, but still ordered his disciples to keep it from being released until after his death. Word inevitably leaked out, and in 1205 the monks at the influential Kōfukuji temple in Nara petitioned the imperial court to ban this heretical teaching.

Hōnen's exclusive practice of the *nembutsu*, which he called the easy path, also began to be accepted by common people as the most suitable religious practice for laypersons, and the rising popularity of this approach caused the opposition to secure an imperial court order for his exile.

At the age of seventy-five, Hōnen was exiled to Tosa for a short time but was still prevented from returning to Kyoto even after his pardon. In 1211 he was allowed to return to Kyoto where he died the following year. In accord with his instructions, his *Selected Passages on the Original Vow* was publicly released, and this full disclosure of his ideas firmly set the doctrinal basis for the Pure Land Sect as well as the grounds for criticism and debate that continued for centuries.

The Decline of Buddhism

Hōnen argued that his radical reformulation of Buddhism was required because of the nature of Buddhist time. His view that Buddhism had declined was not a matter of the moral condition of temples and priests, though there certainly were critics who charged that Buddhist monks were degenerate, but a metaphysical concern for the very nature of time itself as it played out its course in history, sweeping Buddhism into a downward spiral. Drawing on previous Buddhist speculations about time and its inevitable entropy, Hōnen accepted what to him was a historical fact: Japan had entered into a period in which Buddhist enlightenment was no longer possible. The golden age of the Buddha was long past, and there was no hope for recreating his ancient enlightenment. Distance was also a factor. Holy India was far away from the frontier land of Japan, a spiritual wilderness in which the Buddhist teachings had come to an end.

This was not a failure of human effort, for no amount of good intention and practice could offset the nature of the times. Any expectation that people could somehow reverse the flow of time was simply foolish and devoid of any understanding of the cosmic history of Buddhism. The logical conclusion to this analysis was that traditional practices were useless, and, since the teachings had come to an end, even an understanding of them was no longer possible.

The Exclusive Nembutsu

Hōnen's solution to this crisis was to declare all religious practices to be a useless waste of time and effort. Only one practice, the recitation of the *nembutsu*, retained its efficacy. Prior to Hōnen, the recitation of the praise to Amida Buddha had been

understood as a chant that aided meditation on and visualization of Amida. Since he rejected meditation and visualization, Hōnen had to distinguish recitation from meditation and limit the use of the *nembutsu* to vocalization of the chant. In his *One Page Testament*, Hōnen also made it clear that unlike previous practitioners of the nembutsu, his followers need not even understand the meaning of the chant. Critics of this interpretation of the *nembutsu* mocked it as a mere moving of mouths and ridiculed the notion that utterance alone could cause one to be reborn in the Pure Land.

Hōnen even rejected the time-honored practice of having the aspiration to become enlightened. This had long been regarded as the first step in the Buddhist path, for without that commitment to the goal of enlightenment the rest of Buddhist teaching and practice becomes meaningless. The very essence of being a Buddhist was to become enlightened, and Hōnen's critics charged that the rejection of that traditional ideal could only be made by one who was no longer a Buddhist.

Having reduced Buddhist discipline to the recitation of a single chant, Hōnen defended his position in two somewhat contradictory ways. At times he proposed that the merit of the *nembutsu* was that it embraced all of the virtues of the other traditional practices, such that to practice it was in effect to practice all the others. Each of the other practices represented only a part of the entire building that was the *nembutsu*. On the other hand, Hōnen argued that the other practices were taught by the Buddha in order to be rejected. The only way the superiority of the *nembutsu* could be demonstrated and established was by having inferior methods to discard.

Hōnen also employed the widely used Buddhist argument that it was out of compassion for the different and limited capacities of people that the Buddha taught the other practices, but now, during the age of the decline of Buddhism, only the *nembutsu* mattered.

The Original Vow

The reason why only the *nembutsu* was effective in this age of the futility of human effort was found by

Hōnen in the Pure Land scriptures describing Amida's original vows. In these scriptures, Amida made several vows, one of which promised that Amida himself should be denied final enlightenment if, his name having been uttered and heard, there were people who did not find themselves reborn in the Pure Land. Hōnen logically exploited this vow: since Amida has gained final enlightenment, uttering and hearing his name will result in rebirth in the Pure Land. Hōnen's justification for his interpretation of the *nembutsu* as recitation requiring no other effort rested on this vow, which explains why human effort is not necessary since Amida's promise of rebirth is not conditional upon anything except uttering and hearing his name.

One of Hōnen's disciples, Shinran (1173–1262), who founded the True Pure Land Sect, went so far as to say that human effort, even in the form of uttering the *nembutsu*, was not a necessary condition for rebirth in the Pure Land since Amida's vow is the only power that can grant such a benefit.

Over and over again in his *Selected Passages on the Original Vow*, Hōnen refers to the mystique and power of Amida's vows to justify his arguments. There is an indisputable authority to the vows, and Hōnen's constant refrain is that his argument is really not his own but is merely the promises of Amida. He further justifies his position by citing Chinese Pure Land masters who praised the *nembutsu* as the best of all practices. Ignoring the fact that in praising the *nembutsu* as superior they did not reject the other practices (and in fact recommended them highly), Hōnen cites these masters approvingly and interprets them to say that the best of practices is really the only one that is needed. That is what it means to be the best.

Hōnen's *Selected Passages on the Original Vow* was a radical simplification of Buddhist thought and practice. Instead of creating the traditional hierarchy of teachings leading up to his own school at the apex, Hōnen simply eliminated them all. He was as single-minded and exclusive as was Nichiren (1222–82), the bombastic priest who publicly denounced all schools but his own, but has escaped censure of his fundamentalism primarily because he kept his teaching a secret for most of his life. There is also a subtlety to Hōnen's argument by which he relates his line of thinking back to scriptures and appeals to the mystique of Amida's vows, the authority of which needed no support by further argumentation. His use of the works of Chinese Pure Land masters was also disarmingly persuasive as he refashioned their praise of the *nembutsu* as the best practice into a recommendation of it as the only practice.

Critics such as his contemporary Myōe (1173–1232) challenged the logic of his arguments and his use of precedents to support what they charged were unprecedented interpretations. These debates about the Pure Land teachings and practices continued for centuries and form as a whole a fascinating strand of philosophical argumentation in Japan. Hōnen's disciples themselves could not all agree on a common interpretation of their master's teachings, and one of them, Shinran, set out to establish his own approach that eventually resulted in a separate school.

Hōnen's basic idea was as powerful as it was simple: a divine initiative must take the place of human effort in the workings of salvation. There are striking similarities between Hōnen's ideas and those of Martin Luther; accordingly, Hōnen and Shinran have often been compared with the Protestant reformer.

GEORGE J. TANABE, JR.

Further Reading

Coates, Harper, and Ryugaku Ishizuka, trans. *Hōnen the Buddhist Saint.* 5 vols. Kyoto: Chion-in, 1925. This is a translation of a fourteenth-century biography written by an admiring follower of Hōnen.

de Bary, Wm. Theodore, ed. *The Buddhist Tradition.* New York: Modern Library, 1969. Chapter 11 gives a good introduction to Pure Land Buddhism in Japan, and contains a translation of the *One Page Testament.*

Kitagawa, Joseph. *Religion in Japanese History.* New York: Columbia University Press, 1966.

This general introduction to religion in Japan contains good material on the history of Pure Land Buddhism.

Tanabe, George J., Jr. *Myōe the Dreamkeeper*. Cambridge, Mass.: Harvard University Press, 1992. An account of the life and thought of Hōnen's main critic, this work contains a summary of the *Selected Passages on the Original Vow*, and a detailed analysis of Myōe's criticism of it.

JIEN (JICHIN)

Born: 1155, Kyoto, Japan
Died: 1225, Higashi Sakamoto, Japan
Major Works: *Gukanshō* (*Miscellany of Ignorant Views*) (1219), *Jichin kashō* [or *oshō*] *jikaawase* (*The Personal Poetry Contest of the Venerable Jichin*) (c. 1199), *Shūgyokushū* (*Collection of Gleaned Jewels*) (compiled in 1346; expanded in 1594)
Note: *Kankyo no tomo* (*Companion for a Solitary Retreat*) (1222), a *setsuwa* collection by the monk Keisei (1189–1268) was until recently attributed to Jien.

Major Ideas

The pattern of historical events can be understood by reference to the Buddhist notion of the Latter Days of the Law (mappō) *and ameliorated by the intervention of the Shinto gods* (kami).

Dōshin (*principle, causation*), *which differs at various times, is the key to understanding the operations of the gods.*

The proper practice of poetry can be a way to Buddhist enlightenment (kadō sunawachi butsudō).

During the four centuries after Saichō (Dengyō Daishi, 767–822) founded Enryakuji Temple (788) on Mt. Hiei in the mountains northeast of the new capital of Heian-kyō (Kyoto), the Tendai Sect was the ideological center of Japan, complemented by Kūkai's Shingon, the older Six Nara Sects, and the Shinto shrines, which preserved indigenous national beliefs and practices. Its main scripture, the *Lotus Sūtra* (Indian: *Saddharmapundarīka*; Japanese: *Myōhōrengekyō*), argued eloquently for religious diversity while providing a wealth of imagery to poets and storytellers, painters, and architects. Jien inherited the meditation tradition of the Chinese sect's Zhi Yi (Chinese: Chih-i; Japanese: Chigi) (538–597), Genshin's (942–1017) faith in Amida's Pure Land, esoteric (*mikkyō*) practices, and a spirit of accommodation (Indian: *upāya*; Japanese: *hōben*) with native Japanese traditions.

Jien's thinking is partly to be defined by reference to those who, in the late Heian and Kamakura periods, developed their religious programs in reaction to traditional Tendai thought and practice, of which Jien was certainly the most conspicuous representative of his age. Among those who began their religious training in the eclectic Tendai fold are the Amidists Hōnen (1133–1212), Shinran (1173–1262), and Ippen (1239–89); Dainichi

Nōnin (late Heian–early Kamakura), founder of the Japanese Bodhidharma (Zen) School (Nihon Darumashū); Rinzai Zen's Eisai (Yōsai) (1141–1215) and Enni Ben'en (1202–80); Sōtō Zen's Dōgen (1200–53); and Nichiren (1222–82). The vigor of the new movements was often purchased at the price of a focused but narrow parochialism, which persists to this day. (As in the story of the blind men and the elephant, some apparently confused their part with the whole.)

Tendai was an active player in the politics of the day, which doubtless contributed to its Kamakura fragmentation as well as to its virtual destruction as a social force by Nobunaga in 1571. For Western readers the interplay between the Christian Church and the secular powers regrouping after the fall of imperial Rome provides an obvious comparison, except that it was an even more effective counterbalance between state and church than existed in Japan. As spiritual leader in the highest levels of the Fujiwara aristocracy—Jien's brother, Kujō Kanezane (1149–1207) was active in government (prime minister in 1189)—the prelate was inevitably involved in the social issues and intrigues of his day, which is reflected in the fact that he was in and out as chief abbot (*Zasu*) of the monastic complex on Mt. Hiei four times, in 1192–96, 1201–02, 1212–13, and 1213–14.

"The Way of Poetry Is the Way of Buddha"

Jien, as a thinker, reveals himself to us not merely in his formal theoretical writings, but perhaps even more forcefully in his poetry—a literary form rarely chosen by Western philosophers as adequate to their purposes. Even though in the West, as with Lucretius, Dante, Milton, and Nietzsche's *Zarathustra*, the act of poetic composition was not itself considered a form of religious exercise, for the Japanese of Jien's period "The way of poetry is the way of Buddha" (*kadō sunawachi butsudō*).

In the *Personal Poetry Contest of the Venerable Jichin* (*Jichin kashō* [or *oshō*] *jikaawase*) (c. 1199) we find the telling critical fragment by Fujiwara Shunzei (1114–1204):

A poem need not always employ witty devices or clearly express its content. . .it should communicate a sense of charm [*en*] and profundity [*yūgen*]. . . .It will have not only diction and form, but carry with it an ineffable vision. (Konishi)

This anticipates Kamo no Chōmei's famous description of *yūgen* in his *Anonymous Notes* (*Mumyōshō*) (1209–10) as a poetic ideal of elegance, surface simplicity, and few words, but a rare beauty. (Although the third and fourth characters in the *Personal Poetry Contest*'s title are commonly read as *oshō*, this is basically a Zen Sect usage. Tendai reads them as *kashō*; Hossō, Ritsu, and Shingon, as *wajō*. The name Jichin is a posthumous title awarded in 1237.)

For the literary masters in the circle of Emperor Gotoba (r. 1183–98), both the aesthetic ideals and attitudes toward composition were grounded in Tendai religious thought, quite apart from poetry with obviously religious content. Their efforts culminated in the *New Collection of Ancient and Modern Times* (*Shinkokinshu*) (c. 1206), whose 1,978 *waka* included 92 poems by Jien, second only to monk Saigyō's 94. The two monks appear in an oft-cited anecdote revealing the seriousness with which clergy and laity alike revered the practice of poetry at the time:

After Priest Saigyō became a recluse, the innermost meaning of the Tendai *mantras* [*shingon*] was transmitted to him. When Abbot Jichin of Yoshimizu asked Saigyō to reveal this to him, he replied, "To begin with, become adept at poetry. If you don't grasp the meaning of poetry, you will not understand the meaning of the *mantras*." It is said that after Jichin became adept at poetry, Saigyō revealed this to him. (Morrell, 1985.)

In addition to Jien's private collection of some 6,000 poems, published posthumously as the *Collection of Gleaned Jewels* (*Shūgyokushū*), fifteen of the twenty-one Imperial Anthologies of *waka* poetry include 254 of his poems, of which 33 specifically address Buddhist topics (*shakkyōka*). Predictably, *Lotus Sūtra* imagery dominates this small but select group of verse, with three specifically referring to Genshin's *Essentials for Birth in Amida's Paradise* (*Ōjōyōshū*) (985). The Hiei establishment did not oppose Pure Land pietism, only its exclusivist claims.

The Miscellany of Ignorant Views

Jien's history of Japan from its mythical founder, Jimmu, to his own day was the first attempt to explain the events which took place in that country in terms of general principles and patterns. Earlier histories such as the *Record of Ancient Matters* (*Kojiki*) (712) and the *Chronicles of Japan* (*Nihon shoki*) (720) were basically chronicles; however, the events described might be selected and shaped to support some political end. The quasi-histories of the Heian period continued as uncritical mixtures of fact and fiction concocted to illustrate the glories of, say, the Fujiwara family.

Although Jien had his own political reasons for writing the *Miscellany*, he presents the sequence of events as the inevitable result of *dōri*—a term variously rendered as "principle" (Brown and Ishida, 1979), "causation" (Konishi, 1991), or "reason, idea, truth, principle, right" (Rahder, 1985). Different principles are applicable in different periods of Japanese history, but all are subject to the decreasing ability of individuals to practice, and eventually even to understand, the Buddha's Teaching during the period of the Latter Days of the Law (*mappō*). The resulting decline in good government, and in social and religious institutions, can be somewhat ameliorated through the help of the native Japanese gods (*kami*). One happy consequence of this for Jien is justification for his Fujiwara family to continue to "assist" the imperial line.

The *Miscellany* is frequently compared with another "interpretative" history that appeared in the following century, the *Chronicle of the Direct Descent of Gods and Sovereigns* (*Jinnō Shōtōki*) (1339) of Kitabatake Chikafusa (1293–1354). Here the focus shifts away from Latter Day theory and Fujiwara prerogatives to the legitimacy of the imperial line as represented by Emperor Godaigo's Southern Court against the Northern pretender supported by the Ashikaga *shogun*, Takauji.

Jien's close ties to the power structure of his time make him an easy target for the charge that his "history" is little more than a self-serving plea for Fujiwara privilege. But what historian or philosopher is not, in greater or lesser degree, a reflection of his particular time in history? Truly "objective" history, social theory, or philosophy are surely unattainable. But few would be willing on these grounds to dismiss, say, Plato's *Republic* as a historical curiosity of no universal philosophic value for us today. And does Freud tell no more than some peculiarities about the mind-set of the Austro–Hungarian Empire? We can also approach Jien's ideas as universally plausible explanations of human experience, just as we do those of Western thinkers. Can we not note the curious correspondence between the notion of the Latter Days of the Law [*mappō*] and the model argued in, say, *The Decline of the West*, without inquiring too deeply into Oswald Spengler's personal reasons for writing that work?

Since Jien writes of events up to his own day, his remarks about contemporaries are often instructive. We know that his brother Kanezane was an early disciple and supporter of Hōnen, and that Jien provided Hōnen with living quarters in Kyoto in 1211 when he was permitted to return to the capital

after exile. Such considerations may lie behind the lengthy account of Jien as Hōnen's disciple in a contemporary biography (Coates and Ishizuka, 1925). But Jien remarks in the *Miscellany* that the exile incident was handled leniently and that Hōnen had been possessed by a "deceptive demon" (*jumma*) (see Brown and Ishida, 1979, pp. 171–173).

Few turning points in Japanese history have had as far-reaching religious, and artistic, and political effects as the change from Heian to Kamakura. And few individuals have been as centrally positioned in all three areas as Tendai's Jien.

ROBERT E. MORRELL

Further Reading

Brower, Robert H. "'Ex-Emperor Go-Toba's Secret Teachings': *Go-Toba in Gokuden*," *Harvard Journal of Asiatic Studies*. 32, 1972, pp. 5–70.

Brown, Delmer M. and Ichirō Ishida. *The Future and the Past: A Translation and Study of the Gukanshō, An Interpretive History of Japan Written in 1219*. Berkeley, Calif.: University of California Press, 1979.

Brownlee, John S. *Political Thought in Japanese Historical Writing: From Kojiki (712) to Tokushi Yoron (1712)*. Waterloo, Ontario: Wilfred Laurier University Press, 1991.

Coates, Harper Havelock, and Ryūgaku Ishizuka. *Honen the Buddhist Saint: His Life and Teaching*. Kyoto: The Chionin, 1925. Painstaking translation into English of a popular Kamakura biography, with voluminous and useful annotations.

Faure, Bernard. "The Daruma-shū, Dōgen, and Sōtō Zen," *Monumenta Nipponica*. 42:1, 1987, pp. 25–55.

Hambrick, Charles H. "The Gukanshō," *Japanese Journal of Religious Studies*. 5:1, March 1978.

Konishi, Jin'ichi. *A History of Japanese Literature: Volume 3. The High Middle Ages*. Edited by Earl Miner; translated by Aileen Gatten and Mark Harbison. Princeton, N.J.: Princeton University Press, 1991.

Kubota, Jun. "Allegory and Thought in Medieval Waka—Concentrating on Jien's Works Prior to the Jōkyū Disturbance," *Acta Asiatica*. 37, September 1979, pp. 1–28.

Kuroda Toshio, "Gukanshō and Jinnō Shōtōki—Observations on Medieval Historiography," *New Light on Early and Medieval Japanese Historiography: Two Translations and an Introduction*. Translated by John A. Harrison. University Florida Monographs, Social Sciences. 4, Fall 1959.

LaFleur, William R. *The Karma of Words: Buddhism and the Literary Arts in Medieval Japan*. Los Angeles: University of California Press, 1983.

Manaka Fujiko. *Jichin Kashō oyobi shūgyokushū no kenkyū* [*Master Jien and the* Collection of Gleaned Jewels]. Kawasaki, Japan: Mitsuru Bunko, 1974. One of several substantial works on Japanese literature and Buddhism by the noted Tendai nun–scholar.

Marra, Michele. "The Conquest of Mappō: Jien and Kitabatake Chikafusa," *Japanese Journal of Religious Studies*. 12:4, December 1985, pp. 319–341.

———. "The Development of Mappō Thought in Japan," *Japanese Journal of Religious Studies*. 15:1, March 1988, pp. 25–54; 15:4, December 1988, pp. 287–305.

———. *The Aesthetics of Discontent: Politics and Reclusion in Medieval Japanese Literature*. Honolulu, Hawaii: University of Hawaii Press, 1991.

Morrell, Robert E. *Early Kamakura Buddhism: A Minority Report*. Berkeley, Calif.: Asian Humanities Press, 1986. "Amidism in Japanese Tendai," pp. 13–22; chapter 2, "Tendai's Jien as Buddhist Poet."

———. *Sand and Pebbles* (*Shasekishū*): *The Tales of Mujū Ichien, A Voice for Pluralism in Kamakura Buddhism*. Albany, N.Y.: SUNY Press, 1985.

Rahder, J[ohannes]. "Miscellany of Personal Views of An Ignorant Fool [*Guk(w)anshō*]," *Acta Orientalia*. XV, 1937, pp. 173–230. "I intend to translate here the appendix [7th chapter] of the *Gukanshō* and those passages in other chapters, which have a more general, philosophical interest." Somewhat dated, perhaps, but by one of the great scholars.

Stone, Jackie. "Seeking Enlightenment in the Last Age: Mappō Thought in Kamakura Buddhism I," *The Eastern Buddhist*. n.s., 18:1, Spring 1985.

———. "Seeking Enlightenment in the Last Age: Mappō Thought in Kamakura Buddhism II," *The Eastern Buddhist*. n.s., 18:2, Autumn 1985.

Swanson, Paul L. *Foundations of T'ien-T'ai Philosophy: The Flowering of the Two Truths Theory in Chinese Buddhism*. Berkeley, Calif.: Asian Humanities Press, 1989.

Varley, H. Paul. *A Chronicle of Gods and Sovereigns: Jinnō Shōtōki of Kitabatake Chikafusa*. New York: Columbia University Press, 1980.

MYŌE

Born: 1173, Wakayama, Japan
Died: 1232, Kyoto, Japan
Major Works: *Smashing the Heretical Chariot* (1212), *Illustrated Account of the Origins of Kegon* (early thirteenth century), *Entering the Kegon Gate of Liberation Through the Practice of Zen Illumination* (1220), *The Meaning of the Divine Influences Received Through the Mantra of Radiance* (1228), *Dream Diary* (1230)

Major Ideas

The mind, aided by meditation, creates the Pure Land and other perfections.
Moral action is a means for gaining enlightenment.
Passion is not to be rejected but transformed into moral action.
Nature is to be read as language.
Explanation through the logic of imagery is more effective than reasoning.

Myōe was a contemporary of several of the great leaders who founded new schools that constitute what is now called the New Kamakura Buddhism. As a Kegon and Shingon monk, his institutional identity was with the old orthodoxy of the Nara philosophical schools and Shingon Esotericism. His learning and practice, however, spanned all elements from the old and the new, and, as a committed pluralist, he found himself opposing those who excluded parts of the Buddhist spectrum. Aware of how monks and monasteries were not living up to the high ideals of Buddhism, Myōe felt that reform was desperately needed, but did not conclude that it was a matter of devising new schools. The trouble with Buddhism was that it had strayed considerably from its pristine past, and the challenge to Buddhists was to return to that past.

The past, for Myōe, consisted of the original point of departure, Shākyamuni, and all of the subsequent schools and traditions. As a devotee of Shākyamuni, Myōe bemoaned the fact that he did not have a chance to meet the original master, and twice he planned to make the arduous journey to India to at least be in the right place if not the right time. A voracious reader and practitioner, Myōe embraced all ideas and methods as having something to contribute to the pursuit of visions, the constant attainment of which convinced him in time that visionary encounters with Shākyamuni and the many other Buddhas made an actual trip to India unnecessary.

Meditative flights from the world did not mean escape from it. Famed for his moral purity, Myōe was concerned about right conduct not only for himself and fellow monks but for laymen and laywomen as well. He recognized that for ordinary laypersons the demands of meditation were not appropriate, and he therefore argued for the possibility of enlightenment through moral action. Morality was necessary not only for good relations between people, but for salvation as well. The physical world was not simply a defiled place from which to flee, but it was also emblematic of the perfect world that could be envisioned. What was needed was a theory of language by which nature could be read, and Myōe used Kegon and Shingon ideas to define how sand, for instance, speaks.

In 1206 Myōe was granted administration of Kōzanji, a Kegon temple on the outskirts of Kyoto. From then until his death, he divided his time between the temple and the area around his birthplace in Wakayama, seeking ever to meditate, read, and write. By the time of his death at Kōzanji, he had produced a large body of writings ranging from technical doctrinal treatises to poetry and a diary of his dreams.

Mind and Meditation

Against the radical manifesto of Hōnen (1133–1212), the founder of the Pure Land Sect who advocated the rejection of all practices except the recitation of the *nembutsu*, Myōe argued in his *Smashing the Heretical Chariot* that the traditional practices, especially meditation, were still effective and necessary even in the age of the decline of Buddhism. Firmly convinced of the efficacy of meditation on the basis of his own experience and the traditional teachings, Myōe argued that the Pure Land was more than a preexistent place out there somewhere—it was a creation of the mind in meditation. To reject meditation, then, is to destroy the Pure Land.

All of the other functions of the mind were also valued as necessities. The aspiration for enlightenment, which Hōnen had rejected, was a prerequisite not only for becoming a Buddha, but also for the proper practice of the *nembutsu*. Noting that the term itself means mindfulness on the Buddha, Myōe explained it showed that mere recitation of Amida's name was useless without empowerment by the mind. Recitation was an aid to meditation and visualization, and by the force of mind it was possible to see the Buddha and be in his living presence. The goal was the attainment of visions that created new realities, which, though momentary, were more authentic than the everyday world. The large number of scriptures and commentaries of past masters writing about a multitude of methods for inducing meditative consciousness corroborated his own experience that meditation was not only effective, but easy as well.

Moral Causation

Though Myōe regarded meditation as the most effective means to enlightenment, he did not think that moral action was merely a supplement to it. Right conduct in and of itself, unaided even by meditation, was a sufficient cause for enlightenment. In his *Illustrated Account of the Origins of Kegon*, Myōe told the story of how a Chinese woman named Shan-miao fell in love with the Korean priest Ŭisang, who was on his way to Changan (now Xian) to study Kegon Buddhism, and how her burning passion transformed her into a dragon that protected Ŭisang on his return trip home and helped him establish the Kegon School in Korea. The transformation of her passion into virtue was the reason not only for her salvation, but for her deification as well. Known as Zemmyō in Japanese, she was regarded by Myōe as a deity and became the central object of worship at the nunnery he built in her name.

Even profligacy can be turned into virtue. Ŭisang's companion, Wŏnhyo, lived an untrammeled life as if he had forgotten propriety, but his virtue was intact though hidden. Addressing the fundamental problem of how to deal with sin, Myōe had an extremely simple answer: Be good. Even better, perform rituals that have the mysterious power to destroy bad *karma*. What is unusual about this ordinary answer is that Myōe considered it to be the epitome of Kegon Buddhism, which in China and Japan always had the reputation for being so profound that it was difficult to understand or practice. Exploiting the Kegon analysis of how mysterious the workings of the causal rise and fall of things and events are, Myōe presented his unlikely formula, which linked mere morality to a supramundane enlightenment.

Nature as Language

If morality worked in mysterious ways, even more strange were the cause-and-effect relationships of ritual. How was it possible, for instance, for the spreading of ritually purified sand on the deceased to cause a blinding but unseen radiance to expiate the sins of that person? Just as the Buddhas are said to transfer their virtue to their disciples by speaking words into their hands and then rubbing their disciples' heads, so is it that spiritual power can be conferred onto natural objects, such as sand.

Myōe was very much aware of the fact that these claims were preposterous and unexplainable in ordinary terms. His method was to argue through the manipulation of images drawn from nature and myth. Sanskrit, the holy language of India, is said to have emerged from the Buddha's body as light or images of light, and this essential linkage between body, word, and light can be found in all bodies or things. The words of chanted *mantras*, therefore, can permeate and purify grains of sand which then release a radiance that dissolves *karma*.

Language and nature are not related to each other simply in terms of linkages, but are in essence objects. Like sand, language is an object that is manipulated by the sensory faculties of the eyes, ears, and mouth. As a perceivable object—and only because it is perceived—language can be read. Nature, too, is a perceivable object and can therefore be read by those who can see its messages. Language can invoke realities that transcend nature, and nature too, as language, can produce realities that exceed itself. Sand, therefore, can expiate sins.

Logic of Images

Pushing reasoning and explanation to its very limits, Myōe, like many Buddhist philosophers, had to resort to ways of thinking that were not always discursive. In explaining the idea of the non-dual interpenetration of all things with all things, Myōe was well aware of how the many previous attempts at explicating non-duality floundered in the shallows of reasoning. How can the coincidence of opposites be explained? How can black be white?

Using the imagery of the *Kegon Sūtra*, a lengthy scripture in which the central Buddha prefers to emit light instead of speaking, Myōe repainted the picture of the Buddha radiating a beam of light that traveled throughout the world gathering everything into its luminescence before reentering the Buddha through his feet. Instead of trying to understand rationally how, for instance, form is emptiness and emptiness is form, Myōe's appeal is to sight: see the light shine on all things, including opposite things. Like the modern philosopher Mary Warnock, who explains that the imagination working with images is of fundamental importance to think-

ing, Myōe presents the image of an all-embracing light as necessary for clear intellectual understanding. This kind of imagistic thinking is not difficult, visions being, like miracles, much easier than philosophy for common folk to understand.

Myōe is best summarized as having been engaged in a lifelong quest for visions. He sought to see Shākyamuni and be in his presence. He created the Pure Land through the force of meditative vision, and argued that Hōnen was no longer a Buddhist since he had given up on trying to attain visions. In explaining how morality can be the causal condition for enlightenment, how sand can be empowered by language to dissolve past sins in a burning radiance, or how opposites can cohere, he resorted to manipulating images, which could more easily be comprehended by sight than abstractions could be understood through discursive reasoning. Poetry was also important, and he used it as he did meditative insight to transform the hillside at Kōzanji into the very places described in the Buddhist scriptures. Dreams too were repositories of thought and feeling, and in several of the many dreams he recorded for over thirty-five years, he wrote his own interpretations to make explicit the connection he saw between the dream visions and their meanings.

GEORGE J. TANABE JR.

Further Reading

Gimello, Robert M., and Peter Gregory, eds. *Studies in Ch'an and Hua-yen.* Honolulu, Hawaii: University of Hawaii Press, 1983. An essay by Gimello examines the thought and practice of Li T'ung-hsüan and Myōe's understanding of him.

Kawai, Hayao. *The Buddhist Priest Myōe: A Life of Dreams.* Translated by Mark Unno. Venice, Calif.: Lapis Press, 1992. The leading Jungian psychoanalyst in Japan examines Myōe's life and in particular his relationship with women both in his dreams and waking moments.

Morrell, Robert E. *Early Kamakura Buddhism: A Minority Report.* Berkeley, Calif.: Asian Humanities Press, 1987. This collection of short essays and translations of key works by leaders of the old orthodoxy contains the last testament of Myōe.

Rasmus, Rebecca, trans. "The Sayings of Myōe Shōnin of Togano-o," *Eastern Buddhist.* n.s., 15:1, Spring 1982, pp. 87–105. This collection of aphorisms by Myōe reveals his ordinary concerns and practical advice for living.

Tanabe, George J., Jr. *Myōe the Dreamkeeper.* Cambridge, Mass.: Harvard University Press, 1992. A study of the life and times of Myōe, this book also contains a translation of his *Dream Diary*.

SHINRAN

Born: 1173, Kyoto, Japan
Died: 1263, Kyoto, Japan
Major Work: *The True Teaching, Practice and Realization of the Pure Land Way* (popularly known as *Kyōgyōshinshō*; draft written in 1224; completed c. 1247)

Major Ideas

The human condition is one of delusional thought and blind passions.
No act undertaken by human beings can bring them to enlightenment.
Liberation arises through the working of Amida Buddha, who vowed that all who say the nembutsu *(Amida's Name) with trust be born in the Pure Land.*
The entrusting (shinjin) of oneself to the Vow is itself the Buddha's mind given to one.
The moment one realizes shinjin, one's birth in the Pure Land is settled.
Birth in the Pure Land at death signifies immediate attainment of enlightenment, upon which one returns to the world of samsāra *(cycles of existence) to work for the liberation of all beings.*
True reality may be described as jinen *(working "of itself"), which is wisdom–compassion actively bringing beings to awakening without any contrivance on their part.*

Shinran's importance as a religious thinker lies in his coherent exposition of the Pure Land Path as being both rooted in general Mahayana conceptions of wisdom or reality and, at the same time, being accessible to all, regardless of intellectual capacity or ability to fulfill religious practices and disciplines.

He was born into the Hino family, a minor branch of the nobility, at a time when warrior clans were gaining power. At the age of nine he became a monk of the Tendai School on Mt. Hiei, where for twenty years he engaged in study and practice. At the age of twenty-nine, however, despairing of attaining awakening through monastic discipline, he undertook a retreat at Rokkakudō temple in Kyoto and, on the ninety-fifth day, Kannon appeared to him in a dream. Taking this as a sign, Shinran visited the monk Hōnen and eventually joined his following. Hōnen had descended Mt. Hiei and was teaching that simple utterance of Amida Buddha's Name, *Namu-amida-butsu* (*nembutsu*), would unfailingly result in birth in Amida's Pure Land at death. He thus opened up the possibility of Buddhist practice to laity and commoners, and was attracting followers from all levels of society.

Shinran studied under Hōnen for six years until 1207 when, in a persecution of the spreading *nembutsu* teaching instigated by the ecclesiastical establishment, Hōnen and a small number of disciples were defrocked and exiled by order of the imperial court. Shinran was banished north to Echigo on the Sea of Japan coast.

After five years Hōnen and his followers were pardoned, but Shinran, having married, remained in his place of exile for several years, then traveled with his family to a developing provincial area in the Kanto region, where he embarked on a twenty-year period of propagation among ordinary people. He established a sizable following in several provinces, with local groups led by close disciples. Then, when about the age of sixty-three, he returned to Kyoto, where he remained for the rest of his long life, devoting himself to written expression of the teaching.

Shinran's extant writings, both in the Chinese of learned Buddhist discourse and in Japanese, were almost all completed during the final third of his life after his return to the capital, but his early training in Kyoto and his extended sojourn living and teaching among the people of the provinces provided the foundations. His study both on Mt.

315

Hiei and under Hōnen concentrated on careful reading of scriptural and commentarial traditions in Chinese, and he maintains this focus in his own writings, whether in Chinese or Japanese. At the same time, however, expulsion from the capital and monastic life and exile to the countryside provided a test of the teaching that all people could attain birth through the *nembutsu*.

On going into exile, Shinran adopted the name Gutoku ("foolish/stubble-haired"), which expresses his awareness both of the inability to cultivate learning or uphold monastic discipline and, at the same time, of their irrelevance to authentic engagement with the religious path. In interpreting the tradition, then, Shinran seeks to communicate not only the conceptual meaning, but the apprehension of reality that lies at their source.

The Pure Land Path Prior to Shinran: Practice, Faith, and the Moment of Death

Pure Land Buddhism developed in India as a relatively quick and easy means of attaining the stage of non-retrogression. According to the teachings this stage is attained when, with the fulfillment of strenuous practice through many lifetimes, one finally awakened to true reality; it signified that thereafter one would progress in one's practice for Buddhahood without ever falling back into the bondage of samsaric existence (existence involving cycles of birth and rebirth). According to Pure Land writings, although attaining non-retrogression in this world is difficult, it can be reached by being born in Amida's Pure Land upon death. Thereafter, in the supportive environment and the presence of the Buddha, one will steadily advance to supreme enlightenment.

In the long history of the Pure Land tradition, various understandings of the practices required for birth in the Pure Land were taught. Hōnen, however, had found himself altogether incapable of accomplishing traditional forms of practice and, in seeking a path he could follow, he discovered the utterance of the name *nembutsu*, which was based on the understanding that Amida Buddha had vowed to bring all who say his Name in trust to

birth in his Pure Land. Hōnen's teaching represents an inversion of ordinary notions of practice, for its effectiveness does not rest in the inherent good of the act or one's effort as viewed within usual frames of reference. Rather, the *nembutsu* is effective because it embodies Amida's virtues. Moreover, with the historical decline in human capacities and the increasing distance from Shākyamuni Buddha, only the *nembutsu* remains effective in our latter age.

Another question arises, however: Is it the utterance that is crucial, or trust in Amida? Hōnen taught that practicers should believe that even one utterance resulted in birth—this being Amida's Vow—and with this trust, they should seek to say the *nembutsu* throughout their lives. For many, it seemed natural that since vocal *nembutsu* was the practice to be performed in the Path, one should try to say it as often as possible. Others, however, argued that endeavor in *nembutsu* as though it were merely another form of practice indicated a lack of trust in the Buddha's Vow.

The emphasis on utterance was linked to concern over a person's mental condition at the moment of death. Sutras taught that Amida Buddha came then to take the dying practicer to the Pure Land. In other words, the point of death was the nexus between this world and the world beyond. It was believed that, because of its significance, one had to be in a proper state of trust and say the *nembutsu* at the very end of life. Thus *nembutsu* during ordinary times was considered preparation for attaining the proper attitude at the time of death.

In addition to these issues debated by practicers, Hōnen's teaching was criticized as heretical by monks of traditional schools. In particular, he was denounced for his classification of the awakening of the mind aspiring for enlightenment (*bodaishin*) as a practice unnecessary for Pure Land practicers.

Shinran's Thought

Shinran's thought developed as an effort to clarify Hōnen's teaching by locating it at the core of Mahayana thought and by elucidating misapprehensions that arose from grasping the teaching within ordinary, egocentric modes of understanding. The basic structure of Shinran's thought may be discerned by considering his major work, *The True Teaching, Practice and Realization of the Pure Land Way*, in which he presents a comprehensive exposition of the Path chiefly by collecting, arranging, and interpreting passages from the scriptures in Chinese.

As indicated in the title, Shinran organizes his presentation by adopting the generally accepted formulation of Buddhism as consisting of the "three pillars" of teaching, practice, and realization. By employing this formula, Shinran asserts that the Pure Land Path conforms to the basic pattern of Buddhist teachings. At the same time, however, he distinguishes the "true essence of the Pure Land way" (*Jōdo Shinshū*) from other forms of Buddhism by stressing the distinction between Other Power and self-power. Other Power refers to the working of wisdom–compassion embodied in Amida's Vow, while self-power refers to reliance on one's own accomplishment of practices and disciplines. Shinran found, however, that this distinction had not been clearly understood by Pure Land practicers themselves, many of whom had taken up Pure Land practice with an attitude of self-power. Shinran employs the term "calculative thinking" or "designing" (*hakarai*) as a synonym of self-power, signifying people's efforts to make themselves worthy of birth in the Pure Land through moral conduct, worship, *nembutsu* recitation, or sincerity of trust. For Shinran, such an attitude manifests a fundamental self-attachment in which one seeks to attain birth through one's own good, rather than through Amida's compassion. Genuine engagement with the Pure Land Path arises when such calculation is overturned and abandoned. In other words, the true essence of the Pure Land Path implies a mode of engagement that differs from the usual conception of studying the teaching, fulfilling practice, and reaching the goal.

To illuminate the special nature of the Pure Land Path, Shinran alters the traditional formulation of "teaching, practice, and realization" in two highly innovative ways: first, he places it within an encompassing framework, the two aspects of Amida Buddha's directing of virtue to beings; and second, in clarifying the element of practice, he adds a consideration of a uniquely developed concept of *shinjin*, the entrusting oneself to the Vow.

Amida's Directing of Virtue

Shinran states that each element of the Path is "directed" or given to beings by Amida. This means that each element is an intersection or fusion of dimensions: the dimension of time or historical existence in this world, and the dimension of true reality, which transcends the conceptual frameworks of time and space. From one perspective, these dimensions stand in mutual opposition; in traditional Buddhist terms, this is the opposition between *samsāra* and *nirvāna*, or blind passions and enlightenment.

One of the salient characteristics of Shinran's thought is his thoroughgoing view of ordinary human life as pervaded by blind passions rooted in clinging to a delusional self. Even in activities ordinarily seen as religious, Shinran detects elements of self-aggrandizement when they are charted and evaluated by the self. In fact, in Shinran's view, all our judgments of good and evil—acts that move one toward enlightenment and acts that bind one further to samsaric existence—are false, being inevitably distorted by egocentricity.

At the same time, however, reality is not simply transcendent of all human conception; since reality is itself wisdom or enlightenment, it is also characterized by movement toward beings. In Buddhist terms, wisdom that is free of the discrimination of self and the other perceives beings in painful existence as not different from itself and undertakes compassionate activity to awaken them. For Shinran, the heart of the Path lies in this compassion working across the boundary between true reality and delusional existence, a boundary that is itself unreal from the perspective of wisdom.

This activity is expressed in Shinran's thought by his framing the elements of the Path within his conception of Amida Buddha's directing of virtue (*ekō*) to beings. *Ekō*, a basic element of the

Bodhisattva Path, is usually rendered "transfer-ring merit," meaning that aspirants dedicate what-ever merit they gain through performing practices toward enlightenment for themselves and for all beings, without discrimination. Shinran, uniquely interpreting scriptural passages that speak of *ekō*, understands the term to refer not to beings turning their own merits toward attainment of the Pure Land, but rather as Amida Buddha directing the virtue of his own aeons of practice to beings.

This reversal in direction is crucial to Shinran's conception of the Path. It may be said that the absolute dichotomy and the compassionate activity of the Real moving into the realm of beings are experienced together when this reversal in direc-tion takes place. That is, it is precisely when the effort of the egocentric self to move itself toward awakening falls away that true reality approaches. Or more precisely, the falling away of the efforts of the self is one face of the working of wisdom–compassion.

Teaching

We may see the fundamental method in Shinran's thought—and the difference of his conception of *shinjin* from a notion of acceptance of doctrine—in his treatment of the element of teaching.

In *The True Teaching, Practice and Realization of the Pure Land Way*, the opening chapter on teaching is not an exposition of doctrine; rather, it argues that Shākyamuni ("Sage of the Shākyas": Siddārtha Gautama, son of a chief of the Shākya tribal republic) appeared in the world specifically to deliver the teaching of Amida (Amitābha), "Buddha of Boundless Light." In other words, it is not simply that Shākyamuni, as a historical figure, performed practices, attained enlightenment, and then sought to guide people to that enlightenment through various teachings. Rather, the Buddha en-tered the world from the realm of enlightenment with the sole purpose of guiding people, by various means, to Amida's Vow; thus, the Pure Land teach-ing is to be understood as emerging into the history of the world and *from* transcendent reality *through* Shākyamuni. This dual configuration of Shāk-

yamuni's appearance in history and emergence from somewhere beyond time is also evident in Shinran's assertion—based on the *Sūtra*'s explanation—that the teaching of Amida expresses Shākyamuni's profound *samādhi*, in which he "abides where all Buddhas abide." Shākyamuni enters profound contemplation in which he attains that which is beyond time and delivers the teaching of Amida from that contemplation.

In a unique interpretation of the nature of Amida Buddha that he explains elsewhere, Shinran delin-eates this same configuration of the intersection of temporality and timelessness. He applies to Amida a concept of two dimensions of Buddha-body: *dharma*-body as *dharma*-nature or true reality, and *dharma*-body as compassion. *Dharma*-body as re-ality is formless and inconceivable, but in order to awaken beings to itself, it manifests form, taking the name Dharmakara Bodhisattva, establishing the Primal Vow, performing practices, and becom-ing Amida Buddha. In other words, the Vow and attainment of Amida Buddha are understood to arise as the appearance in the form of formless reality. These two dimensions of Buddha—(1) Amida as characterized by form that can be grasped conceptually and (2) true reality that tran-scends all conception—differ but are not separ-able, are one but are not identical. Because of the non-duality, the Path based on Amida's Vow leads beings to supreme enlightenment.

Practice

The relationship between beings and Buddha is understood in terms of practice and *shinjin*, and the significance and consequences of this relationship in terms of realization.

Practice, for Shinran, is to say the Name of Am-ida Buddha. This act is not, however, undertaken as a spiritual discipline or means of accumulating merit. Thus Shinran states that saying the *nembutsu* is not a person's own good act, for it does not arise out of his or her efforts and designs. Rather, it is the manifestation of Amida's practice that is given to beings, and it is precisely for this reason that the *nembutsu* has the power to result in birth in the Pure

Land. In other words, saying the *nembutsu* is genuine practice leading to Buddhahood because it shares the nature of the intersection of dimensions that we have seen above. It is an act occurring in a person's existence, and at the same time it embodies the Buddha's practice fulfilled in the infinite past.

Through developing this understanding Shinran sought to resolve the debate that remained unclarified in Hōnen's thought over the preferability of one utterance or many utterances. Such counts relate only to utterances viewed as human acts and are not applicable to the *nembutsu* in its genuine nature as Amida's practice.

Shinjin

In order to elucidate how the act of saying the Name is given by Amida, Shinran developed a distinctive understanding of the concept of *shinjin* (entrusting mind), which became the core of his teaching as the true cause of birth in the Pure Land.

There are three central points concerning *shinjin* that are important for our concerns: First, it is the pure mind of Buddha. Genuine trust cannot be an attitude that beings awaken in themselves, for all their thoughts and motives are self-centered. Nevertheless, Amida gives them his own pure mind, which they realize in the form of the entrusting of themselves to the Vow. Second, since *shinjin* is directed to beings and not generated by them through practices, realization of it occurs in the shortest instant of time. Third, genuine utterance of the *nembutsu* arises from *shinjin*. In other words, saying the Name is the Buddha's practice, manifesting Amida's virtues in beings' existence, because it emerges from the Buddha's mind in them.

We see here that attainment of *shinjin* is the point of intersection of a person's existence and transcendent reality; it is the fusion of transtemporal reality as the working of Amida's wisdom-compassion with temporal existence. Shinran therefore states that, at the moment of attainment, the ocean of Amida's virtues fills the practicer, and

that the practicer's mind is like a river flowing into the ocean of the Vow and becoming one with it, even while Buddha and being remain in the opposition of enlightenment and ignorance. Further, he states that *shinjin* is the mind aspiring for enlightenment, which Hōnen was criticized for ignoring, and itself is Buddha-nature.

Realization

Shinran's explanation of the significance of attaining *shinjin* is also innovative, emphasizing as it does the intersection of mundane life—which is carried on with delusional thought and blind passions—and true reality as entrusted to Amida's Vow. There are two aspects: attainment of *shinjin* at the moment true reality emerges in one's existence and fuses with it; and one's existence in the world, because of *shinjin*, as necessarily moving toward birth in the Pure Land and enlightenment. These aspects are integrated in Shinran's concepts of transformation and attainment of non-retrogression in the immediate present.

Shinran describes attainment of *shinjin* as an irreversible transformation in which "all the practicer's past, present, and future evil karma is transformed into good...without being nullified or eradicated." That is, one continues to live as an unenlightened being motivated by self-attachment. However, even though one is unable to perceive and act with wisdom–compassion because one has attained the Buddha's mind as *shinjin*, each moment of one's life is pervaded in its depths by the Buddha's working. Hence, Shinran states that when *shinjin* is attained, "we are quickly brought to realize that blind passions and enlightenment are not two in substance." Moreover, where self-power has collapsed, the apprehension of samsaric existence arises, and in turning to the Vow, one may gain a perception like that of Shinran, who states,

All living things have been our parents and brothers and sisters in the course of countless lives in many states of existence; on attaining Buddhahood in the next life, we must save every one of them.

Based on the non-duality of samsaric existence and true reality resulting from the attainment of the Buddha's mind as *shinjin*, Shinran fundamentally altered the temporal understanding of realization in the Pure Land Path. Prior to him, Pure Land masters taught that practicers say the *nembutsu* in the present life and attain non-retrogression with birth in the Pure Land at death. Shinran, however, declares that non-retrogression is attained at the moment of realizing *shinjin*, for *shinjin* itself signifies suchness or reality. Thus, whatever may occurs in one's life, one's birth in the Pure Land at death is settled; one does not remain uncertain until the moment of death.

Furthermore, in Shinran's thought the conception of the Pure Land is also altered. It ceases to be a realm where one first enters the Buddha's realm, for realization of *shinjin* already signifies Amida's presence. Rather, Shinran conceives the Pure Land itself as wisdom, indistinguishable from Buddha, and birth there at the moment of death in this world signifies attainment of supreme Buddhahood or nirvana. Thus beings do not remain in the Pure Land performing practices but, having attained wisdom–compassion, immediately return to the world of samsaric existence to work for the liberation of all beings.

Although he employed the symbols and narratives of the Pure Land teachings, Shinran initiated many fundamental changes on the conception of the Path based on the dynamics of absolute opposition between being and Buddha, together with non-duality and interfusion from the side of Buddha. Late in life, he developed an original conception of the active, non-dual reality that manifests itself as the working of the Vow using the term *jinen* (activity occurring "of itself"), meaning the spontaneous working of wisdom–compassion, free of any deliberate intention by the practicer. It is by *jinen* that beings realize *shinjin*, attain birth in the Pure Land and enlightenment, and compassionately return to this world. Further, *jinen* signifies the Pure Land itself and inconceivable Buddha or reality.

DENNIS HIROTA

Further Reading

Translations

Translations of Shinran's most important works are available in the Shin Buddhism Translation Series (Kyoto: Hongwanji International Center): *The True Teaching, Practice and Realization of the Pure Land Way* (*Kyōgyōshinshō*; in four volumes, 1983–90), *Letters of Shinran* (*Mattōshō*, 1978), *Notes on "Essentials of Faith Alone"* (*Yuishinshō mon'i*, 1979), *Notes on Once-Calling and Many-Calling* (*Ichinen tanen mon'i*, 1980), *Notes on the Inscriptions on Sacred Scrolls* (*Songō shinzo meimon*, 1981), *Passages on the Pure Land Way* (*Jōdo monrui jushō*, 1982), *Hymns of the Pure Land* (*Jōdo wasan*, 1991), *Hymns of the Pure Land Masters* (*Kōsō wasan*, 1992), and *Hymns of the* Dharma-*Ages* (*Shōzōmatsu wasan*, 1993).

The Ryukoku Translation Series (Kyoto: Ryukoku University Translation Center) includes somewhat stiff annotated translations with original texts of the following works: *Shōshin Ge* (a hymn included in *Teaching, Practice and Realization*, 1961), *Kyō Gyo Shin Shō* (an abridgment of *Teaching, Practice and Realization*, focusing on Shinran's own comments, 1966), *Jōdō Wasan* (1965), *Kōsō Wasan* (1974), and *Shōzōmatsu Wasan* (1980).

D. T. Suzuki translated the first four (of six) chapters of Shinran's major work, *Kyōgyōshinshō* (Kyoto: Shinshū Ōtaniha, 1973; includes editors' annotations).

One of the most widely read religious works in Japan is *Tannishō*, a record of Shinran's spoken words. Among the many translations are: *Tannishō: A Primer* (Translated by Dennis Hirota. Kyoto: Ryukoku University, 1982; includes original text) and *Tannishō: A Shin Buddhist Classic* (Translated by Taitetsu Unno. Honolulu, Hawaii: Buddhist Study Center Press, 1984).

Related Studies

Bloom, Alfred. *Shinran's Gospel of Pure Grace.* Tucson, Ariz.: University of Arizona Press,

1965. Outline based on traditional Jōdo Shinshū dogmatics.

———. "The Life of Shinran Shonin: The Journey to Self-Acceptance," *Numen*. 15, 1968, pp. 1–62. Basic summary of what is known with some certainty of Shinran's biography.

Dobbins, James C. *Jōdo Shinshū: Shin Buddhism in Medieval Japan*. Bloomington and Indianapolis, Ind.: Indiana University Press, 1989. Historical account of the movement founded by Shinran through its first three centuries.

Hirota, Dennis. *Plain Words on the Pure Land Way: Sayings of the Wandering Monks of Medieval Japan*. Kyoto: Ryukoku University, 1989. A translation of the *Ichigon Hodan*, a collection of sayings of the *Nembutsu hijiri* (the *Nembutsu* monks) of the Kamakura period. Provides a vivid glimpse into the lives and practice of Pure Land monks during the period of Hōnen and Shinran, with an introduction that sets the tradition of the wandering *nembutsu* monk into its historical context.

Suzuki, Daisetz Teitaro. *Collected Writings on Shin Buddhism*. Kyoto: Shinshu Otaniha, 1973. Insightful essays on religious life based on Shinran's Path.

Takahatake, Takamichi. *Young Man Shinran: A Reappraisal of Shinran's Life*. Waterloo, Ontario: Wilfrid Laurier University Press, 1987. Highly interpretive study of the first four decades of Shinran's life, for which documents are scarce.

Ueda, Yoshifumi and Dennis Hirota. *Shinran: An Introduction to His Thought*. Kyoto: Hongwanji International Center, 1989. Traces the continuity of Mahayana and Pure Land thought and sets forth central themes in Shinran's thinking. Includes an annotated selection of important passages from his writings with original texts.

DŌGEN

Born: 1200, Kyoto, Japan
Died: 1253, Kyoto, Japan
Major Works: *Shōbōgenzō* (*Treasury of the True* Dharma-*Eye*) (1231–53), *Shōbōgenzō Zuimonki* (*Miscellaneous Talks*) (1233), *Eihei Kōroku* (*Recorded Sayings at Eiheiji Temple*) (1243–53), *Fukanzazengi* (*Universal Recommendation for Zazen Practice*) (1227)

Major Ideas

Philosophy of religion must reflect personal existential experience of transient reality.
The theory of "original enlightenment" (hongaku) leads to a doubt about the importance of religious practice.
Religious practice or training and realization or the attainment of enlightenment occur simultaneously and are inseparable in the experience known as "the casting off of body–mind."
The methods of zazen meditation and kōan interpretation are equally conducive to realization.
The ultimate reality of the universal Buddha-nature is not beyond but is conditioned by impermanence.
There is a fundamental unity of being-time (uji) in that all beings occur as temporal manifestations.
The naturalist dimension of being-time and impermanence-Buddha-nature is expressible through poetry and aesthetics.
The realm of karmic or moral conditioning and retribution is inherent to, rather than outside of, the experience of enlightenment.

Dōgen, the founder of the Sōtō Zen Sect in medieval Japan, is often referred to as the leading classical philosopher in Japanese history and one of the foremost exponents of Buddhist thought. His essays on numerous Buddhist topics included in his main text, the *Shōbōgenzō* (*Treasury of the True* Dharma-*Eye*), reflect an approach to religious experience based on a more philosophical analysis than is found in the writings of most thinkers in Zen, which is known as a "special transmission outside the scriptures, without reliance on words and letters."

Dōgen's works are frequently cited by the pre-eminent philosophers of modern Japan, especially representatives of the Kyoto School, including Nishida Kitarō, Nishitani Keiji, and Abe Masao, and he has also been compared to the leading figures in modern Western philosophy, including Martin Heidegger, Friedrich Nietzsche, Alfred North Whitehead, and Jean-Paul Sartre.

The single main element in Dōgen's unique approach to Buddhist theory and practice is his emphasis on the meaning of impermanence in personal experience and as the basis for Buddhist metaphysics. The notion of impermanence or the transiency of all aspects of human and natural existence has always been a fundamental feature of the Buddhist teaching of the insubstantial, selfless nature of reality. However, Dōgen repeatedly cautions against any subtle tendency to view ultimate reality—*nirvana* or the universal Buddha-nature—as an eternal realm separable from or independent of impermanence. Instead, he stresses that a full, unimpeded, and perpetually renewed experience of impermanence and of the unity of being-time (*uji*) is the touchstone and framework of every aspect of Buddhist meditative training and spiritual realization.

Dōgen's Philosophical Development

Much of Dōgen's emphasis of impermanence is based on his own personal experiences as recorded in his traditional biographies. Although many of the details of these records have been called into question by recent historiographical studies, the symbolism of the main events is still important for understanding the meaning of his philosophy of Zen. According to the traditional accounts, Dōgen was born into an aristocratic family at a time when Japan was beginning to be plagued by repeated civil warfare. Dōgen experienced profound sorrow and tragedy even at an early age—his father died when he was two, and his beautiful mother, a mistress of the father, died when he was seven. It is said that when Dōgen saw the smoke from incense rising and vanishing during his mother's funeral, he was deeply moved by an awareness of the inevitability of death and the pervasiveness of ephemerality.

The orphaned Dōgen had the opportunity through members of his noble family to be trained for a court career. However, he decided to renounce secular life in pursuit of the Buddhist *Dharma*. At first, he studied on Mt. Hiei outside the capital city of Kyoto in the dominant Japanese Tendai church, in which the central doctrine was an affirmation of "original enlightenment" (*hongaku*) or the inherent potentiality of all beings to attain the universal, primordial Buddha-nature. However, at the age of thirteen Dōgen had a fundamental "doubt" about the doctrine of original enlightenment: If everyone is already enlightened in that they possess the Buddha-nature, he thought, then what is the need for sustained meditative practice as required by the Buddha's teaching?

Unable to resolve this doubt in Japan, Dōgen traveled to China, where the contemplative path of Zen had become the dominant sect. At first, Dōgen was disappointed in the laxity of the Chinese Zen monks of the Rinzai Sect, who failed to inspire him to resolve his doubt. Then, on the verge of returning to Japan unfulfilled, he met the Sōtō teacher, Rujing (Ju-ching), who insisted on an unrelenting approach to meditation. Under the guidance of his new mentor, Dōgen attained an awakening experience of "the casting off of body–mind" (*shinjin datsuraku*), or a continuing process of liberation from all intellectual and volitional attachments, which signified the resolution of his doubt about the necessity of sustained practice.

Once he returned to Japan, Dōgen founded the

Sōtō Sect in the Kyoto area, but because of sectarian disputes with Tendai and other Zen factions he eventually moved to the remote, pristine mountains of Echizen (now Fukui) Province where he established the Eiheiji temple, the center of the Sōtō Sect today.

The Temporal Basis of Zen Theory and Practice

The resolution of Dōgen's doubt about original enlightenment was based on his new understanding of the meaning of a fully unified conception of time in relation to enlightenment. Prior to his breakthrough experience, Dōgen apparently presumed the conventional dichotomies between past, present, and future, now and then, life and death, impermanence and nirvana, time and eternity, and finitude and Buddha-nature. He thought that human beings were bound to a realm of death and impermanence and that enlightenment was beyond this realm. However, in casting off body–mind, he realized that a single moment encompasses the unity of practice and attainment, so that practice is not prior to—nor does it lead up to—enlightenment, and enlightenment is not a teleological goal reached only at the end of practice. Rather, Dōgen writes in the *Shōbōgenzō*,

> Practice and realization are identical. Because one's present practice is practice in realization, one's initial negotiation of the Way in itself is the whole of original realization. . . . As it is already realization in practice, realization is endless; as it is practice in realization, practice in beginningless. (Terada and Mizuno, 1971)

The identity of time and eternity, and of practice and realization, is also the key to Dōgen's resolution of another dilemma concerning Zen theory. Prior to Dōgen's arrival in China, Zen was divided on the issue of the relation between *zazen* meditation and *kōan* interpretation. The Sōtō Sect tended to favor a gradualist approach to *zazen* known as "silent illumination," whereas the Rinzai Sect favored the Sudden Path based on "*kōan* introspection." For Rinzai Zen, the quixotic *kōan* riddles or puzzles represented barriers to language and thought that catapulted the practitioner into a subitaneous awakening to nonconceptuality and silence.

Although Dōgen emphasized the priority of "*zazen*-only" or "just sitting," he also stressed the importance of analyzing and interpreting the multiple perspectives of the paradoxical kōans as fully identical with sustained *zazen* meditation. For example, the Rinzai approach to the *kōan*, "Does the dog have Buddha-nature?", which is the first case in the famous *Mumonkan* (*Gateless Gate*) collection, emphasizes that the answer, *Mu* (literally "no"), puts an end to discourse and cognition. Dōgen, however, interprets *Mu* as suggesting many implications, including the ontological significance of emptiness or nothingness in addition to the skeptical epistemology implied by a silent response to all inquiries.

The Multidimensional Nature of Temporality

Dōgen, as first and foremost a Zen master, was primarily concerned with attaining and expressing enlightenment. His philosophy of time was aimed not at developing a speculative or abstract metaphysical theory but at clarifying and refining his existential experience of the casting off of body–mind. According to Dōgen, the unity of temporality harbors a complex, multidimensional experiential structure. First, Dōgen asserts the absolute identity of all beings or forms of existence with time in that whatever exists is a temporal manifestation. Nothing—including the ultimate reality of Buddha-nature—exists apart from the temporal domain that is actualized by sustained religious practice. According to the *Shōbōgenzō*,

The Buddha-nature is not incorporated prior to attaining Buddhahood; it is incorporated upon the attainment of Buddhahood. The Buddha-nature is always manifested with the attain-

ment of Buddhahood. (Terada and Mizuno, 1971)

That is, the Buddha-nature is neither an innate potentiality nor an attainable endpoint, but is fully integrated with the continuing dynamism of impermanent reality.

But, Dōgen stresses, it is also important to clarify the meaning of the impermanence of being-time encompassing Buddha-nature so that it is realized in a way that is free of delusions or misconceptions. Impermanence for Dōgen should not be conflated with the mere passing away of time in the sense that "time flies like an arrow," which implies that time is separable from existence, a fleeting yet substantive movement passing from the past through the present and inexorably into the future towards a specific goal. Rather, impermanence is a dynamic, comprehensive nonsubstantive process that is coordinated with the dimension of continuity embracing the identity of all three tenses.

The unity of being-time can be provisionally distinguished in terms of two inseparable levels. The first is the level of spontaneity, suddenness, or immediacy that occurs in each and every holistic moment right here and now, that is, in the eternal now that is beyond relativity to before and after, now and then, or life and death. However, this level of spontaneity should not be understood as mere quickness or rapidity in the conventional sense that time is flying by. Rather, spontaneity is supported by the second level of continuity, which includes the irreversible sequence of past, present, and future in addition to the reversibility and mutual interrelation of the three tenses. In one of the most paradoxical passages in Buddhist philosophy Dōgen writes,

There is continuity from today to tomorrow, from today to yesterday, from yesterday to today, from today to today, and from tomorrow to tomorrow. (Terada and Mizuno, 1971)

In other words, time is ever moving backwards as well as forwards so that spontaneity is sustained by a multidimensional continuity. The fullness of the moment realized in the casting off of body–mind is not passing away, but instead it harbors the unity of the tenses.

Dōgen repeatedly stresses that the unity of being-time does not function in the human or anthropocentric dimension alone, but it is fully trans-anthropocentric in encompassing all forms of existence, and it is especially evident through a contemplation of the beauty of nature and the cyclicality of seasonal rotation. Like many Zen masters in China and Japan, as well as other Far Eastern mystics in the Daoist (Taoist) and Shinto traditions, Dōgen seemed most content after he moved from the secular, highly politicized strife in Kyoto to the splendor of the Echizen mountains, where he experienced a constant state of communion with the natural environment. In his writings he frequently equates the Buddha-nature with natural phenomena such as mountains, rivers, and the moon, and he eloquently expresses an aesthetic naturalist rapture in which the rushing stream is experienced as the voice of the living Buddha, while the mountain peak synesthetically becomes Buddha's face.

A central feature of aesthetic realization is Dōgen's use of poetic language, especially elaborate metaphor and philosophical wordplay, to convey a sense of emotional fulfillment that enhances rather than opposes the enlightenment experience of detachment from worldly, materialistic concerns. One of Dōgen's most eloquent poems was written near the end of life as he returned from Echizen to the capital city for medical care. Making the journey to Kyoto for the first time in ten years, but for what would prove to be the last time, Dōgen wrote in the five-line, thirty-one-syllable *waka* form:

Like a blade of grass,
My frail body
Treading the path to Kyoto,
Seeming to wander
Amid the cloudy mist on the mountain path.

(HEINE, 1989)

Here, the phrase "a blade of grass" expresses a convergence of departure and return, of feeling and detachment, and of the particularity of an individual sense of frailty with the universal insubstantiality and impermanence of phenomena.

Ethics and Karma

In the last few years before his death, Dōgen shifted his philosophical concerns from an emphasis on the metaphysics of the temporality of Buddha-nature to more concrete ethical questions of the rewards and punishments for one's deeds and intentions. Perhaps because he was primarily occupied at this stage of his career with initiating new monks from the Echizen countryside who were relatively unschooled in the subtleties of Buddhist doctrine, Dōgen stressed a very literal interpretation of the notion of *karma* (moral causality). According to Dōgen's writings of this period, every action generates a retributive consequence, and only authentic repentance and acknowledgment of one's guilt can offset the effects of evil *karma*. Yet, by emphasizing the moment-to-moment cause-and-effect process of karmic retribution—which is inseparable from nirvana as part of the *Bodhisattva's* commitment to compassion—Dōgen is consistent with his earlier philosophy, which stressed impermanence and being-time.

The impact of Dōgen's philosophical works remains strong for several reasons. As the founder and author of the main text of the Sōtō Sect, his writings are continually studied and interpreted by Buddhist practitioners and scholars. As an expression of a view of impermanence that seems to capture the essence of Buddhist teaching and also anticipates the emphasis on temporality, death, and finitude in modern Western philosophy, the *Shōbōgenzō* stands at the forefront of international comparative philosophy. In addition, Dōgen's poetic writings on aesthetic experience as well as his later writings on *karma* and morality will be examined for their contributions to philosophical discussions of mystical awareness and the issues of commitment and responsibility involved in authentic religious practice.

STEVEN HEINE

Further Reading

Translation

Terada, Tōru and Mizuno Yaoko, eds. *Dōgen.* 2 vols. Tokyo: Iwanami, 1971. The primary source. Used for quotations in this chapter.

Related Studies

Abe, Masao. *A Study of Dōgen: His Philosophy and Religion.* Edited by Steven Heine. Albany, N.Y.: SUNY Press, 1992. A philosophical study by one of the major contemporary Japanese philosophers of the Kyoto School, this volume includes discussions of Dōgen's notion of being-time in relation to Heidegger's phenomenological philosophy of time and to Shinran's Pure Land Buddhist thought.

Bielefeldt, Carl. *Dōgen's Manuals of Zen Meditation.* Berkeley, Calif.: University of California Press, 1988. A thorough historical textual account of the influences of Chinese meditation manuals on the formation of Dōgen's philosophical and psychological approach to meditation.

Heine, Steven. *Dōgen and the Koan Tradition: A Tale of Two Shōbōgenzō Texts.* Albany, N.Y.: SUNY Press, 1993. A literary analysis of the relation between Dōgen's philosophical essays in Japanese and his collection of kōans in Chinese, both known as the *Shōbōgenzō*, by comparing Dōgen's interpretation of *kōans* to those of other leading thinkers in the Zen *kōan* tradition.

——— . *A Blade of Grass: Japanese Poetry and Aesthetics in Dōgen Zen.* New York: Peter Lang, 1989. The source of the Dōgen poem quoted in this chapter.

Kim, Hee-Jin. *Dōgen Kigen—Mystical Realist.* Tucson, Ariz.: University of Arizona Press, 1975. One of the first major works in English on Dōgen, this remains the most comprehensive study of the Zen master's life and writings.

LaFleur, William R., ed. *Dōgen Studies.* Honolulu, Hawaii: University of Hawaii Press, 1985. Discussions of the philosophical implications in Dōgen's thought by a number of the leading scholars in the field, including Masao Abe, Carl Bielefeldt, Francis Cook, Tom Kasulis, Hee-Jin Kim, and John Maraldo.

Tanahashi, Kazuaki. *Moon on a Dewdrop: Writings of Zen Master Dōgen.* San Francisco: North Point Press, 1985. An excellent translation of some of the most important fascicles in the *Shōbōgenzō*, as well as selected portions of other key texts.

NICHIREN

Born: 1222, Kominato, Japan
Died: 1282, Ikegami, Japan
Major Works: *Risshō ankoku ron* (*Treatise on the Establishment of the Orthodox Teaching and the Peace of the Nation*) (1260), *Hokke daimoku shō* (*Treatise on the Recitation of the Title of the* Lotus Sūtra) (1264), *Kaimoku shō* (*Opening of the Eyes*) (1272)

Major Ideas

The Lotus Sūtra *contains the highest truth of Buddhist teaching and is the only sutra with effective teachings for the "Latter Days of the* Dharma*" (mappō), the religious era which most Japanese believed began in the mid-eleventh century.*

Peace and prosperity are dependent on the establishment of the preeminence of the true teaching of the Lotus.

Belief in the Lotus Sūtra *is symbolized by, and religious practice can be reduced to, recitation of the title of the* Sūtra.

The Buddha Shākyamuni was a manifestation of an eternal, all-pervading Buddha-nature that reappears at intervals in the world in human form.

The Buddha-nature exists equally within all beings and Buddhahood is obtainable for all.

It is the duty of those who accept the teachings of the Lotus Sūtra *to preach it to others regardless of persecution.*

Born into an era of religious, political, and social turmoil in Japan—a time when the aristocratic court had been supplanted by military rule and when the various sects of Buddhism competed, sometimes violently, with seemingly contradictory teachings and practices—Nichiren was one of a number of dedicated and imaginative Japanese Buddhist leaders who worked to make the teachings and practice of Mahayana Buddhism more accessible and open the possibility of salvation to a larger audience by simplifying practices and emphasizing the message of universal salvation. He combed the various Buddhist texts and studied the teachings of the major sects of Japanese Buddhism for explanations of the turmoil within Buddhism and for ways to alleviate the suffering of a country torn by war and natural disasters.

Nichiren found in the philosophy of the Tendai Sect, as articulated by its Chinese founder Zhiyi (Chih-i) (538–597) and transmitted to Japan by Saichō (767–822), an interpretation of the seeming contradictions within Buddhism. He came to understand them as a pedagogical device of the Buddha Shākyamuni, who had preached a series of partial truths designed to lead his varied audiences with differing needs and capacities for understanding gradually toward the absolute truth. According to the Tendai doctrine, the teaching suited to the last "degenerate age," lay in the *Lotus Sūtra*. Nichiren came to feel it his mission to alert his fellow Japanese to the critical need to abandon all other beliefs and practices for acceptance of the teachings of the *Lotus Sūtra*.

Nichiren attempted to convert the Japanese rulers, in the hope that they would suppress other religious beliefs and practices and promote faith in the *Lotus Sūtra*, which he believed to be the only efficacious teaching for contemporary Japan. Twice exiled for his increasingly strident attacks on other sects of Buddhism and for his prophecies that the entire country must convert or face certain disaster, Nichiren was pardoned in 1274.

Failing once more to convince the rulers that only acceptance of the *Lotus Sūtra* and suppression of other teachings could save the nation from the threat of Mongol invasion, Nichiren counted this as his third warning as a loyal adviser to his ruler. He followed the precedent set by Confucian sages in China in withdrawing to live the last few years of his life on Mt. Minobu in central Honshu, surrounded by disciples and converts who were as convinced as he that the Mongol attacks on Japan in the late thirteenth century validated Nichiren's warnings and portended Japan's imminent destruction.

In addition to doctrinal treatises written early in his career as he was engaged in study of the various philosophical traditions and later as explications for his disciples, Nichiren's large body of writings includes many written for a lay audience: memorials to government officials and letters of counsel, support, and consolation addressed to followers in various parts of the country.

Risshō ankoku ron

The *Risshō ankoku ron* (*Treatise on the Establishment of the Orthodox Teaching and the Peace of the Nation*) represents the type of writing at which Nichiren excelled: explication of doctrine for an individual, by means of analogy, anecdote, and detail chosen to speak to that person's particular experiences and understanding. Presented in 1260 to the former military regent, Hōjō Tokiyori, who had retired to a Zen temple but who still held considerable power, it takes the form of a dialogue between a wise man (identifiable as Nichiren himself) and his visitor.

The conversation thus presented elaborates Nichiren's view of the relationship between religion and national welfare and argues that Japan's rulers must take responsibility for propagating faith in the *Lotus Sūtra* and eradicating other beliefs and practices in order to ensure peace and prosperity throughout the land.

Buddhist texts taught that after the death of the Buddha the world would pass through three eras in which the teaching would be variously received: in the first the True Law would flourish; in the second it would be practiced but not understood. In the final degenerate age, called the *mappō* in Japan, it would decline altogether. In the late 1250s Japan had faced a series of natural disasters that con-

vinced Nichiren that the *mappō* had indeed begun. In *Risshō ankoko ron* he cites various sutras that describe the disasters that will devastate a country that turns against true Buddhism and slanders the true teaching: famines, epidemics, plagues, fires, floods, civil strife, and foreign invasion. Several of these had already occurred, and Nichiren warns that the other two—civil strife and invasion—are sure to come about if his words are not heeded.

The Mongol invasions as well as other disasters that soon befell Japan seemed to confirm to Nichiren and his followers the truth of Nichiren's words and to increase their sense of urgency in proselytizing. They particularly focused their attacks on the sects currently enjoying the most success in attracting converts—Pure Land Amidism and Zen—denouncing them ever more forcefully as heretical.

Hokke daimoku shō

The *Hokke daimoku shō* (*Treatise on the Recitation of the Title of the* Lotus Sūtra), written in 1264 during a missionary visit to his native province, contains Nichiren's first statement that the title of the *Lotus Sūtra* is the repository of the *Dharma* and mystically encompasses all Buddhist teaching, and that recitation of the phrase "*Namu Myōhōrengekyō*" (*Homage to the* Sutra *of the Lotus of the Marvelous Law*) and meditation on it can lead to enlightenment. In this essay Nichiren advises his correspondent that she should recite the title, even if only once in her life and even if only between repetitions of the *nembutsu*, a competing practice of expression of faith in the Buddha Amida that was spreading rapidly at the time. He asserts that "if someone does not know the real meaning of the *Lotus Sūtra* and does not understand its import," mere recitation of the phrase "*Namu Myōhōrengekyō*" will ensure salvation.

The essay also contains assurances that it is possible for women to attain salvation, a matter of some controversy in Buddhist thought. Schools of Buddhism that emphasized religious discipline had not only denied that women could attain Buddhahood (without first being reborn as men), but had denounced women as impediments to the salvation of men. Basing his interpretation on the account of the enlightenment of the daughter of the serpent king in the *Lotus Sūtra*, Nichiren proclaimed that "enlightenment will be swifter than the great rivers, faster than the rain falling from the sky" for any woman who prays to the *Lotus Sūtra*. He was alone among the religious leaders of his day in asserting that women could attain salvation in this lifetime without rebirth in another form, merely by recognizing their innate Buddhahood as expounded in the *Lotus Sūtra*.

Kaimoku shō

The *Kaimoku shō* (*Opening of the Eyes*), which was written in 1272 during Nichiren's three-year exile on the island of Sado, contains Nichiren's vow to play the role, or, as he termed it, "to live the life," of the *Bodhisattva* Jōgyō (Vishistacāritra), who promises in the *Lotus Sūtra* to proselytize in the *mappō*, and to withstand persecution like the Bodhisattva Jōfukyō (Sadāparibhūta), who was reviled for his faith.

With this essay Nichiren hoped to open the eyes of Japan to the truth of the *Lotus Sūtra* and to the role he himself played in preaching it. After suffering in a dilapidated hut through a cold winter on this remote island, Nichiren sought to encourage both himself and his followers to withstand the persecution they were facing. He discusses Confucianism, Daoism (Taoism), Brahmanism, and the various Buddhist teachings culminating in the *Lotus Sūtra*, and notes that the Buddha Shākyamuni himself stated that the *Lotus Sūtra* was doubted when he first preached the *Sutra*. Those who first heard the Buddha preach the *Lotus Sūtra* wondered if a devil had not taken on the form of a Buddha, so it was not surprising that Nichiren and his followers should be met with disbelief, calumny, and abuse.

The *Lotus Sūtra* predicts three types of enemies of the *Lotus*—ignorant men, heretical monks, and hermits who claim falsely to be walking the True Path—all of whom Nichiren felt he had encountered. Having understood the truth of the *sūtra* and

the role he was destined to play because of that unique understanding, Nichiren felt it incumbent upon him to preach the truth despite persecution, and he urged his followers not to lose faith because he had been exiled and attacked. Precisely because he was suffering the trials predicted in the *Sūtra*, Nichiren was confirmed in the accuracy of his comprehension of the teaching.

In *Kaimoku shō* Nichiren describes "three categories of people all men and women should respect": the sovereign who protects all living beings, the teacher who leads others to enlightenment, and the compassionate, nurturing parent. He concludes that he himself must be sovereign, teacher, father, and mother to the people of Japan, protecting, teaching, and nurturing, and he vows to be the "pillar of Japan, the eyes of Japan, the great ship of Japan."

LAUREL RASPLICA RODD

Further Reading

Translations and Studies

Anesaki, Masaharu. *Nichiren, the Buddhist Prophet.* Cambridge, Mass.: Harvard University Press, 1916. Reprint, Gloucester, Mass.: P. Smith, 1966. Excerpts from Nichiren's writings woven into a narrative account of his life, with a detailed presentation of his revolutionary vision.

Renondeau, Gaston. *La doctrine de Nichiren.* Paris: Presses universitaires de France, 1953. Translations of six of Nichiren's major treatises written during his exile on Sado with an introduction to the teachings of the *Lotus Sūtra* and the Tendai Sect, and an overview of Nichiren's thought.

Rodd, Laurel Rasplica. *Nichiren: Selected Writings.* Honolulu, Hawaii: University Press of Hawaii, 1980. Review of Nichiren's life and teachings with focus on his methods of communication with his followers. Includes translations of *Risshō ankoku ron* and fifteen letters.

Yampolsky, Philip B., ed. Translated by Burton Watson and others. *Selected Writings of Nichiren.* New York: Columbia University Press, 1990. Translations of six treatises and six letters with brief introductions and extensive notes.

IPPEN

Born: 1239, Kitajō City, Ehime Prefecture, Japan
Died: 1289, Kobe City, Japan
Major Works: "Sacred Poem on the Unity of the Ten and One" (1271), "Sacred Poem on the Six Hundred Thousand People" (1274), "Hymn on the Specific Vow [of Amida]" (1287)

Major Ideas

Salvation is achieved through Rebirth in the Pure Land of Amida Buddha.
Rebirth can be experienced equally in this life and at death.
Rebirth in this life is experienced with and for the duration of every invocation of Amida's name or nembutsu.
The Rebirth of each sentient being is at one and the same time the moment at which Amida achieved full Enlightenment.
Rebirth and Enlightenment are both achieved through the absolute power of the six-character nembutsu *or Name.*
The Rebirth of sentient beings and the Enlightenment of Amida are mutually dependent.

Ippen is numbered among the six main religious figures of the Kamakura period (1185–1333). Along with Hōnen and Shinran, he is rightfully classified as Pure Land. But the Pure Land Buddhism he espoused, unlike that of Hōnen and Shinran, maintained that one could achieve Buddhahood—full enlightenment, release from suffering—in this world. This was also taught by Eisai (Yisai), Dōgen, and Nichiren.

Born into a famous warrior family in decline, Ippen spent his entire youth in formal religious training before succeeding to his father's modest estate. After about seven years as a householder, he shaved his head. His subsequent religious life was a series of pilgrimages, retreats, and revelations, which can be mistaken for a random sampling of the smorgasbord of popular religious practices current at the time. However, Ippen is best understood as a mystic: his life was a walking meditation culminating in occasional and varying mystical experiences, which his teachings describe. His uniqueness was his ability to express this experience in terms of existing religious traditions and to make this experience accessible by reconfiguring popular beliefs and practices into the discipline of meditation.

Pure Land Buddhism

Ippen's mysticism is expressed in terms of the esoteric doctrines he had formally studied as a child and youth in the Seizan School of Pure Land Buddhism. Established by Hōnen's disciple Shōkū (1177–1247), the Seizan School maintained very close ties with the Tendai School. Tendai Buddhism teaches the unity of Buddha, all Buddhas, and all other sentient beings (*shujō*), based on the Buddha-nature inherent in all. This Buddha-nature is what makes beings strive for enlightenment and makes enlightenment possible for all. Pure Land Buddhism confirms the principle of universal salvation, but through Rebirth in the Western Pure Land Paradise (*ōjō*) of Amida Buddha, who has vowed to save all beings who invoke or reflect on his name (*nembutsu*). And the Seizan School, identifying Amida with Buddha-nature, maintains the unity of Amida's enlightenment and the Rebirth of all beings past and present through the invocation of Amida's Name.

For Ippen, this sense of unity, of Rebirth in the Pure Land, of seeing Amida and all other Buddhas and *Bodhisattvas* face-to-face, had to be experienced body and soul, and not simply apprehended intellectually. Thus, he represented the tradition of meditation in Pure Land Buddhism, a practice rejected by Hōnen and Shinran.

Pure Land Buddhism emerged first in China. Under Tanluan (T'an-luan) (Japanese: Donran) (476–542), Daochuo (Tao-ch'o) (Japanese: Doshaku) (562–645), and Shandao (Shan-tao) (Japanese: Zendo) (613–681), Pure Land Buddhism advocated Rebirth as the best way for the weak and sinful to achieve salvation in this the Latter Age of Buddhist Doctrine, a period of religious and social decline. One could not rely on one's own efforts (*jiriki*), but only on the strength of another (*tariki*), on Amida Buddha and his Vow. The marked preference for the invocational (chanting Amida's name) over the meditational (reflecting on Amida's name and his Pure Land) was made absolute only in Japan.

Pure Land practices were adopted by the Tendai School in Japan. The Tendai monks Genshin (942 1017) and Hōnen (1133–1212) were principally responsible for the rise and then independence of Pure Land Buddhism. According to Hōnen, the onset of the Latter Age, calculated to have begun in 1052, made meditation impossible and invocation was the practice of choice (*senjaku*)—that is, the exclusive practice. Amida chose it, he argued—so must we.

Pilgrimage and the Nembutsu

Hōnen and Shinran were willing to wait until death before seeing Amida and his entourage coming out to welcome them into the Pure Land (*raigo*). But Ippen sought to find Amida Buddha and other Buddhas in the shrines and temples where they had manifested themselves. In pilgrimage, Ippen found a concrete expression of traditional Pure Land practices, purification and meditation, necessary to achieve or merely to preview Rebirth. Purification was considered necessary for Rebirth. Preserving the precepts and saying the *nembutsu* would negate sins and lead to purity. Maintaining purity keeping one's priestly vows—was proof of Rebirth in a Buddha's land. As *via purgativa*, the pilgrimage purifies the individual before the approach

to the divine. The dangers of the road (and Ippen faced hunger, slept in the rough, and even risked attack) operate like tribal initiation ordeals to prepare an individual for a new state in respect to a previous social life—in this case, for Rebirth in the Pure Land.

The community one forms with fellow pilgrims constitutes another form of purification. Pilgrims tend to share a common lifestyle for the duration, one which creates a group not divided by wealth, status, or goals. This achieved unity is a state of purity because it is not connected with the reality of social life: it is whole (holy), not divisive, not divided. Ippen did not form an order, but a community of wayfarers, of equals on the same spiritual path. Taking his inspiration from a passage in Shantao's *Hymns on the Hanju Meditation*, he called his followers "fellow practitioners" (*dōgyō*).

Pilgrimage, as part of the contemplative life, is a walking meditation. In Chinese and Japanese Pure Land Buddhism, walking meditation consisted of circumambulating an image of Amida for ninety days while reading sutras and chanting the name of Amida; it was meant to result in full visualization of Amida and other Buddhas. It entered the practices of the Tendai School as *jōgyō nembutsu* (perpetual *nembutsu*), *nembutsu zanmai* (*nembutsu* meditation), and *fudan nembutsu* (continuous *nembutsu*). Shōkū promoted the continuous *nembutsu*.

Ippen's version of the continuous *nembutsu* tradition was the dancing *nembutsu* (*odori nembutsu*): going around and around chanting the *nembutsu*. It started in 1282, spontaneously, at the end of a service in a layman's house: this was the first and probably the last "ecstatic" version of this meditation. Although typically analyzed against the background of folk practices involving dancing and funerals, driving out pestilence, and planting crops, the dancing *nembutsu* should also be understood in the context of Tendai/Pure Land walking meditation that was meant to result in a mystical experience.

But the whole of Ippen's life was a walking meditation in the Tendai/Pure Land tradition. As a spiritual exercise called *yugyō*, Ippen's pilgrimages were preparations for visions and for Rebirth in the

Pure Land itself. Pilgrimage culminated for Ippen in communication with the divine, in revelations through Amida Buddha, Amida's incarnations, and other Buddhas and their incarnations. These experiences confirmed him in his doctrines and practices.

Ippen first experienced this confirmation as revelation in 1271 after a pilgrimage to Zenkōji temple in Shinano Province, which enshrines an image believed to be the living body of Amida in this world. He brought back to his native province a picture of the Buddhas Shaka and Amida guiding a poor soul through fire and flood to the safety of Amida's Pure Land. After some eight months of contemplating this picture and invoking Amida's name, Ippen produced the "Sacred Poem on the Unity of the Ten and One."

"Ten" refers to the ten *kalpas* (aeons) ago, when the Indian king Dharmākara (Japanese: Hōzō), an aspirant to Buddhahood (*Bodhisattva*), achieved full enlightenment (*shōgaku*) and became the Buddha Amida after making and fulfilling forty-eight vows to make a Buddhaland or Paradise and bestow upon all who wished or invoked or meditated on his Name Rebirth in this Paradise. "One" refers to the single chanting of the *nembutsu* by which the practitioner achieves Rebirth. The poem presents the relationship between Amida's enlightenment and the individual Rebirths of Sentient Beings (*shujō*). Amida, in his vows, makes two conditions: one for himself, that he will fulfill his vows or not achieve full enlightenment; and one for Sentient Beings, that they reflect on Amida or that the desire to be Reborn rise up in them. For Hōnen and Shinran, this means that, since Amida has indeed achieved full enlightenment, Rebirth at death is promised if not guaranteed. For Ippen, following Shōkū, if Amida has achieved enlightenment, then all Beings past, present, and future (since Amida is the Buddha of infinite life) have already achieved Rebirth. For Ippen especially, Rebirth in Amida's land is achieved in and for the moment of a single *nembutsu*. There is no question of one and many invocations: the very problem suggests effort on the part of the individual, which is not reliance on another, Amida, and therefore not Rebirth as un-

derstood in the Pure Land School. Rebirth is now and not at death, but "now" must be understood from the point of view of the mystic's experience.

Ippen, as a mystic, transcends time. The word Ippen uses for "one," *ichinen*, means a short moment, the very opposite of aeon (*kalpa*). Yet Amida's enlightenment ten aeons ago and the moment of chanting the *nembutsu* are one and the same. Ippen is speaking of an experience, a state of consciousness in which the single moment and the eternity of the kalpa are fused in a *nembutsu*.

The mystic also transcends life and death in his experience. For Shōkū, rebirth in life was achieved through belief (*sokuben ōjō*) while rebirth at death (*tōtoku ōjō*) was manifested in the appearance of Amida and his train to welcome the believer into Paradise. For Ippen, there is no difference in the experience.

The mystic also transcends space. For Shōkū and Ippen, this world and the Pure Land into which one was Reborn were one and the same. As Ippen expresses it, they are equal in terms of seeking enlightenment.

The revelation expressed in this poem left Ippen secure (*anjin*) in his beliefs and doctrines handed down from Shan-tao, Hōnen, and Shōkū. This sense of security would be confirmed by further revelations.

In 1274, trailed by two women and a child, Ippen went to Kumano. On the way, he was tested when a monk refused to accept from him a slip of paper (*fuda*) printed with the invocation to Amida. Because the monk told him that he could not believe, Ippen told him to take it without believing. At Kumano, Ippen had a vision of the main god enshrined there, a manifestation of Amida, who gave him instructions to make no conditions for accepting the *fuda*. Confirmed now in his mission, Ippen sent the women and child back home and formally began his career of handing out these slips of paper (*fusan*). They read: "*Namuamidabutsu rokujūmannin ketsujō ōjō*" or "I entrust my soul to Amida Buddha, rebirth in paradise determined [for] six hundred thousand people." Four characters (*rokujūmannin*) are the first characters in the four lines of the sacred poem that Ippen composed after his revelation.

Sacred Poem on the Six Hundred Thousand People

The "Sacred Poem on the Six Hundred Thousand People" is a statement of Ippen's experience that Amida and the practitioner become one in the chanting of the *nembutsu*. Shōkū, in the Tendai tradition, maintains that Amida and Beings become one at the moment of salvation. This unity is expressed in the six-character Name (*myōgō*), "*Namuamidabutsu*." "*Namu*" (also read as *kimyō*) is the vow of ordinary sentient beings to achieve salvation, to be reborn, to become a Buddha. "*Amidabutsu*" is the vows made and fulfilled by Amida to save Beings; becoming Amida Buddha is the reward for the specific vows (*betsugan*) he made. Thus, all are Buddhas, all are the same through the mutual accomplishment of making and fulfilling vows to become Buddhas.

The poem is Ippen's first statement on the absolute power of the Name to save. Traditionally, from Shan-tao to Hōnen, the Name was "*Amida*" or "*Amida butsu*." For Shōkū, the name was the six-character "*Namuamidabutsu*." The difference was based on the interpretations of the source of the Name's power to save. In the Tendai School the Name was not seen as having a power to save that was superior to other aspects or manifestations of the Buddha. Shandao and Hōnen saw the source of power as Amida's transcendent, eternally blissful body, the reward for merits earned as a *Bodhisattva*; therefore the source of the power of the Name was Amida himself. Shōkū regarded the source of the power of the Name to be in the merits Amida had earned and turned over to sentient beings, not in Amida himself. Amida and sentient beings were mutually dependent in seeking enlightenment and Rebirth.

Thus Ippen saw that something transcending Amida himself was the source of his power, as it was the source of his enlightenment: the six-character Name. Ippen maintains that Dharmākara was saved and became Amida precisely when and because human beings chanted the six-character Name. Both Amida's enlightenment and rebirth for beings were made possible by the six-character Name, *Namuamidabutsu*. All three—Amida, Beings, and Name—are one when the practitioner chants the *nembutsu*. The practitioner becomes Amida; the practitioner becomes *Namuamidabutsu*. Ippen himself was *Namuamidabutsu* because he chanted "*Namuamidabutsu*."

Ippen gave an absolute and transcendent position to the six-character Name. As he saw it, Amida had been rewarded for the six-character Name itself. Amida was not only *within* the Name (Namu Amida butsu), but he was Amida *by* the Name—the Name or *nembutsu* was said for Amida, too, who is Amida only as long as beings say the Name. As the god of Kumano said to him, "The Rebirth in paradise of mankind was determined with *Namuamidabutsu* when Amida attained enlightenment ten *kalpas* ago."

The power of the Name was present in the slips of paper printed with the Name. Although one can read the "six hundred thousand people" as the number Ippen initially intended to save, one must also recognize that the characters for "six hundred thousand people" are the first characters of the four lines of the poem: with them, Ippen was also declaring the absolute power of the Name. Printed on the slips of paper, the Name works in and of itself. One does not need even to chant the *nembutsu*; the full benefit is obtained merely by coming in contact with it. This is the ultimate expression of "reliance on the power of the other." As Ippen has it elsewhere, the Name chants the Name, the *nembutsu* chants the *nembutsu*.

Distributing these paper slips (*fusan*), Ippen acted as if he indeed were *Namuamidabutsu*. He saw his mission, as mandated by the god of Kumano, to save the Beings of this world without making any conditions—whatever personal reservations he might have had about believers and nonbelievers. Distribution was to be with as little consciousness (a form of self-reliance) as chanting the *nembutsu* itself: the *nembutsu* could not be chanted with any conscious calculation of benefits or results—even Rebirth in the Pure Land.

This poem expresses the meaning of Ippen's name. The word, like its variant *ichinen*, has two meanings: the single invocation of Amida's name, the single *nembutsu*; and the single moment of a *nembutsu*. Ippen is *Namuamidabutsu*, which is Amida, which is rebirth in the Pure Land; it is life, it is death, it is transcending life and death as experienced in the moment the *nembutsu* is chanted. "Ippen" expresses the all-inclusive sense of unity experienced as a mystic.

"Hymn on the Specific Vow [of Amida]"

The "Hymn on the Specific Vow [of Amida]" was composed in 1287 in Harima, when Ippen visited the shrine to Hachiman (also a manifestation of Amida) at Matsubara. Simply put, the hymn describes the suffering of human life, the inability to look to the Buddha in any form for salvation because of the enormous sinfulness of Beings, and the sole opportunity for salvation in the Name.

Again, the Name is posited as the primary and most efficacious way to obliterate sins. The first *nembutsu* results from suffering; the last *nembutsu*, death, ends suffering. The end of suffering is to become a Buddha, which is *Namuamidabutsu*. Life is death; every minute is death; every *nembutsu* is the last *nembutsu*; every *nembutsu* is Rebirth in the Pure Land. Abandon everything, even thought of Rebirth, and say the *nembutsu* continuously. For Ippen, life was a continuous *nembutsu*. The community he founded was dedicated to preserving a constant state of Rebirth.

Speaking in the language of the Pure Land tradition in which he had been educated, Ippen offered no new revelation. In fact, his affirmation of the Tendai and Seizan teachings led to the power and prestige during the next three centuries of the order that claimed him as founder. What Ippen offered was a religious path in which traditional practices such as pilgrimage gave concrete expression to highly esoteric teachings on the meaning and method of achieving Rebirth in this life.

S. A. THORNTON

Further Reading

Foard, James Harlan. *Ippen and Popular Buddhism in Kamakura Japan*. Ph.D. dissertation, Stanford University, 1977. Ann Arbor, Mich.: Xerox University Microfilms. The first and still the best study of Ippen's life and place in Japanese Buddhism.

Kaufman, Laura S. *Ippen Hijirie: Artistic and Literary Sources in a Buddhist Handscroll Painting of Thirteenth-Century Japan*. Ph.D. dissertation, New York University, 1980. Ann Arbor, Mich.: University Microfilms International. An important study of the production of the first and most important biography of Ippen.

Hirota, Dennis. *No Abode: The Record of Ippen*. Kyoto: Ryukoku University, 1986. A translation of the *Ippen Shonin Goroku*, a compilation of Ippen's thought, with a very helpful introductory essay.

Turner, Victor W. and Edith Turner. *Image and Pilgrimage in Christian Culture: Anthropological Perspectives*. New York: Columbia University Press, 1978. The present chapter is heavily indebted to this work for its identification of pilgrimage with meditation for the analysis of Ippen's understanding of wayfaring.

Turner, Victor W. *Process, Performance, and Pilgrimage: A Study in Comparative Symbology*. Delhi: Concept, 1979. The present chapter is also indebted to this seminal work for its characterization of pilgrimage.

KITABATAKE CHIKAFUSA

Born: 1293
Died: 1354
Major Work: *Jinnō Shōtōki* (*Chronicle of the Direct Descent of Gods and Sovereigns*)

Major Ideas

Japan is a divine land, superior to other countries because it has been ruled by an unbroken dynastic line since its founding.
Commencement of Japan's Age of the Gods antedates China's.
Japan's line of emperors will rule eternally.
The ideal government is an oligarchy of courtiers governing in the name of a nonacting emperor.

Born into a high-ranking family at the imperial court of Japan, Kitabatake Chikafusa served Emperors Godaigo (r. 1318–39) and Gomurakami (r. 1339–68) during a tumultuous age of change in Japanese history that witnessed the overthrow of the country's first military government (the Kamakura Shogunate) in 1331, Godaigo's unsuccessful "imperial restoration" (the Kemmu Restoration) of 1333–36, and commencement of the protracted "war between the Northern and Southern Courts," 1336–92.

Establishment of the Kamakura Shogunate in 1185 marked the start of the medieval age of Japanese history, when warriors (*samurai*) displaced courtiers as the rulers of the land. The displacement, however, was gradual. At the time of Chikafusa's birth in 1293, the Shogunate in Kamakura completely dominated the imperial court in Kyoto politically, but the court, consisting of imperial and courtier families, still possessed considerable economic wealth in land and hence the possibility of reviving its political fortunes. Apart from the Shogunate itself, the major obstacle to such revival was the division—which had occurred two decades earlier—of the imperial family into two contending lines that descended from brothers who had both served as emperor. The line of the older brother was called the "senior line" and that of the younger brother the "junior line."

Godaigo, into whose service Chikafusa entered, acceded to the throne in 1318 in accordance with an arrangement whereby the emperorship alter-nated every ten years between the senior and junior lines. A member of the junior line, Godaigo became determined to end the practice of alternate succession and to transmit the emperorship to his own descendants. Opposed by the Shogunate, he schemed to overthrow it. In 1333, after several years of fighting between *samurai* who backed Godaigo's loyalist cause and the supporters of the Shogunate, the Shogunate was destroyed and Godaigo announced the reinstitution of "direct imperial rule."

But Godaigo's imperial restoration failed to deal effectively with the most pressing problem of the day—the struggle among warrior families in the provinces for the control of land—and in 1336 his restoration government was overthrown by the military chieftain Ashikaga Takauji. Fleeing from Kyoto to Yoshino in the mountainous region to the south, Godaigo established there what came to be known as the "Southern Court." Meanwhile, Ashikaga Takauji had a member of the senior branch of the imperial family appointed emperor at the court in Kyoto—now called the "Northern Court"—and founded a new Shogunate in the same city (the Ashikaga or Muromachi Shogunate). Thus began the period of war between the Northern and Southern Courts.

Jinnō Shōtōki

Kitabatake Chikafusa served the Southern Court and became its principal leader after Godaigo's death in 1339 and the accession to the Southern throne of the youthful Gomurakami. He wrote the book for which he is famous, *Jinnō Shōtōki*, in the early years of Gomurakami's reign. A record or chronicle of Japan from its mythical origins in the Age of the Gods to Gomurakami's accession, *Jinnō Shōtōki* is one of two major interpretative works on Japanese history written during the medieval age. The other is Jien's *Gukanshō* (1219), composed a century earlier.

Jinnō Shōtōki must be seen, first of all, within the context of the Shinto revival that began in Japan during the late thirteenth century. For centuries Buddhism had been the dominant intellectual force among Japan's religions; Shinto—although it consisted of the religious beliefs native to Japan before the introduction of Buddhism from the Asian continent and provided the basis for Japan's imperial institution—had been intellectually stagnant over the same time period. But when the Mongol rulers of China undertook two invasions of Japan in 1274 and 1281, Shinto belief was powerfully rekindled in the conviction that the typhoons that inflicted great damage on both Mongol invasion fleets and forced them to return to the continent were *kamikaze*, or "divine winds," sent by the gods (*kami*) of Shinto. Whereas Buddhism had long been regarded as the "protector of the state," Shinto now began to assume that role.

"Japan . . . the Divine Land"

The idea that Shinto was the new protector of the state marked the first phase of the Shinto revival in the early medieval age. The second phase unfolded in the early fourteenth century and was a product of the dynastic dispute in the imperial family discussed above. Discord over succession to the emperorship focused attention anew on the central myth of Japanese history: the Shinto belief that the imperial family had been mandated by the Sun Goddess, Amaterasu, to rule Japan eternally. In the famous opening lines of *Jinnō Shōtōki*, Kitabatake Chikafusa proclaimed:

> Great Japan is the divine land . . . bequeathed [by the Sun Goddess] to her descendants to

rule eternally. Only in our country is this true; there are no similar examples in other countries. This is why our country is called the divine land.

> (VARLEY, 1980)

Thus in *Jinnō Shōtōki*, the most important writing of the medieval Shinto revival, Chikafusa defined Japan as a unique "divine land" (*shinkoku*) because it had been ruled by an unbroken line of sovereigns from its founding by a descendant of the Sun Goddess. Other countries, such as India and China, were inferior because they had often undergone dynastic changes and—especially in the case of India—had also suffered protracted periods of disorder without centralized rule. Chikafusa further asserted Japan's superiority to China by presenting a genealogy of Japanese gods preceding the Sun Goddess, Amaterasu, whose origins were of greater antiquity than those of the putative founders of China.

Chikafusa's chronicle of Japan is organized by reigns, first of gods and then of human sovereigns, and contains much discussion of the process of imperial succession through the ages. By stressing succession and the Shinto belief that the imperial dynasty would rule eternally, Chikafusa rejected the prevalent Buddhist idea—reflected, for example, in *Gukanshō*—that the world had entered a dark and degenerate age of the "end of the Buddhist Law" and that even the imperial dynasty was in danger of extinction.

It is commonly believed that Chikafusa wrote *Jinnō Shōtōki* primarily to argue the legitimacy of the Southern Court over the Northern Court in the dynastic dispute of his time. Yet Chikafusa actually said little in *Jinnō Shōtōki* about the issue of legitimacy in this dispute, probably because he and most of his contemporaries simply accepted as fact that Ashikaga Takauji had mistreated Emperor Godaigo, who never willingly abdicated, and that the Southern Court was therefore the legitimate seat of imperial authority. In short, Chikafusa apparently did not think that the question of the Southern Court's legitimacy required much argumentation.

Rather than concerning himself with imperial legitimacy, Chikafusa devoted his attention in *Jinnō Shōtōki* mainly to the revival of rulership by the court. The ideal government, to his mind, was the kind that had existed during the middle Heian period—the tenth and early eleventh centuries—when the court was administered chiefly by members of the Fujiwara family acting as regents to the emperor. As understood by Chikafusa, this was essentially an oligarchic form of government headed by a nonacting emperor. Since Chikafusa himself belonged to one of the ranking court families that would participate in any such oligarchic government if it were effectively revived, his argument for its reestablishment as the true center of government in the country clearly served the interests of his social class.

Although Chikafusa wanted a revived oligarchic government at court with an emperor who need only appoint the right ministers and then leave all affairs to them, Emperor Godaigo sought, in his imperial restoration, to establish himself as an absolute monarch. The fact that Chikafusa played no significant role in the restoration government during its brief life was very likely because he disapproved of Godaigo's autocratic ways. Chikafusa became active politically only after the establishment of the Southern Court at Yoshino, when Godaigo was no longer in a position to assert himself so forcefully as a ruler.

The Rise of the Warrior Class

Chikafusa devoted much space in *Jinnō Shōtōki* to discussing the rise of a warrior class to power in the medieval age. His belief was that the courtier class, in seeking to regain control of the country, should assume a military function and thus become warrior–courtiers. He extolled as a model of the warrior–courtier his own son Akiie, who led an army in fighting against Ashikaga Takauji after the failure of the Kemmu Restoration.

Chikafusa was a political reactionary. Although he was realistic in stressing the need for courtiers, if they aspired to power, to acquire military skills, his rigid insistence on the maintenance of traditional class distinctions—for example, his demand that warriors should unquestioningly accept subordination to courtiers—made little sense during an age when warriors were in fact in the process of stripping the imperial court and the courtier class of the last vestiges of national rulership. *Jinnō Shōtōki*, and hence Chikafusa's thought, exerted far less influence on his contemporaries than it did on Japanese of later ages. In modern Japan until the end of World War II, *Jinnō Shōtōki* was regarded as one of the principal repositories of the ideology of imperial loyalism.

PAUL VARLEY

Further Reading

Varley, H. Paul, trans. *A Chronicle of Gods and Sovereigns:* Jinno Shotoki *of Kitabatake Chikafusa.* New York: Columbia University Press, 1980. Introduction to and translation of *Jinnō Shōtōki.*

———. *Imperial Restoration in Medieval Japan.* New York: Columbia University Press, 1971. Study of the Kemmu Restoration and the war between the Northern and Southern Courts.

FUJIWARA SEIKA

Born: 1561, Harima Province, Japan
Died: 1619
Major Works: *Bunshō tattoku kōryō, Chiyo motogusa* (1591), *Kana seiri* (*Plainly Written Truths and Principles*), *Seika mondō* (*Seika's Dialogues*), *Suntetsu roku* (*A Record of Pithy Sayings*) (1606), *Daigaku yōryaku* (*Epitome of the Great Learning*) (1619)

Major Ideas

Neo-Confucian ideas should serve as the official court political philosophy.
Neo-Confucian ideas should be applied to the goal of spiritual and moral cultivation.
The Neo-Confucian teachings must be experienced in order for self-cultivation to occur.
An experience of inner enlightenment results from following and practicing Neo-Confucian teachings.
The different Neo-Confucian schools are fundamentally similar.
Buddhism must be rejected as a false teaching removed from the daily concerns of human existence and therefore destructive of the duties that regulate human affairs.
Human beings are innately endowed with illustrious virtue.
Neo-Confucianism and Shinto have the same essence and teach the same virtues.
Human society is hierarchical.
The ruler must cultivate the Confucian virtues in order to rule in a just and benevolent manner.
Learning should be in the hands of secular, rational Neo-Confucians, not Buddhist scholars.

Fujiwara Seika, a Zhu Xi (Chu Hsi) School (Shushigaku) Neo-Confucian scholar, lived during the time of transition from the turbulent Muromachi period (1333–1600) to the peace of the Tokugawa period (1603–1868). His social and political ideas became one of the foundations for the Tokugawa Shogunate (military government). Seika became a Zen monk from an early age but eventually abandoned Buddhism to concentrate on Chinese thought and literature, seeking to establish Neo-Confucian morality as the ethical foundation for government and society. This marked the beginnings of an important shift away from Buddhist priests as the epitome of learning and scholarship, to that of the Neo-Confucian scholar. He was an occasional adviser to the military government of Tokugawa Ieyasu (1542–1616). His most famous student, Hayashi Razan (1583–1657), became an important Neo-Confucian adviser to the Tokugawa *shōguns* (military rulers).

Seika was born in Harima Province into the aristocratic Reizei branch of the Fujiwara family, who were noted specialists in classical Japanese poetry (*waka*). Seika, himself a well-known poet, was a twelfth-generation descendant of Fujiwara Teika, the great thirteenth-century poet. Because of his family connections, Seika was known to powerful warrior leaders.

Seika studied Buddhism and Chinese thought and literature from the age of seven at Zen temples in Kyoto. He held the rank of chief seat (*shuso*) at the Shokokuji, a Rinzai Zen temple that was part of the *gozan* or Five Mountains temple system, remaining a monk until age thirty-seven. His interests eventually turned from Buddhism to Neo-Confucian thought, which had originally been introduced into Japan by Zen monks in the Kamakura period (1185–1333). During the Muromachi period, Zen and Neo-Confucian ideas were studied together within the Zen *gozan* (Five Mountain) temple system. Such ideas as Confucianism, Neo-Confucianism (both the Zhu Xi and Wang Yang-ming [Yōmeigaku] Schools), and Zen were all influences on Seika's thought. In his day,

Buddhist priests were the holders of knowledge and learning—to be learned was to be a Buddhist, especially Zen, priest.

As Seika became increasingly interested in things Chinese, he attempted to travel to China in 1597, but a storm forced him to give up this journey. His interest in China led him to associations with Chinese envoys to Japan and with Koreans who had been taken prisoner during Japanese invasions of Korea. One Korean captive was the scholar Kang Hang (1567–1618), who influenced Seika's interest in the Neo-Confucian ideas of the Chinese philosopher Zhu Xi. Together they edited the "Confucian Classics" on the basis of Neo-Confucian ideas. Seika was aware from his study of China that Neo-Confucian ideas had supplanted Buddhism as the basis for Chinese education and government. Buddhism was held to be a negative doctrine in a world of pressing secular concerns. Seika left the Buddhist monastic life around 1598 to concentrate on his Neo-Confucian interests.

Because of his contacts with powerful warriors, Seika's Neo-Confucianism gained political support from Tokugawa authorities, particularly Tokugawa Ieyasu, the founder of the Tokugawa Shogunate, who periodically attended Seika's lectures in Kyoto. In 1600 Seika had an audience with Ieyasu. He appeared in the attire of a Confucian literatus in order to impress upon Ieyasu that he was a man of learning even if he was no longer a Buddhist priest. Seika declined an invitation to serve in Ieyasu's government, although he did serve as an adviser to him from time to time. Ieyasu found in Neo-Confucian thought, especially the ideas of Zhu Xi expounded by Seika and his disciple Hayashi Razan, a basis for social control and political legitimation. Ieyasu wanted to establish a new social and political order. To this end, Ieyasu wanted the *samurai* to resemble the Chinese scholar–official. Thus *samurai* were to be proficient in both the martial arts and in Neo-Confucian thought.

Seika attempted to establish Neo-Confucianism as an independent philosophical school by liberating it from the Zen Buddhist monk–scholars who had originally studied and disseminated its ideas. He declared that Buddhism was removed from the daily concerns of human existence and therefore destructive of the duties that regulate human affairs. He thus declared Buddhism a false teaching. Nevertheless, and perhaps not surprisingly—given Seika's experiences as a Buddhist monk—Buddhist ideas do influence his Neo-Confucian thought.

Despite Seika's eventual break with Buddhist ideas, he always preferred the reclusive life to the public spotlight of government service. Seika, as a member of the Kyoto aristocracy, looked upon the warrior class with contempt. This explains, in part, his refusal to serve in the warrior government. In 1615 he retired to the mountains north of Kyoto, supported by students and friends. Although Seika eschewed the bureaucratic life himself, he produced important students, such as Hayashi Razan, who became influential Neo-Confucian thinkers, teachers, and governmental advisers.

Principle and "Ether"

Seika's thought was based on his interpretation of Zhu Xi's Neo-Confucian ideas. Briefly summarized, Zhu Xi argued that Heaven, Earth, and humankind are regulated by a universal Principle (Chinese: *li*; Japanese: *ri*). Principle is the spiritual aspect of the universe. The material world is composed of "ether" (Chinese: *qi/ch'i*; Japanese: *ki*). All people have Principle as an innate part of their being, but ether is uniquely different for each individual and accounts for human differences, especially moral differences.

A person's moral character is measured by his or her ability to fulfill social and familial duties in the proper way. This ability is determined by the purity/impurity and clarity/turbidity of their ether. Since the ether of the sages is pure, their Principle is therefore directly revealed. The ether of ordinary humans has some degree of impurity and turbidity, thereby generating desires that obfuscate Principle and lead to evil. The quality of a person's ether is not permanently fixed, however. Those who eradicate the impurity and turbidity from their ether will revert to their original nature based on Principle.

Thus the moral character determined by ether can be cultivated, which in turn allows Principle to clearly emerge and sagehood to be attained.

Morality, then, is necessary in order to clear up the impurity and turbidity of the ether. This is accomplished by cultivating what Neo-Confucians refer to as "the extension of knowledge through the investigation of things." Understanding Principle allows one to live in accord with it and to follow the Way of Heaven. Adherence to such ethical injunctions as the Five Relationships (*gorin*: lord and minister, parent and child, husband and wife, elder and junior, friend and friend) maintains an ordered society that reflects an ordered universe. The moral activity of individuals is necessary to the actualization of a just and moral society and government. All must attempt to cultivate themselves, from the emperor to the lowliest subject.

Spiritual and Moral Cultivation

Seika was particularly concerned with directing Neo-Confucian ideas to the goal of spiritual and moral cultivation. He was less interested in their application to the new political and social order of early Tokugawa Japan. Seika's life and teachings were punctuated by a tension between his Buddhist reclusive and contemplative side on the one hand, and on the other hand the necessity for political involvement in order to implement Neo-Confucian thought as the foundation for a just government. Thus he moves between the inward quest for self-cultivation and the external application of Neo-Confucian thought to social and political issues. His early Buddhist training, and his roots as a Kyoto aristocrat and poet, were juxtaposed against the political reality of rule by warriors who were to benefit from his promotion and teaching of Neo-Confucian morality and social hierarchy. Seika's thought thus blends ethical and spiritual concerns.

Seika believed that one had to experience the Neo-Confucian teachings, not simply treat them as an intellectual exercise. This experience, as explained by Seika, has an almost meditative quality about it. He said that scholars must experience the truth for themselves and thereby cultivate their minds. Such an experience leads to a stillness of mind, reminiscent of the Zen notion of mental cultivation, that allows one to suddenly and fully know the highest truth. Seika was suspect of those who feigned virtuousness as a cover for ulterior motives of personal gain.

There are, then, religious aspects to Seika's Neo-Confucianism. He talked about the attainment of "untrammeled spontaneity" (*sharaku*), an experience of inner enlightenment that results from following and practicing Neo-Confucian teachings. One mean for attaining this experience, according to Seika, is to enter into a relationship with the "Confucian Classics" such that the mind of the individual interpenetrates with the truths the "Classics" teach. Seika was, in effect, combining the Zen Buddhist quest for enlightenment with the Confucian goal of sagehood. Seika found this mystical Neo-Confucianism expressed especially in the poems of Wang Yang-ming, to which he was particularly drawn. Thus Seika was influenced not only by Zhu Xi's Neo-Confucianism, but also by the so-called "idealistic" Neo-Confucian School of Wang Yang-ming.

Seika, unlike his student Hayashi Razan, wanted to underscore the fundamental similarities between different schools within the Confucian tradition and to contrast these with ideas that were antithetical to Neo-Confucianism. For this reason, and because he was attracted to Wang Yang-ming's poetic spirituality, Seika argued that the orthodoxy of Zhu Xi and the idealist Neo-Confucian thought of Wang Yang-ming were compatible. Further, he argued that Confucius and Mencius should be venerated, while Daoism (Taoism) and Buddhism are to be rejected. He also viewed Confucian cosmological principles to be operant in the realm of social and political discourse, which he contrasted with the private aspect of human desires.

Seika's *Chiyo motogusa* (1591) explains the fundamental principles of his Neo-Confucian thought. It was written for his mother, who was a devout Buddhist. In this text he explains the significance of such key Neo-Confucian terms as humility (*kenjo*), "illustrious virtue" (*meitoku*), sincerity (*makoto*), heart or essence (*kokoro*), and reverence (*kei*). He also explains the meaning of the Five Constant Virtues (*gojō*): humaneness (*jin*), righteousness (*gi*), propriety (*rei*), wisdom (*chi*), and faithfulness (*shin*), and the Five Relationships (*gorin*): lord and minister, parent and child, husband and wife, elder and junior, friend and friend.

According to Seika, human beings are endowed with "illustrious virtue" (*meitoku*), that is, absolute goodness free from all evil thought. A sage, he says, is one who polishes illustrious virtue so that it regains the clarity it originally had. Like Zhu Xi, Seika says that when desires arise in human beings, virtue declines. But because *meitoku* is innate in human beings it can be cultivated. Remove desire, likened to a clouded mirror, and illustrious virtue will reappear, likened to a clear mirror. Thus Seika teaches that if one clarifies illustrious virtue, exhibits sincerity (*makoto*), and upholds the Five Constant Virtues and the Five Relationships, then they will attain sagehood in accord with the Way of Heaven.

Seika attempted to square Neo-Confucian ideas with Shinto theology, thereby giving Shinto an intellectual foundation. In the *Chiyo motogusa* he equates Confucianism and Shintō, arguing that they are essentially the same, just with different names. This is true, Seika argues, because Neo-Confucianism and Shinto share the same *kokoro*, heart or essence. Both have as their ultimate objectives the rectification of the heart and benevolence and compassion towards all people.

Seika's ideas about the moral life and how to live in accord with it are found in the *Suntetsu roku* (*A Record of Pithy Sayings*) (1606) and the *Daigaku yōryaku* (*Epitome of the Great Learning*) (1619). Both of these works were written in response to requests by feudal lords (*daimyō*). The *Suntetsu roku* is a commentary on thirty-two sayings taken from the "Classics." In it Seika discusses fundamental Confucian concepts. Of particular interest is his discussion of the hierarchical nature of human beings. Seika distinguishes between the person who follows the principles of the Way (*dōri*), thereby establishing peace and harmony as a result

of knowing and following one's duty (*giri*) and station in life, and the person who ignores the Way in quest for personal gain and profit at the expense of others. He held that one must first cultivate the ethical Way within oneself—it will then have a cultivating effect on other people.

In government the same ideas also apply because, according to Seika, the principles that operate in an individual are the same that operate in the external world. Thus the propriety (*rei*) that governs human activity is in fact a principle of the Way. Seika thus posits the notion that the ruler must cultivate the Confucian virtues in order to rule in a just and benevolent manner, that is, in accord with the Way of Heaven. In general, Japanese Zhu Xi Neo-Confucianism stressed the notion that Principle and Heaven are connected. Thus they could by extension argue that since all things are governed by Principle, the emperor, as the go-between between Heaven and Earth, governs in accordance with Principle. It is necessary, therefore, for people to obey the imperial will. Seika believed that if the government acted with benevolence it was ethically correct and should therefore be successful.

The *Daigaku yōryaku* (*Epitome of the Great Learning*) is a treatise based on some of Seika's lectures on the Confucian classic the *Great Learning*. In a Zen-like, non-dualistic interpretation, Seika argues that the *Great Learning* does away with any distinction between oneself and others. This occurs because "illustrious virtue" (*meitoku*), innate within the Five Relationships that maintain an ordered society, consists of the care and nurturing of all people. For Seika, ideally one needs to cultivate the ability to maintain a peaceful, still mind in the midst of worldly activities. Thus the warrior or bureaucrat needs to fulfill their duties with a quietude and selflessness that maintains an ordered, hierarchical society that by extension nurtures the people. This selfless activity is characterized by Seika as non-dualistic thought. Seika's spiritual virtues are tempered by his admonition that if the people do not obey these teachings, then the government can coerce compliance through force and punishment.

WILLIAM E. DEAL

Further Reading

Translation

Tsunoda, Ryusaku, Wm. Theodore de Bary, and Donald Keene, comps. *Sources of Japanese Tradition*. Vol. 1. New York: Columbia University Press, 1964 (1958), pp. 336–341. A useful selection of Fujiwara Seika's writings in translation.

Related Studies

Maruyama, Masao. *Studies in the Intellectual History of Tokugawa Japan*. Translated by Mikiso Hane. Princeton, N.J.: Princeton University Press; Tokyo: University of Tokyo Press, 1974. Although some of the premises of this classic work have been challenged by more recent scholarship, it nevertheless provides a useful overview of major Tokugawa period thinkers and ideas, including Fujiwara Seika.

Ooms, Herman. *Tokugawa Ideology: Early Constructs, 1570–1680*. Princeton, N.J.: Princeton University Press, 1985. This important study questions many of the long-standing assumptions about the dominance of Neo-Confucianism on Tokugawa-period thought through an examination of the diverse ideas that constituted Tokugawa state ideology. Includes coverage of the life and thought of Fujiwara Seika.

SUZUKI SHŌSAN

Born: 1579, Mikawa Province, Japan
Died: 1655
Major Works: *Banmin tokuyō* (*Right Action for All*) (1661), *Ninin bikuni* (*Two Nuns*) (1664), *Roankyō* (*Donkey Saddle Bridge*) (1648), *Mōanjō* (*A Safe Staff for the Blind*) (1619)

Major Ideas

Daily work is religious practice leading to salvation.
Religious meaning is found in the selfless pursuit of one's occupation.
Appropriate religious practices allow one to maintain worldly duties and responsibilities.
The government should assist in restoring Buddhism's true meaning and significance.
There is no difference between worldly teachings and the Buddha's Dharma—*to act properly in the world is to act according to the* Dharma.
People owe a debt of gratitude to their lord as protector and peacemaker of the state, and for establishing a just and ordered society.
Fear of death can be overcome by "practicing death."

Suzuki Shōsan was a warrior-turned-Zen-Buddhist-priest who combined Buddhist practice with a strong social ethic. He lived during the transition to the Tokugawa warrior government, which was concerned with unifying Japan and establishing a centralized government. Shōsan's ethic was at least partly directed to establishing a moral foundation for Tokugawa-period Japan. His *samurai* background, with its stress on loyalty to one's lord and the selfless conduct of one's duty, is clearly evident in his emphasis on religious practice conducted within the context of daily work. Thus Shōsan eschewed the Buddhist notion of the renunciation of the world in favor of acting selflessly in the world. The audience for his ideas consisted primarily of lower-ranking *samurai* and common people, but the ruling authorities clearly stood to benefit from a workforce that would labor without concern for personal gain.

Shōsan was born into a *samurai* family from Mikawa Province. As a warrior he fought at the Battle of Sekigahara (1600)—which gave Tokugawa Ieyasu (1542–1616) control of Japan—and during the sieges of Osaka Castle in 1614 and 1615. In 1620, after a stint as a guard officer at Osaka Castle, he took the tonsure as a Zen monk, but because he refused to have a master, he never was

fully a part of either the Sōtō or Rinzai Zen traditions. He was, nevertheless, sympathetic to the Sōtō School, with which his family was affiliated. He returned to the former fief, the Asuke domain, that his family was connected with and spent the next twenty-eight years there, spending the final seven years of his life in Edo.

In the Asuke domain Shōsan built a temple network that included Sōtō Zen temples as well as a Pure Land temple. One of the agendas of this temple system was to teach against Christianity, which had gained some important converts in this area of Japan and was perceived as a threat by some in the ruling class. Thus Shōsan was involved with the attempt by the *bakufu* (military government) to shore up its political control over Japan.

Later in Edo Shōsan expounded his ideas to people regardless of their social background. He had a particular following among warrior-class families. He is noted for his attitude toward death—he wanted to live without any fear of death. He also wanted to get his version of Zen Buddhism accepted as the national morality by getting the shogun to embrace his teachings and implement them throughout Japan. This he never succeeded in achieving. His ideas never led to the founding of a formal Buddhist school.

Shōsan's Occupational Ethic

Shōsan taught an occupational ethic leading to enlightenment. He believed that work performed as a warrior, farmer, artisan, or merchant (the four Tokugawa-period social classes) could lead to enlightenment. Thus he connected his occupational ethic to the actual conditions of people in society, offering up the possibility of enlightenment outside the control of the Buddhist monastic hierarchy. Some scholars of Shōsan's life and writings refer to this as a Japanese version of Max Weber's notion of the "inner-worldly asceticism" indicative of the Protestant work ethic. The idea is that although one is *in* the world, one is not *of* the world if one's actions in the world are performed for a higher, transcendent purpose. Weber's notion of inner-worldly asceticism suggests that transformation to self-abnegation can be conceived in terms of commitment to the quest for salvation that occurs physically within the confines of society, but which spiritually has transcended those very boundaries. One participates in the world but does so only in order to attain a higher religious state, not to amass wealth and power.

In light of this ethic, Shōsan would not ordain monks. He believed that one could gain salvation through one's occupation and could therefore dispense with the rituals that required a specific institutional identity or the backing of the Buddhist monastic tradition. Everyday work itself becomes one's religious practice. This occupational ethic, when viewed in the context of his times—that is, the new political order of the early Tokugawa period—can be seen as a way for the common people to find a meaningful (and religious) existence within this new order. Commoners could play a religiously sanctioned and hence important role in the new Tokugawa order. Conversely, the Tokugawa ruling elite potentially had a powerful rhetoric for keeping people anchored to the work required by their social status.

Shōsan strongly believed that Zen Buddhism was important to the new society being crafted in the early seventeenth century and especially more so than Neo-Confucianism. Shōsan reinterpreted Zen in order for it to be effective in this new social ethic he was trying to formulate. His Zen was eclectic—he also advocated the Pure Land practice of recitation of the *nembutsu*, the chanting the name of Amida Buddha. Shōsan's criterion for the selection of appropriate religious practices was that they must allow one to maintain one's worldly duties and responsibilities. This was not an eremetic ideal, a call for retirement from the world, but rather a reminder of the possibility of religious practice conducted within the context of everyday existence. Thus, despite his self-identification with Zen, he most often advocated the practice of reciting the name of Amida Buddha (*nembutsu*), an easy practice that does not require long hours sitting in a meditation hall. Institutional Buddhism, with its monastic requirements, was therefore rejected by Shōsan as being without worldly benefit. Shōsan viewed with contempt those who sought after Buddhist rank and learning, and saw such pursuits as a source of evil in the world. He believed that the government should assist in restoring Buddhism's true meaning and significance for the world after the many years in which Buddhism had been wrongly understood and taught.

In accordance with these ideas, Shōsan was also suspicious of Buddhist philosophical thought because it took people away from practice in everyday life and concentrated unduly on the intellectual. The intellectual was of dubious value for Shōsan. In addition, Shōsan was concerned that the goal of enlightenment overly emphasized some future accomplishment rather than the necessity, as he saw it, of concentrating one's mind on the present so that one can act effectively in the world, now. Shōsan argued that there was no difference between worldly teachings and the Buddha's *Dharma*, that is, there was no distinction between *buppō* (the Law of the Buddha) and *ōbō* (the laws of humankind). Thus, to act properly in the world is to act according to the *Dharma*.

The important implication of this view is that Shōsan was able to use it as a way of supporting the military government and its new social order—one had to achieve enlightenment within the context of the world so that there was no other ground for action other than this world. There was, in more modern terms, no distinction between sacred and profane. Spiritual benefits derived from everyday work were interfused with the material benefits that work had for society as a whole.

Shōsan found great ethical and spiritual import in fulfilling one's moral obligations that naturally occurred from the generosity (*on*) that is given to one by Heaven and Earth, one's lord, one's teachers, and one's parents. Of particular importance for Shōsan's agenda was the debt of gratitude that one owed to one's lord as protector and peacemaker of the state and for establishing a just and ordered society. Thus Shōsan viewed the Tokugawa *bakufu* as a "sagely government" (*seiō seiji*) that established an ordered society from which one could successfully engage in proper ethicoreligious practice. Shōsan viewed the sufferings of others—for instance the suffering caused by poverty—as the result of their karmic past and not the result of government oppression or flawed policy.

Shosan was attempting, in part, to establish a social ethic relevant to society at large but one based on a *samurai* ideal of unswerving duty to one's lord and also on the idea that what one had in the world was a direct result of the generosity of one's lord. Moreover, from a warrior perspective, one owed one's very life to one's lord to the extent that the warrior must be willing to sacrifice body and life for one's lord. There were many debts of gratitude (*on*) owed in one's life to one's lord. By extension, duty and self-sacrifice were viewed by Shōsan as applying to all people no matter what their occupation or social status. Shōsan coupled this social ethic, obviously based in Confucian relational ideals, with the Buddhist view that the purpose of religious practice is to lose one's clinging and desirous ego and instead to live a selfless life.

Work as the Means to Salvation

Shōsan connected everyday actions to Buddhist religious practice. For instance, Shōsan called worldly service a form of religious asceticism vastly superior, for example, to the life of a monk. This, in part, was why Shōsan refused to ordain monks—he did not want people retiring from the world or thinking that there was some greater spiritual benefit to such activity. Similarly, he valued the warrior life over the monastic life because it involved service in the world, rather than the renunciation of the monastic. Thus Shōsan believed that one should seek to perfect oneself from within the occupation inherited from one's family. Service is the way to the Buddhist Path and is a part of the will of Heaven. To seek to change one's occupation—for instance, by becoming a monastic—is to violate the will of Heaven.

This selfless attention to one's occupational place in the world is also a means to a stable, if oppressive, society in which there is little formal allowance for social mobility. Shōsan, however, holds out the dual reward of selfless action—one will attain Buddhahood and attain the blessings of Heaven. Thus work is the means to salvation, and any work constitutes Buddhist practice. All work can be an act of meditation. It is meditation in the world, not a reclusion from the world. The Zen goal of attaining no-mind, for instance, is to achieve the ability to act in a selfless way in the world, unaffected by the vicissitudes of human existence. To extend the military metaphor, Shōsan views the no-mind as the mind that has conquered or defeated the desires and selfish cravings that prevent our cultivation of spiritual attainment.

The discipline that Shōsan's system required was reminiscent of the kind of discipline and self-sacrifice expected of a warrior. But it is also pragmatic—such a well-ordered social order would also be an economically productive one. Thus Shōsan's religious worldview is also a political view as well. The person who is selfless in occupational pursuits, who understands that the world operates on the basis of *karma* and the will of Heaven, will attain to a spiritual purity but also be serving the warrior-class government and helping to maintain the ideal of the four social classes, with the warriors at the head of the hierarchy.

Given Shōsan's samurai background, it is not surprising that he viewed death as something to be overcome. To this end he advocated the idea of "practicing death," that is, engaging in religious practices that would result in one's losing any fear of death. This could be accomplished by imagining oneself in life-threatening situations. The repetition of such thoughts would eventually lead one to overcome the fears that these images might initially impart. Shōsan also encouraged people to meditate on the foulness of the human body. He viewed human desires as an impediment to selfless action in the world, and one of the most pernicious desires was the attachment to the body and life itself. In order to scare off the demon of desires, he had people meditate with clenched fists, gritted teeth, and a frightening glare. Because this body posture resembled that of the fierce-looking *Niō*, or Buddhist protective deities, his Zen is sometimes called Niō Zen.

WILLIAM E. DEAL

Further Reading

King, Winston L. *Death Was His* Kōan: *The Samurai-Zen of Suzuki Shōsan*. Nanzan Studies in Religion and Culture, Vol. 5. Berkeley, Calif.: Asian Humanities Press, 1986. An introduction to Suzuki Shōsan's life and thought from the perspective of his synthesis of Zen and warrior values.

Nakamura, Hajime. "Suzuki Shōsan, 1579–1655, and the Spirit of Capitalism in Japanese Buddhism," *Monumenta Nipponica*. 22:1–2, 1967, pp. 1–14. An interesting discussion of Suzuki Shōsan as an early Japanese capitalist.

Ooms, Herman. *Tokugawa Ideology: Early Constructs, 1570–1680*. Princeton, N.J.: Princeton University Press, 1985. This important study questions many of the long-standing assumptions about the dominance of Neo-Confucianism on Tokugawa-period thought through an examination of the diverse ideas that constituted Tokugawa state ideology. Includes coverage of the life and thought of Suzuki Shōsan.

Tyler, Royall, trans. *Selected Writings of Suzuki Shōsan*. Cornell University East Asia Papers, no. 13. Ithaca, N.Y.: China-Japan Program, Cornell University, 1977. Translations of some of Suzuki Shōsan's important writings with a brief but useful introduction.

HAYASHI RAZAN

Born: 1583, Kyoto, Japan
Died: 1657
Major Works: *Hai Yaso* (*The Anti-Jesuit*) (1606), *Santokushō* (*Notes on the Three Virtues*) (c. 1629), *Honchō jinja kō* (*Study of Our Shinto Shrines*), *Honchō tsugan* (*Comprehensive Mirror of Our Nation*), *Shintō denju* (*Shintō Initiation*), *Shunkanshō* (*Spring Mirror Notes*) (1629)

Major Ideas

Neo-Confucianism is the foundation for government and society.
Divine retribution occurs when one transgresses the Neo-Confucian ethic.
The Confucian Way of Heaven is the same as the Shinto Way of the Gods.
People express their public conformity to the dictates of the Way of Heaven by obeying the samurai *laws.*
An ordered and ethical universe is achieved by acting in accord with the Five Constant Virtues and the Five Relationships.
Human society is inherently hierarchical.
An ordered society is an expression of eternal, universal principles.
Shinto is an important foundation for the social order of the nation.
Buddhism leads people away from the Neo-Confucian truth.
Japanese mythology can be interpreted using Neo-Confucian concepts.
It is humankind's responsibility to maintain the ethical order.

Hayashi Razan was an important early Tokugawa-period Neo-Confucian scholar. Originally a Buddhist monk, he quickly developed an interest in Zhu Xi (Chu Hsi) Neo-Confucianism, and later became a student of Fujiwara Seika (1561–1619). As adviser and teacher to four shoguns, he drafted diplomatic documents and legal ordinances, thereby contributing to the maintenance of the military government. He published many commentaries on the "Confucian Classics" and wrote a history of Japan from a Neo-Confucian perspective. Razan also synthesized Neo-Confucianism with Shinto theology, arguing that the Confucian Way of Heaven is the same as the Shinto Way of the Gods. His private school later became the official government college for Neo-Confucian studies known as the Shōheikō.

Razan was born into a family that claimed a *samurai* background, but whose fortunes as warriors had already waned. He was adopted by his father's elder brother, who was a rice dealer. Razan studied Zen in Kyoto, entering the Kenninji, a Rinzai Zen temple, in 1595 at the age of twelve. He never took the tonsure, leaving the temple two years later in 1597. He began to study Zhu Xi's interpretations of the "Confucian Classics."

In 1604 he became a student of Fujiwara Seika, even though the two did not always agree on the correct interpretation of Neo-Confucian thought. Seika and Razan were both concerned with separating Zhu Xi Neo-Confucianism from its connection with Buddhist scholarship. To this end, they were interested in promoting Zhu Xi Neo-Confucianism as the official orthodoxy whereby Tokugawa rule could be legitimated and warriors could be trained for civil administration.

In 1605 Razan, on the basis of his great knowledge of Chinese scholarship, was employed by the retired military ruler Tokugawa Ieyasu (1542–1616). He remained in service to the military government for the next fifty-two years, until his death in 1657. In 1606 he was appointed first secretary to the Tokugawa government. In accordance with the traditions of the times—a reflection of the earlier Muromachi period connection between Zen, Confucianism, and government service—Razan was ordered to take the Buddhist tonsure and assume the Buddhist name of Dōshun. It is unclear the extent to which Ieyasu, a Buddhist, was actually interested in Zhu Xi Neo-Confucianism or in Razan's expertise as a Neo-Confucian scholar. He may have been more concerned with applying Razan's scholarship, especially his competence in the Chinese language, to the problems of securing a unified polity and a centralized government. Razan, for instance, rarely ever gave lectures on Neo-Confucian themes to government officials. Thus Razan never succeeded in making Neo-Confucianism the official orthodoxy of the military government.

In 1629 Razan was given the honorary Buddhist rank of Seal of the *Dharma* (*hōin*). In 1630, in recognition for his service to the military government, he was given money and land to establish a private academy (*shijuku*) in Edo (now Tokyo). Along with his brother Nobuzumi, he drafted the second *Buke Shohatto* (*Laws for the Military Houses*) and the *Hatamoto Shohatto* (*Laws for the Shōguns Vassals*) in 1635.

Razan is noted for his efforts to claim independence for Zhu Xi Neo-Confucianism from Buddhism. Under Razan Neo-Confucianism became an important part of the government orthodoxy. To this end he published numerous critical editions of the "Confucian Classics" and commentaries on the thought of Zhu Xi. Razan began work on an officially sponsored national history in 1644 that was intended to legitimate the political authority and morality of the warrior government. This text was finally completed in 1670 by Razan's son and titled *Honchō tsugan* (*Comprehensive Mirror of Our Nation*). The book covers Japanese history from the Age of the Gods through the early part of the Tokugawa period, evaluating this history from a Neo-Confucian perspective. Not surprisingly, this history evaluates Buddhism in negative terms. Razan was a critic not only of Buddhism, but also of Christianity and Wang Yang-ming's Neo-Confucian School (Yōmeigaku). His *Hai Yaso* (*The Anti-Jesuit*) (1606) is an account of his debate with Fabian (1565?–after 1620), a Japanese Jesuit.

The position of Confucian adviser to the shogun

became hereditary in the Hayashi family after Razan's death. After Zhu Xi Neo-Confucianism was formally adopted as the official orthodox government teaching (1790), the Hayashi family private academy begun in 1630 became the official shogunal college for Neo-Confucian studies known as the Shōheikō. Razan's writings were collected by his sons and published posthumously in 1662.

The Way of Heaven

Razan was particularly concerned with his own political career and to that end he applied Neo-Confucian ideas to bureaucratic ends. He was an advocate of Zhu Xi Neo-Confucianism (Shushigaku) and promoted it as the foundation for government and society. Following Zhu Xi, Razan taught that there is a universal Principle (Chinese: *li*; Japanese: *ri*) that governs the universe. Principle is the spiritual aspect of the universe. The material world consists of "ether" (Chinese: *qi/ch'i*; Japanese: *ki*). All people have Principle as an innate part of their being, but ether is uniquely different for each individual and accounts for human differences, especially the moral differences between people. Each person is endowed with a moral character that, if cultivated, allows one to fulfill their social and familial duties in the proper way. When this occurs, one purifies and clarifies one's natures and allows Principle to be clearly revealed. Principle can be cultivated, according to Zhu Xi Neo-Confucianism, through what is known as "the extension of knowledge through the investigation of things." Understanding Principle allows one to live in accord with it and to follow the Way of Heaven.

Adhering to such ethical injunctions as the Five Relationships (*gorin*: lord and minister, parent and child, husband and wife, elder and junior, friend and friend) is necessary for maintaining an ordered society that reflects an ordered universe.

According to Razan, the ordered and ethical universe consists of acting in accord with the Five Relationships and the Five Constant Virtues: humaneness (*jin*), righteousness (*gi*), rites or propriety (*rei*), wisdom (*chi*), and faithfulness (*shin*).

Razan conceived of his Neo-Confucian ethic as a cosmic system that, if violated, would result in divine retribution. Transgression included not only violating the Five Constant Virtues and the Five Relationships, but also selfishness and other behavior that causes human suffering.

A Buddhist sense of karmic consequence is suggested by Razan's conception of Heavenly punishment as an inviolable law of the universe. He believed that Heaven's punishment would eventually be meted out, if not to one in their own lifetime, then later on to their descendants. Although Razan was highly critical of Buddhism, the presence of Buddhist ideas in his thought suggests the extent to which it was impossible to fully extricate himself from the Buddhist ideas embedded in the cultural and linguistic context of his day.

Razan was concerned not only with individual human responsibility and actions, but with the fortunes of powerful families and the conduct of government. He believed that a true and ordered society derives from a virtuous government. Heaven is actively involved in the governance of human society. For instance, it is Heaven that decides who will rule, and it is the ruler who oversees what rightly belongs to Heaven. The ruler is to act towards his subjects in the way that caring parents act toward their children.

Razan connected the Way of Heaven to the needs of the military government in his notion that subjects expressed their public conformity to the dictates of the Way of Heaven by obeying the *samurai* laws. An ordered public is one that follows the Way of Heaven without need for military coercion, but Razan believed that the use of military power was appropriate to restore order to a society that had fallen into disorder.

For Razan, as for other Neo-Confucians, the universe—and by extension, human society—was inherently hierarchical. This is expressed in the Five Relationships, which are variations on the cosmic hierarchy of a superior Heaven and a subordinate Earth. This hierarchy is maintained by obeying the Five Relationships and exhibiting virtuous behavior exemplified by the Five Constant Virtues, and by loyalty, filial piety, and reverence.

Razan argued that Shinto was an important foundation for the social order of the nation. In Razan's thought there is a connection between the gods and the Way of Heaven. If one is ethical, that is, if one abides by the Five Constant Virtues and Five Relationships, then one will be rewarded or blessed by Heaven. Similarly, if one obeys the gods, one will be acting in accord with the Way of Heaven.

Criticism of Buddhism

Razan was critical of Buddhism because he viewed it, in part, as leading people away from the Neo-Confucian truth and for holding to an inconsistent theory of the mind. Razan also accused Buddhism of being a foreign teaching that leads to unjust governments when they follow Buddhist teachings. Jimmu, the first Japanese emperor, ruled justly over an ordered society that was destroyed by Buddhism. In order to avoid the Buddhist rejoinder that Neo-Confucian teachings are also foreign, Razan equated Neo-Confucian thought with Shinto theology. Razan argued that Emperor Jimmu ruled according to the just dictates of the Chinese sage—kings Yao and Shun. To follow the Way of the Gods is to follow the Way of Heaven. Razan equated Shinto and Neo-Confucianism on the basis of their foundation in Principle (*ri*), even though their practices differ. Razan claimed Shinto was not different from the "Way of the Kings" (*ōdō*), a term used to refer to Confucianism. Thus, claimed Razan, Neo-Confucianism was in accord with the Way of Heaven and the Way of the Gods, but Buddhism was heretical.

Razan established a Shinto school known as *Rito Shinchi Shinto*, which was openly hostile to Buddhism. In his *Shinto denju*, Razan's Shinto ideas echo the metaphysics of Zhu Xi when Razan equates Shinto with Principle, the truth of the universe outside of which nothing can exist. In this text he also draws a connection between Principle and the Shinto deity *Ame no minaka nushi no mikoto*, thereby concretizing what had otherwise been an abstract concept. The idea of the Kingly Way was also expounded in Razan's *Honchō jinja kō* (*Study of Our Shinto Shrines*).

Part of his attempt to meld Shinto and Confucian ideas was realized in his readings of the ancient Japanese mythology from the standpoint of the rational, humanistic language of Neo-Confucian thought. For instance, he interpreted the myths in the *Nihon shoki* along Neo-Confucian lines, explaining the *kami* in terms of Neo-Confucian concepts. Thus gods (*kami*) are without shape, but they have a spirit, or Principle, that is animated by the material aspect of *ki*. Gods are the foundation of both Heaven and Earth, and are Principle, or spirit of the mind (*kokoro*). The mind, in turn, is where the gods reside. Razan uses the metaphor of the house to express these ideas: just as a lord rules his house, the mind rules the body. And just as people live in a house, so gods reside in the mind.

Razan argued that it is humankind's responsibility to maintain the ethical order. This responsibility can be met by achieving purity of mind and utilizing it as the foundation for acting in the world. The mind has to be pure before one can make one's body pure. Therefore mind is primary and the physical or material, *ki*, is secondary. The mind becomes impure through evils that disrupt the mind through the five senses. Important to the attainment of purity is the concept of humaneness (*jin*). Heavenly Principle is characterized by humaneness, and this moral quality is also found within human beings. Humaneness, in turn, gives rise to compassion (*jihi*), which can be threatened by human desires (*yoku*). When this occurs, it is through proper attention to rites and obligations (*reigi*) that one quells the disorder and impurity that desires generate in the mind.

For Razan, Heavenly Principle (*tenri*) does battle with individual human hearts in order to make one ethical and therefore capable of acting in accord with the Way of Heaven.

WILLIAM E. DEAL

Further Reading

Translation

Tsunoda, Ryusaku, Wm. Theodore de Bary, and Donald Keene, comps. *Sources of Japanese Tradition*. Vol. 1. New York: Columbia University Press, 1964 (1958), pp. 341–352. Includes a useful selection of Hayashi Razan's writings in translation.

Related Studies

Maruyama, Masao. *Studies in the Intellectual History of Tokugawa Japan*. Translated by Mikiso Hane. Princeton, N.J.: Princeton University Press; Tokyo: University of Tokyo Press, 1974. Although some of the premises of this classic work have been challenged by more recent scholarship, it nevertheless provides a useful overview of major Tokugawa-period thinkers and ideas, including Hayashi Razan.

Ooms, Herman. *Tokugawa Ideology: Early Constructs, 1570–1680*. Princeton, N.J.: Princeton University Press, 1985. This important study questions many of the long-standing assumptions about the dominance of Neo-Confucianism on Tokugawa-period thought through an examination of the diverse ideas that constituted Tokugawa state ideology. Includes coverage of the life and thought of Hayashi Razan.

NAKAE TŌJU

Born: 1608, Ogawa, Japan
Died: 1648, Kyoto, Japan
Major Works: *Okina mondō* (*Dialogues with an Old Man*), *Jikei Ausetsu* (*The Diagram of Holding Fast to Reverence, Explained*), *Genjin* (*Inquiry into Man*)

Major Ideas

Innate knowledge is the key to wisdom and to virtue.
Filial piety is a fundamental virtue having both cosmic and personal dimensions.
The Supreme Lord (Shang di/Shang ti) can be known by innate "good-knowing."

Nakae Tōju, the founder of the Wang Yang-ming School of Confucianism in Japan, was born in Ōmi Province on the western shore of Lake Biwa in central Japan. He was born into a period called Tokugawa (1603–1868), when Japan closed itself off from the outside world to maintain its internal peace and prosperity. At the age of nine he was adopted by his grandfather, who was instrumental in his early education. When his grandfather moved to Osu near Matsuyama on the island of Shikoku, Tōju went with him. From an early age he expressed a strong sense of gratitude to his family and to his feudal lord in Osu. His grandfather's death when he was sixteen and his father's death a year later were enormous losses for Tōju.

It was at this time, however, that he heard a visiting Zen priest lecture on the Confucian *Analects*. Tōju attended these lectures faithfully and shortly afterwards began an intensive study of the "Four Books," namely the *Analects*, *Mencius*, the *Great Learning*, and the *Doctrine of the Mean*. At the age of twenty-one he wrote his first work, *Notes and Commentary on the* Great Learning (*Daigaku Keimo*). During these years he also became enamored of the thought of the twelfth-century Chinese Neo-Confucian, Zhu Xi (Chu Hsi), and avidly read his major works.

In 1634 Tōju decided to leave his feudal lord in Osu and return to his mother's home on Lake Biwa. There is some debate as to whether this was motivated by purely altruistic concerns as popular legend relates. His own claim was that he was prompted by reasons of poor health, in addition to

his concern for his mother's well-being. It is also possible that the move may have been due to political entanglements that had arisen in Shikoku. Nonetheless, the conflict that he described between loyalty to one's lord and filiality to one's parent had enormous appeal in his time.

Two years after returning home he opened a school using the Chinese "Four Books" as his basic texts. He is said to have had a stern sense of self-discipline and study, which he passed on to his students. During this period, at the age of thirty-one, he began studying the Chinese "Five Classics" and wrote two volumes of commentary on them. He also began reading the Chinese text *On Filial Piety* (*Xiao jing/Hsiao ching*) and he made a practice of reciting it aloud every morning. His growing reverence for these Chinese classics marked a turning point in his attitude toward the later Chinese Song (Sung) and Ming Neo-Confucian thinkers.

His interest in Zhu Xi had been as strong as his devotion to Confucius, yet he sought to transcend the formalism of Zhu Xi's thinking. Hence he had made a thorough study of the "Four Books," which Zhu Xi had advocated as central for the study of Confucianism. In his early thirties, while reading the "Five Classics," he underwent a gradual conversion to the thought of the Ming Neo-Confucian, Wang Yang-ming (1472–1529). This has been described as a movement in his thinking from a rationalist and formalist position of Zhu Xi to an increasingly mystical and theistic path. In the early Chinese classics he found support for his theistic beliefs and in Wang Yang-ming and other Ming thinkers he found confirmation of his idealist philosophy.

His study of the "Five Classics" has been described as a return to earlier forms of Confucian religiosity. In reading the classical *Book of Odes* and *Documents*, Tōju was no doubt influenced by the recognition of the existence of the Lord of Heaven (Shang di/Shang ti) and of a need for belief in him. Like many Neo-Confucians, Tōju was also interested in the Chinese classic *The Book of Changes*. Here Tōju sought a means of discerning the will of the divine and harmonizing one's action with the changes in the universe. In the *Analects* what became especially striking for Tōju was the "Xiang dang (Hsiang tang)" chapter (10), which describes Confucius's ritual activities and reverential attitude.

Tōju's shift to Wang Yang-ming's thought reflected how his deeply religious concerns had turned him away from Zhu Xi's rationalism. For example, Zhu Xi interpreted the ghosts and spirits in the *Doctrine of the Mean* as two aspects of *qi/ch'i* (Japanese: *ki*) (material force), namely the operations of *yin* and *yang*. Tōju, however, links the Supreme Ultimate, *yin* and *yang*, and the five agents with Supreme Lord. There are also distinctions between Zhu Xi and Tōju with regard to the interpretation of reverence. While for Zhu Xi abiding in reverence primarily meant controlling the mind, for Tōju it also meant fearing the Mandate of Heaven and honoring the virtuous nature. Tōju—and Ogyū Sorai after him—felt the need for an object of reverence in the religious practices. Tōju advocated a devotion to the Supreme Lord while Sorai later urged a respect for ghosts and spirits.

This movement in a more overtly religious direction was brought to a completion with his reading of Wang Yang-ming. In 1645, at the age of thirty-seven, Tōju acquired Yang-ming's complete works. These he read with great enthusiasm and for the last three years of his life he became an ardent exponent of Wang Yang-ming's thought.

Although he taught for only some twelve years before he died, Tōju's influence on subsequent generations of students was remarkable. Indeed, he

became known as the "sage of Ōmi." His school in Kyoto was maintained for a century after his death and his disciples also spread his teachings to the Osaka area. Some of the noted Tokugawa Confucians who acknowledged his influence were Kumazawa Banzan (1619–91), Arai Hakuseki (1657–1725), and Dazai Shundai (1680–1747). Even in the late Tokugawa period such illustrious figures as Sakuma Shōzan, Yoshida Torahiro (Shōin), and Ōshio Chūsai cited him as an example of single-minded devotion to personal and social rectification.

After his death his school divided into two branches, one emphasizing introspection and cultivation of personal morality, the other more interested in applying his ideas to state affairs and to improving public morality. For Tōju, as for Wang Yang-ming, there was an essential unity of these two dimensions, namely thought and action, personal cultivation and public reform.

The Supreme Lord

Nakae Tōju has been described as a monist with respect to his cosmological thought, a theist with respect to his religious beliefs, and an idealist with respect to his doctrine of the mind. Despite the inadequacies of these terms to convey the nuances of Tōju's ideas, they will serve as a framework in which to begin a discussion of his work.

Tōju believed in one unifying principle—the Supreme Vacuity—as the fountainhead of the universe. Identity with this principle is not simply a vague experience of monistic unity, however. Rather, humans are directed towards a Supreme Lord who is both an impersonal absolute and a personal presence.

Indeed one of the distinctive features of Tōju's thought is his reverence for a Supreme Lord (*Jotei*). This Divinity is the principle of absolute truth, the primary agent of creation and an active sustaining presence. These aspects of the divine, namely the unmanifested, the Supreme Vacuity, the enduring Supreme Ultimate, and the manifold creator and sustainer of the world are combined in Tōju's thought. There emerges a unique sense of reverence for this numinous force, which is simultaneously behind and within the universe. This ground of being and cause of life is seen as the source of the unity and continuation of life.

Tōju describes this unified role of the Supreme Lord as the Self-Sustaining Absolute principle and benevolent creator presence. Tōju's sense of reverence for the Supreme Lord is revealed in a passage that is a litany of praise to the marvelous qualities of the divine as a cosmic presence pervading the universe. In Tōju's thought the way human beings pay homage to the Supreme Lord is by awakening the Divine Light within them.

Innate Knowledge

Nakae Tōju felt that in all human beings there is "a divinity like a clear mirror." This he identified as the source of "good-knowing," or conscience. Similarly, it is the root of enlightenment and is united to the divinity of Heaven.

Tōju indicated that this inner light of conscience was divine reasoning in contrast to worldly desires. When the mind is ruled by conscience and not swayed by desires, then we can abide in a state of sincerity and authenticity. From this balanced harmony, the mind is filled with joy and delights. Tōju distinguished between the mind of the sensible world and the inner mind of conscience. He equated conscience with a formless, transcendent reason. By acting in harmony with conscience he felt we will become the incarnation of this timeless principle.

Tōju believed that the mind itself is neither good nor bad but that evil arises through the will. The source of desires is the will, which may lead one to become confused and bewildered. Without the interference of will "virtue brightens and things get restored to their original positions." The fact that all human beings have this innate knowledge is one of the primary reasons that Nakae Tōju espoused the doctrine of human equality and brotherhood.

Filiality as Cosmic Principle and Human Virtue

Although the innate knowledge of the mind links the human being to the universe, the virtue of filial piety is at the center of this process. Tōju's teaching may be seen as a further elaboration of filiality as discussed by earlier Confucians and ultimately as an extension of the Chinese Neo-Confucian Zhang Zai's (Chang Tsai) "Western Inscription." The practice of filiality distinguishes the human being, and yet filiality is part of the very life-giving power of the universe.

This cosmic reciprocity between all things is the dynamic lifeblood of creation. Tōju described the eternal quality of filiality and saw it as part of the Divine Way of Heaven before creation, yet he also felt it was instrumental in the creation process itself and in the continuing cycle of the seasons.

He discussed the all-pervasive presence of filial bonds of the older and the younger in the natural world, which he saw as part of the underlying structure of reality. Indeed, filiality for Tōju is comparable to the principle of gravity, which binds the elements to one another. Thus just as filiality has a cosmic dimension in the natural order, it is the root of social relations in the human sphere. Indeed, Tōju recognized that the "seasons of filiality" in the human order are the Five Relations, which mirror the reciprocity already evident in the natural world.

The activation of filiality in accordance with the underlying filial bonds of the universe was the overarching goal of Tōju's thought. Tōju identified filiality with the "illustrious virtue" cited in the Chinese classic *The Great Learning* and saw both virtues as being at the heart of innate knowledge. The practice of the illustrious virtue of filial piety was a means of preserving the life force in the individual, which was inherited from the ancestors. Tōju further recognized that this life force was essentially linked with the life force of the universe, namely the Supreme Vacuity. Thus to practice filial piety meant to nourish the very life force of the universe. For Tōju, then, filiality was both a personal and a cosmic virtue, sustaining human relations and supporting the cosmic order itself.

MARY EVELYN TUCKER

Further Reading

Translation

Tsunoda, Ryusuku, and Wm. Theodore de Bary and Donald Keene, comps. *Sources of Japanese Tradition*. New York: Columbia University Press, 1958. (Also in paperback in two volumes, 1964.) An excellent source book, with very helpful introductions.

Related Study

de Bary, Wm. Theodore, and Irene T. Bloom, eds. *Principle and Practicality*. New York: Columbia University Press, 1979. An informative collection of critical essays about the Japanese Neo-Confucian thinkers.

YAMAZAKI ANSAI

Born: 1618, Kyoto, Japan
Died: 1682
Major Works: *Hekii* (*Refutation of Heresies*) (1647), *Bunkai hitsuroku* (*Reading Notes*), *Hakurokudō gakukishūchū* (*Collected Commentaries on Zhu Xi's [Chu Hsi's] Regulations for the White Deer Grotto School*) (1650), *Yamato shōgaku* (*Japanese Elementary Learning*) (1658)

Major Ideas

Reverence is the central value of all human relationships and activities.
Both Neo-Confucian thought and Shinto theology teach moral cultivation by following the Way of Heaven and practicing virtue.
The Five Relationships are constitutive of the human condition and are established by the Way of Heaven.
It is incumbent on human beings to carry out their moral obligations.
The imperial line must always be preserved.
Japan is a divine country, unique in the world.
The ancient texts must be studied in order to learn how to properly follow the Way of the Gods.
The Way of Heaven is eternal and transcendent, and functions to regulate and order the universe.

Yamazaki Ansai was the founder of the Shikoku School of Zhu Xi (Chu Hsi) Neo-Confucianism (in contrast to the Kyoto School of Zhu Xi Neo-Confucianism of Fujiwara Seika and Hayashi Razan). He combined Neo-Confucian ethical ideas with Shinto religious thought to articulate a Japanese nationalism that revolved around the divine descent of the emperor and the necessity for imperial rule. He was particularly interested in Zhu Xi's ideas about individual moral training and argued that people should strictly adhere to the moral precepts. To this end, he insisted that his own students undergo rigorous moral training. He also forbade his students from reading texts that he deemed superfluous to the goal of moral cultivation. He placed special emphasis on the concepts of loyalty to one's lord and self-restraint. He argued that his form of Neo-Confucianism was more authentic than that of his rivals, especially Hayashi Razan. He became particularly interested in harmonizing his interpretation of Neo-Confucianism with Shinto teachings. He wanted to make Shinto into a political doctrine applicable to the needs and goals of the Tokugawa government in their efforts to create a centralized political and social order throughout Japan. To this end, he founded the

Suika (Suiga) School of Shinto. His ideas gained him employment as an adviser to warrior government authorities. He expressed these views through his voluminous writings.

Ansai was born into a family with a *samurai* background, but his father had terminated service to his lord and had moved to Kyoto, supporting the family by practicing acupuncture. Ansai's father sent him to become a Buddhist priest at the Enryakuji, the headquarter temple of Tendai Buddhism on Mt. Hiei, when he was about ten years old. A year later he entered the Myōshinji, a Zen temple in Kyoto. At seventeen he entered a temple in Tosa Province. At Tosa Ansai studied the Nangakuha (Southern Learning) School of Neo-Confucianism, which led him eventually to abandon Buddhism.

Ansai's studies eventually brought him to the teachings of Zhu Xi Neo-Confucianism, a move which put him in conflict with the Tosa authorities who had long supported the Southern Learning School. He returned to Kyoto where, in 1646, he formally reentered secular life. In 1647 he published his *Hekii* (*Refutation of Heresies*), praising the truth of Zhu Xi Neo-Confucianism and denouncing Buddhism. Subsequently he wrote numerous texts in support of Zhu Xi's philosophy. In 1655 he began lecturing about Neo-Confucianism, attracting many students to his private school, called Kimon, which thrived in both Kyoto and Tokyo. Ansai's fame caught the attention of the senior adviser to the *shogun*, and his teachings had some influence in the military government. He became associated with the Tokugawa government through his role as adviser and through the patronage of Hoshina Masayuki, who was influential in the government and was half-brother to the third shogun, Tokugawa Iemitsu.

Ansai became interested in Shinto after leaving Buddhist orders, a study that resulted in the formulation of Suika (Suiga) Shinto. Suika Shinto was a mix of Watarai Shinto (Ise Shinto) and Yoshida Shinto, combined with Zhu Xi Neo-Confucian concepts. Suika Shinto attempted to reconcile Shinto and Confucianism. Ansai understood Zhu Xi Neo-Confucianism as the True Way in China and Shinto as the True Way in Japan. Because he considered both systems as the truth, he promoted the simultaneous study of Neo-Confucian and Shinto thought.

Ansai was criticized by some of his disciples, who saw an inherent conflict in combining the rational ideas of Neo-Confucianism with the religious emotionalism of Shinto. Nevertheless, Ansai continued to work toward the integration of Neo-Confucian and Shinto thought, striving to make Shinto into a political doctrine usable by the Tokugawa government.

The success of Ansai's undertaking can be measured in part by the later influence of his ideas—especially his Suika Shinto theology—on some of the ideas of the Kokugaku scholar Hirata Atsutane, on the leaders of the Meiji Restoration (1868), and on the rhetoric of pre-war Japanese nationalism.

The Central Value of Reverence

Ansai's thought is a blend of Shinto and Neo-Confucian ideas. He was deeply interested in the life and ideas of Zhu Xi, which he later blended with his interpretation of the importance of the Shinto tradition. Ansai, in typical Neo-Confucian fashion, viewed human virtue as a reflection of the cosmic virtue, or Principle (*ri*), that naturally controls the universe as a whole. In his system of thought, reverence (*kei*) was the value that he considered to be most central to all human relationships and activities. Ansai compiled and interpreted Zhu Xi's ideas in his *Bunkai hitsuroku* (*Reading Notes*).

Ansai was an ardent Neo-Confucian and highly intolerant of anyone he perceived as having misinterpreted the Neo-Confucian message. His critique of others, therefore, was not limited only to Buddhists. He regularly attacked those he thought expressed a shallow understanding of the Way, claiming his own interpretation to be the sole Neo-Confucian orthodoxy. Ansai, for instance, attacked the famous Neo-Confucian scholar–bureaucrat Hayashi Razan (1583–1657) in part because Razan was both a proponent of Neo-Confucianism while at the same time a high-ranking Buddhist cleric. This synthesis of Buddhist and Neo-Confucian values was relatively common in this period, yet it was a combination that Ansai found offensive. From Ansai's perspective Razan's Buddhist monastic rank went against the Confucian ethic of filial piety.

Ansai's *Hakurokudō gakukishūchū* (*Collected Commentaries on Zhu Xi's Regulations for the White Deer Grotto School*) (1650) is his commentary on one of Zhu Xi's less well-known texts that expounds the significance of the Five Relationships. The Five Relationships (*gorin*: lord and minister, parent and child, husband and wife, elder and junior, friend and friend) and the behaviors that demonstrate the proper understanding of the relationship between them were central to Neo-Confucian thought. In his commentary Ansai claims that the Five Relationships and the ethical imperatives they imply are not simply manufactured by human beings in some arbitrary fashion, but rather are constitutive of the human condition, established by the Way of Heaven. They are a natural part of our very being. Education, says Ansai, is meant to elucidate and cultivate the Five Relationships, and particularly the need for respect toward others. From this an ordered and just society is produced.

Ansai stressed the necessity of carrying out one's fixed moral obligations. This was exemplified, according to Ansai, by the duty that pertains between lord and subject. This is not an arbitrary human construct, but a duty that is a part of the fabric of the universe and hence in accord with Heaven. Ansai applied this moral obligation to the dutiful relationship that exists between the emperor and the Japanese people. The Japanese people had an obligation to uphold the imperial way. Thus Ansai's concept of the virtue of duty that exists between lord and subject was used to bolster the nationalist agenda that characterized his synthesis of Shinto and Neo-Confucianism. Ansai coupled his emphasis on duty (*gi*) with the idea of reverence (*kei*). These, he argued, were essential to enacting Neo-Confucian values in the world. These values were also expressed in Ansai's formulation of Shinto concepts.

Ansai's Shinto theology was called Suika Shinto. He claimed it to be a teaching originally taught by Amaterasu, the Sun Goddess, herself and passed down through a succession of *kami* (divine beings) to humans. Thus Ansai believed in the divine origins of this teaching. *Suika* was a term derived from an honorific name given to Ansai by his teacher. *Suika*, which means "divine descent and protection," was for Ansai the essence of Shinto. The term itself appears, for example, in the *Yamatohime no mikoto seiki*, a Watarai Shinto scripture. The text records this passage:

Human beings are the divine beings under Heaven. They must do no harm to their heart-*kami*. The gods come down [*sui*] . . . for those who first pray; divine protection [*ka*] is for those who make uprightness their base. Thus, relying on one's original mind, everyone must obtain the Great Way. Therefore gods and humans have to preserve the beginning of primeval chaos. . . .

(OOMS, 1985)

Ansai combined this notion with the Neo-Confucian concept of reverence (*kei*), which he insisted should be the ethical foundation for all human behavior. He applied the concept of reverence, in this case, to the idea that one should revere the gods and the emperor. Reverence became in some sense synonymous with worship when applied by Ansai in this Shinto context. Reverence, or worship, was not simply something that one applied to objects of devotion in the external world, but was a virtue that led to moral cultivation within oneself. Ansai also utilized the Neo-Confucian concept of Principle (*ri*), innate in all things, to argue the essential unity between Shinto *kami* and humans, and between emperor and subjects. Ansai's nationalism is apparent in his emphasis on the divinity of the emperor because of his descent from the gods. He insisted that the imperial line must always be preserved.

Ansai was adamant in his claim that the ancient Shinto texts contained the literal, historical truth. Thus the stories of the creator gods in the *Kojiki* were believed by him to have really occurred, rendering the descent of the imperial line from the gods as an actual historical event. Like other proponents of the primacy and uniqueness of the Shinto gods, Ansai argued that Japan was a divine country, unique in the world. This was proved, in part, by the divine origin and unbroken succession of Japan's imperial line. There was even a linguistic proof for this divinity: Ansai claimed that the word *kami* antedated written language and was produced naturally by the human voice, further evidence of the primal sacredness of the term itself.

Ansai favorably compared Shinto to Confucianism, in contrast to his unfavorable view of Buddhism, because he interpreted early Shinto—that is, Shinto before the arrival of Buddhism—to be the same as Confucianism. Ansai combined Neo-Confucian thought with Shinto theology by arguing that both systems teach moral cultivation by following the Way of Heaven, which he equated with the Way of the Gods, and practicing virtue. Ansai tended to view Shinto as necessary for one's devotion to the gods and Neo-Confucian values as necessary for the proper conduct of society. He looked for similarities between the two and sometimes found them in some unexpected places. For instance, he noted the correspondence between

Confucian and Shinto tradition in their similar injunctions against cremation, the usual practice in Buddhist funeral rituals. This was but one of many examples Ansai used to prove that Shinto was co-equal with Neo-Confucianism.

Ansai's *Yamato shōgaku* (*Japanese Elementary Learning*) (1658) was his initial attempt to synthesize Neo-Confucian thought with Shinto, especially by arguing that the Way of Heaven was active in Japan in the native Japanese Way of the Gods. He equates Shinto with the kingly way (*ōdō*) found in ancient China. Similarly, Ansai locates in Amaterasu's pledge to always provide protection to the imperial line a kingly way in Japanese Shinto as well. He viewed this kingly way as having been tainted by Buddhism; the only place it remained in its pure essence was at the Ise Shrine. Further, Ansai argued that the Age of the Gods had never ended and that it still operated in seventeenth-century Japan as a regulatory principle in human lives. Thus, admonished Ansai, we must study the ancient texts in order to learn how to properly follow the Way of the Gods. Ansai saw it as one of his tasks to reclaim Shinto in its pristine form.

Ansai's refutation of Buddhism in his *Hekii* is a critique based on Neo-Confucian ideas. It is part philosophical treatise and part confession about his own discovery of the truth of Neo-Confucian thought and the falsehoods of Buddhism, and his hope of showing others the veracity of Neo-Confucian teachings. In it, Ansai argues that the Way of Heaven is eternal and transcendent, and functions to regulate and order the universe. Ansai reiterates the primacy of the Neo-Confucian idea of social hierarchy expressed especially in the Five Relationships. Ansai also argued that the teachings of the Confucian sages are the complete truth, that they have left nothing unsaid. In light of this, Ansai viewed himself as merely a transmitter of the truth and not its architect, just as Confucius himself had done.

WILLIAM E. DEAL

Further Reading

Translation

Tsunoda, Ryusaku, Wm. Theodore de Bary, and Donald Keene, comps. *Sources of Japanese Tradition*. Vol. 1. New York: Columbia University Press, 1964 (1958), pp. 354–362. A useful selection of Yamazaki Ansai's writings in translation.

Related Studies

Maruyama, Masao. *Studies in the Intellectual History of Tokugawa Japan*. Translated by Mikiso Hane. Princeton, N.J.: Princeton University Press; Tokyo: University of Tokyo Press, 1974. Although some of the premises of this classic work have been challenged by more recent scholarship, it nevertheless provides a useful overview of major Tokugawa-period thinkers and ideas, including Yamazaki Ansai.

Okada, Takehiko. "Practical Learning in the Chu Hsi School: Yamazaki Ansai and Kaibara Ekken." In *Principle and Practicality: Essays in Neo-Confucianism and Practical Learning*, edited by Wm. Theodore de Bary and Irene Bloom. New York: Columbia University Press, 1979, pp. 231–305. This article presents a brief but useful introduction to some of the major themes found in Yamazaki Ansai's thought.

Ooms, Herman. *Tokugawa Ideology: Early Constructs, 1570–1680*. Princeton, N.J.: Princeton University Press, 1985. This important study questions many of the long-standing assumptions about the dominance of Neo-Confucianism on Tokugawa-period thought through an examination of the diverse ideas that constituted Tokugawa state ideology. Includes coverage of the life and thought of Yamazaki Ansai.

YAMAGA SOKŌ

Born: 1622, Aizu-Wakamatsu, Japan
Died: 1685, Edo (now Tokyo), Japan
Major Works: *Bukyō shogaku* (*Little Learning of the Warrior's Creed*) (1656), *Seikyō yōroku* (*Essential Teachings of the Sages*) (1665), *Gorui* (*Classified Discourses*) (1665), *Chūchō jijitsu* (*True Facts of the Central Kingdom*) (1669), *Haisho zampitsu* (*Autobiography in Exile*) (1675)

Major Ideas

The purpose of the warrior is to exemplify the virtue of duty to the rest of society.
The special nature of Japan derives from its divine creation.
Japan's superiority over other countries is demonstrated in the fact that it has been ruled from the beginning by one imperial line.

If the entire intellectual history of Japan in the modern period could be represented by the ideas of one man, that man would be Yamaga Sokō. And if Yamaga's teachings could be distilled to one word, that word would be duty: duty to lord as the supreme expression of humanity, duty to emperor as the supreme lord, duty to Japan as the supreme land. Yamaga worked like a prism on the entire available learning of medieval Japan—Chinese and Japanese—to produce a refraction of distinct but related ideas that became the ideological foundation of first the hereditary military class and later of Japanese society as a whole. His influence was a force in Japan for nearly 300 years. He is identified with the forty-six vassals of Akō (where Yamaga spent ten years) who avenged their lord in 1702. Yoshida Shōin, *guru* and martyr of the movement that restored the imperial house to rule in the mid-nineteenth century, was a teacher of his school of strategy and was profoundly influenced by his ideas. General Nogi Maresuke, an army commander during the Russo–Japanese War of 1904–05, secured posthumous court rank for Yamaga in 1907 and in 1913 caused a sensation when he and his wife committed suicide to follow his lord the emperor in death. In Yamaga one finds the first expressions of the intellectual basis of emperor worship, racism, and militarism, which would underpin Japan's failed attempt at imperialism and bring her to defeat in World War II.

Yamaga's dedication to the ideal of duty might seem hardly congruent with his reputation for intellectual independence and his status as one of the three great *rōnin* (unemployed warrior) of the period. However, it can be traced to a profound sense of longing for the opportunity to serve.

Yamaga's father was a former *samurai* who had killed a man and been forced to flee his domain. Taking refuge in Aizu-Wakamatsu, he eventually took up medicine, but never again entered service. He was befriended by the high-ranking Machino family, who, among other things, apparently provided him with a second wife from among the young women in their service. Sokō was not the eldest son, but the one on whom his father pinned his hopes and whose education he personally undertook. Yamaga's father followed his patrons to the shogunal capital of Edo (now Tokyo). There, through their powerful connections to the wet nurse of the third *shogun* Tokugawa Iemitsu—Kasuga no tsubone—and her son, they secured for Yamaga introductions to the leading scholars of the day.

Yamaga was first sent to study with the Confucian scholar Hayashi Razan, chief secretary to the Tokugawa shogunal house. He studied classical Japanese and Imbe Shinto with Hirota Tansai, poetry with Asukai Masanobu and Karasuma Mitsuhiro, Ryōbu Shinto with the priest Kōyō of the Azcchi chapel at Mt. Kōya, and military science with Obata Kagenori and Hōjō Ujinori, from whom he received his license to teach. Yamaga was always sensible to the privilege of the education afforded him as the son of a mere unemployed *samurai*-turned-doctor. On the other hand, he was fully aware of his own enormous talents: late in his career, he dreamt that the family of Toyotomi Hideyoshi, the second great hegemon of the sixteenth century, had turned over the rule of Japan to himself.

Essential Teachings of the Sages

Yamaga started his own school of strategic studies and had as students many of the great lords of Japan. It was principally as a strategist that he was known, and he dedicated his intellectual endeavors to the service of the hereditary military class. In 1665, however, he published the *Essential Teachings of the Sages* (*Seikyō yōroku*), a dictionary of Confucian terms that was hardly as radical as the response it evoked: Hoshina Masayuki, brother of the shogun Iemitsu and patron of Neo-Confucianist Yamazaki Ansai, had the book banned and Yamaga exiled to Akō. Other considerations may have come into play: Yamaga's influence, his reputation as a strategist, and even his status as a self-employed member of the military class in an age suspicious of such independents. Ten years later in 1675, after Hoshina's death, Yamaga was permitted to return to Edo, where he continued teaching and eventually died.

Yamaga's training in a school of strategy extending back to the generals of the famous Takeda house informed and unified a range of diverse intellectual interests. Yamaga's dedication to the military class is demonstrated by his efforts to provide them with a legitimization of their rule and a program of training and indoctrination that would ensure their continued preeminence in society: Yamaga was the first to codify what came to be called the "way of the warrior" or *bushidō* (although he never used this term). This was made possible by carrying through a fundamental proposition of the relationship between military science and political science. As spelled out in the *Little Learning of the Warrior's Creed* (*Bukyō shogaku*), war was simply an unavoidable method employed in the pursuit of correct government, whose basis was the relation-

ship between lord and vassal. It was important for the warrior to cultivate clean and sober habits in his everyday life and to discipline himself in his dedication to duty in preparation for his role as leader of society. A warrior was expected to start out his day by brushing his teeth, combing his hair, and greeting his parents, and to end it by laying down his life for his master. Being a warrior was a way of life, not just an expedient method for winning wealth and glory, and it carried with it certain obligations.

As expressed in the *Classified Discourses* (*Gorui*), the warrior was indebted to society for his livelihood. In the previous centuries the warrior had earned his stipend through his service in battle. Now that peace had come with the establishment of the Tokugawa regime (1603), the warrior needed to justify his existence. This he did in cultivating morality, that is, a feeling of responsibility for rule and administration. The peasant, the artisan, and the merchant were too heavily occupied by their labors and concerned with their self-interests to consider other problems. It was the role of the military class to regulate the conflicting interests of the other classes and to secure a peaceful society. By virtue of his stipend, only the warrior had the leisure and opportunity to realize fully duty to one's lord, the fundamental principle of rule; it was his obligation to exemplify this ideal, to act as a model and teacher for others, to act constantly in accordance with duty. The warrior dedicated himself to personal discipline, the guidance of others, the maintenance of peace and order in the world, and winning honor and fame thereby.

This monopoly of duty, an ethical value, represented and legitimated the monopoly of power for the military class. Moreover, not only did it legitimate the rule of the country by the military, but it enabled the medieval professional fighting man to convert himself into a nine-to-five civil servant: by seeing his responsibility to his lord as effecting good government, he could appreciate the necessity for acquiring learning as well as martial skills to put to the service of his lord.

Yamaga's pursuit of an ethical basis for the rule of the military class and the obedience of vassal to lord led him to challenge the accepted interpretation of what in Chinese studies or Confucianism was called the "Path of the Sages" or the "Way." The ortho-dox interpretation of the Way described in the "Chinese Classics," called Neo-Confucianism, had evolved in the eleventh century as an approach to personal cultivation by addressing and co-opting Buddhism and even Buddhist practices such as meditation. Neo-Confucianism entered Japan with full force in the 1590s, when Toyotomi Hideyoshi's armies stripped the libraries of the Korean court and nobility and brought them home.

Yamaga, concerned as ever with practical considerations, redefined the Way as government or administration. In the *Essential Teachings of the Sages*, which so incurred the enmity of Hoshina, Yamaga rejected the interpretations of the Han, Tang (T'ang), and especially the Song (Sung) periods upon which the schools of his teacher Hayashi Razan and Yamazaki Ansai were based, and he simply went back to the original texts of Confucius and Mencius. Yamaga's concerns were government, not the cultivation of the seriousness and stillness he thought made for a very narrow-minded and even sour individual (as typified by Ansai).

Thus, along with Itō Jinsai, Yamaga was an early proponent of a movement in Confucian studies of a kind of textual fundamentalism called "Ancient Learning" (*kogaku*), whose most famous exponent was Ogyū Sorai. In this work Yamaga also prefigured Motoori Norinaga in his defense of human nature by refusing to subject it to moral judgment: the moral man, the sage, is one who follows the Way of Heaven; the function of the sage is the regulation of human relations (*rei*) or government. And the contemporary sage is the product, not of nature, but of education in the Way of the ancient sages of China.

The fact that Yamaga actually published his works during his lifetime, while his contemporary Jinsai's works were published by his son in 1705 (the year of Jinsai's death) and later, may have made him an easier target for Hoshina.

The Cult of the Sun Goddess

Yamaga's greatest contribution—to legitimizing the position of the Tokugawa shogunal house in particular and that of the military class in general—was his fusion of the cult of the Sun Goddess with the Way of the Sages. The *Classified Discourses* and the *Autobiography in Exile* (*Haisho zampitsu*) summarize points that Yamaga fully delineated in works such as the *Buke jiki* (one of the first Japanese histories to use documents), the *Takkyō dōmon*, and the *True Facts of the Central Kingdom*. In these texts Yamaga identifies the native court rites, Shinto, or worship of the emperor (*matsurigoto*) with the Way of the Sages transmitted from China. According to Yamaga, little was known of early Shinto because records had been lost in the great revolt of Soga Iruka in the seventh century, which necessitated a dependence on the Chinese transmission or Confucianism. Government had passed from the court to the military houses with the establishment of the first shogunate in the twelfth century, but the military houses had ever revered and served the imperial house and thus the tradition of the teachings of the sages.

Yamaga anticipated Matsudaira Sadanobu by 100 years by legitimizing the Tokugawa regime on the basis that it maintained the correct rule of the military tradition in maintaining the proper lord–vassal relationship to the imperial line. The fact that the land of Japan had been ruled by an unbroken lineage of emperors was due in fact to the military houses who had upheld the cult of the Sun Goddess, ancestress of the line and origin of their mandate to rule; this exemplified the teachings of the Chinese sages concerning rule and duty. Japan, created by the gods and ruled by their descendants, was special among all the lands of the Earth—even to its water and soil—by virtue of its divine creation and unbroken lineage of rulers. Japan was superior to all other lands. Japan, in fact, ought to be studied! Yamaga was perhaps the first to advocate Japanese studies beyond Shinto, a call that was taken up in 1728 by Kada Azumamaro in a petition to the *shogun* Yoshimune for the support of National Learning.

In his preoccupation with the place of Japan in the world, Yamaga anticipated the National Learning or Shinto Revival movement of the eighteenth century as exemplified by Kamo Mabuchi, Motoori

Norinaga, and Hirata Atsutane. His justification of Japan's special status as based on its unbroken lineage of emperors was transmitted to the Mito School and the development of the theory of national essence (*kokutairon*). Certainly his concept of the duty shown to the imperial line by the military houses combined with Yamazaki Ansai's concept that duty was an obligation due only to the emperor, and became a basis for the Restoration of 1868 and the emperor-centered ethics of the late-nineteenth and early-twentieth centuries.

For Yamaga, effecting successful government depended on the indoctrination of the entire military class, employed or not, in the ethical ideal of duty or duty (*gi*). For Yamaga, the very profession of the military class was ethics or morality, especially that of duty. As outlined in the *Classified Discourses*, the teaching of the sages is government, and government is the way of the vassal absolutely loyal to his lord. From the study of strategy Yamaga learned to integrate ideology, ethics, and government and thus lay the foundation for the conversion of the medieval soldier to the modern bureaucrat. For Yamaga, indoctrinating the entire military class in Confucian ethics was the key to the overall strategy for maintaining power over the country. Education was at the heart of Yamaga's program for good government, the heart of government was the entire warrior class, and the heart of the warrior class was absolute duty to one's lord.

The corpus of Yamaga's works taken together can be reduced to one formula: Japan is superior to all other countries in the world because it alone has maintained the fundamental principle of correct rule, the duty of vassal to overlord. This is demonstrated by the fact that Japan was created and ruled by a single, divine, imperial line. This was made possible by the warriors of Japan, who had undertaken the rule of the country throughout a succession of regimes including the Tokugawa regime, but who had maintained and served the imperial line. Therefore the military class of Japan were, in their adherence to duty, the fullest expression of humanity and uniquely qualified to rule the country.

Universal conscription during the modern period extended warrior status to nearly the entire male population and the education system introduced this formula to the nation as a whole: the entire country was thereby effectively co-opted into Japan's militarist projects. Very little was needed to make this formula the ideological basis for Japan's attempt to bring Asia under the four corners of the emperor's roof.

S. A. THORNTON

Further Reading

Translation

Tsunoda, Ryusaku, and Wm. Theodore de Bary and Donald Keene, comps. *Sources of Japanese Tradition*. Vol. 1, pp. 385–401. New York: Columbia University Press, 1964 (1958). Contains a brief discussion of Yamaga Sokō, together with selected passages from his most important works.

Related Studies

Earl, David Margery. *Emperor and Nation in Japan: Political Thinkers of the Tokugawa Period.* Seattle: University of Washington Press, 1964. See "Yamago Sokō and the Emphasis on Patriotism," pp. 37–51. A revealing account of Yamaga's political views and influence.

Maruyama, Masao. *Studies in the Intellectual History of Tokugawa Japan.* Translated by Mikiso Hane. Princeton, N.J.: Princeton University Press; Tokyo: University of Tokyo Press, 1974, pp. 43–50. Yamaga Sokō is discussed in his historical context.

ITŌ JINSAI

Born: 1627, Kyoto, Japan
Died: 1705, Kyoto, Japan
Major Works: *Dōjimon* (*Boys' Questions*) (1707), *Go-Mō jigi* (*The Meaning of Terms in the* Analects *and* Mencius) (1683)

Major Ideas

The Way is the moral cultivation of the individual.
The Way of man is not the Way of Heaven or the Way of nature; morality has nothing to do with nature.
Humanity is worked out in society; the individual is evaluated on the basis of action, not character.

There was a reaction common among some of the second generation of Japanese intellectuals of the Tokugawa period (1603–1868) to the Neo-Confucianism propagated during the first half of the seventeenth century. They resented the deprecation and even rejection of Japanese customs and political institutions implicit in the high esteem in which the culture and civilization of ancient China were held. They were extremely suspicious of the idea that the locus of absolute truth could be found in the mind of the individual. Not only did that diminish the authority of society and its mores, but it eliminated education (external to the individual) as a source of source of authority and a route of advancement for those who were unable to inherit position or power but were ambitious for it. Finally, they tired of the priggish moralizing of the humourless paragons of perfection who denied the validity of any human feeling: sexual love, ambition, even the appreciation of a good poem, or the pleasure in a puff of tobacco. Men as different as Yamaga Sokō and Itō Jinsai helped to break the back of Neo-Confucianism—and its grip on the intellectual world—by going back to the basics, the texts of Confucius and Mencius. They were the precursors of Ogyū Sorai, who completed the process by developing a school of philology that challenged the ability of the Neo-Confucianists to understand, let alone interpret, the meaning of the classical texts.

Jinsai was the son and heir of a lumber merchant. Although fond of learning from an early age, he was expected to become a physician, of which there were many on both sides of the family—one had

even treated an emperor. But Jinsai resisted for years, even to the point of nervous exhaustion, until his family relented. Only with the death of his younger brother, who had taken over Jinsai's responsibilities as head of the family, did Jinsai return to take his rightful place. His sense of independence was also reflected in his refusal to take employment in the service of a feudal lord. Rather, he maintained a private academy, the School of Ancient Meanings (Kogidō), which drew many students but which provided him only a very modest living. The school did, however, survive as an academy under the leadership of his able son Tōgai, well into the modern period. It was one of the great academies serving the merchant community and was influential in shaping the content and vocabulary of the ethics of the common man. (Jinsai's term for humanity and righteousness [*jingi*] was taken up in a sixties' gangster film as a slogan for a value system opposed to the social code demanding obedience and even murder signified by the term "rules" [*okite*].)

Jinsai's reputation reached the imperial court: in 1702 the imperial library acquired his *Letter to Dōkō*, as well as other works later. Even the nobility sent their sons to the school to study literature and history.

The Way and the Virtues

Like Yamaga Sokō, Jinsai challenged the Neo-Confucian system by redefining the concept of the Way. As interpreted by the Song (Sung) Chinese

scholar Zhu Xi (Chu Hsi) (1130–1200), the Way
was the process of organizing and regulating the
whole of society, which began with the individual:
study of the external world and meditation would
effect a recovery of one's Original (good) Nature
(*honshō*) and eliminate the passions (*jinyoku*).
Those with perfect, unclouded knowledge were
called sages (*seijin*).

The original, perfect nature of the human being,
although governed by the same Principle (*ri*) according to which the physical world of the universe
operates (*tenjin goitsu* or *tendō jindō*) and therefore
natural, could be realized only through participation in society. That is, innate in the human mind
were the Five Constant Virtues (*gojō*) realized in
five corresponding social relationships (*gorin*):
righteousness or duty (*gi*) between prince and minister (*kunshin*) or, in the Japanese context, between
lord and vassal; *intimacy* (*shin*) between parent and
child (*fushi*); *distinction* (*betsu*) between husband
and wife (*fufu*); *precedence* (*jo*) between elder
brother and younger (*chōyō*); and *trust* (*shin*) between friends (*hōyu*).

The type of society prescribed by these five natural relationships was hierarchical (as were four of
the five relationships) and absolutely static. In
seventeenth-century Japan this meant that birth determined one's position in the social hierarchy and
kept one there; there was no civil service examination by which one could jump the hurdle between
samurai and commoner. There was no room for
improvement, either socially or morally. Education
enabled one to discover what one was, not what one
could become. One's situation was the way it ought
to be.

A principal assumption, especially among the
samurai, was than an individual's capacity for intellectual and moral achievement was determined
by his class and rank. One's identity was one's
function in society (*yaku*), which was portioned out
according to one's place in society, one's lot (*bun*).
This meant that because of his birth and the impla-
cable laws of nature, a farmer's son could not have
the intellectual or moral capacity that would entitle
him to serve in the government. Only those born to
be *samurai* had that capacity.

Jinsai circumvented the entire Neo-Confucian
system, integrating nature and society by going
back to Confucius and Mencius. Like Sokō, Jinsai
acknowledged the role of history in the transformation of Confucian thought, but Jinsai homed in on
the essential problem of Neo-Confucianism. As
transmitted by his son Tōgai in his *Changes in
Confucian Teaching, Past and Present* (*Kokon gak-
uhen*), Neo-Confucianism was Buddhist or Daoist
(Taoist), not Confucian. Indeed, in response to the
malaise of Song society, the Neo-Confucian masters found themselves confronting Buddhism,
which advocated the retreat from society as a
source of suffering and an impediment to full realization. This resulted in a co-opting of Buddhist
concepts and practices, such as the relationship of
Principle (*ri*) and Material Force (*ki*); the recovery
of original Buddha-nature (*busshō*) converted to
Original Nature (*honshō*); the translation of the
Way of the Buddha and enlightenment (*butsudō*) to
the Way of the Chinese Sages (*seidō*); and the
transformation of meditation practices to the
"quiet sitting" and "sustained reverence" of Neo-
Confucian practice. None of this was to be found in
the *Analects* or the *Mencius*.

The Essential Goodness of the Human Being

Jinsai relied heavily on Mencius to guide his study
of Confucius. He followed Mencius's assertion that
the human being was essentially good, but with
qualifications. The human being, indeed, was possessed of four innate Beginnings or Impulses (sympathy, shame, reverence, and sense of right and
wrong), but a person became good only when these
Impulses were extended and developed (*kakuju*)
into four corresponding virtues or aspects of the
Way. Personal morality consisted of humanity (*jin*),
righteousness (*gi*), decorum (*rei*, the respect for
difference in status), and wisdom (*chi*, the knowledge of the order of the universe). This goodness in
the human being was—for Jinsai—only a start, a
possibility. Without nurturance or proper development and education, this possibility would simply
remain that.

Although Jinsai held that human beings have the possibilities of goodness, he denied that this goodness had anything to do with nature as understood by the Neo-Confucianists. As stated in the *Meaning of Terms in the* Analects *and* Mencius, it is false that the human being was good because humanity's Original Nature operated by the same Principle as that running the natural and moral world of the universe; the Way of the human being had nothing to do with the Way of nature or Way of Heaven. The Way was the Way of the human being, a set of transcendent ideals external to and existing independent of man—ideals to strive for. The Way was individual moral cultivation and development. One did not return to good; one developed it.

The human being did indeed have an affinity with nature, but not with the Neo-Confucian Way of nature. Jinsai's authority was the *Book of Changes*, one of the "Five (existing) Classics" of the Chinese canon and its description of the movement of *yin* and *yang*. For Jinsai the world was characterized by change and growth (*ichidai ka kubutsu*). The human being was no different. In contrast, the Neo-Confucians looked upon change as a move away from good; the good was what did not change. Good was not active; it was always quiet, static.

However, even though Jinsai rejected the metaphysical underpinnings of Neo-Confucianism, he was in total sympathy with the practical aspects of Neo-Confucian thought. Individual moral development had to be worked out in society and in social relationships; virtue was useless unless others benefited from it. Individual motives were not as important as the results. Personal ethics meant maintaining the proper relationship between master and servant, parent and child, husband and wife, elder brother and younger brother, and friend and friend.

Jinsai's interest in practical morality can be seen in his elevation of the four virtues of benevolence or humanity (*jin*): loyalty, good faith, reverence, and forgiveness. These four virtues, combined with righteousness (*gi*) or duty, formed the core of Jinsai's ethics for the common person—the definition of a good human being.

Benevolence: The Cardinal Virtue

Whereas duty became the cardinal virtue of so many thinkers—such as Sokō—and thus served the warrior class, benevolence was Jinsai's cardinal virtue. He insisted that benevolence permeate each action and inform each relationship. In a sense, he was asserting the Chinese priority in values: the primary relationship was that between parent and child, and the benevolence and love that characterized that relationship was supposed to be developed and extended to the community; government was in a sense the extension of benevolence. For Jinsai, a truly and fully realized human being treated everyone with benevolence—those less perfect as well as those as perfect and moral as oneself.

Jinsai extended his benevolence equally to the people living in the Japan of his day. It was so easy for many intellectuals, yearning for the golden days of China's mythical past and its saintly sages, to sour on the realization that seventeenth-century Japan was no Age of Sages and never would be. But for Jinsai, since human nature had nothing to do with the Way, human feelings had nothing to do with morality. A person might be ambitious, jealous, covetous, or depressed; Jinsai judged him on the basis of how others benefited at his hands. Jinsai began the tendency to leave room for the individual to exist independently of society. Feelings were distinct from actions; one could have and even indulge emotions and even physical desires that were not subject to inspection or criticism, especially if they caused no one harm. Jinsai could not consider those who were intolerant and even cruel in their harsh judgment of others less perfect than themselves to be humane. Ogyū Sorai would finish the job of separating human feelings and desires from social action and morality, and Motoori Norinaga would create an ethos out of human feelings.

Jinsai's prescription to treat one and all equally benevolently also meant accepting the customs and institutions of the times. Hardline Neo-Confucianists, committed to the absolute value of principle and stasis, could only seek to emulate the

Chinese sages and to replicate ancient institutions. In contrast, committed to change, development, and growth as the properties of the physical world, Jinsai also accepted change in time, the property of history. Like Sokō, Jinsai saw no need to reject the historical development of Japan and accepted the contemporary social and political realities that were the precipitates of that history (*Boys' Questions*). It is important to recall that Jinsai principally rejected Neo-Confucianism, not because it had undergone historical changes, but because it was Buddhist.

Jinsai expressed the sentiment that moral development was not the purview of a ruler. In *Changes in Confucian Teaching, Past and Present* his son Tōgai conveyed Jinsai's stress on the historical development of the separation of the Way from government by the time of the Han (206 B.C.–A.D. 220); he pointed out that there were no sage–kings after the Duke of Zhou (Chou) and the destruction of the Way of the early sage–kings by the Qin (Ch'in) emperor who had burned books and killed Confucians. The unity of moral development and statecraft was central to Neo-Confucian ideology. Unlike Sokō and Sorai, Jinsai was convinced that the Way, personal moral cultivation, had nothing to do with government. He emphasized the responsibility to society of the individual for his actions, not the responsibility of society for the actions of individuals.

Perhaps that is one explanation for the fact that, although offers were made, Jinsai never accepted a position with a domainal lord. Perhaps, too, with his own meticulous concern for distinction in rank, Jinsai felt that the already hidebound traditions of the Japanese caste system and power represented some transcendent ideal intractable to the properties of growth and development characteristic of nature. But, by identifying the Way as personal cultivation and personal ethics, Jinsai established an ethical sphere in which all men could operate and be acknowledged as fully realized human beings independently of the constraints of the restrictive social system.

S. A. THORNTON

Further Reading

Translation

Tsunoda, Ryusaku, and Wm. Theodore de Bary and Donald Keene, comps. *Sources of Japanese Tradition*. Vol. 1. New York: Columbia University Press, 1964 (1958). Chapter 18, "The Rediscovery of Confucianism," contains a section on Itō Jinsai in which his views are discussed and selections from his works are presented.

Related Study

Spae, Joseph J. *Itō Jinsai, a Philosopher, Educator and Sinologist of the Tokugawa Period*. Monumenta Serica, Monograph 12. Peking: Catholic University Press of Peking, 1948. Still the standard study of Jinsai and the only full-length work.

KAIBARA EKKEN

Born: 1630, Fukuoka, Japan
Died: 1713, Fukuoka, Japan
Major Works: *Yamato zokkun* (*Precepts for Daily Life in Japan*) (1708), *Yamato honzō* (*Plants of Japan*) (1709), *Yōjōkun* (*Precepts on Health Care*) (1713), *Taigiroku* (*Record of Grave Doubts*) (1714)

Major Ideas

Principle (ri) *and Material Force* (ki) *are not dualistic.*
Material Force is the vital, dynamic component of nature that has Principle within.
Filial piety should be extended to the whole natural order.
Humaneness (jin) *is the principle of creativity corresponding to origination in nature.*
Humans are the soul of the universe and participate in the transformation of Heaven and Earth.
Nature should be studied and respected as part of a program of practical learning.

Kaibara Ekken was born on the island of Kyushu in southern Japan. His father was a physician to the local *daimyō*, Kuroda. Like many Confucian scholars he began his studies with medicine under his father's tutelage. He also studied the traditional ideas of Buddhism and Confucianism. Although he appreciated Buddhism as a youth, at the age of fourteen his interest in the Chinese classics grew under the tutelage of his elder brothers. At the age of twenty-six he left for Edo (now Tokyo) to become a physician.

Two years later he went to Kyoto to study Confucianism in greater detail. Here he immersed himself in the thought of Zhu Xi (Chu Hsi), the great twelfth-century synthesizer of Chinese Confucianism. He studied with some of the leading scholars of his day, including Kinoshita Jun'an and Nakamura Tekisai. Although Kinoshita was quite comprehensive in his interests, Nakamura was an ardent Zhu Xi defender. Yet both were firm advocates of practical learning (*jitsugaku*). Ekken also attended lectures by Yamazaki Ansai, although he remained critical of his severe and serious approach to learning. Although they were clearly of different temperaments, it was primarily in terms of their respective emphases in the interpretation of Zhu Xi that they parted company. Ansai was interested in developing the inner life in terms of spiritual practice, while Ekken tended to be more concerned with the investigation of principle in the natural world.

During these years Ekken was also studying the thought of the Chinese Neo-Confucians, Lu Xiangshan (Lu Hsiang-shan) and Wang Yangming. After reading Chen Jian's (Ch'en Chien) attack on these thinkers he rejected their ideas as being too Buddhistic. Ekken also disliked the excesses of some of Wang's followers. Thus in 1660, at the age of thirty, he became an ardent advocate of Zhu Xi's thought. His feeling for Zhu Xi approached a religious reverence. He published selections of Zhu Xi's work with punctuation so that they could be read by the ordinary Japanese. He also wrote the first Japanese commentary on Zhu Xi's *Jin-si Lu* (*Chin-ssu Lu*) (*Reflections on Things at Hand*).

By the time he was forty he had read widely in the Chinese sources, including the texts of the early classical period and those of the later Song (Sung), Yuan, and Ming Neo-Confucians. He was especially influenced by the Ming scholar Luo Qin Shun (Lo Ch'in-shun) and eventually adopted his monism of *qi* (Chinese: *qi/ch'i*; Japanese: *ki*) (Material Force). This essentially implied a rejection of the dualism of Principle (Chinese: *li*; Japanese: *ri*) and Material Force (*qi*). Ekken wished to affirm the vitality of the natural world as manifest in *qi* and wished to avoid abstract intellectualizing. This vitalistic naturalism (monism of *qi*) became the basis for both study of nature and cultivation of oneself.

Like Luo Qin Shun, Ekken came to have certain

reservations about Zhu Xi's thought. He felt it relied too heavily on Buddhist and Daoist (Taoist) sources and that its emphasis on self-cultivation tended to be too quietistic. Ekken set forth these reservations in his treatise *Record of Grave Doubts* (*Taigiroku*). It was clearly difficult for Ekken to disagree with Zhu Xi or to make a complete break with Zhu's thought. For these reasons *Grave Doubts* was not published until after his death. In addition to the intellectual debt he felt to Zhu Xi, Ekken wished to avoid being identified with the Ancient Learning School (*kogaku*) of Itō Jinsai. Although he and Itō both taught a monism of *qi*, he remained critical of Itō's rejection of Zhu Xi and his call for a return to the classics. He also disagreed with Itō's strong emphasis on moral cultivation without the same balanced concern for practical learning that so interested Ekken.

Ekken might be best understood, then, as being a reformed Zhu Xi thinker who derived much of his sensitivity toward nature from Zhu Xi and other Song thinkers. This reverence toward nature becomes the primary motivating force in the development of his own type of practical learning (*jitsugaku*) and filiality toward Heaven and Earth.

Practical Learning: Content and Methods

Ekken's thought was of a broad and comprehensive nature spanning both the humanities and natural sciences with an end toward personal moral cultivation and alleviation of larger social ills. Ekken's motivation in undertaking practical learning was to carry out Zhu Xi's injunction and to investigate things and examine their principles. To facilitate this process he advocated a method of investigation that was adapted from Zhu Xi's directives to his students at the White Deer Grotto. He suggested that a correct methodology should be marked by characteristics, which may be seen as elaborations of Zhu Xi's instructions, namely: study widely, question thoroughly, think carefully, judge clearly, and act seriously.

With regard to the first principle of the need for broad knowledge Ekken felt that one must not eliminate either traditional learning or practical contemporary concerns. What is particularly striking about Ekken's breadth is his conscious effort to include knowledge pertinent to the ordinary Japanese of this day. Indeed he felt it was his mission to study useful popular customs and agricultural techniques as well as to transmit Confucian moral values to the ordinary person.

Yet Ekken was aware of the need to maintain objectivity and rationality in the analysis of principles. He was not interested in simply collecting data or in becoming a specialist or a technician of knowledge. He wanted to be able to bring together specialized research and popular education and to see empirical investigation and ethical practice as part of a single continuum.

Like many Confucians before him Ekken warned against the limitations of methods used by both the humanist scholar and the scientific researcher. For him Confucian learning as an essentially ethical path must be distinguished from textual studies or technical skills as becoming ends in themselves. He urged scholars to maintain a reflective and contemplative posture when reading the classics so as not to fall into the traps of linguistic analysis and empty exegesis. Similarly, he rebuked the scholarly specialists who were interested only in personal recognition and the technicians who were obsessed with manipulative processes.

Yet in terms of the content of education, he sought to bring together both the study of classical texts and the natural world. He advocated a practical learning that would foster self-cultivation while also assisting others. He urged that learning should be "preserved in the heart and carried out in action." Traditional humanistic values and specifically technical skills should be used for the benefit of both self and society. In this way the scholar would be assisting in the Confucian aspiration to participate in the transformation of Heaven and Earth.

In order to bring together humanistic and scientific concerns Ekken felt that a physician, for example, should practice humaneness while helping to "nourish life" (*yōjō no jutsu*). His skills could not be dispensed without an understanding of his larger ethical role. Similarly, to study horticultural techniques or to cultivate plants only because of their beauty was to trivialize their larger role in the natural world. By being concerned with manipulative processes of cultivation a person could fall into the danger of "trifling with things and losing one's sense of purpose." Rather, horticulture and agriculture ought to be undertaken with a broader understanding of "the proclivity of nature to give birth to living things." An appreciation of nature's mysterious fecundity as the source of life was essential to Ekken's form of practical learning in fields as diverse as linguistics, medicine, botany, zoology, agriculture, food, sanitation, law, and mathematics. From this basic premise Ekken undertook a remarkably diverse range of research projects.

Finally, at the heart of this attempt to join the humanistic and scientific modes of learning was his understanding of the unity of Principle (*li*) and the diversity of its particularizations. An important extension of this idea was his belief in both the constancy of Principle and its myriad transformations. Thus although Principle is a unified and constant source of value in human society, it is similarly the source of order in the natural world. Yet at the same time and without contradiction, Principle is manifested in a diversity of forms and in a myriad of transformations. Thus both continuity and change are embraced by Principle. The elucidation of this idea became a motivating force of his own form of practical learning.

Because Ekken, following Luo Qin Shun, collapsed the distinction between Principle (*li*) and Material Force (*qi*), his practical learning was directed toward finding Principle within the transformations of Material Force itself. In terms of moral cultivation this meant a rejection of the distinction between one's original heavenly nature and one's physical nature. He saw them as essentially the same; therefore one's original nature or Principle was to be sought within one's own mind or Material Force. This same monism could be applied to the natural world to undertake empirical studies uncovering the Principle within Material Force.

The Creative Principles of Filiality and Jin

Ekken's practical learning was inspired not only by his monism of *qi*, but also by his doctrine of humaneness (*jin*) and filial piety (*ge/kō*), as extended to the natural world. From Zhang Zai's (Chang Tsai) doctrine of forming one body with all things Ekken elaborated his unique understanding of assisting in the transforming and nourishing powers of Heaven and Earth. Although his contemporary, Nakae Tōju, saw filiality as having a counterpart in the human and natural worlds, Ekken took this understanding a step further by stressing the need for humans to activate a filial reverence for the natural world.

A primary motive in this activation of filiality was a sense of the debt to Heaven and Earth as the parents of things. Ekken recognized the importance of loyalty and reverence to one's parents as the source of life and he carried this feeling of respect to the cosmic order. He maintained that since nature is the source and sustainer of life, one should respond to it as to one's parents, with care, reverence, and consideration. Indeed, a person must serve nature as they would their parents in order to repay their debt for the gift of life. He urged people to cherish living things and avoid wantonly killing plants or animals. This care for nature was a motivating force behind his own scientific research, for he saw it as connected with filiality.

Central to his doctrine of a cosmic filial relationship was an all-embracing humaneness. His scientific and spiritual pursuits are further linked by his understanding of a direct correspondence between humaneness in persons and the origination principle in nature.

Indeed, he recognized that the operation of Principle in the Supreme Ultimate *tai ji* (*t'ai chi*) had the unique purpose of creating the myriad things and thus can be termed "the heart of nature" (*tenchi no kokoro*). Just as birth and origination are the supreme attributes of the natural world, so humaneness is the supreme attribute of the human. Thus birth or origination is the counterpart in nature of *jin* or humaneness in persons.

In this way the creative dynamics of the universe find their richest expression in the creative reciprocity of human beings. The fecundity of nature and the well springs of the human heart are seen as two aspects of the all-embracing process of change and transformation in the universe. Ekken asserted that humans have a harmonious energy granted by nature, and this principle governs their lives. When extended to others this is the creative virtue of humaneness.

For Ekken, then, the human was the "soul of the universe" and thus has both great privileges and awesome responsibilities in the hierarchy of the natural world. He wrote, "It is a great fortune to be born a human; let us not fritter away our lives meaninglessly." One can do this through studying the classics, investigating Principle, developing practical learning, and activating humaneness. He also added the significant directive to "follow the example of nature" in achieving inner wisdom and contentment. With great detail he described the seasonal changes with which one should harmonize one's own moods and activities. He saw this as participating in the process of transformation, which for the human is the key to both knowledge and practice.

As part of his understanding of the human as the soul of the universe, Ekken adopted Zhu Xi's doctrine of total substance and great functioning *ti yong* (*t'i-yung*). To achieve this unique balance of theory and practice meant both an exploration of Principle and an activation of humaneness.

Briefly stated, then, these are some of the central ideas in Ekken's thought: filial piety should be extended to the whole cosmic order, humaneness is the principle of creativity corresponding to origination in nature, and human beings are the soul of the universe and participate through great substance and total functioning in the transformation of Heaven and Earth.

With Ekken, we have arrived at the threshold of a proto-scientific methodology dynamized by a Neo-Confucian religiosity. The understanding of the cosmic dimensions of reverence that was hinted at in earlier Japanese Neo-Confucian thinkers was transformed into a reverent investigation of nature. Similarly, the cosmic filiality of Nakae Tōju and other earlier Neo-Confucians was seen as a reason for both protecting and studying nature.

MARY EVELYN TUCKER

Further Reading

de Bary, Wm. Theodore and Irene T. Bloom, eds. *Principle and Practicality.* New York: Columbia University Press, 1981. A collection of interesting and helpful articles about Japanese Neo-Confucianism.

Graf, Olaf. *Kaibara Ekken.* Leiden, Netherlands: E. J. Brill, 1942. An informative account of Kaibara Ekken's life and thought, published in German.

Tucker, Mary Evelyn. *Moral and Spiritual Cultivation in Japanese Neo-Confucianism: The Life and Thought of Kaibara Ekken (1630–1713).* Albany, N.Y.: SUNY Press, 1989. An intensive treatment of Kaibara Ekken's thought.

Tu Wei-ming. *Confucian Thought: Selfhood as Creative Transformation.* Albany, N.Y.: SUNY Press, 1985. A comprehensive treatment of Neo-Confucian thought, with particular attention to the religious dimensions of the tradition.

OGYŪ SORAI

Born: 1666, Edo (now Tokyo), Japan
Died: 1728, Edo (now Tokyo), Japan
Major Works: *Bendō* (*Distinguishing the Way*) (1717), *Seidan* (*Discourses on Government*) (1725?)

Major Ideas

The Way is the Way of the Sage–Kings of ancient China, that is, government.

The Way has nothing to do with the Principle governing the operation of the natural world; it was invented by the sage–kings.

Realizing one's full humanity is to meet one's obligations to assist in the government of the land according to one's talents and place in society.

The Way is public; everything that does not concern public life belongs to the private sphere of the individual.

Of the three seminal thinkers of the Tokugawa period (1603–1868), Yamaga Sokō was the most influential in the shaping of political ideology, Itō Jinsai in the sphere of personal ethics, and Ogyū Sorai in the development of Japanese scholarship. Sorai, for all intents and purposes, established in Japan the discipline of philology, the study of language. He himself was the foremost scholar of ancient Chinese and his efforts sparked the study of ancient Japanese—the Shinto Revival or National Learning School. In addition, Sorai has attracted attention because of his pivotal role in the development of Japanese Confucian thought: he completed the work of Yamaga Sokō, Itō Jinsai, and others in the establishment of a kind of textual fundamentalism, a return to the ancient classics of China (Ancient Learning or *kogaku*), as a challenge to the privilege of orthodoxy enjoyed by Neo-Confucianism.

Like Sokō and Jinsai, Sorai came from that gray area of Japanese society occupied by physicians. Medicine was a respectable profession for unemployed members of the warrior class, as well as a route of social advancement for the brightest sons of the middle class. Sorai's father was a physician to the future shogun Tokugawa Tsunayoshi, who, for some reason, was sent into exile in 1679 for eleven years. Like Sokō, Sorai spent his youth under a cloud of insecurity, which was channeled into ambition. Sorai began his career by giving lectures

on the street outside the gate of the temple Zōjōji, which was important to the Tokugawa family, and attracting the attention of the temple's abbot. From 1696 until 1709, he was in the service of the shogun chamberlain, Yanagizawa Yoshiyasu. Later, he was called on directly by the shogun Yoshimune to offer advice on the financial and other ills besetting the government. Legend has it that his opinion was the basis for the sentence handed down to the forty-six vassals of the Lord of Akō, who had avenged their lord's death by taking the head of the shogun master of protocol.

Sorai's combined emphasis on practical administration and the refutation of Neo-Confucianism is demonstrated in his *Distinguishing the Way* (*Bendō*). Whereas Jinsai attacked the Neo-Confucian unity of nature and social organization through Principle (*ri*) by denying Principle, ignoring government, and focusing on nature, Sorai did the same by denying Principle, ignoring nature, and focusing on government. The Way, for Sorai, was exclusively government (social institutions) by which peace and contentment were brought to people.

Like Jinsai, Sorai insisted that the Way was external and he denied the Neo-Confucians' assertion that the truth could be found in one's own mind. The Way was culture, institutions, and the art and techniques of poetry, prose, rites, and music, and only these had been passed down by Confucius. Their purpose was to nourish each individual and to secure his fulfillment, peace, and contentment. The purpose of the moral individual was, in return, to nourish the Way, that is, to work for the perfection of the Way, government and social institutions, which would secure the peace and contentment of others.

While Jinsai externalized the Way by claiming absolute ontological status for it (it exists even without man), Sorai externalized the Way by making it the product of men. The Way was something created or invented by men called sages. It was created not by one man, but through the efforts of many. There was no one quality that made a sage; sages were not even perfect—they made mistakes.

The sages (*seijin*) or sage–kings (*sen'o*) are the legendary, great cultural heroes of China—those who invented human institutions. Fu Xi (Fu Hsi) taught fishing, hunting, herding, and the use of tools. Shen Nong (Shen Nung) taught agriculture and medicine. Yao and Shun invented rites and music, by which people were drawn into the proper correspondence with nature. And the great Yu (Yü) controlled the floods. Tang (T'ang), Wen, and Wu Wang overthrew monstrous tyrants. And the Duke of Zhou (Chou) was famed for his devotion to public service.

According to Sorai, the sages had invented the rules of morality by which society regulated itself. In contrast, the Neo-Confucianists maintained that the Five Relationships of society (*gorin*) were natural and inborn in human beings as part of their Original Nature (*honshō*), itself identical with Principle (*ri*). For Sorai, all except that between parent and child had been invented, especially that between king and minister (or as it was known in Japan, between lord and vassal). Or again, the aspects of hierarchy in society were not natural; they were a necessary technique and artifice for establishing rule and order (as well as a guide for distributing wealth and resources). Even the four orders of society (scholar, farmer, artisan, merchant) had been set up by sages.

Morality had been dictated by the sages; it was not natural. What, then, gave the sages their absolute authority? According to Sorai, the sages had no particular quality; their status depended on their accomplishments. The sages were the sages because they had invented human institutions; they had done so because they had been endowed to do so by Heaven. In operating according to their endowment, then, they had been following the will of Heaven and thus creating the rules of the social order. An intense religiosity pervades this aspect of Sorai's thought, so that an irrational feeling provides the authority for an entirely rational intellectual system. Sorai raised the sages to gods, to equality with Heaven itself.

If the sages were responsible for the invention of the Way, transmission of the Way was the responsibility of teachers. Transmission was not the Way itself, only government was the Way. Confucius himself had been unable to enter government service as he wished but had prepared his students to do so. Teaching, like rule, was based on trust. Those teachers who, like the Neo-Confucianists, taught their students to cultivate their inner selves, but not to take up government service, failed them. It was equally a betrayal to induce them to change their natures. One could not change one's nature; the attempt would only lead to resentment. One could not learn to become a sage, only a benevolent person.

The Way was sustained by benevolent human beings. Benevolence was nourishing and manifested itself only in a social context: people "nourished" each other, protected each other, helped each other to develop their individual natural talents. Heaven has endowed individuals with their natures and talents. Heaven has willed the social order. And, when an individual has played his role in society according to his endowments, he has followed the will of Heaven. Moreover, everyone was, broadly speaking, an "official" of the government and obligated to assist in the peaceful governance of the country. This one did according to one's talent and social position, both of which, of course, were endowed by Heaven.

The Way and the Six Classics

The Way was embodied in the "Six Classics" transmitted by Confucius: the books of *Odes*, *History*, *Changes*, *Music* (lost), and *Rites*, and the

Spring and Autumn Annals. They were the repositories of the civilization and culture of the golden age of China, the Zhou (Chou) period (1350?–770 B.C.). Constituting the canon, they remained the primary object of intellectual activity in China until 1911, when the last dynasty fell. In Japan during the seventeenth and eighteenth centuries, they were looked to as the ideal prescription for a perfect state. The master of the "Chinese Classics" was considered a master of public administration, statecraft, and even propaganda.

The "Six Classics" comprised the database of the customs, institutions, and etiquette of ancient China. Heaven had caused the creation of perfect institutions in the past. The transition from past to present history, for Sorai, was a process of degeneration, of fall from a paradise. The history of institutions was the story of their decline. In China the feudal structure had given way to centralized control. Actual administrative power had been transferred from king to officials in the bureaucracy. Authority had been transferred from the benevolent paternalism of the family system to harsh laws. (Jinsai would have added that the functions of government and education had been separated and divided between rulers and teachers.) And the rise of civil service exams had led to the rise of a certain scholarly tradition (represented by the Neo-Confucians). This tradition was characterized by disputation or forcible suasion instead of leading by example, the Way of the Sages.

The decline in institutions was accompanied by a decline in languages. Successive generations found it harder to understand the "Six Classics" after Confucius. If one could not live in the world that had produced the institutions, one could not expect to know or understand those institutions. Without understanding the language of the texts in which those institutions were preserved, one could not expect to read those texts. Neo-Confucian masters of the Song (Sung) period (ninth to twelfth centuries) did not write in the style of the classics; therefore they did not understand the classic texts and their interpretations were invalid.

The only way to recover the Way was philology, the study of language. Sorai had learned from Ming scholars Li Pan-long (Li P'an-lung) and Wang Shizhen (Wang Shih-chen) to distinguish classical prose from later prose styles; the return to classical prose led to the return to thinking about the content of the classical texts. The knowledge and mastery of ancient language was essential to understanding the texts. Sorai made it a point to learn the meanings of the words of ancient China as they were understood in that time and sought thereby to reconstruct the original meanings of the texts. Sorai studied not only the Confucian texts, but all texts in which he might find the "ancient words." Sorai urged diversity and range in scholarly studies. In this way he affirmed the return to Confucius of Sokō and Jinsai and established the School of Ancient Learning. (However, in *Distinguishing the Way*, he criticized Jinsai for not being able to read the *Analects* of Confucius as it would have been read in ancient China.)

As stated in *Distinguishing the Way*, the Way of the Sages is the way to bring peace and happiness to the people. The Way is government. Sorai sought to use philology to reconstruct the institutions and ceremonial, the rites and music, of the sage–kings. These were an absolute value for Sorai: not only were they models for emulation, but they were the source of virtue. By practicing writing in classical Chinese and rehearsing ancient Chinese etiquette, one could discipline oneself to achieve virtue. Sorai insisted on the role of the classics in personal cultivation: as Confucius said, one who did not know the *Book of Odes* simply was not fit to talk with.

In championing ancient Chinese ceremonial, Sorai was insisting on the absolute value of customs and institutions as standards of conduct: one could not look to one's own mind to know the right thing to do. Like Jinsai, Sorai rejected the Neo-Confucian concept of the Principle (*ri*) existing in the human mind. There was nothing in common among the minds of different people; if people followed their own minds, anarchy would result. Therefore one needed to look outside oneself to the laws, to custom, to social mores to find the objective standard of conduct.

By confining the definition of the Way to government and to the exclusion of personal morality or ethics, Sorai divided human activity into two spheres: public and private. The Way was government and public; everything else was private. Thus, when in 1703, the forty-six vassals of the late Lord of Ako were tried for the murder of the shogun's master of protocol, Sorai gave the following opinion: That the men had followed their duty (*gi*) in avenging their lord was only honorable. Therefore they should be allowed the dignity of dying as honorable men, of committing ritual suicide. But their relationship to their lord, this duty, was a private matter. They had broken the law and there could be no question of escaping punishment for their crime against the public good. The laws, not personal virtues, were absolute.

In distinguishing the public sphere from the private and by drawing a line between them, Sorai was able to create a place for the individual in a world that recognized only social groups. Sorai was quite happy to accept the validity of selfishness, physical desires, poetry, and even Buddhism as long as they were kept in the private sphere and the individual met all public responsibilities. "Private" did not mean "evil" to Sorai as it did to some Neo-Confucianists.

In considering Sorai's dedication to the rites and music of ancient China and his commitment to reviving and implementing them in Japan, it is worth exploring how Sorai felt about Japanese institutions. For example, Sokō's sense of Japan's historical development allowed and, moreover, supported the changes that made up the society he lived in; but he never saw them in decline or faced with such massive problems as confronted Sorai. Called upon to advise the shogun Yoshimune in a time of financial crisis for the entire warrior class (who controlled everything except the exchange rate between silver or gold and the rice with which they were paid their stipends), Sorai produced the *Discourses on Government* (*Seidan*). He analyzed the problem of the warriors who had to pay for everything with money "like guests at an inn."

With the models of ancient China in mind, he advised returning the warriors to the land and making them earn their own living—living in the country would also insulate them against the expensive temptations of urban life and thereby keep their incomes and expenditures in line. Sorai advised raising men of talent to position in the government rather than entrusting government to those with hereditary rights. (Considering the rate of adoption in the warrior class, whose individual and collective survivals depended on the performance of sons and heirs, this argument seems moot.) Sorai was even bold enough to suggest further centralization—even the taxation of the feudal lords.

All of these suggestions were vigorously resisted by conservatives unable to accept any changes to the system established by the ancestors of the Tokugawa house. Ironically, reformers of later times would look back to these proposals and lament that the Tokugawa house had lost its last opportunity to save itself.

S. A. THORNTON

Further Reading

Translation

Ogyū, Sorai. *Distinguishing the Way* [*Bendō*]. Translated by Olof G. Lidin. Monumenta Nipponica Monograph. Tokyo: Sophia University, 1970.

Related Studies

Lidin, Olof G. *Life of Ogyū Sorai*. Lund, Sweden: Student Litteratur, 1973.
——— . *Ogyū Sorai's Journey to Kai in 1706; With a Translation of the Kyōchūkikō*. Scandinavian Institute of Asian Studies Monograph Series, No. 48. London: Curzon Press Ltd., 1983.
McEwan, J. R. *The Political Writings of Ogyū Sorai*. Cambridge: Cambridge University Press, 1962.

MOTOORI NORINAGA

Born: 1730, Matsuzaka, Japan
Died: 1801
Major Works: *Ashiwake obune* (*A Small Boat Punting Through the Reed Brake*) (1756), *Shibun yōryō* (*The Essence of the* Tale of Genji) (1763), *Isonokami sasamegoto* (*My Personal View of Poetry*) (1763), *Kuzubana* (*Arrowroot Blossoms*) (1780), *Uiyamabumi* (*The First Step on the Mountain of Learning*) (1799), *Naobi no mitama* (*The Rectifying Spirit*) (1771), *Tamakushige* (*The Jeweled Comb-Box*) (1786), *Kojikiden* (*A Commentary on the* Kojiki) (1798), *Genji monogatari tama no ogushi* (*The Small Jeweled Comb: A Study of the* Tale of Genji) (1796)

Major Ideas

Human emotion is to be prized.

People in tune to deep emotion will naturally give rise to a feeling of mono no aware.

The authentic human life is one in which one is able to express and act on mono no aware.

Deep emotion is an expression of a pure human heart.

Buddhism is inherently antithetical to the development of deep emotion because it requires that one put aside their feelings and renounce the world.

Poetry is the natural product of one in touch with their deepest feelings.

True human emotion is spontaneous, so that we cannot control whether it is good or evil that moves us.

If people act in accord with natural Shinto, they will naturally be moral and society will be well-ordered.

There is no way for human beings to fully comprehend the actions and intentions of the gods.

One should learn about the past directly from the ancient texts.

Motoori Norinaga was a Tokugawa-period Kokugaku, or National Learning, scholar. Kokugaku was a Shinto movement that attempted to reclaim Japan's spiritual past from the overlay of foreign, especially Buddhist and Confucian, ideas. Norinaga was one of this movement's most articulate spokespersons, as his voluminous writings attest. He applied literary critical and philological methods to try to recover from Japan's ancient literature, especially the *Kojiki*, a unique Japanese cultural identity that he associated with the Age of the Gods. He found expressed in Japan's national literature a pristine, original Japanese spirit that placed enormous value on honest human emotions as an expression of the Ancient Way (*kodō*) of the Gods (*kami*).

Norinaga was born into a prosperous merchant family that resided in Matsuzaka, near the Ise Shrine. His father died when he was ten. His family were devout Pure Land School Buddhists, and this exposure to Buddhism had an impact on Norinaga, who studied and practiced Pure Land Buddhism at the family temple. His early spiritual life also included the worship of Shinto deities. This synthesis of Buddhist and Shinto rituals was common in Norinaga's day. Norinaga's education included the study of Chinese and Japanese philosophy and literature. Norinaga's first career was short-lived. He worked in the paper business, having been adopted into another merchant family without a son to preserve the family line. After little more than two years Norinaga severed this adoptive tie. Norinaga himself notes that business was contrary to his wishes, and that he preferred reading and studying.

With his mother's approval, Norinaga went to Kyoto at the age of twenty-one to study medicine, where he stayed for nearly six years. Norinaga not only pursued his medical studies, but read the Chinese classics with a noted scholar, Hori Keizan (1688–1757), who further exposed Norinaga to a combination of Japanese literature, Kokugaku thought, and Confucianism. It was during this time that Norinaga was also introduced to the works of Ogyū Sorai (1666–1728)—a famous *Kokugaku* (Ancient Learning, Confucian studies) scholar— and of the Buddhist monk and literary scholar Keichū (1640–1701). Keichū's writings acquainted Norinaga with the application of philology to literary studies. In particular, Norinaga was influenced by Keichū's attempt to interpret what he construed as the original meaning of ancient Japanese poetry (*waka*) stripped of later, erroneous meanings.

Norinaga returned home to Matsuzaka in 1757 and began a medical practice, which supported his continued study of the literary classics. His studies led him to begin lecturing on Japanese literature initially for members of a literary club he had joined. The three texts that were to become the foundation for Norinaga's lifelong study, the *Kojiki* (eighth-century history of Japan that included the creation of Japan and the activities of the gods), the *Man'yōshū* (eighth-century collection of ancient Japanese verse), and the *Genji monogatari* (*Tale of Genji*) (an early eleventh-century novel), were often the topics of his lectures. His erudition attracted a wide audience and gained Norinaga his first students.

In 1763 Norinaga completed two works that represent his maturing view of Japanese literature. The *Shibun yōryō* (*The Essence of the* Tale of Genji) argues that the Japanese aesthetic concept of *mono no aware*, or the "pathos of things," was of central importance to the *Tale of Genji*. Norinaga extended his discussion of *mono no aware* to Japanese poetry in his *Isonokami sasamegoto* (*My Personal View of Poetry*), in which he uses *mono no aware* as the basis for understanding Japanese poetry. In this text he argues that when a person is overwhelmed by the deep emotion that is *mono no aware*, then that person naturally gives expression to the emotion in poetic form.

The year 1763 was also a turning point for Norinaga. That year he had a single meeting with the great Kokugaku scholar, Kamo Mabuchi (1697–1769), but this had a great impact on Norinaga, who in effect became Mabuchi's disciple through correspondence. Norinaga often inquired of his master's thoughts on Japanese literature, especially

Mabuchi's specialty, the *Man'yōshū*. Mabuchi encouraged Norinaga's study of the *Kojiki* because it was Japan's oldest text and therefore contained the least foreign influence; hence, from a Kokugaku viewpoint, it was closest to Japan's original spirit. Norinaga's subsequent extensive study of the *Kojiki* was a result of this imperative. His monumental *Kojikiden* (*A Commentary on the* Kojiki) (1798), begun soon after his meeting with Mabuchi, took him thirty-four years to write.

Norinaga devoted much of the rest of his life to the study of Japan's ancient past, seeking a return to antiquity (*fukko*) in order to regain its significance for the Japan of his day. Norinaga's fame spread and he had many students who came to study with him. Norinaga also attracted the attention of political leaders. He accepted a position in the Kii *daimyō* to serve as a Kokugaku teacher. His *Tamakushige* (*The Jeweled Comb-Box*) (1786) presented his Shinto thought in relation to political philosophy.

Norinaga spent the last three years of his life lecturing on the topics he had pondered throughout his lifetime. His influence on subsequent Japanese thought was great. His literary criticism and study of the *Tale of Genji* had a strong impact on literary studies. His Shinto views became central to later Kokugaku scholars and were taken up by some of the leaders of the Meiji Restoration (1868). Japanese nationalism in the twentieth century also looked to Norinaga's ideas for ways to legitimate their rhetoric of Japan's unique place in the world.

Mono no aware

Norinaga's Kokugaku, in contrast to the rationality and control of human emotions that marks Neo-Confucianism, can be characterized in terms of emotion and its necessary and proper expression. The concept of *mono no aware* is central to Norinaga's understanding of the emotional significance of ancient Japanese literature and its impact on Japanese identity. Thus *mono no aware* was central to his literary theory and to his view of human nature.

Norinaga's ideas about *mono no aware* were developed as a result of his study of the *Tale of Genji*. This term is an important Japanese aesthetic category, but for Norinaga it was also a foundation for his view of human nature. The term itself can be translated as the "pathos of things," but this only begins to touch on the aesthetic of emotion it describes. Norinaga himself understands *aware* as originally referring to the spontaneous expression of deep emotion. This term, he argues, came to refer in the *Tale of Genji* to a lovely melancholy, an aesthetic pathos, that results from an awareness of the fundamental ephemerality (*mujō*) of existence, a Buddhist sensibility. By Norinaga's day, the term was most often used to refer to pathos or sorrow. Norinaga, seeking to reclaim what he viewed as the true or original meaning of the term, used the many occurrences of *aware* in the *Tale of Genji* (it occurs some 1,044 times) to understand that this concept was central to the aesthetic ideals of the Heian society in which *Genji* was written. Norinaga attempted to reclaim this court aesthetic from the meaning of *aware* used in his day by using the term *mono no aware* to refer to this older, "special" sense of the term. The term *mono*, "things," and the possessive particle *no* gave Norinaga the rhetorical possibility of extending the meaning of the "pathos of things" beyond the intense emotion of an individual to the idea that this *mono no aware* referred to a universal aesthetico-emotional response. This was accomplished by Norinaga by interpreting *mono* as referring to "things," not as specific objects, but in the more general sense of things of the world. Thus, anyone who is in tune to deep emotion will naturally give rise to a feeling of *mono no aware*. Things have pathos intrinsically and any sensitive person will clearly perceive and feel this. Otherwise, one is without real human emotion and is ignorant of *mono no aware*. There is an ethical conception here—the authentic human life is one in which one is able to express and act on *mono no aware*.

Norinaga's notion of *mono no aware* is also related to the idea that deep emotion is an expression of a pure human heart (*kokoro*). This concept of human nature is viewed by Norinaga as feminine. He argues, for instance, that the human heart is feminine and weak, qualities he relates descriptively to women and children. Wise men do not attempt to conceal the feminine aspects of their hearts.

Norinaga's ideas about *mono no aware* appear in such works as *Ashiwake obune* (*A Small Boat Punting Through the Reed Brake*) (1756), *Shibun yōryō*, *Isonokami sasamegoto*, and the later *Genji monogatari tama no ogushi* (*The Small Jeweled Comb: A Study of the* Tale of Genji) (1796). These works are both vehicles for his articulation of his aesthetic category, but they are also literary criticism, understood through the concept of *mono no aware*. For Norinaga, good literature is able to convey deep human emotion, to express *mono no aware*. A Buddhist view of poetry, for instance, might revolve around the idea that poetry helps one to gain enlightenment. But Norinaga's literary criticism rejects such ideas and instead focuses on literature as a vehicle for the expression of deep emotion. In the *Shibun yōryō* Norinaga argues that literature has significance only as conveyor of *mono no aware*, and one should only attend to this essence. It should be noted that Norinaga also claims that Buddhist practice is inherently antithetical to the development of *mono no aware* because it requires, for instance, that one put aside their feelings about their family by requiring one to renounce the world.

Norinaga's View of Poetry

Norinaga's first work, *Ashiwake obune*, elucidates his view of poetry (*waka*), and is influenced by Keichū's ideas. This work first articulates Norinaga's emphasis on the importance of human emotions. He argues that *waka* is produced only when the poet's emotions are properly expressed. Thus, poetry is the natural product of one in touch with their deepest feelings. As such, Norinaga viewed poetry as morally and politically neutral. Norinaga, in a comparison of Japanese and Chinese poetry, values Japanese verse as the necessary vehicle of expression for a Japanese person moved by intense emotion. It is, then, the natural literary expression for Japanese poets.

Norinaga's concept of good and evil is also based on his understanding of *mono no aware*. He argues that things which deeply moves us can be both good and evil. True human emotion is spontaneous, so that we cannot control whether it is good or evil that moves us. From Norinaga's view human beings have little control over the matter: even if we would wish not to be moved by evil, we are helpless to resist in the face of an overwhelming, spontaneous emotional response. Norinaga claims that his view of good and evil is different from such concepts as they occur in Buddhist and Confucian texts. The attempts of Buddhism and Confucianism to lead people from evil to good often goes against natural human emotion and is therefore harmful to the basic value of *mono no aware*. Thus the value of a text such as the *Tale of Genji* lies in its sincere and authentic expression of *mono no aware*, regardless of whether in response to good or evil, and not on the quality of its moral instruction.

Along with the development of ideas concerning human emotions, Norinaga also developed ideas about the importance of Shinto. He speaks of a "natural Shinto" (*shizen no shinto*), described in the *Kojiki*, that has existed since the Age of the Gods, and which differs from the idea of Shinto used in his contemporary world. If people act in accord with natural Shinto, they will naturally be moral and society well ordered. This was the situation in ancient Japan. It is only because people fell away from natural Shinto that it was necessary to impose morality through foreign teachings such as Confucianism. Norinaga promoted a return to the Ancient Way (*kodō*) of the Age of the Gods as revealed in the *Kojiki*, which expressed the Way of the Kami (*kami no michi*). Norinaga's magnum opus, the *Kojikiden*, and other works, such as the *Naobi no mitama* (*The Rectyifying Spirit*) (1771), present his arguments for the necessity of reclaiming the glory of Japan's ancient and divine past, and the philological and other methods by which this can be accomplished.

In such works as the *Naobi no mitama*, *Kuzubana* (*Arrowroot Blossoms*) (1780), and the *Kojikiden*, Norinaga addressed the issue of the nature of the *kami*. He explained that the power of the

kami is ultimately incomprehensible to people who cannot understand their sometimes irrational behavior. Even the gods may appear to do evil, but these actions may turn out to be good. Conversely, the good a god may appear to perform may turn out to be evil. There is not any way for human beings to fully comprehend the actions and intentions of the gods. Thus Norinaga dismissed rational thought as ineffective to the task of understanding the gods.

Norinaga attempted to define the word *kami*. Rejecting existing etymological explanations of the derivation of the term, Norinaga explained the significance of the concept by reference to such feelings as awe, superiority, and a sense of the unusual that irrupt in one who is in the presence of the power of the *kami*. The *kami*, he notes, can take myriad different forms, including humans, animals, and natural objects such as waterfalls, mountains, and trees. Norinaga was particularly interested, however, in the *kami* described in the *Kojiki*, and among these he paid special attention to Takami-musubi, Izanagi and Izanami, and Amaterasu. Amaterasu was especially important because she founded the imperial lineage as Japan's legitimate ruling authority that served as the basis for the Ancient Way.

Norinaga's *Uiyamabumi* (*The First Step on the Mountain of Learning*) (1799), written soon after completion of the *Kojikiden*, sets out his method for the study of the Ancient Way. In essence he wanted to jettison interpretations of ancient texts that he thought were colored by foreign ideas, and to directly study, in detail, the texts in question. One therefore should learn about the past directly from the ancient texts, not through intermediary interpretations. Norinaga suggests that students should themselves write *waka* in order to cultivate an intuitive understanding of the past.

WILLIAM E. DEAL

Further Reading

Translations

Brownlee, John S. "The Jeweled Comb-Box: Motoori Norinaga's *Tamakushige*," *Monumenta*

Nipponica. 43:1, 1988, pp. 35–61. Presents a brief introduction to and translation of Motoori Norinaga's *Tamakushige.*

Nishimura, Sey. "First Steps into the Mountains: Motoori Norinaga's *Uiyamabumi,*" *Monumenta Nipponica.* 42:4, 1987, pp. 449–493. Presents a brief introduction to and translation of Motoori Norinaga's *Uiyamabumi.*

Tsunoda, Ryusaku, Wm. Theodore de Bary, and Donald Keene, comps. *Sources of Japanese Tradition.* Vol. 2. New York: Columbia University Press, 1964 (1958), pp. 1–5; 15–35. A useful selection of Motoori Norinaga's writings in translation.

Related Studies

Harootunian, H. D. *Things Seen and Unseen: Discourse and Ideology in Tokugawa Nativism.* Chicago: University of Chicago Press, 1988. This challenging work utilizes a new historicist perspective to discuss the ideological nature of Kokugaku thought. Includes discussion of the ideas of Motoori Norinaga.

———. "The Consciousness of Archaic Form in the New Realism of Kokugaku." In *Japanese Thought in the Tokugawa Period, 1600–1868: Methods and Metaphors,* edited by Tetsuo Najita and Irwin Scheiner. Chicago: University of Chicago Press, 1978, pp. 63–104. This article-

length study of Kokugaku thought covers ideas that are more fully developed in the author's *Things Seen and Unseen.*

Harper, Thomas James. "Motoori Norinaga's Criticism of the *Genji Monogatari*: A Study of the Background and Critical Content of His *Genji Monogatari Tama no Ogushi.*" Ph.D. dissertation, University of Michigan, 1971. A study of Motoori Norinaga's scholarship on the *Tale of Genji* with a translation of his *Genji monogatari tama no ogushi.*

Maruyama, Masao. *Studies in the Intellectual History of Tokugawa Japan.* Translated by Mikiso Hane. Princeton, N.J.: Princeton University Press; Tokyo: University of Tokyo Press, 1974. Although some of the premises of this classic work have been challenged by more recent scholarship, it nevertheless provides a useful overview of major Tokugawa-period thinkers and ideas including some coverage of Motoori Norinaga.

Matsumoto, Shigeru. *Motoori Norinaga, 1730–1801.* Cambridge, Mass.: Harvard University Press, 1970. A biography of Motoori Norinaga and interpretation of his major ideas from a psychological perspective.

Yoshikawa, Kōjirō. *Jinsai, Sorai, Norinaga: Three Classical Philologists of Mid-Tokugawa Japan.* Tokyo: Tōhō Gakkai, 1983.

HIRATA ATSUTANE

Born: 1776, Akita, Japan
Died: 1843
Major Works: *Kōdo taii (Summary of the Ancient Way)* (1811), *Koshichō* (1811), *Shitsunoiwaya* (1811), *Tama no mihashira (Pillar of the Soul)* (1812), *Tamadasuki* (1829), *Koshiden (Commentaries on Ancient History)* (1825), *Shutsujō shogo (A Laughing Discourse on the Everyday World)* (1811), *Hongyō gaihen (Supplementary Compilation of Shinto)* (1806)

Major Ideas

The Age of the Gods is a paradigm for how to live and work in the present.
The Ancient Way must be reclaimed so that the pure and true Japanese spirit can be actualized in the present.
Daily work and family duties are the expression of one's insight into the Ancient Way.
Study of the past illuminates the meaning and significance of the present.
Proper government is rule according to the wishes of the gods.
Everyday work recreates the original act of creation by the gods and constitutes an offering to the gods in a repayment of the blessings they have bestowed upon human beings.
Takami-musubi is the creator god.
The Japanese heart can be better understood if it is known where one's spirit journeys at death.
Confucianism and Buddhism are false, foreign teachings that corrupt the purity of the Ancient Way.

Hirata Atsutane was a Kokugaku (National Learning) scholar and an ardent nationalist, who led the Shinto movement known as *Fukko Shintō* ("return to antiquity" Shinto), which sought to reclaim a pristine Shinto purged of foreign, especially Buddhist and Confucian, ideas. A disciple of Motoori Norinaga (1730–1801), he further developed Norinaga's concept of the Ancient Way (*kodō*), providing it with a more political and ideological value than his teacher had. Atsutane's quest for the Japanese Ancient Way emphasized the divinity of the emperor. These ideas were particularly influential among leaders of the Meiji Restoration (1868), who sought the return of direct rule by the emperor. The emperor, they argued, was the rightful ruler because of the divine descent of the imperial line from the *kami* (gods). Despite the fact that Atsutane was sometimes strident in his condemnation of foreign influences in Japan, ideas culled from Buddhist, Confucian, and other foreign systems made their way into his theory of Shinto. Although he frequently reviled Western culture, he also studied Dutch medicine and other

Western sciences, and he was familiar with Christian ideas.

Atsutane was born into a *samurai* family of low rank in the Akita domain. From an early age he studied Yamazaki Ansai's (1618–82) Shikoku School of Zhu Xi (Chu Hsi) Neo-Confucianism. At nineteen he ran away to Edo (now Tokyo), where he engaged in menial labor and studied Daoist (Taoist) thought. Some time after this, Atsutane was adopted into a *samurai* family in Bitchu Province. Atsutane first studied the Kokugaku works of Motoori Norinaga in 1801, and from that time on dedicated his life to the study of Shinto. Although Norinaga died before Atsutane could study with him, he nevertheless considered himself Norinaga's student.

Despite the influence that Norinaga had on Atsutane's ideas, Atsutane developed his own distinctive way of interpreting the foundational texts of Kokugaku, such as the *Kojiki*. Atsutane was more interested in the religious practice that a study of the Ancient Way implied, rather than the philological and aesthetic orientation of his mentor Norinaga. To this end Atsutane argued that the religiosity of the Ancient Way had been lost because of the centrality that had been given to poetry and aesthetics in the conceptions of Norinaga and other Kokugaku scholars. Whereas Norinaga had advocated a study of ancient Japanese poetry (*waka*), Atsutane advocated an emphasis on daily work and family duties as an expression of one's insight into the Ancient Way. One was to live the Ancient Way, not simply "feel" it through an aesthetic appreciation of ancient poetry. Because of his emphasis on work and family, Atsutane had a strong following among farmers and local officials. His ideas were rejected by some Kokugaku scholars attempting to maintain the orthodoxy of Norinaga's views, but prized by those advocating a strong Shinto view and the nationalism that accompanied it.

Atsutane is often described as xenophobic and ethnocentric. His strong distaste for things foreign, evident in his treatises attacking Confucianism and Buddhism, would seem to bear out these evaluations. For instance, he viewed Japan as superior to all other countries because only Japan had its origins in the Age of the *Kami*. Other countries did not share in this unique origin and therefore did not share in the blessings the gods bestowed on Japan. He also enthusiastically endorsed the centrality of imperial rule and the divine descent of the imperial family from the gods. He suggested that daily worship of the gods should begin by facing the Kyoto Imperial Palace where the emperor, a living god, resided.

Atsutane's impassioned opinions gained him notoriety. A lecture tour at Shinto shrines throughout Japan was sponsored by the Shirakawa family, who had a long association with the Shinto clerical hierarchy. The Yoshida family, important Shinto proponents, invited him to teach. His strident views also caused him trouble. He was censured and confined to the area of his home by the Tokugawa government for his advocacy of direct imperial rule, which was at odds with the political interests of the Tokugawa. Atsutane wrote numerous treatises and attracted a large number of students to his private school, known as the Ibukinoya. His interpretation of the Ancient Way as a template for

living in the present proved to be a powerful discourse that had a far-reaching impact on later Japanese nationalists. His ideas were important to the anti-foreign sentiment and nationalism that punctuated much of Japanese history until 1945.

The Ancient Way

Atsutane's Kokugaku and Shinto thought centered on the concept of the Ancient Way (*kodō*). For Atsutane, this meant reclaiming the essence of the divine time known as the Age of the Gods, described in the *Kojiki*. This was a period in which the true Japanese spirit existed in a pure fashion, unsullied by the falsehoods of Confucian, Buddhist, and other foreign influences. Atsutane viewed the *Kojiki* as the most important resource for reclaiming and understanding Japan's ancient and divine past. The past, for Atsutane, was not an object to be observed, a museum piece, but rather a way of living to be reinstituted in the present. The past served as a paradigm for how to live and work in the present, and it explained the values and sensibilities that made actualizing the Way of the Gods in the present a possibility. Thus he believed that the *kami* are present and intervene in daily life and, conversely, that human work recreates the past. In this sense, Atsutane viewed past and present as interfused. It was not that the past needed to be interpreted—Atsutane believed that the *kami* had long ago named and specified the significance and meaning of the things in the world—but rather it must be properly recognized and lived.

Atsutane's *Tamadasuki* (1829) was written to assist the people in understanding the Way of the Gods. In it, he rejects the emphasis that Motoori Norinaga and other Kokugaku scholars had placed on the proper aesthetico-emotional response to poetry that was meant to express the affective truth and purity of the ancient Japanese spirit. For Atsutane knowledge of the Ancient Way consisted not in the abstract study of ancient texts, but in the concrete understanding of the intentions and activities of the gods that could be put to use in one's own life.

To this end Atsutane negated the value of studying poetry as a means of understanding the Ancient Way. Atsutane's Kokugaku agenda, therefore, singled out work, and agricultural work in particular, as that which upheld the Ancient Way. In so doing, Atsutane moved away from the aesthetic sensibility of *mono no aware*, or the "pathos of things," that characterized Motoori Norinaga's notion of Shinto. Atsutane's response was a reaction against the earlier nativist interpretations of Motoori Norinaga, who had championed poetry as the way to "feel" what it meant to be Japanese. Thus Atsutane wanted to move from feelings to work or family duties. Atsutane's Shinto can thus be characterized as concerned with practical matters in the world. This emphasis on the quotidian as the ground for acting in accord with the sacred past was, at least in Atsutane's ideal, not directed toward a social elite, but rather to all Japanese. Atsutane sometimes equated the Ancient Way with the everyday lives of the common people.

Atsutane legitimated his views by referring back to textual authority. For Atsutane and many other Kokugaku scholars this was the *Kojiki*. The Ancient Way was made known through the creation of the universe by the gods. This divine activity was reproduced in the creation of the habitable world of humans. Further, this past activity of the gods was still active and accessible in the present. Atsutane's Japan was analogous to ancient Japan. Thus an important aspect of Atsutane's reading of the *Kojiki* was his interpretation that the past served to illuminate the meaning and significance of the present.

Important to these conceptions was the role the emperor was to play in the governance of human affairs. Atsutane argued that the emperor descended to rule the world because of the divine intention of the heavenly deities. But what kind of governance had the *kami* intended? Atsutane's view revolved in part around his analysis of the concept of *matsurigoto*. Although this term had been variously understood as both political and religious administration, Atsutane tended to see it in terms of the idea of religious ritual. He placed great importance on people with the kind of knowledge that enabled them to conduct religious rituals and honor the gods. This, he insisted, was the aim

of proper government, that is, rule according to the wishes of the gods. Japan was a divine land (*shinkoku*) in which the wishes of the gods were actualized through imperial rule.

For Atsutane the concept of *matsurigoto* suggested that religion and government were one and the same. Further, the everyday work of the people, re-creative of the original act of creation by the gods, was in effect an offering to the gods, a repayment of the blessings that the *kami* had bestowed upon human beings. This, of course, amounted to an ethical injunction to work that was linked to a cosmically significant authority. Atsutane viewed the world as the creation of the gods that was meant explicitly for humans to utilize for their well-being.

Atsutane's reading of the *Kojiki* led him to single out the *kami* Takami-musubi as the creator god. In the *Kodō taii* (*Summary of the Ancient Way*) (1811) Atsutane credits Takami-musubi with the creation of Heaven and Earth and endows him with power that surpasses the others gods. Atsutane claimed that it is because of the influence of foreign ideas that the import of Takami-musubi has been lost. Atsutane was, in part, trying to prove that Japan's mythology is not merely a collection of legends of dubious veracity, as some asserted, but rather an account of ancient truths. This proof was relevant to Atsutane's need to legitimatize other aspects of his interpretation of the Ancient Way, especially the special place of the imperial line. Atsutane finds support for his view of a single creator god in his comparison to the creation stories of other cultures that also assert a primary creator deity. He argues that the existence of such stories in other lands authenticates his claims for Takami-musubi. Not only is this *kami* the supreme creator god in Japan, but he also stands as the most divine of all the gods in the world.

Atsutane, in his *Tama no mihashira* (*Pillar of the Soul*), articulated a cosmology that explained the relationship between Heaven, Earth, and the underworld. He also clarified the nature of the afterlife and its inhabitation by the souls of the dead. Atsutane, concerned with the Japanese heart (*yamatogokoro*), believed it was important to contrast this with the Chinese heart (*karagokoro*). One could better understand the Japanese heart if one understood where one's spirit (*tama*) journeyed at death. Without this investigation, Atsutane feared that one might have to settle for a foreign explanation of such matters. Whereas Motoori Norinaga had suggested that souls travel to the underworld (*yomi*), Atsutane rejected this notion. Instead, he attempted to prove that because the underworld was separated from Earth at the time of creation, it was cut off from the light of Heaven and hence was permanently separated from the Earth. Thus it was impossible that the souls of the deceased could travel there. The souls of the deceased were of a different substance from the underworld because they were created by the gods and therefore necessarily traveled to Heaven. Atsutane conceived of a hidden or invisible realm that coexisted with the visible realm of the Earth and was the final abode of the souls of the dead. According to Atsutane, if one virtuously followed the Way of the *Kami*, then one would receive the blessings of the gods in the next life. This was significant to Atsutane because he believed that people were unable to work in an efficient and productive manner if they were constantly dogged by fears and anxieties about death. Atsutane offered up a cosmology that acted to quell such concerns.

Atsutane was a relentless critic of Confucianism and Buddhism because he viewed these as false, foreign teachings that corrupted the purity of the Ancient Way. In the *Shutsujō shōgo* (*A Laughing Discourse on the Everyday World*) (1811), for instance, Atsutane criticized Buddhism as a collection of foreign falsehoods and fabrications. He questioned the authenticity of words claimed to have been spoken by Shākyamuni (Siddhārtha Gautama) and argued that they were later forgeries. Atsutane expanded his attack to include a description of India, the Buddha's birthplace, as vulgar and ignorant, thereby casting aspersions on the cultural origins of Buddhism. Atsutane laments that such vulgarities ever found their way into Japan. He argues that it is only the Ancient Way that can purify Japan from such detrimental teachings and restore the true Japanese spirit.

WILLIAM E. DEAL

Further Reading

Translation

Tsunoda, Ryusaku, Wm. Theodore de Bary, and Donald Keene, comps. *Sources of Japanese Tradition.* Vol. 2. New York: Columbia University Press, 1964 (1958), pp. 35–46. A useful selection of Hirata Atsutane's writings in translation.

Related Studies

Harootunian, H. D. *Things Seen and Unseen: Discourse and Ideology in Tokugawa Nativism.* Chicago: University of Chicago Press, 1988. This challenging work utilizes a new historicist perspective to discuss the ideological nature of Kokugaku thought. Includes discussion of the ideas of Hirata Atsutane.

———. "The Consciousness of Archaic Form in the New Realism of Kokugaku." In *Japanese Thought in the Tokugawa Period, 1600–1868: Methods and Metaphors*, edited by Tetsuo Najita and Irwin Scheiner. Chicago: University of Chicago Press, 1978, pp. 63–104. This article-length study of Kokugaku thought covers ideas that are more fully developed in the author's *Things Seen and Unseen.*

NISHIDA KITARŌ

Born: 1870, Ishikawa, Japan
Died: 1945, Kamakura, Japan
Major Works: *A Study of Good* (1911), *Intuition and Reflection in Self-Awakening* (1917), *From the Acting to the Seeing* (1927), *The Self-Conscious Determination of Nothingness* (1932), *Logic and Life* (1936), *The Logic of Basho and the Religious World View* (1945)

Major Ideas

"Pure experience" is the experience of knowing facts just as they are.

Human beings as creative elements have "absolute free will" in the center of the creative world.

The basho *(place) is "a predicate of predicates," a truly universal, transcendent place in which subject and predicate are mutually inclusive.*

The more conscious one is of oneself as a singular existence, the more God stands over one in the "inverse correlation."

Absolute nothingness actualizes itself through the instrumental nature of our bodies in the "acting intuition."

The world is the "self-identity of absolute contradictions."

Through the death of the self, we encounter the absolute God, who saves us through absolute negation of itself.

Nishida Kitarō struggled over many years to transform Eastern intuitive experience based on his own Zen practice into the Western philosophical mold of thinking, and in doing so he succeeded in establishing an original Japanese philosophy. Especially important was Nishida's contribution in presenting a logical analysis of Eastern nonverbal, nonrational attitudes towards metaphysical matters, probably for the first time in Japanese intellectual history. His universal philosophy had a significant influence on many Japanese philosophers of the modern period, including Tanabe Hajime (1885–1962) and Nishitani Keiji (1900–90). Their philosophical movement, called the Kyoto School, has produced a number of unique thinkers in various fields of study, who attempted to synthesize the invaluable insights of the East and West.

A Study of Good

Inspired by English empiricism and the psychologically oriented philosophy of William James, Nishida created his own concept, "pure experience," in order to define the value of religious experience. Nishida's "pure experience" does not contain any cognitive perception of oppositions, such as those of subject and object, body and mind, and time and space. By transcending the dichotomous standpoint, he opened a new metaphysical passage to the consideration of immediate experience absent of all intervention by judgmental reflection.

For Nishida the good does not mean moralistic human conduct but rather the existential state of being unified with ultimate reality. Nishida always had a serious concern with ethics in human society, but did not consider ethical problems as separate from the problems of self for each individual, and accordingly he understood that "pure experience" is nothing but the realization of true selfhood. For him, the good is the perfection of true individuality, the only foundation from which the well-being of all humanity can be constructed.

Intuition and Reflection in Self-Awakening

Confronting the theories of the French philosopher Henri Bergson (1859–1949) and other Neo-

Kantian philosophers, Nishida attempted to eliminate psychological and epistemological trends from his speculation and to pursue strictly logical thinking. Deepening his understanding of "pure experience," he developed the metaphysical idea of *jikaku*, "self-awakening," in order to explain the inseparable relationship between intuition and reflection. "Self-awakening" as the reality of the self is a truly concrete and universal experience in which subject and object are identical.

Nishida further explored his concept of "self-awakening" and found in the core of the self the "absolute free will," which emerges from and returns to absolute nothingness. The "absolute free will" becomes the center of the creative world and lives in the "eternal now." Thus the focus of Nishida's philosophy moved away from the psychological experience of the individual toward a metaphysical system of the universe in which the individual represents the "creative nothingness."

From the Acting to the Seeing (1927)

Nishida viewed human existence as essentially self-contradictory. Human existence contains within itself absolute contradictions, such as instinct and reason, body and mind, and self and the world. Nishida tried to explore the ground of self-identity at the bottom of contradictory human existence by breaking through the dichotomy of the subject–predicate relation, the paradigm of human perception. Because Nishida was not satisfied with the Aristotelian anthropocentric worldview, he formed his own logic, namely the logic of *basho*, or *topos*, as the only rational way to approach ultimate reality. Nishida's painstaking consideration brought a totally different meaning to the idea of *topos*, which was originally suggested by Plato. Nishida defines *basho* as "a predicate of predicates," a truly universal, transcendent "place" in which subject and predicate are mutually inclusive.

According to Kosaka Masaaki, Professor of Philosophy at Kyoto University, there are three categories in Nishida's *basho*: "*basho* of being," "*basho* of relative nothingness," and "*basho* of absolute nothingness." The "*basho* of being" is a ground that supports all beings existing in space. Because all beings of form and matter in the phenomenal world, including human beings, need the space that they occupy, they are dependent on the "*basho* of being" as a fundamental restriction of their existence. There is, however, another, invisible *basho*, the "*basho* of relative nothingness," at the bottom of the "*basho* of being." It is referred to as "relative nothingness," because it exists only in relation to the "*basho* of being." Only the "*basho* of absolute nothingness" is truly transcendent and truly universal. It is the place where the authentic self turns around and becomes the "self without self." Nishida defines this existential transition as one "from that which functions to that which sees." This means that the "self as the *basho*" can reflect objects just as they are by truly emptying itself, and can see things "by becoming things." Thus the "self as the *basho*" identifies itself with all beings in the absolute contradictory mode of the world. With his idea of *basho* Nishida established a philosophical framework for describing the unfathomable realm of human experience that is normally considered mysticism in the West.

The Self-Conscious Determination of Nothingness

Absolute nothingness permeates all things and all things exist as the self-determination of absolute nothingness, Nishida argues. Through intensive suffering one may suddenly reach the point in which all contradictions of the world, such as inside and outside, one and all, the evil and the good, are united in the "*basho* of absolute nothingness." This discovery of the "absolute contradictory self-identity" as true selfhood in the midst of contradiction may be called conversion in Christian terms, or *kensho* (enlightenment) in Zen terms. The relationship between the absolute nothingness (or God) and the human is characterized by Nishida with the notion of "inverse correlation," in which "the more conscious I am of myself as a singular existence, the more God stands over me." The more the ego-self denies itself, the more absolute nothingness obtrudes into the self. Only through the self-negation of both absolute nothingness and the self do they become genuinely one, a state described by Nishida as the "continuity of the discontinuity." It is only when self-consciousness is completely extinguished in the *basho* that the newborn "self as the *basho*," embodying the "unifying force" of absolute nothingness from within, can fully exert its intrinsic nature as instrument to become a creative force in the world.

Logic and Life

In order to articulate the instrumental nature of the human being, Nishida developed the notion of "acting intuition," a state of total immersion in the present activity when one becomes the "self without self." Most commonly, "acting" means to become active in the world by means of a body, and "intuition" means a certain sensitivity to accept passively the world through the body's perceptual functions. In Nishida's "acting intuition," the relation of active "action" and passive "intuition" is completely reversed and here the "self as the *basho*" truly becomes the creative element. Absolute nothingness actualizes itself through the instrumental nature of our bodies and forms its "expressive world." Finally we realize that our "everyday mindedness," while utilizing the body physically and the intuition intellectually, is essential for the construction of the historical world. Hence, in his metaphysics Nishida always emphasizes the historical role of the individual.

The Logic of Basho and the Religious World View

In this final work Nishida offers critical insight on the philosophy of religion from his standpoint of the logic of *basho*. His lifelong ontological concern with the very existence of the self naturally led him to philosophical speculation on the religious issues of both Christianity and Buddhism, particularly those concerning the salvific power of the Absolute or, more simply, "Other Power" in Buddhist terms. For Nishida the death of the self (or ego) can occur

only in the *basho*, and the everyday self becomes the "self as the *basho*" by embodying thoroughly the transcendent within its own body. The experience of transcendence within oneself is called by Nishida "immanent transcendence."

It is in the so-called "Great Death" that we encounter the absolute God as the deepest contradiction in our existence. The absolute God includes absolute negation of itself and reaches each of us, struggling through life full of suffering and agony. In the depths of despair, even the most wicked and sinful individual can receive unconditional salvation by the grace of the absolute God.

Essentially, Nishida's logic of absolutely contradictory self-identity is a universal way to approach the ultimate truth in all religions. Throughout his life Nishida maintained deep respect for his mother, a devout Pure Land Buddhist, and as his life drew to its close, he succeeded in developing a philosophical perspective on the Pure Land Buddhist idea of Other Power.

SOHO MACHIDA

Further Reading

Translations

Nishida Kitarō. *Art and Morality*. Translated by D. A. Dilworth and V. H. Viglielmo. Honolulu, Hawaii: University of Hawaii Press, 1973.

———. *Fundamental Problems of Philosophy: The World of Action and the Dialectical World*. Translated by D. A. Dilworth. Tokyo: Sophia University, 1970.

———. *Intelligibility and the Philosophy of Nothingness*. Translated by R. Schinzinger. Tokyo: Maruzen, 1958. Reprint: Westport, Conn.: Greenwood Press, 1973.

———. *Intuition and Reflection in Self-Consciousness*. Translated by V. H. Viglielmo, with Y. Takeuchi and J. S. O'Leary. Albany, N.Y.: SUNY Press, 1987.

———. *Last Writings: Nothingness and the Religious Worldview*. Translated by D. A. Dilworth. Honolulu, Hawaii: University of Hawaii Press, 1987.

———. *A Study of Good*. Translated by V. H. Viglielmo. Tokyo: Government Printing Bureau, 1960.

Related Studies

Carter, Robert E. *The Nothingness Beyond God: An Introduction to the Philosophy of Nishida Kitarō*. New York: Paragon House, 1989. This book presents succinct discussions on Nishida's major ideas, comparing philosophies of religion in both the East and the West.

Nishitani, Keiji. *Nishida Kitarō*. Berkeley, Calif.: University of California Press, 1991. Nishitani provides a complete picture of Nishida by presenting both a personal profile and an examination of his philosophical thought; in particular, the ideas discussed in *A Study of Good*.

TANABE HAJIME

Born: 1885, Tokyo, Japan
Died: 1962
Major Works: *Collected Essays on the Logic of Species* (1932–41), *Philosophy as Metanoetics* (1946), *The Dialectics of the Logic of Species* (1946), *A Dialectical Demonstration of the Truth of Christianity* (1948)

Major Ideas

Philosophy has an essentially moral and social responsibility.
No state or nation can identify itself with absolute truth.
Philosophy is capable of being transformed by religious experience.

Along with Nishida Kitarō and Nishitani Keiji, Tanabe Hajime can be counted among the founders of the Kyoto School of Philosophy. This places him among some of the first Japanese to use Western intellectual methods to elucidate the philosophical foundations of his own cultural tradition. Tanabe's thought is particularly noteworthy to the degree it relies on Pure Land, Zen, and Christian thought in articulating a philosophy of religion very much concerned with social and historical existence.

Tanabe was born in 1885 and died in 1962, a life that witnessed the early years of Meiji Restoration, the tumultuous years of Japan's rapid assimilation of Western technology, the nationalist interlude, and World War II. After beginning studies in mathematics at Tokyo Imperial University, he later changed to philosophy, taking a position in the philosophy of science at Tōhoku Imperial University after graduation. In the post-World War I period, philosophers in Japan were concentrating on Neo-Kantianism. In this period Tanabe hoped to remake transcendental philosophy by means of Edmund Husserl's phenomenology, Henri Bergson's vitalism, and the Zen-inspirited philosophy of pure experience being advanced by Nishida Kitarō in Kyoto. Eventually Nishida brought Tanabe to Kyoto Imperial University and sent him to Europe for further studies. In Europe, Tanabe studied with Husserl but was more interested in the thought of the young Martin Heidegger, his tutor. Tanabe returned to Japan in 1924 as Nishida's most promising student, to begin years of lecturing on Kant and Hegel.

The Logic of Species

Tanabe's first major work is the *Collected Essays on the Logic of Species* (based on essays published between 1935 and 1940). During these years of social upheaval and political violence, Tanabe's intellectual interests were focused on the meaning of the Japanese nation in the modern world. In an increasingly nationalistic atmosphere, Tanabe turned his attention to the logical status of the nation as the concrete historical context of individual human existence. Since the individual's relationship to the universal is always mediated concretely by society and history, Tanabe argued that formal logic had not focused sufficiently enough on the logical status of "species" as the necessary mediation between the individual and the universal.

As the universal has no existence apart from its concrete instantiation as species (that is, as tribal or national communities), so also does the individual comes in contact with universal truths only in the limited nexus of concrete historical and social existence. The species transcends the individual as the concrete mediation of the universal. The universal transcends the species, yet has no existence apart from it. The species, however, cannot be directly identified with the universal. In order for the species to mediate the universal, it must undergo a death and resurrection in which the nonidentity of the species and the universal is acknowledged. This is to guard the specific national community from any pretense about being absolute. In this way national existence is able to mediate between the individual and the universal. Notice that Tanabe's "logic of species" is clearly a theory of national existence, but intended to serve as a critique of the blind nationalism rampant at the time.

Metanoetic Philosophy

Tanabe's next major contribution, *Philosophy as Metanoetics*, appeared immediately after World War II (1946). This work offered a commentary on the evils of Japanese nationalism, including his own complicity in it, and a program for the spiritual renewal of Japan in the years to come. During the time of hostilities, Tanabe underwent a personal crisis of meaning eventually resolved by what he called a "metanoia" (*zange*). In an act of repentance and self-surrender, the meaninglessness of his life came to be healed by "a wondrous power," which he eventually identified with the Pure Land Buddhist notion of "other-power" (*tariki*). Tanabe's reflections about his metanoia were shaped significantly by his reading of the *Kyōgyōshinshō*, a thirteenth-century Japanese Pure Land Buddhist text written by Shinran. In Tanabe's metanoetic philosophy, four ideas are outstanding.

First, Tanabe argues that philosophy itself should be understood as the path of metanoia or "metanoetics" (*zange-do*). Metanoetics is not a philosophy about the phenomenon of repentance, but philosophy itself, the only possible form of philosophy. In metanoetics there is the transcendence of noetics (knowledge based on the autonomous power of reason) in which philosophy based on the autonomous power of reason dies in self-contradiction and is resurrected by a power or grace which is its "other" (*tariki*).

Second, Tanabe elaborates the logical structure of metanoetics in what he calls the "absolute critique." For Kant, reason is not infinite and thus cannot establish a foundation for knowledge of the absolute. In this respect, the antinomies of reason (developed in Immanuel Kant's *Critique of Pure Reason*) are unavoidable. In trying to grasp the absolute, reason becomes subject to the crisis of its own death in self-contradiction. Moving beyond Kant, however, Tanabe held that reason is capable of being resurrected by the absolute after passing through the jaws of self-contradiction. In this rebirth of reason philosophy continues, but now as a "philosophy that is not a philosophy" or a philosophy whose discourse has undergone a religious transformation. Metanoetics is not an arbitrary route to be taken by some philosophers, but rather philosophy itself most profoundly understood. The ultimate conclusion of Kant's critique of reason is that when speculation is taken to its limit, philosophical inquiry undergoes a transformation by other-power.

Third, it was incumbent on Tanabe to explain the relationship between autonomous reason and the philosophy that is not a philosophy—the relationship between "self-power philosophy" (*jiriki tetsugaku*) and "other-power philosophy" (*tariki tetsugaku*). Tanabe accomplished this task with his concept of absolute mediation. In the resurrection of reason by other-power, philosophical discourse continues, but now a discourse transformed by the absolute. The other-power of the absolute cannot work on the relative directly. It must be mediated by what is an other-power to it—the free will. In this sense, metanoia is the medium of other-power. The absolute works through the relative by becoming immanent in it. Therefore, metanoia is an act of self-power (free will) even as it is an act of other-power. Similarly, the philosophy that is not a philosophy is a discourse which mediates absolute truth by constantly negating its own claim to be absolute.

Fourth, there is Tanabe's notion of human subjectivity as action-faith. This concept can be contrasted with action-intuition, Nishida's model of human subjectivity. In keeping with a Buddhist rejection of a substantial self, Nishida understood subjectivity as the concrete intuition of reality in which both subject and object arise as the self-determination of absolute nothingness. For Tanabe this would indicate that truth can be known contemplatively as an encompassing totality. In contrast, for Tanabe, truth is fragmented, not total. Thus for Tanabe, knowing is a matter of grace, not contemplation; subjectivity is action based on faith, not intuition.

After the war Tanabe returned to his interest in the logical status of species, publishing *The Dialectics of the Logic of Species* soon after *Philosophy as Metanoetics*. If we think of the logic of species as Tanabe's material logic, then we can think of metanoetics as an interlude in his intellectual itinerary in which he developed a formal logic.

Despite Tanabe's considerable accomplishments, he can be criticized on a number of points. First, although the split between Tanabe and Nishida was acrimonious, perhaps Tanabe exaggerated his differences from his teacher and early mentor. Second, Tanabe's use of scriptural texts is often careless and ahistoric. For instance, he quotes Christian scripture with little interest in theological interpretations of these texts. Jōdoshinshū scholars (specializing in Shinran's Pure Land views) note that his reading of Shinran's *Kyōgyōshinshō* is highly original but critically dubious.

JAMES FREDERICKS

Further Reading

Translations

Tanabe Hajime. "The Logic of Species as Dialectic." Translated by David Dilworth and Sato Taira. *Monumenta Nipponica*, vol. 24, no. 3, 1969, pp. 273–288.

———. *Philosophy as Metanoetics*. Translated by Takeuchi Yoshinori. Foreword by James Heisig. Berkeley, Calif.: University of California Press, 1986.

Related Studies

Ozaki, Makoto. *Introduction to the Philosophy of Tanabe: According to the English Translation of the Seventh Chapter of the Demonstration of Christianity*. Amsterdam/Atlanta, Ga.: Editions Rodopi, 1990.

Taitetsu Unno and James W. Heisig, eds. *The Religious Philosophy of Tanabe Hajime*. Berkeley, Calif.: Asian Humanities Press, 1990.

Takeuchi Yoshinori. "Hegel and Buddhism." *Il Pensiero*, vol. 7, no. 1–2, 1963, pp. 5–46.

UEHARA SENROKU

Born: 1899, Kyoto, Japan
Died: 1975, Kyoto, Japan
Major Works: *Shishin-shō* (*The Heart of History: Selections*) (1940), *Gakumon he no Gendaiteki Danso* (*Contemporary Reflections on Scholarship*) (1946–55), *Heiwa no Sōzō: Jinrui to Kokumin no Rekishiteki Kadai* (*Building Peace: Historical Tasks of the Human Race and of the Japanese People*) (1950), *Sekaishi-Ninshiki no Shin-Kadai* (*New Tasks Toward a Global Historical Consciousness*) (1963–68), *Shisha Seisha: Nichiren Ninshiki no Hassō to Shiten* (*The Dead and the Living: The Notion and Standpoint of Nichiren Consciousness*) (1970), *Kureta no Tsubo: Sekaishi-zō Keisei no tame no Shidoku* (*The Cretan Jar: Readings Toward the Formation of Global Historical Consciousness*) (1975)

Major Ideas

Scholarship involves a person's total engagement as subject.

Genuine peace is grounded in the cultivation of a global historical consciousness as peoples of the world forge their own ethnic–national identity.

To read religious texts is to accept an invitation to enter into the mind of the author and to put this mind into the context of the reader's present world.

The religious experience of transcendence bears fruit in a person's engagement with one's historical tasks.

In the aftermath of the Second World War Japan faced the tremendous task of rebuilding itself almost from scratch, as its people sought to rediscover its ethnic–national identity in the light of the devastation it had experienced. It was during these crucial years that Uehara Senroku came into the scene and made his voice heard as an educator, historian, social critic, civic activist, and religious (Buddhist) philosopher.

As none of his works has been translated from the Japanese, he is of course a virtual unknown outside of his country. Within Japan his major ideas, though they exerted influence among small circles of intellectuals, cultural reformers, and religious groups, failed to make any impact on the actual directions taken by his people in the postwar years and the period of Japan's surging economic growth in the sixties and seventies. Uehara Senroku died in 1975 with a sense of tragic disappointment and self-proclaimed defeat.

His writings are now in a process of republication, however, newly edited in a twenty-eight volume collection. His thought is thus being given the second look it deserves for the significance it carries, not only for Japanese, but for all peoples, as the global community comes to an awareness of the critical world situation at the onset of the next millennium.

Scholarship as Engagement

The earlier work of Uehara consisted of scholarly volumes on European medieval social and economic history, based on years of research and reflection that commenced in 1923 with graduate studies in Europe and continued after his return.

This period of Uehara's career coincided with the surge of Japan's aggressive militarism and territorial expansion into other parts of Asia. On the domestic scene it was characterized by the imposition of repressive measures against the populace by the military authorities. It was thus a time when all sectors of society, not excluding intellectuals and scholars, were given incentives on the one hand and subjected to pressures, including persecution and imprisonment, on the other to win support for the militarists' program. This program consisted of the propagation of absolute allegiance to the *Tenno* (Japanese emperor), proclaimed to be of divine origin and authority. Uehara's decision to devote his full attention to the world of texts of European medieval history for nearly two decades can thus be seen as his way of passive resistance to such an oppressive situation. The time spent in this way bore fruit in his widely acclaimed scholarly writings, published between 1942 and 1948.

It was this rigorous academic regimen he had dedicated himself to during those wartime years—which was accompanied by a continued inner struggle as he observed the events going on around him—that provided the context for his thinking on the nature of engaged scholarship.

In a noted writing, *Shishin-shō* (*The Heart of History: Selections*) (1940), Uehara describes the process of learning, in whatever field of endeavor it may be, as one that involves the "totality of one's sentiments and one's whole experience," and for which one "assumes full personal responsibility." With this description he offers a pointed negative criticism of the prevalent academic style characterized as "objectivism," wherein one deals with objective data that are neutral for all observers and require no value judgment or commitment on the researcher's part, except to lay these out and analyze them according to the proper methods of one's field of investigation.

In contrast to the purportedly "value-free," impersonal, and compartmentalized kind of scientific enquiry that dominated the academy of his time, Uehara proposes and actually succeeds in exemplifying in his own work a mode of scholarship that gives full recognition to the role of the subject in the search for truth, and underscores the responsibility of the inquirer to carry out the implications of that truth in the different areas of human existence that it inevitably involves. In this respect he stood far ahead of many in both the Eastern and Western hemispheres who later came to emphasize the same idea from different angles. (Uehara's approach to scholarship has been given systematic grounding in works such as Hans Georg Gadamer's *Wahrheit und Methode* [*Truth and Method*], published in 1960, and Jurgen Habermas's *Erkenntnis und Interesse* [*Knowledge and Interest*], published in 1968.)

Subjecthood, Ethnic Identity, and Global Historical Consciousness

A key theme that runs through Uehara's thinking is the notion of "subjecthood" (*shutaisei*). On the individual level it is reflected and given expression in Uehara's understanding of scholarship as personal engagement, as well as in his way of reading of religious texts (see below). The idea is also extended to the collective level and provides the basis for Uehara's treatment of Japanese ethnic identity in the context of the world's historical situation.

In addition to his duties as a scholar and educator (including a term as chancellor of a prestigious university in Tokyo), Uehara also devoted time and energy to helping form the renowned Kokumin Bunka Kaigi (Conference on People's Culture), a gathering of intellectuals concerned with the present and future directions of Japanese society and culture. As chair of the conference for many years, he had occasion to present papers on contemporary issues. This was a time when Japan was faced with crucial decisions in reentering the family of nations after its defeat in the Second World War, and in his papers and public addresses Uehara repeatedly emphasized the need for the Japanese to read the signs of the times, be sensitive to the global historical situation, and make decisions as a collective subject in the light of this global historical consciousness (*sekaishi-ninshiki*).

This was also a time when peoples of many countries of Asia, Africa, and Latin America that had been under Western colonial domination were "coming of age" and regaining political independence, and were beginning to join together to become a major force to reckon with in world affairs. Uehara saw great significance in these movements, which were leading to a turning point in human history, and he called upon his own people to discern the implications of these movements in the making of decisions regarding their future as a people. He outlined five key considerations, based on ethical/moral concerns and fundamental human rights, as a set of ground rules for making such collective decisions. These revolve around issues of (1) survival, (2) livelihood, (3) liberty and equality, (4) progress and prosperity, and (5) autonomy and independence.

In other words, as the Japanese people faced the task of forging their own ethnic–national identity in the postwar period, Uehara urged that these issues be addressed in the context of the current global historical situation, that is, to reclaim their subjecthood in a way that took into account the struggles and aspirations of the majority of the peoples of the world relating to those issues, and he warned them not to make decisions based merely on a selfish Japan-centered idea of "national interest."

Unfortunately Uehara's voice was largely ignored in the clamor of the Japanese people, who were interested in seeking economic security in a consumer society patterned after Western models, an interest that political leaders were quick to capitalize on to entrench themselves in power for several decades.

A Hermeneutics of Appropriation: Reading Religious Texts

Uehara found religious grounding for his worldview and his self-understanding with his reading of Nichiren, a thirteenth-century Buddhist prophet who called the attention of the Japanese people and its leaders to the crisis they were facing at the time.

Uehara's religious interests had received an initial spark in his twenties with a reading of the *Lotus Sūtra* and the works of Shinran and Nichiren, but it was only in his sixties that he was able to pursue these with his full attention, having retired from his public duties. He led a small study group that met regularly to read texts of Nichiren, and it was within the context of this study group that his religious vision took shape and found expression.

In several passages of his later writings, Uehara refers to himself, in a modest way, as an offspring—*bunshin* (embodiment)—of Nichiren. These references are to be understood against the background of his understanding of "subject-hood," and find explanation in his descriptions (in several of his essays and interview articles) of the different ways of approaching and understanding Nichiren.

In a public lecture (1970) addressed to followers of Shinran, Uehara also presents the same guidelines he had been applying in his own reading of Nichiren, and thus gives a systematic outline of basic principles of a "hermeneutic of religious texts." In brief, the reading of religious texts involves an entry into the world of the text, an appropriation of the author's mind, and an appreciation of this mind considered in the context of the reader's present situation.

Nichiren himself refers to his own "bodily reading" (*shiki-doku*) of the *Lotus Sūtra* (Mahayana Buddhist text), that is, a way of entering into the world of this text, and a way of relating text to the circumstances of his day. Nichiren's religious vision based on this reading is what prepared him for his engagement with the historical tasks he confronted in his own day. Thus, for Uehara the reference to himself as an "offspring" or "embodiment" of Nichiren is an acknowledgment of his indebtedness to the latter and, having accepted for himself Nichiren's religious vision, is also a profession of Uehara's readiness to take up the historical tasks of his own day in the way Nichiren did in his own. For Uehara this commitment entailed the obligation to help in the awakening of his people toward the forging of their ethnic–national identity as enlightened by a global historical consciousness.

Engaged Buddhism: Religious Experience and Historical Consciousness

Uehara's fundamental religious insight is a crystalization of years of reading and reflection on the texts of Nichiren, a reflection based on Nichiren's "bodily reading" of the *Lotus Sūtra*. Genuine religious experience, Uehara realized, does not result in a separation of oneself from worldly realities, but finds its fruit in a person's reengagement with one's historical tasks, which are enlightened by a global historical consciousness.

This religious insight is consonant with a basic Mahayana Buddhist vision—also a central theme of the *Lotus Sūtra*—of an awakened person (Buddha) as one who does not leave the world to remain in a transcendent state (nirvana), but returns to the world to take up the different tasks of helping sentient beings liberate themselves from their suffering. Uehara has appropriated this vision by way of Nichiren and has given it concrete expression in his own life and writings.

Although he died disappointed and with a sense of not having succeeded in his own historical tasks (very much in the way Nichiren also withdrew from public life and retired to a mountain retreat, meeting a lonely death), Uehara's work remains as an invitation to later generations and to people of all ethnic–national groupings, calling upon them to recover their own individual and collective subjecthood and religious identity and to act in a way that is enlightened by a global perspective and aims toward a creative engagement with historical tasks.

RUBEN L. F. HABITO

Further Reading

Dehn, Ulrich. "Towards a Historical Consciousness of Japanese Buddhism: Uehara Senroku." *Japanese Religions*, 17–2, July 1992, pp. 126–141. This is a summary of a larger study with the same title (in German) submitted as a Habilitation thesis to Heidelberg University.

Habito, Ruben L. F. "Uehara Senroku's Hermeneutic of Shinran: Prospects for Shin Studies." *The Pure Land*, n.s., 8 and 9, December 1992, pp. 47–63.

Maruyama, Teruo. *Tatakau Bukkyo (Militant Buddhism)*. Tokyo: Hozokan, 1991. A collection of essays by a disciple of Uehara, with several references to the latter's influence in his understanding of an engaged Buddhism.

Note: The works of Uehara Senroku are now being reedited and reissued in Japanese in a twenty-eight volume collection, which includes his published or hitherto unpublished writings, under the title *Uehara Senroku Chosaku-Shu* (Tokyo: Hyoronsha, 1987 ff).

NISHITANI KEIJI

Born: 1900, Ishikawa Prefecture, Japan
Died: 1990, Kyoto, Japan
Major Works: *Kongenteki Shutaisei no Tetsugaku* (*The Philosophy of Fundamental Subjectivity*) (1940), *Nihirizumu* (*The Self-Overcoming of Nihilism*) (1946; English translation, 1990), *Shūkyō to wa Nanika* (*What Is Religion?* Translated as *Religion and Nothingness*) (1961; English translation, 1982), *Nishida Kitarō* (1985; English translation, 1991); *Zen no Tachiba* (*The Standpoint of Zen*) (1986)

Major Ideas

Nihilism is the central philosophical problem of the twentieth century.

Modern science is one factor contributing to this nihilism, as it is based on a faulty epistemology linked to a fundamental rift in human consciousness.

The standpoint of Emptiness (shūnyatā) *heals the rift in human consciousness, and is the key to the overcoming of nihilism.*

The standpoint of Emptiness is a field wherein opposites converge; transcending history, it is firmly rooted in and finds its field of manifestation within it.

The standpoint of Emptiness offers a challenge to major categories of Western thought, including the notion of God, the self, time, and history.

Born in 1900, Nishitani Keiji's life and philosophical career concerned itself with the fundamental questions of existence in a way that echoes the struggles and stirrings of the human spirit in the twentieth century. Beginning with a personal struggle with nihilism and despair that led him to read the works of Nietzsche, Dostoevsky, and others in his early life, he found a clue to the overcoming of this nihilism in following the philosophical directions laid out by his mentor Nishida Kitarō (1870–1945).

Having graduated from the department of philosophy at the prestigious Kyoto Imperial University in 1924, he taught ethics and German at another college until 1935, when he was appointed professor of religion, and subsequently of modern philosophy, at his alma mater. Retiring from formal academic duties in 1963, he continued to write and lecture and contribute in various ways to seminars and study groups in the Kyoto area. He held terms as president of the Eastern Buddhist Society (founded by D. T. Suzuki), the International Institute for Japanese Studies, and the Conference on Religion in Modern Society (CORMOS).

After the passing of his mentor Nishida Kitarō in

1945 and of his elder colleague Tanabe Hajime in 1962, he emerged as the representative figure of the Kyoto School of Philosophy for almost three decades until his death in 1990.

Confronting Nihilism as a Philosophical Problem

Throughout Nishitani's numerous writings, a key issue that continues to reappear as the impetus for Nishitani's philosophical reflections is the question of nihilism. This issue was for him not merely a theoretical one, but a living, existential question that confronts one at the roots of one's very being. He describes his decision to study philosophy as the natural outcome of his own struggle with nihilism and despair as a young man.

He tackles the question of nihilism in a work first published in 1946, examining especially the works of Friedrich Nietzsche, Max Stirner, and Martin Heidegger, among others. He characterizes their thinking as a "creative nihilism" as opposed to a "nihilism of despair," in that these thinkers came to grips with the radical finitude of human existence—the awareness of which confronts one with the real possibility of the nihilism of despair—and found instead the basis for a new affirmation and creativity. Noting nihilism as a feature of the historical situation of Europe, Nishitani wrote of how it had come to take hold on Japanese society as well.

In his 1961 work *Shūkyō to wa Nanika* (*What is Religion?*, translated later as *Religion and Nothingness*) he continued his reflections on nihilism and related it to the problematic nature of modern science. Science as understood in the age of modernity, Nishitani notes, involves an objectification not only of the natural world, but likewise of the human subject itself, and thereby results in the depersonalization of the human being as well as in the denaturalization of nature. Such a situation leads to an acute sense of alienation and of derootedness in the human consciousness—features of the *nihil* that cuts through human existence. The almost worship-like attitude with which moderns regard science, an attitude that is corollary to a stance of atheism, only aggravates the issue.

This attitude of scientism, Nishitani claims, is based on the classic but faulty epistemology that separates subject and object, and which tends to create the illusion of the subject ("I," "me," "mine") as an independent entity standing apart from the rest of the world. This illusion is what causes the rift in human consciousness, and for Nishitani it is this rift that lies at the roots of the nihilism confronting modern humanity.

The Standpoint of Emptiness

The key to overcoming the nihilism that continues to loom over humanity especially since the modern age is "the standpoint of Emptiness [*shūnyatā*]," according to Nishitani. A synonym for this is a term derived from Nishida that is echoed throughout the works of the thinkers of the Kyoto School, used with varying nuances in their respective philosophical frameworks: "absolute nothingness" (*zettai-mu*).

Evaluating the thought of Nietzsche, Heidegger, and others, Nishitani gives them credit for drawing out the basic philosophical problem of nihilism and for attempting in their respective ways to overcome this nihilism that poses a fundamental threat to

human existence. But Nishitani points out that these thinkers were not able to go far enough. True, they proposed ways to overcome nihilism via the radical affirmation of the human subject confronted with the abyss of its finitude. But such a stance is based on what Nishitani calls "relative nothingness," that is, a nothingness understood still in terms of its opposite: the notion of being. What Nishitani offers in his work is a way of double negation that opens to the realization of "absolute nothingness."

It is not an exaggeration to say that in this key term is the clue not only to understanding Nishitani, but also to appreciating the religious philosophies of the other thinkers of the Kyoto School as well. And, needless to say, at its background is the worldview of Zen Buddhism.

The realization of absolute nothingness—in other words, "the standpoint of Emptiness" in Nishitani's terms—is nothing short of a religious conversion that leads to a transformation of consciousness. It begins with a doubt that wells up from the depths of human existence, a doubt that leads one to ask the fundamental questions of our being: What and who am I? Why do I exist? Why does anything exist? What is the meaning of all this?

This doubt is described by Nishitani as a growing bean seed that begins to crack and break apart the shell of the ego ("I," "me," "mine," imagined as an entity separate from the rest of the world), awakening this ego from its blissfully ignorant slumber and making it aware of its radical finitude, its nothingness. For Nishitani this is the experience of nothingness; seen in this light, such an experience is recognized as a positive step toward the individual's attainment of greater freedom from the confines of one's small (and illusory) self (ego).

It becomes the Great Doubt as one is led further into the core of one's being, there to meet the Great Death. This Great Death is the dissolution of the small self. This is "the point of its passing away and ceasing to be self . . . it is the moment at which self is at the same time the nothingness of self . . . ," as he writes in *The Religion of Nothingness*.

What emerges in the wake of this dissolution of the small self is no other than "a new heaven and a new earth," a mode of being characterized by total openness and total freedom, wherein the self is no longer separate from, but realizes its oneness with, all the myriad things of the universe. This is the arrival at the standpoint of Emptiness, the entry into a mode of being where everything is seen in full relief "just as it is," in its "suchness." This is the mode of being that enables one to see one's "original face," the face before even one's mother and father were born, and that enables one to see "the oak tree in the garden" *as* the oak tree in the garden and yet also as interpenetrating with all other particular existents in the universe. In other words, it is a standpoint that cuts through boundaries of time and space and yet is nevertheless firmly rooted in the here and now, in the this-and-that of ordinary human life.

The standpoint of Emptiness is a field wherein opposites converge—self and nonself, being and nonbeing, the personal and the impersonal, the unique and the universal—transcending and yet fully grounded in and manifested within history. It is a recovery of the fullness of the present moment that is open to eternity.

Absolute Nothingness and Its Challenge to Western Thought

A thoughtful work introducing Nishitani's ideas to Western readers as well as indicating some significant areas of their possible significance for religious understanding was published in German in 1976: *Das Absolutes Nichts* (in the English translation, *Absolute Nothingness: Foundations for a Buddhist-Christian Dialogue*) (1980) by Hans Waldenfels. In this work the author lays out the backgrounds of Nishitani's religious philosophy, tracing it in the enlightenment experience of Gautama Buddha (Siddhārtha Gautama), the dialectic of Nāgārjuna, the tradition of Zen Buddhism, and then in the thought of Nishida Kitarō. He presents key themes in Nishitani's thought that provide suggestive hints for philosophers of religion and for Christian theologians in considering the questions

of God, the world, history, human destiny, and related issues.

Since the appearance of Nishitani's work *Shūkyō to wa Nanika* in an English translation as *Religion and Nothingness* (1982), more and more philosophers, theologians, and religious scholars have taken up his thought, considering its challenge and the implications of his key ideas on fundamental issues in philosophy, religion, and spirituality. Nishitani's own familiarity with the Western philosophical tradition has enabled him to set his own thinking in the light of such issues and to present his ideas in the context of a conversation with Western philosophical themes.

RUBEN L. F. HABITO

Further Reading

Translations

Nishitani, Keiji. *Religion and Nothingness.* Translated with an Introduction by Jan van Bragt. Berkeley, Calif.: University of California Press, 1982.
———. *The Self-Overcoming of Nihilism.* Translated by Graham Parkes, with Setsuko Aihara. Albany, N.Y.: SUNY Press, 1990.
———. *Nishida Kitarō.* Translated by Yamamoto Seisaku and James W. Heisig. Berkeley, Calif.: University of California Press, 1991.

Related Studies

Mitchell, Donald. *Spirituality and Emptiness: The Dynamics of Spiritual Life in Buddhism and Christianity.* New York: Paulist Press, 1991. A consideration of themes of spirituality in the context of conversations between thinkers of the Kyoto School and Christian spiritual writers. The second chapter considers Nishitani Keiji's contribution.
Unno, Taitetsu, ed. *The Religious Philosophy of Nishitani Keiji.* Berkeley, Calif.: Asian Humanities Press, 1989. A collection of essays and papers from a symposium on the thought of Nishitani Keiji, held at Smith College, North-

ampton, Mass., in 1984, with sections on God, science, ethics, history, and Buddhism.

Waldenfels, Hans. *Absolute Nothingness: Foundations for a Buddhist-Christian Dialogue*. Translated by James W. Heisig. New York: Paulist Press, 1980. A thoughtful work relating Nishitani's religious philosophy to the work of other thinkers, both in the East and West, and showing the bearing of his ideas on fundamental philosophical questions.

KOREA

WŎNHYO

Born: 617, Amnyang, Korea
Died: 686, in a cave temple near Kyŏngju, Korea
Major Works: *Commentary and Supplementary Notes on the Awakening of Faith in Mahāyāna* (c. 622–676), *Treatise on Ten Approaches to the Reconciliation of Doctrinal Controversy* (date unknown), *Arouse Your Mind and Practice!* (date unknown), *Exposition of the Adamantine Absorption Scripture* (c. 685)

Major Ideas

The One Mind is the ontological ground of two aspects of things, the absolute and the conditioned.

All theories are free from any limitations; any theory is valid and not contradictory to any other.

Various levels of the Buddhist teachings are culminated in such Buddhist scriptures as the Lankāvatāra, *the* Awakening of Faith in Mahāyāna, *and the* Adamantine Absorption Scripture.

The One Mind includes all practical approaches to the Buddhist dharma *and shows that they are of the "same one taste."*

One should not waste time but strive diligently to achieve the Buddhist enlightenment from this very moment.

Wŏnhyo was active during the turbulent historic period of the unification war among the Three Kingdoms in seventh-century Korea. When Wŏnhyo was born, only ninety years had passed since the first martyrdom of Ich'adon (527). Considering the adversity of time and the paucity of materials, it is remarkable that Wŏnhyo could master all the advanced Buddhist theories and produce a huge amount of scholarly exegetes on almost all Mahāyāna Buddhist scriptures, and yet at the same time engage himself to spread Buddhism to the masses to the extent that everyone in the Silla could recite the name of Buddha. Although he is revered as the founder of the uniquely Korean Buddhist sect Haedong-jong, he is known more for his syncretic vision and passionate involvement in Buddhist practice. He is considered to be the most important seminal philosopher and religious practitioner in the history of Korean philosophy.

Wŏnhyo was born from a noble family of Sŏl in the vicinity of the Silla capital city Sŏrabŏl (now Kyŏngju). It is believed that he had his hair shaved and became a Buddhist monk at the age of fifteen. *The Samguk Yusa* (the *Memorabilia of the Three Kingdoms*), compiled by a Koryŏ Buddhist monk Iryŏn (1206–89), relates that at the occasion of his ordination he made his old home a Buddhist tem-

ple, Ch'ogae-sa (literally "temple first opened"). From his childhood name Sindang or Sŏdang we can surmise that the name Wŏnhyo is a Chinese character rendering of the indigenous Korean name, probably meaning "dawn" or "morning glory." Such a name is appropriate since Wŏnhyo's achievement is exactly comparable to the dawn of the Korean Buddhism. Throughout the history of East Asian Buddhism, Wŏnhyo's effort toward ecumenism to synthesize all the divergent theories into a unifying whole from the absolute perspective is appreciated by all those who seek harmony among differences and tolerance toward others. His brand of Buddhist philosophy is termed "ecumenical" (Korean: *t'ong*) and is identified as the characteristic mark of Korean Buddhism in general.

From Iryŏn's account we can divide Wŏnhyo's life into six stages: birth and adolescence (617–631); ordination and early vocation (c. 632–661); textual exegesis (c. 662–676); popularization of Buddhism (c. 677–684); return to scholarship (c. 685); death and funeral (686).

In Wŏnhyo's life we can find a classical example of the contemplative life of meditation and a search for truth, alternated with another cycle of active participation and engagement in furthering Buddhist truth; hence a complete harmony of theoretical speculation and practical application in Wǒnhyo's life and work.

In order to understand Wǒnhyo's philosophy, it is necessary for us to be acquainted with the famous story believed to reflect his experience of the Buddhist enlightenment on his way to China.

Wǒnhyo and his junior companion Ŭisang (625–702) decided to travel to China to study under translator-master Xuanzang (Hsüan-tsang) (596–664), who had just returned from India in 648 after sixteen years of study. The first attempt (in 650) failed when they were arrested as spies by the Koguryǒ boarder guards and set free to return home.

Ŭisang's biography in the *Lives of Eminent Monks During the Sung* (988) by Zanning (Tsanning) relates that on their second trip in 661 Wǒnhyo and Ŭisang traveled to a port in Paekche territory and intended to board a ship from there. At dusk they were caught in a heavy downpour and were forced to stay in an earthen sanctuary, which in the next morning's light was revealed to be an old tomb littered with human skulls. The next day the rain kept them in the same tomb, but before daybreak they were haunted by a host of demons. Wǒnhyo learned from this experience that "because thought arises, all types of *dharmas* arise; but once thought ceases, a sanctuary and a tomb are not different. The three realms of existence are mind-alone." Recognizing the futility of seeking understanding through travel, Wǒnhyo returned home. That drastic change of his thought is the foundation on which Wǒnhyo later built his entire edifice of Buddhist philosophy.

Commentary on the Awakening of Faith in Mahāyāna

Once he realized the fundamental truth of Buddhism—that the world is made by the mind alone—Wǒnhyo embarked upon an entirely new life in Silla to write, preach, and edify people transcending the boundary between the sacred and the profane. Wǒnhyo had no special teacher, but he read widely and interpreted every Buddhist text he could find regardless of its doctrinal affiliation.

Wǒnhyo especially depended upon the *Flower Garland Sūtra* and the *Awakening of Faith in Mahāyāna*, and established a unique syncretic Buddhist philosophy.

Wǒnhyo's favorite text, however, was the *Awakening of Faith in Mahāyāna*, for he wrote five different kinds of commentaries on this text alone. Only two out of these five are extant and are known as the *Haedong-so* (*Korean Commentary*). According to the late Pak Chong-hong, the *Haedong-so* offers a theoretical system resolving the controversy between Mādhyamika and Yogācāra Buddhist sects based upon the all-inclusive absolute *tathāgatagarbha* (Korean: *Yǒraejang*). Wǒnhyo prefers to call this absolute the One Mind (*ilsim*). Wǒnhyo, drawing on the innovative explication of the *tathāgatagarbha* doctrine in the *Awakening of Faith in Mahāyāna*, believed the One Mind to be the ontological ground of two diametrically opposed approaches in Mahāyāna Buddhism: first, the true thusness (*chinyǒ-mun*, Madhyamika apophatic) approach and second, the production-and-extinction (*saengmyǒl-mun*, Yogacara kataphatic) approach.

Treatise on Ten Approaches to Reconciliation of the Doctrinal Controversy

It would be safe to say that Wǒnhyo is more ambitious in his intention to harmonize, not just the above two, but all the variant descriptions in Buddhist texts concerning the "perfect and universal sound" of the Buddha's teaching. He believed that variations would cause controversies that would eventually threaten to obscure the fundamental consistency of the religion's message. Hence Wǒnhyo wrote a *Treatise on Ten Approaches to the Reconciliation of Doctrinal Controversy*. Only some fragments of it were recently discovered in a broken memorial stela in honor of the monk Sǒdang (Wǒnhyo) at the Kosǒnsa Temple.

Wǒnhyo's syncretic concern actually permeates all of his exegetical writings. Wǒnhyo was fond of summarizing the thematic essentials (*chong-yo*) of each text in order to capture the essential teachings of each Buddhist scripture. One of the best summaries that reveals Wŏnhyo's syncretic concern appears in the *Thematic Essentials of the Nirvāna Sūtra* (*Yŏlban'gyŏng chong'yo*). When the question arises whether the absolute reality is material or nonmaterial, emptiness or essence, and so forth, Wŏnhyo would answer that

> If taken literally, both views fail to do justice to the reality. The two varying views bring about disputes by failing to grasp the original meaning of the Buddha. If free from any dogmatic position, both views are helpful. In the ultimate sense, they are not contradictory to each other.

Even though Wŏnhyo himself believed in the equal validity of all scriptures based upon his ecumenical perspective of harmonizing all controversies from the absolute standpoint of *tathāgatagarbha*, he was obliged to condescend himself to present a sort of three levels of scriptural taxonomy.

To the first level belongs the *Perfection of Wisdom* scriptures, which explain only the absolute aspect of existence or true thusness, unspeakable and immutable; therefore the *via negativa* approach is adequate on this level.

To the second level belongs such texts as the *Nirvāna Sūtra* and the *Flower Garland Sūtra*, which is replete with the positive description of the conventional nature of the world, that is, the production-and-extinction aspect governed by the principle of causal interdependency.

The above two diametrically opposed levels are amalgamated in the third level of the teachings, which is adaptable and yet motionless, represented by such texts as the *Lankāvatāra Sūtra*, the *Awakening of Faith in Mahāyāna*, and the *Adamantine Absorption Scripture*, where the *tathāgatagarbha* concept is used to synthesize the various Buddhist doctrines.

According to Wŏnhyo, it is the nature of One Mind itself that allows the possibility of syncretism. The One Mind, being distinct from both the non-dual essence and phenomenal appearances, may adapt in various ways depending on the individual *karma*. Free from appearances, the One Mind is neither defiled nor pure, neither one nor many; its non-dual nature allows a radical apophasis, where nothing is posited as the absolute. But the One Mind, distinct from the essence, is both defiled and pure, one and many; its dual nature allows thoroughgoing kataphasis, where all things in the world are affirmed. The One Mind can take any form: ordinary person or saint, the Buddha or *Bodhisattva*. By the same token, the Buddhist teachings are free from limitations and can accommodate any partial perspective.

In sum, from the synthetic standpoint of Wŏnhyo, all religious positions have at least some validity. To those who argue against Wŏnhyo's comprehensive syncretism as being at odds with formal logic and contradicting the very principle of contradiction, Wŏnhyo would answer that one would need only to have an experience of the unconditioned state of enlightenment beyond words and names. To an imaginary critic who insists that what Wŏnhyo describes as neither existence nor nonexistence cannot be found anywhere in the world, Wŏnhyo answered that he used words and speech to point out the *dharma* that eradicates words, just as one would use a finger to point to the moon, which has nothing whatsoever to do with the finger.

But Wŏnhyo believed that once any Buddhist adept is free from all the hindrances to correct understanding and deep experience beyond words, he will no longer conflict with the world, since he will have the all-inclusive perspective that will allow him to find what is of value in all limited perspectives. Wŏnhyo's syncretic philosophy starts from the fundamental experience that he had on his aborted trip to China and ultimately rests on that unspeakable experience of enlightenment.

But he was not content with mere silence; he was most vocal in advocating the Buddhist truth and helping people on all levels of the Silla society to realize the futility of doctrinal bickering. In line with his syncretic concern, Wŏnhyo wrote a total of 119 titles of Buddhist works in 260 volumes, but only 21 of his works remain. Wŏnhyo's reputation as a scholar rests on his syncretic logic in particular, which accounts for the influence on the philosophy of Fazang (Fa-tsang) (643–712), the third patriarch of the Chinese (Huayan) Hua-yen Sect of Buddhism. *The Treatise on Ten Approaches to the Reconciliation of Doctrinal Controversy* was translated into Sanskrit in India. But resolving doctrinal bickering by writing scholarly treatises was not enough for Wŏnhyo; he also advocated and acted out in person what he said and wrote.

Arouse Your Mind and Practice!

In addition to his exegetical writings, Wŏnhyo made a personal commitment to popularize Buddhism among the common people of Silla Korea. Wŏnhyo's concern for ordinary "sentient beings" made him dance around the country with a gourd that he called *Muae* (Unhindered) and sing, "All unhindered persons leave birth and death along a single path," his favorite passage in the *Flower Garland Sūtra*. After an affair with a widowed princess, Wŏnhyo exchanged his monk's robe for lay clothes and referred himself as Householder Sosŏng, repenting his breach of the monastic vow of celibacy. Sometimes he sat in meditation in the mountains or by the rivers; he even visited bars and whorehouses. He was absolutely free and flexible under any circumstances; there were no fixed norms for his actions.

Arouse Your Mind and Practice! is a short but poignant admonition to the novitiates in Buddhism, as well as to the ordinary people of his day. Here Wŏnhyo urges everyone not to waste precious time while alive as a human being, for the days, months, and years will fly by before each person reaches the inevitable mortal destiny. The peculiar phraseology suggests that it might originally have been a song to be circulated throughout the land, recorded in vernacular Korean *idu*, putatively invented by his son Sŏl Ch'ong. Probably composed between 662 and 676, this "song" is Wŏnhyo's most edifying work and one of the strongest admonitions about the urgency of the religious practice to be found in all Buddhist literature. Today it is among the first works, together with Chinul's (1158–1210) *Admonitions to Beginning Students*, read by Korean pos-

tulants who have just joined the Buddhist monastic community.

There are passages that seek to arouse people to understand and practice Buddha *dharma* immediately:

> Everyone knows that eating food soothes the pangs of hunger, but no one knows that studying the *dharma* corrects the delusions of the mind. . . . A broken cart cannot move, an old person cannot cultivate. . . . How many lives have we not cultivated? Yet still we pass the day and night in vain. How many lives have we spent in our useless bodies? Yet still we do not cultivate in this lifetime either. This life must come to an end; but what of the next? Is this not urgent? Is this not urgent?

Exposition of the Adamantine Absorption Scripture

Although the range of Wŏnhyo's scholarly exegesis covers virtually all of the Mahayana scriptures, only Wŏnhyo's *Exposition on the Adamantine Absorption Scripture* was elevated to the status of *non* (treatise) by a Chinese cataloger who believed that the author was a *Bodhisattva* and not a mortal man. Tsan-ning's account of Wŏnhyo's life devotes more than half of its length to the mysterious occasion whereby the text is discovered from the sea near Korea, and to Wŏnhyo's peculiar way of writing a commentary on a table held between two horns of a cow. Here Wŏnhyo or Tsan-ning obviously is punning, for the Chinese words for "horn" and "enlightenment" sound exactly the same in both Chinese and Korean.

More importantly for Wŏnhyo, the *Adamantine Absorption Scripture* was an ideal text for establishing a firm praxis foundation for his ecumenical vision based on his unique theory of reconciling all doctrinal controversies. Wŏnhyo's profound explication of the relationship between the original innate enlightenment (*pon'gak*) of the Buddha and the non-enlightenment (*pulgak*) apparently assumed to be the state of ordinary people, finally finds its appropriate place to be concretely applied in actual practice. Hence Wǒnhyo renounced his retirement and worked one final time on a commentary to the *Adamantine Absorption Scripture* barely one year before his death.

Wǒnhyo must have seen in the *Adamantine Absorption Scripture* an ideal vehicle for amalgamating the syncretic principle with the "unhindered" practice that he committed himself to for the preceding ten and more years. Employing the same sources for writing commentaries on the *Awakening of Faith in Mahāyāna* and others, Wǒnhyo this time focused his hermeneutical structure on the "contemplation practice that has but a single taste." His explication of each chapter of the *Adamantine Absorption Scripture* is correlated with particular type of meditative practice, finally culminating in the "single taste contemplation." This is a fundamental contribution he made to Korean Buddhist philosophy. In the preface to his commentary, Wǒnhyo clarifies the progressive relationships between the different chapters by correlating the "single taste contemplation" with the One Mind.

Thus Wǒnhyo finally succeeded in synthesizing the contemplative practices of the various intellectual and religious currents prominent in Silla Buddhism at that time. To substantiate his interpretation, Wǒnhyo gives four hermeneutical schemata for examining the *Adamantine Absorption Scripture*, each of which culminates in the "essence of the One Mind" or "the fountainhead of the *tathāgatagarbha* that has a single taste."

First, contemplation of the signless *dharma* is employed to negate all signs of deluded thoughts originating from non-enlightenment. Second, the practice of non-production is explicated to help annihilate the rising of even the contemplating mind. Upon practicing nonproduction, one reaches the third level of original enlightenment that inspires and transforms sentient beings, who then can naturally approach the edge of reality devoid of true nature. Relying on this true nature, one finally approaches the *tathāgatagarbha*'s fountainhead that has a single taste.

Since Wǒnhyo's intent was not to form a school like his contemporary Ǔisang, who is revered as the founder of the Korean Hwaǒm Sect, he was ac-

corded less esteem in Silla than in China and had fewer disciples than Ǔisang. Only Ǔich'ǒn (1055–1101) in the Koryǒ dynasty appreciated Wǒnhyo's contribution for harmonizing all the doctrinal controversies and consequently bestowed upon Wǒnhyo the posthumous title "National Preceptor of Harmonizing Controversies" (*Hwajaeng Kuksa*). Since then, whenever Korean Buddhism and Korean society are embroiled in the quagmire of political and religious controversy, Wǒnhyo's name and his spirit of reconciliation are recalled.

JAE-RYONG SHIM

Further Reading

Buswell, Robert E., Jr. *The Formation of Ch'an Ideology in China and Korea: The Vajrasamadhi-sūtra, a Buddhist Apocryphon.* Princeton, N.J.: Princeton University Press, 1989. This is not only a thorough examination of Wǒnhyo's commentary on the *Adamantine Absorption Scripture*, which forged a syncretic outlook toward Buddhist doctrine, but also a wholesale reevaluation of the work itself.

Lee, Peter H., ed. *Sourcebook of Korean Civilization.* New York: Columbia University Press, 1993. For an understanding of the general intellectual milieu of Wǒnhyo's time, and Korean Buddhism in general, this is an essential reference.

Oh, Young B. *Wonhyo's Theory of Harmonization.* Ph.D. dissertation, New York University, 1988. This is a modern attempt to reconstruct the *Ten Approaches to the Reconciliation of Doctrinal Controversy.*

Park, Sung-bae. *Wǒnhyo's Commentaries on the "Awakening of Faith in Mahāyāna."* Ph.D. dissertation, University of California at Berkeley, 1979. This is a thorough examination of Wǒnhyo's *Haedong-so.*

Pak, Chong-hong. "Wǒnhyo's Philosophical Thought." In *Assimilation of Buddhism in Korea: Religious Maturity and Innovation in the Silla Dynasty*, edited by Lewis R. Lancaster and C. S. Yu. Berkeley, Calif.: Asian Humanities

Press, 1991, pp. 47–103. This is a classic in the field.

Rhi, Ki-yong. *Wonhyo sasang 1: segye kwan* [*Wǒnhyo's Thought 1: His World View*]. Seoul: Hongbobwon, 1967. This is the first attempt made by a Korean scholar to expound Wǒnhyo's exegetical expertise on the *Awakening of Faith in Mahāyāna*.

Shim, Jae-ryong. "On the General Characteristic of Korean Buddhism: Is Korean Buddhism Syncretic?" *Seoul Journal of Korean Studies*, Vol. 2, pp. 147–157. This article critically examines the "syncretic" issue in Korean Buddhist philosophy facing contemporary Korean scholars.

CHINUL

Born: 1158 in Kaegyŏng (now Kaesŏng, Kyŏnggi Province), Korea
Died: 1210 at the Songkwang-sa Monastery, Sunch'ŏn, South Cholla Province, Korea
Major Works: *Encouragement to Practice: The Compact of the Concentration and Wisdom Community* (1190), *Secrets on Cultivating the Mind* (1203–05), *Admonitions to Beginning Students* (1205), *Straight Talks on the True Mind* (c. 1205), *Abridgement of the* Commentary of the Flower Garden Sūtra (1207), *Excerpts from the Dharma Collection and Separate Circulation Record with Personal Notes* (1209)

Major Ideas

An ordinary person must have a correct faith that he or she is already identical to the enlightened Buddha.
Sudden awakening/gradual cultivation is the true path of all Buddhas.
According to each person's capacity, one can follow any one of the following three meditative techniques: (1) the dual cultivation of concentration and wisdom, (2) the faith and understanding according to the Hwaŏm School, and (3) the distinctively Sŏn investigation of the critical phrase, hwadu *or* kongan.

Buddhism was already an entrenched ideology of the Koryŏ kingdom as a major religious and intellectual force during the latter half of the twelfth-century Korea. Throughout the dynasty, Buddhism had close ties with the royal court, as monarchs allowed one son to enter the priesthood. They sought advice on both political and religious affairs from learned monks. Two major schools, Kyo (Doctrine) and Sŏn (Meditation), dominated the Koryŏ Buddhism. Prior to Chinul, Ŭich'ŏn (1055–1101), the fourth son of King Munjong (1046–83), tried to fuse the two schools into one by absorbing most of Sŏn monks to Ch'ŏnt'ae doctrinal school. Apart from the intellectual vigor, Buddhism thrived economically through its monasteries, which held large tracts of land and thus became inevitably tainted by corruption and misuse of power. With the rise of the military class, Buddhism underwent a significant reform with the growth of the meditation-inspired Chogye Sŏn School.

At this critical juncture in the middle of the Buddhist Koryŏ dynasty, Chinul had to deal with serious signs of moral and spiritual decline within the fully developed Buddhist *sangha*, in which a major split had occurred between Kyo and Sŏn sects. Relying upon his vision of fundamental unity of Sŏn and Kyo, Chinul developed a unique approach to Buddhism in which the speculative meta-physics of the Hwaŏm doctrinal school can be effectively employed to support the Sŏn soteriological views. This unique combination of Chinul's is considered the most distinctive Korean contribution to Buddhist thought. Later Korean Buddhists have generally followed the basic principles outlined by Chinul. Hence Chinul is revered as the founder of the uniquely Korean Sŏn School, the celibate Korean Buddhist Chogye Order of contemporary Korea (South Korea, officially the Republic of Korea.)

Chinul

Chinul was born to a gentry family of Chŏng at the Tongju district to the west of Kaegyŏng, the Koryŏ capital. His father, an administrator in the royal academy and a pious Buddhist, vowed before the Buddha that if his ailing son was cured of his chronic illness, he would be made a monk. Chinul's illness vanished, and at the tender age of seven he was ordained into the Sagul-san lineage of the Nine Mountains School of early Korean Sŏn; at fifteen he received the full precepts.

But Chinul never studied formally under a Sŏn master, nor did he receive transmission from a recognized teacher. Hence he was eager to find any spiritual guidance in the sutras, commentaries, and records of Ch'an masters as the only authentic source available to him. Chinul's accommodating attitude toward the scholastic schools and a certain eclecticism developed out of his independent study made him borrow helpful hints from the teachings in the scriptures. Chinul's system of three major approaches in the Sŏn meditative practice stems entirely from his three major spiritual experiences while reading scriptures. Hence it is essential to know the kind of spiritual experiences earned from reading books that led Chinul to forge a unique combination of Hwaŏm theory and Sŏn practice that served as the foundation of later Korean Sŏn Buddhism.

Spending nine years in his home monastery, Chinul traveled to Poje-sa at the capital to take the Sŏn *sangha* examination, and he passed it in 1182 when he was twenty-four. However, during his sojourn at the capital he was disenchanted at the worldly climate there and he aired his intention to form a retreat society dedicated to the development of concentration and wisdom. It was eight more years before the retreat society was actually established.

In the meantime, Chinul left the capital and began a spiritual journey to seek for scriptural guidance for the formation of the society. While staying at Ch'ŏng'wŏn-sa, he had the first of a series of three awakenings that affected his attitude toward Buddhist cultivation. Reading the *Platform Sutra of the Sixth Patriarch* (*Liuzu tan-jing/Liu-tsu t'an-ching*), Chinul was struck by a passage that said,

The self-nature of suchness gives rise to thoughts. But even though the six sense-faculties see, hear, sense, and know, it is not tainted by the myriad images. The true nature is constantly free and self-reliant.

Astonished and overjoyed at gaining what he had never experienced, he walked around the hall, reflecting on the passage while continuing to recite it. His heart was satisfied. This experience was Chinul's initiation into Buddhism; an initial awakening to the self-radiating light of mind-nature that ensured his continued practice.

In the autumn of 1185, while residing at Pomun-

sa at Haga Mountain and browsing through piles of Buddhist canonical writings, Chinul was struck again by a textual passage in Li Tong-xuan's (Li T'ung-hsüan) *Commentary of the Flower Garland Sūtra*, which could confirm the Sŏn approach.

If the mind is brightened and your wisdom purified, then one hair and all the universe will be interfused, for there is nothing that is outside the mind. . . . The wisdom of the *tathāgatas* is just like this: it is complete in the bodies of all sentient beings. Merely ordinary, foolish people do not recognize it.

Chinul put the book on his head and unwittingly began to weep. Chinul's second realization led to his later incorporation of Hwaŏm theory and Sŏn practice in the posthumously published treatises *The Complete and Sudden Attainment of Buddhahood* and *Resolving Doubts About Observing the Hwadu*.

In the spring of 1188 Chinul was invited by Tŭkjae, one of the signatories of the original vow to form a retreat society, to join Kŏjo-sa on Kong Mountain. The retreat began formally in 1190.

Encouragement to Practice

In commemoration of the founding of the retreat society, Chinul composed his first major work, *Encouragement to Practice: The Compact of the Concentration and Wisdom Community*. It is full of youthful enthusiasm and sarcastic criticism against the "famous" Buddhist monks thriving within the established order. The community emerges as a reform movement outside of the order to reorient monks toward the proper practice of the Buddhist *sangha*. Conspicuous is his criticism against the Pure Land practice of reciting Buddha's names under the pretext that, in the degenerate age, people of inferior capacities cannot help but depend on the other power of Amitābha Buddha to receive them into his Pure Land. Through copious quotations based upon his personal experience from reading scriptures, Chinul persuades them to have faith in that one is originally an Enlightened Buddha and that recovering this fundamental essence is all that is necessary to perfect one's Buddhahood.

Seven years after its formation, the community at Kŏjo-sa had achieved widespread renown. The number of people who were studying under Chinul had grown to that of a city. The small size of the temple made it inevitable to expand it. But due to the limited areas available at Kŏjo-sa, Chinul sent one of his disciples, Suu, into the Kangnam region to search for a major meditation center to accommodate the growing number of students. Suu arrived at Songkwang Mountain in the southwest region of the peninsula, where he found a small dilapidated temple, Kilsang-sa. But the site was outstanding, the land fertile, the spring sweet, and the forests abundant—truly a place appropriate for cultivating the mind. While the construction of new buildings were going on, Chinul made a final retreat, on his way to the newly designated center, at the Sangmuju Hermitage near the top of the Chiri Mountain in order to consolidate his own practice with a few attendants before assuming the responsibility as spiritual leader of the large community. Miraculous occurrences took place, which indicated to his companions that Chinul had attained final enlightenment. Chinul himself relates the last of his series of three experiences as follows:

> I had not yet forsaken passion and views—it was as if my chest were blocked by something, or as if I were dwelling together with an enemy. . . . I went to Chiri and found a passage in the *Records of the Sŏn Master Ta-hui*: "Sŏn does not consist in quietude nor in bustle. It does not involve the activities of life nor logical discrimination. Nevertheless, it is of first importance not to investigate Sŏn while rejecting quietude or bustle. . . . If your eyes suddenly open, then Sŏn is something which exists inside your home." I understood this passage. Naturally nothing blocked my chest again. From then on I was at peace.

Ta-hui Tsung-kao (1089–1163) and Chinul were only one generation apart. The encounter with *Rec-*

ords of the Sŏn Master Ta-hui profoundly affected Chinul's later adoption and emphasis on the direct "shortcut" approach in Sŏn practice. In fact Chinul was the first Korean master to be influenced by Ta-hui's approach. Since then this *hwadu* observation, which was emphasized even more by Chinul's direct heir in the community, has been the hallmark of Korean Sŏn and is still practiced widely today in all monasteries.

Three years after his sojourn at Sangmuju Hermitage, Chinul arrived at Kilsang-sa in 1200 along with Yose, an influential Pure Land practitioner converted to Chinul's Sŏn, and his other companions. In 1205, after nine years of work and with the reconstruction complete, King Hŭijong (r. 1204–11), an ardent follower of Chinul, proclaimed 120 days of celebration in honor of the occasion. Hŭijong also ordered the name of the community be changed to Susŏn-sa (the Sŏn Cultivation Community), and he renamed the surrounding mountain from Songkwang to Chogye. Lectures were held during the day on the *Records of the Sŏn Master Ta-hui* and meditation was conducted during the evening. Chinul also wrote an outline of the training rules to be followed by the members of the society.

Admonitions to Beginning Students

Chinul's *Admonitions to Beginning Students*, comparable to the *Po-chang's Pure Rules* in China, was eventually adopted as the standard of conduct for all Sŏn monasteries, and it helped to establish ethical observance as the basis of indigenous Korean Sŏn cultivation. It is first of three basic works on the monk's life by three different Korean masters. As such it is the first text given to Korean postulants today. Like Wŏnhyo's *Arouse Your Mind and Practice!* (see the chapter on Wŏnhyo in this volume), Chinul's little work urges all beginners to realize the importance of ethical behavior.

It is essential for us to understand the moral quality of the monk's life as the foundation of their further cultivation. Careful and detailed admonitions abound. A few quotations illustrate Chinul's penchant for emphasizing the importance of moral instruction:

Do not think slightingly of your *dharma* instructors. By so doing, you will create obstacles on the path and your cultivation cannot progress. You must be careful about this! It is like a man traveling at night with a wicked person carrying a torch to show the way. If the man will not accept the service of his light because the carrier is bad, he could fall in a hole.

Secrets on Cultivating the Mind

The *Secrets on Cultivating the Mind* is an outline of basic Sŏn practice written between 1203 and 1205 to instruct the throngs coming to the newly completed Susŏn-sa. This seminal text of Korean Sŏn contains two elements of Chinul's thought: sudden awakening/gradual cultivation and the simultaneous practice of concentration and wisdom.

Lost in Korea during the Mongol invasions two decades after the death of Chinul, the book was reintroduced into Korea from the Northern Ming edition of the Buddhist discourses, the *Tripitaka* (Three Baskets) and translated into the vernacular Korean language by using the newly invented Korean script *han'gŭl* alphabet in 1467. Since then it remains the most popular and influential Sŏn text in Korea today. The modern Korean translation of this text, entitled "Do Not Seek Outside [Your Mind]," captures the basic spirit of the text.

Straight Talk on the True Mind

Straight Talk on the True Mind is Chinul's most accessible exposition of the Sŏn meditation techniques. Probably written around the same time as *Secrets*, this *Talk* represents the median stage in the development of Chinul's thought. Moving away from the primary method explored in his early work *Encouragement to Practice*, Chinul investigates the more sophisticated cultivation of "no-mind" as the most effective means of controlling the deluded mind. A synopsis of ten different techniques is given: any one suitable to one's capacity can be selected and perfected so that delusion will be vanished of itself and the true mind will instantly manifest itself.

Excerpts from the Dharma Collection

Chinul was fortunate to have a bright disciple, Hyesim (1178–1234), posthumously called National Master Chin'gak. In 1208, at the age of fifty, Chinul had sufficient confidence in Hyesim's leadership and decided to go into permanent retreat at Kyubong Hermitage near the Susŏn-sa community. By then Chinul's two major works were all but complete: *Abridgement of the* Commentary of the Flower Garland Sūtra in 1207 and *Excerpts from the Dharma Collection and Separate Circulation Record with Personal Notes*, finished in the summer of 1209 just one year prior to his death.

The latter—the magnum opus of Chinul and a product of his mature thought and lifelong study—is in fact the best work through which we can approach the entire range of Chinul's thought. Intended to be a handbook for Buddhist students under his tutelage, its treatment of the fundamentals of the Korean Buddhist tradition was so influential, comparable to Saint Thomas Aquinas's (1224 or 1225–74) *Summa theologiae* in Western medieval Christianity, that it became one of the basic texts used in the lecture halls of Korean monasteries and is still studied avidly today.

By carefully weighing the merits and demerits of the four major Chinese Chan (Ch'an) schools reconstructed by Gui-feng Zong-mi (Kuei-feng Tsung-mi) (780–841), the fifth patriarch of both the Huayan (Hua-yen) doctrinal sect and the He-ze (Ho-tse) School of Chan, Chinul was able to focus on the different taxonomies of sudden and gradual approaches to enlightenment. Chinul finally recommends "sudden awakening/gradual cultivation" as the most plausible choice for all the Buddhist aspirants, which since then has become the hallmark of Korean Sŏn Buddhist tradition.

Chinul's discussion is an excellent example of the scholarly writing produced by any exegetes in the various Buddhist schools. Chinul's exposition eschews the impression of Zen as often portrayed in the West as bibliophobic and anti-theoretical. While developing the central theme of sudden awakening/gradual cultivation, Chinul also discusses the simultaneous cultivation of concentration and wisdom, the cultivation of no-mind, the faith and understanding of the complete and sudden school—that is, the Hwaŏm thought—and he completes his systematic treatise by including, for the first time in Korea, the *hwadu* meditation, a new type of practice developed by Ta-hui Tsung-kao. As the most comprehensive of Chinul's works, this *Excerpts* (Korean Buddhists often refer to this work as *Chŏryo*) is a good illustration of the syncretic trend of Chinul's thought, in which the convergence of Sŏn practice and doctrinal theories is demonstrated.

To sum up Chinul's prescription for the Buddhist approach to enlightenment, we can analyze three levels of awakening:

First, initial intellectual awakening: at this level one can suddenly be awakened to the fact that one is already a Buddha. This intellectual awakening allows the practitioner to find the entrance to the Buddhist Path.

Second, the stage of gradual cultivation: this stage is necessary because the initial, intellectual awakening or correct faith has to be continuously refined in order to remove past defilements and develop salutary qualities of mind.

Third, the level of realization–awakening: this is attained as the result of gradual cultivation.

Chinul carefully orchestrated even his death, with a certain premonition, which occurred on 22 April 1210. For eight days Chinul, showing signs of illness, conducted carefully organized conversation in the format of questions and answers with his disciples as usual. Finally, picking up his staff, he struck it on the ground several times and said, "A thousand things and ten thousand objects are right here." King Hŭijong conferred on the master the posthumous title "National Preceptor *Puril Pojo*" (Buddha Sun Shining Universally) and named his stupa the *Kamno* (Sweet Dew Reliquary).

The efforts of Chinul and his successors at Susŏn-sa community over the next 108 years established the monastery as a major center of Korean Buddhism for the rest of Koryŏ period. From

Chinul to National Master Kobong (1350–1428), a series of sixteen national masters are reputed to reside at the Susŏn-sa. Due to the monastery's strong orientation toward practice as instructed by Chinul, Songkwang-sa has traditionally been regarded since the Chosŏn (Yi) (1392–1910) dynasty as the temple representative of the *Sangha*-jewel in Korea. It is no wonder Chinul's system of instructing Sŏn monks became the model of all later Korean Buddhist monastic institutions. Recently, however, the present patriarch of the Chogye order, Sŏngch'ŏl (1912–), challenged the long-held tradition of Chinul's syncretism as heretical, claiming that only sudden-awakening/sudden-cultivation through *hwadu* investigation is the orthodox practice of Sŏn Buddhism.

JAE-RYONG SHIM

Further Reading

Translation

Buswell, Robert E., Jr., trans. and ed. *The Korean Approach to Zen: The Collected Works of Chinul*. Translated with an introduction. Honolulu, Hawaii: University of Hawaii Press, 1983. This is a complete English translation of Chinul's extant works. An abridgment of it was published under the title of *Tracing Back the Radiance: Chinul's Korean Way of Zen* by the Kuroda Institute for the Study of Buddhism and Human Values in 1991.

Related Studies

Buswell, Robert E., Jr. *The Zen Monastic Experience*. Princeton, N.J.: Princeton University Press, 1992. A firsthand account of the institutional structure, daily life, and modes of religious practice of the contemporary Songkwang-sa monastery founded by Chinul.

Keel, Hee Sung. *Chinul: The Founder of the Korean Son (Zen) Tradition*. Ph.D. dissertation, Harvard University, 1977. A revised version appeared under the title *Chinul: The Founder of*

Korean Son Buddhism (Berkeley, Calif.: Institute of South and Southeast Asian Studies, 1984). This traces the background of Chinul's thought and its system and influence on Korean Sŏn Buddhism.

Kim, Ing-sŏk. "Puril Pojo kuksa," *Pulgyo hakpo* [*Journal of Buddhism*]. Vol. 2, 1964, pp. 3–39. Seoul: Tongguk University Press. This is the first classic study on Chinul by a Korean Buddhist scholar.

Shim, Jae Ryong. *The Philosophical Foundation of* *Korean Zen Buddhism: The Integration of Sŏn and Kyo by Chinul*. Ph.D. dissertation, University of Hawaii, 1979. An account is made of Chinul's interpretation of nature origination in Li Tong-xuan's thought and its ramification for Chinul's reconciliation of the Sŏn and doctrinal schools.

Yi, Chong-ik. *Korai Fusho kokushi no kenkyu-sono shiso taikei to Fushozen no tokushitsu*. Ph.D. dissertation, Taisho University, 1974. This is the first book-length study on Chinul in Japanese.

YI T'OEGYE

Born: 1501, Dosan, Korea
Died: 1570, Dosan, Korea
Major Works: *Chyonmyongdo* (*Revision of Chong Chi-Un's* Old Diagram of the Mandate of Heaven) (1553), *Chujasojolyo* (*Essentials of Master Chu's Letters*) (1556), *Jasongnok* (*Self-Reflections*) (1558), *T'oegye Kobong Wangbokso* (*The T'oegye–Kobong Correspondence*) (1559–67), *Songhakshipdo* (*Ten Diagrams of Confucianist Learning*) (1567)

Major Ideas

The Four Beginnings emanate from principle and the Seven Emotions from material force. [Early view.]
There is a reciprocal emanation of principle and material force. [Revised view.]
Single-mindedness can be achieved only by unceasing moral effort and self-cultivation.
Everyone is capable of achieving sagehood (becoming fully human) through firm determination, serious self-cultivation, study and inquiry, and right action.

Yi T'oegye (Yi Hwang) was born into a patrician family in Dosan, Korea, where he died sixty-nine years later. The Potters' Mountain Academy (Dosan Sowon), which he founded in Dosan, still stands at the original site. By the age of six T'oegye had mastered the basic 1,000 Chinese characters, and by twelve he was perusing Confucius's *Analects* and making an earnest inquiry into the meaning of principle (Korean: *i*; Chinese: *li*) in the overall scheme of Confucianism. Even at a very early age T'oegye began to compose philosophical poems, making good use of apt metaphors. Throughout his life T'oegye produced over 3,000 poems, in addition to his more formal philosophical writings. At twenty he became totally engrossed in a critical study of the *Book of Changes* and the *Great Learning*. He was intent on developing an all-encompassing vision integrating theory with practice within the Neo-Confucianist framework, and he drew his inspiration mainly from the Chinese Neo-Confucianist Zhu Xi (Chu Hsi) (1130–1200).

After brilliantly passing the state examinations, T'oegye began his career as a public servant, occupying various positions including the presidency of Songkyunkwan, which was at the time the most prestigious research institute of the nation. T'oegye's probity and brilliance enthralled the king; disenchanted as T'oegye was with the strife-torn court, he was called back time and again by the king to serve the country.

T'oegye spent the final decade of his life at the Dosan Sowon training many outstanding scholars. Just before he died, T'oegye bade farewell to his disciples and, having straightened his hat and gown while contemplating his favorite plum flowers in the midst of the pure white snow, he simply died.

T'oegye is noted mainly for his singular contribution to the systematic completion of Neo-Confucianism in East Asia. T'oegye's lasting legacy is embodied in the Four–Seven Debate with Kobong Ki Dae-Seung (1527–72) and his refinement of the concept of single-mindedness (Korean: *kyong*; Chinese: *jing/ching*). The Four–Seven Debate is characterized not only by sharp points and notable advances made on substantive philosophical issues, but also by the highly civilized manner of discourse and its irenic ambience. The Debate is a living example of the Confucian way of life.

The Four–Seven Debate

What is the Four–Seven Debate? The Debate centers around the relationship between the four beginnings (commiseration, shame, deference, and discernment) of the four virtues mentioned in the *Book of Mencius* (humanity, righteousness, propriety, and wisdom) and the seven emotions (joy, anger, sadness, fear, love, hatred, and desire) first alluded to in the *Book of Rites*. The Chinese philosopher Cheng Yi (Ch'eng I) (1033–1107) made the first attempt at giving a systematic examination of the seven emotions. Following his mentor Cheng Yi, Zhu Xi linked the four beginnings to principle and the seven emotions to material force (Korean: *ki*; Chinese: *qi/ch'i*), and said that the four beginnings emanate from principle and the seven emotions from material force. According to the Mencian theory that all the major Confucianists—except Xunzi (Hsün Tzu) (fl. 298– 238 B.C.) and his followers—have espoused, the four virtues are innate in human nature, which is originally good.

What precipitated the Four–Seven Debate was T'oegye's proposed revision of Chuman Chong Chi-Un's *Old Diagram of the Mandate of Heaven*. Chong Chi-Un (1509–69) expressed the view, derived from Zhu Xi, that while the four beginnings emanate from principle, the seven emotions emanate from material force. In commenting on Chong Chi-Un's view, T'oegye proposed that Chong's point be revised as follows: While the four beginnings emanate from principle, the seven emotions emanate from both principle and material force. This leads to the implication: whereas that which emanates from principle is purely good, what emanates from principle and material force can be either good or bad. At this juncture, T'oegye asked for Kobong Ki Dae-Seung's comment, and hence the Debate. The *T'oegye–Kobong Correspondence* consists of three sets of Kobong's letters and T'oegye's responses.

In the first letter Kobong begins by acknowledging that T'oegye has made a notable advance over Chong Chi-un by locating a link between principle and material force. Yet Kobong says that T'oegye's view is still overly dualistic. Further, if T'oegye's view were true, according to Kobong, the four beginnings would be totally unrelated to material force and could not possibly become phenomenally manifest, for it is only in virtue of material force that the metaphysical (original nature), namely principle, could be concretely schematized and made manifest.

In lieu of T'oegye's view, Kobong advances the alternative interpretation that the seven emotions contain the four virtues (*chiljongposadan*). In Kobong's view material force is the only source of emanation, principle is the ground or reason (*soiyonjili*) for being and becoming, and principle is "immanent" (*tajae*) in material force. The four beginnings and the seven emotions are, as a matter of fact, indistinguishable in that they are both emotions. Since there is only one species of emotions of human nature (*songjong*), there is only one source of emanation, and principle and material force are inseparable. The only difference between the Four (Beginnings) and the Seven (Emotions) is that after emotions are aroused, if they attain due measure and degree, as defined in the *Doctrine of the Mean*, they are construed as the Four; if they do not, they are interpreted as the Seven.

What Kobong means by human nature (*song*) is the mean, as defined in the *Doctrine of the Mean*, namely emotions before arousal. This contrasts with T'oegye's understanding of human nature in the Mencian sense, that is, the four virtues. Kobong's monism is, however, in keeping with the Neo-Confucian view that the heart/mind is the fusion of principle and material force, and that harmony—that is, the attainment of due measure and degree of emotions after their arousal—is goodness. Since the heart/mind is the fusion of principle and material force, when it is aroused, material force becomes emanant, and principle "rides" it. If material force is neither excessive nor lacking in emanation and does not hinder principle from properly manifesting itself, harmony is attained. The distinction between the Four and Seven is neither intrinsic nor ontological, but is contingent on the manner in which material force does or does not properly function by way of a schematizing principle.

In response to Kobong's first letter, T'oegye responded as follows: Admittedly, the Four and Seven are, in some sense, both emotions. However, if we are to hold on to the distinction between the metaphysical (original nature) and the physical (physical nature), as drawn originally by the Chinese Neo-Confucianist Zhang Zai (Chang Tsai)

(1020–77) and later refined by Cheng Yi and Zhu Xi, it is only apposite to impute the four beginnings (qua moral) to the former and the seven emotions (qua natural) to the latter if we are to be mindful of "conceptual genealogy." Since the Four and the Seven play different conceptual roles, they should not be conflated. T'oegye came up with the twin phrases "identity-in-difference" (*ichungdong*) and "difference-in-identity" (*dongchungi*); if identity-in-difference is characteristic of Kobong's position, then difference-in-identity is apposite for his own view.

If Kobong propounded a naturalistic monism in assimilating the four virtues to the seven emotions, T'oegye wished to highlight the distinctly moral nature of principle and four virtues. Put differently, if Kobong insisted on the stark fact that the virtues are "contained" in the emotions, T'oegye's view was that although Kobong might be right in making the factual point, it does not follow that the distinctly moral concept of the virtues can be defined in terms of the empirical concept of the emotions.

T'oegye's conception of emotions derived from the *Book of Rites* and Kobong's conception from the *Doctrine of the Mean*. In the former, emotions are conceived as being precarious unless they are guided by principle. In the latter, emotions are viewed from a value-free sort of naturalistic perspective.

In the second letter, Kobong argues first that the Four and Seven emanate from the same human nature. Second, the Four and Seven are alike responses to external stimuli, as in the example of a person rushing to the rescue of a drowning child. Third, the arousal even of the Seven is caused in part by the presence of principle; it is wrong to say that the arousal of the Seven is caused by material force alone. Principle and material force are inseparable. Fourth, the distinction between what is purely good and what is not should not be drawn by attributing what is purely good to principle alone. Rather, how emotions become good and when they do should be explained in terms of their attaining due measure and degree. Fifth, since principle is weak and material force is strong, the fact that emotions do not always attain due mea-

sure and degree after their arousal should be explained in terms of the inability of principle to "ride" material force properly on some occasions. Last but not least, the distinction between original nature and physical nature is not ontological, but functional.

T'oegye begins his response by reiterating the point already made in the first response, that in some sense both the Four and the Seven are emotions. Now, admittedly the seven emotions are responses to external stimuli, and T'oegye further agrees that the four virtues also become evident, in a way, in response to external stimuli. But as a general response to Kobong, T'oegye proposes reciprocal emanation of principle and material force by adopting and adapting to his dualistic use Kobong's notion that principle "rides" material force.

This creative response shows T'oegye's dialectical dexterity as well as his irenic ability for reconciliation. According to the theory of reciprocal emanation, with the Four, material force "follows" principle when principle becomes emanant; with the Seven, when material force becomes emanant, principle "rides" material force. To use a metaphor, just as a person cannot take a trip without riding a horse, the horse will be without a sense of direction if the person does not guide it. However, just because the person and the horse complement each other, it does not follow that they are identical. Hence the vindication of T'oegye's dualism.

At this point, Kobong rightly perceived T'oegye's dualistic conception of human nature to be at the heart of their disagreement. So in his third and final letter, Kobong set himself the task of criticizing this conception by using a new metaphor: original nature (principle) may be likened to the moon in the sky and physical nature (material force) to the moon reflected in water. But just because we talk about the moon in the sky and the moon reflected in water, it does not mean that there are two really different moons. Similarly, there is no real duplication of nature: physical nature is the same original nature qua "immanent" in physical (concrete) entities. What gets aroused is the heart/

mind, which is due to the fusion of principle and material force. The four beginnings are the seven emotions qua good. But the seven emotions include morally indeterminate emotions as well. So the four beginnings constitute a subset of the seven emotions. And the seven emotions become good emotions, namely, the four beginnings when they attain due measure and degree. Kobong goes on to say that what he meant by emotions attaining due measure and degree and thus becoming good was the same as what T'oegye meant by talking about material force "following" principle and principle "riding" material force.

But this view seems to contradict the time-honored Mencian doctrine that the four beginnings are innate, which implies that they are not a consequence of an empirical process as the emotions attaining due measure and degree seem to be. This is precisely the point T'oegye seized on. Having made this very point in his third response, T'oegye goes on to say, in effect, that without assuming a moral point of view, one could not act as a moral agent. In his own way T'oegye was asserting the "primacy of practical reason" and was saying that what he considered to be a jejune sort of naturalism could not do justice to a moral point of view.

Though there were further maneuverings on the part of each, in the end Kobong agreed with T'oegye's conception of a moral point of view, which eventually led Yi Yulgok (Yi I) (1536–84) to synthesize T'oegye's moral point of view with Kobong's naturalistic monism.

Single-Mindedness

In his various writings and notably in *Self-Reflections* and *Ten Diagrams of Confucianist Learning*, T'oegye refined and perfected the Neo-Confucian concept of single-mindedness (*kyong*). Being single-minded means being engaged in unceasing moral efforts and self-cultivation. If looking upward one is to have no occasion for shame and looking downward no occasion to blush, one should render one's inner self upright and act righteously in one's outward conduct. T'oegye

took seriously the Confucian idea that what a person becomes depends largely on self-efforts. T'oegye was committed to the idea that everyone is capable of attaining sagehood (becoming fully human) through firm determination, serious self-cultivation, and study and inquiry, as accompanied by commensurate praxis.

T'oegye's preoccupation with *kyong* was a manifestation of his humanism. For T'oegye, heavenly principle (*chonli*) had only an ethical meaning. T'oegye's *kyong* may be said to be the synthetic composite of the primeval Korean sense of supreme efforts-cum-utmost devotion (*chisong*) and the Confucian notion of "holding fast to mind" (Korean: *jikyong*; Chinese: *chi jing/ch'ih-ching*). Being a thoroughgoing humanist, T'oegye believed in human autonomy; he believed that it is only through self-efforts that one can create a meaningful life. T'oegye's concept of single-mindedness had a lasting influence not only on the subsequent major Korean Neo-Confucianists, including Yulgok, but also on the Japanese Neo-Confucianists of the Tokugawa period.

KWANG-SAE LEE

Further Reading

Translation

Kalton, Michael C., ed., trans., commentator. *To Become a Sage: The Ten Diagrams on Sage Learning by Yi T'oegye*. New York: Columbia University Press, 1988. An excellent translation of T'oegye's last major work, together with an extensive commentary providing the historical and philosophical background.

Related Studies

Choi, Min-Hong. *A Modern History of Korean Philosophy*. Seoul: Seong Moon Sa, 1983. This is a useful survey of the development of Neo-Confucianism during the Chosŏn (Yi) dynasty (1392–1910).

Chun, Shin-yong, ed. *Korean Thought*. Seoul: The Si-sa-yong-o-sa Publishers, Inc., 1982. A collec-

tion of essays on Shamanism in Korea, the Four–
Seven Debate, the rise of Practical Learning
(*Shilhak*), the reception of Western Learning
(*Sohak*), and Korean nationalism. This book is a
concise introduction to Korean thought.

de Bary, Wm. Theodore and JaHyun Kim Haboush, eds. *The Rise of Neo-Confucianism in
Korea*. New York: Columbia University Press,
1985. This helpful collection of essays on
T'oegye Yi Hwang, Yulgok Yi I, and other prominent Neo-Confucianists of the Chosŏn dynasty
and the various issues addressed by them is particularly illuminating concerning the Four–
Seven Debate.

HYUJŎNG

Born: 1520, Anju, P'yŏngan Province, Korea
Died: 1604, Mt. Myohyang, P'yŏngan Province, Korea
Major Works: *The Mirror of the Three Teachings*, *The Mirror of the Meditation School* (1564)

Major Ideas

The essential teachings of Buddhism, Confucianism, and Daoism (Taoism) are the same.
Meditation is the Buddha's mind, and doctrine is the Buddha's words.
Meditation is better than doctrine as a way of finding truth.
Everyone possesses the potential for salvation.

Hyujŏng was a meditation monk of the Chosŏn (Yi) dynasty (1392–1910) of Korea. He was born into a local literati family and, when young, lost his parents. When he was ten, he was adopted as a son of a local magistrate. Hyujŏng entered the National Academy in the capital when he was twelve. He studied there the Confucian classics and military arts for three years. When he was fifteen, Hyujŏng took the civil service examination, but he failed. He wandered around the country and studied Buddhist canonical texts under *dharma* masters until he was twenty-one. For the next several years, he meditated, visiting many places in the country. In 1549 he passed the recently reinstituted monastic service examination, by which monks were selected for positions in the administrative hierarchy of the Buddhist establishment, at the top of his group. He was offered an important monastic title. In 1557 he resigned that post and went back to the mountains to engage in religious cultivation. Thereafter, Hyujŏng concentrated on his religious practice for about thirty years. In 1589 he was falsely accused of sedition and was arrested by the government, but he was soon released. He was appointed by the government the head of the monks' militia and fought during the Japanese invasion of 1592. He died in 1604 at Mt. Myohyang, Korea.

During his lifetime Neo-Confucianism flourished and such representative Confucian scholar-officials as Yi T'oegyc (Yi Hwang) 1501–70) and Yi Yulgok (Yi I) (1536–84) were active. The Neo-Confucian literati entered government service in the capital and dominated the political process. The social position of monks declined and Buddhism withered in a society where Confucianism was paramount. During the reign of King Myŏngjong (1545–67), under the regency of Queen Dowager Munjŏng (1501–65), Buddhism again displayed some vitality. With the death of the queen dowager in 1565, however, Buddhism again suffered suppression, becoming a faith practiced principally by women.

The major works of Hyujŏng are the *Mirror of the Three Teachings* and the *Mirror of the Meditation School*. Hyujŏng also left such other works, "Excerpts of Mind Teaching," "Essentials of Meditation and Doctrine," and "Interpretation of Meditation and Doctrine," as well as his letters, his eulogy records of meditation masters, essays on spells and rituals, and inscriptions to Buddha and eminent Korean monks.

The Mirror of the Three Teachings

The Mirror of the Three Teachings consists of three parts: "The Mirror of Confucianism," "The Mirror of Daoism," and "The Mirror of Meditation Buddhism." In this work Hyujŏng brings out the harmony of the Three Teachings by showing that, although they differ in their religious practices, in essence the three religions are not different.

Hyujŏng notes that the religious characteristics of the Three Teachings differ. He claims that when the Three Teachings are viewed in their functional aspects, Buddhism is the most profound among the three. He argues that Buddhism has much in reserve while Confucianism does not; Daoist (Taoist) thought manifests the essence of emptiness, but does not explain the function of self-nature and numinous knowledge. Meditation Buddhism, on the other hand, clarifies both the nonexistence of self and the existence of the true self.

Hyujŏng, however, does not degrade Confucianism and Daoism, and he praises the two teachings: "Confucius is not the beginning [of the Way]; how can Laozi be the end [of it]? They transform themselves into eternity [truth]." "Confucius planted the root of truth, Laozi nurtured it, and Buddha pulled it out"; thus, according to Hyujŏng, they are not different". For Hyujŏng, what is more important than specific differences among the Three Teachings is their ultimate agreement in essence. Thus he emphasizes the importance of not becoming attached to names and letters, because they lead the practitioners to discriminating thoughts.

The theoretical basis of Hyujŏng's harmonization of the Three Teachings rests in the idea that their essence is mind and that mind is the same among all three.

The Confucian concepts of virtue, benevolence, respect, and sincerity are expressed in different words, but they have the same content: the expression of mind transmitted to Mencius by Confucius. Concerning the relationship between Confucianism and Buddhism, there is no difference in essence between the two: Hyujŏng says,

True men do not differentiate Buddhism from Confucianism. Ch'oe Ch'iwon [857–?], an eminent Korean Confucian scholar, and Chin'gam [774–850], an eminent Korean Buddhist monk, are exemplars of such people.

Therefore, Hyujŏng advised his disciples to learn silence from Confucius and an unmoving state of mind from Mencius. His idea of the harmony between Confucianism and Buddhism transformed itself into action: he held the memorial service of his parents according to the Confucian style and advised the king to respect Confucianism and Buddhism together for three generations' peace.

Hyujŏng was interested not in religious Daoism,

but in philosophical Daoism, the teachings of Laozi (Lao Tzu) and Zhuangzi (Chuang Tzu). In his writings Hyujŏng regards the ultimate purpose of Daoism as that of following the metaphysical way (*Dao/Tao*), and he identifies the Daoist Way with the Buddhist mind. Thus Hyujŏng harmonized the Three Teachings by claiming that the essence of the three is mind and that the concept of mind is identical in all three.

The Mirror of the Meditation School

Written in 1564, *The Mirror of the Meditation School* was composed to teach the essence of Buddhism to monks of his day who were more interested in secular learning and poetry than in Buddhist thought. This work comprises three parts: collections of Buddhist canonical texts regarded by Hyujŏng as essential, Hyujŏng's interpretations on that collection, and his eulogies of that collection.

Hyujŏng's motive for harmonizing meditation and doctrine lay in his attempt to resolve the conflict that divided meditation monks from doctrinal monks. His theoretical foundation for harmonizing the two is that both ultimately derive from the Buddha. Hyujŏng claims that "meditation is the Buddha's mind and doctrines are the Buddha's words; they are not different"; thus they are inseparable and are essential paths to enlightenment.

However, Hyujŏng's harmonization scheme does not treat meditation and doctrine equally: meditation is primary because doctrine is just a gate to it. For Hyujŏng, letters, names, forms, and even the Buddha's words are obstructions to enlightenment. Because doctrinal monks do not depend on "live words" (*hwadu*)—"critical phrases" used as topics of contemplation in the Meditation School— but only on intellectual knowledge to gain enlightenment, Hyujŏng warns them not to become attached to names and letters.

However, for him doctrinal understanding is also useful for cultivation, provided that the monks do not attach themselves to Buddhist texts.

Hyujŏng emphasizes that though each Buddhist soteriological method differs in the time it takes for a practitioner to gain enlightenment, all men possess the potential for salvation. He claims that there are two approaches to enlightenment: by "self-power" and "other-power": a person of high spiritual faculty can get enlightened quickly by self-power, but a person of low spiritual faculty gets enlightened slowly through other-power.

As for the shortcut to enlightenment through self-power, Hyujŏng first emphasizes the importance of believing that one's own mind is the Buddha's mind and the Buddha's mind is none other than one's mind; outside of mind there is no Buddha and outside of the Buddha there is no mind. After enlightening one's mind, a person has to keep cultivating oneself because one's words and actions should be in harmony and his understanding should materialize through praxis. Although all people originally have the Buddha-nature, their actions may differ because they are filled with greed and desire.

To harmonize theory and action, practitioners should meditate with great faith, great eagerness, and great doubt. For right meditation, monks should avoid discriminative thought, and instead focus on *hwadu*. However, students should not study dead words, which cause mere intellectual understanding, but the live phrases of the shortcut approach, which leads to enlightenment.

As for the long-term cultivation by other-worldly power, Hyujŏng argues that the shortcut approach is not ideal for all monks. This is because Hyujŏng viewed his time as a degenerate age during which few monks had the spiritual faculty necessary to complete the shortcut approach. Thus, to lead them to their religious goal, additional alternatives such as recitation of spells (*mantras*) to get rid of past karmic obstructions of religious practitioners and chanting the Buddha's name are suggested by Hyujŏng. However, chanting the Buddha's name for Hyujŏng does not refer simply to reciting the Buddha's name with the mouth, but to harmonizing that name with what is in one's mind; then one's pure mind will be none other than the Pure Land of the Buddha. Thus the essence of religious praxis does not rest in form, but in inner convictions.

Hyujŏng harmonized Buddhism, Confucianism, and Daoism from the perspective afforded by the conviction that the essence of their teachings is identical: all teach the truth of mind. He also harmonized meditation and doctrine by seeking their origin in the Buddha's own experience and upon this basis he claimed that all men are qualified for salvation. Ignorance caused by differentiation based on subjective ideas brings conflicts among human beings. Hyujŏng's approach to find a way to resolve the dichotomy between theory and practice is based on intuition, which is different from the approach of the West, which focuses on intellectual comprehension. In this respect, Hyujŏng's ideas can shed new light on human understanding.

Hyujŏng's thought had little effect on the Chosŏn dynasty Confucian society in which he lived. His influence has been greatest in contemporary Korean intellectual circles: his idea of harmonization among religions affected the new religions that arose in Korea since the mid-nineteenth century, and his idea of the harmonization of meditation and doctrine has had a profound impact on the contemporary Korean Buddhist tradition.

JONG MYUNG KIM

Further Reading

Note: No translation in English is yet available.

Hyujŏng. *Chosŏn sidae p'yŏn. Han'guk Pulgyo chonso* [*Comprehensive Collection of Korean Buddhism*], Vol. 7, 1990 (1986). Seoul: Tongguk Taehakkyo Ch'ulp'anbu. This collection includes the photolithographic reprint of all of Hyujŏng's extant works in classical Chinese.

———. "Sŏn'ga kwigam, Sŏsan taesa chip" ["Hyujŏng: Mirror of Meditation Teachings, Literary Collection of Great Master Sŏsan"]. In the *Han'guk myongjo tae chonjip* [*Great Comprehensive Collection of Excellent Korean Works*]. Translated by Pŏpchŏng and Pak Kyonggun. Seoul: Taeyang Sŏjŏk, 1986. This work in Korean is a partial, annotated translation of Hyujŏng's works.

Song, Ch'onun. "Hyujŏng no sangyŏ kan" ["Hyujŏng's View of the Three Teachings"], *Indogaku Bukkyŏgaku kenkyu.* 41–2, March 1993, pp. 70–76. This article (written in Japanese) discusses Hyujŏng's philosophical analyses of Buddhism, Confucianism, and Daoism.

U, Chŏngsang. "Hyujŏng: Son kwa Kyo ŭi t'ongilchŏm" ["Hyujŏng: Harmonizer of Meditation and Doctrines"], *Han'guk ŭi in'gan sang* [*The Human Mirror of Korea*], Vol. 3, 1966, pp. 202–217. Seoul: Sin'gu Munhwasa. This article (written in Korean) deals with Hyujŏng's views on meditation and doctrine.

YI YULGOK (YI I)

Born: 1536, Kangneung, Korea
Died: 1584, Seoul, Korea
Major Works: *Donghomundap* (*Conversations on Politics Between Host and Guest*) (1569), *Hyangyak* (*On the Community Pact*) (1571), *Dap Songhowon* (*The Yulgok–Ugye Correspondence*) (1572), *Songhakjibjo* (*Essentials of Confucianist Learning*) (1575), *Kyokmongyokyol* (*A Primer of Neo-Confucianism*) (1577), *Sohakjipchu* (*Collected Annotations on the Small Learning*) (1579), *Kyongyonilki* (*A Diary of Royal Lectures*) (1581)

Major Ideas

Only material force emanates, and principle is the reason for emanation.
The distinction between the moral and the human mind is not ontological but ethical.
Sincerity can be achieved through single-mindedness.
The motif of political philosophy should be striving for and realizing the substantial and the practical.

Along with Yi T'oegye (Yi Hwang) (1501–70), Yi Yulgok (Yi I) was one of the two greatest Korean Neo-Confucianists of the Chosŏn (Yi) dynasty (1392–1910). Yulgok was born in 1536 in Kangneung, Korea, and he descended from a prominent family. Yulgok's mother Shin Saimdang was a notable woman who is regarded even now as the paradigm of Korean motherhood. In her own right, Shin Saimdang was a highly respected writer, a splendid landscape painter, and an expert on embroidery. She was the embodiment of virtuous womanhood and exerted a singular influence on her son. Yulgok was a prodigy who mastered the basics of Chinese characters by the age of three. At the age of seven, he composed a piece entitled *A Tract for Clarification of the Meaning of Ancient Writings* (*Komunchinhuchangjon*). When Yulgok was sixteen, his mother died. After the customary three-year mourning period, he went to Mt. Diamond (Keumgangsan), where he sojourned for a year to study Buddhism. Then he returned home to pursue Confucianism. Yulgok became a brilliant philosopher, outstanding educator, and dedicated statesman.

Yulgok was in a sense a Korean Hegel who endeavored to synthesize the thoughts of his predecessors. In particular, Yulgok was enthusiastic about T'oegye and Hwadam Soh Kyong-Dok (1489–1546). Hwadam had propounded Great Harmony (*Taehwa*) by way of moving to integrate principle (Korean: *i*; Chinese: *li*) and material force (Korean: *ki*; Chinese: *qi/ch'i*). Hwadam's conception of material force monism as manifest in Great Harmony had a palpable influence on Yulgok. Yulgok's theory of the concurrent emanation (*kyombal*) of principle and material force was an adaptation of Hwadam's prototypal version as modified by Kobong Ki Dae-Seung (1527–72).

The Four–Seven Debate

One issue that figures prominently in Yulgok's philosophy is the continuation of the Four–Seven Debate between T'oegye and Kobong. Yulgok's view on the four beginnings (commiseration, shame, deference, and discernment) of the four virtues (humanity, righteousness, propriety, and wisdom) and the seven emotions (joy, anger, sadness, fear, love, hatred, and desire) is to be found, for the most part, in his correspondence with Ugye Song Hon (1535–98). The correspondence between Yulgok and Ugye consists of seven sets of Ugye's letters and Yulgok's replies. The main exchanges took place in 1572.

The correspondence began when Ugye raised certain questions about the heart/mind (Korean: *shim*; Chinese: *xin/hsin*). Ugye was a close friend of

Yulgok's, but philosophically he tended to agree, though with reservations, with the main drift of T'oegye's views. Ugye felt that though ontologically speaking, the heart/mind is one, it seems to be two as viewed from a moral point of view, which is due to the difference between principle and material force. For, in Ugye's view, principle generates the moral mind (Korean: *doshim*; Chinese: *daoxin/taohsin*), and material force sires the human mind (Korean: *inshim*; Chinese: *renxin/jenhsin*). Ugye then correlated the moral mind with the four beginnings and the human mind with the seven emotions.

In dealing with the problem of the Four (Beginnings) and the Seven (Emotions), Yulgok disagreed with T'oegye's adumbrated solution of the problem. According to Yulgok, since principle and material force are originally inseparable, though they should not be confused, their reciprocal emanation as propounded by T'oegye is impossible, for reciprocal emanation presupposes their separability. The inseparability of principle and material force is cosmic in significance, in that the Great Ultimate (ultimate principle) is already "immanent" in *yin* (Korean: *cum*) and *yang*, both of which are tied up with material force. At the specifically human level, the seven emotions already "contain" the four beginnings.

While being critical of T'oegye's reciprocal emanation of principle and material force as being dualistic, Yulgok nevertheless espoused T'oegye's notion that principle "rides" material force, and he combined this thesis, as adapted to his own view, with Kobong's idea that only material force emanates and that principle is the reason for the emanation of material force. Without material force emanation is impossible; without principle there is no ground or reason for emanation. According to Yulgok, principle is the "master" (*chujae*) of material force. But without material force principle has no roots; without material force principle has nothing to hang on to. Principle is formless, and material force is tangible. Principle is "no-action" (*muwi*), and material force is "action" (*yuwi*). In fine, they complement each other. Yulgok disagrees with T'oegye on the

question of emanation and denies that principle can emanate.

Even if Yulgok held the view that it is only material force that emanates, he insisted on the primacy of principle not only for the reason of being, but also for the structure of the phenomenal world. Here he clearly disagreed with Zhu Xi (Chu Hsi), for Zhu Xi had insisted on the primacy of material force over principle for the phenomenal world, even though he had affirmed the primacy of principle over material force for the reason of being. It seems then arbitrary, as is often done, to classify Yulgok as a Founding Father of the School of Material Force (*chukipa*) of Korean Neo-Confucianism, at any rate, without further qualifications. In fact, if we note Yulgok's reference to principle as the "central thread" (*chunyu*) or "basis" (*keunjob*), it seems more apposite to view him as a member of the School of Principle (*chulipa*).

The point is that Yulgok did not dogmatically affirm the primacy of either principle or material force. He only tried to sort out the different functions that principle and material force play, thus clarifying the conceptual and ontological relationship between the two, a matter that had been left unclarified by the Chinese. Though T'oegye's theory of reciprocal emanation was better than Zhu Xi's dualism as a way of locating a link between principle and material force, Yulgok felt that T'oegye's ontological dualism was still cumbersome.

The Korean Neo-Confucianists' ways of handling the problem of principle and material force are variations on the East Asian Neo-Confucian theme of one substance and many functions, which is the Confucian counterpart of the one–many problem in Western philosophy.

In his correspondence with Ugye, Yulgok said that the principle of unity is the substance of principle, and the principle of "one thousand differentiation" (*mansueuii*) is the function of principle. Ten thousand things are variegated and uneven. Principle and material force are "neither two things nor one thing," and "Two is one and one is two," which is what is meant by the "wondrous fusion" (*myohap*) of principle and material force.

Yulgok appealed to an aesthetic sense of unity and plurality for his adumbrated solution of the counterpart problem. According to Yulgok, even if there is only one principle, if it "rides" material force, principle becomes differentiation and variegation in myriad uneven forms. That is why the Great Ultimate and *yin* and *yang* are in fusion. The nature of specific entities is constituted by the fusion of principle and material force. If the invisible and formless principle is all-pervasive, the visible and tangible material force occasions the differentiation and limitation of specific entities. Thus in the midst of protean changes and uneven differentiations prompted by material force, principle retains the "equanimity of original wondrousness" (*bonyonjimyoeuijayak*).

Yulgok used the metaphor of water and a vessel: Just as water assumes a concrete form as it is contained in a vessel, so principle becomes manifest in concrete entities in virtue of material force. That the nature of the human being is different from the nature of other entities is due to the differentiating and limiting effect of material force, and that the principle of man is the same principle as the principle of myriad other things is due to the all-pervasiveness of principle. According to Yulgok, the kind of principle not "immanent" in material principle is a myth. Just as there are good and bad aspects of material principle, there are good and bad aspects of principle as well. In other words, Yulgok rejected T'oegye's view that whereas principle generates what is purely good, material force generates what can be either good or bad. Yulgok raised a question concerning T'oegye's view that the four beginnings which emanate from principle are purely good and the seven emotions which emanate from material principle are not without good elements. If so, queried Yulgok, what would be the relationship between the two kinds of goodness? Why multiply entities beyond necessity? (At this point, one wonders whether Yulgok was not wielding the Neo-Confucian Occam's razor.)

The Moral and the Human Mind

From a dialectical point of view, Yulgok set out to do justice to T'oegye's moral point of view. In addressing Kobong's point that emotions become good when they attain due measure and degree, a legitimate question that arises from T'oegye's perspective is: What is it that causes emotions to attain due measure and degree? Is this not where a moral point of view becomes relevant? Is it not the moral will that brings about some such harmony? Yulgok set himself the task of answering this question by fitting out his monism with the notion of will. In other words, Yulgok strove to synthesize Kobong's monism with T'oegye's moral point of view. For Yulgok, the heart/mind before arousal is "nature" (Korean: *song*; Chinese: *xing/hsing*). Emotions are the heart/mind after arousal. The heart/mind qua comparing, sifting, and weighing (*kyekyosangnyang*) after its arousal is will. It is will that should carefully monitor and control the emanation of the seven emotions, so that they may become not selfish desires (*inyok*) but the four beginnings. Whether one's heart/mind becomes the moral mind or the human mind depends largely on the way in which one exercises one's will.

In attempting to illuminate how one attains the moral mind, Yulgok expatiated upon the analogy, first used by T'oegye, involving a man riding a horse. If the man rides the horse well, the horse follows the will of the man—which can be compared to attaining the moral mind. But if the man is carried along by a horse that is not tame, it is the horse, not the man, that is in control—which can be compared to the (uncontrolled) human mind becoming dominant. However, even if the man is carried by the horse, if the horse is tame, the horse follows the will of the man—which can be compared to the human mind's becoming the moral mind. The "moral" mind originates in the correctness of nature and destiny (Korean: *songmyong*; Chinese: *xingming/hsing-ming*) and the "human" mind in the "partialness" of physical being. A person rushing to the rescue of a drowning child is being moved by the moral mind. But is he or she later tries to exploit the deed for profit, the moral mind turns into the human mind. Every person, including sages, has selfish desires such as hunger and thirst. If a person is hungry, he or she is initially moved by the partialness of the human mind; but if the person seeks the satisfaction of the natural desire in a morally correct way, the human mind becomes the moral mind.

According to Yulgok, there is only one heart/mind. If material force hinders principle, the heart/mind becomes the human mind. But if material force lets principle manifest itself, the heart/mind becomes the moral mind. The distinction between the moral and the human mind is not ontological, but ethical and functional. And will plays a crucial role in determining which direction one's heart/mind takes at a given moment. For it is will that makes a moral choice after deliberation. This is where Yulgok's dialectical consideration for T'oegye's moral point of view becomes evident. The distinction between the moral and the human mind is not made once and for all; rather, the determination of one's heart/mind—whether it becomes moral or human—in a contingent situation hinges largely on one's will. There is neither eternal salvation nor eternal damnation. Just as the moral mind can lapse into the human mind, the human mind can be transformed into the moral mind in any contingent situation. That is why it is important to make one's will sincere. For by striving to make one's will sincere, one can increase the probability of rendering one's heart/mind moral in many and varied situations.

Though Yulgok made the dialectical move of assimilation of T'oegye's moral point of view to his philosophy, he made it quite clear that espousal of a moral point of view does not entail, as is the case with T'oegye, commitment to ontological dualism.

Sincerity and Single-Mindedness

Even if Yulgok disagreed with T'oegye on the Four–Seven issue, Yulgok shared T'oegye's preoccupation with "single-mindedness" (Korean: *ky-ong*; Chinese: *jing/ching*), which signaled new interest in praxis in the development of Korean Neo-Confucianism. Yulgok attempted to make an advance over T'oegye by integrating "sincerity" (Korean: *song*; Chinese: *cheng/ch'eng*) with single-mindedness. Yulgok adumbrated an all-encompassing ontological and ethical theory within Neo-Confucianism. The core of Yulgok's philosophy is that through single-mindedness one can achieve sincerity. According to Yulgok, the sincerity of will is the source of self-cultivation and governance of fellow beings. Without sincerity, will shall not be established; without sincerity, principle will not be thoroughly explored; without sincerity, one's constitution (*kijil*) will not be changed. In fine, sincerity is the axis of one's being.

The Substantial and the Practical

In Yulgok's writing, the term "the substantial and the practical" (*shil*) recurs, as evidenced by such phrases as "substantial and practical principle" (*shilli*), "substantial and practical heart/mind" (*shilshim*) and "substantial and practical will" (*shileui*). Yulgok emphasized the sincerity of substantial and practical principle (*shillijisong*). In *Conversations on Politics Between Host and Guest*, Yulgok propounded the notion of striving for and realizing the substantial and the practical (*mushilyokhaeng*). He strove for the synthesis of the investigation of knowledge and the extension of knowledge, on the one hand, and the sincerity of will and the rectification of mind, on the other. With Yulgok Korean Neo-Confucianism decidedly took the practical turn. The basic concern of Yulgok's political philosophy was the economic welfare of the people. Yulgok was alive to the historical contingency of the positive laws and in a letter to the king he emphasized the importance of making drastic revision of these laws to meet the needs of the times. In *Essentials of Confucianist Learning*, Yulgok propounded a way of politics that is *for* the people and *of* the people, if not *by* the people.

Yulgok's thought naturally led to the efflorescence of Practical Learning (shilhak) in eighteenth- and nineteenth-century Korea. In many ways, Yulgok's thought antedated Practical Learning in seventeenth-century China.

KWANG-SAE LEE

Further Reading

Choi, Min-Hong. *A Modern History of Korean Philosophy*. Seoul: Seong Moon Sa, 1983. This is a useful survey of the development of Neo-Confucianism during the Chosŏn dynasty.

Chun, Shin-yong, ed. *Korean Thought*. Seoul: The Si-sa-yong-o-sa Publishers, Inc., 1982. A collection of essays on Shamanism in Korea, the Four–Seven Debate, the rise of Practical Learning, the reception of Western Learning, and Korean nationalism. This book is a concise introduction to Korean thought.

de Bary, Wm. Theodore and JaHyun Kim Haboush, eds. *The Rise of Neo-Confucianism in Korea*. New York: Columbia University Press, 1985. This helpful collection of essays on T'oegye Yi Hwang, Yulgok Yi I, and other prominent Neo-Confucianists of the Chosŏn dynasty and the various issues addressed by them is particularly illuminating concerning the Four–Seven Debate.

HAN YONGUN

Born: 1879, Hongju (Ch'ungch'ong Province), Korea
Died: 1944, Seoul, Korea
Major Works: *Treatise on the Reform of Korean Buddhism* (1913), "A Discourse on the Independence of Korea" (1919), *The Silence of Love* (1926)

Major Ideas

What determines one's fate is not Heaven, but oneself.
The ideals of Buddhism rest in the equality and salvation of human beings.
Meditation practice and doctrinal study should have equal emphasis.
Buddhism should be brought out of the mountains to the people in the cities and villages.
Philosophical theory should be in harmony with social action.
Freedom and peace are essential to human welfare.

Han Yongun's major emphasis was on the goal of achieving freedom and equality for all human beings, a state of affairs that he regarded as required by Buddhism. For him, freedom and peace are secured by independence. Han Yongun's ideas aimed at the restoration of lost freedom and peace through the independence of Korea from Japanese rule.

Yongun was Han's *dharma* name as a Buddhist monk; his childhood name was Yuch'on; his courtesy name, Chongok; his precept name, Pongwan; and his *dharma* pen name, Manhae. Han was of middle-class origins, but his life in infancy is unknown. When he was young, Korea was in sociopolitical chaos. Korea's opening to foreign countries in 1876 caused the inundation of Korea by foreign civilizations. Opposing such a state of affairs, the Tonghak (Eastern Learning) Movement arose in 1894, the first nationalist movement in Korean history. The inability of the Choson (Yi) dynasty of Korea (1392–1910) to defend against foreign imperialism led to increasing Japanese influence on the peninsula. This influence was sanctioned by the great powers through the Anglo–Japanese alliance of 1904 and the Taft–Katsura agreement with the United States in 1905 and ultimately led to Japan's annexation of Korea in 1910, which lasted until 1945. Under such circumstances, Han flourished as a man of many talents: a reform-minded Buddhist monk, an independence movement leader, and a great poet.

Han Yongun studied the Chinese classics for ten years until he was eighteen (1896), when he participated in the Righteous Army movement against foreign invasion. As a political refugee, he fled to a hermitage on Mt. Sorak and became a monk in 1905. Han then studied doctrinal Buddhism for four years and after that he devoted himself to Meditative (Son) Buddhism. He also studied Western ideas through works translated into Chinese. In this endeavor, he was much indebted to the *Yin-bingshi wenji*, an encyclopedic work on Western countries, by Liang Qichao (Liang Ch'i-ch'ao) (d. 1929), an eminent Chinese thinker. Han thus understood the world situation of his time and was introduced to the Western philosophical views of Immanuel Kant, Francis Bacon, and others. As one of the Korean monk representatives in 1908 who visited Japan to observe the modernization process of the Buddhist church for about six months, he had the opportunity to study more Buddhist and Western thought.

Han Yongun left voluminous works written throughout his life: poems, treatises, a compiled canon, essays, expositions, annotations, records of historic relics of a monastery, and novels. His works were published in six volumes as the *Collected Works of Han Yongun* (1973): volume 1 includes the *Silence of Love*, short lyric poems, Chinese poems, stray notes and articles; volume 2 deals with the *Treatise on the Reform of Korean*

Buddhism and various essays; volume 3 consists of *A Canon of Buddhism* (1914), *An Exposition on the Vimalakīrti Sūtra*, and the *Annotated Ten Profound Talks* (1925); volume 4 is composed of *Selected Discourses on the Cai-gen tan* (1917), which discusses the Ming author Hong Yingman's (Hung Ying-ming's) famous guide to spiritual culture, and the *Records of Historical Remains in Konbong Monastery and Its Branch Temples* (1928); and volumes 5 and 6 consist of his novels: *Black Wind* (1935), *Remorse* (1936), and *Iron Blood Beauty* (1937) in volume 5; *Evil Fate* (1938–39), and *Death* (1924) in volume 6.

Among these works, the *Treatise on the Reform of Korean Buddhism*, "A Discourse on the Independence of Korea," and the *Silence of Love* are the representative works of Han as a monk, a nationalist movement leader, and a poet. The *Treatise on the Reform of Korean Buddhism* is Han's most inclusive work as well as his earliest; the book reveals Han's major ideas and reveals the literary characteristics of his later career. The work also marked an important milestone in the development of modern thought in Korea. "A Discourse on the Independence of Korea" consists of responses addressed to the Japanese prosecutor and reveals Han's view of life and the world: Han asserts that freedom and peace are essential to human well-being. The *Silence of Love* is a representative collection of modern Korean poetry, which consists of eighty-eight poems. In this work, Han sought to bring enlightenment to the harsh life of Koreans under oppressive Japanese rule and found the most adequate Buddhist contemplative poetry for this task.

Treatise on the Reform of Korean Buddhism

Originally written in 1910, the *Treatise on the Reform of Korean Buddhism* was published in 1913. In this work, Han advocated the reformation of traditional Korean Buddhism, which he regarded as unable to cope with modern realities, and he aimed at the restoration of freedom and peace, that is, the restoration of Korean sovereignty under Japanese rule, and by extension, a contribution to world peace. Though this treatise was composed for Buddhist monastics, its wider audience was all Korean people living under Japanese rule.

The *Treatise* consists of seventeen chapters. Chapters 1 to 4 provide the theoretical basis for solving impending problems of Korean Buddhism and they thus reveal Han's major ideas. Chapters 5 to 16 discuss urgent issues in Korean Buddhism, focusing on the three teachings of Buddhism (precepts, meditation, and wisdom).

Han defines his time as a period of world imperialism based on militarism, which was corrosive and destroyed the freedom and peace of human beings. Han attributes the responsibility for the misfortunes of Korea under foreign rule to Koreans themselves by saying that what determines the fate of human beings is not Heaven, but human beings themselves. It is wrong, he argued, to believe that humanity plans and Heaven determines. The truth is that it is human beings who both plan and determine. Human beings are responsible for human affairs and thus should not believe in Heaven but in themselves. Therefore, Han concludes, the responsibility for the reform of Korean Buddhism does not rest in others but in the Buddhist monks themselves.

For Han, the purpose of religion is to ensure the happiness of human beings. He asserts that Buddhism can be a soteriological path to the goal because Buddhism is the religion of enlightenment and wisdom as well as the philosophy of truth ("suchness," Buddha-nature). For him, Buddhism teaches that the origin of the self and the universe lies in one's own mind, which is inexpressible and inconceivable. Buddhism does not depend, he argues, on superstitious other-worldly places and deities such as the Christian God and Paradise, the Judaic God, and Islamic Eternal Life, all of which he regards as reflective images of one's own mind.

According to Han, philosophically speaking, only Buddhism explains the distinction between true "suchness" and ignorance; it discusses ways of overcoming ignorance and restoring personal freedom. Han appraises the ideas of philosophers of both East and West and argues that philosophical ideas other than those of Buddhism fail to clarify the essence of all sentient beings.

Equality and Salvation

For Han, there are two fundamental ideals of Buddhism: (1) the equality of human beings, and (2) salvation for all human beings. "Equality" refers to the essence of Buddha-nature (truth) and "salvation" to its application. The Buddhist teaching that all human beings inherently possess the Buddha-nature leads to the idea of the equality of all human beings. Equality produces the idea of freedom. The ignorance of the equality in essence of all human beings leads to the oppression of others. Therefore, what is important is to get enlightened concerning one's mind, the origin of wisdom, the self, and the universe.

Han's term "salvation" is the antonym of egoism. Therefore the salvation of human beings is possible only through the *Bodhisattva* spirit of enlightenment. Buddhism, Han emphasizes, is not a religion of egocentrism, but the religion for the salvation of all sentient beings, and it should actively participate in the reform of society.

Han advocates as the practical way for achieving the equality and salvation of human beings, the reform of outmoded Korean Buddhism through "destruction," arguing that reform is the "son of destruction" and "destruction is the mother of reform." However, his "destruction" does not refer to the wholesale abolishment of traditional Buddhism, but to changing its outdated customs to adapt them to modern life.

Han argues that Buddhist precepts should adapt to the changing circumstances of modern life and he advocates that monks be allowed to marry. The survival of the tradition of celibacy would be wrong, he claims, because celibacy is a practice in violation of human ethics.

Han advocates the mental and institutional reform of meditative practice and chastises the monks for their misunderstanding of meditation and their inability to cope with reality; he points out that they just live in a secluded place and do not move their bodies, and continue to enjoy economic benefits from believers.

As for reform from the perspective of Buddhist wisdom, Han cites the improvement of monastic education through broader knowledge, including liberal arts, science, and foreign study; abolition of the chanting hall tradition; the modernization of religious images, paintings, and the simplification of rituals. He claims that

> misfortunes and happiness depend on oneself; happiness is not the product of prayer, and Buddha is not the happiness-giver; true monks should devote themselves to enlightenment.

Meditation and Doctrine

In order for Buddhism to flourish, Han contended, equal stress should be put on meditative praxis and doctrinal study. He stated that one of reasons for the decline of Buddhism in his day was that there was an overemphasis on doctrinal Buddhism, which was inclined to exegetical studies. Thus he says,

> As for Buddhism, meditation and doctrine are inseparable because the former refers to metaphysical principle and the latter to verbal expressions of Buddhism; while intensive contemplation is obtained through meditation, wisdom is gained through doctrine; contemplation leads people to liberation from life and death, and doctrine is a tool for saving sentient beings; meditation and doctrine are like the two wings of a bird and neither can be lacking.

Thus, based on the theory of the need for harmony between the two, Han suggests changing the balance within the curricula for the future of Korean Buddhism.

Han Yongun was deeply concerned until his death in 1944 with the development of Buddhism for the masses. In its initial period, this idea was expressed by his injunction, "Change the temple location from the mountains to urban centers" and by his efforts to translate Buddhist texts into the Korean language. Later this idea developed more concretely through the youth Buddhist movement, publication of a Buddhist journal, and popularization of doctrines, Buddhist texts, institutions, and properties under such slogans as "From monks to the masses" and "From mountain Buddhism to street Buddhism."

Han Yongun did not view Buddhism as only a metaphysical idea, but interpreted it from the historical and social perspectives of his time, resulting in a new position that he later expressed by the term "Buddhist socialism." The creative feature of Han's idea rests in the harmonization of theory and action. With the rise of the March First Independence Movement of 1919 against Japanese dictatorship, his idea based on the Buddhist concepts of equality and salvation developed into a program for independence.

"A Discourse on the Independence of Korea"

Han Yongun was one of the thirty-three signatories to the March First Declaration of 1919 against Japanese imperialism and he helped draft Korea's "Declaration of Independence." He was arrested for sedition and imprisoned for three years. "A Discourse on the Independence of Korea" was written in 1919, while he was in jail, as responses to the Japanese prosecutor. This work expounded the importance of Korean independence in the preservation of peace in East Asia and reveals his view of life and of human beings: freedom and peace are essential elements to human well-being.

After his release from imprisonment in 1922, Han extended his activities to the public as well as to Buddhist intellectuals. The *Silence of Love* was one of the first collections of modern poetry written in Korean and was an expression of his protest against world imperialism.

"A Discourse on the Independence of Korea" consists of five parts: The preface, an account of the motive behind the declaration of Korean independence, the giving of reasons for the declaration of independence of Korea, a discussion the policies of the Japanese Governor-General in Korea, and an expression of confidence in the future of an independent Korea.

In the preface, Han repeats his claim that freedom and peace are essential to the welfare of human beings. He explains that his concept of "freedom" does not allow for self-indulgence, but calls for refraining from actions that infringe upon the freedom of others. Freedom is always accompanied by peace, he insists; the two are inseparable. He points out that his ideas of freedom and peace are different from those of Immanuel Kant and Liang Qichao. Han criticizes Kant and Liang because although Kant defends individual freedom, he does not mention the universal freedom of all human beings; Liang, on the other hand, advocates the latter, but ignores the former.

Han Yongun viewed his time as a period of world imperialism backed by a militarism that destroys the happiness of human beings. The representatives of world militarism were Germany in the West and Japan in the East. Han regarded Japan's annexation of Korea as a clear example of world militarism.

Han maintained that national independence and self-determinism are the root of human happiness. Han also viewed his time as the right time for the independence of Korea, given the spiritual ability of the Korean people, the change of world powers, and the post-World War I self-determination in Poland, Czechoslovakia, and Ireland. Therefore, while criticizing Japanese dictatorship, Han declared that the Korean people were confident that they would achieve independence.

Han thought that the defeat of Germany in World War I was not the result of the action of the Allied forces because they also used military weapons, relics of militarism, for fighting the war. Rather, the defeat of Germany was the victory of the righteousness and humanism of the people who lived in the most militarist of countries—as shown, for example, in the German revolution that occurred during wartime. Han's confidence in the restoration of Korean sovereignty was drawn from his faith in the power of humanism.

Han Yongun became a progressive reformer by incorporating the modern idea of liberalism into the Buddhist concept of equality. While rejecting egoism, Han adopted the *Bodhisattva* spirit, an idea of altruism, as the ideological basis of social reform.

The Silence of Love was published in 1926. Though profoundly influenced by Rabindranath Tagore (1861–1941), a great Indian poet, Han wrote these poems out of dissatisfaction with Tagore's Hindu notion of Absolute Self. The *Silence of Love* was a mosaic of poetic expressions of Han's outlook on life and the world. In this work Han protested against world imperialism.

The Silence of Love

This collection of poems is linked by such themes as separation, conflict, hope, and reunion. While the separation from his beloved symbolizes the loss of Korea's sovereignty, the rendezvous with his beloved refers to its liberation from foreign rule. His poems also have negative tones, which suggests that Han viewed his time as a period of the loss of freedom. Through personification and the metaphorical use of the expression "beloved" with a Buddhist tone, Han advocated the salvation of human beings through Buddhism, by liberation from Japanese rule and, by extension, a contribution to world peace. However, nowhere is God mentioned. In place of God is Emptiness, Infinity, Eternity, and highest of all, the "Beloved," an undivided Korea.

Han Yongun's dedication to what he regarded as the two main principles of Buddhism—equality among all people and the salvation of human beings—developed into the championing of Korean independence thought and the restoration of freedom and peace lost by the imposition of foreign rule. His idea of salvation developed into a Buddhism that would appeal to the masses, not to the monastic elite. Thus the main characteristic of Han Yongun's thought lies in the harmony of his thoughts and actions.

Though his ideas could not flourish during his lifetime due to the loss of national sovereignty, since the 1970s his reform ideas have a great influence on intellectual and literary circles as well as on contemporary Korean Buddhism.

JONG MYUNG KIM

Further Reading

Translations

Lee, Peter H., ed. *The Silence of Love: Twentieth-Century Korean Poetry.* Honolulu, Hawaii: The University Press of Hawaii, 1980. This work includes a short biographical introduction to Han Yongun and translations by Sammy E. Solberg of selected poems by Han Yongun.

Rockstein, Edward D. "Your Silence—Doubt in Faith: Han Yongun and Ingmar Bergman," *Asian Pacific Quarterly.* 6, No. 2, Autumn 1974, pp. 1–16. A translation of fourteen of Han's poems, with a brief discussion.

Related Studies

An, Pyŏng-jik. "Han Yongun's Liberalism: An Analysis of the *Reformation of Korean Buddhism*," *Korea Journal.* Vol. 19, No. 12, December 1979, pp. 13–18. This article views Han Yongun's liberalism from the standpoint of the social thought of his day, but needs careful reading.

Buswell, Robert E., Jr. *The Zen Monastic Experience.* Princeton, N.J.: Princeton University Press, 1992. Chapter 1 discusses Han Yongun's design for the establishment of married monks and the schism that resulted between celibate and married clergy.

Kim, Uch'ang. "Han Yong-un: The Poet in Time of Need," *Korea Journal.* Vol. 19, No. 12, December 1979, pp. 4–12. This article describes Han's works as more than political and celebrates the possibility of hope for man by the negating of negativity.

Mok, Chŏngbae. "Han Yongun and Buddhism," *Korea Journal.* Vol. 19, No. 12, December 1979, pp. 19–27. This essay discusses Han Yongun's view of Buddhism and his efforts to harmonize meditation and Buddhist doctrines.

Yu, Beongcheon. *Han Yong-un and Yi Kwang-su.* Detroit: Wayne State University, 1992, pp. 11–83. Along with offering a biographical sketch of Han Yongun, this work discusses his major works, focusing on *The Silence of Love*.

THE WORLD OF ISLAM

RĀBI'A AL-ADAWIYYA

Born: 717, Basra, Iraq
Died: 801, Basra, Iraq
Major Works: Sayings compiled by later biographers, especially Fariduddin 'Attar (d. c. 1230) in his *Memorial of the Friends of God.*

Major Ideas

Affirmation of divine unity entails obliviousness to anything but the Divine Beloved.
One should love and worship without fear of punishment or hope of reward.
A true lover of the Deity has no room for despising the world or hating Satan; one's consciousness is focused only on love for the One Beloved.
Affirmation of unity entails absolute trust (tawakkul) *in the Divine Beloved.*
Trust-in-God rules out any planning or hoarding for the future.
Affirmation of unity entails absolute acceptance (rida) *of divine will.*
To ask anything from any creature is to betray affirmation of unity.
To ask anything of the Deity is to betray such acceptance of divine will.
Acceptance is active and leads to an authentic life, not to passivity or fatalism.

At the end of the first century of Islam, the Islamic world was beginning one of the more explosive moments in human intellectual history. While theologians and philosophers applied rationalist perspectives to central issues of human existence and the interpretation of the Qur'an (Koran), groups of ascetics began to appear, challenging the emergent imperial culture. Rabi'a (Rābi'a) 'al-Adawiyya is presented by Sufi tradition as central in forging the new synthesis of theology and ascesis that would come to be know as Sufism.

What we know of Rabi'a is almost exclusively dependent upon the sayings attributed to her and the anecdotes about her in the works of biographers of a later period. She was born of a poor family in the Basra area of southern Iraq and was sold into slavery as a girl. She was released when her owner saw her engaged in all-night vigils after her full day's work. She led a life of intense religious activity and intellectual conversation and refused numerous offers of marriage.

Rabi'a's role in the development of Sufi thought is illustrated in numerous anecdotes concerning her relationship with Hasan of Basra (d. 728). Hasan was the most famous religious authority of his time, an expert on *hadīth* (traditions of the Prophet)

and an acquaintance with many of the Prophet's companions. He was one of the first advocates of ascetic piety in Islam and at the same time one of the first critical investigators into the issue of divine predetermination and human free will. Indeed, Hasan is considered by many to be the founder of both Sufism and Islamic scholastic theology (*kalām*).

If, as the anecdotes suggest, Rabi'a knew Hasan, he must have been very old at the time, and she very young. The crucial point in the Hasan and Rabi'a stories is not their objective historicity, however, but the key Sufi concepts that are illustrated through them and represented in the person of Rabi'a. The anecdotes are built upon the medieval Sufi convention of the spiritual joust in which two sages compete verbally with one another, one of them coming out as the wiser or more sincere. The humble former slave Rabi'a continually wins in her jousts with Hasan, the most famous religious and intellectual figure of his time. What binds these stories together, and what links them with other anecdotes and sayings, is Rabi'a's ability to synthesize ascetic piety with theological concerns (two areas that seemed to remain compartmentalized with Hasan) into a new way of thinking that was to become the ground of Sufism.

Sincerity (Sidq) and the Affirmation of Divine Unity

This synthesis combined the Qur'anic doctrine of the unity of God (*tawhid*) with ascetic impulses and a continuing investigation of the issue of human free will and divine predetermination. For Rabi'a, affirmation of one God was not a matter of mere verbal correctness. Divine unity could be authentically affirmed only by turning one's entire life and consciousness toward that one deity. To consider anything else was, in effect, a form of idolatry. She constantly criticized Hasan and other spiritual leaders for become attached to their ascetic piety and treating it as an end in itself. She offered a devastating critique of those claiming to despise the world for the sake of God; if they had truly achieved an affirmation of one God, they would not be paying enough attention to anything else to bother despising it.

Thus the doctrinal affirmation of one God as a theistic principle was combined with a spiritual quest in which only one thing could be the object of one's concern. This combination led to Rabi'a's celebrated notion of sincerity (*sidq*), or sincere love. For Rabi'a, sincerity is not compatible with acting out of hope for reward or fear of punishment.

The passages in the Qur'an on the day of judgment or moment of truth are among the most compelling and most beautiful examples of prophetic discourse. They are open to many interpretations. Yet by Rabi'a's time, it is clear that they had become associated in the popular mind with a complex topography of Heaven and Hell (with seven levels in each and various descriptions of the joys and torments of the inhabitants) and with a psychology of reward and punishment. Hasan of Basra was famous for his continual intensification of fear of Hell in meditation as a way of motivating an overcoming of the appetites of the carnal self.

Rabi'a rejected the entire edifice of reward and punishment. In numerous prayers she is quoted as asking the Deity to deny her Paradise if she desires worships out of hope for Paradise, and to condemn her to Hell if she worships out of fear of Hell. The most famous anecdote represents Rabi'a as running down the path with fire in the one hand and water in the other. When asked what she was doing, Rabi'a responds that she wishes to burn Paradise and douse the fires of Hell, so that no one will ever love God except out of pure love, devoid considerations of reward and punishment. To be concerned with anything (even Heaven and Hell) beside the one God is in effect affirm something else as God.

Rabi'a was implacably consistent in her articulation of this notion of sincere love. When asked if she hated Satan, she responded no, she was too busy loving God to think about Satan. When asked if she loved the Prophet Muhammad, she said no, with the most profound respect to the Prophet, she had room for only One Beloved. To love another would be to take another being as one's God.

Absolute Trust and Active Acceptance

Connected with this conception of sincerity was Rabi'a's rigorous understanding of the virtue of trust-in-God (*tawakkul*). In numerous anecdotes, Rabi'a is depicted as not only refusing to plan for the future, but even to consider it. To make plans for the future, hoard up supplies, or build up furnishings is to fail to puts one's full trust in the Deity. It is also a contradiction of the rigorous affirmation of one God; to put one's trust in one's own plan is to make of that plan one's God.

The resultant way of life and thought can be characterized as one of active acceptance (*rida*), that is, absolute acceptance of the infinite divine will. It is crucial to distinguish between Rabi'a's active notion of acceptance and passive resignation or fatalism. In several anecdotes, Rabi'a refuses to ask anything of any human creature, because to do so would violate the principle of trust-in-God and the unity of God. She goes on to refuse to ask the Deity for anything, on the grounds that the Deity knows her condition already, and has forewilled it (inasmuch as nothing happens without the will of the all-powerful God). Such petition then would violate the principle of acceptance. Rather than leading to passivity or fatalism, this absolute acceptance—as is the case with the Christian mystics Hadewijch (fl. 1240), Marguerite Porete (d. 1310), and Meister Eckhart (c. 1260–1327)—is viewed as the key to authentic action. In the anecdotes about Rabi'a it is this active acceptance that is the proof of her authenticity to those around her.

The authenticity that comes from acceptance and from the loss of the ego-self in union with the one object of consciousness, the Divine Beloved, is exhibited in a number of miracle anecdotes. In one, the famous early Sufi ascetic Ibrahim Adham has just made a fourteen-year pilgrimage to Mecca, praying at every possible prayer site along the way. When he gets to Mecca, he finds that the object of his pilgrimage, the sacred Ka'ba, is not there. He asks why, and is told that the Ka'ba has gone to see a humble slave-girl. It turns out that Rabi'a had made the pilgrimage and when she got near the precincts of Mecca, the Ka'ba went out to greet her. She was unimpressed, stating that what she came for was not the house, but the master of the house. In the meantime, the great ascetic Ibrahim Adham is led to anger and jealousy that his ascetic feat has been ignored in favor of a simple woman from Basra.

The depth of Rabi'a's sincerity acted as a protection for her in an often insecure world; as a freed woman she had more prerogatives for refusing marriage than other women, but she could not have led the public and vocal life she lived had she not been, in the words of 'Attar, veiled by the veil of sincerity.

Self-Extinction (Fanā') in Mystical Union

Ultimately, the major concepts of Rabi'a's thought are tied together in the ultimate intellectual and spiritual goal: extinction (*fanā'*) of the ego-self in union with the Divine Beloved. It is only in such extinction that the extreme versions of trust, active acceptance, sincerity beyond hope for reward and fear of punishment, and true affirmation of divine unity can be attained. In such extinction, the Deity works in and through the human in the state of the annihilation of the ego-self.

This concept of the annihilation of the self in mystical union, central for all subsequent Sufi philosophy, would be further developed by the other major thinkers of early Sufism: Junayd (d. 910), Bistami (d. c. 875), Tustari (d. 896), and Hallaj (d. 922). They would link it more explicitly to the famous divine saying:

> When my servant draws near to me through ritual devotions and free devotions, I [Allah] love my servant, and when I love him, I become the hearing with which he hears, the seeing with which he sees, the feet with which he walks, the hands with which he touches, and the tongue with which he speaks.

Later Sufis such as Qushayri would go on to place concepts of trust, sincerity, acceptance, poverty, and divine unity into dialectical and complex categories of "stations" (*maqamat*) and momentary states (*ahwal*), but the essential configuration is, according to the biographers of Rabi'a, the achievement of a self-educated former slave girl of Basra.

In the aphorisms and anecdotes of Rabi'a there is a consistent reformulation of the two central issues of Islamic theology: the tension between divine predetermination and human free will, and the tension between the affirmation of divine unity and the plurality of divine attributes. By grounding both issues in the moment of mystical union, Rabi'a transformed them from a locus of scholastic disputation based upon syllogistic logic and grammatical categories language into a realm of mystical thought in which the standard dualisms (self and other, past time and present time, subject and predicate, the reflexive and the nonreflexive) are themselves subject to critical scrutiny, a critical scrutiny that has continued in Sufi thought down to the present day.

MICHAEL A. SELLS

Further Reading

Translation

Sells, Michael A. *Foundations of Islamic Mysticism.* Classics of Western Spirituality. Paulist Press, 1994. Major texts of early Islamic mysticism are translated here, with critical introductions. The book includes a translation of the full text of 'Attar's biography and the sayings of Rabi'a.

Related Studies

Attar, Fariduddin. *Muslim Saints and Mystics* [*Memorials of the Saints*]. Translated by A. J. Arberry. London: Routledge and Kegan Paul, 1966. Arberry offers abridged versions of 'Attar's bi-ographies of early Sufis such as Hasan of Basra, Rabi'a, Bistami, and Junayd.

Schimmel, Annemarie. *Mystical Dimensions of Islam*. Chapel Hill, N.C.: University of North Carolina Press, 1975. This volume presents a helpful historical survey of Sufism, with biographical material on all the major figures.

Smith, Margaret. *Rabi'a the Mystic*. Cambridge: Cambridge University Press, 1928, 1984. This book is still the most complete account of the life and sayings of Rabi'a.

AL-KINDĪ

Born: c. 185 A.H./801 A.D., Basra, in what is now Iraq
Died: c. 252 A.H./866 A.D., Baghdad, in what is now Iraq
Major Works: *Fī al-Falsafat al-Ūlā* (*On First Philosophy*), *Risāla fī Kammiyyat Kutub Arisṭūṭālīs wa mā yuḥtāj ilaih fī Taḥṣīl al-Falsafa* (*Treatise on the Number of Aristotle's Books and What Is Needed to Attain Philosophy*), *Risāla fī al-Ḥīla li-Dafʿ al-Aḥzan* (*Treatise on the Device for Driving Away Sorrows*), *Risāla fī Alfāẓ Suqrāṭ* (*Treatise on the Utterances of Socrates*)

Major Ideas

Prophetic knowledge is superior to human reason and easier to attain.
Through assiduous study of mathematics and Aristotle's books it is possible to acquire knowledge of what is true.
We must strive to overcome the calamities of this life in order to attain the happiness of the life to come.

Abū Yūsuf Yaʿqūb Ibn Isḥaq al-Kindī was born in Basra and educated in Baghdad. It was in the latter city that he spent his life and died. Acclaimed "the philosopher of the Arabs," he is said by one famous medieval biographer to have been renowned for his excursions into Greek, Persian, and Indian wisdom and for his detailed knowledge of astronomy. Another medieval biographer claims that al-Kindī was exceedingly knowledgeable in medicine, philosophy, arithmetic, logic, and geometry, in addition to being skilled as a translator and editor of Greek philosophical works. Moreover, in a famous medieval collection of wisdom literature, it is reported that al-Kindī served in the Abbasid court under the caliphs al-Maʾmūn (813–833 A.D.) and al-Muʿtasim (833–842 A.D.) as a tutor and was preeminent as an astrologer. The list of his books is extensive and, though he is not known to have been schooled in the traditional Islamic sciences, includes works that focus on subjects of a theological and jurisprudential character.

The biographers are nonetheless somewhat reserved in their assessments of al-Kindī's intellectual acumen. Thus one observes that although no one was more renowned in the Islamic world for his efforts in the philosophical sciences or wrote as many famous long essays and short treatises in most of the sciences, he depends upon indecisive proofs and rhetorical, even poetical, arguments.

This biographer also faults him for an inadequate grasp of syllogistic argument.

To date, scholarship has failed to vindicate al-Kindī. In part, this is due to less than a tenth of the nearly 270 works attributed to him by the ancient biographers having come down to the present. And, in part, it is due to his being known today primarily as the author of a treatise on metaphysics, *Fī al-Falsafat al-Ūlā* (*On First Philosophy*). His single treatise on Socrates is all but ignored, and his few treatises on ethical matters have been studied primarily by philologists desirous of identifying the putative sources of his various pronouncements.

The treatise on Socrates, one of the ethical treatises, and two other extant works do, however, contain the germs of a political teaching. It can be characterized as a turning back from the apparent assuredness of Aristotle to the tentative probing of Socrates. Differently stated, al-Kindī's reflections on Plato and Aristotle led him to praise the life of Socrates, the Socrates who had renounced physical and metaphysical speculation in order to concentrate on the day-to-day speech and actions of his fellow citizens. This choice allowed al-Kindī to provide for a limited kind of philosophical inquiry and at the same time to vouchsafe the claims of revelation. We will never know whether he worked out the details of the choice in those political treatises of his that are no longer extant, but we can see how al-Kindī's observations about Aristotle and Socrates may have influenced al-Rāzī's (865–925 A.D.) later portrait of Socrates in the justly famous *Kitāb al-Sīra al-Falsafiyya* (*Book on the Philosophic Life*), thereby setting in motion the series of reflections that lead to al-Fārābī's founding of Islamic political philosophy.

In the *Risāla fī Kammiyyat Kutub Arisṭūṭālīs wa mā yuḥtāj ilaih fī Taḥṣīl al-Falsafa* (*Treatise on the Number of Aristotle's Books and What Is Needed to Attain Philosophy*), al-Kindī admits his inability to provide a rational account of human existence or its end and thus to ground political inquiry. Even his charming *Risāla fī al-Ḥīla li-Dafʿ al-Aḥzān* (*Treatise on the Device for Driving Away Sorrows*), with its delightful allegory of human existence, ends in a similar aporia.

The Allegory of the Ship

The allegory of the ship in al-Kindī's *Treatise on the Device for Driving Away Sorrows* makes the broad point that all possessions, not merely superfluous ones, cause sorrow and threaten to harm us. Our passage through this world of destruction, al-Kindī says, is like that of people embarked upon a ship "to a goal, their own resting-place, that they are intent upon." When the ship stops so that the passengers may attend to their needs, some do so quickly and return to wide, commodious seats. Others—who also tend quickly to their needs but pause to gaze upon the beautiful surrounding sights and enjoy the delightful aromas—return to narrower, less comfortable seats. Yet others—who tend to their needs but collect various objects along the way—find only cramped seating and are greatly discomforted by the objects they have gathered. Finally, others wander far off from the ship, so immersed in the surrounding natural beauty and the objects to be collected that they forget their present need and even the purpose of the voyage. Of these, those who hear the ship's captain call and return before it sails, find terribly uncomfortable quarters. Others wander so far away that they never hear the captain's call and, left behind, perish in horrible ways. Those who return to the ship burdened with objects suffer so, due to their cramped quarters, the stench of their decaying possessions, and the effort they expend in caring for them, that most become sick and some even die. Only the first two groups arrive safely, though those in the second group are somewhat ill at ease due to their more narrow seats.

For al-Kindī, those passengers who endanger themselves and others by their quest for possessions are like the unjust we encounter in daily life. Conversely, the just must be those who attend to their needs or business quickly and do not permit themselves to become burdened with acquisitions or even to be side-tracked into momentary pleasures. The passengers are all bound for their homeland, but it is not clear where they are heading. At one point, al-Kindī claims that we are going to "the true world" and at another that the ship is supposed to bring us to "our true homelands." There is no doubt, however, that whether the destination be one or many, it can be reached only by acquiring the habits that eschew material possessions.

The allegory emphasizes the voyage and the conduct of the passengers. But the vessel is no ship of state nor the captain its governor. The ship is merely a vehicle of transport here, and the captain evinces no desire to police the passengers. Nor is anything said about the route followed by the ship. As one who calls to the passengers, however, the captain may be compared to a prophet. Like a prophet, he calls only once. Those who do not heed the call are left to their misery, even to their perdition. Yet the content of the call is empty: it merely warns about the imminent departure of the ship. The captain offers no guidance about what to bring or leave; he merely calls.

Perhaps more precision is not needed. Al-Kindī presents his tale merely as a likeness of our earthly voyage and within a larger argument that plays down learning about our end in order to favor making our way comfortably in this life. His enumeration of the habits we need to acquire to accomplish this goal seems unduly ascetic. Yet the insensitivity to externals, even to the natural beauty upon the earth, bears closer scrutiny: our use of the complete freedom accorded us about how we conduct ourselves determines whether we reach our goal comfortably or suffer throughout the voyage and perhaps perish. Only those who consistently refuse to become subject to possessions travel in ease. If unable to renounce them completely, they at least are not preoccupied about caring for them nor so enamored of them as to long for them and become sad or angry over their loss.

This tale and the treatise of which it is part are no more able to provide an indication of the purpose of human existence than does the treatise on Aristotle. Lacking knowledge of an end, the means—virtue and moral virtue, above all—becomes primary. There is more. As much as the virtue praised here resembles moderation, it is presented so as to seem preliminary to courage. Moreover, the tale's insistence on the way others commit injustice by amassing possessions provides an indirect indication of what the all-important political virtue of justice requires.

But al-Kindī's teaching goes no further. The primary lesson is that virtuous habits such as these provide comfort during our "earthly voyage" and preserve us so that we may eventually arrive at "the true world" and our "homeland," wherever they may be. Although the treatise points to our lack of wisdom as a problem, it tells us nothing about that most important virtue. Nor does al-Kindī make any attempt here to tell us how we can act to improve our condition or that of those around us. He provides strategies for coping—personal coping—and accepts the milieu in which we live as a fixed variable; that is, as something not worth trying to alter. We learn to put up with it, even to come to terms with it in such a way that we improve our own life. At best, al-Kindī's tale provides a muted call for citizen education—teaching others the importance of reducing their possessions.

The compilation of sayings ascribed to al-Kindī in the *Muntakhab Ṣiwān al-Ḥikma* and those he sets down in his *Risāla fī Alfāẓ Suqrāṭ* (*Treatise on the Utterances of Socrates*) lead a little closer to something resembling a political teaching. Socrates and al-Kindī are portrayed in each as men aloof from the worldly concerns of most people, as men who have learned to turn their thoughts away from possessions and to think about how to live a truly free

human life. Each account consists of anecdotes and pithy statements attributed to Socrates and to al-Kindī respectively, some of which reinforce things said in the treatise about Aristotle's philosophy and in the treatise about the avoidance of sorrows.

In the end, however, al-Kindī must be understood as paying insufficient attention to the political milieu and the ways it can be changed. For him the tensions between the claims of the philosophers and those of the divinely inspired lawgivers take greater prominence than their commonality of purpose. The latter becomes clear only when the larger human good aimed at by both philosophers and lawgiving messengers or prophets can be brought into focus. Differently stated, the moral virtues of courage and moderation, justice as something more comprehensive than paucity of possessions, and the object of wisdom, become clear only when that larger human good, the goal of prophecy, is clarified. Even if eventual disagreement between divine science and human philosophy must be acknowledged, the two have much in common. The tradition of political philosophy to whose development al-Kindī contributes, even if he does not bring it to bloom, concentrates on what is similar in the ways the two address the well-being and development of the individual and the governance and improvement of the group. It does so almost to the exclusion of explaining what separates the two.

al-Kindī's emphasis on personal development and resigned acceptance of the world around him point to these larger questions. He is intent upon balancing the claims of pagan Greek philosophers and faithful followers of a new, apparently more readily accessible, wisdom. Alert to the wisdom and examples of human excellence set forth in the writings of the Greeks as well as in the revelation accorded such respect in his own community, al-Kindī has the merit of discerning how the two complement one another with respect to individual well-being. And in dwelling so thoroughly on these questions of individual excellence, he points clearly to the broader issue even while failing to address it directly himself.

CHARLES E. BUTTERWORTH

Further Reading

Translations

Al-Kindī. *Alkindī's Metaphysics, A Translation of Ya'qūb ibn Ishāq al-Kindī's* Treatise on First Philosophy [*fī al-Falsafah al-Ūlā*]. Translated by Alfred L. Ivry. Albany, N.Y.: SUNY Press, 1974. A translation, with an introduction and commentary, of al-Kindī's famous metaphysical treatise.
———. *al-Kindī, Cinq épîtres*. Edited by Jean Jolivet and Daniel Gimaret. Paris: Éditions du CNRS, 1976. French translation of five small treatises on logic and metaphysics by al-Kindī.

Related Studies

Atiyeh, George N. *al-Kindī: The Philosopher of the Arabs*. Rawalpindi, Pakistan: Islamic Research Institute, 1966. A thorough account of the writings and general teaching of al-Kindī. Appendix III contains the sayings of al-Kindī found in the *Muntakhab Ṣiwān al-Ḥikma*.

Butterworth, Charles E. "al-Kindī and the Beginnings of Islamic Political Philosophy." In *The Political Aspects of Islamic Philosophy: Essays in Honor of Muhsin S. Mahdi*, edited by Charles E. Butterworth. Cambridge, Mass.: Harvard University Press, 1992, pp. 11–60. An analysis and interpretation of those works by al-Kindī that indicate his political teaching.

Jolivet, Jean. *L'Intellect selon Kindī*. Leiden, the Netherlands: E. J. Brill, 1971. An edition and translation, plus a thorough analysis of the teaching and possible sources of al-Kindī's treatise *Letter on the Intellect*.

ABŪ BAKR AL-RĀZĪ

Born: 251 A.H./865 A.D., Rayy, in what is now Iraq
Died: 313 A.H./925 A.D., Rayy, in what is now Iraq
Major Works: *Book of the Philosophic Life, Book of Spiritual Medicine*

Major Ideas

Nothing in revealed religion prohibits philosophical inquiry.
The goal of philosophy is to make oneself as much like God as is humanly possible.
Passion should be suppressed and resisted.
In the pursuit of pleasure, a kind of mean—an upper and lower limit—should be observed.
The afterlife will be praiseworthy or blameworthy depending on the way we have live here below.
Human life should be directed towards acquiring knowledge and practicing justice.

Abū Bakr Muḥammad Ibn Zakariyyā' al-Rāzī was born in Rayy in what is now Iraq. He lived in Baghdad in his early thirties and again from about 901 to 907 A.D., while the Abbasid caliph al-Muktafi was in office. Just as earlier, so later, he returned to Rayy as soon as possible, and it was there that he died. A man of imposing stature, al-Rāzī was predominantly a physician and teacher of medicine, but he also served as a sometime adviser to various rulers and was a prolific author. Indeed, his writings include over 200 treatises, pamphlets, and books. Though his writing apparently led to a paralysis of the hand and impaired eyesight, he nonetheless continued with the help of secretaries and scribes.

It is difficult to form an appreciation of al-Rāzī's thought because so few of his writings have come down to us and because the major source for our knowledge of what he believed is an account his archenemy, the Ismaili missionary Abū Ḥātim al-Rāzī, presented of their different positions. Fortunately, we do have an important work Abū Bakr al-Rāzī wrote late in his life. It seeks to justify his conduct against contradictory criticisms leveled against him by unnamed individuals he describes as "people of speculation, discernment, and attainment." These critics first accuse al-Rāzī of turning away from the life of philosophy, especially insofar as that life is exemplified by the man upon whom he is said to model himself—Socrates. Because al-Rāzī socializes with others and busies himself with

acquiring money, activities shunned by the Socrates known to them, they think he has abandoned the way of Socrates. Yet they also blame the ascetic life of Socrates for its evil practical consequences. So, according to them, al-Rāzī is as wrong to have turned away from Socrates as he was to have followed him in the first place.

Book of the Philosophic Life

In his *Book of the Philosophic Life*, al-Rāzī answers these charges and provides insight into his fuller teaching. The treatise teaches us little about why Socrates made his famous conversion, that is, changed from a youthful asceticism to a mature involvement in all-too-human activities. Even though he could present the turn as evidence that Socrates also deemed it wrong, al-Rāzī treats Socrates's asceticism as merely a zealous excess of youth. Since Socrates abandoned it early on, he sees no need to consider whether a life so devoted to the pursuit of wisdom that it ignores all other concerns is laudable or whether the good life is the balanced one he describes as his own at the end of the treatise. al-Rāzī refrains from blaming Socrates for his ascetic practices because they led to no dire consequences. He sees no reason to simply blame asceticism.

Still, the issue cannot be ignored, for it points to the broader question of whether the pursuit of philosophy must be so single-minded that it takes no account of the needs of human beings or, differently stated, whether the proper focus of philosophy is nature and the universe or human things. al-Rāzī does not immediately distinguish between the two, for he identifies practicing justice, controlling the passions, and seeking knowledge as characteristic of the pursuit of philosophy and praiseworthy in Socrates's life. By emphasizing that Socrates abandoned asceticism so as to participate in activities conducive to human well-being, al-Rāzī avoids examining whether it is wrong per se or against nature. He judges it instead in terms of its results—in quantitative terms, rather than in qualitative ones—and deems it wrong only when following it threatens the well-being of the ascetic or of the human race. Such a tactic also allows al-Rāzī to avoid having his critics impugn him for being sated with desires just because he does not imitate Socrates's earlier asceticism.

The point is eminently sensible, but al-Rāzī weakens it by contending that however much he may fall short of Socrates's early asceticism (a position he has now made defensible), he is still philosophical if compared to nonphilosophical people. He would have been on more solid ground had he acknowledged that asceticism is always a threat to the world we live in and then praised the salubrious consequences of the life of the reformed Socrates. It is not an appropriate argument, however, for Socrates's subsequent begetting, warring, and merrymaking are not at issue for al-Rāzī's critics. The question is, rather, whether doing those things prevents one from being philosophical, and al-Rāzī passes over it in silence.

By phrasing his defense in quantitative terms, he fails to give an adequate account of the balanced life. What al-Rāzī needed to do was show that, despite Socrates's later involvement in worldly activities, he continued to be as interested in philosophy as before. Or, even more to the point, al-Rāzī needed to argue that Socrates's earlier asceticism kept him from pursuing philosophy fully insofar as it prevented him from paying attention to the questions related to human conduct.

He takes up neither line of argument because either one would take him away from his major

goal, namely, setting forth the argument that completes his depiction of the philosophical life. It in turn depends upon his full teaching, and he offers a summary of it by listing six principles, all taken from other works. Nonetheless, he develops only two in the sequel. One, phrased almost as an imperative, asserts that pleasure is to be pursued only in a manner that brings on no greater pain, and the other insists upon the way the Divinity has provided for all creatures.

This latter principle necessarily obliges human beings not to harm other creatures. In his elaboration of this principle, al-Rāzī leads the reader to issues of political importance: the natural hierarchy between the different parts of the body and between the various species, then a presumed hierarchy among individuals within the human species.

Such distinctions allow him to formulate a provisional definition of morality, something he calls the upper and lower limits. Briefly, accepting differences in birth and habit as fixed and as necessarily leading to different pursuits of pleasure, al-Rāzī urges only that one not go against justice or intellect (understood naturally and according to revelation) on the one hand, nor come to personal harm or excessive indulgence in pleasure on the other. The point is that since some people can afford more ease than others, the rule must be flexible. Though he urges that less is nonetheless generally better, the disparities caused by differences in fortune do not provoke him to suggestions about the need to strive for a more equitable distribution of wealth or to regulate the way it is passed on. Completely eschewing such excursions into politics and political economy, al-Rāzī notes merely that the less wealthy may have an easier time of abiding by the lower limit and that it is preferable to lean more towards that limit.

Making Oneself Similar to God

All of this is captured in what al-Rāzī calls the sum of the philosophical life, "making oneself similar to God . . . to the extent possible for a human being." This summary statement is extraordinarily subtle and inventive. It consists of four basic parts:

al-Rāzī begins by asserting certain qualities of the Creator; he then seeks a rule of conduct based on an analogy between the way servants seek to please their sovereigns or owners and the way we should please our Sovereign Master. Next he draws a conclusion from that analogy about the character of philosophy, and he ends with the declaration that the fuller explanation of this summary statement is to be found in his *Book of Spiritual Medicine*.

The interested reader must turn to the *Book of Spiritual Medicine*, al-Rāzī says, because in it he mentions (1) how we can rid ourselves of bad moral habits and (2) the extent to which someone aspiring to be philosophical may concern himself with the gaining of a livelihood, acquisition, expenditure, and the seeking of rulership. In other words, the definition of the philosophical life set forth here raises questions that he identifies elsewhere as relating to moral virtue, especially moral purification, and human affairs—economics as well as political rule. For al-Rāzī, then, philosophy consists of three basic concerns: moral virtue or ethics, household management or economics, and political rule. Allusion to the *Book of Spiritual Medicine* only underlines what had already been made clear by al-Rāzī's introduction of the two principles from his larger teaching. As al-Rāzī notes almost in passing, confident that the reader discerns how divine providence for all creatures warrants some serving others, it is perfectly justifiable to distinguish between human beings in terms of how essential they are to the well-being of the community.

Such reflections allow al-Rāzī to defend himself against the calumnies of his nameless critics. The defense goes beyond mere exculpation to an explanation of philosophy itself. Thus, in the concluding words of this treatise, as part of his final self-justification, al-Rāzī asserts that philosophy consists of two parts, knowledge and practice, and that anyone who fails to achieve both cannot be called a philosopher. His own role as a philosopher is vouchsafed: his writings testify to his knowledge, and his adherence to the upper and lower limits proves his practice. Still, there is no doubt that he prizes knowledge more. It is here, after all, that he explains how his pursuit of knowledge has led him to injure his hand and eyes.

CHARLES E. BUTTERWORTH

Further Reading

Translations

al-Rāzī. "Abū Bakr Muḥammad Ibn Zakariyyā al-Rāzī: The Book of the Philosophic Life," translated by Charles E. Butterworth, *Interpretation*. Vol. 20, No. 3, Spring 1993, pp. 227–236.
——— . *The Spiritual Physick of Rahzes*. Translated by Arthur J. Arberry. London: John Murray, 1950.

Related Studies

Butterworth, Charles E. "The Origins of al-Rāzī's Political Philosophy," *Interpretation*. Vol. 20, No. 3, Spring 1993, pp. 237–257.
Walker, Paul E. "The Political Implications of al-Rāzī's Philosophy." In *The Political Aspects of Islamic Philosophy, Essays in Honor of Muhsin S. Mahdi,* edited by Charles E. Butterworth. Cambridge, Mass.: Harvard University Press, 1992, pp. 61–94.

AL-FĀRĀBĪ

Born: 257 A.H./870 A.D., Farab, Turkestan
Died: 339 A.H./950 A.D., Damascus, Syria
Major Works: *al-Madīna al-fāḍilah* (*The Opinion of the People of the Virtuous City*), *Short Commentary on Aristotle's* Prior Analytics, *About the Scope of Aristotle's* Metaphysics, *On the Intellect, The Harmony Between the Views of the Divine Plato and Aristotle, The Attainment of Happiness, Aphorisms of the Statesman*

Major Ideas

God created the world by the emanation of the Ten Intellects.
The logic of Aristotle provides a secure foundation for reasoning.
The prophet who has mastered both philosophy and spirituality is the perfect ruler for the state.
Happiness results from fulfilling one's function as a rational human being: theoretical and practical perfection.

Abū Naṣr Muḥammad al-Fārābī, one of the greatest Muslim Peripatetics, received the title of "Second Teacher," the first teacher being Aristotle. Having studied with Yūhannā ibn-Ḥaylān, a Nestorian Christian, Fārābī also studied mathematics, philosophy, astronomy, and music with another Christian master, Abū-Bishr Matta ibn-Yūnus, in Baghdad.

Fārābī, like many other Muslim philosophers, traveled widely, visiting centers of learning and meeting with the learned masters of his time. He spent the last few years of his life in Allepo, at the court of Ṣayf-ad-Dawlah.

Fārābī's philosophy represents the first serious attempt in Islamic philosophy to bring about a rapprochement between the teachings of Plato and Aristotle. It was toward this end that he wrote many commentaries and expositions on Plato's and Aristotle's treatises. Despite such commentaries, he came to be known for his works on logic and political philosophy. In logic, ethics, and metaphysics he followed Aristotle; in politics he preferred Plato.

Existence, Emanation, and the Intellects

Fārābī argues that all existing beings are divided into necessary and possible existents. Necessary beings exist by virtue of themselves and need no external cause of their existence. Possible beings are those that can exist or not exist, and their exis-

tence requires an external cause. Fārābī then goes on to argue that if one were to strip all the accidental (unnecessary) attributes of a existent thing, what would be left is the essence of that thing. Therefore, all existent beings for Fārābī consist of an essence to which existence is added. It is only God, Fārābī tells us, for whom essence and existence are one and the same.

Fārābī's views on the origin of the world seem to have been influenced by the Neoplatonic doctrine of emanation. According to Fārābī, God, in contemplating himself, emanates an intellect from himself and from this intellect, which contemplates itself, emanates the Second Intellect, and so forth until the Tenth Intellect, which Fārābī calls the "Agent Intellect." These intellects, for Fārābī, provide the intermediary world between the incorporeal world and ours, the world of generation and corruption.

Fārābī, who interprets Aristotle's account of the intellects in his own way, argues that Aristotle believes in four different intellects. These intellects are: Intellect in Potentiality, which he identifies with the human soul and its ability to think; Intellect in Actuality, which is the realization within the corporeal world of the intelligible; the Acquired Intellect, which to him is attained when the intellect in actuality reflects upon the intelligible; and finally there is the Agent Intellect, which is the cause of thinking.

Fārābī's Logic

Fārābī is perhaps the greatest logician of Islam. He undertook an extensive study and critique of the entire Aristotelian *Organon*. His principal contributions to logic were his analysis of principles of syllogistic reduction, his emphasis on hypothetical and disjunctive syllogisms (arguments involving "if . . . then . . ." and "either . . . or . . ." premises), his discussion of induction, and his account of the use of the categorical syllogism in arguments by analogy. In addition to these significant contributions, he has offered an in-depth treatment of the status of future contingencies and the determination of future events.

Post-Fārābī Muslim logicians remained under his influence; even those who modified or criticized his views often came to know of Aristotle through his eyes. The most notable example is Avicenna, who was highly influenced by Fārābī's view on logic.

The Prophet as Philosopher and Statesman

Fārābī believed that there is but one fundamental religion and that the various religions were manifestations of it. Affirming the truth of all religions, Fārābī maintained that each religion is applicable to its particular milieu. All religions, therefore, are like points on the circumference of a circle aiming at the center, which is God. What differentiates people is not the variety of religions they profess, but ignorance of the fact that all persons are manifestations of God on different planes of reality and at different stages of spiritual progress.

Expanding upon the oneness of truth, Fārābī elaborates on the notion of prophecy. Fārābī's interpretation of prophecy, a view that brought condemnation from orthodox scholars, led him to consider a prophet as someone who has mastered philosophy as well as spirituality. A prophet in Fārābī's view is a perfect human being, one who has actualized all of that person's intellectual and spiritual potentialities. According to Fārābī, the traditional concept of prophecy, in which God chooses a prophet based on his own will, is incorrect.

Once human perfection is attained, the prophet assumes two responsibilities, being a philosopher and being a statesman. The acquired intellect of the philosopher through its contact with the Agent Intellect brings about illumination, which Fārābī identifies as revelation (*wahy*). The prophet, in addition to being a perfect philosopher, is a perfect statesman whose primary responsibility is to govern the state justly. In order to govern, the prophet must use his illuminated intellect to make decisions that will insure the common good of the people.

For Fārābī, the philosophical mind at the peak of its development becomes like matter to the Active intellect. Prophets are those who have attained this state and go beyond the philosophical truth to imaginative truth, which is then transformed into symbols, figures, and actions, through which societies can be moved towards a greater degree of moral insight and ethical practice.

Since all things come into being from a single cause, Fārābī declares, a good state follows the principle of having a prophet–philosopher as the ruler, and hence the cause of the good state. The prophetic aspect of the ruler enables him to communicate with the masses, who understand only the language of persuasion. The prophet's philosophical side, on the other hand, allows the prophet as ruler to speak to the intellectual elite, who can understand reasoning and will accept only that which is rationally justifiable. This view of the prophet as ruler also implies that the principles of religion ultimately are consistent with philosophical principles and that the apparent inconsistency between religion and philosophy stems from the failure to realize that each one is designed for a different task.

Fārābī's Political Philosophy

The human being, according to Fārābī, has an innate yearning for community life, and as such attains happiness only within the state. Following Plato, Fārābī believes that people are happy if and only if they fulfill the function for which they were created. Since human beings are unequal in that they have various capacities for service, it is therefore the responsibility of the state to ensure that its citizens are placed where their true nature can best be utilized.

Like Plato in the *Republic*, Fārābī models his ideal state after the human body; as a natural model in which there exists a hierarchy consisting of mind, spirit, and body. The highest level in this hierarchy—the mind—has a natural right to dominate and harmonize the lower levels. In government, accordingly, the prophet is the "unruled ruler," who governs by virtue of his divine wisdom.

Some historians of philosophy argue that Fārābī may have been a Shi'ite, since he was patronized by Ṣayf ad-Dawlah, a Shi'ite king, and therefore his political philosophy should be viewed in that context. That is, the ruler of the Fārābian state would resemble a Shi'ite Imam, who as possessor of divine wisdom, with access to esoteric truth, is therefore qualified to rule.

Since a good state is a natural state and it is only natural for human beings to want to be happy, it is the responsibility of the state to insure that its citizens be happy, according to Fārābī. He treats the subject of happiness and its attainment extensively.

There are three alternative interpretations of the nature of happiness according to Fārābī: happiness as a purely theoretical activity, happiness as practical activity exclusively, and happiness as a harmonious combination of the theoretical and the practical.

Arguing that theoretical excellence brings about practical excellence, Fārābī concludes that it is the task of philosophy to actualize the perfection of the theoretical. Accordingly, Fārābī argues that human perfection as the ultimate goal is achieved by a rapprochement of theoretical and practical reason. Although Fārābī contended that theoretical perfection is to be sought through metaphysical inquiry, there are indications that Fārābī believed that, practically speaking, theoretical perfection could not be attained even in the best of cases.

Although the practical component of happiness is presented by Fārābī as a private activity of a moral nature, true happiness, according to him, is possible only within the context of a society. Thus Fārābī emphasizes the necessity of a perfect political order and a supreme ruler whose virtuous character can bestow happiness upon the citizens. The purpose of life for Fārābī is the full development of the rational faculty and the attainment of truth through philosophical contemplation. Such an end in life can be fulfilled only in well-organized societies wherein just rulers govern. However, to be just one needs the type of theoretical wisdom that makes it possible to devise practical laws. Fārābī states that those societies that are governed by rulers who are the repositories of philosophical wisdom are "good societies," while others the others are "ignorant" or "misguided societies."

MEHDI AMINRAZAVI

Further Reading

Fackenheim, E. "The Possibility of the Universe in Al-Farabi, Ibn Sina, and Maimonides," *Proceedings of the American Academy for Jewish Research.* XVI, 1946–47, pp. 39–70. This essay explores various theories of the creation of the incorporeal world.

Hammond, Robert. *The Philosophy of al-Farabi and Its Influence on Medieval Thought.* New York: Hobson Book Press, 1947. The role of Fārābī as one of the greatest interpreters of Aristotle and his impact on medieval philosophy is discussed.

Lerner, R., and M. Mahdī, eds. *Medieval Political Philosophy.* New York: Cornell University Press, 1963. In this book, Fārābī's political philosophy and its impact on medieval political thought are discussed.

Mahdi, M. "Remarks on Alfarabi's Attainment of Happiness." In *Essays on Islamic Philosophy and Science*, edited by G. Hourani. Albany, N.Y.: SUNY Press, 1975, pp. 47–66. The concept of happiness and its relationship to philosophy, as well as the Aristotelian elements in Fārābī's views, are discussed.

Rescher, N. *Al-Farabi, An Annotated Bibliography.* Pittsburgh, Pa.: University of Pittsburgh Press, 1962.

AVICENNA (IBN SĪNĀ)

Born: 370 A.H./980 A.D., Bukhara
Died: 428 A.H./1037 A.D.
Major Works: *Kitāb al-shifā* (*The Book of Healing*), *Kitāb al-Najāt* (*The Book of Deliverance*), *Risālah fi'l-'ishq* (*Treatise on Love*), *Ḥayy in Yaqzān* (*The Son of the Awake*), *Risālah al-ṭa'īr* (*Treatise on Birds*), *Fountains of Wisdom*, *al-Ishārāt wa'l tanbīhāt* (*The Book of Directives and Remarks*), *Manṭiq al-mashriqiyīn* (*Logic of the Orientals*)

Major Ideas

The universe emanates from God.
The Active Intellect governs the sublunary world.
There are three substances: intellect, soul, and body.

Abū 'Ali Sīnā, known as Avicenna or Ibn Sīnā, was by far the most influential of all Muslim philosophers, both in the tradition of Islamic philosophy and that of medieval Christian philosophy.

Avicenna was born into an Isma'ili family, and his father, who was himself a man of learning, paid special attention to his son's education. Having demonstrated an exceptional ability in learning, Avicenna began his education at an early age. By age ten he had memorized the whole of the Qur'an (Koran) and a great deal of Arabic grammar. He went on to study logic and mathematics with Abū 'Abdallah al-Natilī, and physics, metaphysics, and medicine with Abū Ṣahl al-Masihī.

Avicenna, who had mastered all the sciences of his time, remained unable to understand Aristotle's metaphysics until he came across al-Fārābī's commentary upon the work, which clarified the difficulties for him. Avicenna at the time was eighteen years old. It was for his vast breadth and depth of knowledge that he later came to be known as al-Shaīkh al-ra'is ("the leader of the wise"), Hūjjat al-ḥaqq ("the proof of God"), or "the Prince of Physicians."

Avicenna, whose life in his homeland had been touched by political turmoil, left for Jurjan in the hope of finding patronage. Having visited several courts and spending a few years as a minister at the court of Shams al-Dawlah, he ended up in Iṣfahān, where he enjoyed fifteen years of peace and tranquility only to be interrupted by the invasion of

Iṣfahān. Avicenna returned to Hamadān where he served as a minister; after he was jailed for his refusal to continue his administrative duties, he died of a colic attack.

It is said of Avicenna that he had an unmatched power of concentration and that he composed many of his philosophical treatises on horseback while following the king to the battle. Rarely have so many intellectual and spiritual facets manifested themselves in a person who was at the same time a statesman, philosopher, and physician; he laid the foundation of medieval philosophy while synthesizing the Hippocratic and Galenic traditions of medicine, a science which he regarded to be shallow.

Creation by Emanation from God

Avicenna, like al-Fārābī (257 A.H./870 A.D.–339 A.H./950 A.D.), argues that the universe is the product of emanation. From God, the source of existence, issues forth a First Intelligence, and it is from this that a Second Intelligence emanates. The process continues until it culminates in the Tenth Intellect, which governs the sublunary world, the Active Intellect which most Islamic philosophers identify with Archangel Gabriel. Through the above scheme Avicenna attempts to resolve the complex philosophical problem of how the world, being a multiplicity, can come from a Unity, namely God.

The above argument entails a division among

existent beings which is as follows: necessary (*wājib*), possible (*mūmkin*), and impossible (*mūmtani'*). For Avicenna these concepts are closely connected to another major distinction among existent beings, that is, the distinction between essence (*māhiyyah*) and existence (*wujūd*). This major distinction between *essence* as that which constitutes the distinctive identity of a thing and *existence* as a common feature of all things was adopted by most of the medieval philosophers, both Christians and Muslims.

Avicenna, who has received the title "the philosopher of Being," argued for the principality of existence over essence. The intricate relationship between various aspects of Avicenna's ontology (theory of being) is designed to demonstrate that from God, the only Necessary Being, comes the world, which on the one hand is *contingent* (in that its existence depends upon emanation) and, on the other hand, is *necessary* since its source is necessary. Avicenna argued that essences have only an abstract existence in that they exist in the mind and not in the external world. When existence is superadded to the essence, the result is an existent being. What then remains to be added are the accidental properties (characteristics that are not necessary)—the whole sum of properties and forms, the outward manifestations of a thing.

In addition to dividing beings into necessary, contingent, and possible beings, Avicenna classifies them on the basis of their substance and accidents. Substance is further divided by Avicenna into three categories, depending on the degree of its dependence on matter. They are as follows:

1. *Intellect* (*'aql*), which is completely separated from matter.
2. *Soul* (*nafs*), which despite its distinctness from the body interacts with it.
3. *Body* (*jism*), which is matter and is subservient to it in that it requires the soul as its mover.

The Tenth Intellect as the "Giver of Forms"

In his cosmology Avicenna attempts to demonstrate the continuity and multiplicity that exists between the one and the many. To do so Avicenna relies on the soteriological function of the angels within a Neoplatonic scheme to explain the existence of the multiplicity that has come from a unity without violating the principle that from the one, only one can come into being (*ex uno non fit nisi unum*).

Avicenna, whose concept of the process of creation and its relation to intellection has been discussed, makes a correlation between the process of emanation from God to the soul and the body of the Heavens. From the First Intellect, which corresponds to the supreme archangel, emanates the Second Intellect, which is the soul and body of the First Heaven. The Third Intellect, which is emanated from the second one, respectively constitutes the soul and body of the Second Heaven. In the process of each emanation the purity to generate another soul and body is reduced until with the Tenth Intellect when the purity necessary for the generation of another Heaven is no longer there. It is here that the corporeal world of generation and corruption comes into being from the remaining possibilities within the Tenth Intellect.

The Tenth Intellect, as the intermediary between the corporeal world and the world of intellects and God, is referred to as the "giver of forms" (*wāhib al-ṣuwar*). Upon the coming into being of an existent being, the Tenth Intellect emanates a form (distinctive character), and when a thing withers away, it takes the form away or replaces it with another form.

The second function of the Tenth Intellect is that of illuminating the minds. Forms in the angelic mind of the Tenth Intellect descend upon matter, and man's mind through the act of illumination is able to conceive the form separately from matter; the combination of matter and form constitutes the outward manifestation of an existent being.

Avicenna, whose use of angels as intermediaries between the one and the many solves the problem of how multiplicity came from unity, lays the groundwork for a sacred cosmology in which he argues for the study of the macrocosm as a means of knowing the microcosm, the world within. This led to the emergence of the science of letters in Islam known as *jafr*, in which the letters of the Arabic alphabet are linked to the principles of cosmology.

Psychology and Theory of Knowledge

Avicenna's views on psychology are directly related to his views on epistemology (theory of knowledge). Like Aristotle, he argues that man has three faculties—vegetative, animal, and rational. These faculties are interconnected and, depending on the external circumstances, they are activated. The vegetative soul rests on minerals, the animal soul on the vegetative, and the rational soul on the animal soul. The highest level of the vegetative soul and the lowest of the animal soul therefore closely resemble each other. Each soul contains the faculties of the previous soul in addition to that of itself. The vegetative soul, for example, contains reproduction and growth; the animal soul possesses the power of desire, lust, and anger. The faculties of the animal soul, however, are divided into two classes, the five external and the five internal senses. The five internal senses consist of reproduction, imagination, estimation, retention, and recollection. The five external senses are those of sight, hearing, touch, taste, and smell.

It is only in the human being, the most sublime example of creation, that the rational soul exists. The rational soul consists of two parts, the practical and the theoretical. The practical soul is the source of movements and oversees the decision-making of the day-to-day affairs of life. The theoretical faculty, which is characteristic only of human beings, consists of four levels.

This classification, which is in line with some of Avicenna's predecessors such as al-Kindī and al-Fārābī, divides the intellects into the intellect in potentiality, the intellect in actuality, the active intellect through which illumination is received, and the acquired intellect, *intellectus adeptus*, through which the intelligible world is realized.

Avicenna's psychology corresponds to his ontology, according to which intellect emanates from pure Being, and this process solidifies as it descends. From the bottom, the mineral level, the more the soul ascends, the purer it gets. Avicenna's psychology therefore attempts to put this scheme into the context of his ontology.

Avicenna in the first chapter of *Kitāb al-shifā* tells us a hypothetical story which serves as the axiom upon which his epistemology is based. He tells us that a person is born and raised in a void such that he or she can not touch, see, smell, or hear anything and therefore cannot conceive of the external world. The only knowledge this person has is that of his or her own self, and the immediacy of this knowledge is such that the person is absolutely certain that if nothing else exists, he or she does.

The presence of different faculties in the human being as described in the foregoing discussion enables one to gain knowledge of the external world. Since by sense perception one can know material objects, the animal soul and human soul are therefore able to know the more abstract objects of cognition.

The Doctrine of Prophecy

The nature of the phenomenon of prophethood in Islam has been the subject of a long discussion by Muslim jurists, philosophers, and theologians. Avicenna divides the notion and the task of prophethood into four levels—the intellectual, the imaginative, the miraculous, and the practical. Relying on Hellenistic intellectual heritage, Avicenna argues that some persons have exceptionally strong intuitive powers through which they come to many discoveries on their own. The discovery of a new religious universe is attributed to the ability of this power.

The faculty of intellectual intuition which Avicenna identifies with the active intellect in the very being of the prophet becomes the acquired intellect. So the prophet remains a human and "humanness" becomes an accident to the active intellect which participates in the person.

Possession of an exceptionally strong faculty of imagination is the second attribute of a prophet through which conceptual images are transformed into real lifelike images, a concretization of the objects of imagination.

The prophet has to have the ability to perform, to

rule over the material domain. A prophet's identification with the active intellect, the giver of forms, enables the prophet to exercise the same power over the corporeal world that the human self, the "I," exercises on the body.

Finally, there is the practical or sociopolitical role of the prophet as a statesman, a lawgiver, and one who bears the responsibility of actualizing the law (*shari'ah*). It is the implementation of the prophet's insight and moral and intellectual concepts that is a testimony to the validity of those notions.

Mysticism

The mystical dimension of Avicenna's thought has received less attention than his Peripatetic (Aristotelian) works. Avicenna is said to have developed the mystical side of his philosophy towards the end of his life. In a treatise called *Manṭiq al-mashriqiyīn* (*Logic of Orientals*), Avicenna states that the bulk of his Peripatetic writings are written for the spiritual elites. His writings concerning mysticism or what he calls the "science of the elites" include such works as *Risālah fi'l-'ishq* (*Treatise on Love*), *Ḥayy in Yaqzān* (*The Son of the Awake*), and *Risālah al-ṭair* (*Treatise on Birds*).

From a study of the above works, the essential components of Avicenna's esoteric philosophy, which is none other than the gnostic perspective, are revealed. The philosophical groundwork for such a view already exists in Avicenna's ontological structure in that God is the only Necessary Being and all else are contingent upon it. The corporeal world, being an antipode of God, represents the prison of the human soul, whose yearning for its abode makes the soul look for a master. The spiritual guide leads the seeker of truth from darkness into light.

Avicenna's symbolic language, which makes use of angelology and cosmology, does not negate the Peripatetic philosophy, but reinterprets it in a symbolic way to suggest the complexity of the spiritual world and the sacred cosmos in which spiritual realization takes place.

MEHDI AMINRAZAVI

Further Reading

Arberry, A. J., trans. *Avicenna on Theology*. Wisdom of the Earth Series. London: John Murray, 1951. This is a translation of extracts of *Kitāb al-Najāt* (*The Book of Deliverance*), with an account of Avicenna's life.

Corbin, H. *Avicenna and the Visionary Recital*. Translated from the French by W. Trask. Princeton, N.J.: Princeton University Press, 1990. This work discusses the more mystical aspects of Avicennian philosophy. Also, it contains some translations, including the treatise *Son of the Awake*.

Courtois, V., ed. *Avicenna Commemoration Volume*. Calcutta: Indo-Iranian Society, 1956. This is a rich collection of essays on different aspects of Avicennian philosophy.

Davidson, H. "Avicenna's Proof of the Existence of God as a Necessarily Existent Being." In *Islamic Philosophical Theology*, edited by P. Morewedge. Albany, N.Y.: SUNY Press, 1979, pp. 167–187.

Goichon, A. *The Philosophy of Avicenna and Its Influence on Medieval Europe*. Translated by M. Khan. Delhi: 1969.

Nasr, H. *Three Muslim Sages: Avicenna, Suhrawardi, Ibn 'Arabi*. New York: Caravan Press, 1976. The essay represents a general survey of Avicenna's philosophy and impact on later Islamic philosophy.

Rahman, F. "Essence and Existence in Avicenna." Medieval and Renaissance Studies, IV, pp. 1–16. London: Warburg Institute, 1958.

Wickens, G., ed. *Avicenna, Scientist and Philosopher: A Millenary Symposium*. London: Luzac Press, 1952. The relationship between the scientific and the philosophical aspects of Avicenna's thought are reflected upon.

QUSHAYRI

Born: 986, Nishapur, the Khurasan area of Iran
Died: 1074, near Nishapur, Iran
Major Works: *Risālah* (*The Treatise on Sufism*), *Lat'aif al-Ishārāt* (*Subtlest Indications*)

Major Ideas

Sufi terms and concepts create a web of meaning in which each key term is made up of and dependent upon all the others.

By completely giving over the self in each moment of intense contemplation, a progression towards a higher mode of consciousness is possible.

Through the experience of intimacy and dread, one experiences the holy.

By the time of Qushayri, Islamic mysticism had moved from a period of explosive growth and discovery, characterized by the great early figures of Rabi'a al-Adawiyya (d. 801), Bistami (d. c. 876), Junayd (d. 910), and Hallaj (d. 922), to a period of more self-conscious reflection on the role of Sufism within Islam and upon Sufi experience and concepts.

This change did not mean an end to the creativity characterized by the earlier figures; such creativity continued for centuries. Parallel to it, however, emerged a new, more synoptic kind of Sufi literature, associated with Sarraj (d. 988), Sulami (d. 1021), and Makki (d. 966). This trend reached its culmination in the masterwork of Qushayri, the *Risālah* (*The Treatise on Sufism*), known simply as *The Qushayrian Treatise*.

Qushayri (Abd al-Karīm ibn Hawāzin al-Qushayri) was born near Nishapur in the Khurasan area during the period of the Ghaznavid dynasty. He received the full Islamic education of the time, memorizing the Qur'an (Koran), studying Islamic law (*fiqh*) and 'Asharite theology, and becoming a disciple to the Sufi master ad-Daqqaq (d. 1021). Qushayri wrote a number of works, including a Qur'anic commentary, but it is the *Treatise* that has marked his enduring legacy. In it Qushayri follows the example of Sulami in presenting a comprehensive set of biographies of early Sufis, based upon the traditional form associated with the *hadīth*. Each Sufi saying is preceded by a chain (*isnad*) of authorities who transmitted the saying. By using

this form, Sulami and Qushayri ground Sufism in the ancient core of Islamic authority.

As important as the biographies of eighty-three Sufis are, the most influential parts of the *Treatise* are the second and third sections. Part 2 is a brilliant essay on the twenty-seven most important Sufi concepts. Part 3 is a longer set of essays on Sufi moral and psychological concepts. No short article can summarize Qushayri's analysis of all these terms and concepts. The examples below are meant to show the mode of thinking exhibited in the *Treatise* as a dialectical, dynamic, and multifaceted approach to Sufi ideas.

Perspectival Approach to Sufi Experience

Qushayri's perspectival approach is at its most condensed and most brilliant in part 2, the section known by the misleadingly dry title of "The Explication of Expressions" (*tafsir alfaz*). The analysis of each major concept is woven around the sayings of earlier Sufis; we encounter the living oral tradition as it is preserved by a literary master who creates within his treatise, as it were, a subtle conversation among the early Sufis. Qushayri is particularly fond of the unattributed proverb, often introduced by the phrase "they say," "some say," or "someone said." When Qushayri does cite named Shaykhs, his citations tend to cluster around a few figures such as his teacher ad-Daqqaq and ad-Daqqaq's teacher, Sulami. The various proverbs and poetical verses are woven into a highly sophisticated analysis. A single term, such as *waqt* (moment), will be defined from various points of view—non-Sufi and Sufi—and as each short essay progresses, deeper understandings of the term gradually unfold. In many cases a term will undergo a progression through various meanings in one essay, only to be viewed in the following essay from the opposite point of view. Multiple reversals can and do occur within a single essay as a term is viewed positively, then negatively, and then in a manner that transcends both or take both aspects up into a new term. This "perspectivalism" keeps the essay in a continual state of dynamic tension; no single static definition stands on its own.

Stylistic and emotive variation provides another element of surprise. The endings of individual sections can range from Junayd's unforgettable account of "constriction and expansion," to the comic episode of two Sufis who, carried away by the experience of ecstatic existentiality (*wujūd*), rip trees out by the roots and wrestle one another into submission in ecstasy combat. The closing episodes, often relating stories of strange behavior and miracles, condense and dramatize the previous, highly nuanced and sophisticated discussion in a story indelibly fixed in the reader's imagination.

The discussion of each term does include an acknowledgment of the common meaning of the term and its basic semantic field, and a discussion of the various ways it is defined and employed by different groups of Sufis. Also included, however, is a probing analysis of the emotive and psychological ramifications of the concept, along with its moral and experiential dimensions; an analysis of the theological implications of the concept, with special attention to the classic tension between human free-agency and divine all-powerfulness; and a careful relation of the term and concept to the dimensions of the lyric (through poetry citations) and the dramatic (through extended anecdotes).

In addition to the multidimensional character of each essay in itself, the various essays are interconnected by both foreshadowing and retrospection. Frequently an essay will explain one term in terms of another not yet introduced; or a later discussion of a new term will cause the reader to reevaluate the understanding of a term previously introduced. Of course, any "dictionary" must explain one term through others, but Qushayri's treatise intensifies the sense that the key Sufi terms and concepts create an interdependent web of meaning in which each key work or nexus is made up of and dependent upon all the others. In this way the treatise is not only a brilliant examination of Sufi concepts, but also an illustration of the dynamic and multiperspectival character of Sufi discourse.

Time and Condition

Qushayri's approach to the understanding of the mystical experience with its objective of coming into union with God and reality is apparent in the opening exposition of the concept of *waqt* (moment, instant) and the relations among time, experience, and identity. In Sufism, the *waqt* is the temporal period of the *hal* (state, condition). There is constant progression through stages of intensity in both moments and states, aiming at a complete giving over of the self to each moment, as if that moment were the totality of one's existence. A further element of the Sufi moment is the lack of self-will or choice. A moment "comes upon" the Sufi independent of any intention or deliberate effort, spontaneously. Qushayri offers a complex set of differing perspectives on time. Ultimately, the moment is presented as a time-out-of-time-within-time, a bringing of the eschatological afterworld into the present.

Qushayri then addresses the topic of the contemplative state or condition (*hal*) in a way that emphasizes the inherent dynamism in Sufi psychology. He begins with the common contrast between the ephemeral state or condition and the more continuous "station" (*maqam*) along the path to mystical union. He then entertains a more complex perspective that maintains the existence of non-ephemeral states that are superior to the ephemeral variety. Qushayri concludes that non-ephemeral states can exist but only as a "taste" of something that can then grow. A person who experiences a continuous state of "taste" will also experience even higher states that are ephemeral. When these higher states become continuous, even higher ephemeral states occur.

Qushayri's favoring of ephemeral states as superior to non-ephemeral states places within the Sufi psychology of contemplation a focus on unending change. He then goes on to examine the content of the states that the seeker encounters in moving along the infinite road to the real. To indicate the content (delight, constriction, longing, anxiety, terror, absence, presence) of a state, he uses the untranslatable term *ma na*, which combines the notions of "meaning," "essence," or "feeling." The word indicates more than a "feeling" and yet something more specific than "consciousness"— what we shall call a "mode of consciousness."

Awe and Intimacy

Qushayri begins his account of constriction (*qabd*) and expansion (*bast*) with a key psychological distinction between conditions involving future expectations (such as hope and fear) and conditions involving immediate experience (such as constriction and expansion). Constriction is a gripping of the heart, an experience analogous to fear, but far more intense in that it is an experience of the immediate and in the present. Expansion is a dilation, an expansive feeling of peace or well-being, again intensified down into the immediate present. Although expansion is originally viewed as the more desirable state, the essay turns—in a typically Qushayrian twist—to a sudden reversal of perspective in which the comfort of expansion is seen as a trap.

The essay ends with Junayd's famous utterances on constriction and expansion. After the sophistication and delicacy of Qushayri, the quoted Junayd is rough and searing. The voice speaks from the point of "I am there." Junayd speaks of the central Sufi experience of "passing away" in union with the divine while undergoing a constant oscillation between the conditions of fear and hope, presence and absence, union and separation. These conditions either come upon the mystic on their own, or are imposed upon the mystic by the deity, referred to with the unattributed pronoun "he":

Fear grips me. Hope unfolds me. Reality draws me together. The real sets me apart. When he grips me with fear, he makes me pass away from myself. When he expands me with hope, he return me to myself. When he brings me together in reality, he makes me present. When he separates me through the real, he makes my witness the other-than-me and veils me from him.

Coming at the end of the sophisticated setting up of the concepts, Junayd's comments resonate down through centuries of Sufi thought and experience.

Beyond constriction and expansion, Qushayri leads us to awe and intimacy. Rudolf Otto, in his influential definition of holy as the *mysterium tremendum* (dread-inspiring mystery), attributed to the human experience of the holy the simultaneous modes of intense desire and intense fear. For the early Sufis, the *mysterium tremendum* is based upon a somewhat different pair of modes of consciousness: the simultaneous experience of intense intimacy and intense dread or awe. Intimacy (*uns*) and dread (*hayba*) are two of the fundamental modes of Qur'anic discourse and classical poetry, and Sufis have taken these modes into a highly sophisticated experiential psychology. Qushayri quite naturally turns to the classical poetical tradition for proof texts on the experience of intimacy.

A Conceptual World: Poetical, Philosophical, Psychological

The above examples suggest a way of viewing the intricate conceptual world of Sufism, which reached one of its culminations in Qushayri. The longer essays from part 3 of the *Treatise* focus on moral psychology (with probing examinations of various forms of egoism: envy, pride, self-display, backbiting) and experiential psychology (with essays on visionary intuition, remembrance, love, and longing), to name only a few examples. As with the more condensed essays of part 2 of the *Treatise*, each concept is intertwined with the others.

The intertwining of concepts entails an intertwining of "modes" as well. Each concept has a psychological, a philosophical, and a poetical context; Qushayri's genius resides in his ability to do justice to the three areas. With the appearance of Qushayri's *Treatise*, Sufi writings arrived at a new historical plateau. The mystical utterances of the great early figures such as Rabi'a and Junayd were now integrated more fully into the sophisticate traditions of the poetical remembrance of the beloved, the classical moral examination of forms of egoism and self-delusion, a new emphasis of a self-reflective and self-critical science of ecstatic experience, and an increasingly sophisticated philosophical reflection on the nature of time, personal identity, illusion, and reality.

MICHAEL A. SELLS

Further Reading

Translations

Qushayri, Abu l-Qasim 'Abd al-Karim b. Hawazin al-. *Risālah al-Qushayriyya*. Translated from the Arabic by Richard Gramlich as *Das Send-schreiben al-Qushayris Über das Sufitum*. Stuttgart: F. Steiner Verlag: 1989. A meticulous modern translation into German with interpolated explanations and comparisons to other Sufi texts.

al-Qushayri. *Principles of Sufism*. Translated from the Arabic by B. R. Von Schlegell. Berkeley, Calif.: Mizan Press, 1990. The only complete English translation of part 3 of Qushayri's *Treatise*.

Related Study

Sells, Michael A. *Foundations of Islamic Mysticism*. New York: Paulist Press, 1994. Includes the only complete English translation of part 2 of the Qushayri's *Treatise*, "The Explication of Expressions," along with extensive commentary.

AL-GHAZĀLĪ

Born: 450 A.H./1058 A.D., Tus, Iran
Died: 505 A.H./1111 A.D.
Major Works: *Intentions of the Philosophers*, *The Deliverer from Error*, *Incoherence of the Philosophers*, *The Just Mean in Belief*, *Revival of Religious Sciences*, *The Elixir of Happiness*

Major Ideas

The world was created in time and has a beginning.
Rationalistic philosophy fails to bring about certainty.
There are twenty fallacies committed by the Peripatetic philosophers.
A mystical vision of truth is the only way towards the attainment of certainty.

Philosophers rarely have an impact on the history of philosophy through their lives as well as through their ideas. Ghazālī, however, is such a figure in that various phases of his life left an indelible mark on the history of Islamic philosophy by strengthening Sufism while curtailing the influence of rationalistic philosophy, particularly in the eastern part of the Islamic world.

Life and Quest for Truth

Abū Ḥāmid Mūḥammad al-Ghazālī was born into a family of scholars and mystics. He was first influenced by his father, who was a pious dervish, and later by a Sufi friend of his father, not to mention his brother, who is recognized as a distinguished mystic. Despite the presence of Sufis around him, Ghazālī showed a great deal of interest in jurisprudence and speculative sciences.

Ghazālī studied with such masters as Mūḥammad al-Radadhkhānī al-Ṭūsī, Abū Naṣr al-Isma'īlī, and al-Jūwainī, known as "Imam al-Haramaīn." Ghazālī, who at this point was studying in the Nizāmīyyah Academy, became the disciple of 'Ali al-Farmadhī al-Ṭūsī, through whom he became further acquainted with the theoretical as well as practical aspects of Sufism. He then applied himself to austere forms of ascetic practices, but to his dismay did not attain the desired spiritual states. This, in addition to the fact that Ghazālī's intellectual thirst was too strong to allow him to forget the intellec-

tual pursuit of truth, contributed to his growing skepticism.

At this point in his life, Ghazālī was the chair at the Nizāmīyyah Academy and one of the supreme judges known for his numerous commentaries on jurisprudence. Although having attained such titles as "the Proof of Islam" (*ḥūjat al-Islam*), "Renewer of Religion" (*mujaddid al-Dīn*), and the "Ornament of Faith" (*Zain al-Dīn*), Ghazālī was inwardly going through an intellectual and spiritual crisis. In his quest for certainty he had begun to question the position of the scholastic theologians who derived the validity of their ideas from dictums of the faith that they considered to be axiomatic. His doubt soon spread to other facets of his belief, and the inner turmoil of teaching the orthodox positions on one hand and questioning them on the other intensified his spiritual crisis.

Assuming that reason leads to certainty and a firm ground upon which one can establish belief, Ghazālī immersed himself in the study of philosophy. To his dismay, he then discovered that reason goes only so far: it fails to bring about ultimate certainty. He alluded to inconsistencies among the philosophers and discussed twenty points on which, according to Ghazālī, they could be proven to be mistaken.

With his hope for attaining certainty dashed, Ghazālī collapsed, physically and mentally going through an intense state of despair, losing his appetite and power of speech. Having become convinced that truth is not attainable through the study of jurisprudence or philosophy, he began a mystical journey in 488 A.H./1095 A.D. when he left Baghdad for Damascus, where he practiced austere forms of ascetic practices. Ghazālī wandered in Islamic lands for eleven years, during which time he meditated and engaged himself in ascetic practices, until he returned to his native city of Tus. From then on Ghazālī either taught or spent time in seclusion.

Ghazālī's intellectual journey was very similar to that of Descartes' methodology since Ghazālī, like Descartes, questioned everything that can be questioned, searching for a truth which is indubitable. In his search for the indubitable truth, Ghazālī questioned the original identity of the self or the "I" before the self is placed within the context of a given religion. Believing himself to have found the "I" which serves as the foundation of knowledge, Ghazālī touched on a number of epistemological issues; he pointed to the dubious nature of sense perception and of reality itself.

Having criticized the traditional views of the Peripatetic's epistemology, Ghazālī went on to offer a critique of four classes of knowers: mystics, Bāṭinīs, theologians, and philosophers. As to mystics, Ghazālī was opposed to those Sufis who did not observe the religious law (*shari'ah*) and who propagated the Doctrine of the Unity of Being (*waḥdat al-wujūd*), which for him had pantheistic implications. Ghazālī was vehemently against the Ismā'īlī Shi'ites, also referred to as the Bāṭinīs (esotericists), for they rejected the *shari'ah* and argued that only an infallible Imam has access to truth.

According to Ghazālī, theologians were blameworthy only for their methodology, and not for the content of their discussion. Ghazālī (who in the opinion of many, remained a theologian for his whole life despite his criticism of them) found the attempt to establish a reason-based theology a futile effort. Theology, he argued, does not begin with axiomatic principles, but with premises whose val-

idity should ultimately be accepted on the basis of faith alone.

The Incoherence of the Philosophers

Having mastered Greek philosophy—in particular Aristotle—as well as his Muslim counterparts, Ghazālī wrote *Intentions of the Philosophers* (*Maqāṣid al-falāsifah*) and a lucid exposition of Aristotelianism entitled *Incoherence of the Philosophers* (*Tahāfut al-falāsifah*), in which by the dialectical method he attempted to destroy the philosophers' positions.

Ghazālī divides the philosophers into three groups: the *materialists* (*dahriyyūn*), who reject the existence of God and argue for the eternity of the world; the *theists* (*ilāhīyyūn*), who accept the existence of God; and the *naturalists* (*ṭabī'iyyun*), who are not necessarily opposed to the existence of a creator, but who argue against the immortality of the soul.

Ghazālī, whose thorough understanding of the philosophers' position had led him to believe that pursuing reason alone would lead to the destruction of religion and morality, considered the philosophers to be heretical on three accounts: For accepting the eternity of the world, for denying God's knowledge of particulars, and for denying bodily resurrection.

Acceptance of the eternity of the world entails making the world coeternal with God, an unacceptable conclusion to the orthodoxy, Ghazālī points out. Philosophers argue that the eternity of the world follows by necessity from three fundamental axioms: (1) Nothing comes out of nothing, or to put it differently, something cannot come from nothing, (2) Given a particular cause, the effect necessarily and immediately follows, (3) A cause is different from and external to the effect.

Ghazālī offers a series of arguments against the axioms that philosophers regard to be self-evident. In numerous arguments he alludes to inconsistencies within these axioms. The denial of God's knowledge of particulars necessitates God's relative ignorance, a position unacceptable by the Islamic credo. Furthermore, the denial of bodily resurrection is contrary to numerous Qur'anic references concerning bodily resurrection. The philosophers, Ghazālī argues, make the following three claims as the basis for denying the belief in bodily resurrection: (1) There is no logical necessity that bodies be resurrected in their physical forms, (2) If there are no bodies in the hereafter, there can be neither pain nor pleasure in the other world, (3) Hell and Heaven in their physical sense do not exist; they are of a purely spiritual nature.

Ghazālī then proceeds to argue against the above premises, using the rationalistic method of the Peripatetics. Ghazālī specifically criticizes the philosophers for holding twenty fallacious opinions to which the use of reason has led them. Among the fallacious views he attributes to the Peripatetics in his *Incoherence of the Philosophers*: The world has no beginning and no end, God did not create the universe ex nihilo, God is simple and has no quiddity (distinguishing character), God can know nothing but himself, God cannot know particulars, heavenly bodies have animal souls that move by volition, miracles are impossible, human souls are not immortal, corporeal resurrection is impossible.

Ghazālī contends in his critique of the above fallacies that through faith and faith alone can one come to the truth; the reliance on reason leads only to frustration and incoherence.

Criticism of the Emanation Theory

Ghazālī undertook a scathing attack against several philosophical positions, among them the theory of divine emanation. Ghazālī meticulously demonstrates that the theory of emanation propagated by philosophers fails to achieve the very purpose for which philosophers have postulated it. First, it does not solve the problem of how multiplicity came from unity and second, it fails to retain the divine unity that the theory of emanation is supposed to safeguard.

On the question of God's knowledge of particulars, Ghazālī is adamant that God knows all the particulars and anything short of that negates God's omniscience. Even Avicenna, who accepts God's omniscience, is criticized by Ghazālī for stating that even though God knows everything, He does so in a universal way, that is, in a way that is beyond the spatiotemporal limitations of human cognition.

Knowing that philosophers base many of their arguments on the law of cause and effect, Ghazālī critically analyzes it. His criticism, which is very similar to David Hume's argument, maintains that the relationship between a cause and the effect is not a logical necessity. Knowledge of the causal relations between fire and burning or water and wetness is not based on reasoning about necessary relations, but on sense observation.

Having argued against the necessary connection between a cause and its effect, Ghazālī uses this to offer an explanation of the phenomenon of miracle. To those who argue for the impossibility of miracles on the ground that a miracle violates natural laws, Ghazālī's critique of causality explains how the continuity of the so-called "laws" of nature can be disrupted without violating any law.

Ghazālī's Ethics

Ghazālī elaborates extensively on ethics and moral problems. Relying on the Qur'anic concepts, he uses Aristotelian notions to shed light on some of the complex issues. One of the issues that Ghazālī was particularly interested in was the problem of free will and determinism and how that is related to the problem of human choices.

Ghazālī, both as a theologian and a jurist, believed that causal determinism is incompatible with moral responsibility. To solve the problem he offers an ingenious argument that contains three levels: first, there is the level of the material world, where events occur out of necessity; second, there is the sensuous world, where there is relative freedom of action; and finally there is the Divine realm, where there is absolute free will.

Ghazālī realizes the significance of having free will, since without it Heaven and Hell would be meaningless. Having established the relative nature of human will, Ghazālī discusses vices and virtues and man's duty to exercise his noble gift of free will to do what is good. He defines vices as desires of the flesh and ego (*nafs*) that lead to bodily excesses such as unrestrained sex; overindulgence in food; misuse of speech; love of wealth, position, name, and self-assertion. There are also sicknesses of the soul that ought to be cured by such virtues as repentance; renunciation of the materialistic world; abstinence from giving in to the desires of flesh; spiritual poverty or emptiness, which signifies a desire and ability to be filled by divine truth; patience; reliance on God as the spiritual center of the world; and finally love, the most important of all virtues. Love, for Ghazālī, leads to an unmediated mode of cognition between the human being and God (*'arif*). This subject was extensively treated in the post-Ghazālī period and it reached its climax in the School of Isfahan during the fifteenth and sixteenth centuries in Persia.

MEHDI AMINRAZAVI

Further Reading

Translations

Kamali, S. A., tr. *Tahāfut al-Falāsifah or Incoherence of the Philosophers*. Lahore: Pakistan Sabih Ahmad Philosophical Congress, 1958, 1963. Provides access to Ghazālī's famous critique of the philosophers.

McCarthy, Richard Joseph, tr. *Freedom and Fulfillment: An Annotated Translation of al-Ghazālī's* al-Munqidh min al-ḍalāl *and other Relevant Works of Ghazālī*. International Studies and Translations Program Series. Boston: G.K. Hall, Twayne, 1980. Includes a reliable and sensitive translation of Ghazālī's *The Deliverer from Error* and other works.

Related Studies

Marmura, M. "Ghazali's Attitude to the Secular Sciences and Logic." In *Essays on Islamic Philosophy and Science*, edited by G. Hourani. Albany, N.Y.: SUNY Press, 1975, pp. 100–111. An investigation of Ghazālī's classification of the sciences and their relation to philosophy.

Shehadi, F. *Ghazali's Unique Unknowable God*. Leiden, the Netherlands: Brill, 1964. This is a study of the unknowability of God according to Ghazālī.

Sherif, M. *Al-Ghazali, The Mystic*. London: Luzac, 1944. A study of Ghazālī in the later phase of his life when he abandoned philosophy and became a mystic.

Urmaruddin, M. *The Ethical Philosophy of al-Ghazzālī*. Published by the author in four parts, 1949–1951. Also in one volume (Aligarh, India: 1962).

——— . *The Idea of Love in the Philosophy of al-Ghazzālī*. Aligarh, India: Muslim University Press, 1941.

——— . *Some Fundamental Aspects of Imam Ghazzālī's Thought*. Aligarh, India: Irshad Book Depot, 1946.

Wensinck, A. J. *On the Relation Between Ghazali's Cosmology and His Mysticism*. Amsterdam: 1933. The sacred cosmology of Ghazālī, and the place of Sufism in it, are discussed.

SHAHRASTĀNĪ

Born: 1076, Shahrastan, the Khurasan area of Iran
Died: 1153, Shahrastan, Iran
Major Works: *Kitab al-Milal wa'l-Nihal* (*The Book of Religious and Philosophical Communities*) (1127); *Nihayat al-'Iqdam* (*The Culmination of Demonstration in Scholastic Theology*)

Major Ideas

Religious and philosophical ideas can and should be studied in a critical, comparative manner.

Scholastic theology can be analyzed by placing schools and sub-schools according to positions on key issues such as divine unity (tawhid) *and divine predetermination* (qadar).

The divisions of Shi'ism can be grouped according to views of authority and the Imamate.

Other traditions referred to in the Qur'an as "communities of the book"—Jews, Christians, Zoroastrians, and Harranians—can be understood through their own interior arguments.

In the analysis of such communities—as well as those of the pre-Socratics, Brahmanists, and worshippers of Kali—analysis can show how central questions shape culture, rather than provide solutions to doctrinal issues.

Within 100 years of the death of the Prophet Muhammad, Muslims found themselves inheriting a vast cultural world stretching from Andalusia to Afghanistan. The next four centuries were a time of explosive intellectual growth, as Muslim thinkers explored their own traditions and the heritages of the peoples they encountered.

Shahrastani Muḥammad ibn 'Abd al-Karīm ash-Sharastānī, who has justly been called the "principal historian of religion in the oriental middle ages" (by Carra de Vaux in the *Encyclopaedia of Islam*), offered a distinctive method of viewing the cultural interaction and conceptual development of world religions and philosophies within the Mediterranean, Near Eastern, and South Asian world. We know little about his biography. He studied jurisprudence and theology, but his personal philosophical and religious allegiances are a matter of controversy. In addition to his masterwork, *The Book of Religious and Philosophical Communities* (*Kitab al-Milal wa'l-Nihal*), he wrote a *Dual of the Philosophers* and a respected work on theology, the *Culmination of Demonstration in Scholastic Theology* (*Nihayat al-'Iqdam*). It is the first work, however, on which his present influence and reputation are based.

Unity and Attributes

Shahrastani's famous discussion of the scholastic theologians (*mutakallimun*) is based upon categorizations of schools and sub-schools with respect to their positions on a number of topical categories, including *tawhid* (the affirmation of divine unity) and *qadar*, the issue of divine predetermination versus human free will.

The affirmation of divine unity is codified in the Islamic *shahada* or testimony (itself encoded in the call to prayer and recited five times a day): "No God but God and Muhammad is his Messenger." The common meaning of such affirmation is of course that there is only one Deity. To affirm any other deities is to be guilty of *shirk* (associationism), that is, the associating of other deities with the one God. To the theological mind, as demonstrated in case studies by Shahrastani, *tawhid* raised further questions. If there is only one Deity, how do the divine attributes in the Qur'an (Koran) (seeing, hearing, knowing, having compassion) relate to the Deity? Are they part of the divine essence? If so, are we to imagine a multiplicity of powers (knowing, hearing, seeing) existing from all eternity, and would that not be a subtle form of *shirk*, asserting

461

the existence of multiple, eternal powers? However, if the attributes are not part of the Deity's essence, then does the Deity change? Is it in a state of not-hearing at one time, and hearing at another, subject to accident and contingency?

Shahrastani demonstrates no particular dogmatic answer, but illuminates, rather, how the debate among various schools led to more profound questions. Shahrastani also takes up Qur'anic references to a Deity that sees, hears, creates "with two hands," and "sits on a throne." Some groups, such as the Mu'tazila, considered a literal interpretation of these images to be a form "likening" (*tashbih*) the Deity upon human characteristics, a procedure that would entail an anthropomorphic image just as idolatrous as idols made of wood and stone. They argued in favor of a figurative interpretation (*ta'wil*) that would explain how such figures of speech can refer to the one Divine Power.

Shahrastani shows us how the theological debate generated new positions, with some scholars arguing that attributes shared by humans (seeing, hearing, and so forth) are intrinsically anthropomorphic, and therefore affirming only those, such as power, knowledge, and will, which in their view belong to the Deity alone. Others argued that figurative interpretation is an "explaining away" of the Qur'anic text based upon the preferences of human rationalizing, and a stripping (*ta'til*) from the Deity of the attributes it has affirmed for itself in its own word.

Predetermination and Justice

Shahrastani's second theological category is divine predetermination (*qadar*). Several passages in the Qur'an emphasize the all-powerful nature of the Deity in a way that seems to preclude human will or choice; the Deity is said to "stop up the ears" of those who have rejected the Qur'anic message, for example. Other passages are urgent prophetic appeals to the hearer to choose the path of prophetic wisdom. If the response of the listener has already been predetermined by an all-knowing, all-powerful Deity, what is the status of such appeals? Is it fair or just for the Deity to then reward and

punish humans on the basis of a decision made from all time by that Deity?

Shahrastani quotes Wasil, the most famous theologian of the Mu'tazilite School of theology, who rejected divine predetermination:

> It is not possible for him [God] to will for his servants what is in disagreement with his command—to control their action and then punish them for what they did.

Later, he quotes 'Amr as asking, "Does he predestine me to do something and then punish me for it?" For the Mu'tazilites, the Deity is all-wise (*hakim*) and therefore must act in the interests of his creatures and with justice (*'adl*). Human beings have an innate capacity for understanding justice, right and wrong, without which they could not receive prophetic revelation in the first place. For their opponents, such statements are denial of divine power and knowledge; what the Deity does is, by nature, just—the Deity cannot be held accountable to fallible human understandings of what is just; and what the Deity imparts by way of revelation is in fact the only knowledge of right and wrong, and the only understanding of justice available to humankind.

Ironically, and confusingly, those who rejected divine predetermination (*qadar*) were called by the epithet the *qadariyya*. Those who affirmed predetermination were called the compulsionists (*jabriyya*). Those who appealed to the interpretations of the earliest companions of the prophets and rejected the theological attempt to apply formal human reason to such questions were called the traditionalists (*salaf*), but even this group finally accepted a form of theological discourse to defend their original anti-theological stance.

Another major group was called the attributionists (*sifatiyya*). This group originally sprang from the position of the theological al-Ash'ari, who vehemently maintained both the literalness of the attributes and the reality of divine predetermination. However, his school, the Ash'arites, later tried to walk a middle ground on both issues and came to be the most widely accepted theological school in

Islam. Some spoke of divine conditions (*ahwal*), which would be neither divine attributes eternally one with divine substance nor accidents that would prevail upon the Deity. In the area of divine predetermination, Shahrastani suggests that they tried to walk that middle ground by speaking of the Deity as creator of all acts, and of human beings as "acquiring" the power of the act at the moment of participation in it.

The Ash'arite School later was considered the "orthodoxy" among some writers, and some consideredShahrastani to be of that school. However, although he was willing to give his opinion, what makes Shahrastani's work reflective of a great thinker is not his argument for any particular position, but rather his ability to expound positions in such a way as to bring out the centrality of key theological issues and show how the Islamic tradition shaped itself around the effort to resolve those issues.

Cosmology, Heavenly Spheres, and Heavenly Ascent

Shahrastani's treatment of cosmology is particularly important. In his discussion of the pre-Socratic philosophers he outlines what we might call "neo-pre-Socratic Islamic thought," that is, the construction of the pre-Socratics by Islamic thinkers who then formed "schools" around them. Although much of the thought is consonant with what we know of Thales, Empedocles, and other pre-Socratics, it carries a new emphasis, with more thematic unity based upon more continued return to the question of the primal element "receptive of all forms." It is difficult to know, given the lack of other testimony, how much of the thematic unity is due to the Islamic schools themselves and how much is the work of Shahrastani.

Shahrastani also brings us the critical texts of the anonymous figure known as the "Greek Master" (*al-shaykh al-yunani*), texts that turn out to be the most radically apophatic passages of Plotinus, passages attempting to express the inexpressible. Shahrastani thus demonstrates that in addition to the more Aristotelian school of Islamic Plotinian

thought centered around the "Theology of Aristotle" (a careful paraphrase of Plotinus's *Enneads* 4, 5, and 6, but without the apophatic passages), there was a more mystically inclined school that focused on those Plotinian passages placing ultimate reality beyond the categories of being altogether.

Perhaps Shahrastani's most brilliant essay is that on the Sabaeans of Harran. Harran, the ancient city near the upper Tigris, was an early Islamic center of alternative philosophies, from the Hermeticists (devoted to Agathodaemon, Asclepius, and Hermes), to those following elaborate ritual calendars. Shahrastani places the Harranians in a debate with the *hanifs*. The word *hanif* was used in early Islam to refer to monotheists, particularly the pre-Islamic monotheists of Arabia; Abraham was considered the archetypal *hanif*.

The Harranians outline a cosmos made up of concentric spheres inhabited by spirits (*ruhaniyat*), and the goal of philosophy is either to ascend through the spheres to encounter the spirits, or to draw the spirits down into temples on Earth. From the spirits one receives true inspiration. The *hanifs* counter that the true bearers of truth are the prophets, who are, as in the *mi'raj* account of Muhammad's ascent through the Heavens, the guardians of the various Heavens.

As Shahrastani unfolds the argument, he demonstrates a fundamental tension in classical Islamic thought between the spiritualists (those who see the goal of philosophy as having become more spiritual—or, as in the case of Avicenna, more intellectual) and the humanists (those who see the goal as having become more human and who see the intermediaries of truth as the human prophets). Shahrastani thus helps us in understanding the symbolic significance of every detail of the cosmos of concentric spheres, the identity of the guardians of the spheres, the way in which human beings can rise through the spheres, the test by which they are tried at each sphere, and the ultimate arrival at the divine throne. This paradigm, which is fundamental not only to medieval Islam, but to medieval Judaism and Christianity as well (and which, indeed, served as one of the meeting places and places of contest among the three traditions) has a coded system of values that, through his debate format, Shahrastani helps to make explicit.

The analysis of theological debates about the unity of the Deity and divine predetermination, the philosophical cosmology of the pre-Socratics (as reconstructed in Islamic philosophy), the mystical dimension of Islamic Plotinian thought, and the symbolic cosmology of the heavenly spheres and their guardians are only some examples of Shahrastani's contributions. In these cases, and throughout his masterwork, he uses a categorization of schools to demonstrate how central questions, dilemmas, and symbols become the matrix for the development of ever more sophisticated versions of Islamic thought.

MICHAEL A. SELLS

Further Reading

Translations

Shahrastani, Muhammad ibn Abd al-Karim. "Kitab al-milal wa-al-nihal." *Les dissidences de l'islam*. Translated from the Arabic to French by Jean-Claude Vadet. Paris: P. Geuthner, 1984. The vast field of Shahrastani's thought has been relatively neglected in Islamic studies. This is one of two recent partial translations.

———. *Muslim Sects and Divisions: The Section on Muslim Sects in* Kitab al-milal wa 'l-nihal. Translated by A. K. Kazi and J. G. Flynn. London and Boston: Kegan Paul International, 1984.

AVERROES (IBN RUSHD)

Born: 520 A.H./1126 A.D., Córdoba, Spain
Died: 595 A.H./1198 A.D., Marrakech, Morocco
Major Works: *The Decisive Treatise*, *The Incoherence of the Incoherence*, *Commentary on Plato's* Republic, *Middle Commentary on Aristotle's* Rhetoric

Major Ideas

Philosophy does not contradict the revealed Law of Islam.
Rule by one or a few is better than rule by many.
Because the understanding of the mass of people is limited, the revealed Law speaks to them indirectly.
Recondite questions of faith should not be discussed in public.

Abū al-Walīd Muḥammad Ibn Aḥmad Ibn Muḥammad Ibn Rushd, or Averroes, as he is more commonly known in the West, differs from his predecessor, Avicenna, in that he wrote no autobiography and had no devoted disciple record his deeds. What little we do know about his life must be garnered from a few personal references scattered throughout his writings and from the Arab biographers as well as two famous historians of the Maghreb. In these sources, he is praised extravagantly for his intellectual excellence and profound accomplishments in jurisprudence, medicine, poetry, philosophy, natural science, and theology. The autobiographical references we encounter in his works serve mainly to explain the imperfect character of the work being offered to the public, but show thereby how busily engaged he was in other activities. Still, the biographical material is such that we know little about the major events in Averroes's life and even less about the circumstances surrounding his intellectual formation—that is, who his teachers were, what books he read, and the order he followed in his studies.

He was born in Córdoba in 520 A.H./1126 A.D., the son and grandson of noted *cadis*—his grandfather having served as the great *cadi* of Córdoba and of Andalusia. During the first twenty years of Averroes's life, there was much political upheaval in Andalusia. Wracked by internal dissension, the ruling Almoravid dynasty fell to the emergent Almohad forces under the famous warrior 'Abd al-Mu'min. The sources describe this as a period of

study for Averroes—one in which he devoted himself to jurisprudence, medicine, theology, and the natural sciences. Averroes is praised so for his devotion to study that he is said to have studied all but two nights of his life, that of his marriage and that of his father's death.

Though known as much for his practical activity as a *cadi* and adviser to rulers as for his theoretical accomplishments, we hear nothing of Averroes's political activity until he was nearly thirty. Called to Marrakech in 548 A.H./1153 A.D. by 'Abd al-Mu'min, then ruler of the Almohad dynasty, Averroes was named adviser to 'Abd al-Mu'min's grandiose project of building schools and literary institutions throughout the realm. By this time, he had already composed some treatises on logic. The most important event in Averroes's life, his presentation by Ibn Ṭufayl to Abū Ya'qub, 'Abd al-Mu'min's successor, as the one most qualified to undertake the task of commenting on Aristotle's works, did not take place for about another fifteen years.

The historians praise Abū Ya'qūb highly as an exceedingly handsome, courteous, intelligent, and well-educated man. He is said to have loved science and to have studied medicine as well as philosophy. Indeed, one account of Averroes's first meeting with Abū Ya'qūb emphasizes this ruler's philosophic learning: having asked Averroes his opinion about whether the world was created or has existed eternally—a question with far-reaching theological implications—and having noted Averroes's confusion about a suitable reply, Abū Ya'qūb turned to Ibn Ṭufayl to pursue the question and displayed such a mastery of the teachings of the philosophers about the problem that he reassured Averroes of the sincerity of his question.

Subsequent to this interview (565 A.H./1169 A.D.), Averroes was appointed *cadi* of Seville and held the post until he was called to Marrakech in 578 A.H./1182 A.D. as personal physician to Abū Ya'qūb. During these thirteen years, he composed middle commentaries on Aristotle's logical works, on most of the major works having to do with physical science, on the *Metaphysics*, and on the *Nichomachean Ethics*. Moreover, he wrote short commentaries or summaries on some of Aristotle's other works in natural science—that is, on the *Parts of Animals*, *Generation of Animals*, and *Parva Naturalia*, as well as two treatises, *On the Application of the Intellect and Intelligibles* and *On the Substance of the Celestial Sphere*. Averroes also composed a large commentary on Aristotle's *Posterior Analytics*. In addition to these writings related to Aristotle and Aristotelian investigations, Averroes composed treatises on topics of more immediate concern to fellow Muslims, namely the *Decisive Treatise*, with its introduction (*al-Ḍamīmah*) and sequel (*Kashf 'an Manāhij al-Adillah*), and the famous refutation of al-Ghazālī, the *Tahāfut al-Tahāfut* (*Incoherence of the Incoherence*).

The treatise *On the Substance of the Celestial Sphere*, dated in 574 A.H./1178 A.D. from Marrakech, and references in the *Meteorologica* to earthquakes occurring in Córdoba show that Averroes traveled extensively during these years. Serving as personal physician to Abū Ya'qūb only a matter of months, he was appointed *cadi* of Córdoba later in 578 A.H./1182 A.D. Abū Ya'qūb lost his life two years afterwards in the siege of Santarem and was succeeded by his son Ya'qūb ibn Yūsuf, also known as Abū Yūsuf and as al-Manṣūr, a ruler praised as a great warrior and a great builder. Averroes had a very close relationship with this ruler—almost one of intimate friendship—but was nonetheless punished, along with other notable scholars, for being overly occupied with philosophy and "the sciences of the ancients." The many

stories told to explain this unusual action on the part of a supposedly philosophically-minded ruler, ranging from desire to punish Averroes's suspected insolence to an attempt to calm zealous partisans of religion within the court, need not concern us here.

The punishment occurred in 592 A.H./1195 A.D., about a dozen years after Abū Yūsuf Ya'qūb began to rule, and involved Averroes being banished to Lucena, a small town near Córdoba. During those twelve relatively tranquil years, Averroes composed large commentaries on Aristotle's *Physics*, *On the Heavens*, *On the Soul*, and *Metaphysics*; a middle commentary on Galen's *On Fevers*; a short or middle commentary on Plato's *Republic*; and a small book entitled *On the Happiness of the Soul*. Averroes's banishment lasted only two years; having returned to the court in Marrakech, he died shortly afterwards in 595 A.H./1198 A.D.

Political Philosophy

Generally speaking, Averroes's works can be classified as (1) commentaries on Aristotle and other important thinkers and (2) occasional treatises written to resolve particular questions. His political teaching is stated most directly in the first kind of writings, especially in his commentaries on Aristotle's *Rhetoric* and Plato's *Republic*. Writings of the second kind develop some of his broader themes—especially the two treatises having to do with the relationship between philosophy and divine law, namely the *Decisive Treatise* and its sequel *Kashf 'an Manāhij al-Adillah*. Here we will focus primarily on what Averroes has to say about the different kinds of political regimes and, above all, the best regime, for his discussion of it leads him to reflect more generally on other major political questions.

From Averroes's *Commentary on Plato's* Republic we learn, above all, that the simply best regime is one in which the natural order among the virtues and practical arts is respected. The practical arts and the moral virtues exist for the sake of the deliberative virtues, and—whatever the hierarchical relationship between the practical arts and the moral virtues—all of these exist for the sake of the theoretical virtues. Only when this natural order is reflected in the organization and administration of the regime can there be any assurance that all of the virtues and practical arts will function as they ought. In order to have sound practice, then, it is necessary to understand the principles on which such practice depends: the order and the interrelationship among the parts of the human soul. He reaches the same conclusion, albeit much more rapidly, by identifying the best regime in his *Middle Commentary on Aristotle's* Rhetoric as the city whose opinions and actions are in accordance with what the theoretical sciences prescribe.

These principles permit Averroes to identify the flaws in the regimes he sees around him more clearly. They are faulted either because they aim at the wrong kind of end or because they fail to respect any order among the human virtues. Thus he blames democracy for the emphasis it places on the private and for its inability to order the desires of the citizens. In his *Commentary on Plato's* Republic, he first emphasizes the need to foster greater concern for the public sphere and to diminish the appeal of the private and then discusses the ultimate happiness of human beings in order to indicate how the desires should be properly ordered.

Some aspects of this teaching are problematic. However persuasive Averroes's arguments about the goodness of the best regime and the evils of the alternatives to it, one cannot fail to notice that he accepts without question the means advocated by Plato's Socrates for bringing it about and then preserving it once it has come into existence—means both immoral and unethical. With no hesitation, he recommends a lie to justify the class stratification fundamental to this regime. Moreover, he endorses deceptions concerning the equitable distribution of marriage partners, the way children will be accustomed to warfare, and the education of the wise. In addition, he approves of the proposition that older citizens who have allowed this regime to come into being will be expelled from it just as it is about to take shape.

Averroes accepts these lies, deceptions, and injustices because he contends that the plain truth is not always persuasive, that reason does not usually prevail. Most adults are like children in that they need to be trained to do what is right, and such training requires compulsion as well as deception. Unless the citizens can be induced to believe in a good that transcends their own immediate well-being, they will not make the sacrifices necessary for the establishment and functioning of the virtuous regime. Though a few may eventually come to understand why they must place the public good before their own private well-being and why they must subordinate their immediate desires to a more distant good, most will not.

In the *Decisive Treatise*, Averroes points to this same problem by referring to a famous Qur'anic passage. Noting that most scholars agree upon the need to address people with different levels of learning in ways suitable to them, he urges that this is precisely what the Qur'an (Koran) recommends. It is because religion, like politics, must take the whole citizen body into account that different kinds of speech and even different kinds of practices are justified. Moreover, those who would deny that the revealed law works in such a manner put the citizenry into danger. By explaining complicated matters of faith to those not able to follow the reasoning, these would-be teachers lead the less gifted into confusion and frequently into disbelief. A broad vision of the variety within the human soul and of what is needed for sound political life leads Averroes to endorse the tactics—and in some respects, the very principles—of Platonic politics.

CHARLES E. BUTTERWORTH

Further Reading

Translations

Averroes. *Averroes on Plato's "Republic."* Translated by Ralph Lerner. Ithaca, N.Y.: Cornell University Press, 1974. An intelligent and intelligible translation of a most important work.

———. "The Decisive Treatise." Translated by George F. Hourani. In *Averroes On the Harmony of Religion and Philosophy*, by George F. Hourani. London: Luzac, 1976. A competent translation accompanied by selections from other relevant texts, all fully annotated.

Related Studies

Butterworth, Charles E. *Philosophy, Ethics, and Virtuous Rule: A Study of Averroes'* Commentary on Plato's "Republic." Cairo Papers in Social Science, Vol. 9, Monograph 1. Cairo: AUC Press, 1986. A careful, fully annotated study of Averroes's *Commentary on Plato's* Republic.

———. "The Rhetorician and His Relationship to the Community." In *Islamic Theology and Philosophy: Studies in Honor of George F. Hourani*, edited by Michael E. Marmura. Albany, N.Y.: SUNY Press, 1983, pp. 111–136, 297–298. A comparison of the rhetorical and political teachings of the three major Islamic political philosophers al-Fārābī, Avicenna, and Averroes.

———. "Averroes: Politics and Opinion," *The American Political Science Review*. Vol. 66, 1972, pp. 894–901. An account of the way Averroes relates his scientific commentaries to his practical political teaching.

Mahdi, Muhsin S. "Averroës on Divine Law and Human Wisdom." In *Ancients and Moderns, Essays on the Tradition of Political Philosophy in Honor of Leo Strauss*, edited by Joseph Cropsey. New York: Basic Books, 1964, pp. 114–131. A study of the treatise usually considered as the appendix to Averroes's *Decisive Treatise*; Mahdi demonstrates that it should properly be considered a preface.

———. "Remarks on Averroes' *Decisive Treatise*." In *Islamic Theology and Philosophy: Studies in Honor of George F. Hourani*, edited by Michael E. Marmura. Albany, N.Y.: SUNY Press, 1983, pp. 188–202, 305–308. A careful exegesis of the political teaching contained in Averroes's masterful *Decisive Treatise*.

SUHRAWARDĪ

Born: 549 A.H./1153 A.D., Suhrawad, Iran
Died: 587 A.H./1191 A.D., Allepo, Syria
Major Works: *Philosophy of Illumination (Ḥikmat al-ishrāq), The Book of Intimations, The Book of Oppositions, The Book of Conversations, The Flashes of Light, The Knowledge of God, Treatise on Illumination*

Major Ideas

Knowing the truth requires the experience of illumination.
God is the Light of Lights (nūr al-anwār).
A rapprochement of discursive philosophy, intellectual intuition, and ascetic practices brings about illumination.
Any act of cognition requires knowledge of the self.
The self knows itself through an unmediated and direct relationship known as "Knowledge by Presence."
Essence is the primary aspect of an existent being; existence is the secondary.

Shihāb al-Dīn Suhrawardī, known as Shaīkh al-Ishrāq ("the master of illumination") as well as al-Maqtūl ("the Martyr"), was a Persian Muslim philosopher who founded the School of Illumination (ishrāq) Because of his controversial ideas, at the age of thirty-eight he was put to death by the order of Ṣalāh al-Dīn Ayyūbī, Saladin the Great, Syrian commander and sultan of Egypt.

Suhrawardī was born in a village near Zanjan, a northern Iranian city. His full name is Shahāb al-Dīn Yaḥyā ibn ḥabash ibn Amīrak Abūl Fūtūh Suhrawardī.

At an early age he went to the city of Maragheh, where he studied *hikmat* with Majd al-Dīn Jīlī, and he then traveled to Isfahan, where he studied philosophy with Zahir al-Dīn al-Fārsī and the *Observations (al-Baṣā'ir)* of 'Umar ibn Ṣālah al-Ṣawī. He then set out upon a long journey through the Islamic lands to meet the Sufi masters, while practicing asceticism and withdrawing for long spiritual retreats. He tells us that he had looked for a companion with spiritual insight equal to his, but he failed to find one.

Since Suhrawardī persisted in advocating a type of wisdom which was inconsistent with the views of the orthodox jurists, the jurists finally asked Mālik Zahīr, son of Ṣaladīn, to put Suhrawardī to death for advocating heretical ideas. When Mālik

Zahīr refused they signed a petition and sent it to Ṣaladīn, who ordered his son to have him killed. Mālik Zahīr reluctantly carried out his father's order and Suhrawardī was killed in the year 587 A.H./1191 A.D.

In light of the above factors, one can view Suhrawardī as a Persian who inherited a rich culture with Zoroastrian elements in it, a philosopher well-versed in Peripatetic (Aristotelian) philosophy, and a mystic who tried to demonstrate that at the heart of all the divinely revealed traditions of wisdom there is one universal truth.

Suhrawardī lived at a time when the two schools of philosophy and mysticism were perceived to be irreconcilable. In fact, the influence of discursive philosophy had been somewhat curtailed following the conversion of al-Ghazālī from a philosopher to a mystic. Suhrawardī argued that mysticism and philosophy are not irreconcilable and that the validity of the immutable principles of philosophy can be verified through the illumination of the intellect.

Suhrawardī and Aristotle

Suhrawardī argued that discursive reasoning is the necessary condition for the attainment of illumination. Toward this end he composed many treatises commenting on a wide range of traditional topics pertaining to Peripatetic philosophy. On the whole, where he speaks as a philosopher, he is a Peripatetic whose opinions are similar to those of Avicenna.

As to the most important debate in Islamic philosophy, the distinction between existence (*wujūd*) and essence (*māhiyyah*), Suhrawardī departs from the traditional Peripatetic understanding of them. Suhrawardī argues that the discussion concerning the principality of existence over essence neglects the fact that essence is a degree of existence.

Suhrawardī also criticizes Aristotle's theory of hylomorphism, arguing that corporeal beings are combinations of form and matter. Suhrawardī defines matter as a simple substance that is capable of accepting the forms of species. He then reduces physical features into qualities which can be expressed in terms of their ontological status.

Finally, Suhrawardī rejects the existing theories of vision that were held in the Middle Ages and proposes his own. He maintains that vision can occur when an object is lit. The soul of the observer then surrounds the illuminated object, and the illumination (*ishrāq*) of the soul (*nafs*) that then takes place through light emanated from the Light of Lights (*nūr al-anwār*) is vision.

Suhrawardī's Logic and Epistemology

Suhrawardī criticizes the traditional Aristotelian notion of categories and reduces them to four. He then criticizes the Peripatetics' concept of "definition" as that which provides us with the knowledge of what a thing is. He rejects the Peripatetics' claim that there is an essential nature of the human being indicated by the definition of the human being as a rational animal. Suhrawardī argues that other attributes of the human being are as important as rationality. Since there is no definition that can adequately disclose all the attributes of the human being, the definition as such remains an inadequate means of understanding. Suhrawardī demonstrates that empiricism and rationalism also fail and that their applications in epistemology are limited.

How a human being comes to know is a mystery, which despite his meditations Suhrawardī could not resolve. In a dream-vision Suhrawardī sees Aristotle, who resolves the mystery of how the self comes to know by telling Suhrawardī that to know anything one has to first know oneself.

Suhrawardī then argues that the fundamental principle of knowledge is that before the self is to know an object, it has to know itself. The self knows itself through a direct and immediate relationship known as "Knowledge by Presence" (*'Ilm al-ḥuḍurī*).

The Light of Lights

Suhrawardī departs from traditional Islamic ontology by arguing that the source of being is not simply being but *light*. Assuming that light is necessary since the cognition of everything else requires it, beings in the world are therefore defined in terms of their ontological status and the degree of their luminosity. The beings closer to the Light of Lights are more transparent and ontologically superior. Light, as an axiomatic truth and thereby self-evident, is made up of an infinite succession of contingent lights, and each light is the existential cause of the light below it. The ultimate light, which is the same as the Necessary Being (*wājib al-wujūd*), is for Suhrawardī the Light of Lights, the ultimate cause of all things. As the ontological distance between the object and the Light of Lights grows, darkness prevails until the object in question becomes impenetrable to light. Suhrawardī identifies the world of such objects with the corporeal world in which we live.

For Suhrawardī, just as light has degrees of intensity, so does darkness. Although he classifies light in accordance with the extent to which light exists by necessity, his criterion for determining the ontological status of beings is whether they are conscious of themselves or not. Self-awareness is absent when a being is impenetrable to light.

Relying on his ontological system, Suhrawardī reduces quantity to quality. According to him, it is not the case that a two-foot stick of wood is "longer" than a one-foot stick. For Suhrawardī, this relation should be expressed in terms of "more" or "less." Therefore, it is the case that a two-foot stick is "more" than the one-foot stick.

This "more" or "less" becomes meaningful within the context of a hierarchical ontology. The closer a being is to the Light of Lights, the more it "is." Some beings therefore "are" more than others, depending on the degree of their closeness to the Light of Light. Applying this concept to human beings, Suhrawardī argues that those who have mastered discursive philosophy and intellectual intuition and have practiced asceticism are more "luminous," in the metaphysical sense of light, and are therefore closer to the Light of Lights.

Angelology

Having used the symbolism of light and darkness, Suhrawardī goes on to develop an elaborate angelology based on a Zoroastrian theory of angels. Thereby, once again, he joined two religious universes, those of Islam and Zoroastrianism.

All beings, according to Suhrawardī, are the illuminations of the Light of Lights, which has left its vice-regent in each domain. The lordly light (*nur ispahbad*), which is the vicegerent of the Light of Lights in the human soul, accounts for the joy of human beings when they see fire or the sun.

Between the Light of Lights and its opposite pole, the corporeal world, there are levels and degrees of light, which Suhrawardī identifies with the various levels of angelic order. Suhrawardī's use of Zoroastrian symbolism is partly done in the spirit of his ecumenical philosophy in order to demonstrate that since the inner truth of all religions is the same, some concepts of a religious tradition can often be used to interpret and clarify the concepts of another tradition.

From the Light of Lights comes the "longitudinal" angelic order, which Suhrawardī identifies with a masculine aspect such as dominance, whereas contemplation and independence give rise to a "latitudinal" order. Suhrawardī identifies the latitudinal angelic order with Platonic ideas. From the feminine aspect of the longitudinal order comes into being the Heaven of fixed stars.

For Suhrawardī there exists a veil between each level of light, which acts as a "purgatory" or *Barzakh* and allows the passage of only a certain amount of light. The primordial, original, and all-encompassing nature of this system, through which Suhrawardī expresses a number of esoteric doctrines, is such that he calls it *al-ūmmahāt* (the mother), since all that exists originates from this hierarchy and, therefore, contains within itself the "ideas" (*a'yan thābita*) whose unfolding is the world.

Angelology in Suhrawardī's philosophy is a two-fold concept: first, it is an attempt to map out the world. Second, through the use of angelic symbolism, the correspondence between the human being as the microcosm and the universe as the macrocosm is further demonstrated.

This new philosophy of angels changes the traditional view of angels as the sustainers of the universe. According to Suhrawardī, angels serve a number of functions, the most important of which is their intermediary role between the Light of Lights and humanity. For instance, the "lordly light" (*al-nūr al-isfahbodī*) is defined by Suhrawardī as that which is "within the soul of man."

Psychology

Suhrawardī relies heavily upon Avicennian psychology. In fact, his classification of the faculties of the soul remains Avicennian, in which the faculty of the soul is divided in three parts, the vegetative soul (*al-nafs al-nabātiyyah*), the animal soul (*al-nafs al-ḥayāwanīyyah*), and the intellectual soul (*al-nafs nāṭiqah*).

Suhrawardī argues that, in addition to the five external senses, the human being possesses five internal senses that serve as a bridge between the physical and the spiritual world. The internal senses, according to Suhrawardī, are: *sensus communis*, fantasy, apprehension, imagination, and memory.

Physics

In putting forth his views on physics, Suhrawardī begins with a discussion regarding the nature of the universe, which from his point of view is pure light. The views of the 'Asharī'te atomists, who were one of the predominant intellectual schools of the time, were based on the principality of form and matter and, therefore, the study of physics for them became the study of matter. Suhrawardī argues against them by saying that since material bodies are constituted of light, the study of physics is the study of light.

Having defined the nature of things as light, Suhrawardī goes on to classify things according to the degree of their transparency. For example, all those objects that allow light to pass through them, such as air, are in a different ontological category from those that obstruct light, such as earth.

In explaining meteorological phenomena, Suhrawardī follows Avicenna and Aristotle, but he rejects their views concerning change within things. For example, whereas Aristotle argues that the boiling of water is caused by the atoms of fire coming in contact with water, Suhrawardī states that boiling depends on a quality in water such that when water comes close to fire the potentiality for boiling is actualized. He argues that when water boils in a jug of water placed over a fire, the fire does not come in contact with the water nor does the volume of water change. Suhrawardī draws the conclusion that there exists a special quality or attribute within water which is receptive to the influence of heat.

It is obvious that such a theory has implications not only for the field of physics but also as an esoteric doctrine that seeks to explain how the association of different things may create qualitative changes within beings. This principle is one of the crucial elements in the development of spiritual alchemy, which appears in Islamic esoteric writings.

Eschatology

Suhrawardī contends that the Peripatetic argument for the subsistence of the soul is weak and insufficient. Using his ontological scheme based on light and darkness, Suhrawardī argues that all souls, depending on the degree of their perfection, seek unity with their origin, the Light of Lights. The degree of one's purification in this world determines the ontological status of the soul in the other world. According to Suhrawardī, the goal of the human being is to become illuminated and return to its origin in the other world. The other world is only a continuation of this one, and the status of the soul in the other world depends on the degree to which a person is purified here and now.

Suhrawardī identifies three groups of people according to the degree of their purity and illumination and establishes a causal connection between their purity and their ontological status in the other world. These three groups are:

1. Those who remain in the darkness of ignorance (*'Ashqīya'*),
2. Those who purify themselves to some extent (*Sūdad*), and
3. Those who purify themselves and reach illumination (*mūta'allihun*).

History of Philosophy

Suhrawardī, who adhered to the notion of *Philosophia Perennis*, or what he called *Ḥikmat al-Ladūnniyyah* or *Ḥikmat al-'Atīqah*, maintains that the eternal truth has existed always among the followers of divinely revealed religions. For Suhrawardī, philosophy is identified with *Sophia Perennis*, the perennial wisdom, rather than with rationalizing alone. From an Ishrāqī point of view, Hermes (Prophet Idris, Enoch, or Khidr) is the father of wisdom who initiated *Sophia Perennis*. From him two chains of transmission branch off; one branch is preserved and transmitted through the Persian masters and the other one through Greco-Egyptian masters, until Suhrawardī, who considers himself to be the reviver of perennial wisdom.

For Suhrawardī there are four types of people within the hierarchy of knowledge:

1. The *ḥakims*, who have mastered both discursive philosophy and gnosis.
2. The class of philosophers who are masters of practical wisdom and do not involve themselves with discursive philosophy.

3. The philosophers who know discursive philosophy but are alien to gnosis, such as al-Fārābī and Averroes.

4. The seekers of knowledge who have not mastered either of the two branches of wisdom, rationalist or practical philosophy.

Influence of Suhrawardī on Islamic Philosophy

Suhrawardī's philosophy was a turning point in the history of Islamic philosophy in that it presents the first serious attempt for a rapprochement between mysticism and rationalist philosophy. Suhrawardī's methodology of reconciling discursive reasoning with intellectual intuition remained the cornerstone of Islamic philosophy, especially in the eastern part of the Islamic world.

Suhrawardī's philosophy gave rise to the School of Iṣfahān during the Safavid era in Persia when such notable masters of the ishrāqī doctrine as Mullā Ṣadrā, who propagated Suhrawardī's doctrine with substantial modifications, established a philosophical paradigm on its foundations.

Ishrāqī philosophy is a living philosophical tradition in many parts of the Islamic world, in particular, in Iran, Pakistan, and India.

The primary concern of Suhrawardī's entire philosophy is to demonstrate the complete journey of the human soul towards its original abode. Having mastered rationalist philosophy, one should then follow the teachings of a master who can direct the disciple through the maze of spiritual dangers. It is only through a combination of practical and theoretical wisdom that one reaches a state where spiritual knowledge can be obtained directly without mediation.

MEHDI AMINRAZAVI

Notes on the Works of Suhrawardī

Suhrawardī was immensely prolific. Fifty of his works have survived and they can be placed in five different categories:

1. The four texts of doctrinal nature written in Arabic, *Talwīḥāt* (*Intimation*), *Maqāwamāt* (*Opposites*), *Mūṭāraḥāt Conversations*) and his magnum opus, *Ḥikmat al-ishrāq* (*Philosophy of Illumination*). The first three books are written in the tradition of the Peripatetics and *Ḥikmat al-ishrāq* is written in the "Language of Illumination" (*Lisān al-ishrāqī*).

2. A number of treatises that are also of doctrinal significance, some of which can be regarded as commentaries on the four major works. These include: *Hayākil al-nūr, Yazdān shinākht, Būstān al-qulūb, Alwāḥ al-'Imādīyyah, Partaū-nāmah, al-Lamaḥāt*.

3. There is a group of highly esoteric narratives, written mostly in Persian. They are: *'Aql-i surkh, Lūqhat-i Mūrān, Āwāz-i Par-i jibra'īl, al-Ghūrbat al-Gharbīyyah, Rūzī ba jamā'at-i sūfīyān, Risālah fī al-Mi'rāj, ṣafīr-i sīmūrgh*. The central theme of the above works is the spiritual journey of humanity and the dangers therein.

4. A number of shorter commentaries and translations into Persian. This category includes the translation of Avicenna's *Risālah al-ṭa'īr* (*Treatise on Birds*) and his commentary upon Avicenna's *al-Ishārāt wa'l tanbīhāt* (*The Book of Directives and Remarks*).

5. A number of litanies, invocations, papers, and what his commentator Shahrazuri calls *al-warīdāt wal-Taqdīsāt*.

Further Reading

Jurji, E. J. "The Ishraqi Revival of al-Suhrawardi," *Journal of the American Oriental Society*. No. 60, 1940. A discussion of the revival of the School of Illumination.

———. "The Illuministic Sufis," *Journal of the American Oriental Society*. No. 57, 1937. This essay discusses the significance and influence of Suhrawardī and his thought on Islamic mysticism.

———. "The Relationship Between Sufism and Philosophy in Persian Culture," *Hamdard Is-*

lamicus, Vol. 6, No. 4, 1983. Another very helpful analysis.

———. "Spiritual Movements, Philosophy and Theology in the Safavid Period." In *Cambridge History of Iran*, Vol. 6. Cambridge: Cambridge University Press, 1986. A general survey of the later developments and the impact of Suhrawardī's philosophy of illumination.

———. "The Spread of the Illuminationist School of Suhrawardi," *Islamic Quarterly*. Vol. 14, No. 1, 1970. An explanatory and historical account.

Nasr, Seyyed Hossein. *Three Muslim Sages*. New York: Carvan Books, 1969. Includes a general survey of Suhrawardī's life and thought.

Tehrani, Kazem. *Mystical Symbolism in Four Treatises of Suhrawardi*. Ph.D. dissertation, Columbia University, 1974. A careful analysis of four treatises written in Persian.

Thackston, W. M. *Mystical and Visionary Treatise of Suhrawardi*. London: The Octagon Press, 1982. A translation of a number of Suhrawardī's mystical narratives written in Persian.

———. "Shihab al-Din Suhrawardi." In *A History of Muslim Philosophy*, Vol. 2, edited by M. M. Sharif. Wiesbaden: O. Harrassowitz, 1966, pp. 372–398. A detailed but general study of Suhrawardī that encompasses various aspects of Suhrawardī's philosophy.

IBN ʿARABĪ

Born: 1165, Murcia, Andalusia, Spain
Died: 1240, Damascus, Syria
Major Works: *Interpreter of Desires* (1214–15), *The Ringsettings of Wisdom* (begun in 1229), *Meccan Openings* (1201–38)

Major Ideas

The Real (al-ḥaqq) *is simultaneously beyond all names and logical categories and immanent in its own self-revelation through them.*

The Real cannot be known dualistically, as an object by a subject.

Human consciousness is the prism and mirror in which the undifferentiated Real reveals and refracts itself into its attributes.

The Real can only be known insofar as the human ego-self passes away and the Real reveals itself at the moment of passing away.

The Real in its transcendent identity is beyond polarities of lord and servant, divine and non-divine.

The manifestations of the Real are in constant flux.

The Real cannot be delimited or fixed in any single manifestation.

True understanding occurs only to those who are themselves in a state of in constant self-transformation.

Ibn ʿArabi (Muḥyiddīn Ibn al-ʿArabī) was born in Murcia, Andalusia. As a boy he was already famous enough for the philosopher Averroes (Ibn Rushd) to request an audience with him. He traveled throughout the centers of learning of his time: Seville, Córdoba, Marrakech, Tunis, Cairo, Konya, Mecca, Baghdad, and Damascus, where he died and where his tomb has become a popular shrine.

Ibn ʿArabi's ideas represent and culminate the third major phase of Sufi thought. In the first phase, thinkers such as Rabiʿa, Junayd, and Bistami articulated the Sufi concept of mystical experience as the passing away of the human ego-self (*nafs*) and a Sufi way of life centered in that experience, and a Sufi affirmation of divine union as the immersion of human consciousness in one divine beloved to the point of obviousness to all other things. In the second phase, represented by Sulami, Sarraj, Makki, Qushayri, and al-Ghazālī, the Sufi experience of mystical union and the Sufi way of life were more explicitly integrated with ritual Islam and Islamic theology.

With Ibn ʿArabi, mystical union becomes not only the central moment in the affirmation of divine union and in the life of the Sufi, but it becomes the central event within mystical language as well, an event that fundamentally transforms all language concerned with ultimate reality, reconfiguring and sometimes shattering the normal dualisms of subject and object, human and divine, before and after, self and other.

Ibn ʿArabi's writings mirror his philosophy of "perpetual transformation." His works—over 200 of them—continually move through the discourses of law, comparative philosophy, Islamic theology, esoteric sciences (alchemy, astrology, number symbolism, and talismans), meditative practice, Qurʾanic interpretation, *hadith* sciences, theory of prophecy, and sainthood. Rather than forming a system, and certainly not forming a static philosophy of "oneness of reality" as the "sum" of all things (a conception that was due to later systematizers and followers of Ibn ʿArabi), his work resists closure and analysis by linear development. Like a moving picture made up of separate frames, it is the moving image that is meaningful, not the series of static frames. This method of writing is a perfect reflection of the dynamism of Ibn ʿArabi's philosophy.

Divine Attributes and Human Consciousness

Ibn 'Arabi's thinking has been labeled as "theosophy," but its originality and most lasting contribution are in the domain of apophatic thought, sometimes called "negative theology" (having to do with matters that are inexpressible). In this sense his thinking and writing put his work alongside that of Plotinus (d. 270), Moses de Leon (d. 1305), Marguerite Porete (d. 1310), and Meister Eckhart (d. c. 1327) within the simultaneous flowering of Islamic, Jewish, and Christian mystical thought of the twelfth and thirteenth centuries.

As with the other practitioners of apophatic thinking, Ibn 'Arabi begins from a critique of any attempt to refer to or name the transcendent, and ends with a dialectically simultaneous affirmation of absolute transcendence and absolute immanence. Ibn 'Arabi's positions are grounded in previous controversies of scholastic theology (*kalam*). After several centuries of growth, Islamic theology had divided into hundreds of schools of thought, all seeking to harmonize the absolute oneness of the Deity with the various attributes (ninety-nine attributes in the Qur'an [Koran]) ascribed to it. Are these attributes ("the hearer," "the seer," "the compassionate," and so forth) the same as the essence of the Deity? If so, then the Deity has a plurality of eternal powers. If the attributes are not co-eternal, then the deity is subject to accident and change, in a state of not-hearing in one instant, for example, and hearing in the next.

The quandary was vividly dramatized in the debate over a *hadith* (a saying of the Prophet Mohammed), parallel to a passage in Genesis, in which the Deity is said to have created Adam "in his image." If the "his" refers to the Deity, then how is one to conceive of a transcendent, infinite Deity confined to an "image"? Some theologians responded that the "his" must refer to Adam, to Adam's being made as a full human, rather than going through a period of gestation, for example. The Deity transcends all images. Ibn 'Arabi's solution to this dilemma was to combine the Sufi concept of mystical union with his concept of the "complete human being." Adam, as the symbol of the complete human, that is, of archetypal human consciousness, is the mirror through which the Deity reveals its own attributes to itself, and the prism through which its undifferentiated unity is refracted into the various attributes.

The attributes of the Deity do not exist in themselves, nor are they purely categories of human imagination. They are actualized only at the point that the mirror of human consciousness is polished and the reflections in it become visible. By combining cosmic and the individual, macrocosm and microcosm, Ibn 'Arabi treats this polishing of the mirror as any human's "passing away" in union with the divine beloved. When the Sufi, following the Sufi path outlined by Qushayri and Rabi'a, achieves a point where his or her ego-self is annihilated, then the Deity reveals itself in the polished mirror of that Sufi's heart. At this point, to paraphrase the crucial *hadith* of mystical union, the Deity becomes

> the hearing with which he hears, the seeing with which he sees, the hands with which he touches, the feet with which he walks, the tongue with which he speaks.

In dialectical terms, this "polishing of the mirror" is a co-creation in which both the Deity and human (as manifested entities endowed with form and categories) are created in the polished mirror of the complete human being. A lord cannot exist without a servant, a creator Deity cannot exist without a creation in which it manifests itself and reflects itself. Ultimate reality, what Ibn 'Arabi calls the identity or self of the Real (*dhat al-haqq*), lies beyond all such dualisms. The antecedent of "his" in "in his image" is neither the Deity by itself nor Adam by himself, but the Deity–human at the moment of mystical union. The image occurs within the polishing of the mirror when the Deity's image is revealed and prismatically refracted in its attributes within the polished mirror of the human heart.

Intellectual Binding and Perpetual Transformation

From the perspective of eternity, this self-revelation always has occurred. However, from the perspective of time, it is ephemeral. It cannot be possessed. Ibn ʿArabi takes the dynamic notion of "the moment" as developed by earlier Sufis such as Qushayri and makes it the centerpiece of his mystical dialectic. Quoting a Qur'anic passage that refers to the Deity as being in every moment in a different condition, Ibn ʿArabi states that the image of the eternal and infinite when it occurs in time is in a state of perpetual transformation. In every moment the image changes. Each image is formed by the linguistic, conceptual, philosophical, and psychological categories of the persons in which it appears. Each is a valid manifestation of the Deity.

The central intellectual error, the cause of religious and philosophical disputes and violence, is the attempt to "bind" the Deity into a particular fixed image. The human analytical intellect functions according to the principle of binding. It constructs both grammar and logic according to bound or delimited categories: self and other, subject and predicate, before and after, here and there. When the binding categories of language and logic are applied to the Deity, an image of the Deity is formed. This image is valid—but only "for the moment."

When the human being clings to the image and reifies it, however, "binding" leads to idolatry. The most disastrous idolatry of all occurs when people bind the Deity into their own affirmations of its transcendence. In his critique of the Qur'anic Noah, who called upon God to annihilate the idolaters, Ibn ʿArabi suggests that Noah himself "bound" the Deity into the idol of the "beyond the world," an image just as limiting (by marking of the Deity from the world) as the polytheists' images of the Deity "within" their images of stones and wood. The unlimited must simultaneously be beyond all things, within all things, other than all things, and identical with all things. This critique applies to Sufis as well those who are tempted to bind the Deity into a particular station, vision, or experience.

The intellectual activity of binding, therefore, must be complemented by "perpetual transformation" (*taqallub*). The polished mirror of the human heart—as locus not of emotion, but of this higher knowledge—is capable of every form. This phrase "capable of every form" becomes the central concept in Ibn ʿArabi's famous collection of love poetry, *Interpreter of Desires*, a volume that together with a later commentary plays upon that creative tension—so important in Sufi thought—between love poetry and philosophical analysis. Ibn ʿArabi evokes the classical motif of the lover's meditation on the lost beloved and his dwelling upon the beloved's departure with the women of her tribe and the "stations" along their journey away from the poet.

For Ibn ʿArabi the beloved and the women of her tribe are aligned with the ephemeral images or manifestations of the Real. The movement *toward* the beloved (symbolized by the movement of the pilgrim through the stations of the *hajj*, the pilgrimage to Mecca) are identical to the movements of the divine manifestations *away* from the human knower. The human being who accepts the condition of fundamental humanity is thus in a state of continual joy and continual sorrow. In every moment he passes away in union with the divine beloved, the beloved appears in the reflection of the polished mirror of his heart, and—most importantly—the human accepts the immediate disappearance of that image so that it can be replaced by a new image. The angels who objected to the creation of Adam, a creature who would "spill blood and cause corruption" (Qur'an, 2:30–33), failed to understand this notion of the role of humanity as the locus of a continuing kaleidoscope of divine manifestation.

When the mystic achieves this state of perpetual transformation, he or she is able to participate fully in the perpetual co-creation. In a Sufi appropriation and transformation of the metaphysics of scholastic theology, the world is annihilated and re-created in every moment. However, instead of the re-creation of the objective world by an independent creator Deity—as we find in scholastic theology—the Sufi re-creation is the mutual construction of the divine attributes and human categories within the polished mirror of the human heart, a construction that is renewed in each moment (*waqt*).

Different people have moments of different lengths. Some never achieve an image of reality. Some achieve one in a lifetime and hold on to it with dogmatic fervor. Some achieve one in a year. Some in a month. In a remarkable parallel to the dynamist notion of transcendence and immanence found later in Meister Eckhart, Ibn 'Arabi, like Eckhart, emphasizes the continual creation of the divine image in every new moment, a creation that simultaneously always has occurred and always is occurring. Ibn 'Arabi identifies the eternal "breath of the compassionate" by which Allah breathed spirit into his creation, through Adam, with the breaths of the individual Sufi. The goal of Sufi meditation and annihilation in mystical union is to make "his/His moment his/His breath." The alternate pronouns show that the referent at any moment is both the divine and the human as they mutually construct one another within the polished mirror and prism. Ibn 'Arabi also speaks of the divine as revealing it(self) to it(self) through it(self), again fusing the two possible pronouns of the pronoun (reflexive and non-reflexive) into one. When Ibn 'Arabi asks who reveals whom in whom and through whom, he stresses the transformation of categories of reflexive and non-reflexive, self and other, at the moment of mystical union.

Ibn 'Arabi proclaimed that the heart capable of every form can receive and affirm all valid manifestations: the Torah, the Qur'an, the Christian monk's cell, the abode of idol, the meadow of gazelles. Wherever the "caravan of love" leads, Ibn 'Arabi writes in his most famous poem from the *Interpreter of Desires*, that is his religion, his faith. This famous statement is not a call for tolerance, a weak virtue in which one agrees to ignore other beliefs or to allow them to exist. Rather, it is a call for a complete immersion in and acceptance of all manifestations of reality.

Such acceptance is perpetually both critical and self-critical of the ways in which delimited images of ultimate reality can be reified and idolized. The heart capable of every form is a conception of a knowing faculty that is dialectical in the sense of seeing each manifestation as the abode of divine immanence which simultaneously points to the Real's transcendence of all images. It is also dynamic in that the joy of receiving one manifestation is accompanied by the sorrow at losing the previous manifestation, a joy and a sorrow that are ultimately part of the one experience of mystical union, perpetually reenacted in each moment.

Ibn 'Arabi's thought was systematized by later followers, and throughout the period of classical Islam, the influence of Ibn 'Arabi was central. In the modern period that influence came under attack from some modernists who were influenced by positivist Western ways of thinking and by dogmatists such as the Wahhabis of Saudi Arabia (where Ibn 'Arabi's works are banned). In recent years there has been a strong worldwide resurgence of interest in Ibn 'Arabi, known as "The Grand Master" (*al-shaykh al-akbar*) of Islamic mystical philosophy.

MICHAEL A. SELLS

Further Reading

Translations

Ibn al-'Arabi. *Bezels of Wisdom*. New York: Paulist Press Classics of Western Spirituality, 1980. Translated by Ralph Austin. This complete translation of Ibn 'Arabi's most influential work also includes very helpful introductions to each chapter.

——— . *Les Illumination de La Mecque* [*The Meccan Illuminations*]. Translated by Michel Chodkiewicz, William Chittick, Cyrille Chodkiewicz, Denis Gril, and James Morris. Paris: Sindbad, 1988. Major scholars in the field have collaborated in this rich selection of translations (with introductory commentaries) from Ibn 'Arabi's greatest work, the *Meccan Openings* (or *Meccan Illuminations*).

Related Studies

Chittick, William. *The Sufi Path of Knowledge*. Albany, N.Y.: SUNY, 1989. This volume offers a synoptic view of Ibn 'Arabi's metaphysics with extensive translations from the *Meccan Openings*.

Hirtenstein, S. and M. Tiernan, eds. *Muhyiddin Ibn 'Arabi: A Commemorative Volume*. Dorset, England: Element, 1993. This collection presents an outstanding set of translations and essays by Ibn 'Arabi scholars from the Middle East, North America, and Europe.

Hirtenstein, S., ed. *Journal of the Muhyiddin Ibn 'Arabi Association*. Oxford: 1981. This journal has become a central source for new scholarship and interpretation in Ibn 'Arabi studies.

Sells, Michael A. *Mystical Languages of Unsaying*. Chicago: University of Chicago Press, 1994. Ibn 'Arabi's mystical language is placed in detailed, critical comparison with selected texts of Plotinus, Erigena, Marguerite Porete, and Meister Eckhart.

SIRHINDĪ

Born: 971 A.H./1564 A.D., Sirhind, India
Died: 1034 A.H./1624 A.D., Sirhind, India
Major Works: *Maktūbāt* (*Letters*), *Mabda'-ō-Ma'ād* (*Origin and Return*), *Ithbāt al-Nubuwwa* (*The Affirmation of Prophecy*)

Major Ideas

The world is not the same as the Divine Being, but has a reality of its own.
Living according to the tenets and practice of orthodox Islam is a prerequisite for traveling the Sufi path of individual purification and realization.
The highest state of spiritual progress is that of the Prophet Muhammad, but spiritual aspirants, by being followers and heirs of the Prophet, can ensure the continuity of the reformist mission in the world.

Shaikh Aḥmad Sirhindī was primarily a mystical thinker and Sufi master. His activities in reformulating major Sufi ideas led to his being given the epithet "Renewer of the Second Millennium" (*Mujaddid-e-Alf-e-Thānī*), since the dates of his life (971–1034 A.H.) spanned the opening years of the second millennium of the Islamic calendar. According to a tradition of the Prophet Muhammad, a great Muslim leader will arise at the beginning of each century to renew the religion. In his thought Sirhindī elaborated on the role of this "Renewer" (*Mujaddid*), and even today he is generally known as the *Mujaddid* while the branch of the Naqshbandī order which he founded is known as the *Mujaddidī*. The influence of this branch eventually spread far beyond India to the Arab Middle East, Central Asia, Turkey, and other regions, and it remains one of the most vital spiritual and occasionally political forces in the contemporary Muslim world.

Scholars generally speak of two phases to Sirhindī's career. The early one featured training in the Islamic intellectual tradition and initiation in two major Sufi orders, Chishtī and Qadirī, after which he attained a respectable position as a scholar of Islam at the court of the Mughal emperor Akbar.

The second phase in his career began in 1598 A.D. in Delhi, where he met Khwaja Bāqī bi'llāh, a Naqshbandī Sufi master from Afghanistan who had recently come to India. Under this master he attained higher states of spiritual realization, which convinced him of the necessity of combining orthodox practice of the Islamic tradition with mystical experience.

Sirhindī became a prominent spiritual teacher in the Naqshbandī order and wrote extensively on matters of Islamic mysticism, theology, and his own spiritual experience. At certain points in these writings he also commented on the religious policies that he felt should be adopted by the Mughal state.

Scholars differ concerning the prominence of political opinions in Sirhindī's thought. The most recent Western academic studies, based on the content of Sirhindī's writings and the response of his contemporaries and successors to them, conclude that he was primarily a Sufi theorist. In South Asia, however, his image has gradually developed so as to portray him as an incipient Muslim nationalist who challenged the syncretistic religious tendencies of the Mughal court. Proponents of this view cite as evidence the fact that he was publicly reprimanded and even imprisoned for about a year in 1619 A.D. before being released and ultimately honored by the emperor Jahāngīr. Those who emphasize the Sufi element of Sirhindī's concerns note that Jahāngīr complains in his memoirs about Sirhindī's arrogance and theories, rather than objecting to any specifically political recommendations on his part.

Following his release from prison he returned to

Sirhind and for the rest of his life continued his literary and spiritual teaching activities. His sons, in particular Muḥammad Maʿṣūm (d. 1668 A.D.), and their successors continued the *Mujaddidī* Sufi line and left their own collections of letters and practical Sufi manuals in the tradition of their illustrious ancestor.

The Letters (Maktūbāt) of Sirhindī

The most important literary legacy of Sirhindī is undoubtedly his three volumes of collected letters, known as the *Maktūbāt*, most of which are written in Persian, although some entire letters and many phrases are written in Arabic. The 534 letters were collected and edited during his lifetime by three of his disciples under his supervision. About a third of the letters are in the form of answers to questions he was asked. About half of the letters run less that twenty lines, although a few of them are as long as twenty pages. The tradition of writing one's major ideas in the form of a personal letter but with a wider audience in mind is quite typical of this period of Sufism, both within and beyond South Asian Islam, and numerous such collections exist. The challenge to the scholar is that the letters must be carefully sifted through, as the doctrines presented in them are not organized thematically or presented systematically.

Among the major points discussed in the *Maktūbāt* are "the unity of appearance," practical mysticism, and the respective ranks of the prophet and the saint. Within each of these topics one may point to a humanistic factor, in the sense of affirming the purpose and significance of human activities in reforming both the inner self and the outer world, which works throughout Sirhindī's thought.

The Unity of Experience (Waḥdat al-Shuhūd)

The concept of the unity of experience essentially concerns the relationship between the Creator and the Creation. One of the more intensely debated issues in Sufism in the later periods was tension between monism and dualism in mystical thought and, more generally, in the Islamic worldview. Since these Sufi philosophical doctrines were often expressed in very abstract symbols and expressions, it is difficult to explicitly characterize figures such as the Sufi philosopher Ibn ʿArabī (d. 1240 A.D.) as having been exclusively monistic. Based primarily on the thought of Ibn ʿArabī's successors and on the popularization of his ideas through vehicles such as mystical poetry, many Sufis came to consider that the doctrine of the "Unity of Existence" (*waḥdat al-wujūd*), which they attributed to Ibn ʿArabī, was uncompromisingly monistic.

In response to this metaphysically monistic and ethically relativistic outlook Sirhindī propounded a complex cosmological system that detailed the relationship between God and the world in such as way as to provide a more positive existential status to the creation and human activities.

His theory came to be known as the "Unity of Appearance" (*waḥdat al-shuhūd*). In formulating it he criticized some aspects of the "Greatest Shaikh's" (Ibn ʿArabī's) teachings, but remained highly influenced by others and often cites him approvingly. Among the features of Sirhindī's philosophical system is the idea that in the creative process the divine names are emanated from the mind of God into the world, where they must encounter their opposites in order to be fully discerned and experienced. The world, therefore, is not the same as the Divine Being, but rather has a shadowy or adumbrated reality of its own. By positing this reality as apart from that of God, Sirhindī is able to assert a real existential status to evil, as opposed to the relativism entailed by absolute monism.

The Mystical Path

For Sirhindī, living according to the tenets and practice of orthodox Islam is a prerequisite for traveling the Sufi path of individual purification and realization. The main purpose of this path is certainty of faith rather than hidden knowledge. However, those who grasp the essence or the inner dimension of the Islamic Law (*sharīʿa*), are at a higher level than those who simply enact the outer formal requirements.

Sirhindī continued to stress the element of sobriety characteristic of Naqshbandī Sufis. In this context he disapproved of mystical practices incorporating dancing, music, or trance states. He advocated the practice of silent *dhikr*, the calm and focused recitation of the names and attributes of God and other pious phrases. According to Sirhindī, the spiritual aspirant, under the close supervision and guidance of a Sufi master, pursues an itinerary of spiritual progress that reverses the process of the descent of the divine reality into physical manifestation.

Each person possesses a subtle body composed of ten spiritual centers known as the *laṭā'if*, including the "heart" and "spirit." These spiritual centers are arranged at two levels, which correspond to the two cosmic levels: (1) The eternal, spiritual realm of God's command (*'amr*), which precedes empirical manifestation, and (2) the temporal world of physical creation (*khalq*).

Through specific practices of contemplation and recitations combined with the interventions of the Sufi master, the aspirant activates the energy focused in these centers in order to initiate and pursue spiritual awakening and ascent.

Prophecy and Sainthood

Another aspect of Sirhindī's perspective on monism and dualism was his exposition of the respective states of the "Prophet" and the "Saint."

All Muslims hold that the Prophet Muhammad was the best of creation. In mystical and Shi'ī thought, however, there tended to be an emphasis on the continuation of charismatic qualities in the world even after the death of the Prophet. The role of the saint (*walāya*) was increasingly elaborated on by Sufis as a kind of metaphysical template for human spiritual progress. Some Sufis had even seemed to suggest, according to Sirhindī, that the status of the saint was existentially higher than that of the Prophet since the saint was conceived of as having remained absorbed in the contemplation of the divine reality rather than descending into the turbidity of worldly matters.

Consistent with his upholding of the value and meaningfulness of human efforts, Sirhindī posited that the level of Prophecy (*nubuwwa*) both incorporated and transcended the saintly level of intoxication and union with the divine in order to return to the world with a sober approach and a focus on a reformist mission. Citing a *hadith* (saying) of the Prophet Muhammad—"My Satan has submitted"—Sirhindī elaborated on the status of the Prophet as one who fulfills a mission of transforming both himself and the world by being willing to descend deeply back into worldly existence even after having attained the highest level of mystical heights of annihilation (*fanā*) in the divine, for, "the descent occurs proportionately to the ascent."

What then, could be the highest state available to the Sufi, since Muhammad was the Last of the Prophets, according to Islamic belief? Today's spiritual aspirants could pursue the state of being followers and heirs of the Prophet in order to ensure the continuity of this reformist mission in the world.

An interesting and controversial aspect of Sirhindī's teaching was his idea of his own special mission. Although alluded to in a fairly esoteric fashion in his works, this stimulated controversy and even some condemnations for heresy among his contemporaries. In an esoteric reference in his work, *Mabda'-ō-Ma'ād*, Sirhindī claims that a new age has been initiated with the coming of the second Islamic millennium in which the cosmological state known as the "Reality of Muhammad" would unite with that of the "Reality of the *Ka'ba*." A new composite higher state known as the "Reality of *Aḥmad*" would be the result, ushering in a new period of fulfillment and spiritual progress for Muslims. This is apparently a thinly veiled reference to his own name, Ahmad. Further, using number mysticism, he spoke of the individual instantiation of the "Reality of Muhammad" in the form of the historical Prophet as having been twofold, spiritual and human. The balance between the human and the spiritual sides of the Prophet had, over time, become disturbed in favor of the spiritual dimension, with consequent detrimental effects on the Muslim community's affairs in the world. He claimed that in the Second Millennium, following the lead of the "Renewer" (*Mujaddid*), the "Perfections of Prophecy" would be restored through the efforts of the heirs and followers of the Prophet.

His more extravagant, almost messianic claims were not entirely alien to the history of Islamic mystical thought, and thus Sirhindī's statements, while clearly controversial, did not result in his being universally condemned for heresy during his lifetime. Over time the image of Sirhindī as a heroic reformer and advocate of uncompromising adherence to Islam became increasingly evocative for the Muslims of India and Pakistan. One can understand the appeal of Sirhindī's more activist, world-affirming outlook to Muslim reformers who partially blame mystically-inspired quietism for the decline of Muslim power and influence in the world in later centuries.

MARCIA K. HERMANSEN

Further Reading

Ansari, Muhammad Abdul-Haq *Sufism and Shari'ah: A Study of Shaykh Ahmad Sirhindi's Effort to Reform Sufism*. Leicester, England: The Islamic Foundation, 1986. This work focuses on how Sirhindī's thought reinforced the exoteric practices of Islam. The second part includes translated selections from his letters and a glossary of terms.

Friedmann, Yohanan. *Shaykh Aḥmad Sirhindī*. Montreal: McGill University, 1971. A groundbreaking study that examines the later construction of Sirhindī's historical image as political activist and reformer in the light of contemporary and later sources.

Rahman, Fazlur. *Selected Letters of Shaikh Aḥmad Sirhindī*. Karachi, Pakistan: Iqbal Academy, 1968. A brief, philosophically-oriented look at Sirhindī's ideas, featuring edited original Persian texts of some of his more important letters.

ter Haar, J. G. J. *Follower and Heir of the Prophet: Shaykh Ahmad Sirhindī (1534–1624) as Mystic*. Leiden, the Netherlands: Het Oosters Instituut, 1992. A recent study that focuses on Sirhindī's mystical thought.

MULLĀ ṢADRĀ (ṢADR AL-DĪN SHĪRĀZĪ)

Born: 980 A.H./1571 A.D., Shiraz, Iran
Died: 1050 A.H./1641 A.D., Basra, Iraq
Major Works: *al-Asfār al-arba'ah* (*The Four Journeys of the Soul*), *al-Mabda' wa'l-ma'ād* (*The Book of Origin and Return*), *al-Shawāhid al-rubūbiyyah* (*Divine Witnesses*), *al-Hikmat al-'arshiyyah* (*Descending from the Divine Throne*), *Commentary on Avicenna's* Shifa', *Commentary on Suhrawardī's* Hikmat al-Ishrāq

Major Ideas

There is a unity of Being.
Being has an independent existence, whereas essences are contingent upon Being and are without a reality of their own.
There is motion in substance.
Becoming is a spiritual journey from the less perfect to the more perfect.
God is the ultimate perfection.
There is a unity of the knower, the known, and knowledge.

Mullā Ṣadrā (Ṣadr al-Dīn Shīrāzī) was born into a noble Persian family. His life coincided with the reign of Shah Abbas the First, during whose rule Shi'ism and the propagation of Islamic law, philosophy, and theology reached its climax in Iran. He devoted himself to the study of the intellectual sciences—in particular, the philosophies of Avicenna, Suhrawardi, and the Neoplatonists, especially Ibn 'Arabi. His intense studies of philosophy intimidated some of the orthodox jurists who held much political power and who regarded philosophy as a heretical activity. Due to the hostility of the orthodoxy to his serious pursuit of philosophy by the studying and teaching of it, Mulla Sadra was forced to leave Isfahan, where he had been studying, and move to a small village outside of the city of Qum. In exile, Mulla Sadra spent twelve years in contemplation and ascetic practices, which led to the strengthening of his intellectual intuition (*dhawq*).

Mulla Sadra is important in the history of Islamic philosophy for several reasons. First, his work, in particular his magnum opus, the *al-Asfār al-arba'ah* (*The Four Journeys of the Soul*), is a compendium of the history of Islamic philosophy. Having presented the ideas of his predecessors in great detail, Mulla Sadra goes on to offer a thorough examination and critique of their philosophical ideas. Second, Mulla Sadra consolidated the School of Isfahan, which his teacher Mir Damad had established. This philosophical school was a turning point in the history of Islamic philosophy in Iran and produced some of the greatest masters of Islamic philosophy. The philosophical tradition of the School of Isfahan that was perfected by such masters as Mulla Sadra came to be known as "transcendental wisdom" (*al-ḥikmat al-muti'āliya*), a rapprochement of discursive reasoning, intellectual intuition and practical wisdom.

Mulla Sadra wrote three distinct types of works: commentaries on the Qur'an (Koran) and *Hadith*, polemical works, and philosophical treatises. His commentaries on various verses of the Qur'an, such as the verses on light, is an indication of his esoteric reading of the scripture. He also wrote a monumental commentary upon the sayings of the Shi'ite Imams, bringing out their more esoteric aspects. His polemics are directed towards the antinomian Sufis and their violations of the religious law. Finally, there are the philosophical writings of Mulla Sadra, most of which were written for the intellectual elite and the learned scholars who had sufficient training in traditional Islamic philosophy.

Theology

Mulla Sadra synthesized the theological (*kalam*) discussions, Avicennian metaphysics, and the mystical thoughts of Ibn 'Arabi. The result is a tradition of wisdom that relates to the traditional concerns of the theologians, the discursive reasoning of the philosophers, and the direct experience of the Sufis. Mulla Sadra in particular was influenced by two figures, Avicenna, the philosopher of Being, and Suhrawardi, the philosopher of light and the founder of the School of Illumination (*Ishraq*) in Islamic philosophy. Mulla Sadra interprets Avicennian philosophy from a Suhrawardian point of view while making some fundamental revisions in Suhrawardi's ontology.

Theology, which by the time of Mulla Sadra was well developed, relied on the same vocabulary as that of the philosophers. Mulla Sadra takes note of the similarity in the use of technical terms by philosophers and theologians and of their methodologies. The second point Mulla Sadra alludes to is that Islamic theology is developed, not as an independent branch of intellectual sciences, but as a discipline that is primarily concerned with Islamic law.

Mulla Sadra, in his treatment of *kalam*, adopts a two-pronged approach, arguing against the theological methodology on one hand while affirming the truth of the objectives of the theologians on the other. Mulla Sadra demonstrates how and why it is that theological arguments fail to prove their purported conclusions while at the same time he is careful not to question the validity of the theological beliefs. In his work on the problem of eternity versus creation in time and the problem of bodily resurrection, Mulla Sadra brings some of the controversial positions of philosophers closer to the views of the theologians.

Mulla Sadra and Avicenna

Mulla Sadra retains the general structure of the Avicennian philosophy that asserts the existence of the Necessary Being and the gradations of Being that emanate from the Necessary Being. However,

he departs from Avicenna by putting more emphasis on the centrality of a personal insight leading to the discoveries of the immutable principles of philosophy. It is precisely these experiences that serve as the foundation upon which Sadrian philosophy is established. Whereas Avicennian principles are derived from discursive philosophy and his logic is based on rationalization of philosophical categories, Mulla Sadra's "logic of transcendence" is derived from his most inward and noetic insight. Mulla Sadra refers to these principles as the "Principles of Oriental Philosophy" (*Qa'ida Mashraqiyah*) and "Transcendental Principles" (*Qa'ida Laduniya*).

Mysticism

Mulla Sadra was profoundly influenced by the mystics of Islam, both by theoretical and practical dimensions of Sufism. With regard to theoretical Sufism, Mulla Sadra was highly influenced by Ibn 'Arabi, the great Andalusian mystic. In fact, a great number of the technical terminologies that Mulla Sadra uses are borrowed from Ibn 'Arabii and his massive commentary upon Islamic gnosticism. In particular, Mulla Sadra finds Ibn 'Arabi's treatment of such issues as human understanding of the experience of the divine and various problems associated with that understanding to be quite illuminating.

As to the practical aspects of the Sufi path, Mulla Sadra endorses asceticism as part of the path of knowledge while he rejects the excesses and the antinomian practices of the Sufis.

Divisions of Knowledge

Mulla Sadra divides knowledge into two types—that which is learned by sense perception or instruction and that which is learned through intellectual intuition, a mode of knowledge marked by directness and the absence of mediation. The knowledge that is learned through the senses or instruction itself is divided into the traditional divisions of knowledge most commonly held by the Peripatetics, namely, theoretical and practical. The theoretical sciences consist of logic, mathematics, natural philosophy, and metaphysics; practical wisdom includes ethics, politics, and economics.

Mulla Sadra goes on to subdivide the sciences, leading to a unified theory of knowledge, which despite the multiplicity of different branches of knowledge leads the intellect to that knowledge of unity that lies at the heart of Sadrian philosophy. This view of knowledge (*hikmah*) integrates various modes of knowing, including that of practical wisdom, since knowledge for Mulla Sadra is not only informative but also transformative.

Theories of Being, Change, and Knowledge

Mulla Sadra, whose encyclopedic knowledge of Islamic philosophy provided him with the basis for illuminating analyses of the philosophical ideas of his predecessors, makes three major contributions to the field of Islamic philosophy. They include (1) his commentary on Being, leading to the Doctrine of the Unity of Being, (2) his account of the occurrence of change in motion, known as "Substantial Motion," and (3) his theory of the unity of the knower, the known, and knowledge itself.

Mulla Sadra takes issue with Suhrawardi, the founder of the School of Illumination, and his own teacher Mir Damad, reversing their scheme based on the principality of essence (*mahiyyah*) over existence (*wujud*). He argues that existence is the primary and principal aspect of an existent being and that essences are accidents of Being. Furthermore, Existence or Being (which for most of the Islamic philosophers, including Mulla Sadra, are the same) has an independent existence, whereas essences are contingent upon Being and therefore without a reality of their own.

Regarding the classical divisions of Being, Mulla Sadra accepts Avicenna's division of Being into necessary, contingent, and impossible. Mulla Sadra also elaborates on copulative and noncopulative Being. Copulative Being is that which connects the subject to the predicate such as in "Socrates is a philosopher." The term "is" here has a twofold function—a copulative one, which connects the adjective of being a philosopher to Socrates, and a second one, namely, the existential

function, which alludes to the existence of an existent being, in this case Socrates. Mulla Sadra, who is interested in the latter use of "is," argues that "is" in the corporeal world is always copulative except for the Being of God, who is pure and without essences.

Mulla Sadra accepts Plato's concept of archetypes as the "master of species" (*arbab al-anwa‘*). According to Mulla Sadra, the corporeal world as a level of Being derives its characteristics from the archetypal world. The separation of the corporeal world from its archetypal world leads to the principle of "the possibility of that which is superior" (*Qa‘ida imkan al-ashraf*), a principle for which Mulla Sadra is known. This principle entails that for everything that journeys from the imperfect to perfect in the material world, there is its cosmic counterpart in the incorporeal world.

Mulla Sadra's criticism of the Illuminationists goes beyond the priority and principality of existence over essence and includes the theory of hylomorphism. Accordingly, matter manifests itself in various domains of existence according to the ontological status of each level. Whereas the world of objects is immersed in the lowest level of matter, the soul belongs to a higher level of matter suitable for it. This process continues until it culminates in the intelligible world, where realities are completely free from matter.

Motion in Substance

Mulla Sadra is unique in the history of Islamic philosophy in that he allows for motion to exist in substance (*al-harakat al-jawhariyyah*). This is a deviation from Avicenna, who considered motion in substance to lead to a continuous change and the loss of that which constitutes the identity of a thing.

Mulla Sadra uses a number of arguments in support of his theory of the existence of motion in substance. When an apple has become ripe, it is not only the accidents that have changed, but the substance of the apple must have changed as well. In fact, when a potentiality becomes actualized, Mulla Sadra argues, it signifies a change both in accidents and in substance. Mulla Sadra states that for every change that occurs in accident, there has to be a corresponding change in substance, for accidents depend on their substance for their properties. Therefore, change in an apple is an example of the created order and signifies several points: first, that the world is like a river that is constantly in a state of flux; second, change occurs out of necessity and nothing remains the same except God; third, this change is not an accident in the universe, but is part of its very nature. This change, according to Mulla Sadra, acts as a force that moves the universe towards becoming; becoming is fundamentally a spiritual journey that all beings yearn for and accounts for both the ripening of an apple as well as for the yearning of the human being for transcendence.

Mulla Sadra uses the notion of Substantial Motion to shed light on the concept of time. For Mulla Sadra, as for Aristotle, time is the quantity of motion, except that for Mulla Sadra the change in quantity is the quantity of change in substance. Time is not to be viewed only quantitatively but has an ontological aspect as well. Motion in substance is also the measurement of perfection and therefore has a purpose and direction, and carries a sense of necessity with it.

The fact that all things are in motion and that motion goes from less perfect to more perfect is an indication for Mulla Sadra that the entire universe is yearning for the ultimate perfection, God. This view also entails that in some sense the universe is conscious of its own state of being and yearns for an eventual unity with its origin. Since Substantial Motion also entails that the identity of the object in question is always changing, Mulla Sadra concludes that this type of motion brings about a type of creation at every given moment. In other words, God through Substantial Motion creates the universe instantaneously at every moment. The Reality of God manifests itself through creation, which then goes through successive creations.

What Mulla Sadra was trying to achieve was to bring about a rapprochement between the Peripatetic who argued for the eternity of the world and the theologian view who insisted on creation ex nihilo. According to Mulla Sadra, the world as an extension of God has always existed, but yet it was created in time that ceases to exist, and is then recreated.

Epistemological Unity

The unity of the knower, the known, and knowledge is deeply embedded in the Sadrian philosophy. Since God's essence and Being are the same and all things emanate from Him, He is at once the knower, the known, and the knowledge.

From the above it follows that in order for any person to achieve a similar status, one has to achieve unity with God. The reverse is also true: anyone who attains the knowledge of unity is in his or her very being the knower, the known, and the knowledge; in knowing unity, one has become unified. It is for this reason that Mulla Sadra's *al-Asfār al-arba'ah* (the *Four Journeys of the Soul*) alludes to the spiritual journey of the soul from the time that it departs from God until it achieves unity once again.

Mulla Sadra not only offers complex philosophical arguments but also uses gnostic imagery as a mirror representing Divine Essence within which God witnesses the essence of all things. Although Mulla Sadra never explicitly states that unity with God is the necessary condition of knowledge, the thrust of his philosophy is such that this notion is implied.

Mulla Sadra and his teachings were a turning point in the history of Islamic philosophy. One of the greatest achievements of Mulla Sadra was the training of several students who themselves became masters of Islamic philosophy and propagators of Sadrian philosophy. Among them we can name 'Abd al-Razzaq Lahiji, Mulla Muhsin Fayd Kashani, and Qadi Sa'id Qummi.

Sadrian philosophy, which had gone through a period of decline, was once again revived in the eighteenth and nineteenth centuries in Iran by such notable figures as Sabziwari, Ali Nuri, Ahsa'i, and the Zunuzi family. The teaching of Mulla Sadra and his students was well received by the Islamic philosophers of the subcontinent of India, and some of his books became the official texts of traditional schools. Islamic philosophy today in Iran and the eastern parts of the Islamic world is still under the influence of Mulla Sadra and his teachings.

MEHDI AMINRAZAVI

Further Reading

Translation

Morris, James. *Introduction to* Wisdom of the Throne. Princeton, N.J.: Princeton University Press, 1981. A translation of Mulla Sadra's *al-Hikmat al-'arshiyyah.* Morris's introduction to Mulla Sadra's philosophy is comprehensive and concise.

Related Studies

Corbin, Henry. *Introduction to Mulla Sadra's* Kitab al-masha'ir [*Le Livre des pénétrations métaphysiques*]. Tehran: A. Maisonneuve, 1963. The introduction provides a general exposition of Mulla Sadra's philosophy.

Nasr, Seyyed Hosssein. *Islamic Life and Thought.* Albany, N.Y.: SUNY Press, 1981. An excellent survey of Islamic thought, covering law and society, cultural and intellectual life, the sciences, philosophy, and Sufism (as well as a number of important contemporary questions). Chapters 14, 15, and 16 present a leading scholar's analysis of the ideas and significance of Mulla Sadra.

——— . "Ṣadr al-Dīn Shīrāzī." In *A History of Muslim Philosophy*, Vol. 2, edited by M. M. Sharif. Wiesbaden: O. Harrassowitz, 1966. A general overview of the components of Mulla Sadra's philosophy.

——— . *Ṣadr al-Dīn Shīrāzī and His Transcendental Theosophy.* Tehran and London: Iranian Academy of Philosophy, 1978. An excellent introductory book on Mulla Sadra's philosophy.

——— . "The School of Isfahan." In *A History of Muslim Philosophy*, Vol. 2, edited by M. M. Sharif. Wiesbaden: O. Harrassowitz, 1966. This essay explains Mulla Sadra's philosophy and puts it within the historical and intellectual context of his time.

——— , ed. *Mullā Ṣadrā Commemoration Volume.* Tehran: Tehran University Press, 1380 A.H., 1960 A.D. This volume contains essays on various aspects of Mulla Sadra, in particular his views on Being.

al-Rahman, Fadl. *The Philosophy of Mullā Ṣadrā.* Albany, N.Y.: SUNY Press, 1975. This study presents a balanced and comprehensive view of Mulla Sadra's philosophy.

SHĀH WALĪ ALLĀH

Born: 1703, Phalit, India
Died: 1762, Delhi, India
Major Works: *Ḥujjat Allāh al-Bāligha* (*The Conclusive Argument from God*), *al-Budūr al-Bāzigha* (*Full Moons Rising*)

Major Ideas

There is a need to coordinate the intellectual approaches of the various Islamic religious sciences.
Study of the reports of the Prophet Muhammad is essential in determining religious practice.
The understanding of specific religious injunctions requires going to the higher level of ideas, the World of Images.
Human societal development involves continuous historical progress through four levels (irtifāqāt) *corresponding to the stages of nomadic life.*

Shāh Walī Allāh lived during that period in the development of the Islamic tradition known as the "wisdom" period, when a synthesis of the traditional religious sciences of philosophy, theology, and mysticism had been effected. In pre-modern times, however, this classical synthesis was showing signs of breaking down under various sectarian, political, and social pressures.

The main thrust of Shāh Walī Allāh's teaching and writing activities was therefore to reintegrate and revitalize the study of the Islamic religious sciences through coordinating the approaches of the main Islamic intellectual disciplines: law, theology, mysticism, and especially Qur'anic and *hadith* studies. To this end he composed some forty books and treatises and served as a religious scholar and spiritual guide.

Shāh Walī Allāh was born into a strongly religious and learned family. His father, Shāh 'Abd al-Raḥīm, was a noted jurist and scholar who founded an Islamic teaching institution, a *madrasa*, in Delhi. He instructed his precocious son in Qur'anic studies, Arabic language, and the Naqshbandī mystical tradition, making him his successor at the tender age of seventeen. Shāh Walī Allāh therefore assumed his father's position at the time of the Shāh 'Abd al-Raḥīm's death in 1719.

A powerful formative influence on Shāh Walī Allāh's thought was the pilgrimage he made to Makkah (Mecca) in 1730. He spent about a year and a half in the Holy Cities of Makkah and Madina studying with most prominent and respected Sufi masters and *hadith* scholars of the time, who, recognizing his abilities, took him into their circle. His fluency in Arabic was such that many of his major works were written in that language. In addition, quite a number were composed in the Persian language, the major vehicle for prose among the Muslims of the Indian subcontinent until the twentieth century.

The period spent in the intellectual, religious, and cultural hub of the Muslim world gave Shāh Walī Allāh a cosmopolitan outlook in matters of Islamic law and practice so that his works address Muslims as a whole, rather than a more parochial audience. Since his Makkan masters were steeped in the tradition of *hadith* studies, Shāh Walī Allāh embraced the concept that the study and interpretation of the sayings of the Prophet were the key to integrating and revitalizing the practice of Islam in his time.

After his return from Arabia Shāh Walī Alāah pursued his scholarly and mystical activities in Delhi, teaching in the Islamic religious school founded by his father and guiding disciples in the intricacies of the mystical path.

The Conclusive Argument from God

His major work, *Ḥujjat Allāh al-Bāligha* (*The Conclusive Argument from God*), was composed after his return from the pilgrimage. In this two-volume study he presents an overview of an entire cosmology. In volume 1 he expounds on the underlying purpose of creation, the dynamics of human psychology, the higher significance of human thoughts and actions, the progressive development of human social and political systems, and ultimately the need for religious revelation and its interpretation. In volume 2 he applies his method for bringing out an understanding of the deeper spiritual aspects of the Islamic legal injunctions to specific *hadith* reports of the Prophet covered in the order of the topics featured in traditional *hadith* compendia. Due to this enterprise of elucidating and reconciling the inner and outer dimensions of Islamic practice, he is often compared to the great thinker and mystic al-Ghazālī (d. 1111).

His metaphysical system is also highly influenced by the philosophical Sufi tradition of both al-Ghazālī and Ibn 'Arabī (d. 1240), who related the Platonic concept of a higher or ideal level of meaning to the events of this world. This somewhat fluid layer, which seems to mediate between the purely spiritual and the purely material dimensions of reality, is known as the "World of Images." This was understood by him to be the realm at which religious symbols were formulated before their articulation in specific religious injunctions. The essential understanding of what it means to follow these specific religious injunctions, then, must ultimately be sought at this higher level rather than in the particular instances of their external occurrence. This led Shāh Walī Allāh to elaborate a theory of symbolization and its expressions in concrete historical situations of meaning and applicability, which argues that the symbols have a kind of objective validity of their own. The conclusion is that the Islamic law must be practiced in its exoteric form in order to obtain its inner spiritual benefits.

In the case of his theory of religious revelation, he conceives of Islam as a universal religion, which, however, naturally had to take on concrete form in the time of the Prophet in the context of seventh-century Arabia. There is therefore somewhat of an unresolved tension in his thought between the concept of an ideal template of a universal religion termed the *dīn*, which is suited to the innate temperaments of all persons, and his asserting the applicability of its particular historical manifestation, Islam, to all times and places.

In his system, human beings are not merely passive receptors of religious laws. Those who strive in the path of moral and spiritual development are able to participate in the shaping of the future course of destiny, for even after death the most evolved among them will join the angels of the "Supreme Assembly" to participate in the task of guiding further human social and spiritual progress.

Qur'anic Studies

Although Shāh Walī Allāh's translation of the Qur'an (Koran) from Arabic into Persian was not the first, as some have claimed, it was pioneering in his conscious intention to go beyond previous translations in striking a balance between an overly literal version and one conveying merely the gist of the text. In the preface to this translation and in a later book called the *Principles of Quranic Exegesis*, he elaborated on the types of divine discourse which constitute the Qur'an, including its legal import, its account of God's favors to human beings, its evocation of God's acts of intervention in human history, and its warning of the eventual reckoning at the end of time.

Works on Islamic Law

Shāh Walī Allāh's sound training in law and *hadith* in the Holy Cities led Shāh Walī Allāh to favor the *hadith* methodology of the school of Mālik ibn Anas (d. 795) and the theoretical tools of the Legal School of al-Shāfi'ī (d. 819). In his own practice, like most South Asian Muslims, he followed the Hanafi School of Law. Such eclecticism was known as *taṭbīq*, or bringing diverse elements into correspondence. Some of his works on law and *hadith* are technical studies of theory and interpretation; in others he considers the historical sources of the disagreements among the four major Sunni schools of law and suggests that the factors leading to these differences should be understood developmentally, so that differences do not become rigidified identifications. His position on the ability of qualified individuals to interpret the main sources, Qur'an and *hadith*, of Islamic legislation is not entirely radical, but signals his willingness to allow a certain level of individual interpretation (*ijtihād*) on the part of the qualified jurist.

Sufism

Shāh Walī Allāh's approach to the practice of Sufism was both eclectic and reformist. His attitude to Sufi practice and theory, as to the other Islamic disciplines, was that each Sufi order had its own unique history and strengths. The individual spiritual aspirant should therefore be taught to practice those elements of Sufism most compatible with his or her inherent nature, whether contemplative, devotional, or intellectual.

Shāh Walī Allāh was influenced by the philosophy of Ibn 'Arabi, which featured the idea of an emanationist cosmology. While many of his contemporaries felt that the implicitly monistic formulations of Ibn 'Arabī and the more dualistic philosophy of the respected Indian Sufi, Shaikh Aḥmad Sirhindī (1625), were insurmountably opposed, Shāh Walī Allāh argued that their differences were essentially those of perspective and orientation rather than rooted in true metaphysical incompatibility.

Shāh Walī Allāh claimed initiation in the major Sufi orders of his age and, rather than stressing affiliation to any one of them, may have attempted to establish his own eclectic sort of practice, which, however, did not take hold. What seems to have been passed on to posterity was a diminishing emphasis on Sufism as a distinct form of practice and discipline, and an attempt by some of his descendants to incorporate Sufi elements so as to spiritualize more mainstream elements of Islamic belief and practice. For example, the Deoband *madrasa*, a prominent Islamic institute of higher learning, was founded by followers of his son, Shāh 'Abd al-Azīz (d. 1823); his grandson, Shah Ismā'īl Shahid (d. 1831), initially composed highly technical works of mystical philosophy, but is most widely known for serving as the ideologue of a militant Islamic reform movement, the "Muhammadan Way" (*Ṭariqa Muḥammadiyya*).

Shāh Walī Allāh as Reformer

Living at a time of transition in the political situation of Muslims in India and experiencing the fragmentation of the Mughal empire and subsequent upheavals on the eve of the colonial period, Shāh Walī Allāh seems to exemplify certain of the trends typical of pre-modern Muslim reform movements. Unlike the Wahhabis of Arabia, however, he did not reject the practice of venerating Muslim saints and believing that they, as well as the Prophet, had a continual spiritual presence that was accessible to the faithful.

In his discussion of human social and political development Shāh Walī Allāh coined the term *irtifāqāt* from an Arabic root meaning "gaining benefit by." According to his view of human societal development, human beings make continuous historical progress through four levels, or *irtifāqāt*, which correspond to the stages of nomadic life, urbanization, the establishment of states, and the consolidation of international empires such as the Islamic Caliphate.

It is interesting that today all major religious movements in Muslim South Asia invoke Shāh Walī Allāh as an intellectual progenitor. His son, Shah 'Abd al-Azīz, was a noted scholar and teacher with a wide circle of pupils. Other South Asian Muslims who have a more anti-Sufi, puritan outlook—such as the Ahl al-Ḥadīth group—and even the followers of Maulānā Maudūdī (d. 1979) find in Shāh Walī Allāh's return to the fundamentals of the Islamic legal system and political rejection of alien influences a precursor to their own reformist beliefs. Islamic Modernists see in Shāh Walī Allāh a thinker who responded to the crisis of his time by accommodating divergent legal and ideological factions, calling for a renewed *ijtihād*, and searching for the spirit behind the literal injunctions of the religious tradition.

MARCIA K. HERMANSEN

Further Reading

Translations

Published English translations of Shāh Walī Allāh's works up to this point have generally lacked a scholarly critical apparatus. This lack is particularly crucial since Shāh Walī Allāh uses a highly technical vocabulary, often in an idiosyncratic way.

Shāh Walī Allāh. *Full Moon Appearing on the Horizon* [*al-Budūr al-Bāzigha*]. Translated by J. M. S. Baljon. Lahore, Pakistan: Ashraf, 1988. An unannotated but readable translation of one of the author's more comprehensive works.

——— . *A Mystical Interpretation of Prophetic Tales by an Indian Muslim: Shāh Walī Allāh of Delhi's Ta'wīl al-Aḥadīth.* Translated by J. M. S. Baljon. Leiden, the Netherlands: E. J. Brill, 1973. An abridged annotated translation of stories about the line of Prophets.

——— . *The Sacred Knowledge* [*Alṭāf al-Quds*]. Translated by G. H. Jalbani and D. Pendelberry. London: Octagon, 1984. A highly mystical text dealing with the Sufi system of spiritual progress through awakening the centers of the subtle body.

——— . *Sufism and the Islamic Tradition: Lamaḥāt and Saṭa'āt of Shāh Walīullāh of Delhi.* Translated by G. H. Jalbani and D. Pendelberry. London: Octagon, 1986. Two works on mystical philosophy.

Related Studies

Baljon, J. M. S. *The Religion and Thought of Shāh Walī Allāh.* Leiden, the Netherlands: E. J. Brill, 1986. The most complete and readable study of major themes of his thought. Contains an annotated list of his works.

Rizvi, Athar Abbas. *Shāh Walī Allāh and His Times.* Canberra, Australia: Maarifat, 1980. A detailed study of the historical environment as well as of Shāh Walī Allāh's major ideas. Notable for its extensive use of manuscript sources.

MUHAMMAD IQBAL

Born: 1873, Sialkot, India (now Pakistan)
Died: 1938, Lahore, India (now Pakistan)
Major Works: *Asrar-i Khudi* (*Secrets of the Self*) (1915), *Rumuz-i Bikhudi* (*Mysteries of Selflessness*) (1918), *Payam-i Mashriq* (*Message of the East*) (1923), *Zubur-i 'Ajam* (*Persian Hymns*) (1927), *Six Lectures on the Reconstruction of Islamic Thought* (1930), *Javid Namah* (*Book of Eternity*) (1932), *Bal-i Jibril* (*Gabriel's Wing*) (1936), *Armaghan-i Hijaz* (*Gift of Hijaz*) (1938)

Major Ideas

The restoration of Muslim glory begins with a rational understanding of the destiny of human beings and will follow their spiritual ascent, which will culminate in the perfect order.

Muslims can truly attain spiritual salvation if that salvation is both individual and social.

History is not the reflection of Divine will and therefore its course can and ought to be changed.

Islam ought to be interpreted rationally, doing away with purely mystical and scholastic approaches to religion.

Sir Muhammad Iqbal was born in 1873 in Sialkot, in the Indian province of Punjab. He was born shortly after the Great Mutiny of 1857 and grew up at a time when Muslim power was on the decline before the rise of British colonialism. Throughout his life Iqbal grappled with the religious, social, and political implications of the occlusion of Islam in his homeland. His rich literary and philosophical corpus was unique in its time— it introduced a most serious effort directed at both understanding this development and charting a way for restoring Islam to its due place in the temporal order.

Iqbal received his early education in Sialkot and Lahore in the religious sciences, Arabic, Persian, and English. It was at Lahore's Oriental College, where he studied with Sir Edwin Arnold between 1893 and 1897, that he first studied modern thought. In 1899 he received a master in philosophy from that college, and began to teach Arabic, compose poetry, and write on social and economic issues. His poetry was in the classical Perso-Urdu style, but also showed the influence of European literature, especially Wordsworth and Coleridge.

In 1905 he left India to study law at the University of Cambridge, but it was philosophy that soon consumed his intellectual passion. At Trinity College he studied Hegel and Kant and became familiar with the main trends in European philosophy. His interest in philosophy took him to Heidelberg and Munich in 1907, where Nietzsche strongly influenced him. It was there that he received his doctorate in philosophy, writing a dissertation entitled *The Development of Metaphysics in Persia*. A year later, in 1908, he was called to the Bar at Lincoln's Inn in England. A lawyer and a philosopher, he returned to India in that year.

Soon after his return he began teaching philosophy at Lahore's Government College. In addition he also took a keen interest in the unfolding plight of Indian Muslims under British rule. Before leaving for Europe Iqbal had been a liberal nationalist, sympathetic to the Indian National Congress Party. He was now communalist in his outlook, supporting Muslim separatism and its chief advocate, the All-India Muslim League. The British, however, saw no danger in Iqbal's politics—for it was always subsumed in his more potent philosophical message—and knighted him in 1922.

Four years later, in 1926, Iqbal was elected to the Punjab Legislative Council, and grew closer to the All-India Muslim League. He showed more and more support for a separate Muslim homeland in lieu of submitting to Hindu rule which was to follow independence. In fact the very idea of a separate Muslim homeland, consisting of the Muslim majority provinces in northwest India, was first proposed by Iqbal in 1930. Still, he never ceased to be first and foremost an intellectual force, and it is his impact on Muslim thought more than his political leanings that have secured his place in Muslim cultural life.

Religious Reform and the Reconstruction of Islamic Philosophy

Iqbal is unique among contemporary Muslim philosophers in utilizing theology, mysticism, philosophy—of the East along with that of the West—and the potent emotional appeal and nuanced style of Perso-Urdu poetry to understand and explain the destiny of humanity. It is Iqbal's ability to traverse the expanse that separates philosophy from sociocultural concerns that has made him both a philosopher and a cultural hero.

Iqbal argued that it is in the realization of their destiny that the spiritual salvation and political emancipation of Muslims can be realized. Islam holds the key to the realization of that destiny, for faith is central to a Muslim's life. It is religion that defines human existence, and it is through religion that man may rise to greater heights.

Much like other Islamic modernists, Iqbal idealized the early history of Islam. It was in the Muhammadan community that Muslims had reached the pinnacle of their spiritual and worldly power—the full realization of human destiny. It was that vision of the past that guided his prescriptions for the future. He became convinced that man was able to realize the full potential of his destiny only in the context of the revival of Islam, in an order wherein the perfection of the soul would be reflected in the excellence of social relations. Yet Iqbal's formulation was not a jejune call to atavism; while he idealized early Islamic history, Iqbal also incorporated modern values and precepts into that ideal, such that the Muhammadan community and the fundamental tenets of the Muslim faith embodied all that he believed to be good in the modern West. The impact of the West on Iqbal was deep-seated and is clearly evident in the fabric of his worldview. His criticisms of many aspects of the Western civilization, especially its secularism, in some of his works such as *Payam-i Mashriq* (*Message of the East*) only thinly disguise his extensive borrowing from Western thought.

Idealization of Islam went hand-in-hand with advocating religious reform. Iqbal argued that Islam can serve humanity only if it is reformed and reinterpreted in the image of its Muhammadan ideal—and Iqbal's understanding of the West—while using the tools of philosophical analysis and mystical wisdom. Iqbal did not view this exercise as innovation or reformation, but as rediscovery and the reconstruction of Islam. He believed that the inner truth of Islam had over the centuries been hidden by obscurantist practices and cultural accretions promoted by Sufi (Islamic mysticism) masters (*mashayakh*), religious divines (*'ulama*), and wayward monarchs. It was they who had produced a view of Islam that had led the faithful astray and sapped that religion of its power, ending its glorious reign.

To reverse their fall from power and to realize their destiny, Muslims must find access to the truth of their religion. They must become aware of the fact that Islam, as it stood before them, was impure; only then would they look beyond popular impressions of Islam—passionate and devotional attachments to the religion—to find its hidden truth. Iqbal's early works, *Asrar-i Khudi* (*Secrets of the Self*) and *Rumuz-i Bikhudi* (*Mysteries of Selflessness*), encouraged Muslims to adopt such an approach by harping on the themes of love and freedom; not romantic love or political freedom per se, but love of the truth and freedom from that view of Islam which had been vouchsafed through cultural transmission.

Still, his most complex philosophical views were argued emotionally in his poetry. He caught the attention of Muslims using the very language and sensibility which he believed they had to abandon if they were to aspire to greater heights. Iqbal is just as towering a figure in Persian and Urdu poetry as he is in contemporary Islamic philosophy.

Iqbal rejected fatalism (*taqdir*). He did not view history as the arena for the Divine will to unfold in, as Muslims generally do, but for humans to realize their potential. He encouraged Muslims to take charge of their own lives and destinies, to shape history rather than serve as pawns in it. To him history was not sacred, and hence was easily changeable. This was a modernist conception that showed the influence of the Kantian notion of "Divine aloofness." It was at odds with the time-honored 'Ash'arite tradition in Islamic theology and philosophy, which teaches that history is the manifestation of the Divine will and is therefore sacred; man can not hope to understand the Divine wisdom and hence should not reject the writ of history, nor seek to interfere with it.

In encouraging Muslims to redirect history and to assume responsibility for its unfolding through a rational interpretation of their faith, Iqbal also echoed the beliefs of Mu'tazalite philosophers who had centuries earlier taken the 'Ash'arites to task but had failed to shape the subsequent development of Islamic thought.

Iqbal understood that there could be no systematic rationalization of Islam unless there was a single definition of a Muslim. As a result he sought to reduce the diversity of the Islamic faith in the hope of underlining the fundamental unity that has bound the various sects, denominations, and schools of thought constituting the Islamic faith. As the eloquent poetry of *Zubur-i 'Ajam* (*Persian Hymns*) shows, he was less concerned with the various expressions of Islam and more with the basic tenets of the faith, the lowest com-

mon denominator among Muslims. It was also to this end that he idealized early Islamic history, the period when there were no divisions in the body of the faith. His vision of Islam was a simple and pristine one.

The Perfection of the Human Being and of Society

The principal aim of the reformation and rationalization of the Islamic faith was to recreate the ideal Muhammadan society—the perfect order in which humanity would attain its highest ideals. This is a task which begins with the perfection of the self—best exemplified in the example of Prophet Muhammad himself—and culminates in the creation of the ideal social order. This meant that the political fortunes of Muslims would once again rise in India only pursuant to a revival of Islam.

Iqbal's perspective, however, was not so much political—although it had great impact on Muslim politics—but philosophical. He combined the Nietzschean concept of "Superman" with the Sufi doctrine of Perfect Man (*al-insan al-kamil*), devising an all-encompassing view of human development and social change. He saw God as the perfect ego, but an ego nevertheless, more near and tangible than God of old. As outlined in the *Javid Namah* (*Book of Eternity*), God is the supreme ideal in which Iqbal's scheme of human development would culminate. This conception of the Divine closely resembles the Sufi notion of *al-insan al-kamil*, and no doubt parallels Nietzsche's Superman.

In describing his views Iqbal used the doctrine—proposed by the Sufi saint, Jalal al-Din Rumi (1207–73)—of the ascent of the human self. Rumi had explained the Sufi experience in terms of an alchemical process which would transform the base metal of the human soul into the gold of Divine perfection. Iqbal echoed Rumi in the *Bal-i Jibril* (*Gabriel's Wing*), where he argued that life continues despite death, for the soul is immortal and life continues as death and later as resurrection. Through this death and becoming human life would perfect itself. Since the rise of humanity was closely tied to the reconstruction of the temporal order, Iqbal relied on Rumi to sanction the passing of the old Muslim order to pave the way for the rise of a new and triumphant one. Human and social development, as such, will continue until they attain the state of perfection as understood by Sufis and pondered upon by Nietzsche. Iqbal defined that perfection as a state where love and science—symbolizing essence of East and the West—happily occupy the same intellectual space.

With every birth man can attain a higher spiritual state in a more perfect society, for man has the essence (*jawhar*) that can be transformed into perfection. That process can only occur through the intermediary of true of Islam, for Islam has the blueprint. Just as meditation and asceticism would prepare the soul of the Sufi for spiritual ascent, activism—abandoning fatalism in favor of an engaged approach to individual and social life— would perform the same function in Iqbal's scheme. That activism would culminate in the "Islamic state," which Iqbal equated with the Sufi conception of spiritual bliss.

The imprint of Sufism on Iqbal here is unmistakable and quite interesting. Iqbal generally rejected Sufism, arguing that it had always been concerned only with the spiritual salvation of the individual, whereas he believed individual salvation could not be divorced from the reconstruction of the temporal order. Yet criticism of Sufism was not tantamount to rejecting those aspects of its teachings and beliefs that he had found quite persuasive. The titles of Iqbal's various divans attest to the influence of Sufi imagery and symbolisms on his thought.

In many ways Iqbal's vision was a modernization of Sufism using the tools of Western philosophy. His innovation lay in introducing social development as a necessary condition for attainment of perfection and spiritual salvation. It is this aspect of his thought that was of relevance to Muslim political activism in India at the twilight of the Raj, and later influenced many revivalist thinkers who have since looked to politics as the medium for effecting individual spiritual salvation.

Iqbal was without doubt a most creative and original thinker, one who sought to bring together many strains of Islamic life and thought together and to reform the Muslim faith, imbue it with modern precepts, and reconstruct it anew. He related Islamic thought to Western philosophy, and linked spiritual salvation to intellectual change and social development. As a poet of exceptional abilities he conveyed these ideas to his audience most forcefully. Although there is no distinct school of thought associated with Iqbal, there is no doubt that many across the spectrum of Islamic thought have been swayed by the wisdom of his agenda and the logic of his method, and have sought to emulate him in reviving their faith and reforming their societies.

SEYYED VALI REZA NASR

Further Reading

Ahmad, Aziz. *Iqbal and the Recent Exposition of Islamic Political Thought*. Lahore, Pakistan: Muhammad Ashraf, 1950. A study of the place of Iqbal's views in modern Islamic intellectual history.

Fernandez, A. "Man's Divine Quest, Appreciation of Philosophy of the Ego According to Sir Muhammad Iqbal," *Annali Lateranensis* (Rome). Vol. XX, 1956. An analysis of Iqbal's arguments about the ego.

Hakim, Khalifah 'Abdul. "The Concept of Love in Rumi and Iqbal," *Islamic Culture* (Hyderabad, India), 1950. A study of Rumi's impact on Iqbal.

Iqbal, Muhammad. *Six Lectures on the Reconstruction of Religious Thought in Islam*. Lahore, Pakistan: Muhammad Ashraf, 1930. The most thorough exposition of Iqbal's vision.

Malik, Hafeez, ed. *Iqbal: Poet-Philosopher of Pakistan*. New York: Columbia University Press, 1971. A most useful collection of essays on various aspects of Iqbal's life and thought.

May, Lini S. *Iqbal: His Life and Times*. Lahore, Pakistan: Muhammad Ashraf, 1974. A thorough examination of the major themes of Iqbal's life.

Schimmel, Annemarie. *Gabriel's Wing: A Study Into the Religious Ideas of Sir Muhammad Iqbal*. Leiden, the Netherlands: E. J. Brill, 1963. This volume is a comprehensive examination of Iqbal's thought.

SAYYID MUḤAMMAD ḤUSAIN TABĀṬABĀ'Ī

Born: 1903, Tabriz, Iran
Died: 1981, Qum, Iran
Major Works: *Al-Mizan fi Tafsir al-Qur'an* (*Balance in Qur'anic Commentary*) (n.d.), *Qur'an dar Islam* (*Qur'an in Islam*) (n.d.), *Rawabit-i Ijtima'i dar Islam* (*Social Relations in Islam*) (n.d.), *Usul Falsafah wa Rawish-i Realism* (*Foundations of Philosophy and Method of Realism*) (1953–85), *Tafsir a-Mizan* (*Qur'anic Commentary*) (1965), *Shi'ah dar Islam* (*Shi'ism in Islam*) (1969), *Shi'ah: Majmu'ah-i Muzakrat ba Professor Henry Corbin* (*Shi'ism: Collection of Discussions with Professor Henry Corbin*) (1976), *Usul-i Falsafah-i Realism* (*Foundations of Realist Philosophy*) (1976), *Falsafah-i Iqtisad-i Islam* (*Philosophy of Islam's Economics*) (1982), *Nahayah al-Hikmah* (*Ultimates of Knowledge*) (1984)

Major Ideas

Realism is the acceptance of the reality of existence.
The realist method leads to acceptance of the existence of the Necessary Being.
Marxism is an expression of human idealism and is therefore a fallacy.
Traditional Islamic philosophy is compatible with realist philosophy, and can be studied using the realist method.
Comparative study of Islamic and Western philosophies is central to the debate between the two.
Islamic philosophy is better equipped to engage Western thought in dialogue and debate than is Islamic jurisprudence or theology.

Tabataba'i (Sayyid Muḥammad Ḥusain Ṭabāṭabā'ī) was born in 1903 in Tabriz, Iran, to a well-known family of Islamic scholars and divines. He completed his early education in Arabic and the religious sciences in Tabriz. In 1923 Tabataba'i left for Najaf, Iraq, where he continued his education at the great Shi'ite seminaries of that city. In Najaf he studied jurisprudence (*fiqh*) and theology (*kalam*), which constitute the core of Shi'ite religious education, with Mirza Muhammad Husain Na'ini and Shaykh Muhammad Husain Isfahani. Still, his main interests were philosophy, the intellectual sciences, and Islamic mysticism and gnosis (*'irfan*), to which he devoted most of his attention as a student. He studied the standard texts of Islamic philosophy with Sayyid Husain Badkuba'i, and mystical texts—notably Muhy al-Din Ibn 'Arabi's (d. 1240) works—with Mirza 'Ali Qazi. After completing his studies in Najaf in 1934, Tabataba'i returned to Tabriz where he began to teach. Although well versed in theology and jurisprudence, he focused all his attention on teaching philosophy.

Tabataba'i belonged to the school of Sadr al-Din Shirazi (Mulla Sadra) (d. 1641), who had fused the main tenets of the Peripatetic and Illuminationist schools of Islamic philosophy to create the *hikamat-i muta'aliyah* (transcendental philosophy). In questions of eschatology the Sadrian perspective followed the Peripatetic School. The principal force and novelty of the Sadrian School lay in its theosophy. Mulla Sadra stipulated that since everything is preceded in its being by nonexistence in time, then there is no individuality of any kind. Every form of existence is renewed and is therefore impermanent. The universe is continuously renewed—ending and originating. Only God, who is infinite and exists separate from all being, is permanent and unchanging. He is the Necessary Being. All other existence is contingent on Him, and forms in gradations away from Him.

Tabataba'i moved from Tabriz to Qum, which is a major center of Shi'ite education, in 1945. Tabriz was then suffering from the impact of the Second World War and was one of the centers of Communist activity in Iran. The hardships of life in Tabriz at the time led Tabataba'i to leave his city of birth.

His choice of Qum, however, had to do with his belief that the emphasis on jurisprudence and theology in the curricula of Shi'ite seminaries ought to be balanced with Islamic philosophy.

Tabataba'i, with the exception of S. M. K. 'Assar (d. 1977), is perhaps the foremost Sadrian philosopher of the contemporary period. As a master of this school he was committed to educating a new generation of thinkers in the *hikmat-i muta'aliyah*, and not only to see to the continuation of the Sadrian tradition but also to preserve the place of philosophy in the education of Muslim religious leaders. Throughout his life—despite objections from some of the 'ulama (religious scholars), who scoffed at philosophy—Tabataba'i openly taught Islamic philosophy and even the mystical and gnostic texts, and generated interest in them among a wide range of Islamic thinkers, divines, seminary students, and lay intellectuals in Iran. In his classes he taught Avicennian philosophy, but more importantly he taught Mulla Sadra's seminal *al Asfar al Arba'ah* (*The Four Journeys*). He was without doubt most effective in popularizing and continuing the tradition of the Sadrian School. He trained a number of philosophers over the years, who have continued in his footsteps. The most notable of these among the 'ulama are S. J. Ashtiyani, S. H. Khosrowshahi, and S. M. Mutahhari (d. 1979); and among lay intellectuals, Seyyed Hossein Nasr and William Chittick.

By the time Tabataba'i settled in Qum he was also gravely concerned with the marginalization of Islam and its ever-more minor role in defining national culture and personal identities, and shaping intellectual discourses in Iran. The government in Iran—and also in Iraq where Tabataba'i had lived and studied—had adopted secularist policies, and had systematically pushed Islam and Shi'ism out of society. The educated classes had become openly secular, and were drawn in greater numbers to Western philosophical perspectives in general, and Marxism in particular. His experiences with life in Tabriz during the Second World War, when Communist activity would culminate in a secessionist movement, had no doubt made him particularly sensitive to the challenge of Marxism. Tabataba'i

believed that Shi'ite jurisprudence and theology were not capable of contending with the intellectual and ideological challenges of Western thought. Islamic philosophy alone had the tools and the sophistication to appeal to educated Muslims and thereby preserve the Islamic character of national culture before the Western onslaught.

Revival of interest in philosophy in Islamic circles was only the first step. For it to have a cultural impact it had to relate to the ambient culture and worldview of lay Muslims. Tabataba'i sought to present Islamic philosophy in terms that would be understandable to modern Muslims, using some of the precepts of Western philosophy. This task began with dialogue with Western thought. It was with this aim that in 1958 Tabataba'i began correspondences and personal discussions with the French scholar of Islam, Henry Corbin. The discussions with Corbin lasted for some two decades and had a profound impact on Tabataba'i. Corbin was not only a first-rate specialist on Shi'ism, but was also a serious student of Islamic and Western philosophies. He was then the foremost authority on Shahab al-Din Suhrawardi (d. 1191) and his Illuminationist theosophy; he had also been close to Martin Heidegger, and was the first to translate his works into French. Corbin thus served as a bridge, enabling Tabataba'i to create an Islamic approach to comparative philosophy as the basis for dialogue and debate with Western thought. Tabataba'i later extended the purview of his comparative perspective to include discussions on Daoism (Taoism) and Hinduism. Some of his students, such as S. H. Nasr, D. Shayegan, and W. Chittick, have been closely tied to this aspect of Tabataba'i's work.

Tabataba'i soon concluded that the most important element of Western philosophy—what accounts for its hold on educated Muslims—is its rooting in realism and its reliance on the realist method. It was this conclusion that led to his influential works on realism in philosophy, *Usul-i Falsafah-i Realism* (*Foundations of Realist Philosophy*), and *Usul Falsafah wa Rawish-i Realism* (*Foundations of Philosophy and Method of Realism*). The first was published in 1976, and the second is a five-volume study that was begun in 1953 and was published in full in 1985. In these works he outlined the precepts of the realist school, and especially its method of philosophical inquiry, for his readers. He then presented Islamic philosophy in the context of his discussion of realism.

In his treatment of realism Tabataba'i argued that the Sadrian perspective, in which God alone is the Necessary Being, is true realism as the term is understood in the West. Realism has meaning only if it accepts the "reality" of existence, as Mulla Sadra had. By this definition Tabataba'i was a realist, and in fact viewed himself as one. It followed from this that Marxism, which was an "idealism," was born of human perception, did not recognize the "reality" of existence and thus could be no more than a fallacy. Tabataba'i was bolstering one aspect of Western philosophy—the one that was most appealing to educated Muslims—and was using its logic to legitimate Islamic philosophy among the lay intellectuals and, by the same token, to dethrone Marxism. It is interesting that he did not seek to reject Marxism for its atheism—for that would not be a strong argument before educated Muslims—but for its lack of "reason." Tabataba'i's approach was, however, more than mere posturing; it was the beginning of a concerted attempt directed at bringing Islamic philosophy and realism in line. He envisioned a symbiotic relation between the two. Just as realism would open educated Muslims to Islamic philosophy, the Sadrian perspective would bolster realism before Marxist idealism. Islamic philosophy did not wish to compete with realism, but to support it. It was for this reason that Tabataba'i was a comparativist and not a rejectionist.

He perceived that there existed perfect harmony between faith and reason, and between Islamic philosophy and realism. In fact, he argued that true faith—and its reflection in Islamic philosophy—is perfectly rational. His aim, therefore, was not to bring about a new synthesis between Islamic philosophy and realism, but to bring out the intrinsic realism of Islamic philosophy. It is important to note that Tabataba'i was not a modernist. He viewed realism as the gateway to relating tradi-

tional Islamic philosophy to contemporary philosophical questions.

The problem that Tabataba'i faced was how to reconcile the mystical dimension of Sadrian theosophy, which perceives of truth experientially, with realism. In his person, the problem was largely resolved. He was an exemplary teacher and religious leader. Just as his persona was a source of emulation and a manifestation of the best in the Islamic tradition of learning and scholarship, it was also the most clear manifestation of the truth of his perspective. In his person the fusion of philosophy and mysticism, and theosophy and realism, was both visible and effective.

Beyond this his formulation avoided the problem of reconciling theosophy and realism because it was essentially Sadrian at its core. Tabataba'i studied realism and imbibed ideas from it, but he always remained true to the Sadrian tradition. Realism was a linguistic and semiological tool in arguing the case of Islamic philosophy before realist minds. Realism was a definition, particularly limited in its scope as it was somewhat politically motivated. Tabataba'i was drawn to realism not by any internal inconsistencies in the Sadrian perspective, but by the political and ideological challenge of modernization on the one hand, and Marxism on the other.

This does not mean that Tabataba'i's experiment was unimportant. To the contrary, it was an important opening in Islamic philosophy. He may have failed to reconcile the tension between Sadrian theosophy and realism, but by using the realist method in analyzing Islamic sources, he made a significant impact on traditional Islamic studies.

His contribution does not lie in convincing all and sundry that Islamic philosophy is through and through compatible with realism, but in instituting the realist method in addressing philosophical questions. In his own works he consciously broke with the traditional style and method of argumentation, relying instead on the realist method. His style has therefore been an important intellectual influence in its own right. He also applied the realist method in addressing theological and jurisprudential questions. His commentaries on the Qur'an

(Koran), the *Nahj al-Balaghah*, and Muhammad Baqir Majlisi's *Bahar al-Anwar*, for instance, consciously sought to incorporate the realist method into traditional Shi'ite religious sciences. His impact is clearly visible on contemporary Shi'ite social thought. He also used the realist method to present more effectively the tenets of Islam and Shi'ism to educated Muslims and, through translation, to non-Muslims. His *Shi'ah dar Islam* (*Shi'ism in Islam*), written in 1969 and published in English in 1975, is a clear example in this regard.

Tabataba'i's impact on Islamic philosophy and Shi'ite thought has been profound. His works have been read widely, and gradually left their mark on the structure of Islamic thought in Iran, and the Shi'ite centers of learning elsewhere. His many students have, moreover, continued in his tradition. Some have remained more closely attached to Tabataba'i the Sadrian theosophist. They have continued to teach and expound on this school of thought, handing down to the next generations the tradition that Tabataba'i handed down to them. Most notable are S. J. Ashtiyani, S. H. Nasr, and W. Chittick. Others—most important among them, S. M. Mutahhari and N. Makarim Shirazi—have carried Tabataba'i's dialogue with the West further to establish a modernist school of Shi'ite thought that used the realist method to rationalize Shi'ism. This school ultimately became engaged in heated debates with Marxism, and was politicized during the course of the Iranian revolution of 1978–79.

The Islamic Republic of Iran has claimed Tabataba'i as one of its ideologues. This is in part a reflection of the high regard in which Ayatollah Khomeini—himself a Sadrian philosopher—held Tabataba'i, and in part a result of the involvement of some of his students in the revolution. Still, he was far from an ideologue. There is evidence that he did not approve of the revolution, and he remained aloof from politics until his death in 1981. To his last days he remained first and foremost a philosopher, and then a Muslim and Shi'ite intellectual, jurisconsult, and theologian.

SEYYED VALI REZA NASR

Further Reading

Translations

Tabataba'i, Sayyid Muhammad Husain. *Islamic Teachings: An Overview*. Translated by R. Campbell. New York: Mustazafan Foundation, 1989. A compilation in English of some of Tabataba'i's writings on Shi'ite thought.

——— . *Shi'ite Islam*. Seyyed Hossein Nasr, trans. and ed. Albany, N.Y.: SUNY Press, 1975. Tabataba'i's classic study of Shi'ism, written for educated and secular Iranians. The English translation served as an introduction to Shi'ism for non-Muslims.

——— . *The Qur'an in Islam: Its Impact and Influence on the Life of Muslims*. London: Zahra Publications, 1987. A study of the importance of the Qur'an in the Islamic faith.

Chittick, William, trans. and ed. *A Shi'ite Anthology*. Selected by 'Allamah Tabataba'i and with an introduction by Seyyed Hossein Nasr. Albany: SUNY Press, 1981. This volume provides a collection of the most important texts of Shi'ism, selected by Tabataba'i.

Nasr, Seyyed Hossein, Hamid Dabashi, and Seyyed Vali Reza Nasr, eds. *Shi'ism: Doctrines, Thought, and Spirituality*. Albany: SUNY Press, 1988. An anthology of primary and secondary sources on Shi'ism, including some of Tabataba'i's teachings on the faith.

Related Studies

Corbin, Henry. "The Force of Traditional Philosophy in Iran Today," *Studies in Comparative Religion*. Winter 1968, pp 12–26. A comprehensive study of the continuity of traditional Islamic philosophy in contemporary Iran.

Dabashi, Hamid. *Theology of Discontent: The Ideological Foundation of the Islamic Revolution in Iran*. New York: New York University Press, 1993. The chapter on Tabataba'i in this volume is one of the most comprehensive accounts of Tabataba'i's life and thought in English. The chapter explores the relation between

Tabataba'i's ideas and Iranian revolutionary ideology.

Nasr, Seyyed Hossein. *Islamic Philosophy in Contemporary Persia: A Survey of Activity During the Past Two Decades*. Salt Lake City, Utah: Middle East Center, University of Utah, 1972. A comprehensive study of expressions of Islamic philosophy in modern Iran, including an examination of Tabataba'i's place in it.

THINKER INDEX